Business Data Processing

Houghton Mifflin Company Boston

Dallas Geneva, Illinois Hopewell, New Jersey Palo Alto London

Business Data Processing

George J. Brabb

Gerald W. McKean

Illinois State University

Printed in the U.S.A.

Library of Congress Catalog Card Number: 81–82556

ISBN: 0–395–31684–7

Contents

5 *Output media and devices* 105

6 *Secondary storage* 127

10 Structured design and structured programming 279

11 Program debug and maintenance 300

Special Option — Ready-made software 316

Special Option — The software industry 325

Part 4 Data processing systems 333

12 Analyzing data processing systems 334

13 System design and implementation 361

Part 5 Data processing and management 437

18 Managing data processing operations 507

Special Option Auditing online systems 532

Special Option The social impact of computers 538

Preface

Business Data Processing is not just a textbook. It is the major unit of an instructional package. This package was developed to meet the following objectives:

1. To introduce students with little or no background to the concepts and related practices being applied in data processing within modern business organizations.
2. To make this process interesting to students by emphasizing the real world and giving them hands-on experience.
3. To make the instructional process more enjoyable and productive for the instructor by providing assistance in course development, with recognition that major course objectives are different for different instructors.

To accomplish these objectives, a total of three elements have been developed.

Textbook

This textbook is the keystone of the instructional package. It comprises a comprehensive introduction to the concepts and practices involved in the manipulation of facts pertinent to business activity. Throughout we stress the purpose of business data processing, that is to successfully plan and carry out business operations.

Five elements make up the text itself. The major subject content is found in 18 chapters organized into 5 parts: Introduction (2 chapters); Data Processing Hardware (4 chapters); Data Processing Software (5 chapters); Data Processing Systems (4 chapters); Data Processing and Management (3 chapters). One or two Special Options follow each part. Each Special Option presents some topic in depth and is designed for one of two purposes. Most Special Options answer questions (often unasked) that bother students just starting to learn about data processing and computers; for example, whether a computer can think, and how mainframes, minicomputers, and microcomputers are different. Other Special Options present some important, but peripheral topics that are often given short shrift in data processing textbooks, for example, the impact of computers on society, the software industry, and security of online systems.

Following each chapter and each Special Option a brief article illustrates some aspect of the chapter or Special Option. These articles are taken from business and trade publications and each was chosen to help show data processing's role in the business world.

Each chapter is introduced by an outline and has an ending summary. Great care has been taken to make the text readable by undergraduates. Discussion questions and exercises at the end of each chapter assist student learning and help to develop student understanding of chapter content. Most of the exercises call for hands-on work or investigation of actual data processing activities. A glossary at the end of the text contains definitions of the technical terms and concepts used in the text.

The organization of the text is modular; it need not be read directly cover to cover. To increase its flexibility, depth of coverage in each area can also be varied. Part 1, Introduction, presents an overview of data processing systems and computers. The first chapter in Part 2 (on hardware) provides the most basic concepts in that part. In Part 3 on software, the first chapter provides an overview. The remaining chapters there could be omitted if programming is not an important element in the course. Each chapter in Part 5 on data processing and management can stand alone. This flexibility in order and depth of use means that the instructor can mold a course reflecting his or her unique objectives.

Study Guide

The Study Guide is designed to assist students in learning the material in *Business Data Processing.* A listing of the learning objectives for each chapter is supplemented by sets of true/false, multiple-choice, and completion questions that check on learning. Essay questions then check on understanding. Answers are provided for all objective questions, but not for essay questions.

Practice Set

The Practice Set that is available for use with *Business Data Processing* will provide students with experience in system design and development. Practice Set assignments ocrrespond to parts of the text, giving students the opportunity to apply what they learn as they learn it. The practice set develops a data processing system (accounts receivable), starting with manual processes and ending with an integrated, computerized system. For courses involving programming, the Practice Set serves as a source of program assignments.

Instructor's materials

Special package items for the instructor are also available for use with *Business Data Processing.* These items will, we hope, assist instructors in developing course materials and in structuring classes.

The authors wish to acknowledge the support of those who have provided special assistance in preparing this instructional package. We appreciate the assistance provided by the College of Business at Illinois State University, where we were allowed access to a computer and to a word processing system as we developed the instructional package. Dr. Timothy Duffy prepared the Study Guide. The following persons provided valuable reviews of the manuscript for the text: Mr. John Bennison, Brown University; Dr. Robert L. Carmichael, University of California at Los Angeles; Professor James C. Hershauer, Arizona State University; Mr. Gary M. Kern, University of Virginia, Professor John J. Neuhauser, Boston College; and Professor Donald Reese, University of Tennessee.

Special thanks go to Betty Brabb, wife of the senior author, who contributed so much while converting his very rough drafts into well-organized manuscripts virtually free of mechanical error.

G. J. B.
G. W. M.

Part 1

Introduction

Chapter 1 The Nature of Business Data Processing

Outline

Business data processing defined

Business **data processing** systems are those procedures, people, and machines devoted to recording and manipulating business data. Business **data** derive most directly from business activity. They are created in the many business transactions taking place daily. Some examples are placing an order for a product or materials, selling a business asset, employing a person to work for a firm, and paying a wage or salary to that employee. Business data arise also from the environment in which a firm operates. Knowledge of environmental characteristics like incomes, tastes, and habits help a business firm to recognize and profit from market demands. Actions of competitors also provide valuable information for business managers.

Like any system, a business data processing system is created and operated for a purpose. That is, it is an organized endeavor with one or more definite objectives in mind. It is the purpose of this chapter not only to define the data processing functions carried on in data processing systems but also to reveal the objectives of these activities.

It seems appropriate to begin our study of business data processing systems by establishing their purposes. After that, we will look at the operations involved in accomplishing these purposes. We will then be prepared to appreciate one view of data processing—the systems view. Finally, we will be able to recognize some desirable characteristics of such systems.

The purposes of business data processing

Every business transaction can be described by a variety of facts. The sale of a suit to a customer in the local department store can serve as an example. Facts concerning this transaction *could* include the following:

1. Name and address of the person buying the suit
2. Whether or not this is a credit transaction
3. If this is a credit transaction, who is to pay the bill
4. The identity of the clerk making the sale
5. The department of the store in which the sale is made
6. A description of the suit (color, size, and style)
7. The selling price of the suit
8. The cost to the store of the suit
9. The color of the purchaser's hair
10. The sex of the salesclerk
11. How the suit was packaged for the customer (box, paper bag)
12. Whether or not the sun was shining
13. The level of bank debits in the community for this month

By the application of a little imagination, the reader could extend this list ad nauseum. It is obvious that all these facts are not of equal value to the management of the store, but some are of vital importance. Trends in colors, sizes, and styles of suits sold are important in planning future purchases. Sales generated by each department and each salesperson in the store are important in planning changes in store layout or personnel assignments, and in evaluating personnel practices. The difference between purchase cost and sales price, when accumulated for all such sales, is important in determining margins of profit and in preparing tax reports and statements to stockholders. Over time, accumulated facts indicate whether the store should be expanded or similar stores should be established elsewhere.

Specific data on the amount of the sale are necessary in order to bill a customer for a credit purchase. Information on factors external to the store (such as bank debits) can be important in explaining why total sales reached the level they did. Planning for future sales may be improved by noting general economic conditions in the community.

The reasons for capturing the facts associated with business transactions and processing them can be grouped in three general categories.

1 Some data must be collected and analyzed to *provide information for management planning and control activities.*

Management must plan for future activity and exercise control over current activity if plans are to be carried out successfully. Such actions determine the profitability (success) of the enterprise. The management of the department store must know if actual sales are below, equal to, or above expected sales. Inventory amounts (numbers of suits by size, color, and style) must be adjusted to actual sales. If fewer suits are being sold than expected, unsold suits will remain in stock. Prices (and profit margins) may have to be reduced in order to move the suits out to make room for faster-selling items.

If sales are equal to expectations, then the suits purchased can all be sold, and future orders can continue at planned levels. In other words, the same plan of action can continue because it is successful.

Obviously, if actual sales are above expected sales, adjustments in plans are called for. The number of suits ordered have not satisfied customer demand; therefore, plans need to be modified and the pace of orders stepped up. It could even be that more salespeople, stock clerks, and tailors are required to handle the increased sales.

2 Some data must be collected as a basis for **custodial** (or maintenance) **processing**.

Just as the buildings, furnishings, and heating systems of an organization must be taken care of, documents (sales slips, paychecks, purchase orders, receiving slips, tax reports, and so on) must be prepared and their contents recorded, manipulated, and compared in order to carry on the daily business routine. Employees must be paid and customers must be billed. Purchase orders must be prepared to obtain supplies for the enterprise, and supplier invoices must be recorded for payment as goods are received. Legal reporting requirements (income tax reports, health reports on employees handling food, and so on) must be met if the enterprise is not to be forced to close down. Such activities are necessary to continued operation, although they may contribute only indirectly to profit (success). Data generated by transactions and contained on custodial documents may serve as the basis for information reports to management; but the processing necessary to their production and use (completing a purchase order, for example), although required to keep the operation going, is not a basic planning or control activity of management.

3 Data must be collected and retained to *provide historical facts* as a basis for the other two types of activity.

Planning cannot be rational without historical data to use in establishing past and current trends and tendencies. Further, adequate management control of any activity requires the recognition of performance standards. Such standards are most often obtained from the analysis of past (historical) behavior. Legal requirements exist for retaining past data as a basis for tax and other reports.

It is not accidental that the three reasons for data processing are listed in the order given. This order reflects their relative importance. The most important use of business data is in providing management with the information necessary to recognize trends and patterns in the activities of the enterprise and in the environment within which it operates. Such recognition is necessary if the business is to adapt successfully and continuously to these changing trends and patterns. Without a well-informed management, the enterprise will almost surely fail. Without preplanning of activities and later control over physical operations to see that those plans are being carried out, day-to-day operations very well may cease.

Emphasis on management information does not really come at the expense of the other needs for data processing. A data processing system that collects and preserves the proper facts to provide adequate information for management planning and control will of necessity perform the custodial processing required to keep the enterprise in operation. However, a system designed primarily for efficient custodial processing may not necessarily provide good management information. The custodial approach tends to put major emphasis on reducing the cost of inescapable processing activities. Putting management information needs first emphasizes the importance of considering profit motives when striving for improvement in data processing procedures.

Operations in business data processing

The specific operations that make up data processing activities are originating, classification and sorting, storage and retrieval, summarization, analysis, and communication. Regardless of how the data processing is accomplished

—by humans using pencil and paper or by the most sophisticated electronic equipment—these basic activities are performed as follows:

1 **Originating (recording).** Data describing a transaction or the conditions of the environment within which the organization operates must be originated, that is, captured (recorded) in some form for processing.

Often transactions data are captured on handwritten or typed forms such as sales tickets, purchase orders, invoices, or checks. In a manual processing system, these documents are passed on to a clerk for sorting and entry into the appropriate accounts. If the data are to be processed by machine, they must be transcribed or converted to some machine-readable form. Increasingly, data are captured by special recording devices and entered directly into some electronic storage medium such as a magnetic disk. Where data are not entered directly into some such device, a machine-readable medium such as a punched card, punched paper tape, or magnetic tape is created as a by-product of the operation producing the original transaction document (sales slip, purchase order, and so on). Sometimes the document itself is prepared in a form that can be "read" by a special input device. Examples are checks with the account identification and amount written in magnetic ink and cash register tapes written in a special kind of type so that they may be read by an optical character reader. Whatever the means of processing, the data must first be recorded on some medium that can be entered into the manual or machine processing cycle. Such media are usually called **source documents**.

2 **Classification and sorting.** Recorded data must be classified by type and then physically arranged (sorted) into particular sequences or groupings if they are to be useful in guiding management decisions.

Classification can take many forms. Data can be classified by source or by immediate importance. Obviously, the most useful classifications are those bearing some logical relevance to the planning and control functions of management. Thus customer records at the department store can be classified by frequency of purchase, average amount of purchase, and whether or not the customer is paying on time. Sales records can be placed in categories (classified) by department, by salesperson, and, perhaps, by specific item.

Data can also be classified by the response they require. **Action data** require a response. Some action data items require an immediate response —for example, a customer request for delivery of a specific item. The occurrence of other facts (the presence of a specific datum) may lead to a delayed action. For example, the fact that a sales clerk reported on time and worked for a full day will mean that he or she will have to be paid for the day's services, but not until the next payday arrives. **Inaction data** require no action. For example, if an employee cashes his or her paycheck, no action is required. However, if the employee fails to cash the paycheck, action could be required, since accounting entries would need to be adjusted, and so on.

The actual physical process of placing data in classifications (arranging data) is called *sorting.* Not all sorting is done for the purpose of classification. For example, the day's credit sales at the department store may be arranged in account-number sequence before being used to update customer account records. The processing can be more efficient when both the input file (the credit sales) and the master file (the accounts to be updated) are arranged in account-number sequence. Having both files in the same sequence makes it easier to match each transaction to the master record it affects. Such ordering has no significance other than the increase in processing efficiency that results.

3 **Storage and retrieval.** Data must be retained in some accessible form after their initial recording until they lose their usefulness.

Returning to the department store example, account records must be maintained to show in detail each customer's transactions with the store. Customers often wish to confirm the details of these transactions. A simple statement of the amount owed is not always sufficient. Management also has need of details concerning when amounts were charged and billed and if and when payment was rendered. Accounts for those who are no longer customers of the store need to be deleted (purged) at periodic intervals.

Planning decisions are apt to be based on analysis of sales trends in total and in detail by department and/or specific items as indicated earlier. This means that these data must be retained (stored) somewhere so that they can be retrieved when needed. The form of the storage medium and the method of retrieval will depend on the frequency with which the data file must be queried and the detail required in each response.

4 **Summarization.** The simplest form of data analysis is accumulating details to obtain totals. This also includes the process of computing an arithmetic average, since such an average is merely a rescaled sum.

The management at the department store needs information on the total amount of income and expense for the whole store, for individual departments, and even for individual employees in order to plan rationally. Such data, when expressed in the form of rates (averages), can be used to check on progress toward a goal (total) as time passes. Standard accounting reports such as income statements and balance sheets also represent this type of processing activity. Note that this process is primarily descriptive and does not usually reveal reasons for (causes of) particular results.

Sums are also a standard method for checking on the completeness of processing. For example, the totals of processed items must be equal to the totals of recorded items. Such control procedures are discussed fully in Chapter 15.

5 **Analysis.** To reveal the full informational content of data, the underlying relationships they contain must be identified.

Mere summations usually reveal little more than the symptoms of success or failure. The underlying causes of such results can only be found by examining underlying relationships. For example, the ratio of liquid assets to liabilities helps to reveal whether or not a firm is able to meet its debts. However, a complete analysis of this question involves a comparison over time of the flows of money into and out of the firm. More basic relationships such as those between advertising expenditures and amount of sales require more sophisticated analysis. Modern management science provides the techniques for such modeling and analysis. Examples of useful analytic tools are regression, mathematical programming, and computer simulation.

6 **Communication.** Processing results are worthless if not sent to and accepted by someone who can use them.

As will be indicated later in defining *information,* facts do not become information until they are received and accepted by someone with the responsibility, ability, and desire to use them in decision making. By the same token, any report, whether its contents are useful in decision making or not, is not a report until reported, that is, until communicated to a responsible recipient.

A systems view of business data processing

The input/process/output system

One way to view business data processing is as a three-phase system of input, processing, and output as shown in Figure 1.1. Data are recorded, which is called **input**, then **processed** (classified, sorted, stored, retrieved, summarized, analyzed, communicated) to obtain desired **outputs** (either management information, custodial documents, or historical records). It should be emphasized that the same basic inputs are required to provide any of the three types of outputs. The processing activities in phase 2 also are required (in varying degrees) to obtain each of the outputs.

Data or information?

An important data processing concept is found in the systems view of Figure 1.1, namely that there is a difference between *data* and *information.* If there were no difference, not all of the activities in phase 2 would be required. Classification and sorting, summarization, and analysis would be superfluous. There would be no need to change the form of data or store them for later use. All that would be required would be to transmit the data to the person or persons needing to use them. Let's look at how data and information differ.

Data are raw facts. They may or may not be information, since they are the raw material from which information is created. Carefully examining Figure 1.1 indicates that information must be some sort of knowledge that is useful to managers in carrying out their planning and control functions; but the mere fact of its usefulness does not make such knowledge information. We need a definition for *information* that will allow us to separate data from information in

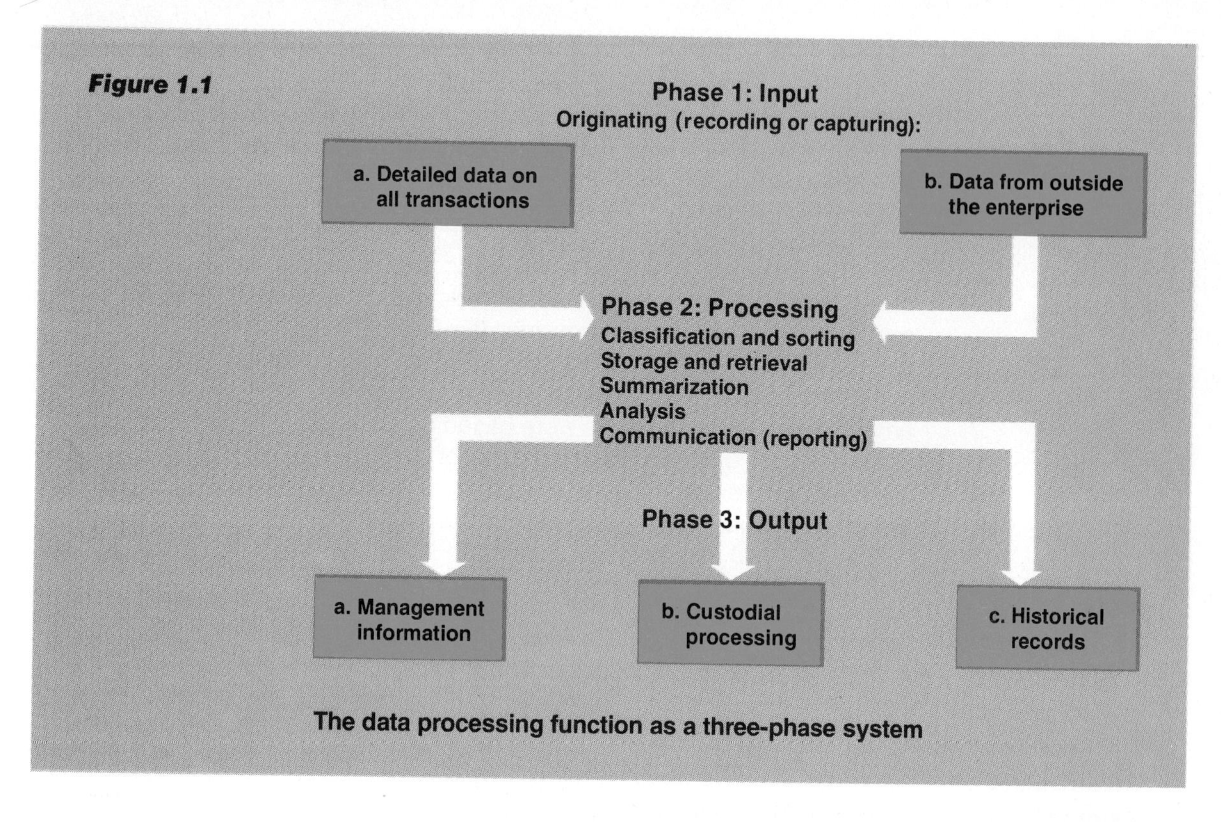

Figure 1.1 The data processing function as a three-phase system

every instance. Such a definition must take into account a further property of information: it is presented to its potential user (communicated) in such a manner that its usefulness is recognized by that user. Thus the definition for *information* in this text will be: **Information** is communicated knowledge expressed in a form that makes it immediately useful for decision making.

This definition is not easy to grasp unless we see what each part of it actually means. First, *knowledge* means a novel or new fact, something previously unknown to the recipient. Second, *communicated* knowledge is a novel or new fact that has been *sent to and received by* the person to whom it is directed, and *recognized and accepted* by that person for use as a basis for action. Third, this knowledge must be so stated that *further processing is not necessary* in order to use the information for decision making.

Consider the manager who receives but does not read a report because the report refers only to what happened two months ago. Information in our sense has not been created. The facts contained in the report are not novel and are not accepted by the manager as information. Consider the sales manager who receives a quarterly report on sales of each product by each salesperson in his or her sales group, then summarizes the data and plots them on a graph to compare them with performance in the same quarter of the previous year. The data processing system that creates information in this case includes the sales manager, undoubtedly a high-priced data processing clerk. Finally, consider the general manager who receives a report stating that production in the previous month totaled 144 tons, a fact this manager was told by an assistant ten days ago. Again, no information was imparted by this fact, since the manager already knew it.

As another example, consider the case of one manager who regularly received a suggested weekly production schedule based on a mathematical programming model of the operation under her control. Unfortunately, this manager had never been trained to interpret the output of such an analysis and also was not familiar with the basic model used in the analysis. This manager continued to use standard charting and rule-of-thumb techniques to schedule the operation. Or consider the factory manager who each month got a detailed report showing production and cost relationships for every operator and machine combination in the factory. This report was filed away, and all cost-control decisions were based on a summary report organized to show cost per unit for producing each of the 12 products manufactured in the plant. In the last two examples, information in our sense has not been created, because the reports were not accepted for use by the recipients.

The last two examples illustrate an important feature of the stated definition of *information.* Information cannot be created unless the abilities and desires of the recipient come into play. The mere transmittal of relevant and timely *facts* is not enough. Unless those facts are accepted as a basis for action, they are *not* information.

The structure of business data processing systems

Another instructive way in which to view business data processing systems is to look at their mechanical structure. All business data processing systems tend to have the same mechanical structure. The basis of the structure is the concept of a file.

A **file** is a set of records relating to a specific business activity. An example of a file is the accounts receivable file at a department store. It is made up of the individual records for the credit (charge) customers of the store. Each individual record shows, basically, the amount of money that a customer owes the store. Each record may also contain some or all of the following facts for a customer:

name and address
credit standing or credit limit
date of the last payment
details on unpaid credit transactions (dates, items purchased, prices and costs, and so on)

The basic accounts receivable file just described is the **master file** of the accounts receivable system. Customer transactions (purchases or payments) are recorded in a **transactions file** and used to **update** the records in the master file. Other changes to the master file are recorded in a **change file** and made as well. Records for departing customers must be **purged** from the file (the record must be closed out and withdrawn from the file). Poor credit risks must also be purged. Customer records change as customers marry, lose family members in death, change address, change credit status,

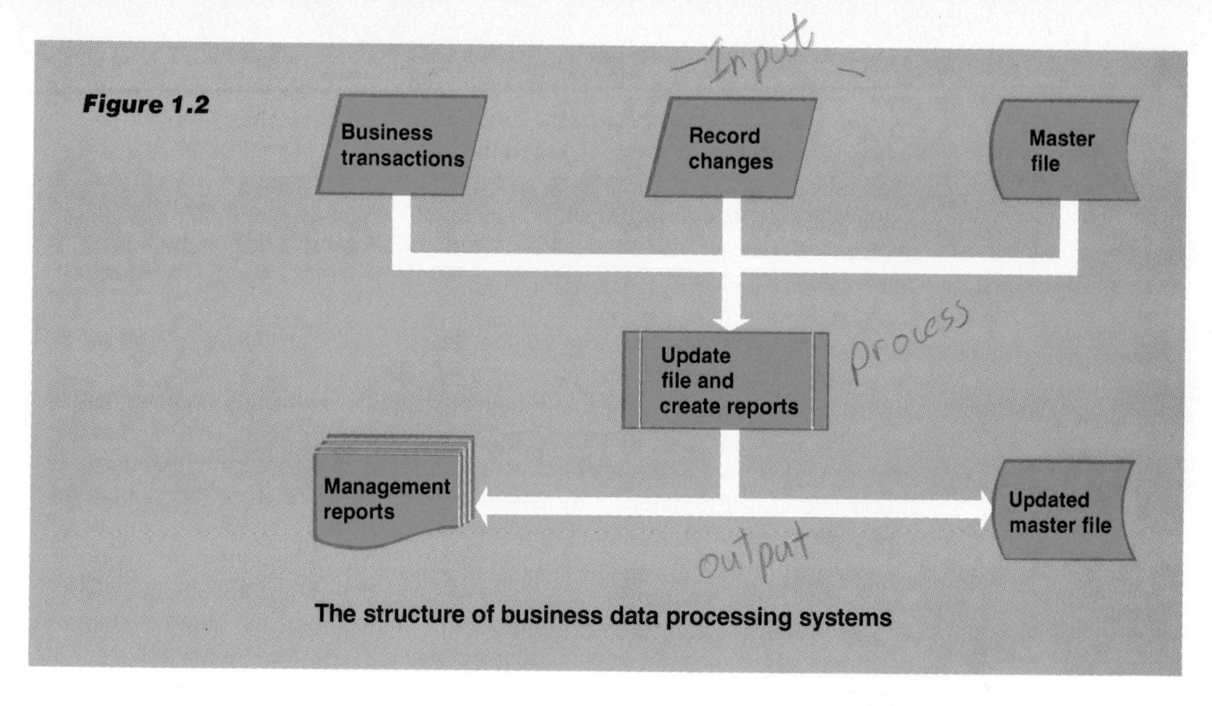

Figure 1.2 The structure of business data processing systems

and so on. We see then that a master file is created; then transactions and changes are recorded and used to change the master file to keep it current.

Obviously, various reports must be created by the system. Management must know the amount and rate of default (uncollectibles) on credit sales. They must know also the volume of such sales in total and by department, and so on. These reports are created from the transactions, the changes, and the updated master file.

In summary, a business data processing system is created and operated by developing a master file and a system for updating it as transactions and changes that affect its contents occur. Management reports are developed from the flow of transactions and changes affecting the master file and from the updated master file itself. This structure is shown in Figure 1.2.

What makes a good data processing system?

An effective data processing system will be timely, pertinent, precise and accurate, and economically feasible and efficient.

A *timely* data processing system will capture current data and output current information. For example, the department store manager who receives an analysis of departmental sales for the previous quarter one month after the close of that quarter is reacting to situations that may very well have changed dramatically since the quarter ended. This manager is in the same position as an automobile driver negotiating the freeway at rush hour but able to see only through the car's rearview mirror. Timely processing that reflects current conditions can help a manager perform his or her duties just as being able to see out the front and side windows as well as through the rearview mirror helps the automobile driver.

Ideally, data should be processed into information fast enough to provide adequate control of the physical operation that generated the data. In such a case, information is fed back in time to affect the situation from which the raw data were generated. Such a data processing system is called a **real-time data processing system**. This concept is discussed more fully in Chapter 7.

A *pertinent* data processing system will produce the proper information and do the proper custodial processing. A system for evaluating performance of the shoe department in the department store should not be overly concerned with reporting the color of each pair of shoes sold. It should, however, attempt to capture data concerning the extent to which customers found shoes in the colors they wanted—that is, the reasons why potential customers were not served. On the other hand, the manager of the shoe department need not receive personnel performance reports relating to the personnel in the women's ready-to-wear department.

The terms *precise* and *accurate* refer to two aspects of what people ordinarily think of as accuracy (correct values). A precise value, for our purposes, is correct within the limits of allowable error. For example, the manager of our mythical department store does not need to know that total sales in the notions department this year were exactly $182,134.69; he or she would probably remember this figure as either "$182,000" or "about $180,000." For the manager's purposes, the $180,000 figure may be sufficiently *precise,* sufficiently close to the exact value. However, he or she would be disturbed to find that through a consistent clerical error, this figure included some sales made in the men's clothing department each month. Such a lack of *accuracy,* that is, the presence of a consistent error, a **bias**, in the reported figures, could be very misleading.

Another example of bias, or lack of accuracy, could arise from charging all indirect costs to the individual operating departments of the store on the basis of total sales in each department. Departments requiring larger or smaller amounts of space, specialized storage and display equipment, or unusual amounts of janitorial services would not be charged with an appropriate portion of the indirect costs.

Just how precise and accurate management information has to be depends on how the information is to be used. For planning purposes, it is definitely important that information be accurate, but it does not have to be absolutely precise. In controlling detailed operations at the department level, however, information must be both very precise and very accurate.

To be *economically feasible and efficient,* a data processing system must do two things: (1) it must not place an excessive burden on the physical operation generating the data to be processed, and (2) it must give the most information possible for the dollars expended. The second statement implies that it would not be possible to change an efficient system to get more information without spending more money. The first statement is more complex. If processing costs are too high, the physical operation will

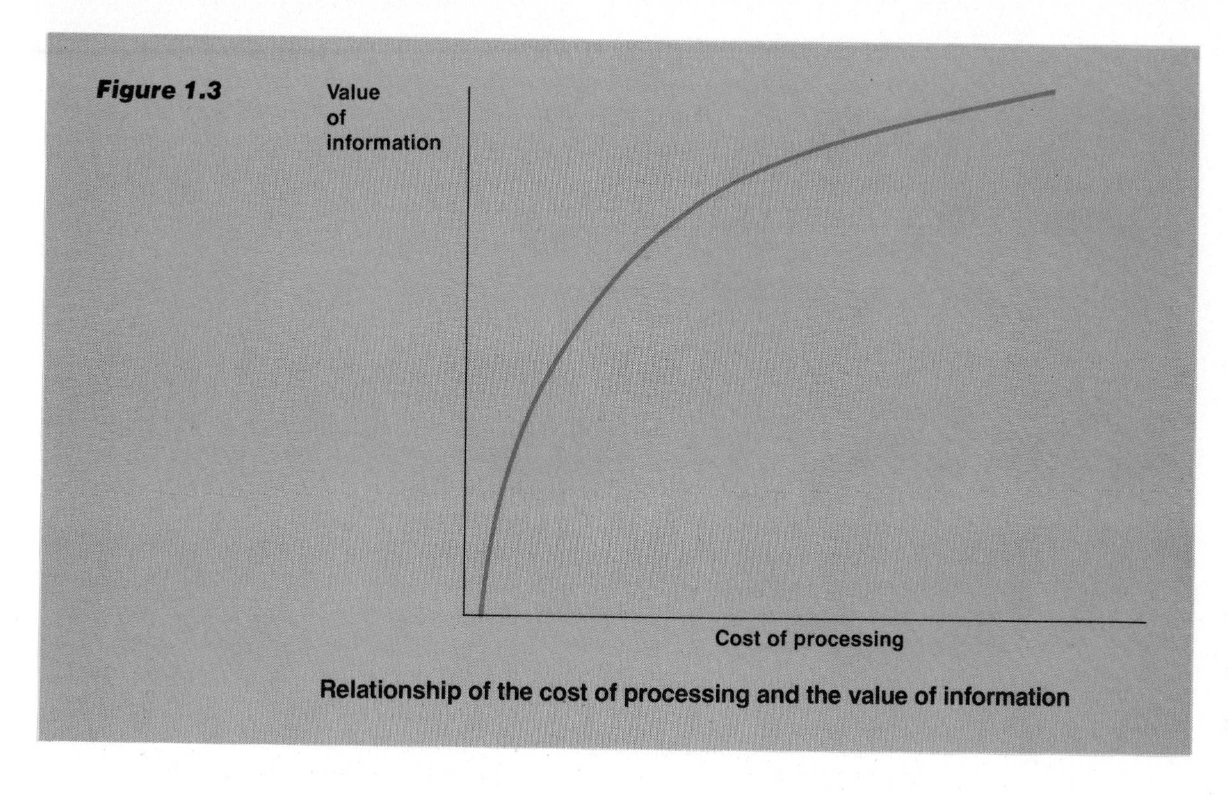

Figure 1.3 Relationship of the cost of processing and the value of information

eventually have to cease. However, just the fact that the returns from the physical operation are sufficient to cover the associated processing costs does not mean that the level of processing is appropriate. The general relationship between cost and value of processing is shown in Figure 1.3. This is an application of the principle of diminishing returns. As cost of processing increases, the value of the information received for each dollar of expense tends to increase, but at a rapidly decreasing rate. Eventually, very little additional information is being obtained for each addition to processing costs. Ideally, investment in the process is stopped at the point where the value of the last unit of information generated is just equal to the cost of obtaining it.

Summary

Data processing consists of a set of procedures [originating (recording), classification and sorting, storage and retrieval, summarization, and analysis] used to process data (raw facts). The data are used to (1) produce information (communicated knowledge expressed in a form that makes it immediately useful for decision making) for management planning and control, (2) produce custodial documents, and (3) provide historical records. The overall process is carried out by setting up master files, using data about business transactions and the business environment to update the master files, and creating reports from the flow of transactions and changes and/or the status of the master files. An effective data processing system will be timely, pertinent, precise and accurate, and economically feasible and efficient.

Key terms

Define the following terms as briefly as possible and then, in a short paragraph, clarify each definition.

Action data
Analysis
Bias
Change file
Classification and sorting
Communication
Custodial processing
Data
Data processing
File
Inaction data
Information
Input
Master file
Originating (recording)
Output
Process
Purge
Realtime data processing system
Source document
Storage and retrieval
Summarization
Transactions file
Update

Discussion questions

1 Explain carefully the difference between the two concepts in each pair listed below. (Note that it is necessary to define each concept in order to identify clearly how it differs from the other member of the pair.)
   - **a** Data and information
   - **b** Classifying and sorting
   - **c** Summarization and analysis
   - **d** Communicating and reporting
   - **e** Precise and accurate
   - **f** Economically feasible and economically efficient

2 List in order of importance the three reasons for processing business data, and briefly justify your choice of order.

3 Why must the concept of information as used here include each of the following characteristics?
   - **a** Novelty
   - **b** Communication
   - **c** Form of information
   - **d** Decision making

4 What are the three basic parts of a data processing system?
5 What makes a good data processing system?
6 What is a business transaction?
7 Business data processing has been characterized as being file-oriented. Justify this characterization.
8 Why are storage and retrieval important in business data processing?
9 Can data be information? Explain.
10 The manager of the shoe department at a local department store receives an analysis of sales by each salesperson for each month two weeks after the end of the month. Would this provide realtime information flow? Explain.
11 Why emphasize informational needs of management in the design of business data processing systems?

Exercises

1 A rancher produces beef cattle by breeding the cows, raising the calves, and, eventually, fattening out two-year-olds in feed lots. He receives an analysis of net gain and feed consumed for cattle in each feed lot for each two weeks at the end of the next week. Would this provide realtime control? If not, how would you suggest it be changed?
2 The rancher of question 1 receives an analysis of birth weight, weaning weight, and feed-conversion efficiency (weight gain/pounds of feed) for each animal marketed, two weeks after marketing. Will this provide realtime control for the breeding operation? If not, how would you suggest it be changed?
3 The local mayor and city council are faced with a decision on whether the city should provide garbage service or leave the provision of this service to private firms.
   a What types of data might be obtained in order to develop information on which to base this decision?
   b What processing might be performed on these data before they are presented to the mayor and city council?

Trusting the Computer for All Reasons

Mesco Metal Buildings Corp., Grapevine, TX, is a fast-growing manufacturer of pre-engineered metal buildings. Having used computers since 1963, the company credits much of its success to aggressive use of modern data processing techniques. Today, the company depends on its multiuser, multiapplication Prime computer system for estimating and engineering applications, as well as a dozen other tasks ranging from payroll processing to planning market strategy.

Mesco markets through factory-authorized "builderships," located predominantly in the Southwestern and Southeastern U.S. To figure the cost of a totally standard building, a builder consults Mesco's price book. Most buildings are not standard, however, so builders routinely telephone Mesco for price quotes. To obtain a quote, the builder provides a Mesco estimator with the building description, which may be a detailed specification or nothing more than overall dimensions. The estimator first writes all the information on a special computer input form, and then enters the data through the keyboard of an input/output terminal connected directly to the Prime system.

In calculating the quote, the system constructs a list of all required components and associated labor costs. For standard items, the system simply selects the correct list price. For non-standard components and assemblies, it extrapolates values from prices of similar standard parts and by using precise estimating formulae.

Trusting the system

According to Randy Cunningham, director, information systems, the computer price quotation system really pays its way. Referring to the system's "smarts," Cunningham says, "We've grown to trust the computer, even when it produces a quote that disagrees with our usual experience." Cunningham notes the computer automatically increases the estimate for a job requiring an unusually high number of welds. Conversely, the system reduces the estimate if the job calls for many duplicate parts. And a discount is automatically applied, based on total weight of the shipment. To account for future inflation of raw materials prices, the system checks how long it will be before the job is delivered. Freight cost is calculated, credit risk evaluated, and the final quote is printed in a clean, easy-to-read document.

Giving fast, accurate estimates is essential to Mesco's success as it competes in the growing metal building marketplace. Cunningham believes computerized estimating is a powerful competitive tool. "It's very flexible. On a competitive job, for example, the system can be told to reduce profit margin, but it does it in a very orderly, precise way, so we still know exactly where we stand on the job," Cunningham explains. "The Prime system also helps us win orders because it lets us turn out quotes faster than the competition," he adds.

The second critical application for Mesco's Prime system is in engineering—designing the steel frame structure of buildings. Cunningham explains, "The computer system lets us optimize the design to take advantage of the inherent virtues of this type of building." Whether working with limited information or with a comprehensive set of specifications, the system automatically defines the basic frame of the building, including the number and spacing of frame members, whether or not additional support columns are needed, and if so, how many and where they are to be located. . . .

But one of the most unusual and valuable programs in the system is used only once a year, for market forecasting. Before the start of each year, county by county metal building sales for the whole country, supplied by the industry's association, is input to the Prime system. The computer constructs detailed sales forecasts for Mesco and all its competitors, and projects sales figures for each company, by county. The result is a valuable industry model that Mesco can use to plan market strategy and to evaluate the strengths and weaknesses of itself and its competitors.

The program is a demanding "number cruncher," according to Cunningham "But it only slightly slows down the system's response time for other interactive users for a few days each year."

Chapter 2

The Computer

Outline

Introduction

The automatic electronic digital computer is a widely used data processing device, which has led to a revolution in data processing procedures. With its help the modern manager routinely applies an ever-widening array of planning and control algorithms of increasing power and complexity. It is also a widely misunderstood tool, underused and improperly used, improperly blamed for human failures and just as improperly praised for human accomplishments. The computer is a tool, a powerful tool that extends the intellectual powers of human beings. If it is to be used properly, it must be understood and must be placed in proper perspective.

It is the purpose of this chapter to define the computer and how it is used in business data processing systems. First, the computer and its principal functions are defined. Then, the development of computers in business data processing systems is reviewed, revealing how computers have changed in response to business data processing needs and how business data processing systems have changed to take advantage of the computer's increased abilities. Finally, the major types of computer systems that have been and are available for business data processing are summarized.

There are two general types of electronic computers, analog and digital. Analog computers use electronic circuits and current flows as a physical representation of a process or system. Analog machines are useful in engineering planning and research and production process control. They are not used in business data processing. Our attention will be devoted to the automatic electronic digital computer, which is what we will mean when we use the word *computer.*

Definition of the computer

The *automatic electronic digital* **computer** is a *machine* that utilizes *electronic circuits to manipulate data* expressed in a *symbolic form* according to *specific rules* in a *predetermined* but *self-directed* way. This complete definition is somewhat hard to absorb as a whole. Let's look at its individual parts.

First of all, the computer is a *machine.* This means that it is inanimate and requires an outside power source. This also means it can perform only those activities for which the basic capabilities have been specifically designed into the machine. In other words, it is limited to its designed capabilities and such outside direction as can be given it. If separated from its outside power source, it ceases to function.

Second, it is *automatic.* This means that once started, it continues to run without outside interference.

Third, it is *electronic;* that is, it is made up of electronic circuits and runs on electrical energy.

Fourth, the computer is a *symbol manipulator.* It manipulates data, not physical entities. These data are represented as electronic impulses within the machine. The electronic impulses are combined to form number (*digital*) representations of data. Electronic circuits are used to manipulate these symbols.

Electronic devices are largely two-state devices. For example, a switch is either on or off, a spot on the surface of a magnetic tape is either magnetized or not magnetized, a particular location on a punched card or punched paper tape is either a hole or it is not, and a particular point on a wire at a particular instant either contains an electrical impulse or it does not. It therefore seems natural and reasonable to use the base 2 or **binary number system** as the basic data-representation method in the computer. Only two digits exist in the binary number system, 0 (zero) and 1 (one). They can easily be matched to the two states of the electronic devices. Combinations of 0s and 1s can be used to represent nonnumeric data as well as numeric data. This coding process is described in Chapter 3.

Fifth, the computer must follow *specific rules* in manipulating data. These rules are, in the main, the rules of Boolean algebra. That is, the computer can perform *only* the processes of *addition, subtraction, multiplication, division,* and *comparison* ($a = b$, $a < b$, $a > b$), in addition to data transfer between components.

Sixth, the computer must follow a *predetermined* sequence of its allowable processes. That is, someone (the programmer) must prepare a finite sequence of the allowable individual operations, a **program**, for the computer to follow.

Finally, the computer can follow the predetermined sequence in a *self-directed* way. It can store the program within its own memory and then follow it through under its own direction, without further outside guidance. This **stored-program** characteristic is what differentiates the computer from other data processing machines. That is, the computer can be made, in effect, to *learn* a process, *store* the instructions in its memory, and *follow* them through *unaided* by further supervision and direction. Since the instructions are stored in the memory and the memory is accessible to a user, the instructions can be changed. The computer can thus be given the ability to handle many different jobs. It is much more flexible than the "programmable" accounting machines because its programs are a sequence of logic and arithmetic operations. The availability of logic (decision-making) powers allows the machine to modify its operations while working on a job, making it more versatile and giving it great power to duplicate human cognitive mental processes.

In summary, then, we find that *the electronic digital computer is a symbol-manipulating machine that can be "instructed" to perform any sequence of logical or arithmetical operations on data.* Further, these instructions are easily modified, either by being totally replaced or by being modified by the machine in accordance with results it obtains during an operation.

How computers work

Five functional elements make up the computer. Each performs one of the basic functions of input, storage, control, arithmetic and logic, and output.

Figure 2.1

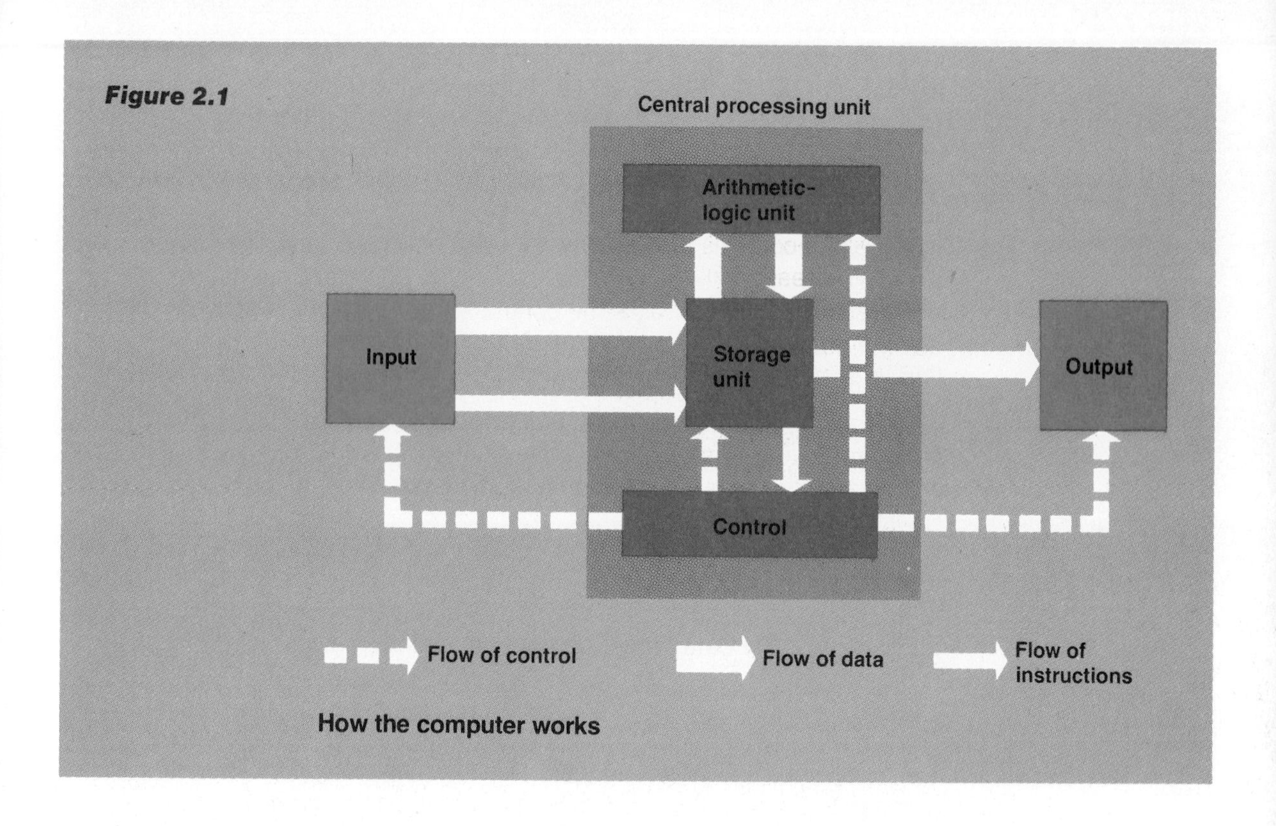

How the computer works

The manner in which the elements are organized is indicated in Figure 2.1. An understanding of these functions is necessary for understanding what a computer is and what it can do for us.

Input element The **input element** of a computer performs a **translation** function. It translates data from the symbols of our language (numbers, letters, and so on) to the symbols (electronic impulses) used inside the machine. For example, the card reader senses the holes in a punched card and converts each hole into a set of electronic impulses which represent the digital meaning of that hole.

Storage element The **storage element's** obvious function of storage has four parts:

1 The storage of program instructions
2 The storage of input (raw) data
3 The storage of intermediate results from processing
4 The storage of final results (processed data) for output

Note particularly that data are passed directly from input to storage and must be in storage to be sent to output or to any peripheral device added to the basic computer.

Control element The **control element** includes the operator's console and several registers and related control circuits. Buttons and switches on the console are used to manually start and stop the machine. Once it is operating, however, the control shifts to a program stored in memory. Instruction registers within the control section are used to select individual program instructions in the sequence specified by the program, interpret each instruction, and cause the proper operating (logic, arithmetic, and transfer) circuits of the machine to be activated to carry out that instruction and proceed to the next. It is the control section working in concert with the storage that makes possible the stored-program concept of machine operation. In summary, the control element performs the following operations:

1 Selects program instructions in the proper sequence
2 Interprets each instruction as it is selected
3 Activates the appropriate circuits (logic or transfer) to carry through the instruction

Arithmetic-logic element The **arithmetic-logic element** is the set of registers and circuits where the actual arithmetic computations and the comparisons (the data processing operations) are performed.

Output element The **output element** performs a translation process that is the reverse of the input function. Data and information expressed in the electronic-impulse symbols of the machine are translated to human-sensible forms or to forms that can be used in further machine processing. Thus, the symbols stored as electrical impulses in an electronic device are used to operate a printer and cause it to print the symbol representations (letters, numbers, and special characters) for which those impulses are a code.

The central processing unit

As Figure 2.1 illustrates, three of the five functional elements of the computer are involved in processing. The processor unit is called the **central processing unit (CPU)**. The CPU includes the control element, the arithmetic-logic element, and the primary storage element. Data are entered into the storage unit. From storage they are taken and processed in the arithmetic-logic unit in accordance with the procedures specified in the program as interpreted by the control unit. Data are then returned to the storage unit for transmittal to the output unit, where they are translated into usable output. Thus the computer has the standard input/processing/output form of any data processing system.

Modern computers, however, are much more involved processors than the previous paragraph implies. Current computers have the capability to perform multiple functions at the same time.

Flow through the computer

It is particularly important to note the various paths through the computer. Refer to Figure 2.1 again. Data to be processed go from input to storage until required for processing. At that point, they are sent to the arithmetic-logic unit and are operated upon. The results are returned to storage, from which they go to output. Instructions (the program steps) start along a similar path, going from input to storage, where they are held until required for interpretation and action. At that time, they go to control and are interpreted and acted upon.

The computer will not take one single action without an instruction to do so. Normally, instructions are found in the computer's own memory. The switches and buttons on the console are only a very inefficient substitute for this normal mode of operation. Note also that instructions (the program) usually do *not* flow to output. The program remains in storage until erased or replaced by data or another program.

It is important to note that data and programs are both stored in the storage unit, represented by the electronic impulses contained there. Each machine represents human language symbols by a particular code. Instruction characters and data characters are both represented in the same code of electronic impulses. Either a data word or a program instruction is stored in each "word space" in the storage section. It is largely for this reason that the storage is organized in an identifiable way and each space is individually identified by an **address**. The address is like the number of a post office box; it serves to identify a specific place in storage so that it can be gone to (accessed). The computer can differentiate data words and program statements because, and only because, the *program* directs the computer from instruction to instruction. The instructions tell the machine where to obtain the data words to be processed. The sequence of the program is maintained by following the program from location to location in the order in which the program steps are to be accomplished.

Overlap of functions

A major reason that modern computers can do so much processing is because they perform several functions at the same time. This **overlap** of functions is made possible by the addition of buffers and controllers on devices outside the CPU. This concept is easiest to illustrate with input and output (I/O) devices. I/O devices usually involve some mechanical or manual processes. For example, cards or tape must be physically moved, keys must be punched, or printing mechanisms activated. The **buffering process** is illustrated in Figure 2.2. On input, the input device, running under independent control, tries to keep the buffer storage reservoir full at all times. The all-electronic CPU gulps data from the reservoir much more rapidly than the input device can load data into the reservoir, but it gulps data only intermittently. The input device can run continuously and thus come closer to satisfying the input demands of the CPU. On output, the output device tries to empty the reservoir into which the CPU is intermittently dumping output. As a result, all the elements of the system run pretty much continuously (see Figure 2.3).

The independent device control units also can supervise the completion of peripheral operations started by the CPU. For example, the CPU may complete a report and store it temporarily on a storage device outside the

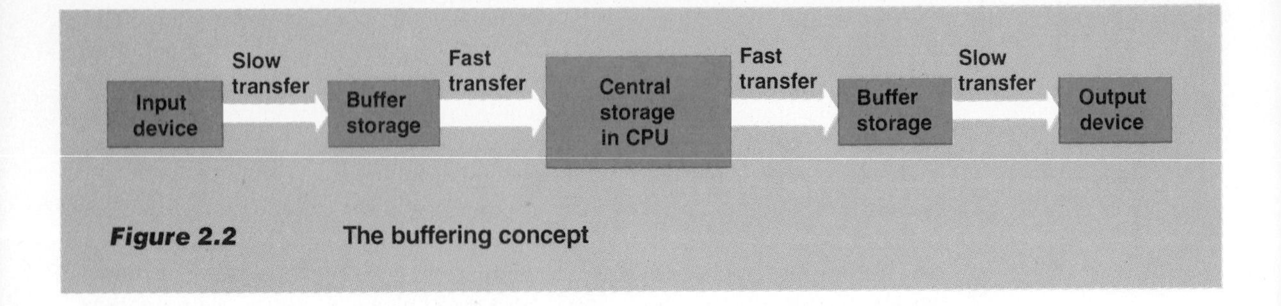

Figure 2.2 **The buffering concept**

CPU (on secondary storage). When a printer becomes available, the CPU directs a control unit to read the report from the storage device and print it on the printer. The control unit supervises the entire process and then reports back to the CPU when the process is complete.

Overlapping of computer functions allows many things to happen at once in a modern computer system. It frees the CPU from some repetitive operations and allows a greater amount of processing to be accomplished on the computer system.

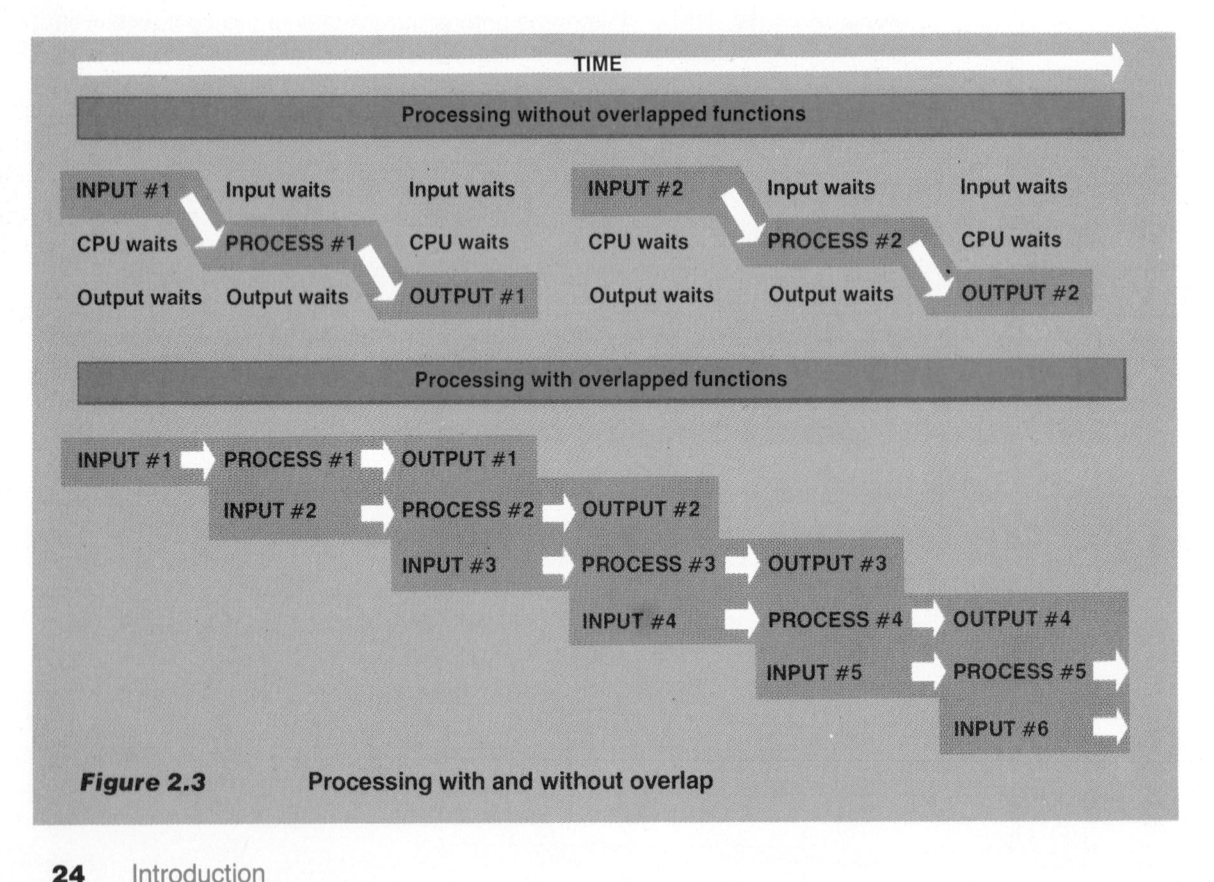

Figure 2.3 **Processing with and without overlap**

The development of computers

First generation (1946–1960)

First generation digital computers were much simpler than their current descendants. Based on vacuum tube technology, they were slow and bulky by today's standards.

Hardware The basic hardware component, or machine part, was the bulky and heat-generating vacuum tube, and the speed of operation was timed in thousandths of a second, called **milliseconds**. Primary (CPU) storage usually consisted of magnetic drums. The surface of a cylinder was coated to allow locations strung along tracks around the cylinder to be magnetized (see Figure 2.4). There was no overlap of functions. The CPU was idle over 90 percent of the time waiting for input or output to be completed.

Input and output media Punched cards were used for inputting and outputting data. Input involved key transcription from documents to cards. Output involved punching cards on the computer and then listing them on an electromechanical lister in a separate operation.

Programming Instructions were entered as a series of binary numbers (0s and 1s) in a code unique to each computer (machine language). Assemblers, which substituted mnemonics (abbreviation-like combinations of letters) for the numbers of machine language, became available during this generation.

Figure 2.4

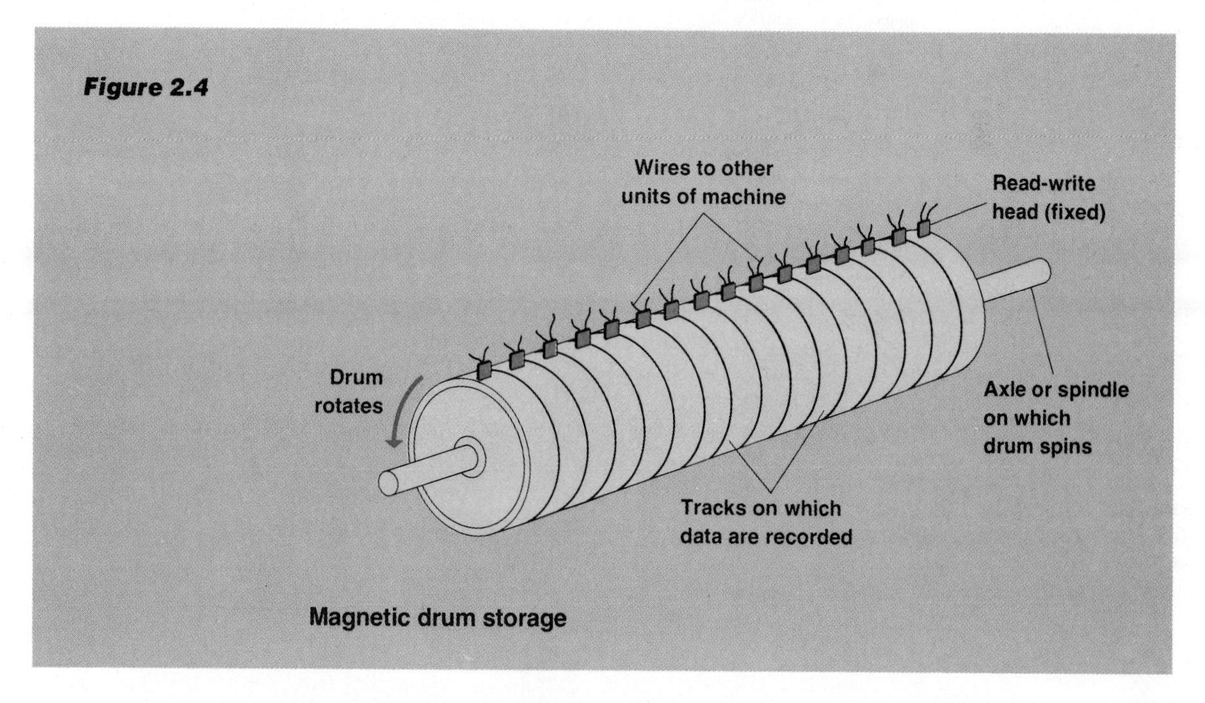

Magnetic drum storage

Applications Accounting and clerical tasks could be performed one application (job) at a time. For example, inventory update and sales analysis both use the same input (sales records) but would be programmed and run as two separate applications, or jobs.

Second generation (1960–1964)

Second generation computers were faster and less bulky, and generated less heat than their predecessors.

Hardware The basic hardware component was the transistor, and the speed of operation was timed in **microseconds** (millionths of a second). Magnetic core was the most common primary storage medium. Tiny doughnut-shaped pieces of ferrite were strung on intersecting wires in a three-dimensional grid (see Figure 2.5). They were faster and more reliable, and could be added in modules to provide an expandable memory. The addition of buffers and controllers on input and output (I/O) devices as described earlier allowed a limited overlapping of functions. Two functions (input and processing or output and processing) could be conducted at the same time, and one controller could control several I/O units so that limited **modularity** (expansion by modules) was possible. By the end of the generation, **peripheral devices** had been developed so that operations such as tape to printer or cards to tape could be started by the CPU and then run to completion without further CPU supervision. Secondary online storage (auxiliary storage directly connected to the CPU) also appeared during this generation. Magnetic tapes and fixed disks (metal platters with magnetizable surfacing) provided online access to large data files at greatly increased speeds.

Input Punched cards and magnetic tape were both used for input. Tape could be read and written much faster than cards.

Output Data was output by line printers with speeds up to 600 lines per minute.

Programming Programming "languages" were created and allowed a program to be developed in terms related to the job being programmed. The two major languages which became routinely available by the end of the second generation were FORTRAN (*FOR*mula *TRAN*slator) for scientific problems and COBOL (*CO*mmon *B*usiness-*O*riented *L*anguage) for business data processing. COBOL was file oriented, making it easier to program business applications.

Control Simple operating systems (programs called monitors) allowed the computer to process stacks of jobs. Input was accepted in stacks and processed either in order or according to some simple priority scheme. Output was similarly controlled.

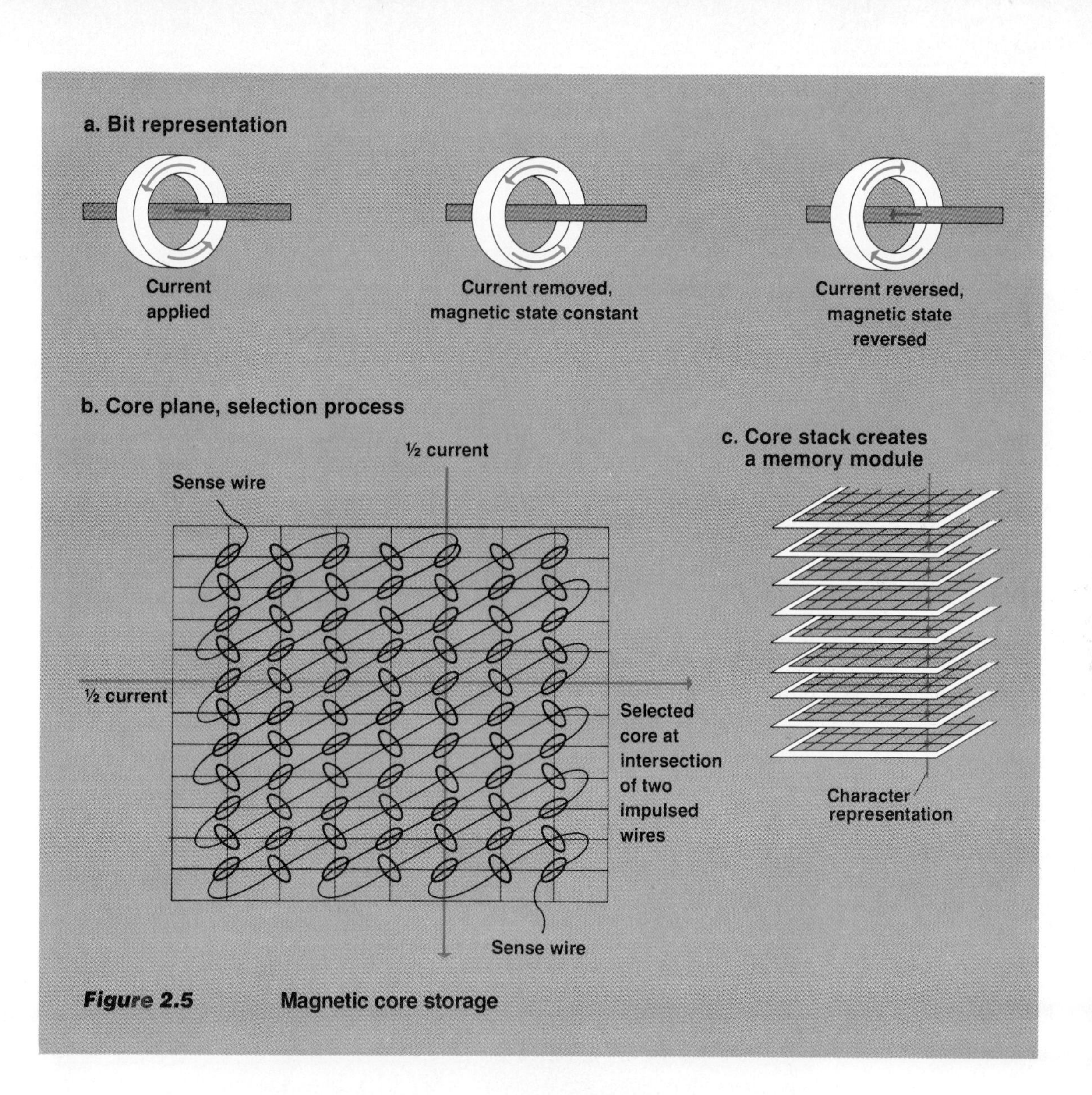

Figure 2.5 Magnetic core storage

Multiprocessing One processor (computer CPU) controlled another. Initially two computers shared a common mass-storage device such as a disk. The "master" computer loaded programs and related data (jobs) onto the disk and then directed the "slave" computer in processing them. The slave loaded results back on the disk for output under control of the master. The most sophisticated master/slave systems were simply two CPUs in the same system. The workload accomplished by the slave could be increased several times.

Applications Larger, more integrated data processing systems began to be developed. Several different applications could be handled by inputting the data only once. Systems began to be justified on the basis of their impact on management effectiveness rather than just their reduction of processing costs.

Third generation (1964–1971-2)

Miniaturization and mass production of components led to smaller, faster, and more capable computers.

Hardware Major hardware components were microcircuits—circuits printed on the coatings of tiny silicon chips (see Figure 2.6). Speed reached the point where operations were timed in **nanoseconds** (billionths of a second), about 1 million times as fast as first generation machines. Figure 2.7 attempts to make such speeds understandable. By the end of the third generation, microcircuits were beginning to replace cores as primary storage.

In this generation, overlap of functions was fully developed; one system allowed as many as 17 different peripheral operations at the same time. Modularity was also developed more fully; it became possible to assemble a complex computer with components from different manufacturers. Manufacturers of plug-compatible devices provided competition to major computer manufacturers in supplying periphal components for input, output, and storage.

Figure 2.6

An LSI chip One of these tiny silicon chips can store up to 64,000 characters of data. The advent of chip technology has reduced the size and cost of computer components and increased the speed with which computers operate. [Courtesy Mini-Micro Systems (Modern Data)]

Input There were major improvements in key input, and terminals for direct entry of data were introduced. Key-to-tape and key-to-disk systems were developed. (It is impossible to print data on a disk or tape character by character, since the tape or disk cannot be moved just one character space at a time. One must key into a buffer and then write the content of the entire buffer onto the tape or disk.)

Output Line printers, both impact type and nonimpact type, were improved to provide speeds up to 3000 lines per minute. The newest widely used output device was the cathode ray tube display. (Think of a television screen.) Computer output was also placed on microfilm.

Programming **Computer families**, sets of computers graduated in size and all from the same manufacturer, could be programmed using the same numerical instruction code (machine language). Users could adjust to a larger computing workload by shifting to a larger computer in the same family. Downward compatibility could not be guaranteed since larger computers responded to a larger set of instructions.

Figure 2.7

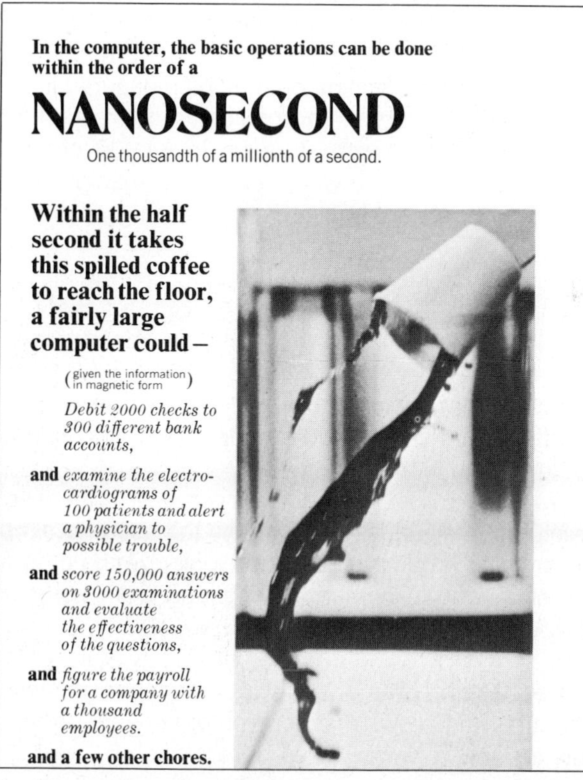

An illustration of modern computer speeds **Nanoseconds were the unit of time used to measure the operations of third generation computers. Fourth generation computers operate at an even faster rate. (Photo courtesy IBM; Design by Charles Eames)**

Control Operating systems programs provided for priority processing of job queues in several different formats. (These sophisticated supervisory programs allow multiple users to have what appears to be simultaneous use of the same computer.)

Applications Online systems and large data bases became common. Input and output from remote terminals and long-distance transfer of data were also common. Data processing systems featuring instantaneous response were widely developed, and users at remote sites could have ready access to a central computer. Figure 2.8 represents one such configuration.

Fourth generation [1973(?)-]

Third generation hardware and systems evolved into the faster, more complex, smaller, and simpler systems of the fourth generation (see Figure 2.9). There is a gray area between the third and fourth generations but, in general, fourth generation systems have the following characteristics.

Hardware Major hardware components are the even smaller and faster large-scale integrated (LSI) and very large-scale integrated (VLSI) circuits. A complete computer, including key input and printed output, can be carried in a large briefcase. Large computers perform millions of transactions per second with basic machine operations measured in **picoseconds** (trillionths of a second). Primary storage takes the form of superminiaturized microcircuits. One tiny chip can store up to 64,000 characters of data. Another development is **bubble memory**, which manipulates what look like microscopic bubbles in a thin film deposited on garnet crystals.

Input Trends established in the third generation continue. There is widespread use of direct online input through a variety of general-purpose and special-purpose terminals that communicate directly with the computer.

Output Faster (nonimpact) printers have been and are being developed. Use of displays and computer output microfilm is increasing.

Programming Better languages continue to be developed. The newest are "structured" languages which allow the use of a simpler logical structure in programming (structured program logic). Some programming features, such as system supervisors and language translators, now are available as hardware components (firmware), particularly for microcomputers.

Control Many types of software that control systems are being offered as hardware. This allows microcomputer vendors, for example, to offer components for only a few hundred dollars each that will greatly increase what a micro can do.

Applications Computers are now so common as to be unavoidable. For example, data from retail sales transactions in most large stores are

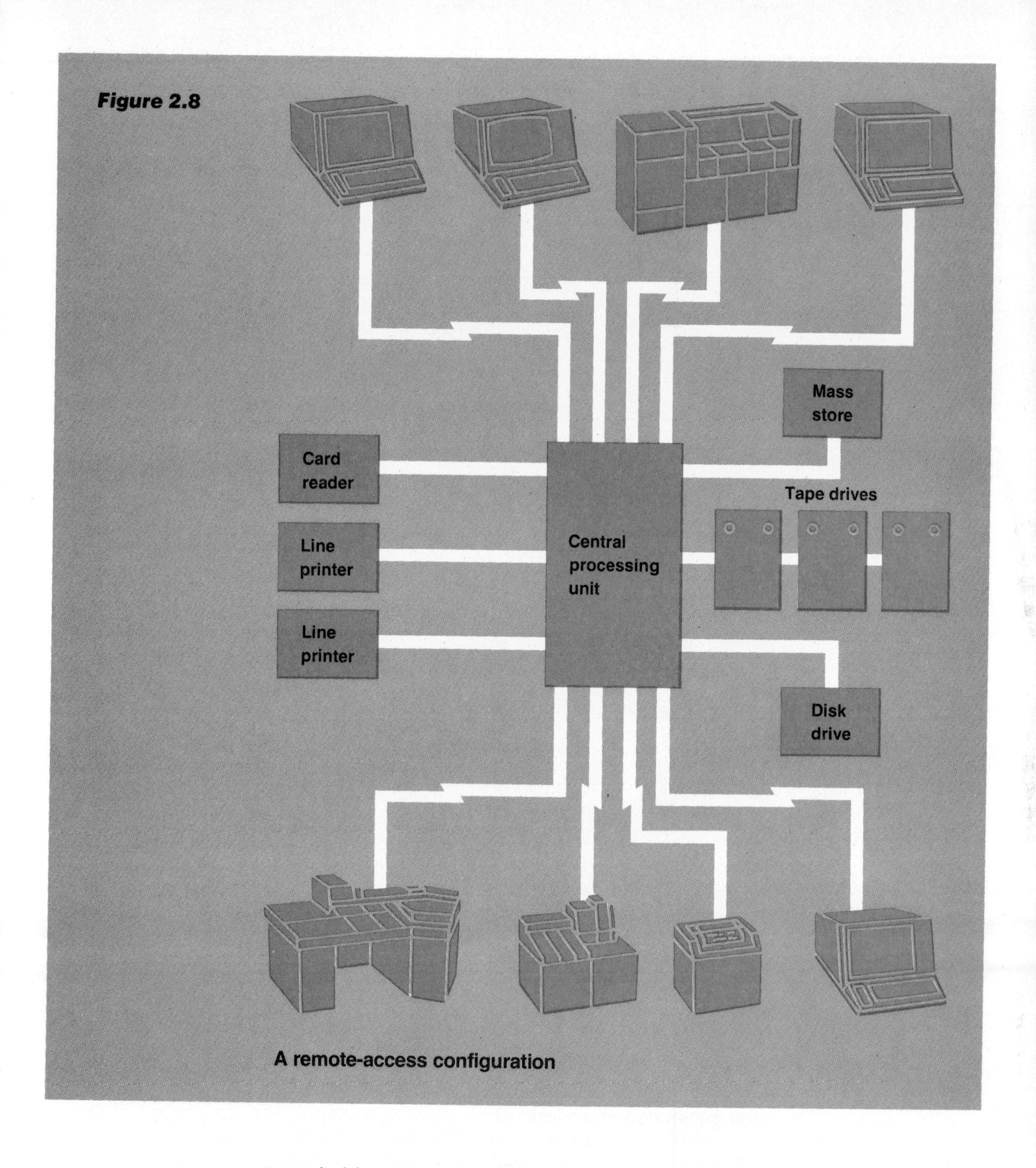

Figure 2.8

A remote-access configuration

recorded by special devices and entered directly into a computer system. Realtors locate appropriate houses for clients by asking a computer to match the client to available properties. Executives, secretaries, and clerical workers all use the computer as a business tool. For example, the executive

Figure 2.9

First generation and fourth generation computers The top photo shows a bulky first generation machine, the Remington Rand UNIVAC, which was introduced in the 1950s. The bottom photo, in contrast, shows a Hewlett-Packard HP-83 desk-top computer, which is not much larger than a conventional typewriter. Note the small cathode ray tube display on the left side of the HP-83. (Top photo courtesy Remington Rand; bottom photo courtesy Hewlett-Packard)

retrieves and analyzes data to obtain information to guide business decisions, secretaries use storage and editing systems to provide word processing support for their activities, and other clerical workers enter transactions data at online terminals. Small businessmen use microcomputers as sophisticated accounting systems which develop and retain valuable management information and accounting reports at a lower cost than accountants and analysts.

Figure 2.10 shows a proposed network for the educational-processing function of a higher education system in a single state. The state contains two major universities and several smaller state colleges in its system. The two largest institutions and the office of education in the state capital each has a large computer, and each of the smaller institutions has a smaller computer. All the computers would be tied together by a network of telephone lines. The power of the big computers would thus be made available to all the institutions of higher learning in the state. In addition, direct transmission of large masses of data between computers in the system would be possible. Research, educational, and administrative functions within the system could be enhanced and coordinated. Excess computing power at the larger installations would be made available to users located at the small installations. This system design can be accomplished easily with current technology. Such networks are already operating in other areas.

Distributed processing Perhaps the most significant change in the fourth generation has been the development of decentralized and distributed data processing systems. In true distributed data processing systems, geographically dispersed computers (usually minicomputers) are connected in a network with each other and (usually) with a central computer (most often a large CPU called a mainframe). The part of the processing that is purely local or has to do only with data acquisition is carried out locally. The basic data that are retained (after the initial local processing) and the results of the local processing are transmitted to the central computer for further processing. A distributed processing network puts some computing power under the control of the local manager. The systems that result are usually more accessible and more acceptable to users in the local unit.

Decentralized processing Minicomputers can now be very powerful computers but are relatively low in cost. This has caused some corporations to develop dispersed data processing systems with essentially independent computer systems at local sites. The expanded power of microcomputers has contributed to this trend and is also providing low-cost intelligent terminals for distributed systems. (Both distributed and decentralized systems will be discussed in Chapter 7.)

Computer generations summarized

The characteristics of computers in each of the four generations are summarized in Table 2.1, where some definite trends can be clearly seen. First, computers have been getting faster. Current machines perform in the

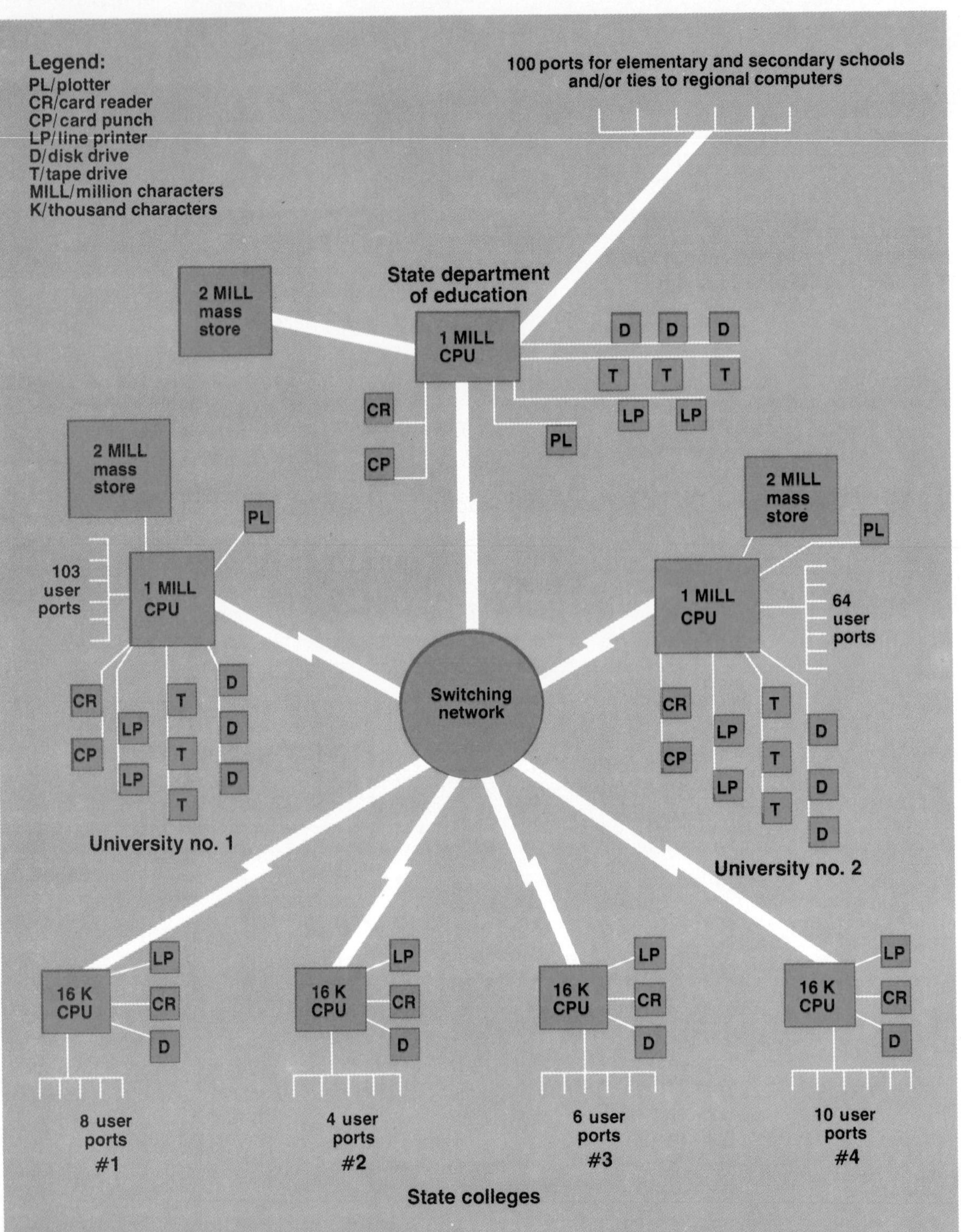

Figure 2.10 A computer sharing network

CHARACTERISTIC	FIRST 1946–1960	SECOND 1960–1964	THIRD 1964–1971-2	FOURTH 1973(?)–
Major electronic component	Vacuum tubes	Transistors	Microcircuits (integrated circuits)	Miniaturized microcircuits (LSI and VLSI)
Internal speed measure	Thousandths of a second	Millionths of a second	Billionths of a second	Trillionths of a second
Primary (CPU) storage	Drum, special devices	Core	Microcircuits, core	Microcircuits, bubble
Secondary storage	Almost none	Tape, fixed disk	Disk packs, fixed disks, drums	Microcircuits, fixed disks, disk packs, bubble
Major input devices	Punched cards	Punched cards, magnetic tape	Key-to-disk and key-to-tape recorders, punched cards, terminals	Terminals, incremental recorders
Major output devices	Punched cards	Punched cards, magnetic tape, line printers (impact)	Impact line printers, nonimpact line printers, displays	Nonimpact line and page printers, displays, impact line printers
Operating control	Manual	Queue monitor	Priority processing (software)	Sophisticated software and hardware
Major programming features	Instructions in binary code, assemblers	Job-related programming (software)	Program compatibility in computer families (software)	Structured languages and firmware (software and hardware)
Modularity	None	Limited	Extensive	Routine
Overlapping	None	Limited	Extensive	Routine
Number of systems installed (end of period)	3,000–4,000	20,000–25,000	80,000–85,000	350,000–375,000 (1981)

Table 2.1 **Characteristics of the Computer Generations**

range of 1 to 10 million instructions per second. First generation machines carried out less than 100 instructions per second. Second, computer hardware is getting smaller. A 64,000-character primary memory was about the upper limit of first generation machines. Most of today's microcomputers can have that much primary memory. Total online storage can store billions of characters available at electronic speeds to the computer or computers in the system. Third, computer systems are becoming more complex, involving multiple peripheral devices and remote online input in many forms within a single system.

One wonders what may come in the future. Bubble memories are increasing in use and may soon be cheap enough to replace microcircuits.

Laser and light memories involving film technology have been touted for some time as the next wave, but several implementation dates have come and gone with announcement of varying degrees of failure to reach full maturity of the processes.

Advantages and disadvantages of computers as data processors

Regardless of the complexity of computers and the uncertainty of what is to come, computer use continues to increase. Businesses large and small are turning to the computer as *the* data processing system. It is undeniable that the popularity of computers grows out of the advantages they offer: their speed, reliability, and ability to perform complex processing. The tools of modern management science would be crude indeed without the computer.

The major disadvantages of computers is that complex programming is difficult and the initial cost of a working system is high. Computers employ such basic logic that using that simple logic to develop sophisticated systems is not easy. The cost of the hardware is now only about one-fourth the cost of the software. Installation, programming, and implementation costs make computers difficult to justify on the basis of cost alone.

Summary

A computer is a symbol-manipulating machine which adds, subtracts, multiplies, divides, makes comparisons, and transfers symbols from place to place. It is controlled by programs—sequences of instructions—stored in its memory, the same memory where it stores raw data and interim and final results. The instructions comprising the program can be modified or replaced even while the machine is operating and even under its own control. This means that the machine can perform any symbol manipulation people can devise. Since it is a machine that operates electronically, it can perform its feats at very high speeds practically without error if the program and the data are correct.

As a data processing system, the computer inputs data, processes them, and outputs results. These basic functions are performed by five basic components: input, storage, arithmetic-logic, control, and output. Current machines are comprised of sets of devices for performing input, output, and storage under the control of a processor which is responsible for following and performing a program of instruction. Buffers and controllers allow several functions to be performed at the same time. These configurations can involve remote input and output, the use of specialized input and output devices, and the sharing of the computer by multiple users, most of whom are located away from the computer room. Individual systems can be joined together in networks, sharing processing chores.

Key terms

Define the following terms as briefly as possible and then in a short paragraph, clarify each definition.

Address
Arithmetic-logic element
Binary number system
Bubble memory
Buffering process
Central processing unit (CPU)
Computer
Computer family
Control element
Input element
Microsecond
Millisecond
Modularity
Nanosecond
Output element
Overlap
Peripheral device
Picosecond
Program
Storage element
Stored program
Translation

Discussion questions

1 List and define the major functional components of a computer, including the exact functions performed by each component.
2 What is the stored-program concept?
3 Both data and program instructions are placed in the storage component of a computer. How are they differentiated by the computer?
4 What is an automatic electronic digital computer? Try to put the answer in your own words even if it requires several sentences.
5 How has the development of input and output buffers extended the ways in which computers can be used?
6 When inputted through the input unit, where do
 a the instructions go?
 b the data go?
7 What is the CPU? What jobs does it carry out?
8 If a mass-storage device such as a large fixed disk unit were added to a computer, would it be part of the CPU? Explain.
9 Turn to Figure 1.1 on page 9 and prepare a parallel diagram of a computer. What are the three corresponding sections?
10 How has the introduction of less expensive, smaller storage devices with larger capacities affected business data processing?

Exercises

1 Locate and visit a computerized data processing installation in your area. Is the computer system providing
   - **a** centralized processing?
   - **b** decentralized processing?
   - **c** distributed processing?

2 Visit a local computer store where microcomputers are sold and obtain brochures and other explanatory material on a microcomputer-based business data processing system.

How to Make a Realtor Smile

Charles Wikoff [of Missoula Mont.] is smiling. He's smiling because automation is enabling him to spend more time evaluating investment possiblities and less time preparing reports.

As a result, his clients at Wikoff Realty are receiving more extensive financial documents including detailed portfolios, cash flow tables, rate of return schedules, tax situation analysis and other vital investment reports. Previously, these reports were prepared manually, involving lots of paperwork, long hours and comparatively small returns. Because paperwork was taking its toll, Wikoff decided to automate his report preparation.

Through Alpha Omega, Inc., the authorized Digital Equipment Corp. distributor in Missoula, Wikoff ordered Dec's microcomputer-based WS78 word processing system. . . . Alpha Omega installed the Real-Estate software package and a freelance programmer developed custom accounting and financial programs.

Wilkoff Realty devotes itself almost exclusively to commercial properties such as office complexes, shopping centers, mobile home parks and industrial buildings. The agency has around 35 clients, all of them repetitive.

Fitting Needs

When a client is interested in purchasing a property, it is up to Wikoff to locate the property that is best suited to that client's needs and financial requirements.

"Before we installed our system, running down all the information needed to take a client through a purchase or a sale was tedious," Wikoff explained. "I had to figure the best move for him to make financially, then decide what he needed for tax purposes, the kind of terms we should go after, the amount of the down payment, everything. That invovlved going through the customer's entire file and doing all the calculations on paper. Then, of course, there was the matter of locating the property that best met his needs."

Installing the DEC WS78 with the new software package changed all that because

Source: "Report Prepared via WP Put Smile on Realtor's Face," *Computerworld,* September 7, 1981, p. 67–68.

all client records and programs are on floppy disks. The programs include cash flow analysis, exchange basis, an exchange worksheet, portfolio analysis, individual tax analysis, an internal rate of return, a financial management rate of return and amortization schedules.

The programs and the forms associated with them may be viewed on the terminal at any time, Initially, Wikoff enters all pertinent data regarding the client: name, address, income tax situation, properties owned and other factors. Information can be deleted, added, moved or duplicated through the use of special keys adjacent to the main keyboard.

Information common to a number of documents, such as name and address, need only be entered once; the WS78 programs automatically insert the information in the correct location on all other records. Similarly, data is appended to all pertinent files as it is keyed.

Routine analysis

Wikoff routinely reviews and analyzes client investments. In the portfolio analysis program, for example, every property is detailed: its description, when it was purchased, amount of purchase, payments remaining and the amount of income it earns the client. A complete examination, which once took several hours, now can be accomplished in about 20 minutes.

The system also makes all calculations. "A cash flow analysis used to take 45 minutes manually," Wikoff noted. "With the WS78, I can now do them in about three minutes." The cash flow analysis program is useful for improving a client's financial standing. Resident in the WS78's files, it details the amount of money each client earns from his various holdings, how much he pays out and his cash position. By comparing cash flow analysis with portfolio rate of return and the tax analysis, Wikoff can deduce adjustments necessary for his clients' portfolios.

"A complete amortization schedule can be prepared and printed in about five minutes."

"We also used to estimate tax brackets," he continued. "Now we enter exact income, dependents, marital status and deductions. The system quickly calculates the person's tax liability so we can judge the impact of a particular investment."

DEC WS78 system has not only expanded Wikoff Realty's capability, it has also improved the efficiency of the company's office management. When he bought the real estate software package, Wikoff looked ahead to increased business volume and had a program written specifically to help run the company.

Wikoff said the unit has more than paid for itself in the time it has saved him and the opportunities it has opened up.

Special Option

Can Computers Think?

Computer "intelligence"

The thinking machine appears frequently in science fiction, and the popular press also often describes large computers as "giant brains." So one wonders, can computers be given independent intelligence? Can a computer think? In Chapter 2, we defined the computer as a machine that manipulates symbols according to the rules of Boolean algebra, but we also indicated that the computer can follow complex instructions stored in its memory even to the point of changing those instructions. The computer is capable of making decisions, choosing its next action on the basis of what is now true. Can it, then, be given the ability to learn, to reflect, and to make independent choices—choices that have not been fully predefined?

Experiments in artificial intelligence have progressed to the point that robots have been designed which have, in effect, a will to live. These mobile microcomputers seek out a power source when their batteries need recharging. Is that intelligence?

Computers also have been programmed to learn from experience in limited ways. For example, computers have been programmed to play checkers and chess. Two basic approaches to playing an effective game are available. One technique attempts to look ahead a given number of moves to judge the effectiveness of each available move at any point in the game.

"Trees" are constructed that can indicate finally which initial move will be most effective. Such a tree is illustrated in Figure S1.1. Note how rapidly the number of alternatives to be considered expands at each level of the tree. Moreover, Figure S1.1 understates the problem since we have allowed no more than three alternatives at each level. This is the major problem with the brute-force approach: it uses up memory at an alarming rate. It also could require years to fully evaluate the possible moves of a chess game.

A more profitable approach is to teach the computer to categorize situations in some fashion that allows the decision tree to be trimmed to a manageable number of branches at each level. If programmed properly, the computer learns to play a better game.

This brief discussion of the computer's limited abilities should not be misunderstood. The computer is still only a machine that does just what it is told. It can only manipulate symbols within a framework of logic provided by its human programmer. It can follow through that logic more accurately, faithfully, and quickly than can its human master. It cannot, however, improve upon the logic reflected by its controlling programs.

Computing versus thinking

These facts lead to one and only one conclusion. Only to the extent that we can define thinking as a step-by-step process can the computer be made to "think." However, we must recognize that the computer is a much better

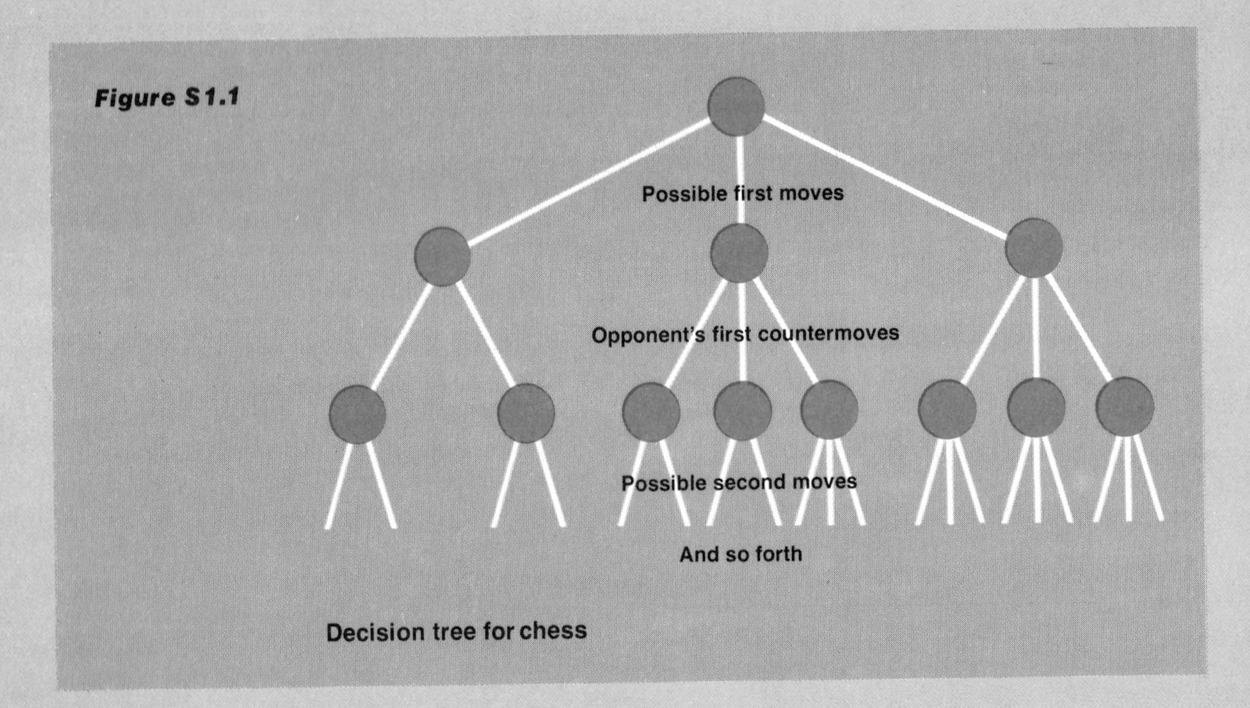

Figure S1.1

Decision tree for chess

manipulator of symbols than human beings. If a person can define tasks involving only symbol manipulation, the computer can perform them. In this way, the computer can extend the power of human intellect. Human beings can often define symbol manipulation processes that they cannot carry through either in a reasonable time or with sufficient accuracy. Without the computer to carry out the necessary voluminous calculations, we could not, for example, adequately plan a trip to another planet, and without the computer to evaluate swiftly the progress of the trip, we could not carry out such a trip after it was planned.

Creative thinking, on the other hand, is more difficult to define. Computers have been programmed to "draw" pictures by random selection of lines or colors subject to broad limits about which combinations of lines and colors are acceptable. Similarly, computers have been programmed to "write" stories and plays by randomly selecting lines of dialogue and action within the constraints imposed by a story line. If the accidental production of acceptable results is creativity, then computers are creative. Again, however, they only manipulate symbols as instructed by some person. The only creative element is the ability to make (within limits) a random choice of symbols.

In summary, a computer can think in only a limited sense because human beings understand the process of thinking to only a limited degree. However, to the extent that thinking can be defined as an explicit manipulation of symbols, computers can be made to think. Therefore, to the extent that thinking can be defined as the rational manipulation of symbols for problem solving, computers can think.

Battling the Electronic Mind

At home on a winter's evening, Burton J. Vincent, founder and chairman of the investment-banking firm of Vincent Chesley & Co. in Chicago, was matching wits over a chessboard with a new opponent named Boris. At a crucial point someone in the next room started hammering, whereupon Boris remarked, "WE COULD USE LESS NOISE!" The comment was coincidental. It is one of 80 quips the Boris 2.5, a computerized chess set, can flash across its electronic display at random. The gimmick, designed to entertain the solitary player, points up how close machines have come to aping humans since the first computer chess game went on sale in 1977. Another game, the Voice Chess Challenger, communicates moves audibly, in any of four languages.

But how well can the computer play chess, a game long described as "the art of human reason"? This question continues to challenge computer scientists, who for 30 years have been using the game to develop artificial intelligence—the computer's capacity to perform operations analogous to human learning and decision-making. In 1977, a program designed at Northwestern teamed up with what was then the world's most powerful computer, Control Data's Cyber 176, to defeat a couple of chess experts. Since then, giant computers have taken games against some of the top-ranked players in the world. Edward Fredkin, an MIT professor who runs a small computer company, is sponsoring a $100,000 prize for the first person to design a program that can win the World Chess Championship.

Chess players have been arguing passionately about whether humans should let cybernetic competitors into their game. The U.S. Chess Federation accepts computers in tournaments but seldom lets them play humans for prize money.

The computer chess games available on the market play below the expert level and so far have failed to entice players of high caliber. James T. Sherwin, GAF's executive vice president for legal and investment services, is one of 32 Americans ranked as international masters. Having defeated such greats as Samuel Reshevsky and Bobby Fischer, Sherwin doubts that a mere machine could provide the competitive stimulus on which he thrives.

"The element of human combat is lacking," Sherwin says. "A really good chess player has got to have a killer instinct like any athlete. You are always thinking about whether you are getting your opponent down. But how do you psych out a computer? You can't exhaust the possibilities in

---

Source: Marilyn Wellemeyer, "Battling the Electronic Mind," *Fortune,* February 23, 1981, 27–37.

chess through scientific analysis. You have to rely on intuition and talent, and ultimately those elements conspire to achieve beauty. Chess is an art form that can only be created with someone on the other side of the board building tension. The distillation of all your experience and some creativity, some unknown factor, are at work, and that would be terribly difficult to program."

Even so, computer specialists keep trying, and talented programmers intimately acquainted with the game are much in demand. Kathe Spracklen, a former tournament player, and her husband, Dan, quit their jobs as computer specialists at Burroughs and Univac to design chess programs. Four products made by three companies now use the Spracklens' programs. These include the Boris 2.5 made by Applied Concepts and the Sensory Chess Challenger just introduced by the company's chief competitor, Fidelity Electronics. While the Spracklens collect royalties on Boris, Fidelity has put them under contract, so they can no longer design programs for other companies.

Some programs run on devices used exclusively for chess; others can be used on general-purpose computers. All play according to the same basic principles.

To choose a move, the computer goes through a two-part process. First it laboriously scans all available moves and considers the opponent's possible responses. The number of moves a computer can examine depends on the size of its memory and the speed of play. If, for example, the computer has a choice of 30 moves and it looks only three turns ahead, it must examine 30 × 30 × 30, or 27,000, possibilities.

Unable to sacrifice

Next the computer evaluates each potential move according to pieces defended or captured and the position attained on the board. The program assigns different values to each piece—a pawn may be worth only 1, while a rook may count for 20. To assess the more complex factor of position, the program assigns a positive value to the squares that are important to control, and it accentuates the positive. It may take ten to 50 times longer to evaluate a position than the gain or loss of pieces. An experienced player sometimes sacrifices a piece to improve his position, but microprocessors can't make this sophisticated trade-off. Computers tend to favor capturing material at the expense of strategic position.

All the programs can compete at several skill levels. Boris, for instance, plays at six levels, from an estimated U.S. Chess Federation rating of 1000 (novice) to 2000 (expert). Playing at a high level, a small computer may take 48 hours to do the millions of calculations required before it can make a move. Players may grow impatient waiting, but this is not the chief complaint of Joseph Callaway, chairman of Montgomery Ward Life Insurance Co. and a highly ranked competitor. In a postal chess game with a convict, he once waited months for a response, only to learn the man had escaped.

Most computers play conservative and predictable opening and middle games and a weak end game. The programs may have surprising faults. The Sensory Chess Challenger can't checkmate an opponent's lone king with its own king and rook—child's play for the human. Ralph Wanger, president of the Acorn Fund in Chicago, occasionally puts a Microchess cassette program on his Commodore Pet 2001 at the office. "At the top level, using an obscure version of the King's Gambit, I have found that I can capture the queen in six moves," he says. "The computer hasn't wised up to that."

For all its shortcomings, the computer's consistency, thoroughness, patience, and availability can make it a good teacher. Burton Vincent started experimenting with computer chess four years ago after his regular opponent died. In the two weeks after he got Boris for Christmas, he spent 100 hours grappling with his new machine. Vincent's rating is 1386, just above the average tournament player's. He always beat early models of the Chess Challenger, but Boris took him in their first game. Now when Vincent wins, Boris acknowledges defeat with several gracious beeps and a flash of CONGRATULATIONS! "Nothing really compares with playing another person," says Vincent, "but playing Boris can be a good substitute."

Part 2

Data Processing Hardware

Chapter 3

Computer Hardware Basics

Outline

Electronic data representation
- Two-state electronics
- Binary number system
- Bits and bytes
- Parity bit
- Octal numbers
- Hexadecimal numbers

Data coding in the computer
- True binary
- Binary-coded decimal (BCD)
- Extended binary-coded decimal interchange code (EBCDIC)
- American standard code for information interchange (ASCII)
- Zone bits
- Packed binary
- Floating-point binary

Primary computer memory
- Fixed- and variable-word lengths
- Volatile and nonvolatile memory
- Read-only memory
- Scratch-pad (cache) memory

Primary memory hardware
- Characteristics of magnetic core memory
- Integrated circuits, LSI, and VLSI
  - Characteristics of integrated circuit memories
- Bubble memory
  - Characteristics of bubble memory

We learned in Chapter 2 that automatic electronic computers manipulate symbolic representations of data with electronic components. These components, together with the devices used for input, output, and storage, constitute computer **hardware**. In other words, computer hardware is the machine devices in a computer system, including the central processing unit, devices for data preparation, data input, secondary storage, and output, and devices for intercommunication among hardware components.

The first part of this chapter explains how data can be represented by the two-state devices of a computer and discusses the binary number system. Data coding within the computer is explained in the second part of the chapter. The last section defines some important characteristics of memory devices (primary memory) within the CPU.

Electronic data representation

Two-state electronics

In Chapter 2 we stated that electronic devices are, by their nature, two-state devices. Vacuum tubes and transistors are really electronic circuits: Just as a switch is either on or off, a circuit is either open or closed. Similarly, we noted, magnetized surfaces (drums, disks, tapes) are partitioned into tiny areas, each of which is either magnetized or not magnetized. A location on a punched card or a punched paper tape either contains a hole or it does not. At a particular moment in time, a point on a wire either has a current flowing through it or it does not. Thus the code used to represent data in electronic systems is the base-2, on-off, or binary number system.

Binary number system

The binary number system, as we learned, uses just two digits, 0 (zero) and 1 (one). In contrast, the decimal system uses ten digits (0, 1, 2, 3, 4, 5, 6, 7, 8, and 9). The decimal system thus uses a base of ten (10), as opposed to the binary system's base 2. Each "place" in the decimal system represents a power of ten. For example, the number 2,943,061,578 can be broken down:

Counter	Counted value	Decimal representation
2	10^9	2,000,000,000
9	10^8	900,000,000
4	10^7	40,000,000
3	10^6	3,000,000
0	10^5	000,000
6	10^4	60,000
1	10^3	1,000
5	10^2	500
7	10^1	70
8	10^0	8
The total is the number		2,943,061,578

Or it can be broken down as follows:

Meaning of place	Billions	100s of Millions	Tens of Millions	Millions	100s of Thousands	Tens of Thousands	Thousands	Hundreds	Tens	Units
	10^9	10^8	10^7	10^6	10^5	10^4	10^3	10^2	10^1	10^0
Counter	2	9	4	3	0	6	1	5	7	8

Binary representation substitutes 2 for 10 as the base, but otherwise works the same way as the decimal (base 10) system. For example, the decimal number 23:

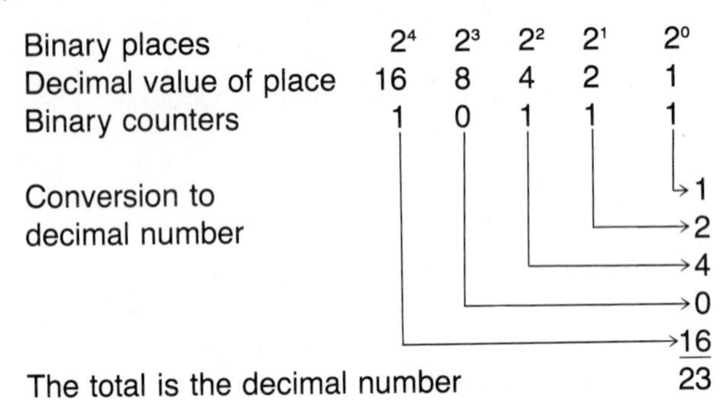

But what about fractions, that is, numbers less than 1? Negative exponents indicate numbers less than 1, so in the decimal system, what the number 0.261 represents is shown at the top of the next page.

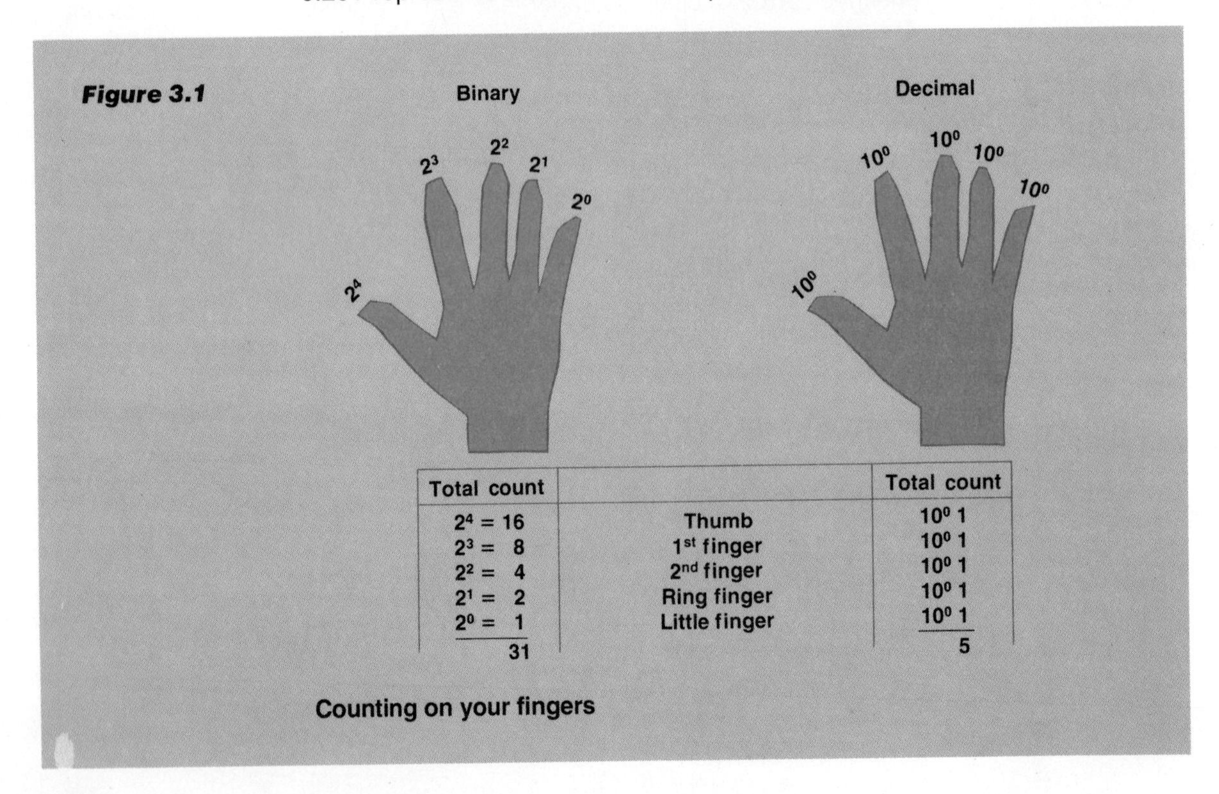

Figure 3.1 Counting on your fingers

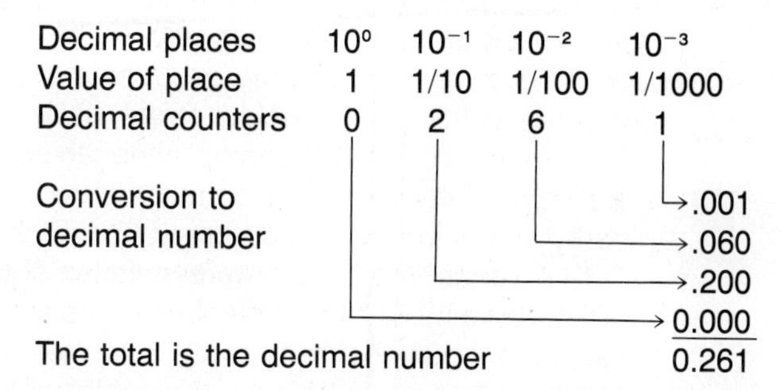

Fractions in binary appear a little more complex but follow the same process. For example:

Place	**Fraction**	**Decimal value**
2^{-1}	1/2	.5
2^{-2}	1/4	.25
2^{-3}	1/8	.125
2^{-4}	1/16	.0625
2^{-5}	1/32	.03125

The decimal number 0.875 would be represented in binary as:

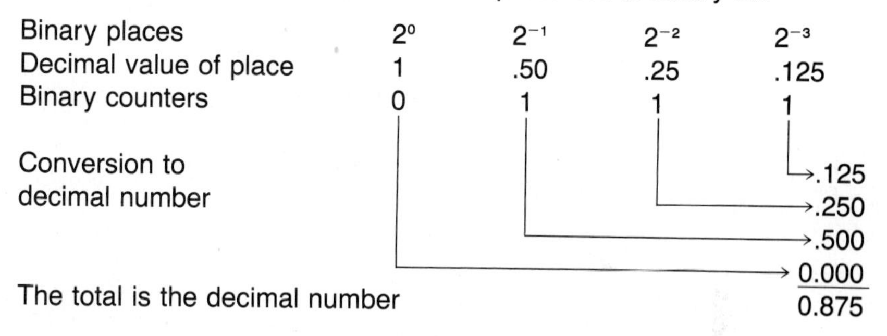

For those of us who have used only the decimal number system, binary seems very cumbersome. But think, how far can you count on the fingers of one hand? In the decimal system, to 5. In the binary system, to 31 as seen in Figure 3.1. When counting on your fingers, you are using a two-state system: a finger up is a 1, a finger down is a 0. So, obviously, binary is a more efficient number system when a two-state representation is used.

Bits and bytes

In data representation, we call the smallest unit of counting a bit. The word *bit* comes from a contraction of *bi*nary digi*t*. A **bit** is a binary 0 (turned off) or 1 (turned on).

A **byte** is a collection of bits, usually 8. Although there are some computer systems that use some other number of bits in a byte, when *byte* is used in this text it will refer to 8 binary digits unless it is specifically stated otherwise. Generally, a byte tends to represent one character, but not always, as we will see below. However, up to this time, we have used the word *character* to mean one 8-bit byte.

Parity bit

In addition to the bits that represent a byte, or character, each byte in most computers has one or more **parity bit(s)** (also called check bits). The purpose of this bit is to detect errors that arise during internal data transfers. Each byte is required to contain either an odd or even number of 1 *(on)* bits. If the representational code contains an odd number of *on* (1) bits and even parity is required, the added parity bit will be turned *on* (set to 1).

To illustrate, the binary representation of the decimal number 25 is 11001 which contains 3, an odd number, of 1 bits. To obtain even parity, the added parity bit would be set as a 1 and we would have 11001 1. Suppose, however, that an *on* bit were accidentally shut off. (This may happen, rarely, when an electrical current is interrupted for a fraction of a second.) We might end up with 10001 1, an odd number of *on* bits. The computer would then indicate that it had received incorrect data.

Octal numbers

The octal, or base-8, number system has been used as a shorthand way of representing binary numbers. In the **octal number system,** each position represents a power of 8 and is counted 0 to 7 times. For example, the decimal number 2,643 would be represented in octal as 5123.

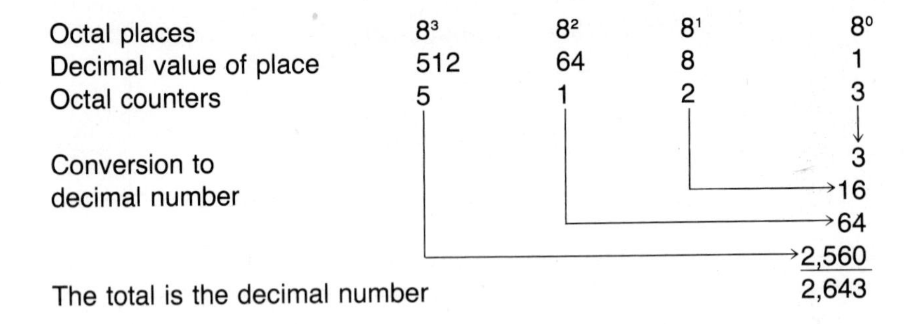

The reason *octal* has been substituted for *binary* is that 1 octal digit can represent 8 different values. Three binary digits are required to represent 8 values. Conversion between them is accomplished by representing each group of 3 binary digits as an octal digit using the following code:

Octal	Binary
0	000
1	001
2	010
3	011
4	100
5	101
6	110
7	111

Thus, the binary number 111010101 would be written as 725 in octal when coded by this method:

111	010	101
7	2	5

Can you show that the decimal equivalent of both these numbers is 469?

Hexadecimal numbers

If a base-8 system represents binary digits efficiently, why not try a base-16 system? *Hexadecimal* is derived from the Greek word for *six* and the Latin word for *ten,* thus it means "sixteen." The developers of the **hexadecimal system** extended the decimal digits, 0 through 9, to 16 counting symbols by using the letters A through F to represent the added values of 10 to 15. Thus, the complete system is as follows:

Decimal	0	1	2	3	4	5	6	7	8	9	10	11	12	13	14	15
Hexadecimal	0	1	2	3	4	5	6	7	8	9	A	B	C	D	E	F

The representation of the decimal number 2,643 in hexadecimal would be A53:

Hexadecimal places	16^2	16^1	16^0
Decimal value of place	256	16	1
Hexadecimal counters	A(10)	5	3
Conversion to decimal number			3
			80
			2,560
The total is the decimal number			2,643

What would the hexadecimal number FADE represent in decimal (base 10)?

$$
\begin{aligned}
F &= 15 \times 16^3 = 61{,}440 \\
A &= 10 \times 16^2 = 2{,}560 \\
D &= 13 \times 16 = 208 \\
E &= 14 \times 1 = 14 \\
\text{Total} & \quad 64{,}222
\end{aligned}
$$

As a shorthand for the binary system, the hexadecimal system converts each 4 binary digits to a hexadecimal digit. Note that 4 binary digits can represent the decimal numbers up to 15. Thus,

Decimal	**Binary**	**Hexadecimal**
0	0000	0
1	0001	1
2	0010	2
3	0011	3
4	0100	4
5	0101	5

Decimal	Binary	Hexadecimal
6	0110	6
7	0111	7
8	1000	8
9	1001	9
10	1010	A
11	1011	B
12	1100	C
13	1101	D
14	1110	E
15	1111	F

The binary number 000111010101 would be 1D5 in hexadecimal and 469 in decimal:

Binary	0001	1101	0101
Hexadecimal	1	D	5

Converting the hexadecimal to decimal:

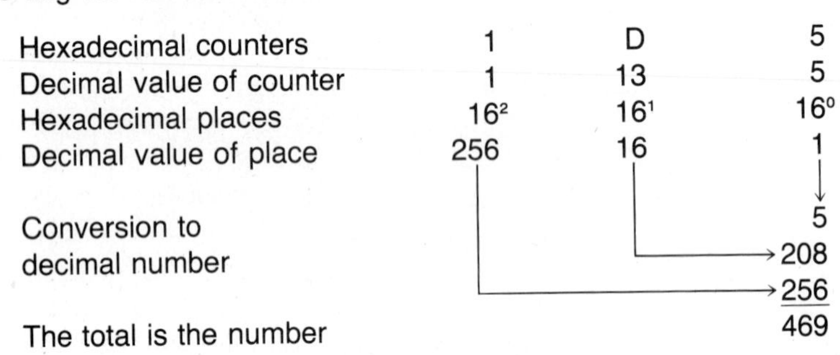

Hexadecimal counters	1	D	5
Decimal value of counter	1	13	5
Hexadecimal places	16^2	16^1	16^0
Decimal value of place	256	16	1
Conversion to decimal number			5
			208
			256
The total is the number			469

It was demonstrated above that the decimal value of the binary number 000111010101 is also 469. Note that the hexadecimal conversion eliminates 6 of the 9 steps that would be needed to convert from binary to decimal. After reading the next section, you will note, too, that the EBCDIC character *A* is much easier to recognize as C1 than as 11000001.

Data coding in the computer

True binary

The most obvious internal coding to use in a computer is simple or **true binary.** In this system, each component state represents a binary digit (bit), a 0 or a 1. A group of bits, usually 8 or 9, makes up a byte. Each byte represents an alphabetic, numeric, or special character. A computer **word** is a collection of bytes handled as a unit within the system. When using binary representation, each word usually contains a fixed number of bits representing an integral number of bytes. The number of bits in a computer word usually varies from 8 to 64, with only a few of the largest machines using more than 36 bits for a word. The maximum decimal number that can be represented by different common word lengths is:

Word length in bits	Maximum decimal number represented
8	255
12	4,095
16	65,535
24	16,777,215
32	4,294,967,295
36	68,719,476,735

Only numeric data (positive whole numbers) can be represented in true binary. Since we need negative numbers, fractions, and alphabetic and special characters as well, other codes have been developed.

Binary-coded decimal (BCD)

Each binary digit (bit) can represent either a 0 or a 1, that is, two things. Adding a bit allows four "things" to be represented, that is four recognizably different combinations of 0s and 1s are possible with 2 binary digits (00, 01, 10, 11). If 3 bits are used, eight recognizable combinations are possible (000, 001, 010, 011, 100, 101, 110, 111). Generally, each time a binary digit is added, the number of recognizable combinations is doubled. If n represents the number of bits, 2^n represents the number of recognizable combinations that are possible. Each of these different arrangements of 0s and 1s can be used to represent a different numeric, alphabetic, or special character. The **binary-coded decimal (BCD)** system is one code for arranging bits in a standard way to represent characters. The most common binary-coded decimal character sizes have contained either 4 or 6 bits. Four-bit BCD has not been widely used because it allows the representation of only 16 (2^4) characters; the 6-bit BCD code has been most common. The 6-bit BCD representation of the alphabetic and numeric characters is presented in column 1 of Table 3.1. Note that a total of 2^6 or 64 characters can be represented in 6-bit BCD. Thus, there can be 28 special characters (+, −, *, ÷, !, and so on) in addition to the 10 numeric digits and the 26 alphabetic characters shown in Table 3.1.

Extended binary-coded decimal interchange code (EBCDIC)

In order to allow for upper- and lower-case alphabetics, certain letters of the Greek alphabet, and added special characters, the BCD code was extended to 8 bits. This new code, the **Extended Binary-Coded Decimal Interchange Code (EBCDIC)**, pronounced "eeb-see-dick," allowed for 256 characters. The EBCDIC representation for the upper-case characters and the 10 decimal digits is shown in column 2 of Table 3.1.

American standard code for information interchange (ASCII)

EBCDIC was developed by one computer manufacturer, International Business Machines (IBM). The American National Standards Institute sponsored a different code, the **American Standard Code for Information Interchange (ASCII)**, pronounced "askey." This code was developed through the cooperative efforts of a number of computer manufacturers in an effort to

CHARACTER	STANDARD BINARY-CODED DECIMAL (BCD)	EXTENDED BCD INTERCHANGE CODE (EBCDIC)	AMERICAN STANDARD CODE FOR INFORMATION INTERCHANGE (ASCII-8)
A	110001	11000001	01000001
B	110010	11000010	01000010
C	110011	11000011	01000011
D	110100	11000100	01000100
E	110101	11000101	01000101
F	110110	11000110	01000110
G	110111	11000111	01000111
H	111000	11001000	01001000
I	111001	11001001	01001001
J	100001	11010001	01001010
K	100010	11010010	01001011
L	100011	11010011	01001100
M	100100	11010100	01001101
N	100101	11010101	01001110
O	100110	11010110	01001111
P	100111	11010111	01010000
Q	101000	11011000	01010001
R	101001	11011001	01010010
S	010010	11100010	01010011
T	010011	11100011	01010100
U	010100	11100100	01010101
V	010101	11100101	01010110
W	010110	11100110	01010111
X	010111	11100111	01011000
Y	011000	11101000	01011001
Z	011001	11101001	01011010
0	001010	11110000	00110000
1	000001	11110001	00110001
2	000010	11110010	00110010
3	000011	11110011	00110011
4	000100	11110100	00110100
5	000101	11110101	00110101
6	000110	11110110	00110110
7	000111	11110111	00110111
8	001000	11111000	00111000
9	001001	11111001	00111001

Table 3.1 **Examples of binary data codes used by the computer**

standardize computer coding. ASCII is also an 8-bit code, but represents each character with an arrangement of bits different from EBCDIC. ASCII representation of the upper-case letters and the 10 decimal digits is shown in column 3 of Table 3.1.

Zone bits

Note that in the ASCII column the three left-most binary digits seem to differentiate the upper-case alphabet and the numbers. But this is not strictly true. The 4 digits on the left in both EBCDIC and ASCII are **zone bits**. Note that the 4 right-most digits for the number representations are merely 4-bit BCD. These positions are valued at 8, 4, 2, 1 reading from left to right. Note that in the 6-bit BCD code, zero (0) is really coded as 10 in the 4 right-most bits. In both EBCDIC and ASCII, the binary representations of the decimal digits in the 4 right-most digits is straight binary for all the numeric characters. The zone bits, the four left-most bits, are used to distinguish numbers from alphabetics, positive numbers from negative numbers, special characters from letters and numbers, and so forth. For example, in EBCDIC, the alphabetic characters A and J are represented by the same digits in the 4 bits on the right; but the digits on the left show that the characters represented are from different sections of the alphabet (zones). Thus, A is the 0001 (first) character from among the letters A through I and J is the 0001 character from among the letters J through R; and S is the first character from S through Z.

Packed binary

So far we have talked about storing single characters in each byte and combining bytes to make words or fields (meaningful groups of characters). In most modern computers, words or fields are defined in the computer as combinations of bytes. In EBCDIC and ASCII each byte contains 8 bits, 4 for the zone and 4 for the digit.

But the zone codes (first 4 binary digits) of the 8-bit byte can be expressed with just one character in hexadecimal. Conveniently, the second hex digit, corresponding to the last 4 bits of an 8-bit byte, represents the decimal digit being stored. For example, this is what the EBCDIC and ASCII representations of the decimal number 438 would look like in hexadecimal:

	zone digit		
EBCDIC	1111 0100	1111 0011	1111 1000
Hexadecimal form	F 4	F 3	F 8
ASCII	0011 0100	0011 0011	0011 1000
Hexadecimal form	3 4	3 3	3 8

Recognition that the zone code repeats in these codings led to the development of **packed binary** decimals. The zone code need be entered only once. Packed decimal notation represents a number as consisting of two parts. Each numeral is represented independently in a 4-bit half-byte.

The repetitious zone code is entered only once as the last half-byte, as follows (in ASCII):

				Zone
Number	4	3	8	3
Binary half-bytes	0100	0011	1000	0011

Each decimal digit is coded in 4-bit binary with the final code on the right identifying the zone value. The zone value cannot be discarded. It indicates whether the number is positive or negative. The zone code would be chosen from EBCDIC or ASCII depending on the choice of the computer manufacturer. We have chosen to use ASCII. In EBCDIC, the zone code would have been 1111. Note the reduction in required storage space that results from this packing. Only numeric data can be packed, however.

Floating-point binary

In discussing the binary coding, we have ignored numbers with a fractional part and numbers less than 1. The format especially useful for storing such numbers is called **floating-point binary**. Floating point is merely a binary representative of scientific notation. In floating point, a number is represented in two parts: a power of 10 (exponent) and a mantissa (the number).

The numbers below are presented in standard decimal and in scientific notation:

Standard	Scientific notation	
Decimal	**Meaning**	**Form**
458	$.458 \times 10^{3}$	.458E3
45.8	$.458 \times 10^{2}$	.458E2
.458	$.458 \times 10^{0}$	.458E0
.0458	$.458 \times 10^{-1}$	.458E−1

Note that in scientific notation, the decimal point is written in the same position for all the numbers. That is a real advantage when storing numbers in the computer. In storing a number, the decimal point need not be stored, it can be supplied by the computational hardware. The exponent, however, must be shown as a separate part of each word. Special circuits make all this possible. Using this floating-point hardware, a computer can perform arithmetic with these numbers and then express the results either in the floating-point form or in the ordinary decimal form.

Primary computer memory

In Chapter 2, we learned that primary computer memory (primary storage) stores input data, instructions, partial results, and final results for output. In order to store all these diverse elements in the same storage device and not get them mixed up, this storage must be carefully organized.

All electronic storage devices are divided into locations, each identified by a unique address (number). Reference to the appropriate address is the process used to keep the different things in storage separated.

Fixed- and variable-word lengths

The size of the location identified by a given address is not the same in all computers. In some computers, the primary storage is organized so that each addressable location contains a fixed number of bytes or characters. Such storage organization is called **fixed-word-length storage**.

Because all the words to be stored into a computer are not of equal length, a fixed-word length is sometimes inefficient. An entire location must be used for words shorter than the available space. Conversely, for words that are longer than the standard word length, two or more locations must be used. The latter situation requires special (program) instructions. Memory could be more efficiently used if the word length could be fitted to the length of the stored word. By addressing the character location at one end of the word and reading toward the other end until a "word mark" (special character) is found, word length can be allowed to vary. Storage devices that provide this facility are called **variable-word-length storage**.

Volatile and nonvolatile memory

Electronic memories provide varying degrees of permanence of the content stored in them. If the content is lost (erased) when electrical power to the unit is shut off, the unit is said to provide **volatile storage**. The content of **nonvolatile storage** is unaffected by interruptions of electrical power to the unit. If all other factors (storage capacity, speed of access, mode of access, reliability, and cost per character stored) are equal, nonvolatile memory is preferable to volatile memory.

Read-only memory

Memory devices that the ordinary user cannot access are common in current computer systems. They are used to store parts of the operating system, routines (simulators), for converting programs written for some other computer into programs that will run on the host computer, and for compilers and other language translators. Such a device is called a **read-only memory (ROM)**, pronounced as spelled. The advantage of a ROM is that the contents are protected against accidental destruction.

Some ROMs are constructed so that their content can be modified using special procedures. These devices are called **programmable read-only memories (PROM)**. A PROM allows the user to convert a read-only memory to a different use rather than buying a new unit. Ordinary users are unable to carry out the special procedures required to allow the ROM to be rewritten.

Scratch-pad (cache) memory

When computers carry out millions of instructions per second, the CPU tends to outrun its ability to transfer data back and forth. When this happens, the CPU might as well be turned off. Just waiting for a previous result or the next instruction to be fetched from a distant memory location may cause the CPU to be idle a significant proportion of the time. In one-billionth of a second, one nanosecond, electricity will flow only about 11 inches, or the length of an ordinary sheet of typing paper. If the data or instruction must travel a number of feet, the CPU waits idly. One way to increase the instructions accomplished per second in modern computers is to provide small auxiliary, **scratch-pad (cache) memories** as part of the arithmetic-logic and control sections. These memories are used as a person uses a scratch pad when carrying out a series of calculations. Interim results and instructions likely to be needed soon are automatically but temporarily entered into the scratch-pad memory for fast, easy accessibility by the processor when they are needed.

Primary memory hardware

As indicated in Chapter 2, first generation computers used a variety of hardware devices for the primary (CPU) storage device. The most popular memory device in the first generation was the magnetic drum. Other devices were nonmagnetic and volatile. One was the vacuum tube which represented binary data much as you count binary on your fingers. A tube was a switch, and each of these switches was either on or off to represent the 2 binary digits. Modern memory devices include magnetic core, integrated circuits (microcircuits), and bubbles.

Characteristics of magnetic core memory

Primary memory devices of the first generation had limited capacity and were quite bulky. Magnetic drums were bulky, slow, and not too reliable. Vacuum tubes were bulky (each tube represented 1 bit), generated a great deal of heat, and were even more unreliable. Magnetic core memory was developed in the early 1950s, and due to its speed, reliability, nonvolatility, and cost, it became the standard primary storage device of second and third generation computers. Before long, however, magnetic core primary storage will become very rare, as integrated circuits can already be considered standard equipment on new machines.

As shown in Figure 3.2, magnetic cores represent binary digits by the direction of the polarity of the core. Strung together on intersecting wires, they form a core plane. Stacks of planes form a memory module. Access to each core is provided by the intersecting wires, plus a "sense" wire which recognizes the change in the state of a core when electrical charges are sent down the two intersecting wires on which the core is strung. This reading process is destructive of the core content since it requires the state of the core to change. Each read of a core must be followed by a write of that same core to put it back to its original state.

As indicated in Figure 3.2, core bits from each core plane in a stack form a byte. This structure is geared to individually addressable bytes and variable-word-length memory.

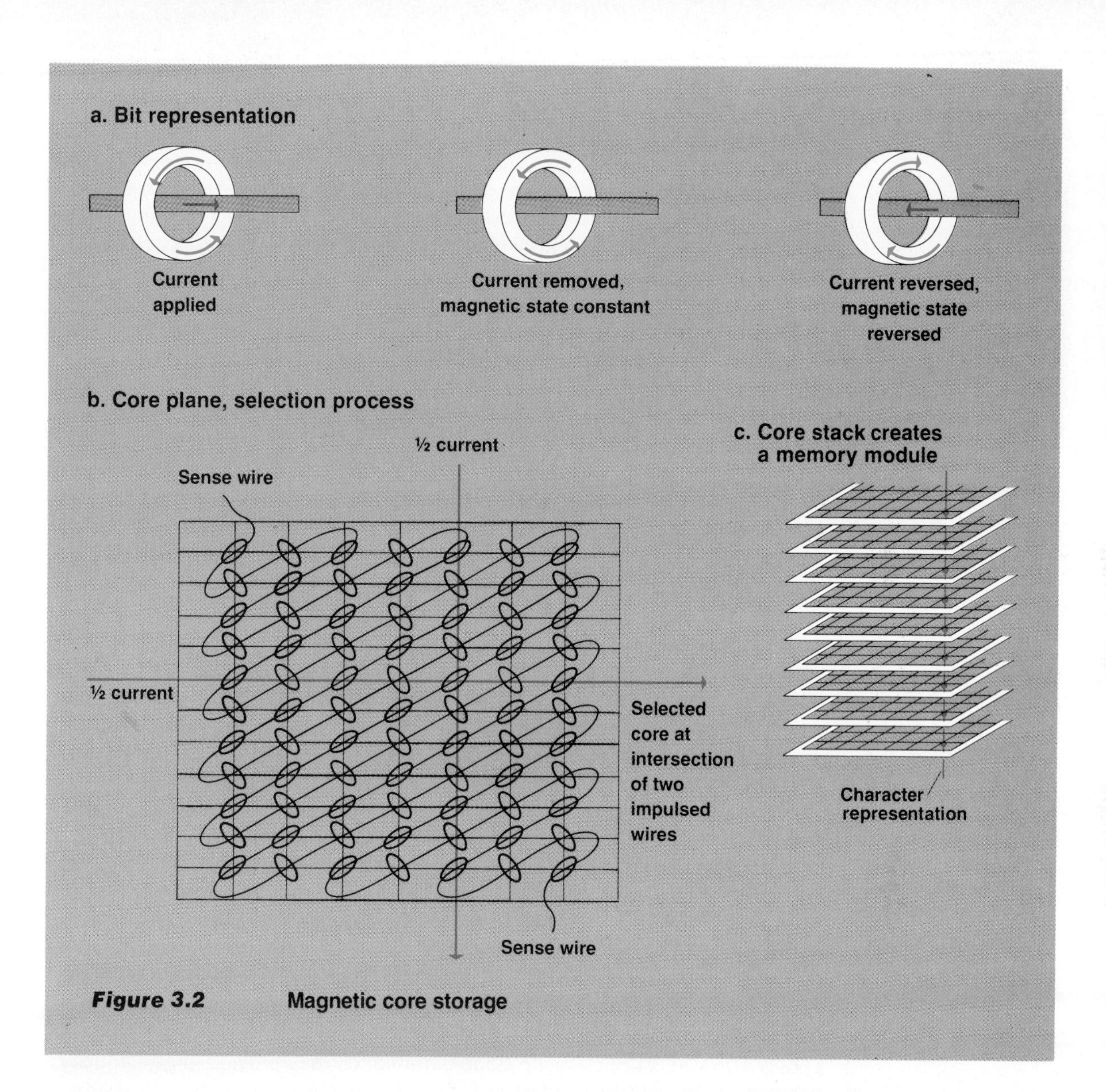

Figure 3.2 Magnetic core storage

Integrated circuits, LSI, and VLSI

Integrated circuits (IC), or microelectronics, were first used in computers in 1971. In this process, electronic circuits containing a number of components in a miniature form are placed on a single chip. The process essentially involves designing a circuit board at regular size and then through a combination of photographic and chemical processes shrinking the circuit and printing it on a silicon chip one-tenth of an inch square.

The number of components per chip has been steadily increased. In 1971, a memory chip might contain 16 complete memory circuits. In 1975, the same size chip contained 64 to 124 memory circuits. The process of shrinking integrated circuits was referred to as **large-scale integration**

(LSI). Current very large-scale integration (VLSI) processes are putting as many as 64,000 bits of storage on a single chip. By 1985, this process is expected to put 1 million components on a chip.

Characteristics of integrated circuit memories Integrated circuit memories involve the electrostatic concepts common in many first generation devices. A bit is represented by the state of a miniaturized circuit. The storage is therefore volatile. It is also very fast, nondestructive, and much, much smaller than the core it replaces. Because they can be mass-produced, they are also cheaper. Mass production is accomplished by building a "mask" and using it to "print" unlimited numbers of additional chips of the same design. LSI and VLSI memory chips have displaced the magnetic core as the most popular primary memory components in today's computers.

One factor that limited the size of core memory modules and also limits the number of components placed on a chip is the heat generated by the components. If components are too closely packed together, the heat they generate will build up to a damaging level unless a cooling system is added.

Bubble memory

As we learned in Chapter 2, the newest storage medium, if examined under a very powerful microscope, looks like tiny bubbles floating in a thin film. Actually, the bubbles are negatively magnetized cylindrical islands in a positively magnetized film spread on a garnet wafer. They are formed by applying an external magnetic force and are read by tiny strips of material whose magnetization changes when close to a bubble (see Figure 3.3).

Characteristics of bubble memory Bubble memories are nonvolatile and very reliable. Reading a bubble is nondestructive, so costly circuitry to replace the bits as they are read is avoided. Bubble memories have very high density. One square inch of garnet can now contain as many as 3 million bubbles and thus store 3 million bits of data. In the laboratory, 1 square inch of garnet has been shown to be capable of storing 100 million bits of data. The more bubbles per chip, the lower the cost per bit. It is expected that bubble memories will provide extremely low-cost memory in the future. In connection with VLSI circuitry, bubble memories may provide large-capacity computers that can be carried in a shirt pocket.

Summary

Electronic components are two-state devices and are therefore most efficient when working with data coded in binary numbers. Binary numbers are base-2 numbers made up as strings of binary digits (bits) consisting of ones (1s) and zeroes (0s). Within the computer, these bits are commonly organized into 8-bit groups called bytes.

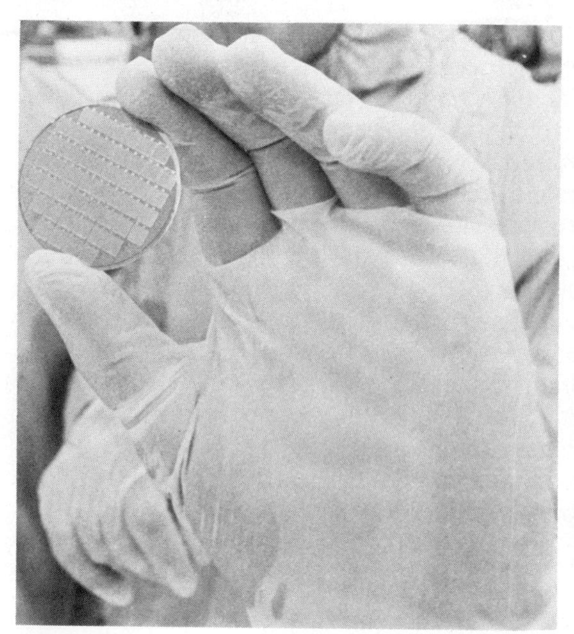

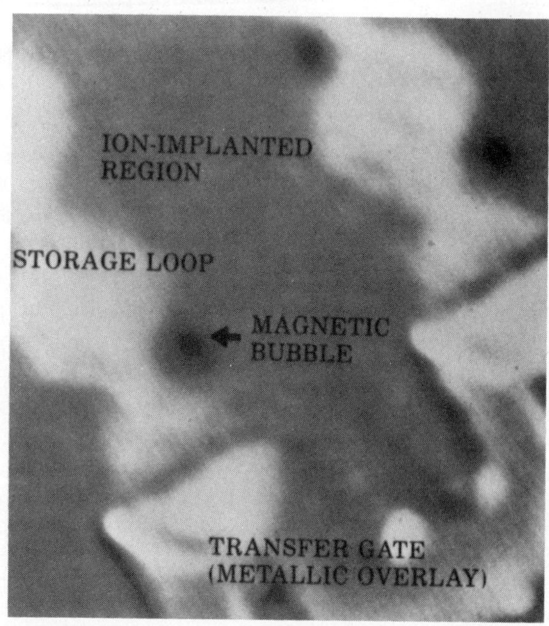

Figure 3.3 **Bubble memory On the left is a slice of garnet, the basic material used in the fabrication of magnetic bubble memory devices. Arrays of forty-eight 70,000-bit bubble circuit chips are fabricated on each slice of garnet. The photo on the right, magnified 3000 times, shows tiny patterns etched in the metal coating on the garnet that serve as avenues for bubble movement. (Courtesy Bell Labs)**

To detect errors that might occur during internal data transfers among computer components, each byte or character is required to contain (most often) an even number of 1 bits. To accomplish this, a parity bit added to each byte or character is set to 1 or 0 as required to obtain the required parity.

Several binary codes are used to represent numbers, letters, and other characters within the computer. True binary is not used as often as some form of binary-coded decimal. Binary-coded decimal codes represent a character with 4, 6, or 8 bits. The most commonly used codes are the 8-bit EBCDIC and ASCII codes. Shorthand codes for binary numbers are the octal (base-8) and the hexadecimal (base-16) systems. Hexadecimal is the more important since it provides the method for obtaining packed decimal. Packed decimal allows storage of data in a little over half of the space required for straight EBCDIC or ASCII.

Special floating-point circuits are used to represent and manipulate fractions and numbers with a fractional part. The floating-point system uses scientific notation to represent such numbers.

Primary computer memory can be made up of words of fixed or variable length. The memories can also be volatile (erased when electric power is cut off) or nonvolatile (permanent, even when the power is off).

Modern computers feature read-only memory (ROM) whose content cannot be altered by the user. One type of read-only memory, programmable read-only memory (PROM), can have its content changed by following special procedures. Both types of fixed memory are used to store simulators so that the host computer can run programs written for a different computer. They also store supervisory programs and compilers.

Scratch-pad memories provide storage that speeds up processing. Placed in the arithmetic-logic or control section, these extra memories store upcoming instructions or partial results where they are easily and quickly accessible.

Miniaturized integrated circuits (IC) on a small silicon chip are the most common component of primary memory in current computer systems. Large-scale integration and very large-scale integration have increased the storage capacity of an IC from 16 bytes per chip to 64,000 bits per chip in only ten years. One million components on a chip are expected by 1985. Bubble memories in which magnetized spots (bubbles) in a thin film are used to represent binary 1s promise to allow 100 million bits on a 1-square-inch garnet wafer. Bubble memory, unlike most IC memory, is nonvolatile. It also provides greater reliability.

Key terms

Define the following terms as briefly as possible and then, in a short paragraph, clarify each definition.

American Standard Code for Information Interchange (ASCII)
Binary-coded decimal (BCD)
Bit
Byte
Extended Binary-Coded Decimal Interchange Code (EBCDIC)
Fixed-word-length storage
Floating-point binary
Hardware
Hexadecimal system
Integrated circuit (IC)
Large-scale integration (LSI)
Nonvolatile storage
Octal number system
Packed binary
Parity bit
Programmable read-only memory (PROM)
Read-only memory (ROM)
Scratch-pad (cache) memory
True binary
Variable-word-length storage
Very large-scale integration (VLSI)
Volatile storage
Word
Zone bits

Discussion questions

1 Why are binary numbers used as the basis for the codes used to represent data in computers?
2 What is the advantage (during processing) of using the hexadecimal number system?

3 What is the purpose of a parity bit? How does it work?
4 What is the advantage of packed binary code? How does it work?
5 Why are floating-point circuits (hardware) used in computers?
6 Name the different types of primary computer memory discussed in this chapter. What is the primary purpose of each type?
7 How are data and instructions kept separate in a computer's memory?
8 What is the major advantage of variable-word-length storage?
9 Why would nonvolatile storage be preferred to volatile storage?
10 What is scratch-pad memory? How is it used?
11 What is the advantage of read-only memory?
12 Refer to Table 3.1 and the related discussion (pp. 55–58) and develop a comparison of the EBCDIC and ASCII codes.
13 What are the advantages and disadvantages of each type of storage component listed below?
   a Integrated circuits
   b Bubble
   c Magnetic core
14 What is the advantage of PROM?

Exercises

1 Assuming hexadecimal notation, indicate the hexadecimal digit represented by each half-byte in the following words:
   a 1101 0101 0010
   b 1110 0011 1101
   c 0010 1010 0001
   d 1010 1010 1100
2 Convert each of the following numbers to packed binary based on EBCDIC code.
   a 4,039
   b 64,185
   c 789
   d 15,385
3 How far can you count on ten fingers using binary? How did you arrive at this number? Did you find the easy way to compute this?

Bubble Memories Find a Niche

Ever since the first commercial bubble memory was introduced nearly four years ago by Texas Instruments Inc., the much-ballyhooed solid-state magnetic storage device for computer data has been a product in search of a market. Prospective users recognized its potential advantages—low price, high capacity, and the capability of not losing stored data when power is cut off—but few were willing to pay the initial high prices charged by the makers of the device to recoup their investments. Also, the vendors had problems in getting the new technology into production, which delayed the price cuts that are counted on in the microelectronics business.

But now production is building up, and it appears that the first volume application is at hand: computer numerical controls for machine tools. In fact, so many manufacturers of machine-tool controls are lining up to buy the bubble memory that there are signs that its price is beginning to take the downward slide that has been forecast for so long. "The emerging machine-tool controls business is a market that can generate significant volume," says a TI official.

Suited to the factory

Orders for machine-tool controls will account for about one-third of the estimated $30 million in bubble memory sales this year, estimates Stewart F. Sando Jr., manager of Intel Corp.'s magnetics operations, one of the handful of bubble memory suppliers. He expects this penetration to increase and push 1981 sales to $40 million. And if the bubble memory finally takes off as expected in other applications, total sales could increase 10-fold in just a few years.

The bubble memory is attractive to machine-tool users because it is well suited to the hostile environment of the factory floor. The control, which directs the metal cutting or forming job of a machine tool, requires a memory to store the program for each task. Enlarging the tool's memory will make it easy to reprogram the machine tool to change operations "on the fly," without having to stop while new instructions are entered into the control's memory.

And unlike the punched-tape units that still control many tools, the bubble memory has no moving parts or paper tape that can be damaged by scraps of metal flying off the cutting machines or fouled by greasy lubricants. Even more important, power interruptions or voltage surges will not erase the data in a bubble memory as they will in the semiconductor memories also used in

Source: "Bubble Memories Find a Niche." Reprinted from the November 24, 1980 issue of *Business Week* by special permission, machine-tool controls. Bubble memories store data in the form of tiny bubbles that move in thin films of magnetic material.

Just one year ago, General Numeric Corp. became the first machine-tool controls manufacturer in the U.S. to use bubble memories. Since then, the Elk Grove Village (Ill.) company has equipped 1,400 controls with bubble memories supplied by Rockwell International. General Numeric's parents—Siemens of Germany and Fujitsu-Fanuc of Japan—have also been selling similarly equipped controls overseas, bringing total worldwide sales to 20,000. "The bubble memory is clearly the way to go," declares Harry D. Mackie, sales and marketing manager of the five-year-old joint venture.

Other controls manufacturers are moving quickly to follow General Numeric. White-Sundstrand Machine Tool Co.'s Controls & Data Systems Div. is offering Intel's bubble memories as an option. Bendix Corp.'s Industrial Controls Div. "is intent on backing up all its controls with bubble memory" by next year, says Stanley A. Berry, director of engineering. And McDonnell Douglas Corp.'s Industrial Control Products Div. has targeted market entry for 1982—or "after the prices come down some more," says Norman R. Timares, director of marketing and engineering for the division.

The price of the new memories is still causing more than a few machine-tool controls makers to move cautiously. That includes the industry leaders. "It is a question of cost and commercial availability of the devices," says Robert W. Breihan, numerical control product manager of General Electric Co.'s Industrial Control Dept., the nation's largest machine-tool controls manufacturer. He points out that backup battery systems can bridge the gap during power outages and protect semiconductor memories.

Still, GE is continuing to develop controls with bubble memories in its laboratories. "We have shown that it is doable," Breihan says. "Now it is just a question of deciding whether it needs to be done." And Charles Carter, technical director at Cincinnati Milacron Inc., which turns out its own controls, worries that prices will not come down "until all users swing over to bubble memories."

But declining prices of the bubble memory devices may hasten their adoption throughout the machine-tool controls business. Intel has taken a bold step by guaranteeing a price reduction during the next year. In August it slashed by 40% the $1,650 price of its 1 megabit bubble-memory kit, which can store 1 million bits of data on a single chip. The quantity price—now $995—will drop another 40% in August, 1981, and then again by half the following year, at which time the semiconductor maker will be offering the kits for as little as $295.

Intel's bubble-memory kit is a package that includes the circuits that drive the memory's magnetic field and also circuits that provide the control logic. Sando believes that bubble-memory sales took off so slowly because most companies neglected to develop such a single-source kit. "The market stalled because some had trouble with manufacturing, and none of us had our support circuits completed," he admits.

Bubble memories are not just affecting new machine-tool controls. Bubbles are also being used to upgrade old control systems. Honeywell Inc.'s Information Systems Div. is so eager to gain the advantage of bubble memories on the machine tools turning out its printed circuit boards that it launched an in-house project to retrofit its 15-year-old machine-tool controls with the new memories. Honeywell is now waiting for control packages from Intel. David W. Behner, project engineer at the Honeywell division in Phoenix, believes that productivity will improve about 20%. "The potential is unlimited, he says"

Chapter 4

Input Media and Devices

Outline

The media and devices that provide the input, output, and storage functions in a computer system are very important. To use computers as parts of business data processing systems, we must be able to enter master files, transaction files, and change files into the system and store them there. Currently, most transactions and change data are being entered online as the transaction occurs or the change is reported. We must be able not only to enter data but also to retrieve stored data and information for use in decision making and in custodial processing. As indicated in Chapter 2, the input and output components provide communication with the storage component of the computer. This chapter will define the media and devices that perform the input functions and discuss some of their important characteristics. It starts with some basic definitions.

Basic concepts

Media and devices

Data to be entered into any processing system must first be captured (recorded). This could be done with pencil and paper—for example, the sales ticket written out by the clerk in a department store. The data-carrying *medium* would be the paper, the recording *device* would be the pencil. In a more advanced system, the data may be printed on paper by a machine. Examples are the typewriter and cash register which print on paper or paper tape. The data medium is the paper or paper tape, the device is the typewriter or the cash register—the machine. In more advanced systems, data may be entered directly into an electronic processing system through a keyboard or through a special reading device. Here the device is the machine, but the medium is the electronic impulses.

The output and storage functions also involve media and devices. Data and information are printed on paper, punched as holes in cards or paper tape, stored as electronic impulses in a machine or displayed on television screens. The media are the paper, the cards, the punched paper tape, and the electronic impulses. The devices are the file cabinets, the typewriters or printers, the cash registers, the electronic machines, and the television screens.

When we speak of media and devices, we mean the following: A **medium** is the physical material, or the configuration thereof, on which data are recorded. A **device** is a machine or unit for performing a data processing function.

Access method

Access method refers to the process used to locate a data item in storage or on an input medium.

In **direct (random) access**, the content of each data location in storage can be accessed directly, and it takes the same amount of time to obtain data from each data location. In **sequential access**, data locations must be accessed in their positional order, in sequence. Thus, to read the data item located at the end of a punched paper or magnetic tape, the read head must be at that last position. If the tape is freshly mounted, accessing the last position will require reading past all the preceding positions on the tape. However, if the last previous access had been to the next-to-last data position, access will be quick, since the read head will be positioned at the beginning of the data location to be accessed.

Transfer rate

Transfer rate refers to the number of characters (or bytes) that can be read out of (or off of) or accepted into (or onto) a device or medium in one second. Transfer rate is determined by several factors. When transferring into or out of a nonrotating storage device such as core, bubble, or microcircuit memories, transfer rate is determined by the carrying capacity of the line on which the transfer takes place. Speed of transfer between storage devices is determined by the slowest device. Thus, transfer from core storage to magnetic disk or tape will be determined by the transfer rate of the tape or disk.

The speed of transfer onto or off of rotating storage devices such as disks and drums is harder to determine. The speed of rotation of the device and the number and location of read/write heads must be considered. For a magnetic tape, the speed at which the tape can be moved past the read head must be considered.

Capacity

The amount of data in bytes that can be stored in or on a medium or device is called its **capacity**. Capacity of a storage device is usually determined in two steps. First, the capacity of a module of the medium is considered, and then the number of modules that can be used on a system is taken into account. For example, the Hollerith punched card stores 80 characters per card. Therefore, module size is 80 characters. Since the number of cards that can be used for offline storage is unlimited, there is no effective limit on this capacity. Any media that can be stored offline (magnetic and paper tape, disk packs, cards, tape cassettes, floppy diskettes) have these same capacity characteristics. Online storage capacity will be limited by the number of devices on which the removable media can be mounted. Offline capacity is technically limited only by physical storage space.

Online and offline

Online and *offline* refer to whether or not a device is attached to the central processing unit of the computer. Specifically, the terms are defined as follows: An **online** device is physically connected to and under the control of the CPU. An **offline** device is not physically connected to and is not controlled by the CPU.

The concepts of online and offline are also used to refer to data processing activities, depending on whether the activity is performed by the computer (online) or in a separate operation (offline). For instance, punching cards on a card keypunch is an offline activity; keyboarding data directly into the computer at a terminal is an online activity.

Fixed online storage (core, bubble, integrated circuit, drum, disk) also comes in modules. The capacity of fixed devices is determined by the combination of module capacity and the number of modules that can be added to the system in total and by the capacity per module and the number of modules on the system at a given time.

Input methods—overview

The input and output elements allow the person to communicate with the machine, translating human language into the electronic impulses of the machine and vice versa. Translation of human-sensible symbols and language into the symbols and language of the machine is accomplished in four general ways.

1 **Key transcription** to a machine-sensible medium involves operators using machines with typewriter-like keyboards to punch data into cards or paper tape or to encode data on magnetic tape or disks. Historically, key transcription has been the most widely used transcription process. Figure 4.1 presents an overview of the three most common key transcription processes.

2 **By-product recording** involves the creation of a machine-sensible medium (punched card, punched paper tape, magnetic tape, magnetic disk, or optically readable printout) as a secondary product of a required operation in the business activity. For example, an optically readable cash register tape is obtained as a by-product of entering transactions at the cash register. By-product recording is gaining in popularity, but is expected to be replaced by direct-entry devices.

The media most widely used in by-product recording are punched cards, punched paper tape, and magnetic tape. These media are prepared as a secondary operation while the recording device (cash register) is carrying out some primary processing operation (totalling the sale and printing the sales slip).

3 **Direct-entry devices** include simple typewriter-like terminals, display devices with a keyboard, devices incorporating various forms of optical readers, display devices capable of accepting input from light pens or from the touch of a human hand, and voice-recognition devices.

Point-of-action, or point-of-sale, devices may perform by-product recording or direct-entry functions. A **point-of-action entry device** records data at the location where a transaction takes place. The optically read cash register tape would be an example of point-of-action recording; so would an airline reservation terminal that is directly connected to a computer.

4 **Character reading** of human-sensible documents allows people to use familiar methods to record data and represents an adaption of a machine

Figure 4.1

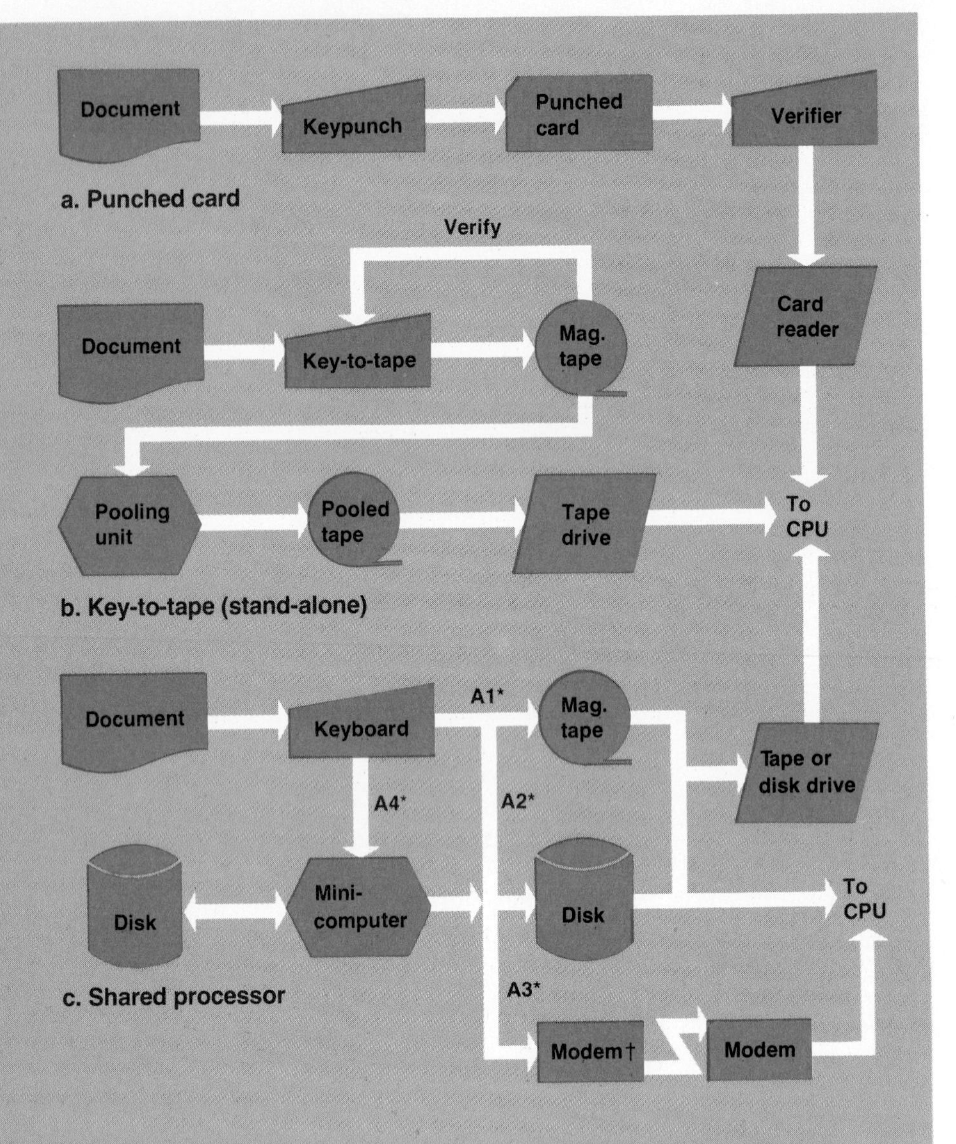

* These are alternatives; normally only one would be present in a given system.

† Modems are remote transmission devices, and will be discussed in Chapter 5.

The three most common key transcription processes

Figure 4.2

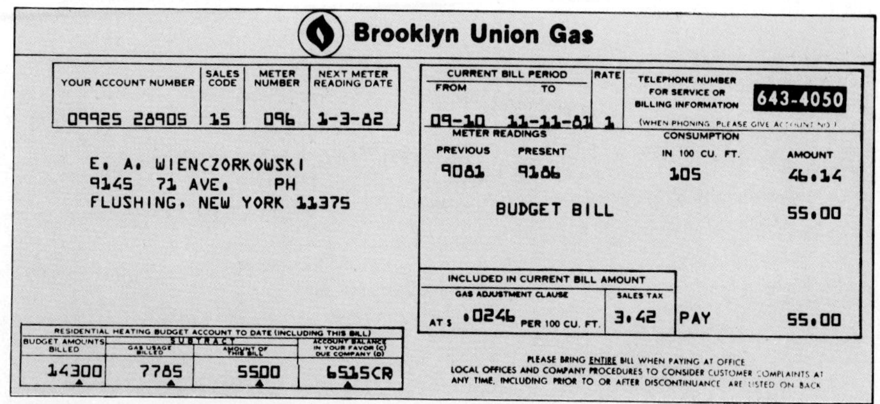

Brooklyn Union Gas

YOUR ACCOUNT NUMBER	SALES CODE	METER NUMBER	NEXT METER READING DATE
09925 28905	15	096	1-3-82

E. A. WIENCZORKOWSKI
9145 71 AVE. PH
FLUSHING, NEW YORK 11375

CURRENT BILL PERIOD FROM	TO	RATE	TELEPHONE NUMBER FOR SERVICE OR BILLING INFORMATION
09-10	11-11-81	1	643-4050

(WHEN PHONING PLEASE GIVE ACCOUNT NO.)

METER READINGS PREVIOUS	PRESENT	CONSUMPTION IN 100 CU. FT.	AMOUNT
9081	9186	105	46.14
BUDGET BILL			55.00

INCLUDED IN CURRENT BILL AMOUNT			
GAS ADJUSTMENT CLAUSE	SALES TAX		
AT $ .0246 PER 100 CU. FT.	3.42	PAY	55.00

RESIDENTIAL HEATING BUDGET ACCOUNT TO DATE (INCLUDING THIS BILL)			
BUDGET AMOUNTS BILLED	SUBTRACT GAS USAGE BILLED	SUBTRACT AMOUNT OF THIS BILL	ACCOUNT BALANCE IN YOUR FAVOR (C) DUE COMPANY (D)
14300	7785	5500	6515CR

PLEASE BRING ENTIRE BILL WHEN PAYING AT OFFICE
LOCAL OFFICES AND COMPANY PROCEDURES TO CONSIDER CUSTOMER COMPLAINTS AT ANY TIME, INCLUDING PRIOR TO OR AFTER DISCONTINUANCE ARE LISTED ON BACK

A machine-readable document **This typical bill from a utility company is an example of a machine-readable document that can also be understood by people. (Courtesy Brooklyn Union Gas Co.)**

to human procedures. **Mark reading** involves codes or use of special forms that make the meaning of the marks clear. The use of these methods is rapidly expanding (see Figure 4.2).

Figure 4.3 gives a general overview of computer input media and devices. The reader should spend a few minutes studying it.

Key input

The common key input media and the associated devices are:

Medium	**Device**
Punched card	Card keypunch, key verifier, card reader, card sorter, card collator, card lister, and card punch
Punched paper tape	Paper tape punch and tape reader
Magnetic tape	Incremental tape recorder (may be recorded on reel or cassette) and tape drive
Magnetic disk pack	Incremental disk recorder (usually in a system involving multiple key stations) and disk drive

Punched card

The oldest of the key-input media and one familiar to most people is the Hollerith 80-column punched card. Other forms are a smaller 96-column card and specially designed cards of various sizes. Only the Hollerith card and the 96-column card will be discussed here.

Figure 4.3

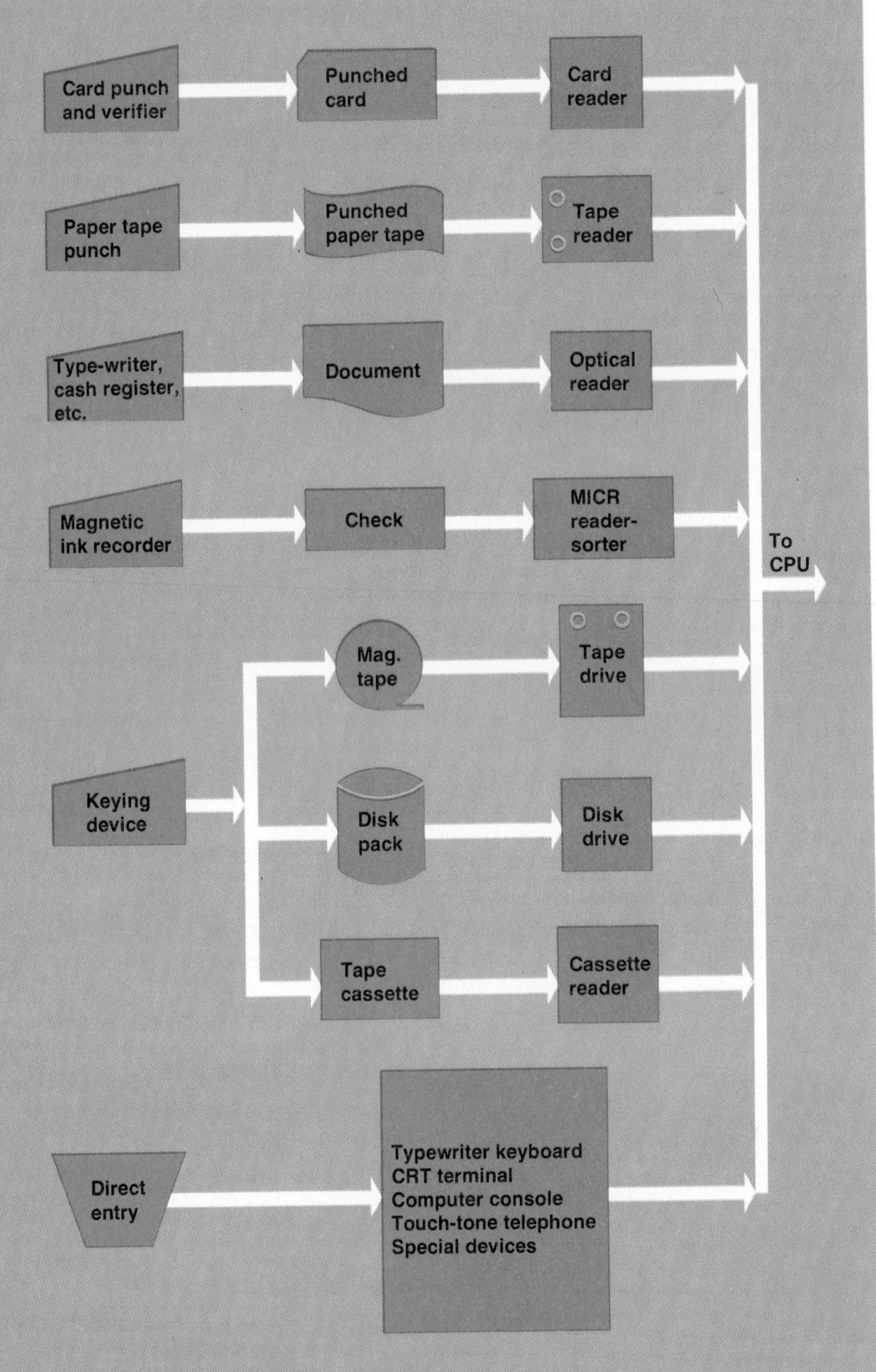

Overview of input media and devices

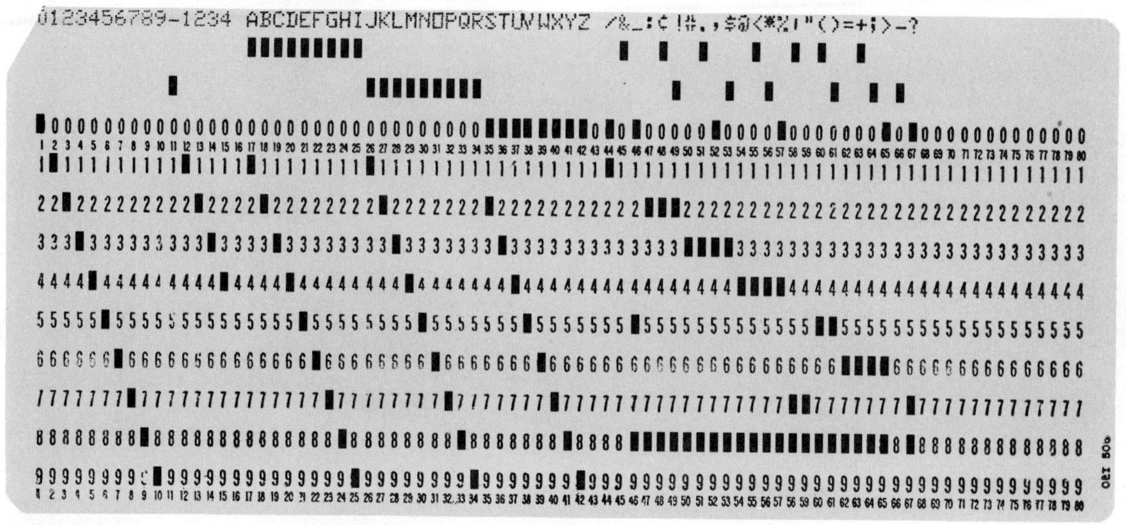

Figure 4.4 The Hollerith 80-column card

Hollerith 80-column card

The **Hollerith 80-column card** is shown in Figure 4.4. Note that the 80 columns across the card are numbered in the line between the 0 line and the 1 line and again at the bottom of the card. Each column represents 1 character.

In total, the card consists of 80 columns each divided into 12 rows. The first 3 rows from the top of the card are zone punches, respectively, the 12 zone, 11 zone, and zero zone. The 9 bottom rows in each column are called the digit, or numeric, punches.

Note the *numbers* punched in columns 1–15. The first 10 numbers require just 1 punch in a column to represent the number. The hole representing the number is like a binary 1; lack of a hole, like a binary 0. Once again a bi-state process is being used to represent decimals. This time, however, it is the physical position of the hole on the card that gives it its decimal meaning.

Plus and minus numbers are differentiated by adding a zone punch in front of a negative number. The last 4 digits (columns 12–15) could be considered a negative number because of the punch in the second zone (row) from the top of the card in column 11. This zone is called both the 11 zone and the minus zone.

The alphabetic and special characters generally require multiple holes to represent each character. Note that most of the multiple punches consist of a zone punch and 1 or 2 numbers. There are exceptions, however. The minus sign is merely an 11 punch, the ampersand (&) is a 12 punch, and the number sign (#), equal sign (=),and double quote mark (") do not use a zone punch.

Finally, note that the content of each column is printed at the top of the card. We say the card has been *interpreted.* The characters were printed on the card as part of the operation of punching the card.

Figure 4.5

The IBM 129 card keypunch (Courtesy IBM)

The 96-column card

A more recently developed punch card is the 96-column card introduced for use with business minicomputers in 1969. The **96-column card** is smaller than the 80-column card, but it uses smaller holes and a binary-coded decimal code to provide more compact data representation. Although 96-column cards may be encountered in business data processing, they are not in very wide use.

Briefly, then, this card is interpreted across the top as was the Hollerith card, but in three rows rather than in one. The portion of the card where holes are punched to represent data is divided into 3 areas. Each area consists of 32 columns. The columns are numbered at the bottom of the areas. Each area contains 6 rows, which are identified from the top as B, A, 8, 4, 2, and 1. The B and A rows are the zone punches for 6-digit binary-coded decimals. The last four rows are the binary digits for 8, 4, 2, and 1.

There are 4 punch zones of 32 characters each across the top of the card for a total of 128 print positions. For certain uses, the extra spaces can provide a better-looking printed message with appropriate spacing.

Punched-card processing equipment

The card keypunch Punched cards are prepared on a machine called the **card keypunch** (see Figure 4.5). The keyboard is much like a typewriter keyboard, but specialized versions are available to accommodate different combinations of characters needed by some users. The machine manipulates and positions the cards automatically and can also be set up to repeat certain keypunching procedures automatically.

Figure 4.6

Digital equipment corporation's CD20-C, CR10-H console model card reader (Courtesy Digital Equipment Corporation)

The correctness of the initial keying is checked by having a second operator key the same data against the card on a machine called a **verifier**. If the second operator keys in data that does not match the holes on a card, the machine stops and a light alerts the operator. A discrepancy means that either the card was incorrectly keypunched by the first operator or the second operator has made a mistake. A quick check allows the verifier operator to correct the error. The latest card punch machines perform both functions, punching and verifying, but not at the same time.

Card reader Punched cards are read into the computer through a machine called a **card reader**. Older readers sensed holes with wire brushes and moved the card with rollers and other mechanical devices. The new high-speed readers sense the holes optically by means of photoelectric cells and move the cards in part with pneumatic (air) devices (see Figure 4.6).

Card sorter The modern **card sorter** senses the holes in a column electronically by a photocell at rates of 1,000 to 1,500 cards per minute. Cards can be sorted, sequenced, or column-selected by directing them into numbered pockets according to the punches in a specific column. To sort an entire field requires that the cards be passed repeatedly through the machine, once for each column contained in the field. Counters record the number of cards placed in each pocket. There are 13 pockets, with one being reserved for cards on which the sorted column is blank.

Card collator Two or more decks of cards (files) can be merged, merged with selection, or matched on a **card collator**. Suppose, for example, that you wanted to make some changes to a master file. The master deck of cards and a change deck of cards giving updated information could be merged with selection. This means that selected cards in the master (those replaced by cards from the change file) are removed to create an updated master file. Most collators have two input pockets and four output stackers and can separate decks as well as merge them. They will also detect and remove cards with blank columns.

Reproducing punch Sometimes called the gang punch, the **reproducing punch** can be used to reproduce a deck exactly or to reproduce all or part of each card with rearrangement of its contents. It can also add the same constant data to each card punched. When attached to processing equipment capable of addition (the accounting machine or a card calculator), it can be used to create updated master cards.

Accounting machine The **accounting machine** is in essence a card lister with the ability to sum fields as it lists the card contents onto a paper form. The subtotals and totals it creates can be used (with the reproducing punch) to create updated master cards and useful totals by categories for activity reports to management.

Advantages of punched cards

Each card is a record, allowing easy addition, deletion, rearrangement, or replacement of individual records. Cards are easily read by human beings when interpreted by having the contents printed along the edge.

Data processing systems using punched cards and card processing equipment are called **unit record systems** in recognition of the fact that each card is normally a record (either master, change, or transaction). Unit record systems are faster and less error prone than manual systems. They are also much slower and more error prone than computerized data processing systems. They do allow limited integration of systems and reduce duplication of recording activities since the same transaction card can be used for input for several different applications.

An example of a unit record system for an hourly payroll system is shown in Figure 4.7. Note that changes to the payroll master records (address

Figure 4.7

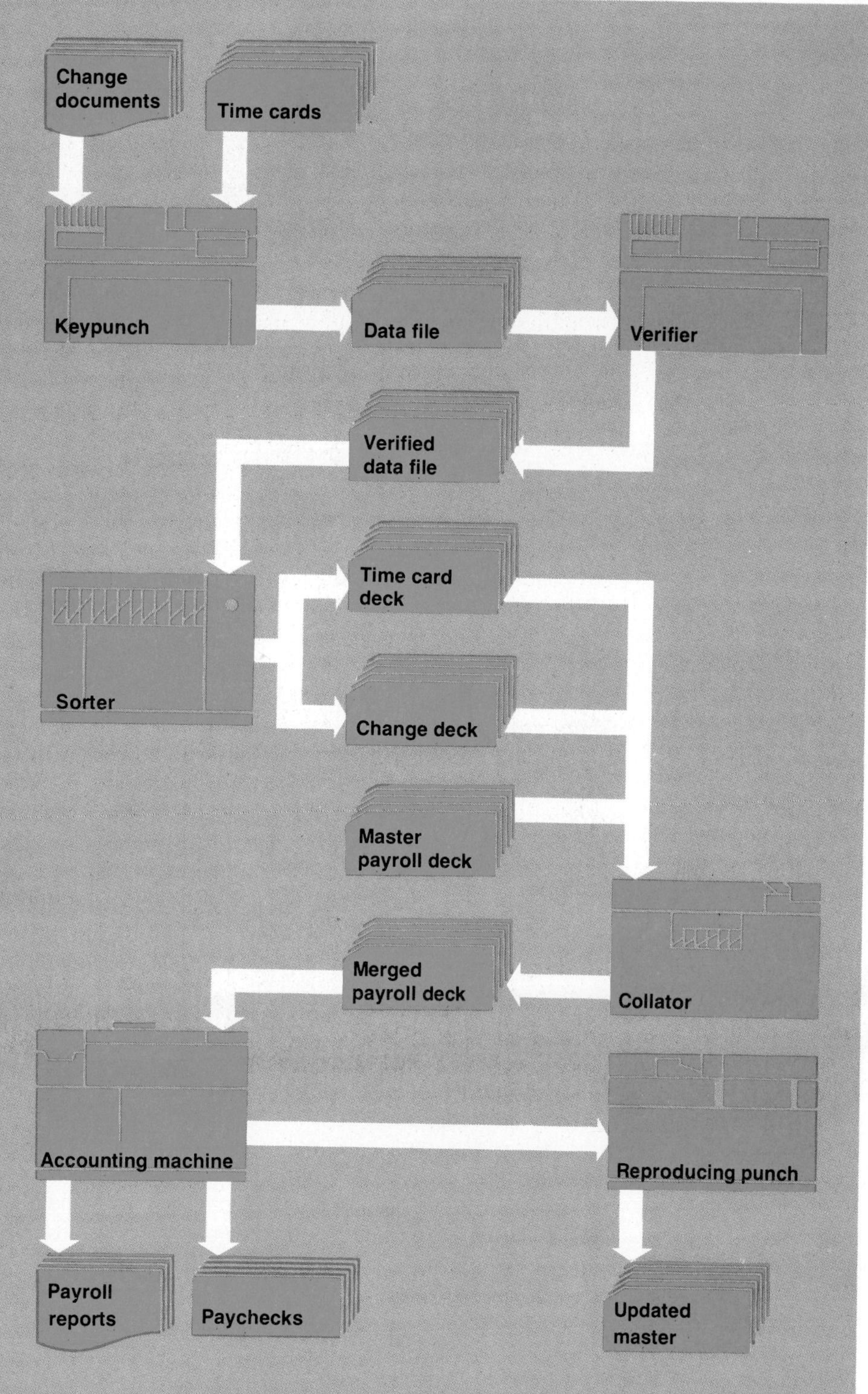

Unit record hourly payroll system

Figure 4.8

A punched card used as a turnaround document (Courtesy New England Telephone)

changes, separations, new hires, and so on) are merged into the master payroll deck to create a preliminary updated master file. Timecards (transactions deck) are then merged with this master to create payroll checks, payroll reports, and a final updated payroll master deck.

Disadvantages of punched cards

Cards limit the record size unless records extend over more than one card. Cards are a bulky storage medium and need a low-humidity environment to prevent them from absorbing moisture and swelling. Also, a card cannot be corrected or reused with different data. When all costs are considered (preparation, handling, storage, and reading time), the punched card must be considered a high-cost data entry medium on modern mid-sized and large-scale computer systems. Cards are economical only in low-volume operations where only a few keypunches are needed or in operations using the card as a turnaround document. When used as a turnaround document, the card is initially punched (usually on the computer) and interpreted to create a bill that is sent to the customer. The customer returns the prepunched card with the payment. The amount paid is then keypunched onto the card to complete the input document for payment processing (see Figure 4.8).

Punched cards were once the standard input medium for most machine processing. However, card costs, human labor costs, and costs of maintaining electromechanical devices have risen substantially. Simultaneously, the costs of electronic equipment (video-display terminals, optical readers, disk drives, and the like) have decreased as speed and reliability have increased. As a result, cards are much less widely used in modern systems. Still, processing concepts associated with cards (sorting by column, fixed fields of data, unit record processing, and so on) persist even on the electronic replacements for card systems.

Punched paper tape

Standard **punched paper tape** is ¾ inch wide (see Figure 4.9). Data bits (1s) are represented by holes in the tape. Holes are punched along five, seven, or nine channels (seven is the most common) running parallel to the tape edges. A character is presented by the combination of holes (1s) and spaces (0s) occurring across the seven channels at a particular point on the tape. Normal density is 10 characters per inch. Punched paper tape has been used as a communication medium about as long as cards have. Nevertheless, tape is not nearly as widely used as cards.

Advantages of paper tape

Advantages of paper tape are its low cost and unlimited record length. The cost of paper tape is only about one-third of the cost of a punched card on a per-character basis. Paper tape punches and readers are light and relatively inexpensive. They are normally marketed as part of a unit including a typewriter that types a copy of all data punched or read. An example is shown in Figure 4.10. Several minicomputer systems do not use paper tape as the input-output medium. The vendors of these systems offer special high-speed readers that use optical sensing. Punched paper tape has been widely used as an input medium for telecommunications systems.

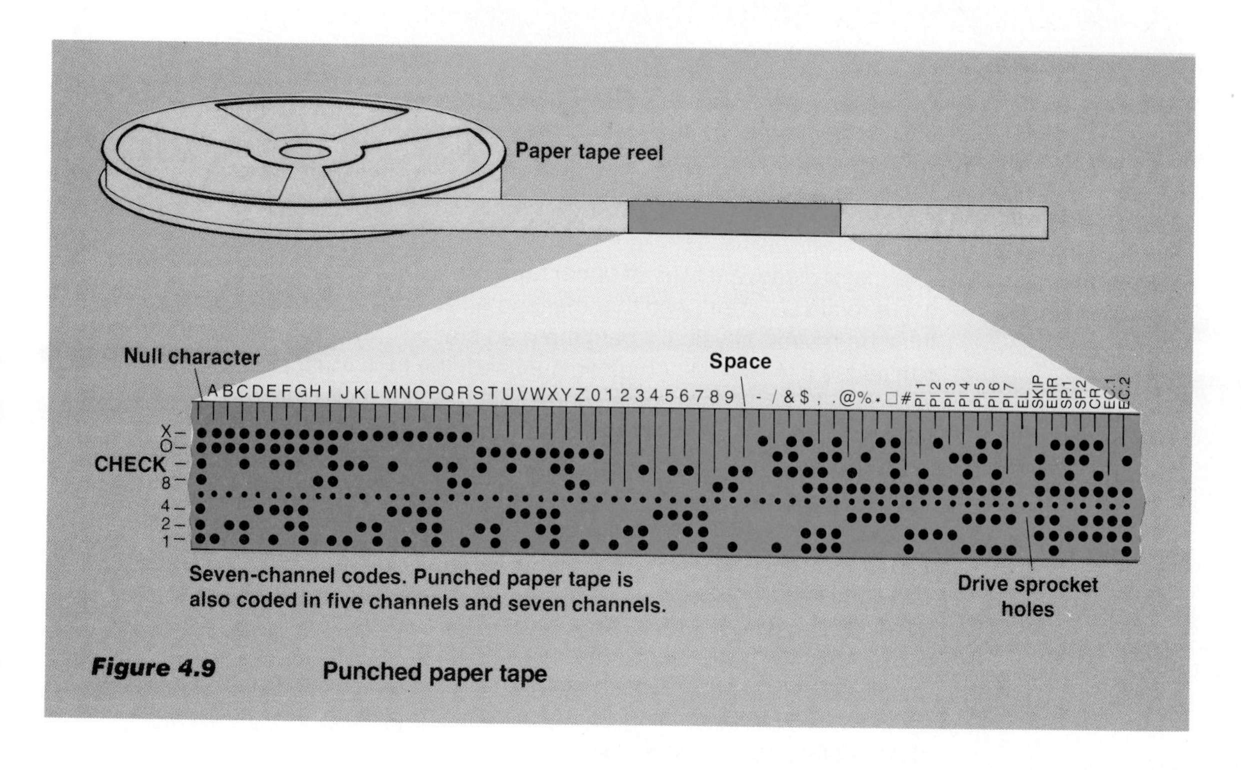

Figure 4.9 Punched paper tape

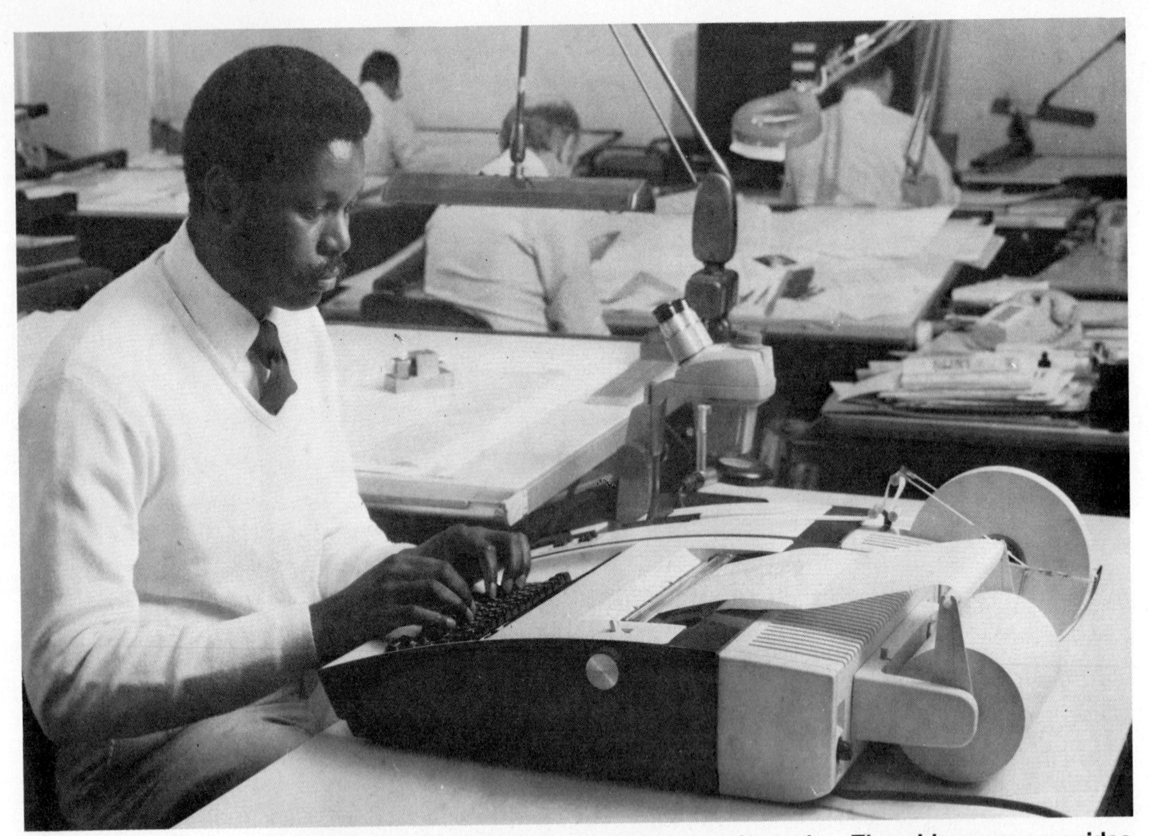

Figure 4.10 **A hardcopy terminal with a paper tape read/punch The wider paper provides a hardcopy record of all data punched or read. On the far side of the machine we can see the paper tape, passing through guides and on into the read/punch. (Courtesy Teletype Corporation)**

Disadvantages of paper tape

The major disadvantages of paper tape are that it is easily torn, that misreads occur relatively often, and that the tape has a limited life. Tape is also slow. It must be moved physically past the read station. Trying to move it too rapidly can cause it to tear. When being punched, the tape must either stop or move very slowly while the holes representing a character are being punched; otherwise, the holes will be stretched or torn. Paper tape is often heavily oiled to give it greater strength, but then it becomes stiffer and more difficult to handle. It also holds dirt more easily. The shelf life of an unused tape is limited, however, unless it is oiled.

Tapes are also difficult to correct. To replace an incorrect character or to add a missing character, the entire tape must be repunched. As magnetic tape drives have become cheaper and tape cassettes have been adapted for computer use, paper tape has declined in popularity. The floppy diskette (small floppy disk) is also a paper tape replacement on microcomputer systems. These technologies seem to be replacing punched paper tape almost totally in the newest systems.

Magnetic tape

Magnetic tape, and magnetic disks, are secondary storage devices and will be discussed extensively in Chapter 6. They are introduced here for purposes of comparison with other input methods.

Standard magnetic tape for use with computers is usually ½-inch-wide Mylar tape coated on one surface with a magnetizable substance. Widths of ¾ inch and 1 inch are also used. Bits are recorded in channels running along the length of the tape. Older tapes had seven channels, newer tapes carry nine. Characters are represented by the combination of bits occurring across all channels at a particular location. Common character densities are 800, 1,600, 3,200, and 6,250 characters per inch. Tapes are read at speeds of from 36 to over 200 inches per second. Their most common length is 2,400 feet. Tape and a tape drive are shown in Figure 4.11.

The original method of recording data on magnetic tape for computer entry was a two-stage process. Data were keyed into punched cards and then transferred from the cards to magnetic tape by a computer. Key-to-tape systems bypass the punched card, allowing initial keying directly onto the

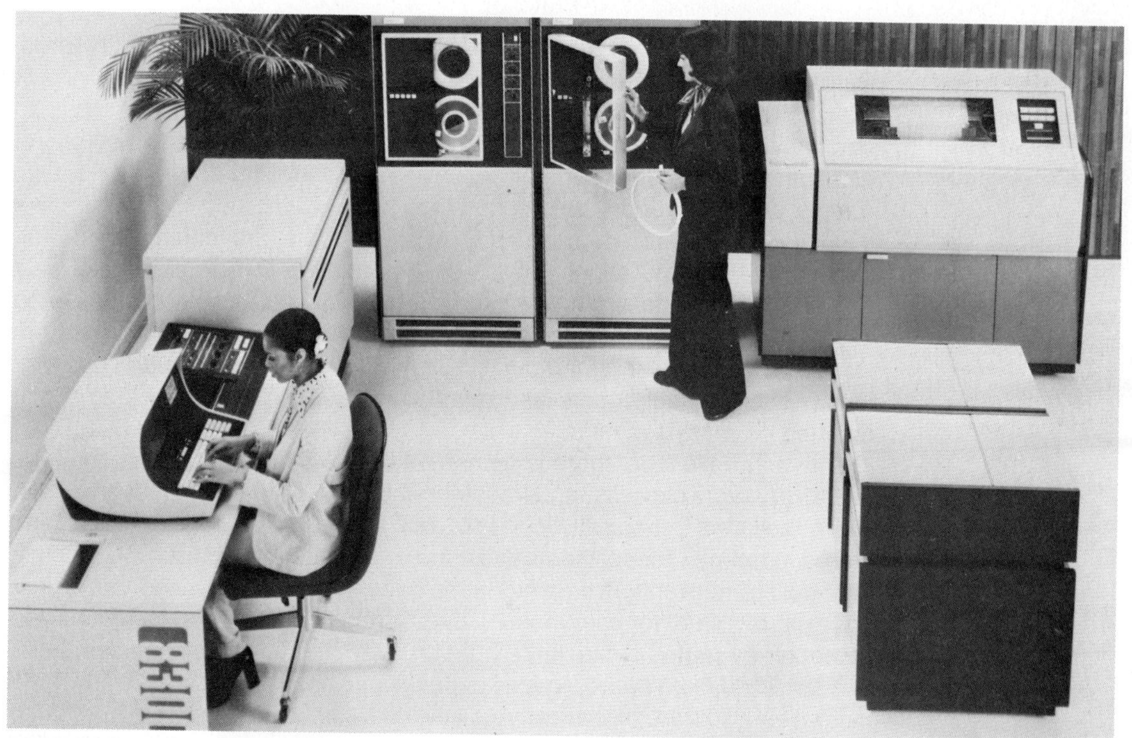

Figure 4.11 **A multiple component computer system with two tape drives As the operator at the rear loads tape onto a tape drive, the operator in the foreground inputs data at a visual display console. (Courtesy National Cash Register Co.)**

magnetic tape. The first key-to-tape system was a buffered, stand-alone unit consisting of a keyboard and a computer-compatible incremental tape drive. The breakthrough was the ability to write on the tape "incrementally," one group of characters (in this case, 80) at a time. Tapes from several recorders could be consolidated on a common tape by a pooling device before processing. Today, systems involving minicomputer controllers with small memories supervising from 1 to 64 individual key stations are available. Other systems record on tape cassettes. The tape cassettes are usually translated to computer-compatible magnetic tape for input to the computer.

The presence of punched cards has been so widespread that early key-to-tape devices recorded data on the tape in a card format of 80 characters at a time. Unit record systems or any system using punched-card input could be converted to magnetic tape input merely by substituting the incremental tape recorder for the card keypunch in the system. Newer systems can overcome this limitation, however. During pooling of tapes from several recorders, smaller-length records can be combined into longer records as necessary.

The use of incremental tape recorders is rapidly expanding the use of magnetic tape as a transcription medium. The cassette tapes, particularly, are being increasingly seen in point-of-action offline data capture systems.

Advantages of magnetic tape

Key entry of data to magnetic tapes is generally faster than entry to cards. Definitive, firm data are not available, but statements by qualified experts in industry publications indicate that average entry speeds are at least 20 percent higher. This increase in entry speed is gained from the lack of handling and the larger number of stored record layouts (formats) available on a system. Several systems now allow key verification of input from a second keying station immediately after the data are entered. In some multiple-station installations, the supervisory station can create new formats while the other stations are keying data. Thus, formats for the next jobs to be keyed can be ready and waiting when the first jobs are completed. Data from individual stations can be automatically merged in preparation for computer input. Batch control counts and totals can be automatically prepared and inserted on many systems.

With magnetic tape, there is no natural limit to the record length, the tape has a very large capacity, and transfer rates are high. Tapes also have a long life if they are periodically cleaned and reconditioned, and handled and stored properly. Tapes themselves are not expensive, commonly costing nine dollars to twenty-five dollars a reel, and they can be reused, but a tape drive is required to use them. Drives are commonly connected to the computer through a controller, a buffering device that usually handles 2 to 8 or 16 individual drives. The prices of drives and controllers vary widely. Price increases with the complexity of the device. Alternatives that add to tape-drive costs include echo read-and-compare for automatic error detection while writing, automatic reread if an error is detected while reading, reading in either direction on the tape, and increased transfer rate.

Disadvantages of magnetic tape

Disadvantages of magnetic tape are its sequential-access characteristics, which make rearrangement or insertion of records difficult, and the need for careful handling and storage. Tapes are easily erased and must not be handled roughly. Tape edges can be bent or creased and bits rearranged by careless handling. Tapes are also damaged by high humidity and by dirt, grease, or oil coming into contact with the magnetized surface. Excess heat can cause the tape to warp and stretch.

Magnetic-disk pack

Magnetic disks are made of thin metal or heavy Mylar coated with a magnetizable material. Data are recorded as magnetic spots along circular tracks (rings) around the magnetic surface. Bits are less densely packed on the outer tracks so that each track contains the same number of bits. Characters are often represented as combinations of the single bits stored along a track. The top and bottom surfaces of the disk pack are not used to record data, but the rest of the disks usually have data on both sides. Access arms mounted in the drive mechanism move in and out between the magnetized surfaces and carry the read/write heads to the various tracks. The disk pack is used by placing it on a drive spindle, which spins it at a high rate of speed. The read/write heads are then inserted to pick up (read) or place (write) data at the proper locations (see Figure 4.12).

Figure 4.12

Magnetic disk drives Here the manager of the data processing department at John Hancock Mutual Life Insurance Co. examines one of the many disk packs that store data about John Hancock's 18 million insurance policies. (Courtesy John Hancock Mutual Life Insurance Co.)

Figure 4.13

A multiple-station key-to-disk data entry system (Courtesy Mohawk Data Systems)

Key-to-disk devices are mostly multiple-station systems, although stand-alone key-to-disk devices are available. A multiple-station system is shown in Figure 4.13. The entry devices are organized much like the key-to-tape systems described above. Standard key-to-disk systems are competitive with card keypunches at volumes requiring six to eight card punch machines.

The newest key-to-disk system involves a so-called floppy disk and is becoming common as a single-unit installation. The floppy disk is made of Mylar without the metal core and is much cheaper. These disks are also being used as secondary storage in minicomputer-centered business systems.

Advantages of disk packs

In general, disks are one of the most popular general-purpose random-access devices. Disk packs are widely used to provide direct-access storage in business data processing. This allows selective updating of individual records in a file. Transactions data can be passed against a sequentially or randomly ordered file without being ordered in the same fashion.

Drives are available that can hold a number of accessible disk packs at one time, giving direct access to many millions of characters online at one time. Switching one disk for another on the drive is simple, requiring less than one minute.

The major advantages of magnetic disk packs arise out of their random-access characteristics and the speed they bring to processing. The greater purchase price of disk packs over tape is offset by the greater processing efficiencies of random-order access. Access speeds are faster and transfer rates higher for disks than tapes. Disks are particularly useful in online systems and are being increasingly used for file storage.

Disadvantages of disk packs

Magnetic disk packs are bulky and (relatively) expensive. Disks are bulkier than magnetic tapes, although much less bulky than cards. More important, normal tape-processing procedures involve the creation of a new tape file, leaving the old file intact to provide reference or system back-up. In disk processing, however, the new file is created by changing the data on the existing disk file, and the old file is lost. Disks are more expensive than tape; a disk pack can easily cost 20 times as much as a reel of tape.

Direct-entry devices

Whenever a human being enters data directly into the computer without using an intervening input medium, direct entry takes place. We have already mentioned several types of direct-entry devices. Three will be described in more detail at this time—typewriter-like terminals, cathode ray tube terminals, and intelligent terminals. These devices are dual-purpose in that they serve as both input and output devices; they will be discussed as output devices in Chapter 5.

Typewriter-like terminals

The most common type of terminal for shared computer systems is the **typewriter-like terminal**, a machine with a typewriter-style keyboard. The user enters data via a keyboard which is connected to the computer by a direct cable or telephone line. The computer responds over the same line. There is no opportunity to key-verify input. Errors are controlled by having the computer edit the input and by proofreading the typed copy produced on the terminal. Most of these terminals operate at 10 to 15 characters per second, although a few can operate at faster speeds (up to 30 characters per second) when outputting from the computer. Some have a paper tape reader and punch for use in offline data preparation, in program input, or in preserving output (such as saving a program developed online for use at another time).

The newest development in these typewriter-like terminals is portability. Models weighing as little as 17 pounds are available. These portable units cost more than the lowest-cost standard models (about $750), but usually not as much as the most expensive standard models (about $3,000). Typewriter-like terminals currently provide low cost and reliable means of communicating directly with a computer via the telephone, and they offer a permanent hardcopy record of both data input and computer output.

Cathode ray tube (CRT) terminals

A **cathode ray tube (CRT) terminal** looks like a TV screen with a keyboard attached. Because the CRT is electronic, its operations are fast and silent, unlike those of typewriter-like terminals. In addition, some CRTs have graphic capabilities that can be valuable in analyzing time flows and relationships of economic variables. Screen and print colors, sizes, and capabilities vary widely, however, and most CRTs do not produce hardcopy or have graphic capabilities. The addition of either adds substantially to the cost of the terminal. Some CRTs can accept input by the use of a light pen, which is discussed later in the chapter.

Transmission speeds for CRT devices vary from 10 to almost 10,000 characters per second, but are usually limited by transmission of data over phone lines. The display area varies from 200 to 2,000 character spaces. Keyboards vary from standard typewriter keyboards through keyboards arranged in alphabetical order to keyboards allowing specialized inquiry or program initiation from a single key.

Intelligent terminals

Combining a minicomputer or a microprocessor (computer on a chip) with a terminal (usually a CRT) allows programming to perform special tasks, thus the phrase **intelligent terminal**. Such a terminal can lead the user through a sequence of entry operations and can perform many of the data-editing activities normally carried out by the central computer. Some also control selected peripheral devices such as magnetic tape cassette handlers.

Use of intelligent terminals is expanding rapidly as more and more data processing systems go online. There is a real advantage in relieving the central computer of the editing burden and providing additional data storage at the terminal. The number of accesses of the central computer decreases, and the amount of data transfer and processing associated with each access increases. This results in more efficient use of CPU time. Intelligent terminals tend to feature larger screen capacities and faster transfer rates, which, together with the processing hardware, make them much more expensive than ordinary terminals.

Source-data automation

By-product recording media and devices

These media tend to be punched cards, punched paper tape, magnetic tape, and magnetic disks. The preparation device (card punch, paper tape punch, incremental recorder, cassette recorder, or floppy disk drive) is hooked to another data processing device such as a cash register or a typewriter, and the keying involved in the basic process is used to enter the data on the medium. Bookkeeping machines have also been adapted to produce punched cards, punched paper tape, magnetic tape cassettes, or optically readable journal tapes as a by-product. The tape cassette is being adapted in an amazing variety of ways for by-product data recording. The magnetic tape cassettes are often translated to computer-compatible magnetic tape in a second offline operation.

The characteristics of these media and devices are discussed in other sections of this chapter. The appeal of by-product recording is that the keying process that creates the initial data-carrying document also produces the machine-sensible data-carrying medium. It can easily be seen in Figure 4.1 how the input process would be shortened and total costs reduced. With the development of optical readers capable of reading manually written documents and those capable of translating the human voice to electronic impulses, the need for transcription keying is reduced still further.

Character reading media and devices

The major advantage of character reading devices is that a human-sensible document can be used as the input medium to the computer.

Magnetic ink character recognition (MICR)

No doubt you've looked at those odd-shaped characters strung across the bottom of your checks. They are printed with a special ink containing iron particles that can be magnetized. After being magnetized, they can be read by special-character readers for computer input. Figure 4.14 shows a **magnetic ink character recognition (MICR)** reader-sorter. These devices read documents (checks, deposit slips, withdrawal slips, and others) at speeds of up to 1,600 documents per minute. The MICR characters on each document are magnetized by the machine, sensed, and used to sort the document into the proper pocket (see Figure 4.15). Validation processes such as the use of check digits can be incorporated into the machine. The documents read can be of different sizes and thicknesses as long as the MICR characters are placed in the proper relation to the bottom edge of the document (see Figure 4.16).

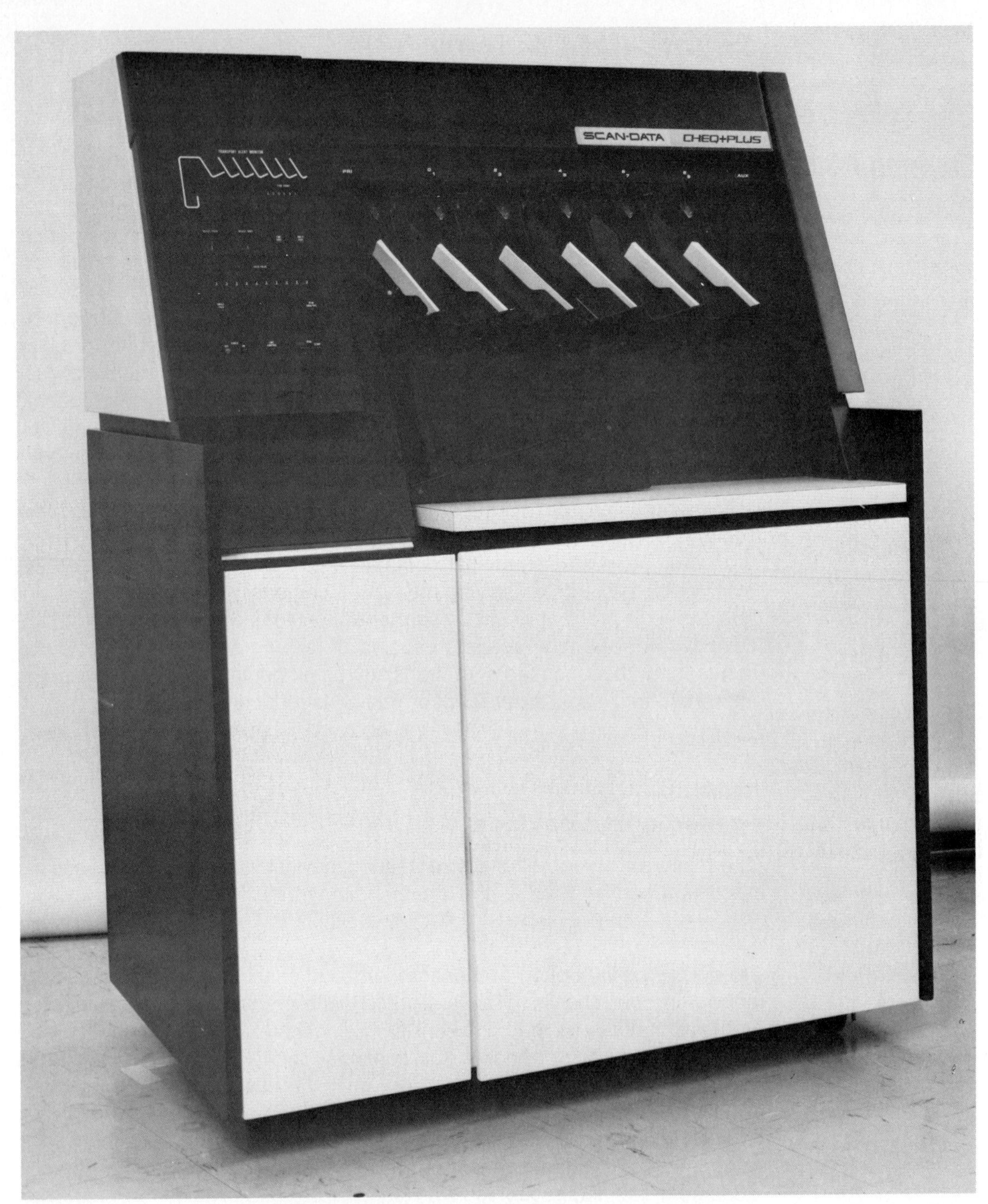

Figure 4.14 **A MICR reader/sorter** **The Scan-Data reader/sorter can be operated online, where it reads and sorts according to commands from a central computer, or it can operate according to its own internal control logic to sort and verify documents. (Courtesy Scan-Data Corporation)**

Figure 4.15

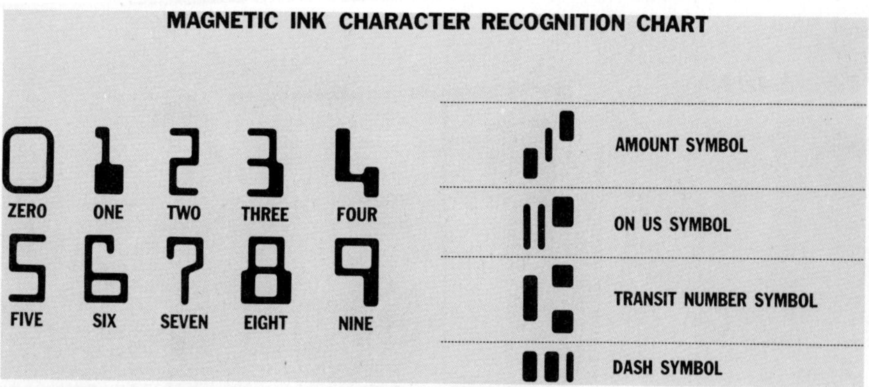

The MICR character set

Figure 4.16

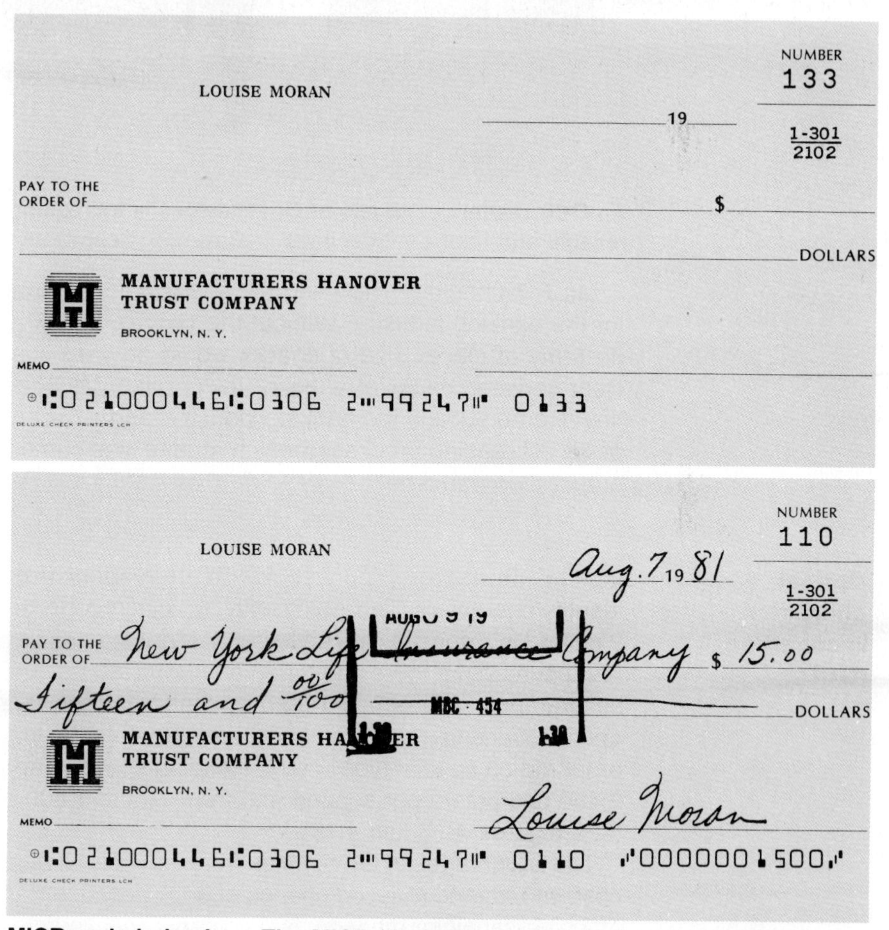

MICR-coded checks The MICR characters along the bottoms of the checks indicate which bank the account holder uses, the account number, the type of transaction the document is used for, and so on. On the second check, which has been processed, the amount of the transaction has been added during processing.

Figure 4.17

An OCR reader **The use of OCR devices is increasing as they become more reliable and their cost declines. (Courtesy Scan-Data Corp.)**

MICR technology, including the shapes of the characters, was developed for the banking industry. Without this process, banks would need to employ an army of clerks, use of checks would be very costly, and checks would clear between banks at a much slower pace. MICR has not been applied to any degree outside the banking industry, partly because of the development of optical reading processes which require less cumbersome and less costly preparation equipment.

Optical character recognition (OCR)

Optical character recognition (OCR) readers use photoelectric cells to identify characters. The least costly devices recognize only the numerals 0 to 9 printed in a special type style (font). More expensive readers can recognize hand-printed numbers and typed numbers, letters, and special characters in several fonts. Input media read by these devices range from cash register and accounting machine tapes in special fonts to page-size documents prepared on special typewriters. Reading speeds vary from less than 100 to 2,400 characters per second and from 180 to 1,800 documents per minute (see Figures 4.17 and 4.18).

The advantages of OCR, aside from use of a human-sensible medium, are cost, speed, and reduced chance of error because transcription to a different machine-sensible medium is avoided. The removal of the transcription operation can result also in greater efficiency and faster throughput for the data processing operation as a whole. However, error control depends on visual proofing and requires well-trained typists and proofreaders and close supervision over the initial recording operation.

Figure 4.18

ABCDEFGHIJKLMN
OPQRSTUVWXYZ,.
$/*-1234567890

The OCR character set

Certain very sophisticated OCR devices can also read handwritten characters. This has obvious advantages in that it eliminates still another transcription step. The quality of the handwritten characters must be carefully maintained, though, because the OCR device cannot read characters unless they are very precise and uniform (see Figure 4.19).

A significant shortcoming of most OCR systems is that they restrict the equipment and paper the user can choose. Most readers require paper that meets stringent specifications for reflectance, blemishes, weight, and so on. Typewriters and ribbons must be of the highest quality with tight control of spacing and quality of printing. Supplies are therefore expensive. OCR readers also may misread or reject a document because of dirt specks or wrinkles. These limitations are being reduced as the process is constantly improved.

Figure 4.19

Guidelines	Right	Wrong
Make characters large	06AT4	06AT4
Make characters simple	275TX	275TX
Don't connect characters	FA2GO	FA2GO
Don't leave gaps	P890B	P890B

Some guidelines for handwritten OCR characters

Optical mark recognition (OMR)

Although not, strictly speaking, a character reader, an **optical mark recognition (OMR)** device is a simpler version of an OCR device. OMR readers optically read marks (lines) rather than characters. A single mark or a combination of marks represents particular characters or other types of data. A wide variety of marks can be read: marks made by computer printers, hard or soft pencils, and special typewriters. These marks are humanly readable after special training (see Figure 4.20).

Optical bar codes are a variation on optical mark recognition. A series of bars and spaces are printed on an item for sale or on its price tag to represent pricing and inventory data and, sometimes, data useful in market research. The bar codes are read by a hand-held scanner or by a scanner fixed on a check-out counter. Probably the most familiar type of bar code is the Universal Product Code (UPC), which is used primarily on items in supermarkets. With the UPC the cash register acts as a terminal, recording and displaying prices, taxes, and totals. (Figure 4.21 shows one use of a bar code.)

OMR devices vary in speed and cost. Some accept only punched-card-size documents; others accept full pages. Also, some OMR readers merely translate to another machine-sensible form such as punched cards or magnetic tape.

Figure 4.20

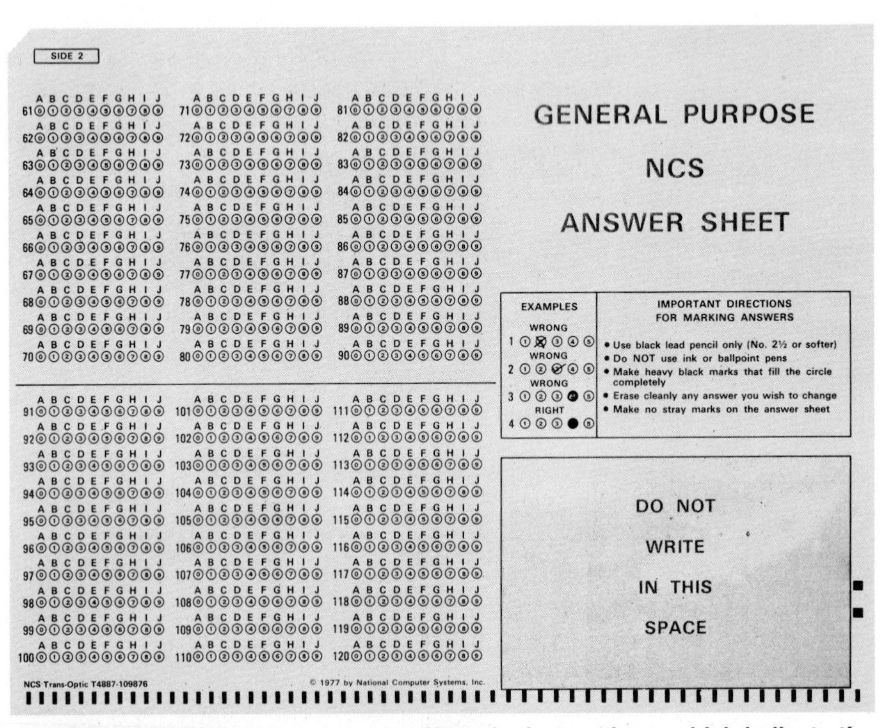
SIDE 2

GENERAL PURPOSE

NCS

ANSWER SHEET

EXAMPLES

WRONG

WRONG

WRONG

RIGHT

IMPORTANT DIRECTIONS FOR MARKING ANSWERS

- Use black lead pencil only (No. 2½ or softer)
- Do NOT use ink or ballpoint pens
- Make heavy black marks that fill the circle completely
- Erase cleanly any answer you wish to change
- Make no stray marks on the answer sheet

DO NOT WRITE IN THIS SPACE

NCS Trans-Optic T4887-109876

© 1977 by National Computer Systems, Inc.

An OMR mark-sense answer sheet Note the instructions, which indicate the restrictions on how the answer sheet may be marked. (Courtesy National Computer Systems)

Figure 4.21

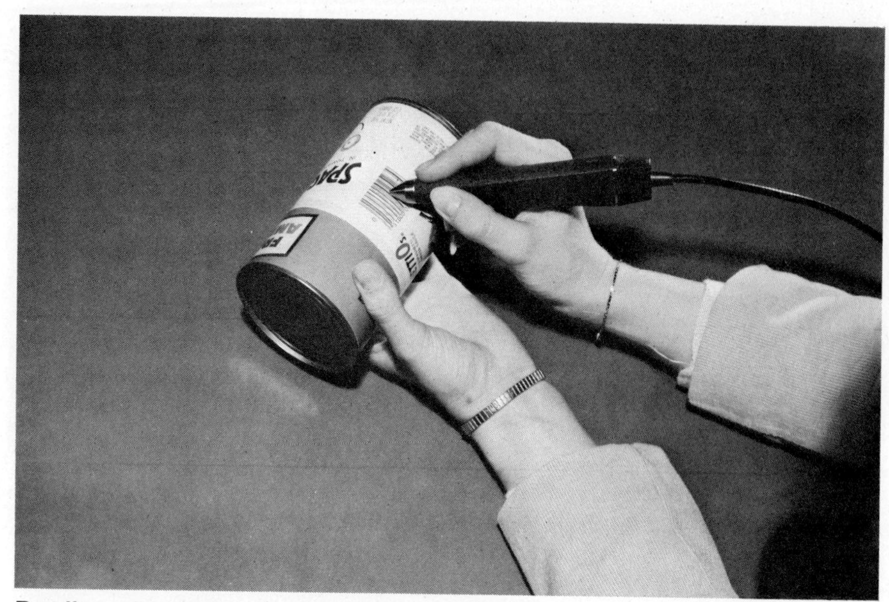

Reading a bar code Here a wand reader is being used to read a bar code for point-of-sale data entry. (Courtesy National Cash Register Co.)

The most extensive use of OMR occurs in educational testing. Bar codes are being used increasingly in point-of-sale recorders. They seem particularly adaptable to any operation, such as meter reading, where limited amounts of data are collected in the field, and to operations where data are prepared by someone outside the data processing department. OMR use is likely to remain limited, particularly as OCR technology improves.

Point-of-action entry

Point-of-action or point-of-sale entry processes are revolutionizing retail data processing and promise to have application in other areas (materials control, transportation invoicing, and others). One device is illustrated in Figure 4.22. Point-of-action entry is also common in systems for factory data collection and credit card transaction recording. Some systems merely involve standard keyboard terminals. Factory data entry systems are now quite sophisticated. Time-and-performance data necessary to job costing and control are captured at online terminals involving combined plastic-card reading and key entry. Less sophisticated (usually older) systems for collecting timecard and job-status data are stand-alone devices that create punched paper tape or punched-card records or activate central tape or card punches via a simple communications network. Most of these networks are now policed by a small computer that edits input and organizes the data on a magnetic tape or disk for later processing. Current small systems handle 4 to 16 remote stations

Figure 4.22

Point-of-sale data entry At this supermarket check-out counter the clerk records each item sold and all sales information through an online "cash register"/terminal. Note the device to the clerk's left, which prints a receipt for the customer. (Courtesy National Cash Register Co.)

and can be more economical than key entry at 7 or 8 stations. Large, shared computer systems generally involve at least 16 stations and may involve as many as 64 in large factories with many work stations.

Now available to supermarkets is an automated check-out counter that includes package-bottom-reading optical scanners, several of which can be controlled by one minicomputer, and a modified cash register terminal accessing the same mini. Currently used systems for point-of-sale (POS) recording online to a central computer provide automatic credit card validation as well as standard transactions processing. Most POS systems have built-in sequence control and instruction routines that guide the sales clerk through each transaction. Terminals can handle up to a dozen different transactions and include such activities as discounts, uneven trade-in, and down payment on the item purchased. Data-capturing mechanisms include optical wands, electromechanical devices (hand-held and fixed) for reading punched tape and cards, and magnetic readers for capturing magnetic ink encoding. Some systems merely store transactions data on tape cassettes or other machine-sensible media, whereas others perform online and enter all transactions into a central computer storage device (disk or drum).

Advanced input media and devices

Light pens

Many CRT terminals accept interactive input from the touch of a light pen on the tube face. Contrary to the implication of its name, the light pen does not really write on the tube face with light. Rather, it contains a photo cell which is activated by lighted areas of the screen to tell the computer where it is being pointed. An example of a light pen in use is shown in Figure 4.23. This device is widely used with interactive graphic CRT displays to rotate and enlarge drawings and to choose elements to be expanded upon or displayed at another level of detail.

Data are transmitted to the computer by pointing to a specific item or area on the screen. The interpretation of light pen impulses is under program control by the computer. Light pens have been used by students to input answers during computer-controlled instruction, by managers to select the reports or graphs to be displayed, and by engineers to create, rotate, expand, contract, and otherwise manipulate geometric figures and engineering drawings.

Figure 4.23

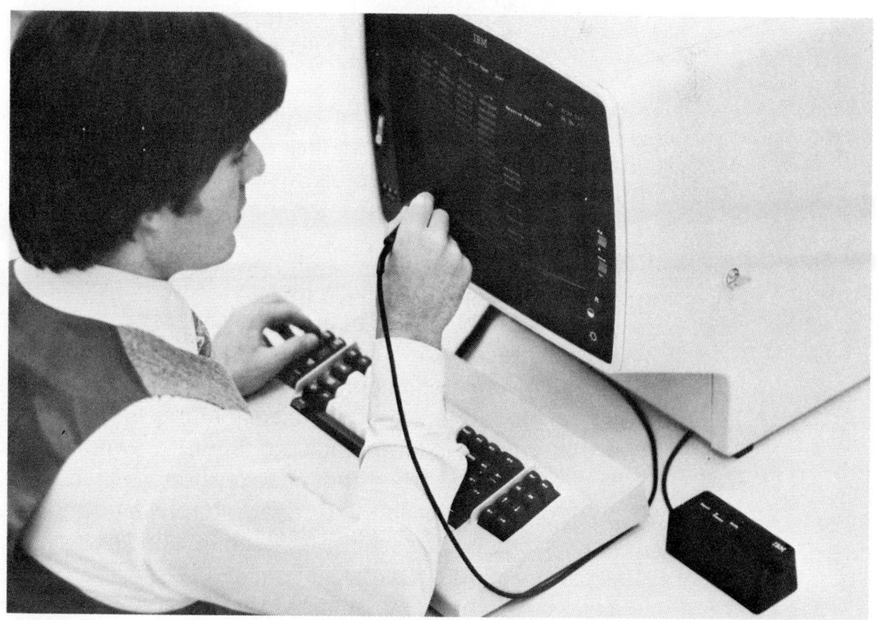

A light pen in use with an IBM 3278 CRT terminal (Courtesy IBM)

Voice input

Sound waves can be converted to electronic impulses. This fact has led to the development of a few devices that accept voice input of the basic decimal numbers and simple words like yes and no. The great limitation of voice input is that the computer must store away the voice patterns of every user. A bad cold may disguise a user's voice, so that the computer fails to respond.

Economics of data entry

Data on the costs of using different entry devices vary by application and according to the users involved. Available neutral studies tend to be fragmented and are seldom scientifically designed to provide statistical measurement of their reliability. However, certain "facts" seem to be widely accepted about costs in this area.

1. Card keypunching is less costly than other means at volumes of less than 10 million characters per month. This is due primarily to the low cost of card preparation and handling devices as compared with the cost of corresponding tape and disk devices.
2. Key-to-tape processes become economically feasible alternatives to card punches at volumes of about 10 million characters per month.
3. Standard key-to-disk processes require somewhat higher volumes before becoming feasible alternatives. The new "floppy disk" systems are competitive at smaller volumes, however.
4. Optical character recognition systems become alternatives to card punch systems in the range of 20 million to 25 million characters per month. When special typing is not required before OCR reading, these systems become alternatives to key-to-tape systems at about 25 million characters per month.
5. Point-of-action recorders would appear to be competitive to card punching at lower volumes than the other transcription processes. However, the popularity of this approach seems to be based more firmly on its speed, accuracy, and fitness for integrated systems design than on its cost advantage.

It is interesting to note that the new minicomputer and microcomputer systems for business data processing tend to favor online entry even if a keying process is involved. The saving from not purchasing, punching, verifying, and storing cards and the decreasing cost of the hardware combine to make direct entry economically attractive. Direct key entry from remote-action stations to larger multiprogrammed systems is also expanding rapidly. These trends indicate that *most* systems will involve direct entry from the point of activity in the very near future. Key transcription will still remain to handle batch processing operations and the initial conversion of files to electronic media. Cards will remain in use as turnaround documents but are likely to be printed mechanically at the point of action and read optically when returned for processing, as is being done with gasoline credit cards.

Improvements in optical readers will further simplify input processes by allowing typewriter or manual preparation of the input medium.

Summary

Media and devices for capturing (recording) data in a machine-sensible form for input to a computer are many and varied. Media carry the actual data record; the device performs a data processing function (in this case, input). Input media and devices are characterized by access method (direct or sequential), transfer rate, and capacity. These devices may be online (attached and under the control of the CPU) or offline.

Input to computers is by either key transcription to a machine-sensible medium, by-product recording on a machine-sensible medium, mark or character recognition, or direct entry. Common media are punched cards, punched paper tape, magnetic tape, magnetic disk packs, and documents for optical reading. Direct entry is accomplished by key entry at terminals. Special devices, such as light pens, special readers, and voice-entry devices, also enact direct entry.

Card keypunching is less costly than other means of data entry only at low volumes. Point-of-action recorders appear to be more competitive with card punching at lower volumes than do other transcription processes. Key-to-tape processes become economical at slightly lower volumes than key-to-disk systems. This latter difference is small enough to be outweighed by other system-design criteria. Optical recognition processes appear to be the most expensive data entry systems because original documents must be transcribed. New minicomputer and microcomputer systems for small businesses tend to favor online data entry even if a keying process is involved. Direct entry by key entry or by special devices is expanding rapidly for all sizes of computer systems.

Key terms

Define the following terms as briefly as possible and then, in a short paragraph, clarify each definition.

Access method	Cathode ray tube (CRT) terminal
Accounting machine	Character reading
By-product recording	Device
Capacity	Direct-entry device
Card collator	Direct (random) access
Card keypunch	Hollerith 80-column card
Card reader	Intelligent terminal
Card sorter	Key-to-disk device

Key-to-tape system
Key transcription
Magnetic disk pack
Magnetic ink character recognition (MICR)
Magnetic tape
Mark reading
Medium
96-column card
Offline
Online
Optical character recognition (OCR)
Optical mark recognition (OMR)
Point-of-action entry device
Punched paper tape
Reproducing punch
Sequential access
Transfer rate
Typewriter-like terminal
Unit record system
Verifier

Discussion questions

1 Compare the advantages and disadvantages of the following as input media:
  a Punched paper tape
  b Punched cards
  c Magnetic tape
  d Disk pack
2 Compare the advantages and disadvantages of key-to-tape and key-to-disk systems for data input.
3 Speculate on the effects on business data processing of the availability of a simple and cheap optical reader capable of reading most persons' handwriting.
4 In what sense are punched cards, magnetic tape, and disk packs dual-purpose media?
5 Contrast the advantages and disadvantages of point-of-action direct entry and by-product recording as means of recording data.
6 What is the main advantage of by-product recording?
7 What is the difference between magnetic ink character recognition and optical mark reading?
8 Speculate on the conditions that would make an optical reader the preferred entry device.
9 Speculate on the conditions that would favor the use of the punched card for data entry.
10 Since intelligent terminals are so much more expensive than "dumb" terminals, why are they used?

Exercises

1 Enter the data record below on the Hollerith card form provided by blacking out the locations where holes would be punched:

Field Name	Columns	Content
Employee Number	1–6	118764
Employee Name	8–34	Samuel A. Seltzer
Hours Worked	36–39	37.5
Department Number	41–43	213
Hourly Pay Rate	45–49	09.73

2 Develop a college student advising and registration system involving the use of OCR input to register the student.

Input Savings at DuPont

At E. I. DuPont Company in Wilmington, Del., a departmental data processing section has found that "small" efficiencies and the contributions of a modern data entry system pay significant dividends when applied on a large scale. Equipment features save the department a million keystrokes a month and have greatly improved operator efficiency and accuracy.

"We've saved as much time and labor costs through improvements in data entry efficiency in the last year as we did when we originally switched over from keypunch to computerized data entry." Dan O'Connor, data processing supervisor of DuPont's Fabrics and Finishes department, says.

Sixth largest of DuPont's 11 industrial departments, Fabrics and Finishes sold approximately $500 million of paints, coatings, and treated fabrics to consumers and industrial customers last year.

The department's data processing division, with 30 employees, formats and preprocesses sales-order, inventory and other accounting data furnished by manufacturing and warehouse distribution points from more than 50 other locations in the United States, Puerto Rico and Hawaii.

"With thousands of product varieties and colors, it requires a massive effort to process orders, prepare invoices and keep inventory levels correct," O'Connor says. "Until three years ago, we used keypunch equipment—including 23 IBM Model 029 and 16 Model 059 keypunches—to preprocess and consolidate data for presentation to management.

"In 1975 we began the switchover, leasing two System 1200 data entry/communications systems from Mohawk Data Sciences, and in three months, we had enough operators fully trained to do all the processing by computer.

"Our workload grew fast, and soon we needed more disk storage, so we upgraded to two MDS System 2400s," he says. "In the meantime, and especially since the 2400 installations in late 1976, we were able to take advantage of features that now save us a million keystrokes a month and have greatly improved operator efficiency and accuracy."

Verified and validated

Operators enter and verify accounting data on disk, then dump to magnetic tape for processing at DuPont's central computer installation, the Information Systems Department, located nearby. Approximately 20 magnetic tapes per night are sent by mail truck to the center's multiple, large-scale

Source: "Data Entry Efficiencies Cut Keystrokes." *Modern Office Procedures*, 24 (© April 1979), 86–88.

IBM computers by O'Connor's data processing staff. One of the MDS processors can also communicate directly with the center, utilizing IBM Remote Job Entry (RJE) protocol and a card reader.

Primary applications involve monthly tabulation and formatting of the department's customer, stock-control and accounting/invoicing master records from reports generated by all distribution points, whether by mail in printout form, by telecopies, or by low-speed communications.

Once batch-processed and validated, the records go to department management for evaluation and/or further processing on a large mainframe computer system. Other jobs requested by internal customers are done on an as-needed basis, with O'Connor smoothly moving four-operator teams into place to handle the ever-shifting workload.

Currently, the section averages from 25 to 30 million keystrokes per month, according to O'Connor, with most work revolving around the very active files of approximately 40,000 customers. A nine-digit customer identification code—which O'Connor programmed using MDS' Self-Interpreting Program (SIP) generator—has resulted in large keystroke savings.

"Using this program," O'Connor says, "a terminal operator can enter the customer's name, industry type and distribution shipping point location into the computer in nine keystrokes—eight digits for identification and a ninth, computer-determined check-digit—rather than the 40 or so it would take otherwise.

"Each of our customers has a plastic card printed with his identification number, so the number can be imprinted on the order form at the point of sale. The number accompanies the product order through the warehouse data processing system and then, by one of several transportation methods, to the central data processing section."

Additional data processing efficiencies have resulted from an MDS operator-statistics software package used to smooth internal billing procedures and work flow in general. The package has been creatively interpreted so that specific operator-convenience improvements, such as color forms, form highlights and automatic ditto marks, could be made.

Degree of difficulty

"The MDS operator statistics package lets me determine not only gross keystrokes numbers," O'Connor says, "but, just as important, the actual degree of difficulty of each procedure.

"By watching keystroke error-rate activity, I can tell when something is taking more time than it should, because the error-rate increases," he explains. "By tracing the error-rate back to the operator, I can find and correct the problem.

"For example, I saw that errors often increased when operators changed from one type form to another, like from debit to credit, because it was difficult for the operator to notice the subtle change printed on the form. Now we use different colored forms—white, blue, yellow and pink—to differentiate between form types, and error frequency is much improved."

Other procedural improvements from the statistics program include highlighting the most critical information on certain very complex forms. "Some errors are more critical than others, so the important information is highlighted to show extra caution is necessary," according to O'Connor. Adding a dittomark capacity to certain form types that demand highly repetitive information further streamlines the data entry operator's task.

"Besides helping us adjust the system to our operators' convenience, the statistics program is appreciated for its fairness, both by our internal customers and the operators themselves," O'Connor says. "Before we had this equipment, I had to judge degree of difficulty somewhat arbitrarily, which didn't help my internal billings to divisions that used our data processing facilities. Now I have absolute numbers that not only make billing precise but also smooth traffic flow in general, by showing me trends that we should adjust to expedite processing.

"And the operators like the equality and fairness of keystroke statistics, because they can see the work they're putting in, and they can see what they're getting out of it, too," O'Connor says.

"In fact, operator comfort is our top priority," he says, "beginning with the team approach to data entry and verification, where the operators decide among themselves who gets what job when, and where we all strive to close working harmony, and ending with a concern for physical comfort. The fact that MDS equipment is designed with rounded rather than sharp and potentially dangerous edges and corners was important to us when we selected it, as was the moveable keyboard on their terminals.

"What else? The temperature stays at 74 degrees consistently, we use static-repellent rugs throughout, we listen to music and we hold weekly meetings on safety and working conditions. We feel elite because we feel efficient, and we get more efficient as we get more experience on the computer system."

Chapter 5

Output Media and Devices

Outline

Output from computerized data processing systems must eventually be recognizable and usable by people. The devices that have been developed to present data and output to people can be grouped into five general types: character printers, line printers, page printers, visual displays, and voice response.

An overview of computer output media and devices is presented in Figure 5.1, which the reader should spend a few minutes studying to get a good idea of how these processes are carried out. Note that each output process involves a medium and a device. The most common medium is paper, and the most common devices are character printers, line printers, and page printers. The next most common device is designed to display information in some way. Media included here are microfilm as well as the electronic impulses of visual display terminals (VDTs) which use a cathode ray tube (CRT), TV-like display. The use of audio (voice) responses is rising rapidly, particularly in specialized situations where only a limited set of responses is needed. Other output media and devices not so widely used include punched cards (listed on paper), graphics involving the use of a plotter, and magnetic tape (used more often as back-up storage, since it must be converted to another medium to provide human-sensible output).

Hardcopy (paper) output

Character printers

The simplest devices, **character printers**, are the computer-controlled typewriters and typewriter-like devices that print 1 character per machine cycle. They are slow devices. Many print no more than 300 characters per minute but the fastest character printers approach 900 characters per minute.

Character printers use four different ways of printing. Early ones like the manual typewriter and early electric typewriters used a different *type bar* for each character. The type bar forced (struck) the ribbon against the paper, transferring the character image to the paper.

Modern character printers more frequently use a *typing element* that has all the characters molded into an element (usually ball shaped). To print a character, the element is indexed into position and struck against the ribbon, transferring the image to the paper. Speeds of up to 15 characters per second are possible. Type fonts and the character set itself are easily changed by mounting a different typing element.

A third method of character printing mounts the characters on a **type wheel**. To print a character, the wheel is rotated to the correct character and then forced against the ribbon and paper.

The fourth method of printing characters, the **matrix character printer**, is rising rapidly in popularity. The matrix is composed of wires or tiny rods

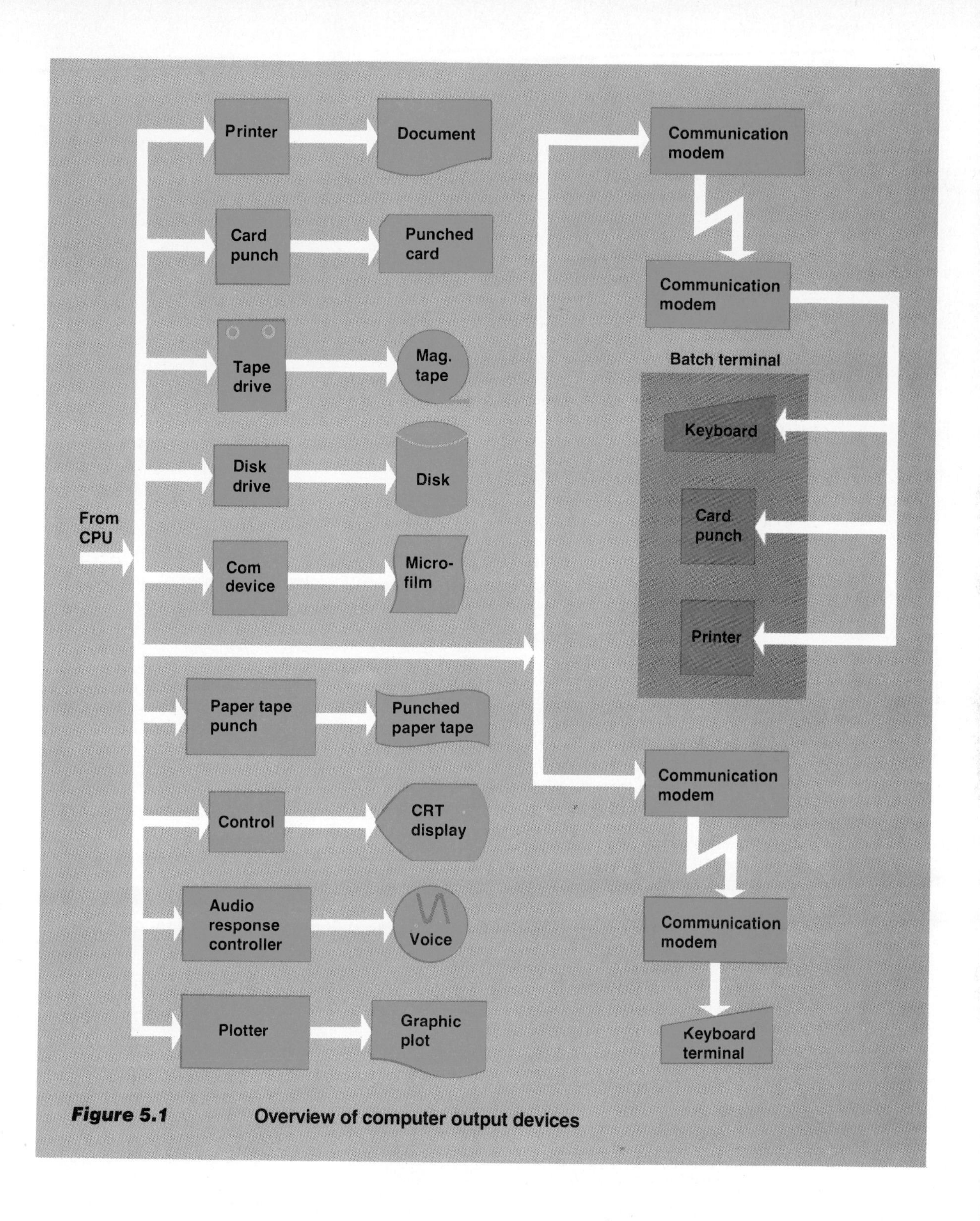

Figure 5.1 Overview of computer output devices

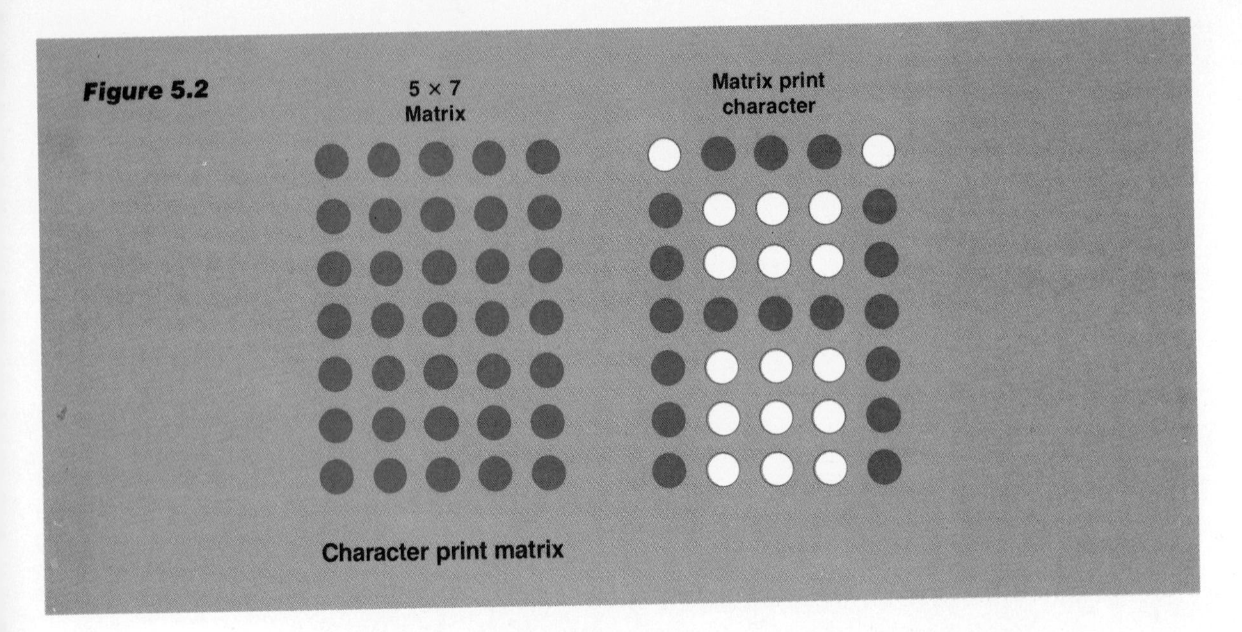

Figure 5.2

arranged in a rectangle. Commonly, the rectangle is composed of 5-by-7 or 7-by-9 rods. To print a character, the rods forming the character are thrust forward to press the ribbon against the paper, and the character is formed by the configuration of dots (see Figure 5.2).

Line and page printers

Line printers print an entire line on each machine cycle. **Page printers** print an entire page in one machine cycle. Line printers are both impact and nonimpact. Page printers are only nonimpact.

Impact line printers

The most common devices used strictly for output are line printers. Most are **impact printers**, which print by forcing (impacting) the type character against the ribbon and paper. There are four major types: the bar printer, the drum printer, the chain printer, and the matrix line printer.

Bar printer The **bar printer** features a vertical type bar at each print position which contains all the print characters. It is the slowest of the impact printers because the bars must move up to position the proper symbol for printing at each character position. At the instant that the desired characters are in position, a magnetically activated hammer pushes paper and ribbon against the bar. Typical speeds are 200 to 300 lines per minute. Line length is usually 120 characters.

Drum printer The **drum printer** takes its name from the horizontal drum, or print cylinder, that contains the possible print characters. Each character is repeated at each possible character position across a row on the drum. Thus, each circular column around the drum contains every possible character. Hammers at each print position strike whenever the proper character is in position, and several may strike simultaneously, so that the entire line is printed in one drum rotation. The number of different characters that can be printed (usually between 50 and 60) varies with drum size. The drum printer usually features 132 characters per line and prints at speeds varying from 200 to 3,000 lines per minute, but most operate at 1,000 to 1,500 lines per minute. Very few operate at speeds above 1,500 lines per minute (see Figure 5.3).

Chain printer The **chain printer** uses a rapidly moving chain whose links are engraved character printing slugs. The chain contains five sections of the characters available (usually 48). As the chain moves continuously at a constant and rapid speed across the paper, hammers at each print position strike when the proper character is at that position. Printing speeds of 2,000 lines per minute are possible. Chain printers commonly operate at about 1,200 lines per minute. Figure 5.4 shows a typical chain printer; Figure 5.5 shows a print chain.

Figure 5.3

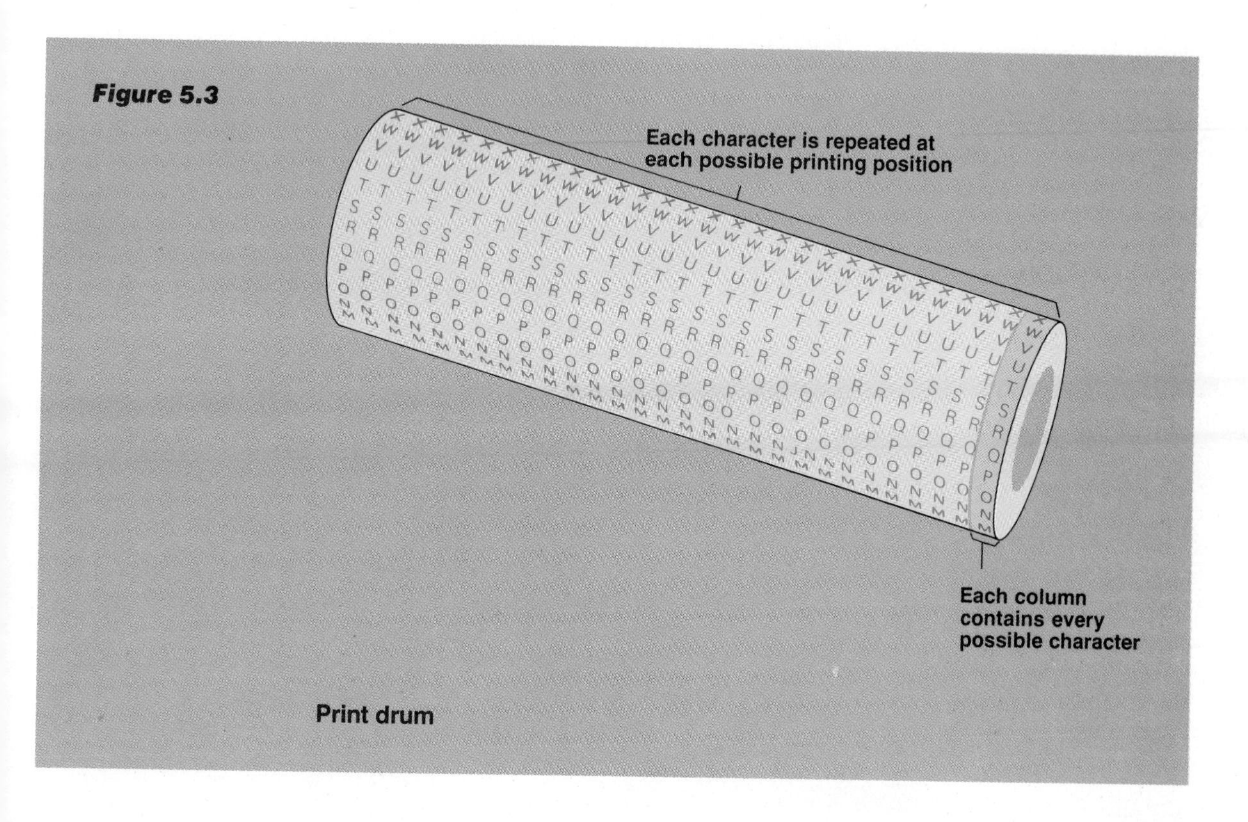

Print drum

Figure 5.4

Chain printer   Note the continuous sheet of paper. The holes along the edges of the paper fit over pins on the paper drive.   (Courtesy IBM)

Figure 5.5

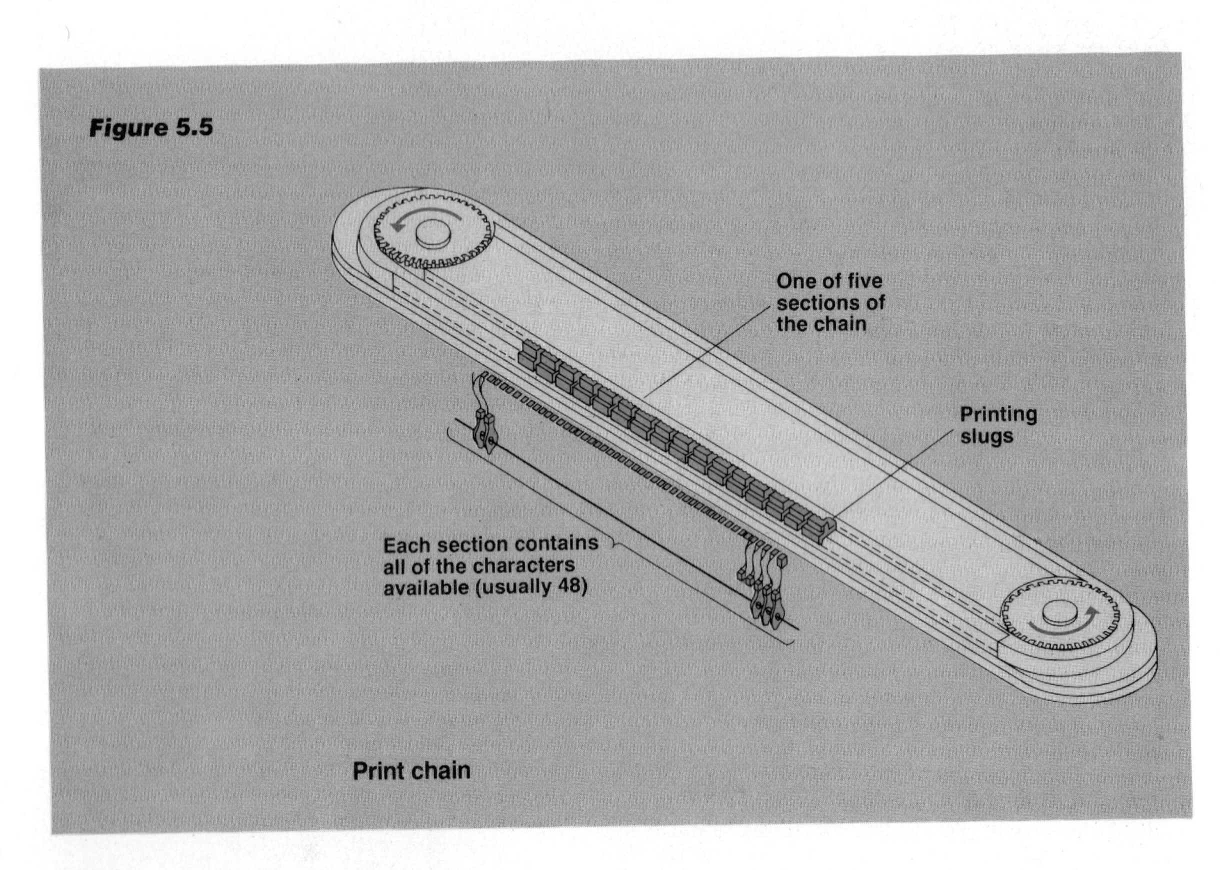

Print chain

Matrix line printer The matrix line printer has a character matrix at each print position across a line, and all are activated on a single machine cycle.

Nonimpact printers

Nonimpact printers use ink jets, electrothermal imaging, electrostatic imaging, CRT/photographic techniques, and laser/xerographic processes, rather than impact methods, to place the image on the page. Ink jet printers are actually character or line printers. The rest of these devices also print either 1 character or 1 line at a time, but they are very fast, and their final output usually consists of single loose pages. Consequently, they are often referred to as page printers.

Ink jet printers The most common type of ink jet printer uses magnetic or electrostatic "steering" to direct a spray of fine droplets of ink. On the paper, the droplets form dots that make up characters in a way similar to matrix printing. The steering process directs the ink jet through the matrix positions to form the character. Another kind of ink jet printer uses a special magnetic ink that is attracted to a magnetically formed character behind the paper.

Electrothermal imaging Electrothermal imaging is also a variant of the matrix printer. A heat-sensitive paper is used, and the rods defining a character are heated and touched to the paper to create the character image. This is a relatively slow and cumbersome technique, which requires special paper. Since the paper is very sensitive, it can be spoiled by exposure to heat, even that from human touch.

Electrostatic imaging In electrostatic imaging, the character shapes are charged onto the paper in the form of dots of static electric charge. When exposed to ink, the static charges cause ink particles to stick to the paper, thus forming the characters. Speeds of 2,000 to 5,000 lines per minute are possible, but special inks (toners) and special paper are required.

CRT/photographic technique The CRT/photographic technique starts with the formation of characters on a cathode ray tube (CRT). The lighted characters are exposed to photographic film or paper, which is then developed by the ordinary photographic process. Again, special chemicals and special paper are required. This technique is not as fast as the electrostatic process, but the characters produced are very clear and true. As a result, CRT/photographic techniques are used mainly to set type suitable for making printing plates.

Laser/xerographic imaging The fastest printer in common use today (1982)—laser/xerographic imaging—uses a low-power laser beam to paint the mirror image of characters on the light-sensitive surface covering a rotating drum. Each character is formed in a dot matrix. Reproduction onto the paper is by the same xerographic process that occurs in office copying machines—the character shapes are negatively charged to attract particles

Figure 5.6

A laser/xerographic printer The Xerox 9700 laser/xerographic printing system can print complex forms and attain speeds of over 20,000 lines per minute. (Courtesy Xerox Corp.)

of toner. Speeds up to 23,000 lines per minute are possible. At that rate, most of this book could be printed in one minute. Figure 5.6 shows such a printer.

Impact printers versus nonimpact printers

Printer output is on paper. Standard paper for use on impact printers is usually wider than standard letter-sized paper, and carbons must be used if multiple copies are desired. To provide positive feed control, impact line printers and the faster impact character printers use pin feed control. Each of the side edges of the paper (beyond the printed sections) contains a row of holes. Pins mounted on the ends of the paper drive or on the printing platen engage the holes in the paper to drive it smoothly forward with little chance of misalignment or wrinkling. Most paper for impact printers comes as a **continuous form**, one long sheet that folds like a fan. A line of perforations separates individual forms. After printing, the individual sheets must be separated and the pin-feed edge holes removed. These tasks are usually accomplished with a machine known as a **forms burster**, which can also separate forms that are less than full-page size. Carbons are removed and multiple copies separated on a **decollator**.

Storage of impact-printed output requires large file drawers and cabinets, although special binders and associated rack-type storage devices are also available.

In contrast, most nonimpact printers produce output on letter-size 8½-by-11-inch paper. However, most nonimpact printers require specially treated paper, which can be costly. Some nonimpact printers are now able to print on both sides of a sheet of paper, which halves paper cost.

A major advantage of nonimpact printers is speed. They are usually so fast that multiple copies of documents can be printed individually, which overcomes the disadvantage of cumbersome carbon paper and limited numbers of copies. Another advantage of nonimpact printers is that they are quieter. There is no need for the clanking hammers of the impact machine, the noise from which usually requires that impact printers be isolated from office work areas. (We should also mention, however, that there is current controversy about certain chemicals used in some nonimpact machines, which are suspected to be potentially hazardous to health. Though not conclusively proven at this time, this potential hazard could influence the operation and use of nonimpact machines in the future.)

Another major advantage of several nonimpact printers is their ability to rotate the paper 90 degrees. This means lines, characters, and words may be printed in almost any direction between horizontal and vertical in one pass through the printer. This allows the use of blank paper stock for all forms. Complex forms are printed and the content entered in one pass through the machine, resulting in significant savings in total paper costs. Finally, the quality of printed output is much better with nonimpact printers, and some nonimpact printers offer multiple type fonts.

By limiting the character set of an impact printer, faster print speeds are possible. Actual speeds for a given printer will vary depending on whether the material being printed is all numeric, all alphabetic, or mixed numeric and alphabetic. In addition, single or double spacing will affect print speeds for line printers. Actual impact-printer production rates will depend on all these factors, plus the factor of idle time caused by the need to change printing forms.

Prices of line printers vary widely. Price goes up for faster print speeds, for larger character sets, and for the ability to print different numbers of lines per inch. Normal line spacing is 6 lines per inch, but some printers can print 8. Prices are lower if only 120 characters per line are printed rather that the more normal 132. Print-quality levels (uniformity of character formation, constant line and character spacing, straightness of lines) can also affect price. Pleasing appearance, good form alignment, and high print quality are desirable in a printer preparing custodial documents.

Thermal printers can be produced much more cheaply than impact printers, but the paper they require is quite expensive. In general, the cheaper the printing device, the more expensive the paper and the cheaper the paper, the more expensive the device, if quality output is to be obtained.

Visual display devices

Cathode ray tubes and computer-output microfilm are the visual display devices in most common use, although other forms exist, such as a plotter that adds a third dimension in the form of vertical wires each clipped to an appropriate length.

Cathode ray tube (CRT) displays

The CRT terminal is used for both input and output. On input, the screen is used for queries, forms display, and visual checking of input. Input is actually keyed through the typewriter-like keyboard of the device. On output, most CRT devices only *display* output, they do not provide hardcopy (printed copy) of that output. The CRT display works much like your TV screen. An electron beam scans back and forth across the phospor-coated inner face of the display tube at high speeds. When a spot is not to be written, the beam is turned off. When the beam is on, the phosphor coating is activated and glows. The glowing spots create the character images, lines, curves, or other figures seen on the screen.

Applications

CRT devices are widely used for individual input/output terminals in interactive, online systems. (**Interactive** means that the person using the terminal interacts with the computer by exchanging questions and answers with the machine.) CRTs can quickly display system status, for example, information on the number of seats available on an airline flight. They can also present complex answers quickly since a display can be filled at rates as high as 10,000 characters per second. They can support management decision making by quickly presenting the results of interactive analysis; for example, can units sold be expected to change and, if so, by how much, if the unit price is dropped 25 cents?

One special use of the CRT is for graphic displays. Figure 5.7 illustrates this capability. Many types of graphic displays are possible, such as graphs, charts, and line drawings that help make complex relationships easier to understand. You will also recall from Chapter 4 that some CRTs, whether displaying graphics or characters, will accept input from a light pen.

With the addition of a microprocessor (computer processor on a single microcircuit board), a CRT terminal can become an intelligent terminal capable of independent processing. This allows complex editing of input and output to reduce errors as well as other independent processing.

Advantages of CRTs

The major advantages of CRT devices are speed and the ability to display graphics. Another advantage can be cost. The cheapest electronic displays are cheaper than the best-quality hardcopy terminals. If hardcopy is occasionally needed, a printing device can be linked to the CRT. Finally, CRT terminals can be located at remote sites accessible only by telephone if a communication device is added.

Disadvantages of CRTs

The greatest disadvantage of the CRT display is the lack of a permanent record of display contents, whether it is input or output. If such a record is required, a printer or microfilm unit must be attached to the CRT terminal.

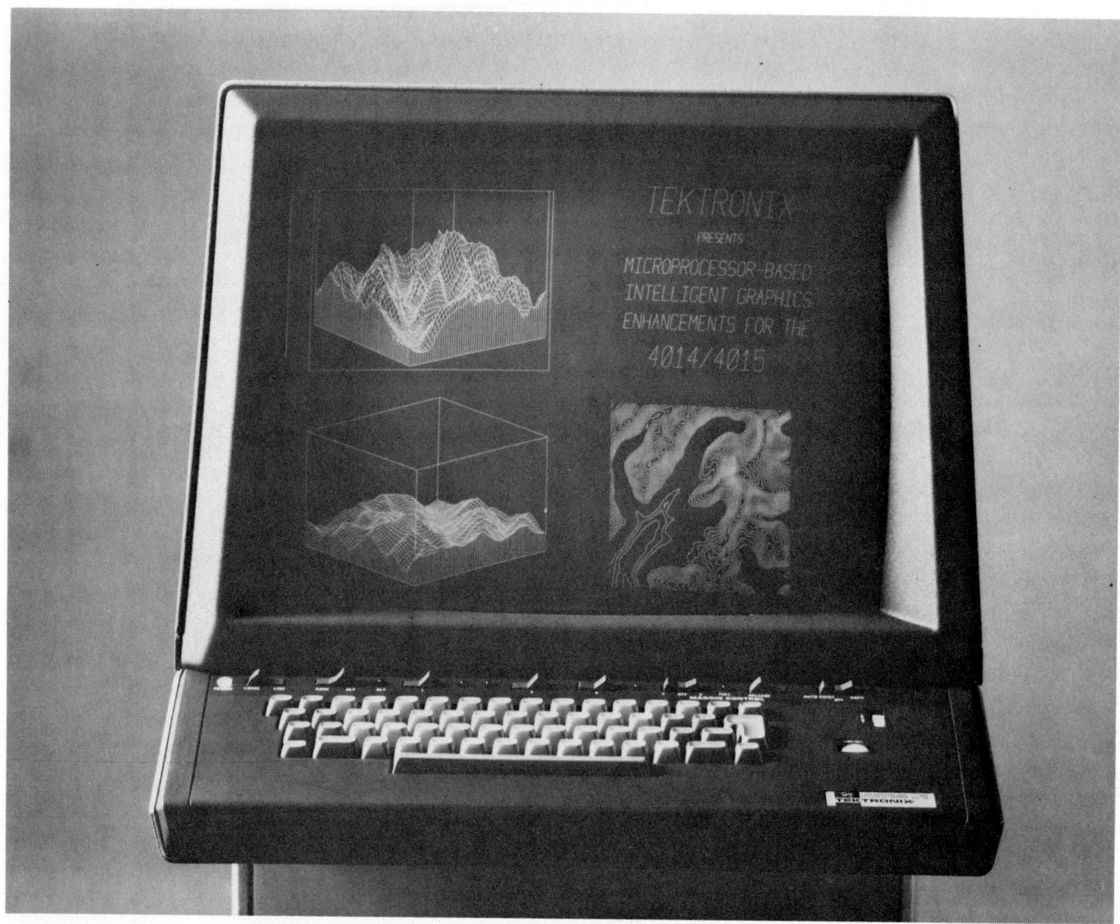

Figure 5.7 **A CRT terminal with graphics capability** **This Tektronix 4014-1 Computer Display Terminal features interactive keyboard control of high density alphanumeric or graphic computer output. It can also provide hardcopy output. (Courtesy Tektronix, Inc.)**

Computer-output microfilm (COM)

One method of speeding output and reducing output-media storage requirements at the same time is to put the output on microfilm. An overview of the **computer-output microfilm (COM)** process is given in Figure 5.8. Part a shows the general process, and part b shows how the film is recorded and used. Fiber optics are substituted for the CRT in some systems. The end of each optical fiber displays a portion of the "picture" to be filmed. A third form writes directly on the film with an electron beam. COM can be produced online from the host computer or offline from magnetic tapes or disks.

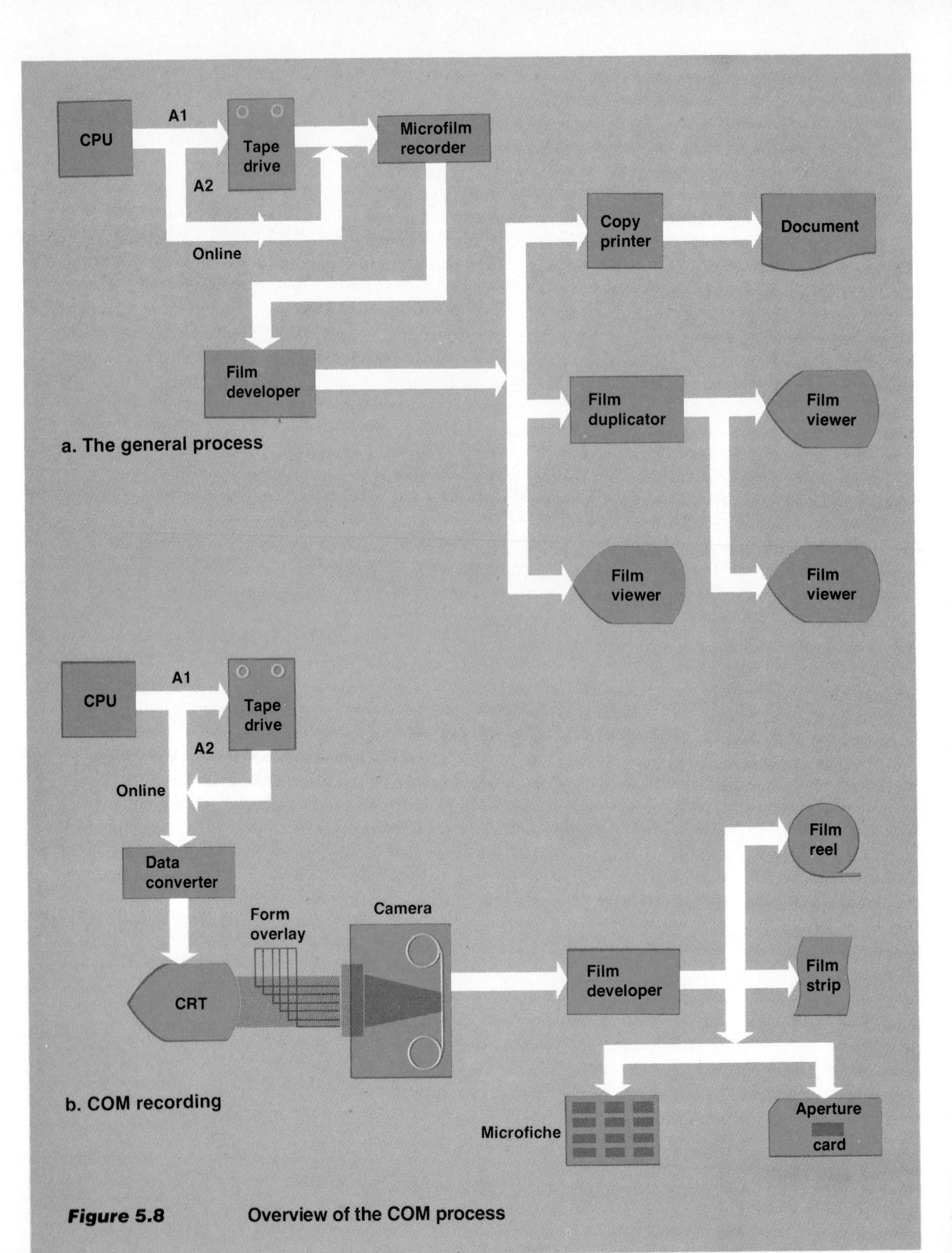

Figure 5.8 Overview of the COM process

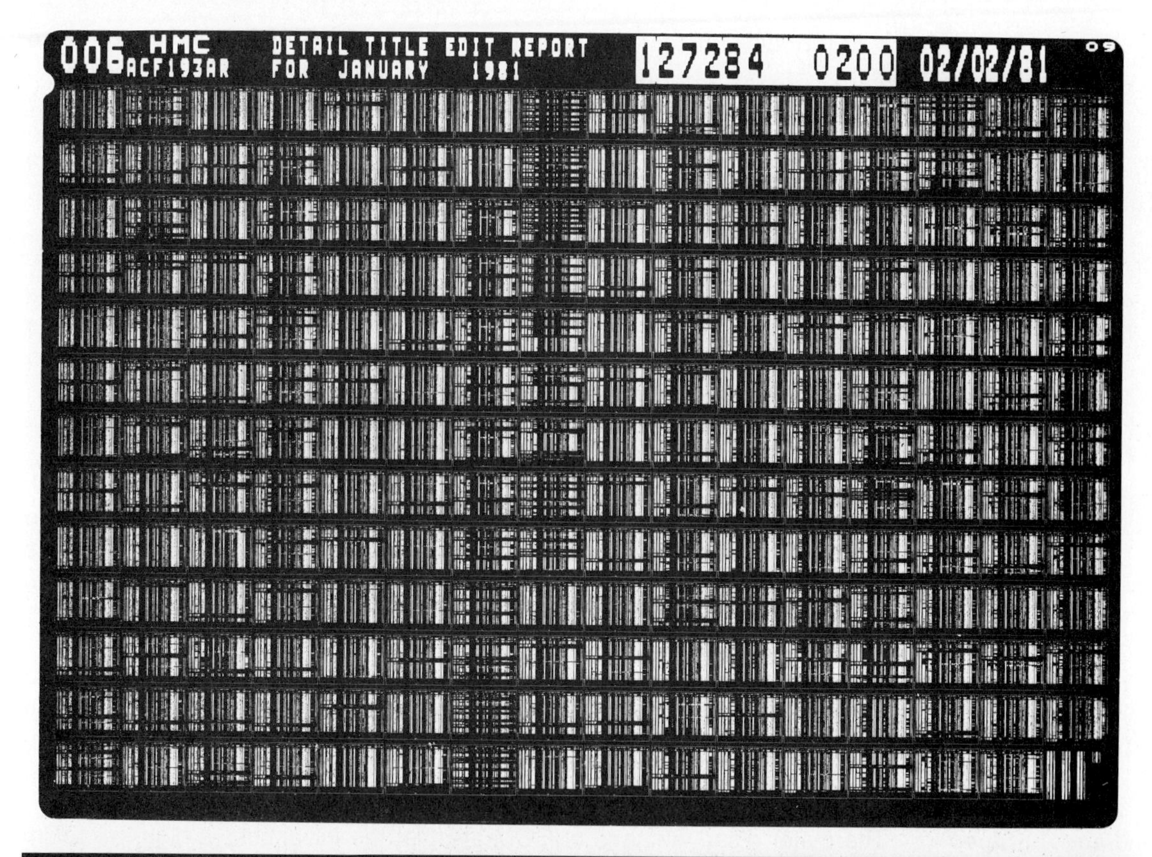

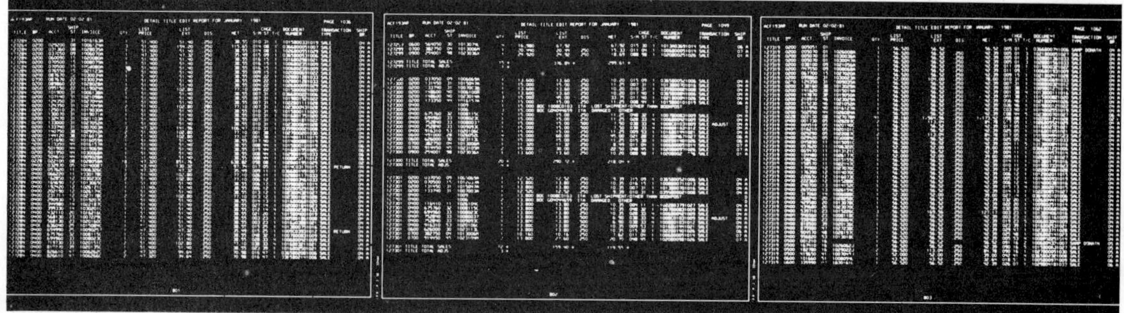

Figure 5.9 **A microfiche card The entire card, shown at the top, contains as much information as would fit on several hundred paper documents. The lower portion shows an enlargement of a segment of the card, and gives some idea of what you see when you view the card through a microfiche reader.**

Applications

Microfilm outputs are of four types as shown in the figure. The film can be used as a reel of film or cut into special film strips, normally containing 12 frames (pictures) per strip. An individual frame can be mounted on aperture cards or photographed onto a small portion of a rectangular microfiche (see Figure 5.9). One 8½-by-11-inch microfiche card can store thousands of printed pages in some systems. Microfiche cards come in several sizes. Through the use of a computer-generated indexing system, stored microfilm, either tapes or fiche, can be quickly retrieved and displayed.

COM saves printer time not only at output time but also in situations where many copies are needed. With the aid of a forms overlay, custodial documents can be produced. Typical COM speeds are up to 60,000 lines per minute, which is closer to the internal transfer rate of the computer than are the speeds of other hardcopy devices. COM-produced files are compact, and retrieval can be mechanized and therefore made rapid and essentially direct.

Advantages of COM

Where output volume is large, COM offers compact storage, reduced handling costs, quick retrieval of stored records, reduced paper costs, fast and simple reproduction of computer output in any number of copies, and efficient system design.

About 40 pounds of computer output can be stored on 25 four-by-six-inch sheets of microfiche at the normal 24-to-1 reduction rate. Thousands of pages of information on a variety of activities can be stored in a small space. Catalogues, inventory lists, and work schedules can be made available to widely dispersed employees. If additional film copies are needed, they are quick and easy to produce. Also, the quality of every copy remains the same. Paper costs are reduced when film reading is substituted for receipt of a printed copy.

A major advantage of COM is speed. Output on microfilm is created at rates of 60,000 lines per minute and up, which is about three times the speed of the fastest available printer.

Disadvantages of COM

The major disadvantages of COM are that the initial cost is high, microfilm cannot be read without a viewer, and microfilm cannot be written upon or modified when evaluating reports. The increasing use of COM attests to the fact that its advantages outweigh its disadvantages.

Plotters

Another visual display device is the **plotter**. A plotter is in reality a special-purpose printer that outlines drawings. There are two general types, the flat-bed plotter and the drum plotter (see Figure 5.10). Drum plotters move the paper past a stylus (pen) that can move only horizontally back and forth across the paper. The combined movement of the stylus and the paper creates curves and can represent three dimensions. Control is either directly from the computer or by instructions the computer has written on magnetic tape. Flat-bed or table plotters spread the paper over the flat bed (table) of the plotter. The stylus can then move in two dimensions above the paper. The table plotter is also controlled by computer instructions either directly or from magnetic tape. Some styles of plotters use multiple styluses to allow for different colors and different line weights.

Figure 5.10 **A drum plotter This particular plotter, the CalComp 1055, is equipped with four styluses and can plot at a speed of 76.2 centimeters (30 inches) per second. (Courtesy CalComp)**

Applications

Plotters have been used in engineering, drafting, and design of styled products such as autos and dresses. They are now being used as part of interactive graphics systems. CRT graphics terminals are used interactively with special software to allow executives to analyze data relationships online. Hardcopy plots may then be prepared on plotters. However, most applications of plotters to data have been for noneconomic analyses. They are not as flexible in use as are the graphic CRT terminals.

Advantages of plotters

Plotters allow visual display of complex relationships, encouraging and supporting the definitions and analyses of interrelationships among problem elements.

Disadvantages of plotters

The major disadvantages of plotters are their cost and their inflexibility. The new micrographics systems on CRT graphic terminals are much more flexible and no more expensive, even when a hardcopy capability is added.

Special output devices

Voice-response output devices

Voice response is being used in computer-controlled inquiry systems to provide a response that does not require the operator to read the response and/or makes telephone inquiry possible. Spoken words (or syllables in more sophisticated systems) are prerecorded on a storage medium (the magnetic drum, the magnetic disk, and photographic-film drums are being used). Each word or syllable is given a code. The computer program composes responses to inquiries in the form of coded messages. The coded reply is sent to the audio-response device, which assembles a proper sequence of prerecorded spoken elements and transmits the message back to the station from which the inquiry came. Use of voice response is expanding rapidly. It is used in a number of credit card validation systems. At the New York Stock Exchange, the computer verbally quotes the latest price and volume information on NYSE stocks in response to telephone inquiries from subscribers to the quotation service.

The major advantage of voice response is that every touch-tone telephone becomes an inquiry station. With the addition of small portable terminals, any telephone can become a terminal. Complicated inquiries can be typed in and an audio response returned.

Hardcopy terminals

Hardcopy terminals are interactive typewriters and typewriter-like devices. Key entry is the method of input, character printing on paper is the output method. An example of a hardcopy terminal is shown in Figure 5.11. As output devices, hardcopy terminals are really just very slow character printers. Their major advantage as interactive devices is that they provide a paper copy of both input and output. Their major disadvantages as both output and interactive devices is their slow speed. CRT terminals are much faster and easier to use in interactive systems.

Figure 5.11

The DECwriter LA-34 hardcopy terminal (Courtesy Digital Equipment Corp.)

Portable terminals

Portable terminals are hardcopy or CRT terminals with built-in modems. The **modem** (*mod*ulator *dem*odulator) is a device for converting electronic impulses representing data in the sending terminal or the computer into sound impulses (data tones) for transmission over a telephone line. The modem also converts the sound back to electronic machine impulses at the receiving end. An example of a portable terminal is shown in Figure 5.12. The main advantage of portable terminals is that they allow access to the computer from any telephone. Their major application has been to provide salespeople in the field with access to customer and inventory files and to computing power. A few executives use the portable terminals to access company data and to tap into the power of the computer when away from the office. Portable terminals have been widely used in education and research to provide computer access at sites away from the campus or research laboratory.

Figure 5.12

A portable terminal **The Texas Instruments model 787 is a hardcopy portable terminal that prints at 120 characters per second. The 787 is equipped with an internal modem that can be plugged directly into a phone line and allows the user to "dial" with the terminal's keyboard. This terminal weighs 17 pounds. (Courtesy Texas Instruments, Inc.)**

Portable terminals are most frequently hardcopy; the printing is accomplished by use of thermal paper and a matrix character printer. Electrothermal matrix printers are less expensive than other smaller printers. They are also lighter and therefore more portable. The terminal in Figure 5.12 weighs less than 20 pounds including the case.

Summary

There are many ways to obtain computer output. Each form involves a medium (data-carrying element) and a device (machine element to produce or use the medium). The most commonly used device is the line printer, which prints a complete line with one machine cycle. Other types are character printers and page printers.

Line printers work either by striking a character- or line-carrying element against the ribbon and the paper (impact printers) or by using ink jets, electrothermal imaging, electrostatic imaging, CRT/photographic techniques, or laser/xerographic imaging (nonimpact printers). So-called page printers use only nonimpact printing processes.

Printing speeds vary from the 150 characters per minute of the slowest character printer to around 20,000 lines per minute of the fastest nonimpact page printer. The most common speeds are 600–800 characters per minute for character printers, 1,200–2,000 lines per minute for impact line printers, and 4,000–13,000 lines per minute for nonimpact line and page printers, with 5,000 lines and up the most common speeds for page printers.

Nonimpact printers can print only one copy at a time, but their speed makes it possible to print multiple copies individually.

Other output methods are cathode ray tube (CRT) displays, computer output microfilm (COM), plotters, and voice response. The CRT terminals are increasingly used for both input and output as interactive online systems have become common. COM is the fastest output process with speeds of 60,000 lines per minute and more. Microfilm output reduces the volume of output, can be easily and quickly reproduced in an unlimited number of copies of constant quality, and reduces storage and distribution costs. Computer-indexed storage systems make microfilm a quick and easy medium for retrieval and display of records.

CRT terminals are being increasingly used to analyze business data. Use of plotters to provide graphic displays is also increasing. Hardcopy terminals are not as widely used as CRT terminals. Portable terminals provide computer access from any telephone and put computing power in the hands of salespeople and traveling executives.

Key terms

Define the following terms as briefly as possible and then, in a short paragraph, clarify each definition.

Bar printer
Chain printer
Character printer
Computer-output microfilm (COM)
Continuous form
CRT/photographic technique
Decollator
Drum printer
Electrostatic imaging
Electrothermal imaging
Forms burster
Hardcopy terminal
Impact printer
Ink jet printer
Interactive
Laser/xerographic imaging
Line printer
Matrix character printer
Matrix line printer
Modem
Nonimpact printer
Page printer
Plotter
Portable terminal
Type wheel
Voice response

Discussion questions

1 What are the major advantages and disadvantages of impact line printers?
2 What are the major advantages and disadvantages of nonimpact printers?
3 Under what conditions should COM be used?
4 Since nonimpact printers are much faster, why do you suppose impact line printers are the most common printer used with the computer?
5 What are the advantages and disadvantages of COM as a computer output device?
6 In what way or ways can punched cards be considered a dual-purpose input/output medium?
7 Which output media can be used for input?
8 What is the fastest computer output device?
9 What is the slowest computer output device?
10 What, in your opinion, is the best type of computer terminal? Why?
11 Speculate on what computerized data processing systems might look like today if printers had never advanced beyond 300 lines per minute.

Exercises

1 Develop a plan for a college student advising system which would use CRT display terminals in the advising and registering of students.
2 A regional auto parts distributor carries approximately 25,000 items in inventory and services about 150 auto dealers and garages and 50 auto parts retailers. How might this distributor use each of the following:
   a COM
   b CRT terminals
   c A laser-imaging page printer

DATA PROCESSING UPDATE

From Line Printers to Page Printer

One of the nation's leading manufacturers of decorative hardware for the home is using a computer page printer to speed the production and distribution of daily reports and to reduce to one-half the floor space formerly needed for paper supplies.

"For several years we had a problem with two very large, very important reports for inventory planning and dispatching," according to George Sundberg, manager of DP operations at Amerock Corp. here. "The reports, which totaled about 1,500 pages, didn't get generated until about 6 a.m. It was physically impossible to get them ready in time for people coming into the manufacturing operations an hour later.

"Because the reports were received late, they were using the previous day's information, with the result that the data they were looking at was about 24 hours out of sync. This caused available components and capacity to be allocated to jobs which were not really of the highest priority," the operations manager said.

In April 1977, Sundberg replaced two 950 line/min impact printers with the Honeywell, Inc. Page Printing System Model I (PPS I).

Operating at 12,000 line/min, the system reduced print time by 25%, enabling the two reports to be ready on time. Unlike the impact printers it replaced, the PPS I prints an original document on standard size paper, reducing the need for forms bursters and eventually eliminating decollators.

Helps upgrade jobs

Not only has the system improved the turnaround time on all reports, it has also helped upgrade the job function of many people previously responsible for collating and distribution tasks, Sundberg said. For example, all reports had previously come from the computer system and were printed out by computer operators. Employees then decollated these reports and determined the distribution list and number of copies to be sent to each individual.

Distribution, number and decollation are now all handled by the PPS I. This has not only trimmed three to four hours a night from the distribution process, but it has also given those employees responsible for distribution the opportunity to operate the PPS I.

Sundberg also pointed out that the use of the PPS I eliminated the need for $10,000 in

Source: "*Printer Speeds* Manufacturer's Reports," *Computerworld,* February 25, 1980, SR3, 12.

labor costs which would have been required if Amerock had continued to use impact printers.

Honeywell's nonimpact printer operates electrostatically, using roll-feed dielectric paper from Crown Zellerbach Corp. Data and forms images are electrostatically conveyed to the paper as it passes through the system.

Format information, such as logos or headings, are flashed onto the paper as it passes over a changeable magnesium cylinder. The data from the tape unit is conveyed to the paper as it passes over a matrix print head.

A liquid ink or toner is then drawn and bonded to the electrostatic images so the images can be read.

The PPS I is compatible with most mainframes. At Amerock, however, the principal systems are Honeywell 6640s with 256K words per machine.

Advantages of system

A primary feature of the system, Sundberg emphasized, is its ability to print general ledger, sales reports, manufacturing priority lists, inventory reports and a myriad of internal reports without the need for messy printout carbons that are often illegible.

"People no longer complain that their light-colored dress shirts have been fogged up by carbon printouts," he noted.

In addition, the roll-feed paper has halved the storage areas previously needed for paper supplies.

The system uses roll-cut paper to provide sheets 8.5 or 11 in. wide and from 3 to 14 in. long. Unlike the odd-sized computer printouts of the impact printer, the roll-cut paper is versatile and convenient to store. Paper waste averages below 2%.

Other advantages Sundberg likes are:

If holes need to be punched in pages for ring-binder storage, this information is easily keyed into the print subsystem's minicomputer. Perforation can also be keyed in as a requirement.

The Honeywell PPS I is a stand-alone system that freed the two Honeywell computers for other jobs. When the mainframes had been used with impact printers, the process occupied a large percentage of their time.

Custom forms on the PPS I cost the same as stock paper after a cylinder for the custom form has been made. This cylinder usually costs about $350 to $500.

Today, Amerock uses the Honeywell PPS I to produce 850,000 pages monthly and is now considering customer catalog production on the equipment. Overall, Sundberg is pleased with the system and the quality of the paper.

Chapter 6

Secondary Storage

Outline

Modern computer systems are complex combinations of a CPU and numerous peripherals (see Figure 2.8, page 31). Their software and hardware systems often provide interactive processing in the "foreground" (highest priority) and batch processing in the "background" (lowest priority). Users are often geographically dispersed—spread around a building or around the entire earth. Access may be by direct cable in the local area and by public telephone circuits or dedicated telecommunication lines for more remote locations. Users may be involved in any number of activities. They may be inputting data, or they may be creating a routine report or a special report. They may simply query a data base, or they may engage in sophisticated data analysis. They may create, edit, and reproduce written material (word processing). All this is made possible by the speed of modern processors and by the use of peripheral storage devices (secondary memory). This chapter focuses on the secondary storage devices necessary to today's systems.

Uses of secondary storage

Secondary storage has many uses. It stores the large masses of data (the data bases) that are the cornerstone of today's integrated data processing systems. It provides libraries of programs for users, both private user programs and the language translators (compilers) that users require to develop and run their own programs. Parts of the system executive (supervisory program) reside in secondary storage and are "rolled into" the CPU only when being used. Finally, the status of every job in the total job stream that is not immediately active in the central processor must be maintained in detail. To reactivate a job when its turn comes, one must know the status of all machine registers, the next instruction to process, the value of the data elements being operated upon, and the results already produced. This information is normally stored in secondary storage.

Common characteristics of secondary storage

The most common media for secondary memory are magnetically recorded tapes and disks. Large-capacity storage devices designed to provide online access to very, very large amounts (masses) of data and information are called **mass-storage systems**. Some mass-storage systems incorporate tape and disk technology, others use magnetic cores, microcircuits, or bubbles as the recording medium. All possess the common characteristic of being attached to the CPU through special input/output controllers. All can be expanded in modules, and all are judged by certain critical operating characteristics.

Channels

Figure 6.1 combines and extends Figures 4.3 (page 74) and 5.1 (page 107) to incorporate the concept of a channel. A **channel** consists of a hardware device and the associated communication links (cables, telecommunication lines) that control and accomplish the flow of data and information between the primary storage in the CPU and the peripheral I/O and storage devices. Data flow into and out of the primary storage through one or more data paths commonly referred to as **ports**. Each channel is attached to a port and can control access to a variety of input, output, and secondary storage devices. A signal from the CPU initiates the transfer of data associated with these devices. The channel then carries the task to completion, operating independently of the central processor which may then return to other processing. When the data transfer from or to a peripheral device is completed, the channel so informs the CPU.

A channel may be a physically separate unit linked to the CPU by an electronic cable, it may be a part of the peripheral device itself, or it may be a special part of the CPU. For efficient operation, a large computer system (mainframe) will require several channels for communication with the peripheral devices attached to the CPU. Channels control the buffering (described in Chapter 2) between the CPU and the input/output devices. It is the buffering concept and channels that make overlapping of functions possible.

Channels are themselves special-purpose computers. Regardless of their location and regardless of what devices they control (input, output, or secondary storage), channels must fill and empty buffers and monitor the flow of data between system components. To do this, they must handle input, storage, data transfer, and output functions. In modern systems, a microprocessor (a computer on a chip) carries out these tasks as directed by the CPU. It is the incorporation of this preprogrammed intelligence that gives channels their ability to perform independently of the central processor. Obviously, each channel can perform only one operation at a time, and the number of operations that can be overlapped depends directly on the number of channels available on the system. A channel that can handle only one device at a time is called a **selector channel**. Channels that can be active with several devices at one time are called **multiplexor channels**, or just multiplexors. A byte multiplexor handles 1 byte at a time from each of its several devices, intermixing the bytes. A block multiplexor works with a group of bytes from each device it controls and intermixes these blocks. (Multiplexors can, in practice, be thought of as performing more than one operation at a time.)

Access methods

Secondary storage can be classified by type of access. As noted in Chapter 4, sequential-access devices do not provide the same access time for each item read. The time to access the input record or input block required next depends on the location of the previous access. Direct-access devices provide access to each location or block in about the same amount of time regardless of the location of the previous access.

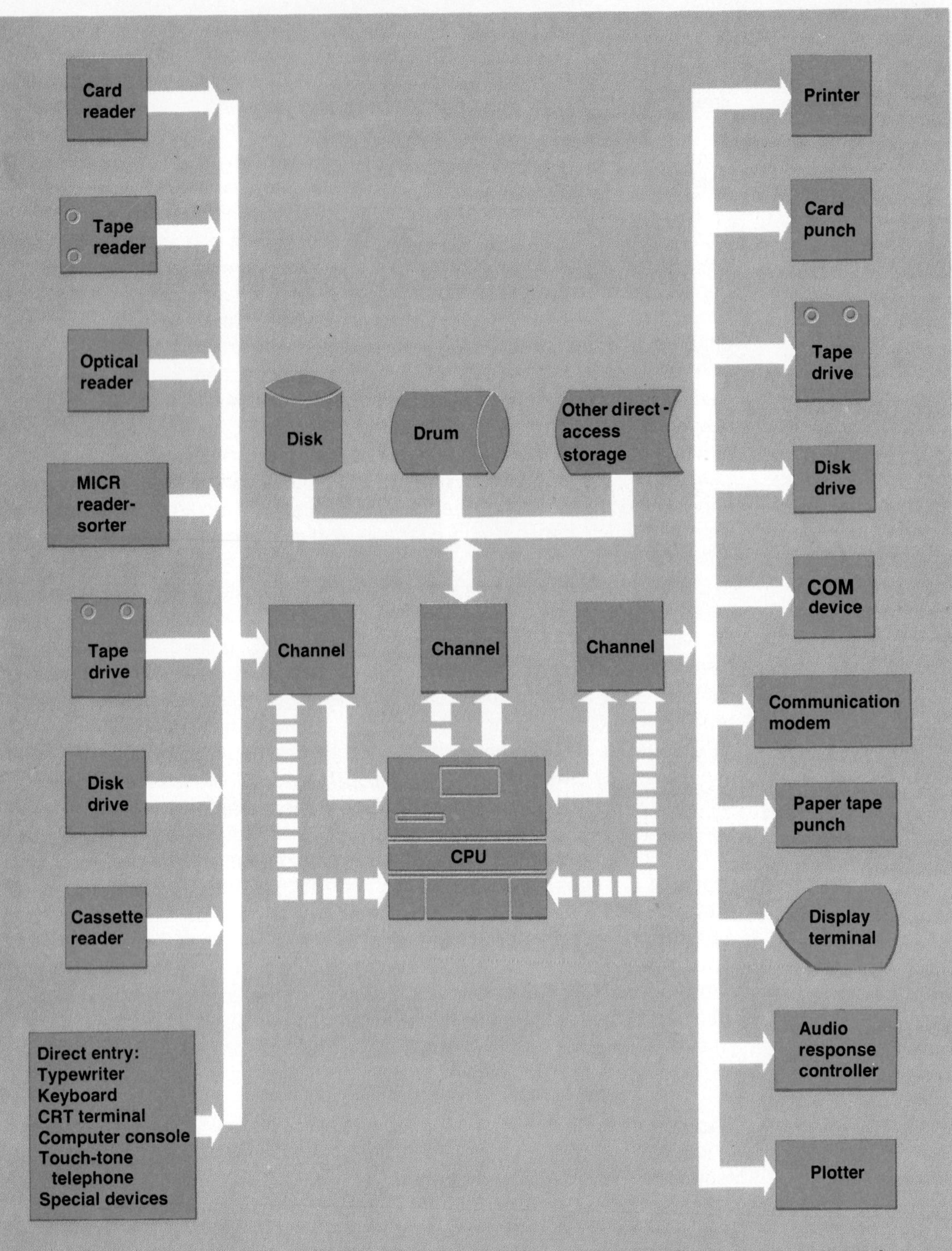

Figure 6.1 Overview of I/O and storage peripherals illustrating the use of channels

Other direct-access techniques usually involve an **indexed sequential access**. The location of blocks of data are identified in an index. Using the index, access to the beginning of a group (block) of locations is direct, but access through the block of locations is sequential.

Transfer rate

Transfer rate, the speed with which data can be transferred once they are accessed, is usually measured in bytes per second. Devices involving only electronics in the transfer are naturally faster than devices involving some mechanical processes.

Access time

An important characteristic of secondary storage devices is how much time it takes to fetch the content of a particular location or block. **Access time** for a system device is generally measured as the time to find a location and return its content to primary memory. This time is a function of access method, device speed, and channel speed (transfer rate). Generally, direct access devices are faster than sequential access devices both for initial access and for transfer rate. Channels for use with direct-access devices and online terminals are generally designed for a higher speed of data transfer.

Volatility

Like primary storage devices, secondary storage devices may be volatile or nonvolatile. As explained previously, the contents of volatile storage devices are erased when electrical power to the device is interrupted; the contents of nonvolatile devices are not affected by power interruptions.

Capacity

An important characteristic of a secondary storage device is its capacity in terms of number of bytes stored per unit and in total number of bytes in all units. Bytes per unit (for example, per reel of magnetic tape) is a function of recording density (bytes per inch or bpi) and the length of the recording track. The modular design of modern computer devices allows a large range of capacity for secondary storage, even on small microcomputer systems. The total secondary storage capacity of the largest mainframes is measured in billions of bytes.

Magnetic storage mechanics

The storage of data on a magnetizable surface is accomplished by exposing the data track on that surface to pulses of a magnetic force field. As seen in Figure 6.2, the **read/write head** emits a magnetic force field when current is passed through the coils. Electromagnetic impulses magnetize spots on the tape to indicate "on" bits. The magnetic coil mechanism that creates the electromagnetic impulses to write on the track can also read the track by

Figure 6.2

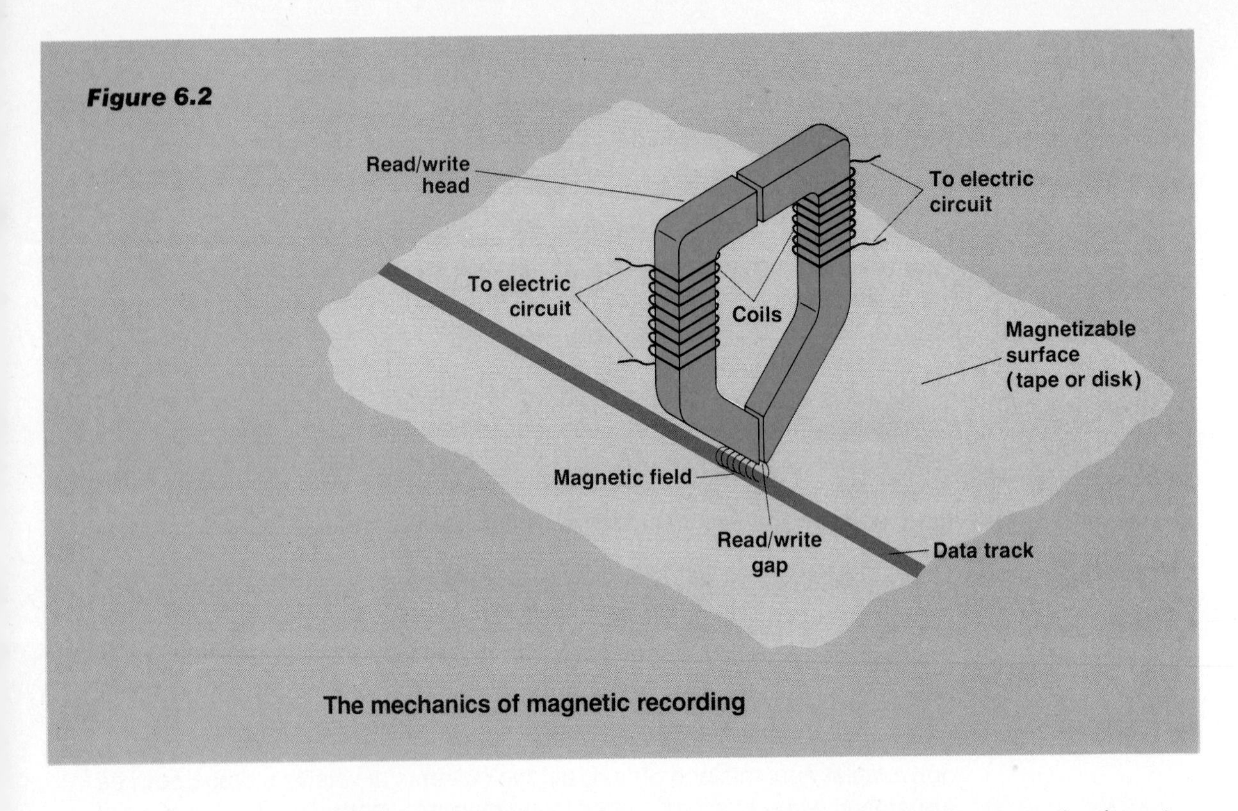

The mechanics of magnetic recording

sensing the electromagnetic impulse given off by each magnetized spot. Current versions of the read/write head are manufactured using semiconductor technology and the coils are imbedded within the head. Also, some types have two sets of heads, one for reading and one for writing.

To obtain narrower tracks and more bits per inch (greater data density), the head must be closer to the recording surface and the gap that creates the magnetic field must be narrower. The narrower gap creates a narrower

Figure 6.3

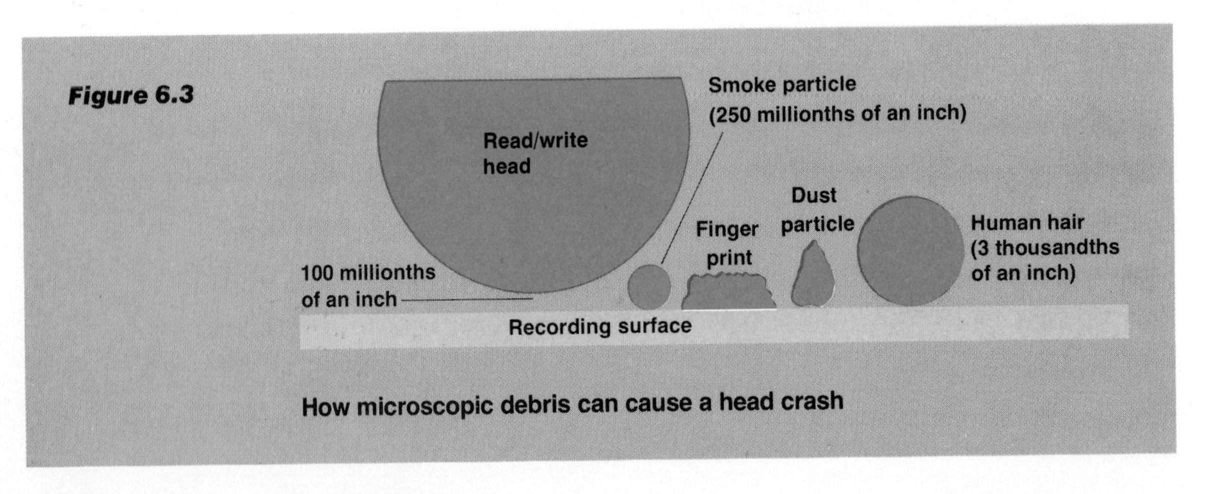

How microscopic debris can cause a head crash

magnetic field. Moving the head closer to the recording surface gives the magnetic field less room to spread. In this way, greater density is attained. In modern disks for example, the read/write head flies only 20 to 100 millionths of an inch above the disk on the air pressure created by the spinning disk.

The greater the data density, the more important it is to keep contaminants out of disk and tape drives. Figure 6.3 illustrates how even the tiniest particle of smoke or the oils in a fingerprint can cause contact between the read/write head and the magnetic surface on modern high-density (double density) disks. Contact between the head and the surface breaks up the film of air that separates the two surfaces and a "head crash" results. In a head crash, the read/write head rubs along the recording surface and physically rearranges or destroys the thin film of magnetizable material. Usually, the surface must be repaired before it can be reused.

Magnetic tape

The first form of secondary memory to be widely used was magnetic tape. In the one-job-at-a-time, applications-oriented atmosphere of the first and second generations, magnetic tape provided some real efficiencies. A computer can read from or write on magnetic tape much faster than it can read or punch cards. The capacity of a reel of tape allowed online access to an entire file on one tape drive. The availability of several tape drives on one computer system allowed some integration of processing. For example, a master file could be updated with both changes and transactions in one operation (see Figure 6.4).

Tape reel

There are so-called mini tapes, tape strips, and tape cannisters, but by far the most common magnetic tape medium is the reel holding 2,400 feet of oxide-coated plastic tape ½ inch in width (see Figure 6.5).

Data representation on magnetic tape

Data coding The most commonly used magnetic tape carries 9 channels (tracks) and codes data in 8-bit bytes plus a parity bit. Spots on the magnetized surface of the tape represent data in the form of on bits and off bits. Each vertical column of 9 bits (8 bits plus a parity bit) represent a byte, or character, of data. Word or record length is variable. Either EBCDIC or ASCII plus a parity bit can be used to represent characters.

Magnetic tapes are available in various lengths and in widths up to 1 inch. Seven-channel tape with data represented in 6-bit binary plus a parity bit are also available. Nine-channel tape ½ inch wide and 2,400 feet long is most common.

Interrecord and interblock gaps The lengths of records on tape may vary according to processing needs. In order to represent records (for

Figure 6.4

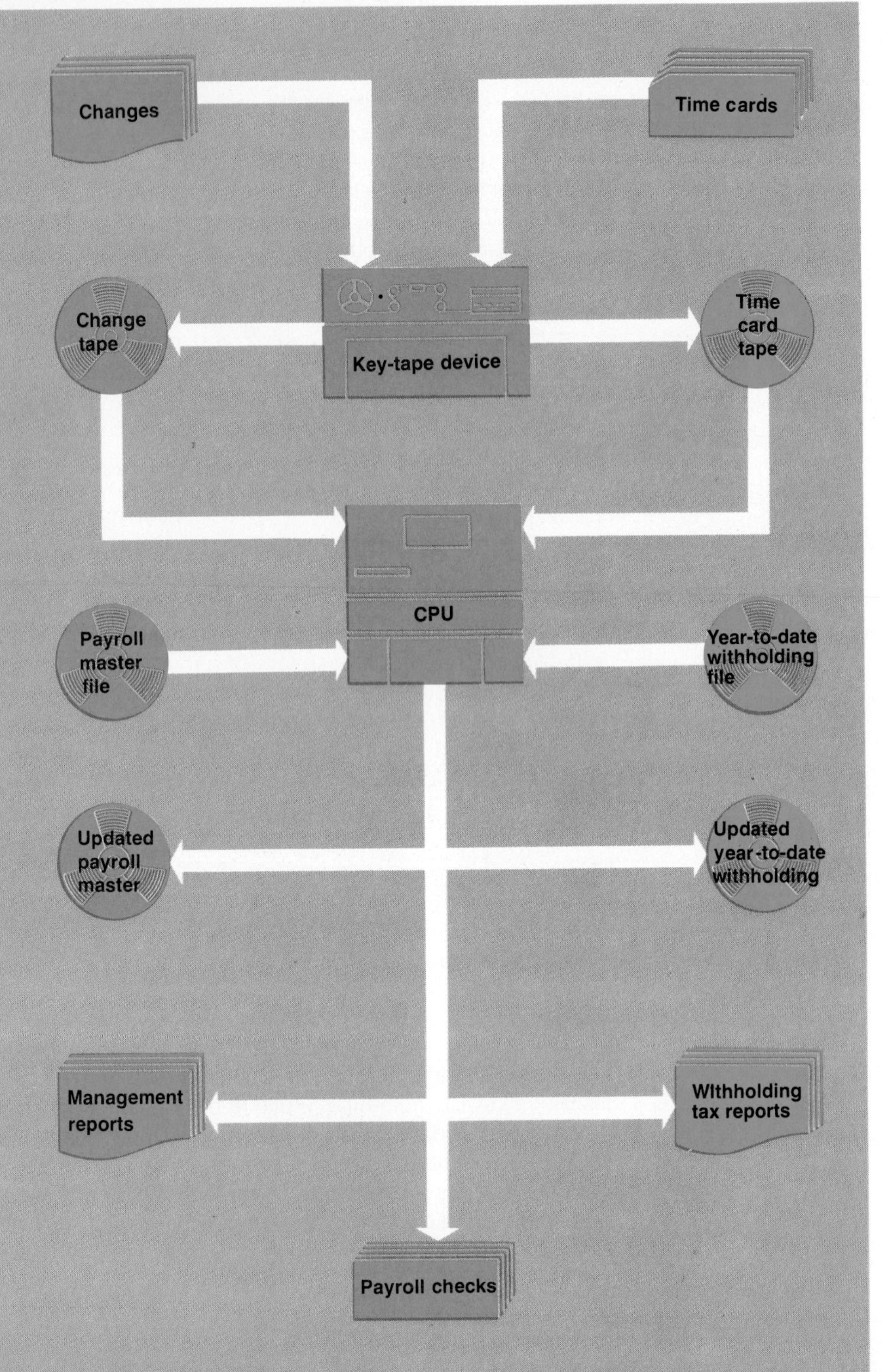

A magnetic tape hourly payroll system

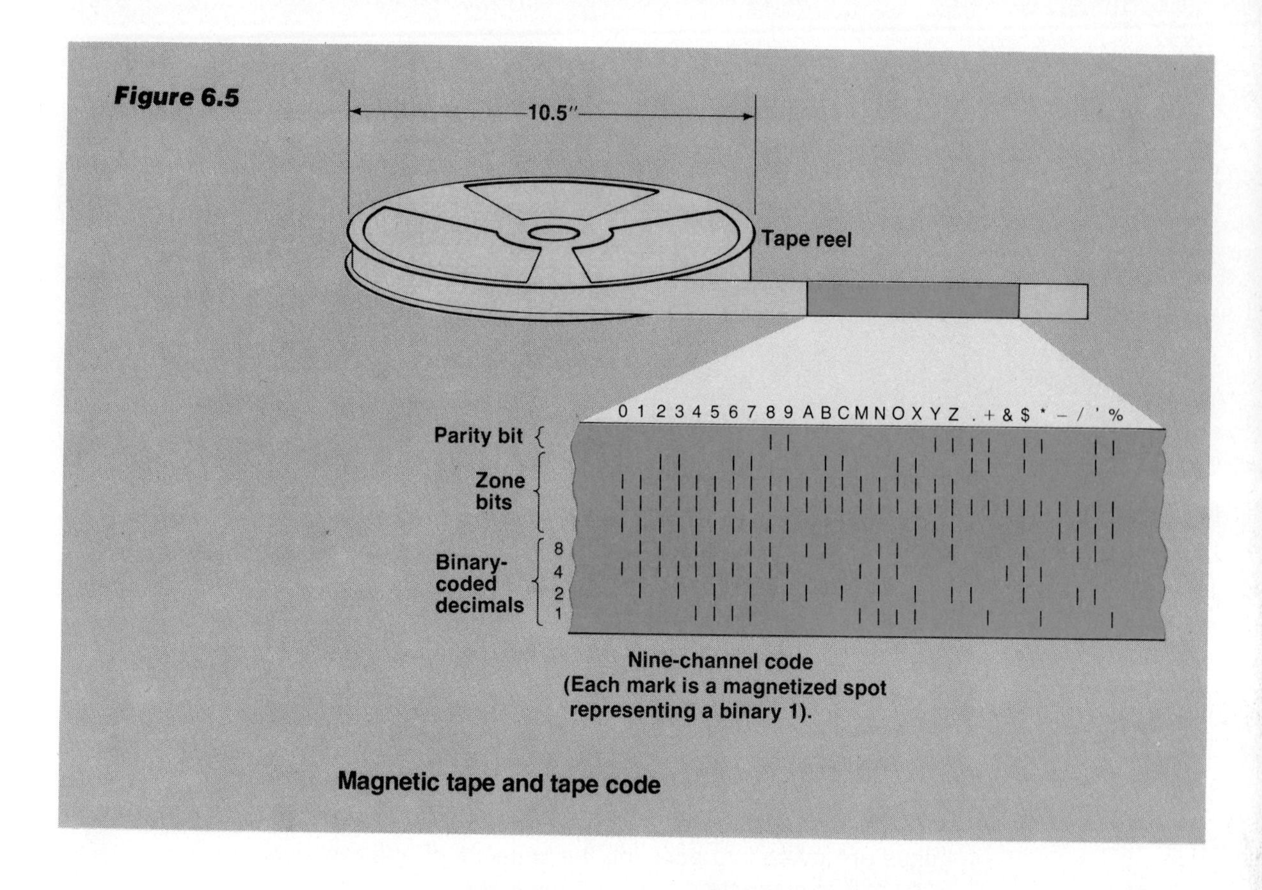

Figure 6.5

Magnetic tape and tape code

example, a timecard) and to process each record separately, there must be a means for determining where one record stops and the next record begins. Most generally, a space is provided within which the movement of the tape can be stopped and restarted. This space is called an **interrecord gap** (see Figure 6.6).

The records next to one another on a tape usually belong to the same file and will be processed by the same program, so it is more efficient to read a group of records at one time, since this eliminates many starts and stops of the tape. These groups, or **blocks** of records are separated by **interblock gaps**. Reading in blocks, the entire content of a block is moved into primary storage with a single read command. If each read command reads only one record, several read commands could be necessary to read the equivalent of one block. Interrecord or interblock gaps vary from .6 to .75 inch depending on the speed of the tape drive. Blocking the records speeds processing and saves tape.

Tape capacity

Each position along the tape across the channels represents one byte. The number of such byte positions (characters) in 1 inch of tape represents **tape density**. Tape density varies from 200 characters per inch (bpi) to 6,250 bpi.

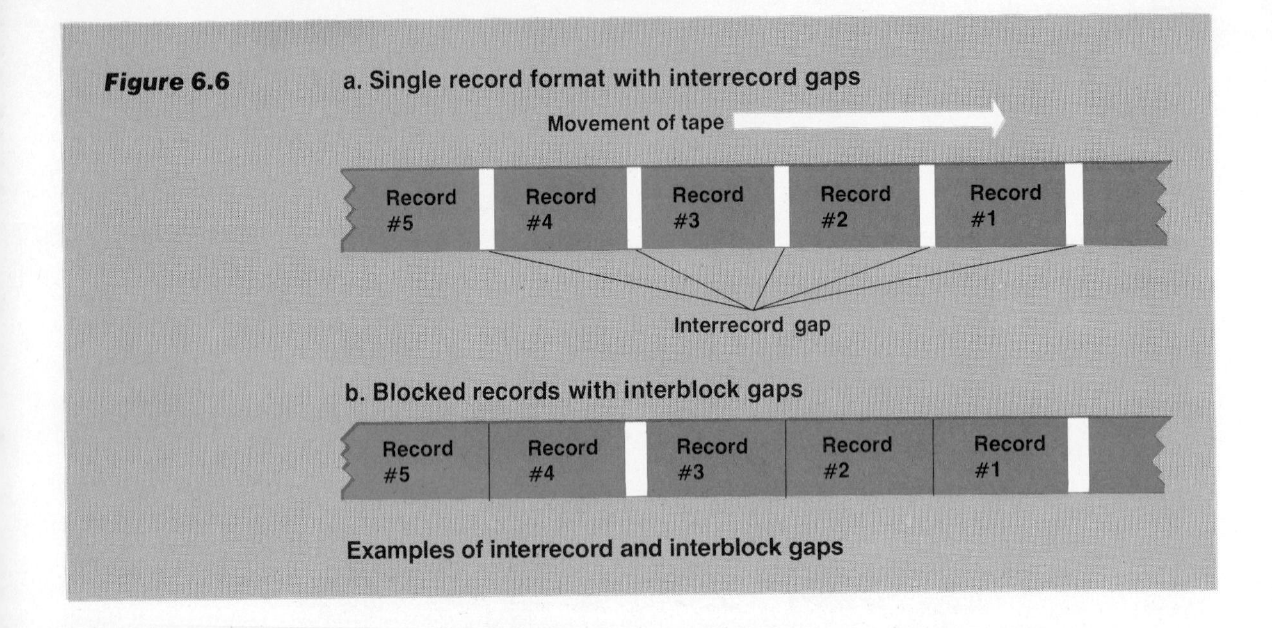

Figure 6.6 Examples of interrecord and interblock gaps

The most common densities are 800, 1,600, and 6,250 bpi. At 6,250 bpi, the contents of almost eighty 80-column punched cards could be stored in 1 inch. One 2,400-foot reel of tape theoretically could store 12 × 2,400 × 6,250 or 180 million characters. Actually, however, when interrecord and interblock gaps are taken into account, the capacity of one reel averages only about 140 million characters.

The tape drive

A magnetic **tape drive** is a device for reading from and/or writing on magnetic tape. As can be seen in the detail of Figure 6.7, the tape is fed between two reels, passing through a read/write mechanism between them. A full reel is mounted on one side and an empty reel on the other side. The start button is pushed and the tape threads through a drive capstan and a vacuum column to the read/write mechanism. The purpose of the vacuum column is to provide slack in the tape so that it can be stopped and started smoothly without jerking it off a reel and tearing or stretching it. Another vacuum column is provided between the read/write mechanism and the take-up reel. Most modern tape drives read the tape in both directions (see Figure 6.8).

The read/write mechanism is made up of nine read/write heads (one for each channel on the tape). Most tape drives contain a controller which can be programmed to rewind a tape when the end is reached, back up one block (record) at a time, skip over a bad section of the tape, or even correct a minor error on the tape without interrupting processing. When a reading error occurs, the tape is backspaced to read the block again. If, after a specified

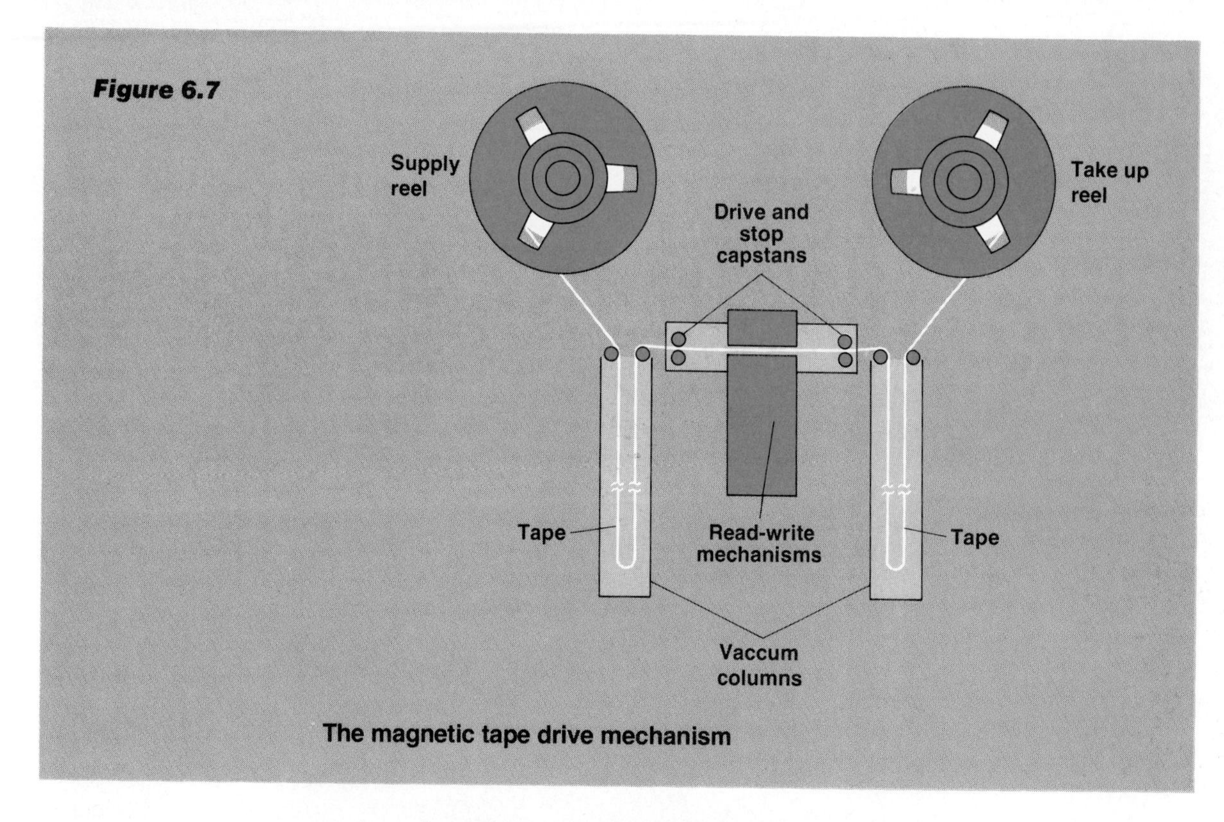

The magnetic tape drive mechanism

number of reading attempts, the data error cannot be read or corrected, processing stops and the operator is informed of the error.

When writing on the tape, most drives immediately reread what has been written to check for errors. If an error is detected, the tape is reversed one block (record) and rewritten. Again, if a specified number of attempts to write without error do not succeed, the operator is alerted to the problem.

Tape control

Since tapes cannot be read by humans beings, it is necessary to label each file carefully to prevent using the wrong tape. Reading a magnetic tape does not affect its content. Writing on a tape, however, does destroy its previous content. It is particularly important that tape files be protected against accidental destruction of files to be preserved. Most tape reels have a control ring inside the hub which can be removed to lock out the writing mechanism on the tape drive. Outside labels should indicate file content, the length of time the file is to be retained, and, in a sensitive situation, the program that is used to process the file. The tape label not only should appear on the outside of the reel in humanly readable form but should also be entered at the beginning of the tape (see Figure 6.9). The last record on the tape should be a trailer record for the file which provides a record count and/or other control data.

Figure 6.8

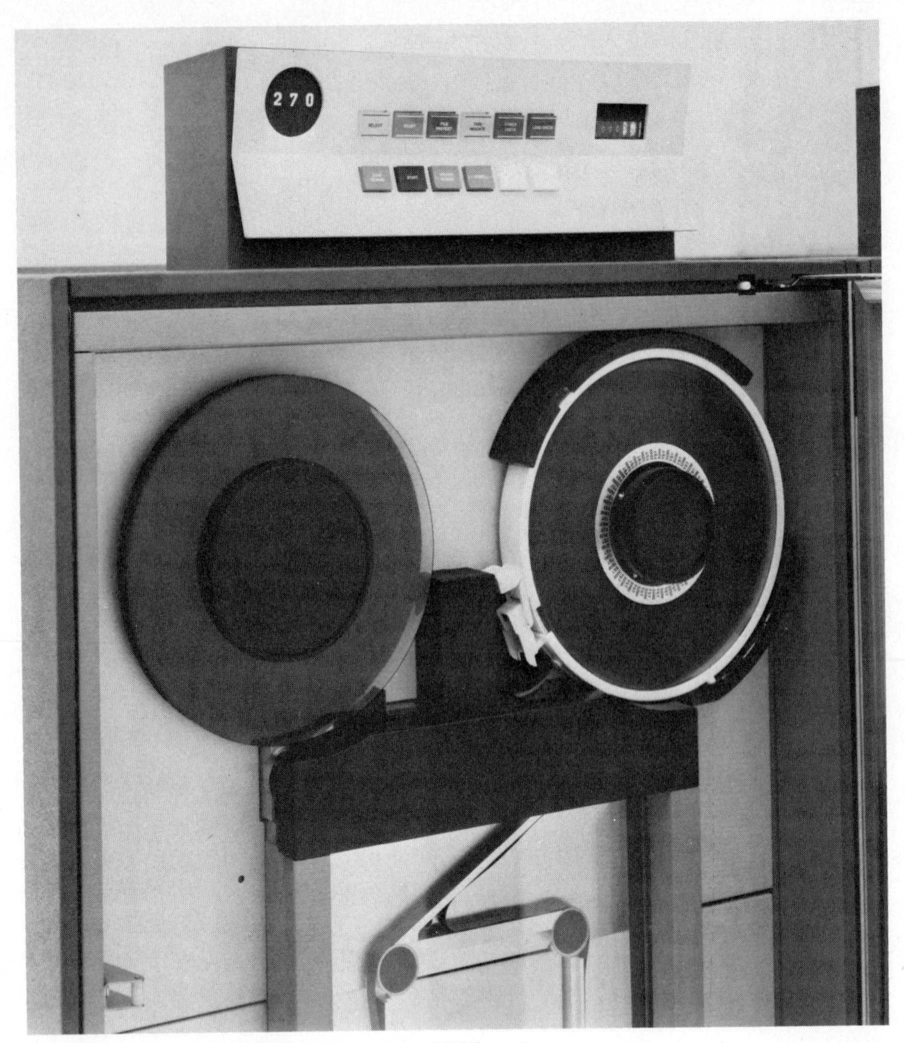

Close-up of a tape drive (Courtesy IBM)

Transfer rates The speed with which data are transferred onto or off of a magnetic tape can vary from 50,000 to 400,000 bytes per second. A transfer rate of 240,000 bytes per second is roughly equivalent to reading 3,000 punched cards in one second. However, the effective transfer rate is often much lower than the rated speed of a tape drive. Suppose, for example, a tape contains a file that is divided into 2,000 blocks, each containing 500 bytes of data. There would be a total of 1 million bytes of data in the file. At 400,000 bytes per second, 1 million bytes apparently could be read in 2.5 seconds. This is not the case, however, for each block would be read separately and the tape drive would stop and start roughly 2,000 times. Stopping and starting the tape requires about .005 second. Two thousand stops would require a total of 10 seconds (2,000 × .005) and the total time required to read the file would be 12.5 seconds: 2.5 seconds reading and 10 seconds stopping and starting. To

Figure 6.9

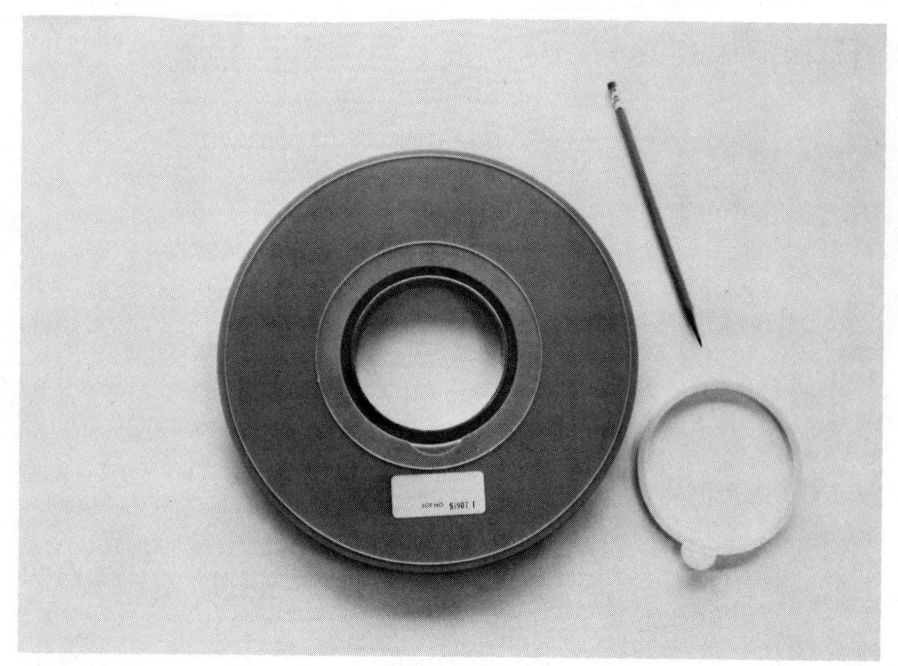

A tape reel   Note the label on the reel and the control ring, which has been removed, to the right.

indicate the efficiency of blocking, suppose each record contained 100 bytes and each record were read independently. Total processing time would increase to 52.5 seconds because of the additional time required to stop and start a total of 10,000 times rather than the 2,000 times when blocks were used.

Applications

Tape files can be a cheap storage medium if sequential access is acceptable. When files are processed at regular intervals (periodically), this is possible. An example is the hourly payroll system illustrated in Figure 6.2.

A second example of a tape-based system is the accounts receivable billing system shown in Figure 6.10. Note that the updated accounts receivable master file would become the input master file on the next billing run.

Magnetic tape is also used for storing back-up files on interactive online systems. At periodic intervals (most frequently at the end of each day's business), the master files stored in online direct-access files are written onto a tape. These tapes provide back-up in case of system failure. In sensitive situations where loss of the file could result in substantial monetary losses or where great accuracy is required, these "snapshots" of the file could be "dumped" onto tape more frequently. Only about three of these snapshots are required to obtain a picture of processing activity that can prove useful in restoring lost files.

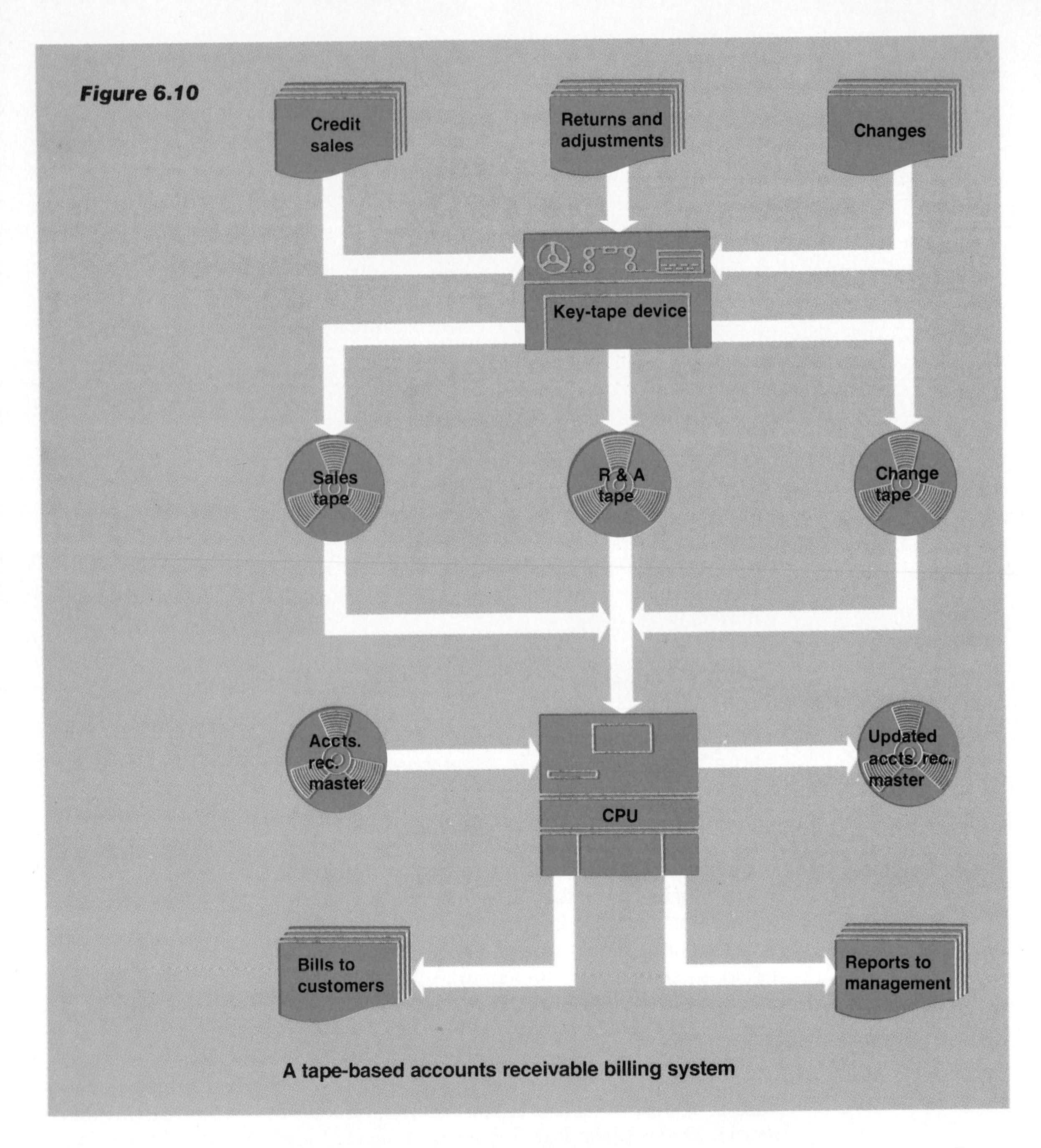

A tape-based accounts receivable billing system

It is hard to sort the nonsequential contents of a tape into a sequence. The primary sorting technique is to merge sequentially ordered sequences alternately on two tapes, then merge the sequentially ordered sequences of those two tapes alternately onto two other tapes. This process requires four tapes and continues until all the records are sequentially ordered on one tape.

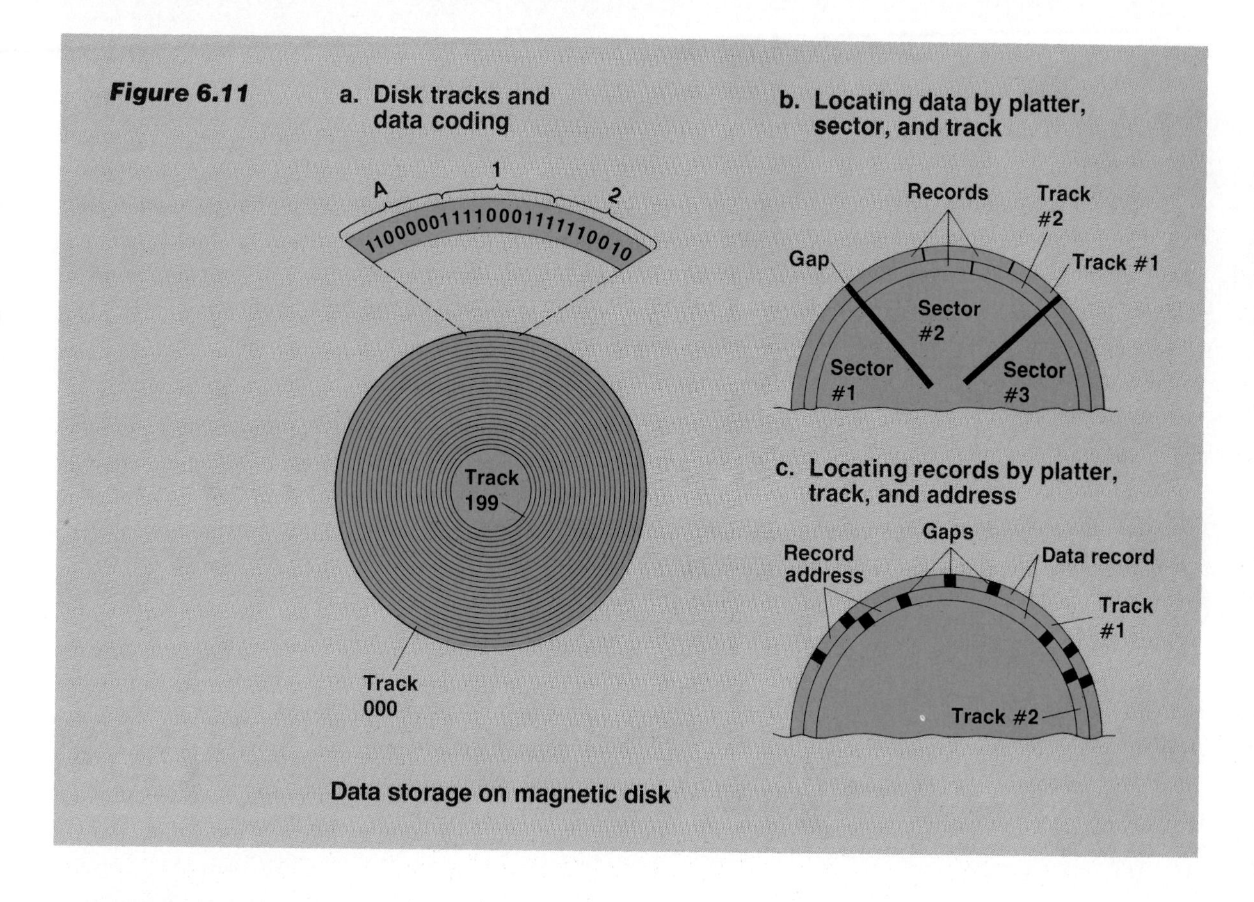

Data storage on magnetic disk

Magnetic disks

The sequential processing limitations of tapes were overcome with the development of magnetic disks. A **magnetic disk** is a round platter with at least one oxide-coated surface which can be magnetized. Only the upper surface was coated on early disks; modern disks record on both the upper and lower surfaces. (Note that *disk* is sometimes spelled as *disc* in EDP.) Data are recorded in rings on the disk which are called **disk tracks**. There are usually several hundred tracks on each disk surface. As is illustrated in part a of Figure 6.11, data are recorded along the tracks as strings of magnetized spots representing 0s and 1s. Each track stores the same number of bytes even though the outer tracks are longer than the tracks nearer the center of the disk. Disks provide for variable record lengths and identify each record with a unique location number as seen in parts b and c of Figure 6.11. Note that in part b, each location is identified by disk number (which platter surface), track number (which circle), and sector number (where on the circle). This is really a form of block addressing. Some disks do not have sectors but address data by disk face and track only. Each track is given a special identifier called a track number, or home address. The specific data is then given a specific (numeric) location along the track. The numeric address becomes part of the record. Interrecord gaps are needed to distinguish record addresses from the real record content (the data) and to distinguish one record from another. Therefore, records are normally combined in blocks with addresses given only to each block in order to speed processing. This addressing scheme is shown in part c of Figure 6.11. Handling records in blocks reduces the number of addresses on each track and thereby reduces the number of gaps along the track. Therefore, blocking increases the capacity of a disk.

Disk pack mechanics

To read or write on a disk the read/write head floats over the track involved. The read/write heads for a disk pack are on arms that move jointly and can be withdrawn to remove the pack. The heads must be moved into position over the track to be accessed. When one read/write head is positioned over a track on one disk, the remaining heads are positioned over the same track on the other disk surfaces. As shown in Figure 6.12, these coordinated tracks are called a **cylinder**. The fact that the various heads are all positioned on the same cylinder at a given time can be used to speed processing. When entering data, all tracks in a cylinder can be filled with data before respositioning the heads to another cylinder. On retrieval, less head seek

Figure 6.12

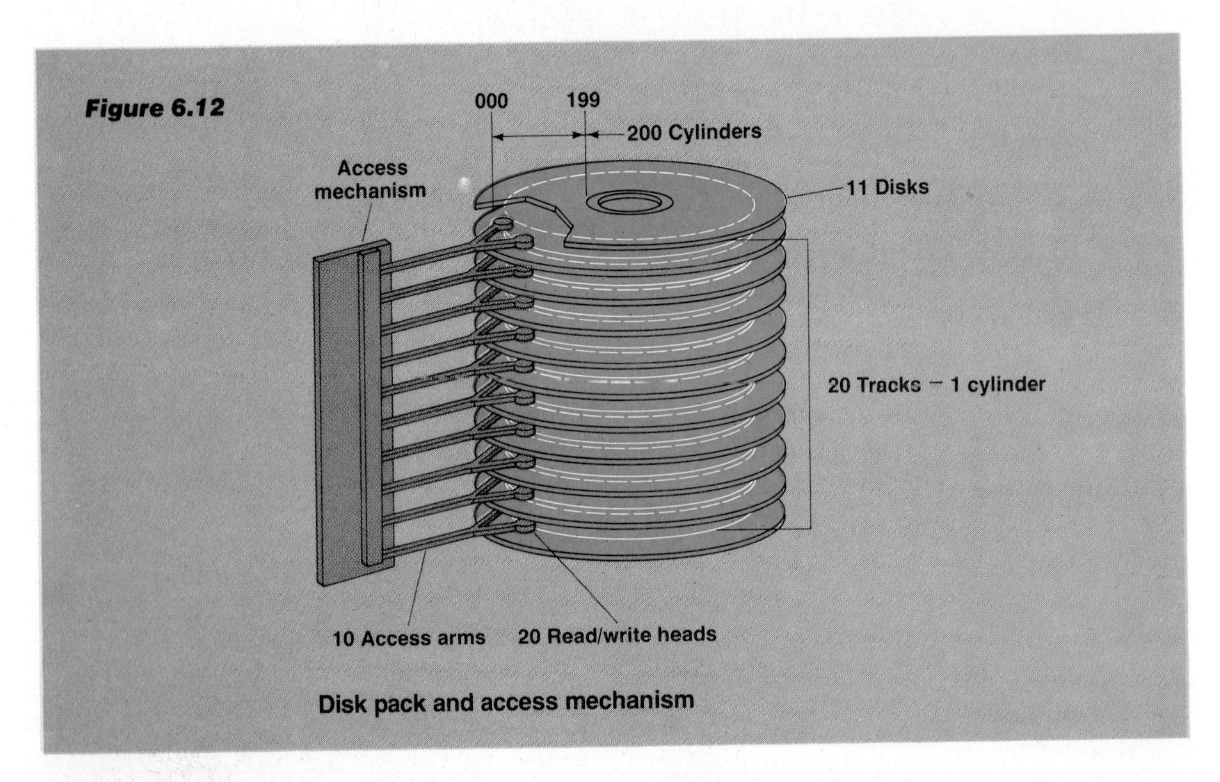

Disk pack and access mechanism

time is required to find needed data. The picture in Figure 6.12 should help to clarify this point.

Types of disks

There are two types of disk storage devices, fixed disks and removable-element disks. **Fixed disks** are permanently mounted on a spindle and usually have a set of read/write heads for each disk surface. Some even have a read/write head for each track. Head-per-track disks are not available for every computer and are extremely expensive. They do, however provide faster access, since there is no wait for heads to be positioned over the track being accessed. Figure 6.13 shows a fixed-disk drive.

Removable-element disks include disk packs, floppy disks, and disk cartridges.

Figure 6.13

Fixed disk drives The stacks of disks in a fixed disk drive cannot be removed. (Courtesy IBM)

Figure 6.14

A disk pack and a disk drive In the foreground is a disk pack in its protective cover ready for storage. Behind it is a disk drive with a disk pack in place and ready for operation. (Courtesy Control Data Corp.)

Disk pack A **disk pack** is shown in Figure 6.14. The disk pack differs from the fixed disk in that the small stack of platters is removable and may be stored offline. It is mounted on a disk drive as shown in Figure 6.14. With its cover removed, the stack of platters is set on the drive spindle, the drive cover closed, and the drive started. A set of read/write heads mounted on access arms are then inserted between the platters in the stack. Moving in and out from track to track, they read the coated surfaces. The outer surfaces of the top and bottom disks are not coated. Note that all the read/write heads move together and are always positioned over the same track on each disk surface. Disk packs usually have one read/write head for each surface. Read heads capable of reading as many as 12 tracks on each surface at the same time are in use, however.

Floppy disks Both fixed disks and disk packs use metal platters coated with iron oxide as the disk. A newer disk uses a plastic platter with coated surfaces. The plastic platter is flexible and becomes flat and rigid only when the disk is spun on the spindle, hence the name, **floppy disk**. Floppy disks are cheaper than the rigid metal disks, costing from $3.50 to $8.00 per disk, but also are more easily damaged by careless handling. Floppy **diskettes** 5 to 8 inches in diameter are a popular direct-access storage medium for microcomputers. (see Figure 6.15).

Disk cartridge When a single disk is sealed inside a plastic housing, a **disk cartridge** is created. Disk cartridges are a common form of direct access device for minicomputers. The new Winchester disk drives which seal 6-to-8-inch diskettes inside a housing can provide as much as 43 million characters of online storage for business microcomputers. Most cartridges can be removed and stored offline like disk packs (see Figure 6.16).

Access time

Disks are direct-access devices. The time it takes to access a disk location, that is, the time it takes for the read/write mechanism to reach a location and return its contents to primary memory depends mainly on two factors; head-seek time and rotational delay.

Head-seek time The average time it takes for the read/write head to be positioned over the track containing the record sought is called **head-seek time**. Only in head-per-track disks is there no head-seek time.

Rotational delay The time required for the beginning of the desired location to move under the read/write head is **rotational delay**. On the average, this is one-half of a disk revolution but it can vary from nothing to the time used for one complete revolution of the disk. Rotation speeds vary from about 1,000 to 3,000 revolutions per minute, with 2,400 revolutions per minute most common.

Figure 6.15

A floppy disk system Here we see an entire interactive/minicomputer system, with a CRT terminal, hardcopy printer, and floppy disk drive. The operator is inserting a disk. It is easy to see the size advantages of such a system. (Courtesy Digital Equipment Corp.)

Data transfer rate Total access time also depends on how fast the channel is over which data are transferred. Data transfer rate is the number of bytes transferred along the channel from the disk to primary storage in one second. It is a function of disk rotation speed and data density. Transfer rates vary from 156,000 to as much as 3 million bytes per second, with rates around 300,000 bytes per second most common.

In sum, figuring in head-seek time, rotational delay, and transfer rate, the access time for magnetic disks ranges from 20 to 600 milliseconds (thousandths of a second), with most in the 20 to 60 millisecond range.

Disk capacity

The capacity of fixed disks and disk packs varies widely. The smallest removable disk, the floppy diskette, provides from .25 to 1.2 million bytes of storage. A single disk pack may store from 4.5 million to 100 million characters. This wide variation arises from the fact that disk packs may contain from 5 to 12 disks and from 8 to 20 recording surfaces. They also vary from about 15 to 18 inches in diameter. The most common packs are 15 inches in diameter, contain 6 disks (10 recording surfaces), and store about 7.5 million bytes. Cartridges store from about 2 million to 80 million bytes per cartridge. Fixed disks may store as much as 300 million bytes on one unit.

In practice, it is difficult to generalize about the characteristics of disk systems because they vary widely and are changing rapidly. For example, the IBM 3350 disk drive, a widely used device that is rather typical of current technology, has a capacity of 6.3 million bytes per unit, a head-seek time that averages 21.8 milliseconds, and a data transfer rate of 1 million bytes per second. IBM's newest device, at this time, though, is the model 3380 disk drive. This unit has a capacity of 2.52 *billion* bytes per unit (each unit consisting of two drives), a head-seek time that averages only 16 milliseconds, and a data transfer rate of 3 million bytes per second.

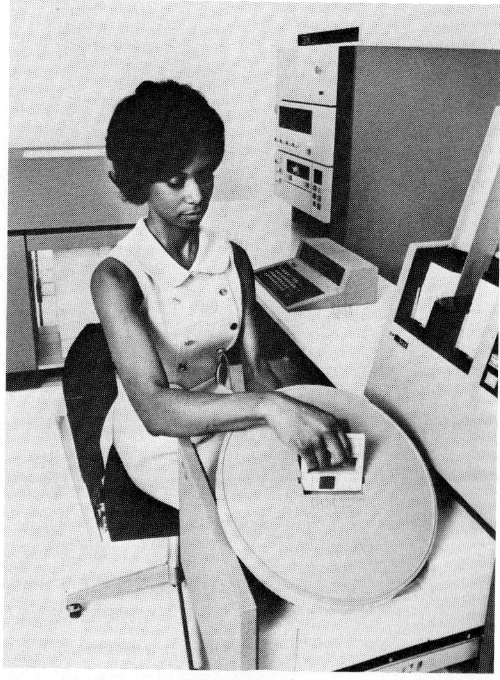

Figure 6.16 **Disk cartridges "Winchester-type" disk cartridges, such as the IBM 3348 Data Module shown on the left, contain a read/write mechanism, as well as the disk. The type of cartridge shown on the right is useful for minicomputer systems that do not need the storage capacity of large disk packs, but do need the flexibility of removable disks. (Courtesy IBM)**

Figure 6.17

An eight-pack disk drive The IBM 3330 mass-storage disk drive is one of the larger-capacity units available. (Courtesy IBM)

Disk drives

Disk drives for disk packs can accept from one to eight packs on a single unit. The multiple-disk-storage drive shown in Figure 6.17 has space for eight disks and can store about 800 million bytes.

Applications

Disks are direct-access storage devices used in business data processing to provide online access to data files. Figure 6.18 is a pictorial representation of an online inventory accounting system. Note that input could be provided by punched cards, magnetic tape, disk packs, or input online from the point of activity. We have assumed input online. Note that the inventory item master file and the customer (accounts receivable) file are both online. They could be stored either on a large fixed disk or on independent removable packs.

Disk systems can be used for almost any application. The direct-access disk can be used as a sequential-access device for applications like payroll as well as for direct-access online interactive systems. If the processing "hit rate" on the master file is low (that is, if few records are accessed on each processing run), direct-access storage is generally preferred, even for applications-oriented systems which are updated periodically. That is, if the percentage of records updated on each run is 25 percent or less, a direct-access master file is usually more efficient. If processing is periodic and the hit rate is high, for example, payroll processing, a sequential-access master file is more efficient.

Other applications of disk files are numerous. Fixed disks are often used to store those parts of the system executive, or supervisory program, not in constant use in the primary memory. Language translators, compilers, utilities, and other parts of the system program library are also stored on fixed disks. In time-sharing and other interactive systems, the users' permanent files and any master data processing files in constant use are usually stored on fixed disks. Disk packs are used for master files not in constant use and for change and transactions files for data processing systems.

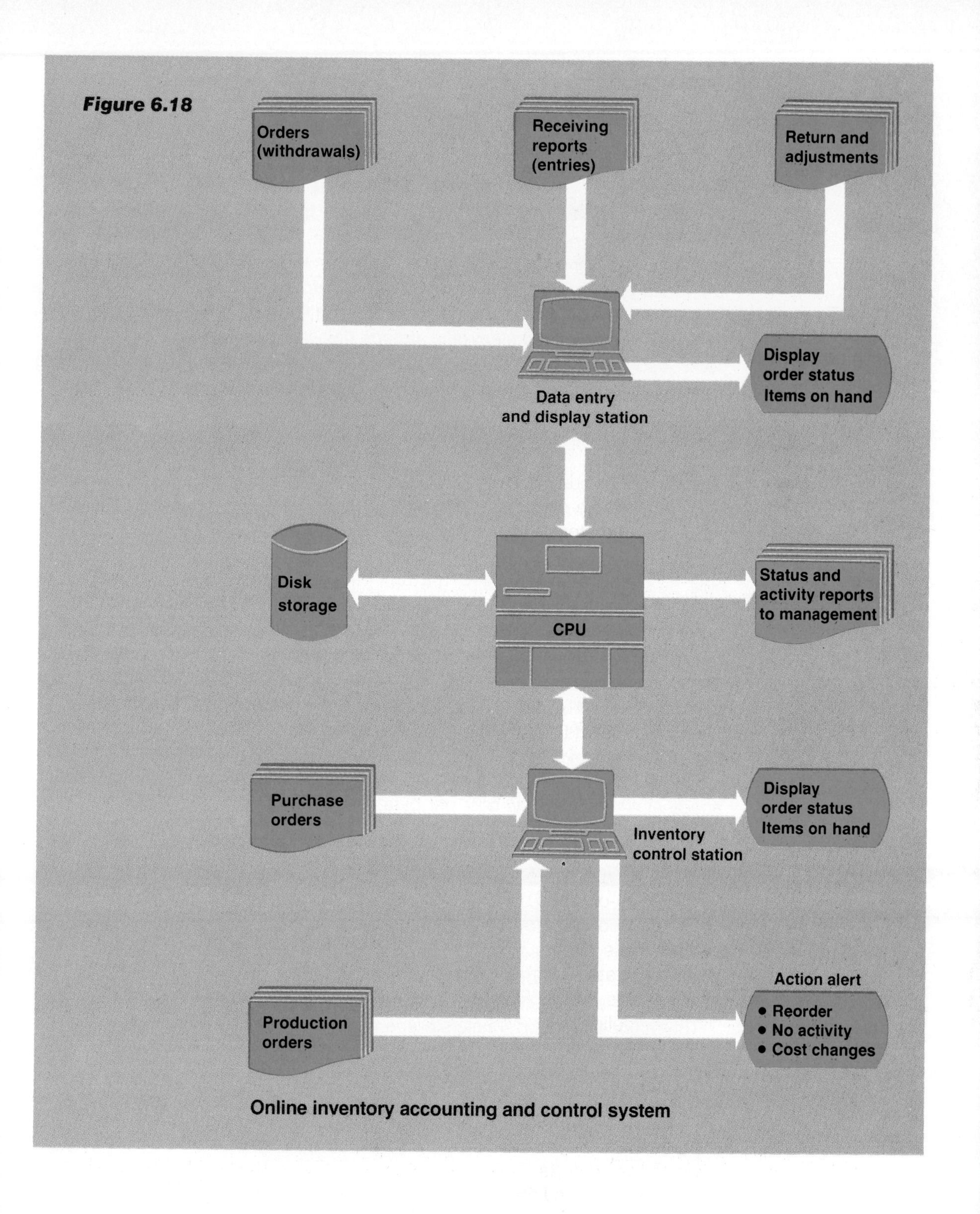

Figure 6.18 Online inventory accounting and control system

Other secondary storage media and devices

Magnetic drums

As described earlier (see Figure 2.4 on page 25), the **magnetic drum** is a cylinder spun rapidly around its longest axis. The outer surface of the cylinder is coated with a material that can be magnetized. Data are recorded in tracks running around the outside of the drum. Fixed read/write heads over each track read from and write to the tracks as the drum rotates. Drums are now used as secondary storage when the user is concerned with relatively fast access to a limited amount of data. Even in this use, however, drums are being replaced by fixed electronic storage devices, such as bubble memory, cores, and microcircuits as well as disks. Disk access is being improved, and in units of about the same physical size, the disk pack can store much more data.

Magnetic strips

Magnetic strips represent an attempt to combine the low cost and high storage capacity of magnetic tape with the advantages of fast online direct access to stored data. A magnetic strip is a length of flexible plastic material with a coated surface organized like short pieces of magnetic tape mounted side by side. Either the strips are hung independently on racks within the storage device or several are placed in each cartridge and the cartridges hung in the storage device (see Figure 6.19). When accessed, a control mechanism removes the strip or the cartridge from the rack to a read station. The strips are wrapped around a cylinder and read or written or the cartridge contents passed by a read/write head. After the reading or writing operation, the strip or cartridge is returned to its place on the rack. Cartridges provide the possibility of offline storage for online access. These devices have relatively long access times but store very large volumes of data in a small space at a relatively low cost per byte.

Mass-storage systems

Modern data processing systems are more frequently online, interactive systems. Data are more frequently recorded and processed as transactions occur; mass storage of files online has made such systems possible.

The major devices for mass storage of data have already been described. In order of current popularity, they are:

1 *Multiple disk drives.* With capacities to 800 million characters or more per unit (Figure 6.13) and the ability to have multiple units online, these devices can provide online access to billions of characters of data and information.

2 *Magnetic strips and tape cartridges.* These devices have been used

Figure 6.19

A magnetic-strip cartridge mass storage system The IBM 3850 ("honeycomb") mass storage device is shown in operation as the control mechanism retrieves a cartridge from offline storage. (Courtesy IBM)

where speed of access is not critical but a very large volume of data must be stored online. For example, they have been used by insurance companies to provide online access to customer policies. Some are used to provide online access to catalogs and reference (library) information.

3 *Integrated circuits.* As the cost of memory chips comes down in relation to their capacity, they are being substituted for practically all types of online memory, both primary and secondary. A total of 1 million bytes per chip is forecast to be a reality by 1985.

4 *Bubble.* Bubble memory is getting cheaper. Its speed of access makes it a likely replacement for cores, microcircuits, and drums as a high-speed, low-volume secondary memory.

5 *Magnetic core.* Cores are being replaced by cheaper devices. Large mainframes of a few years back often used an extra core as secondary memory, but this is no longer occurring.

Mass-storage applications

The ease of adding a mass-storage secondary memory has changed the nature of data processing. Online, direct-access memories of seemingly unlimited size have removed the limitations on both program size and online file storage.

The availability of secondary random-access storage, large-capacity data channels, and improved supervisory programs and supporting hardware features make it possible to write a program of almost any size that manipulates data from files of almost any size. This "virtual" storage allows automatic paging and overlay of programs, which in turn allow large programs to be broken up with only the portions (pages) in immediate use residing in primary memory. Data files can be handled in much the same way.

Mass storage has made it possible to store more data files online in the form of multiple data bases (integrated sets of interrelated files). The effects of a single transaction can be reflected throughout all these files almost instantaneously. For example, a sale at the department store can be recorded online to update immediately the accounts receivable file (if it is a credit sale) or the cash file (if it is a cash sale), the inventory file, the sales record file, and the salesperson and/or department performance file(s). Large data libraries not only are assisting in responding to queries from customers, salespeople, and executives but are providing online access to research data for engineers, chemists, operations researchers, market researchers, and planners. Researchers and executives are also being provided with online access to reference libraries containing the results of prior research.

Virtual storage, multiprocessing, and other characteristics of today's advanced data processing systems will be discussed in detail in Chapter 7.

Summary

Secondary storage devices are peripheral devices located outside the CPU but connected to the primary memory through channels. Channels control secondary storage devices and the buffers designed to overcome the difference in speed between the slower external device and the faster CPU.

Secondary storage devices provide either sequential or direct (random) access. Like primary storage, secondary storage is either volatile (stored data disappears if power to the device is interrupted) or nonvolatile (interruptions in power do not destroy the contents). The time required to find a storage location and return its content to the CPU is called the access time of a device. The number of bytes that can be transferred from or to the device in one second is called its transfer rate. All these characteristics are important when choosing a secondary storage device.

The most common media for secondary storage are magnetic tape and magnetic disk. Tapes provide sequential access, are nonvolatile, and have a transfer rate of 50,000 to 400,000 bytes per second, but they seldom attain that speed because the drive reads either one record or one block of records at a time, stopping at the gaps between the records or blocks. Tape capacity also is affected by these gaps, and although data density may be 6,250 bits per inch, only about 140 million bytes can be stored on a 2,400-foot reel of tape. Tapes are relatively inexpensive storage devices but are being replaced by direct-access devices such as disk packs.

Magnetic disks are metal or plastic platters shaped like phonograph records. Data are recorded on circles or tracks on the magnetizable surfaces of the disk. Disks provide direct access and have a faster access time than magnetic tape. The fastest access and greatest transfer rates are provided by fixed disks with a read/write head for each track on each disk surface.

The disk pack is the most common type of disk device in use. Six to twelve disks form a stack which has a removable cover. The uncovered stack is mounted on a drive spindle and accessed by arms containing a read/write head for every recorded surface. Disk packs can be stored offline as well as online. Some packs can store 100 million bytes or more. When mounted on a multiple-drive unit holding as many as 8 packs, over 800 million bytes of secondary online storage is provided. The use of disks is expanding rapidly because of their ability to provide direct-access files and the more efficient processing systems derived from the use of such files.

Other secondary storage devices include magnetic drums and magnetic strips.

Mass-storage systems providing from many millions to billions of bytes of online storage capacity are common. These systems use magnetic disks, integrated circuits, and bubble and magnetic core memory devices. Software and related hardware allow the use of the virtual-memory concept wherein limits on the size of computer programs are effectively removed. Multiple sets of integrated files (multiple data bases or data banks) and online reference libraries not only speed business data processing but assist engineers, scientists, and researchers in their work.

Key terms

Define the following terms as briefly as possible and then, in a short paragraph, clarify each definition.

Access time
Block
Channel
Cylinder
Disk cartridge
Disk drive
Diskette
Disk pack
Disk track
Fixed disk
Floppy disk
Head-seek time

Indexed sequential access
Interblock gap
Interrecord gap
Magnetic disk
Magnetic drum
Magnetic strips
Mass-storage system
Multiplexor channel
Port
Read/write head
Rotational delay
Secondary storage
Selector channel
Tape density
Tape drive
Transfer rate

Discussion questions

1 What is the difference between primary memory and secondary memory?
2 How do channels relate to the concept of overlapping?
3 When disk packs are available to provide both online and offline storage, why do you think fixed disks would ever be used?
4 What do you think is the best storage medium to use for each of the following? Why?
   a Primary storage
   b Scratch-pad
   c Offline storage in machine-sensible form
   d Random-access online secondary storage
5 Which storage media can be used for storing sequential-access files?
6 Speculate on the effects on business data processing of the availability of a low-priced storage device with almost unlimited capacity (perhaps 100 billion bytes) and very fast access (perhaps 10 nanoseconds).
7 Speculate on the possible uses in business data processing of a cheap, noneraseable memory of almost unlimited capacity. That is, the memory contents could not be changed after being written on once.
8 Is there any storage medium used with computers for input, output, or storage which is noneraseable and almost unlimited in capacity?
9 How can you explain the popularity of each of the following?
   a Floppy disks
   b Floppy diskettes
   c Disk packs
10 Speculate on what modern large computers might look like if cheap mass storage had not been developed.

Exercises

1 What storage medium would you suggest for storing the master payroll file for each of the following companies? Justify each choice.

a IFM Insurance Company which pays all its employees a monthly salary. (IFM's policies are sold by independent agents who are not employees of the company.)

b The hourly payroll system of MAFM Company which manufactures consumer appliances in six different plants with a total of 8,600 hourly employees.

c SAFM Department Stores sales clerks who are paid a combination of base salary and commission based on total sales during the previous two-week pay period.

2 What storage device would you suggest for storing the master file in each of the following systems? Justify each choice.

a Master reservation file for the reservation system of FA International Airlines. The system must be able to indicate within 30 seconds seat availability on any flight scheduled within the next 90 days and to respond to a reservation request within 30 seconds.

b The master inventory file for each store in the GFM Grocery Stores Chain. Each inventory is updated daily (actually, overnight).

c The master file for an online inventory control system for WAFM Wholesalers, wholesalers of drugs and pharmaceuticals.

d The transactions file for the accounts receivable system of Local Department Store. Local has approximately 3,000 charge customers, about one-third of whom make a credit purchase during any one month. All 3,000 customers receive a bill each month even if they owe nothing.

IBM's Coming Disk-Drive Surge

International Business Machines Corp. has long called the tune in disk drives, the mass-memory systems that operate much like a phonograph to provide the bulk of the on-line data storage in large computers. But in recent years the giant has seen its share of the disk-drive market for its own computer systems steadily eroding to a point where outsiders have taken nearly one-third of this $1.5 billion business.

Now, however, these IBM competitors are growing increasingly worried that IBM is about to pull the rug out from under them. The so-called plug-compatible manufacturers (PCMs) have built up their sales with what are basically copies of IBM disk drives at lower prices. IBM is about to make that job tougher.

The big computer maker has come up with the new 3370 disk drive, announced in January along with its new 4300 series of mainframe processors, which competitors believe will revolutionize their business. It would do this by employing a new thin-film technology that analysts say would eventually cut memory costs by 90% and improve the storage capacity of a single 14-in. disk by as much as 30 times over the IBM 3350, the current industry standard. "Figuring out where IBM is going becomes a guessing game with damned high stakes," says Arthur Withop, manager of recording technology components for Memorex Corp., the largest disk-drive PCM.

IBM itself has never admitted that it is using thin film in any of its new products, saying only that the 3370 uses semiconductor technology in its construction. But one analyst comments, "That's just another way of saying thin film." Now, competitors are anxiously awaiting the first shipments of the 3370 so that they can open one up and look inside. "While we're not exactly scared by what we hear along the grapevine about IBM's new disk drives, we are a trifle nervous," admits one competitor.

The technology that is creating all this tension is simply a means of getting the magnetic head closer to the spinning disk's surface where the data are stored. The head reads or writes the bits of computer data, which are in the form of magnetic signals. The closer the head and disk are, the better the head can focus on individual bits of information without being confused by magnetic interference from neighboring recording tracks. In that way, more data can be squeezed into the same disk area. "It's like the difference between writing with a crayon or writing with a pen," says Memorex's Withop.

There are several ways to apply a thin

Source: "IBM's Coming Disk-Drive Surge." Reprinted from the June 11, 1979 issue of *Business Week* by special permission, film to either the head or the surface of a disk. One of these is similar to electroplating: A metallic film, just a few molecules thick, coats a substrate when a current is passed through a chamber filled with an inert gas, such as argon. But any of these processes can achieve a thinner or smoother surface than the present practice of grinding down ferrite materials mechanically.

Sales targets

Memorex has been researching thin film for disk-drive application for four years, and last year established a center devoted to recording technology at its Santa Clara (Calif.) site. The company plans to use the thin-film technology as a key part of its product strategy to go after what it calls the "true-blue shops" that buy only IBM products (which are always painted blue). "We're going to be spending a lot of time talking to them this year," says Withop.

The timing of Memorex's first thin-film disk drive will depend—as it will with all of the PCMs—on how long it takes the company to tear apart the new IBM drive and design and build its version. In any event, Memorex has to be on the market within 18 months to be competitive, industry experts say. The other PCMs are also gearing up to meet the IBM challenge.

"There's no doubt that thin film is on the way," says Steve S. Popovich, who is the director of corporate technology for Storage Technology Corp., "and we're ready for it." The Louisville (Colo.) company, which is the No. 3 PCM, is preparing to produce its own thin-film heads, possibly by as soon as August, he says. And Control Data Corp. and the ISS Div. of Sperry Rand Corp. both say that they will be able to match IBM with their own thin-film disk drives within the next 18 months.

Still, some industry observers are less than sanguine about the prospects for the PCMs, pointing out that IBM has invested at least 10 years and $50 million in thin-film R&D—an effort no other company can match. Says one analyst: "This time IBM is going to leave them in the dust." He predicts a move by PCMs away from direct competition with IBM and toward the "friendlier" markets of other computer-systems makers. James N. Porter, A Cupertino (Calif.) consultant, says that IBM's disk-drive competitors are in for "some surprises," but he does not foresee a major shake-out in the market.

Bright future?

If the PMCs are not able to move into thin film fast enough, however, there are a growing number of subcontractors that would like to sell them thin-film components. As many as a dozen little companies—some less than two years old—are putting their R&D budgets into thin film in the belief that the PCMs will be unable to catch up with IBM in the memory technology race this time around.

Magnex Corp., an Oklahoma City affiliate of Exxon Enterprises, is one company that is looking forward to a bright future supplying thin-film heads. "Most of the plug-compatible companies have visited us," says President Fred S. Lee, "and several of them have had R&D programs for three or four years—so far, we haven't been much impressed."

Neither is Everett T. Bahre, president of Information Magnetics Corp., a Goleta (Calif.) head maker that has been providing customers with prototype thin-film heads since late last year. He predicts that the PCMs will drop behind when it comes to getting their products out of the laboratory and into the marketplace in any kind of commercially important volume. "You can easily get the first unit out," he says, "but it's the first 10,000 that count."

The new IBM 3370 disk drive, which competitors expect will have a thin-film head, is certainly not the end of the bad news for disk-drive PCMs. Executives from the IBM competitors read the giant's recent price reductions on its present top-of-the-line drives as an indication that another disk-drive product—code named Whitney—is on the way. It is expected to use thin-film technology in the fabrication of both the head and the disk, and to be announced within a year, along with the company's new H series of mainframe processors.

Beyond that, there is another IBM disk-drive development called McKinley, industry observers say, and something called System R—the ultimate system for the time when the computer becomes nothing more than a big memory manipulator. So it seems unlikely that the day will ever come when the managers of disk-drive PCMs are not casting anxious looks at what is going on at IBM.

Special Option

Mainframes, Minis, and Micros

Introduction

Since 1951, many, many models of computers have been produced. As of 1981, there were probably 200 different models available for purchase or rent. One hears these computers referred to as mainframes, minicomputers, and microcomputers. The implication is that mainframes are the larger-than-mini computers found in data processing systems in large data processing centers. Microcomputers, on the other hand, are "computers on a chip" which are used to *feed* the bigger system as intelligent terminals and preprocessors. Micros are also used as stand-alone computers in small business systems and as so-called home or hobby computers. The minicomputer falls between the large mainframes and the small microcomputer but overlaps both of the other sizes. It is the purpose of this Special Option to identify the real differences among these three size categories. We'll describe them from the small (micros) to the large (mainframe) and then compare their features. But first, let's take a look at the integrated circuit on a chip.

Chip technology

Integrated circuits (ICs) were first announced in 1959. These ICs were single semiconductor chips less than ¼ inch square containing several complete electronic circuits. They were put into use in the 1960s, and by 1970, the capacity of each chip had been increased to a stage referred to as large-scale integrated (LSI) circuits wherein the number of components on a chip is numbered in the thousands. Today, we are in the age of very-large-scale integrated (VLSI) circuits wherein 100,000 transistors are contained on a single chip. By the mid-1980s, the number of components on a chip may exceed 1 million.

Most LSI producers use a "dip and wash" technique to produce chips. The first step is the designing of a diagram of electronic circuitry by a scientist. This diagram is photographically reduced in size until the individual components in the diagram are in the micron (1 millionth of an inch) range. A photographic negative, or "mask," is made of the pattern and reproduced many times. Ultraviolet light is then passed through the negatives onto a 4-inch silicon wafer that has been treated with a light-sensitive material. The patterns are thus etched on the surface of the wafer. The wafer is then dipped in an acid which eats away the surface material where it has not been etched. Next a very thin layer of metal is laid on to connect the components. Another layer of photo-sensitive material is etched, washed, and covered with metal and so on. Some chips require ten or more etched layers. Once all the layers are formed, the individual chips are sawed apart, fine wire leads are attached, and each chip is mounted on a "card" or "board" for inclusion in a system.

VLSI production is more complex, substituting processes such as electron-beam lithography (drawing with a beam of electrons) to create the patterns on the light-sensitive layers.

The beauty of these developments is that less is more. As chip components become smaller and denser, power and packaging requirements shrink and costs go down. For example, one current super computer, Control Data Corporation's Cyber 205, can carry out 800 million instructions per second, which is about eight times as powerful as its two-year-old predecessor. The 205, however, is significantly smaller and costs about the same as the machine it replaced as "the world's most powerful computing system."

Microcomputers

The basis of the microcomputer is the microprocessor. The microprocessor is a "processor on a chip." Specifically, a *microprocessor,* as its name implies, is a general processor created using microcircuit technology (LSI and VLSI) without any of the supporting circuitry and devices to provide memory, input/output, and control capabilities present in a computer system. A *microcomputer* is a true computer built around a microprocessor by adding circuitry and devices to provide memory, input/output, and control functions.

Microcomputers are full computers, with CPU, memory, and I/O, and are physically packaged on one or more printed circuit boards. These boards are commonly about 12 inches by 7 inches. Some systems are built by combining smaller boards (cards) each of which contains one or two subcomponents. The cards are inserted into a card frame which provides the necessary electrical interconnections. When packaged in a chassis with a power supply and connectors for I/O devices, the system is complete. Many microcomputers for the hobby trade look like TV sets with a keyboard attached by a cable. The chassis containing the CRT display also contains the card frames and power supply. The keyboard provides input; the CRT provides output. When these systems are provided with devices for reading tape cassettes or portable floppy diskettes and some sort of printer, business data processing systems are created.

Microcomputers are priced from about $800 to almost $10,000 and are available through retail outlets. Software is also available through retail outlets and is being provided by software houses, moonlighting programmers, and computer hobbyists. Complete accounting systems for small companies are available at minimal cost from a variety of firms. In this area, microcomputers are starting to invade the former domain of the minicomputer as the basis for small business systems. The latest move is to connect several microcomputers to produce a powerful and flexible multiprocessor computer system.

Microcomputers generally operate with 8-bit to 16-bit word sizes. This limits primary memory sizes to 64,000 bytes or less. Input is usually through the keyboard of a CRT display. Output is by display tube and by character printers. Secondary storage is most commonly provided by floppy diskettes. These 5-to-8-inch flexible platters are capable of storing 500,000 to almost 2.5 million characters. Winchester disk drives are now available which can store from 3 to 80 million characters per drive. Magnetic tape cassettes are also a common secondary storage medium.

System software for these small systems is usually provided on hardware read-only memory chips called firmware. A variety of programming languages are available, with BASIC the most common high-level language.

Minicomputers

This category of computers is hard to define. It might actually be divided into microminis, miniminis, and megaminis (small, medium, and large). Minis overlap micros at the small end, starting with 8-bit and 12-bit word size machines whose primary memory will not exceed 32K words. At the high end, the minis overlap mainframes, with 32-bit word sizes and 2 million bytes of primary memory. Most minis have 12-bit to 24-bit word sizes and a smaller instruction set than most mainframes. Their architecture differs from micros in that whereas the micro has an entire processor on a chip, the mini has only a single logic function on each chip.

Minicomputers tend to use the full range of I/O devices available for computers. Random-access memory (RAM) capability is usually provided by secondary storage in the form of disks (both fixed disks and disk packs), often combined in a single drive.

The differences between minicomputers and microcomputers become more obvious as the size of the system expands. The larger word size of the minicomputer allows for a larger primary memory (more locations can be addressed) and more complex configurations of peripherals. Specialized interfaces and controllers, often built using microprocessor technology, make it possible for minicomputers to invade the domain formerly reserved for large mainframes. They are no longer restricted to use as intelligent terminals and small data processing systems. Minicomputers are now common as the core of systems supporting 64 or more simultaneous users. They are connected in networks to provide on-site processing for users located away from the central data processing installation. (These distributed data processing systems are described more fully in Chapter 7.) Minicomputers are often no longer mini; they possess most of the characteristics of large mainframes, except the ability to directly address large primary random-access memories. This, too, is changing as minicomputers with larger word sizes and virtual memory capability become more common.

Minimal minicomputer systems can be purchased for as little as $5,000. The largest minicomputer systems include banks of peripherals controlled by sophisticated executive programs and can cost over a quarter of a million dollars.

Mainframes

Mainframes and mainframe systems vary widely in size, speed, and complexity. Some systems are relatively simple with only a few input and output devices and limited secondary storage. Other systems serve hundreds of users simultaneously, feature multiple processors, many millions of bytes of primary memory, billions of bytes of online secondary storage, and almost every conceivable type of input/output device.

Word sizes on these systems vary from 24 to 36 bits with 32 bits most common, but 36 bits not unusual. Primary memory sizes vary from about 128K to 12 million bytes; the most common size is in the 3- to 5-million range.

Technologically, the modern mainframe is not greatly different from the large minicomputer. The generally greater word size on mainframes means a larger instruction set as well as a larger primary memory. It also means that fewer functions can be squeezed onto one chip. However, it is now estimated that an entire mainframe CPU will be contained on just three chips by the end of the 1980s.

Summary

The significant characteristics of mainframes, minicomputers, and microcomputers are summarized in Tables S2.1 and S2.2. To make the comparison clearer, the minicomputer and mainframe have each been broken into small,

Table S2.1

COMPUTER TYPE	WORD SIZE IN BITS (MOST COMMON)	PRIMARY MEMORY SIZE (BYTES)	PRICE (DOLLARS)
Microcomputer	8–16	4K–64K	1.5K–10K
Minicomputer			
Small	8–12	4K–48K	10K–25K
Medium	16	24K–256K	25K–70K
Large	24–32	256K–2M	75K–300K
Mainframe			
Small	32	128K–1M	40K–100K
Medium	32–36	1M–5M	100K–2M
Large	36	5M–8M	2M–5M
Superlarge	36	8M–12M	5M–8M

Comparison of computer size categories

Table S2.2

COMPUTER TYPE	INPUT	OUTPUT	SECONDARY STORAGE
Microcomputers	Keyboard	CRT display, character printer	Floppy diskette, Winchester disk drive, tape cassettes
Minicomputers			
Small	Keyboard terminal	CRT display, character printer	Floppy diskette, disk packs
Medium	All devices	CRT display, line printer	Fixed disks, disk packs
Large	All devices	All devices	Fixed disks, disk packs
Mainframes			
Small	Keyboard, punched card reader	Line printers, CRT display	Disk packs, fixed-disk packs
Medium to superlarge	All devices	All devices	All devices

Comparison of device use by computer size categories

medium, and large categories, with a further category of superlarge for mainframes. The overlap among the three classes is apparent. These tables make it clear why some experts identify a minicomputer as any computer that a manufacturer labels mini. Note how the small minicomputers correspond to the microcomputers. Conversely, the large minicomputers overlap even the medium-sized mainframes. As computer users, we can be indifferent to these classifications, but as technicians, we appreciate differences in architecture that lead to only minor differences in capability.

Growth of a Computer System

What does a small business do when it is faced with a 200% increase in gross sales, an accounting machine in its death throes and a service bureau gently nudging its clients to seek processing power elsewhere?

For the Hayward Lumber & Home Supply Co. [of Salinas, Cal.] the answer to these problems was found in a carefully designed growth plan mapped out with and including Datapoint Corp. minicomputers.

Hayward Lumber has five retail lumber and building material centers, a kitchen cabinet outlet, a prehung manufacturing center, and warehousing and land development divisions. The firm has been in business since 1919, with current gross revenues of about $21 million.

Previous planning had prepared management for an upgrade of its processing methods, which in 1976 consisted of an NCR Corp. 400 accounting machine, a leased IBM keypunch and the utilization of an IBM Systems/3 service bureau [a separate company hired to process a client's date on its own computer system].

The decision to automate all accounting was hastened, however, by the reluctance of the service bureau to continue indefinitely the processing of Hayward's payroll and voluminous accounts receivable. A consultant firm's survey of the entire company operations yielded two recommendations: convert to a completely in-house DP department immediately with a Hewlett-Packard Co. HP 3000 installation, or make the conversion gradually with Datapoint equipment, which could include an interface with System/3 through specially formatted diskettes.

The second choice was considered more feasible because it would give management and the accounting department a chance to absorb the impact of automation more easily, was more desirable costwise and would permit the training of experienced employees rather than necessitate hiring a technical operations manager. The IBM service bureau agreed to assist in the gradual conversion process. . . .

A vendor specializing in Datapoint systems, Virginia Winn Software Co., was contracted for all systems design and customized software. Winn also provided staff training, in addition to the Datapoint customer education classes in which two employees participated.

System installed

The initial installation in December 1976, consisted of 16K processor, 5M bytes of

Source: "Mini Helps User Weather 200% Sales Increase," *Computerworld,* August 25, 1980, p. special report/33.

disk storage, the diskette controller, three terminals and a small printer. This provided accounts payable data entry to System/3, as well as accounting systems that remained resident on the Datapoint.

A major consideration in all programming was the establishing of good internal audit controls and system security, which had been recommended by the company's auditors.

Another priority was to keep the accounting centralized and to have as little impact on the branches' daily operations as possible.

The first installation proved so successful that more and more demands were forthcoming from users. An upgrade to a 48K processor with 40M bytes of disk storage, six terminals and a 600 line/min printer was made barely a year later.

The configuration allowed elimination of the keypunch because all data entry was now done through the Datapoint terminals. Processing costs were reduced at the service bureau when accounts payable and payroll came inhouse.

The credit department gained flexibility with on-line account inquiry, and the conversion helped it absorb the impact of restrictive credit legislation. Many other accounting functions were augmented, including the development of a data base to support Lifo inventory valuation, which generated additional working capital from substantial tax savings.

Time demands

Because of the heavy time demands made on the newly founded DP department to accommodate the continued increase in sales and unit volume, the plans of operating totally in-house were accelerated. Housekeeping routines, including the formatting of the IBM diskettes for System/3, were taking up data entry time because the formatting could be done only when Datashare (dispersed data processing) was not operating. Program development for new systems was also having to wait its turn, and heavy overtime hours resulted.

A second stand-alone system was considered for processing and development, but it was at this time that Datapoint announced its Attached Resource Computer (ARC). By this combination of hardware and software, separate processors are dedicated to applications execution, disk I/O and the interchange between the two. . . .

The ARC system would therefore support the data entry functions under Datashare and the processing of data or program development with all users having access to a common data base without conflict. ARC also allows almost unlimited growth because additional processors can be added to the system as needed.

ARC installation

ARC was installed in June 1979, with three 120K-byte processors, 80M bytes of disk storage and an additional terminal. No software changes were necessitated by either upgrade, and downtime for each installation was held to one day until the system was up and running.

By December 1979, all systems had been developed, and Hayward DP was operating totally in-house, with dependence on the outside service bureau terminated. Data entry is now available to the input clerks for eight hours daily. The entire system is down one hour for security backup, and the bulk of the end-of-day processing is run unattended at night utilizing a print spooler.

By making the conversion in relatively slow steps, and with top management providing input and support during each phase of implementation, the upgrade from the

1976 situation to the present-day operation has been easily absorbed in both cost and personnel factors. With a 50% increase in sales dollar volume since 1976, and a 24% increase in personnel company-wide, the accounting department has added only one employee.

A DP committee has been formed, comprised of the chief executive officer, the controller, the assistant controller and the DP director. This committee is responsible for all systems design, the formation of both short- and long-range goals concerning data processing, and the effective communication between senior executives and the DP function.

Special Option

The Computer Hardware Industry

The growth of business data processing

Since the first commerical application of computers in 1954, their use in business data processing has grown phenomenally. As shown in Table S3.1, a primary reason for this growth is that hardware has steadily declined in cost and increased in capability, causing a continuous, more or less twofold drop in hardware costs. The expansion in business data processing that has resulted has developed its own braking system, however. More capable computers have made possible a greater number of systems of increasing complexity, but this growth has created a shortage of technically trained personnel, particularly systems analysts and programmers. This shortage, in turn, has driven development costs upward. As can be seen in Table S3.1, while hardware costs per instruction have declined to a very low level, the cost per instruction of design and development has more than doubled.

The data in Table S3.1 should not be taken as absolutely correct; they combine a number of estimates and measurements initially developed for a variety of purposes. They are intended to show only the basic trends of growth in business data processing.

Elements of the hardware industry

The computer hardware industry is made up of several hundred manufacturers. A few of these manufacturers are very large and produce mainframes, minis, and micros. Others specialize in only one size computer (for example, micros). Still others produce only storage devices or peripherals (tape and disk drives, printers, terminals, and so on).

The top ten companies in size of sales in 1979 are shown in Table S3.2. Obviously the leader, with over seven times the dollar sales of number two Burroughs, is International Business Machines Corporation (IBM). IBM accounted for about 60 percent of the sales dollars generated in the data processing industry. The sales of the tenth-ranked firm in the industry, Data General, amount to less than 3 percent of IBM's sales.

The top five companies (IBM, Burroughs, NCR, Control Data, and Sperry Rand) are all mainframe producers. In sixth place and closing fast is the top minicomputer manufacturer, Digital. Number seven, Honeywell, is again a mainframer. Hewlett-Packard in eighth is a minicomputer manufacturer. Number nine, Memorex, sells a variety of peripherals. Data General (tenth) is another minicomputer manufacturer. Minis didn't really take off until the middle 1970s, and all the mainframers also produce systems that compete for the mini dollar. Finding three minicomputer manufacturers among the industry leaders clearly indicates how their use has been expanding.

Table S3.3 presents a breakdown of sales for 1977 and 1979 into industry categories. It is interesting that the largest category is peripherals and terminals, with mainframes a distant second in 1977 but service and software second in 1979. Note the almost perfect reversal in standing

YEAR	NUMBER OF COMPUTER SYSTEMS INSTALLED	INSTRUCTIONS PER SECOND	COST PER MILLION INSTRUCTIONS	TOTAL COST/INSTR. OF DESIGN AND DEVELOPMENT
1951	10	100	$250.00	—
1955	250	500	165.00	4.20*
1960	5,400	.4M	18.00	4.40
1965	23,000	1M	2.75	5.50
1970	90,000	2M	.20	7.00
1975	210,000	4M	.08	8.00
1980	350,000*	10M*	.04*	9.10*
1985	550,000*	80M*	.01*	9.75*

*Estimated by the author

Table S3.1 Trends of growth and related cost data for the computer industry

1979 RANK	COMPANY	1978 RANK	1979 DP REVENUES ($M)	PERCENT OF TOTAL REVENUES	1979 NET INCOME ($M)
1	IBM (International Business Machines)	1	18,338	80	3,011
2	Burroughs	2	2,432	87	306
3	NCR (National Cash Register)	4	2,404	80	235
4	Control Data	5	2,273	70	124
5	Sperry Rand	3	2,270	49	259
6	Digital Equipment Corp.	6	2,032	100	208
7	Honeywell Information Systems	7	1,453	35	240
8	Hewlett-Packard	8	1,030	42	212
9	Memorex	9	664	90	32
10	Data General	11	540	100	50

Source: *Datamation,* July 1980, pp. 97–126.

Table S3.2 **The ten top firms in the data processing industry**

between mainframes and service and software in the two years. Media and supplies, in last place both years, is even further behind in 1979. These changes reflect the increasing use of remote access and various forms of processing networks. The increasing use of display terminals is reducing the need for media and paper supplies.

	1979		1977	
	$M	% TOTAL	$M	% TOTAL
Mainframes	7,185	16	7,387	24
Minicomputers	4,360	10	2,502	8
Peripherals & terminals	20,507	45	13,766	44
Service & software	11,828	25	5,685	18
Media & supplies	1,807	4	1,771	6
Totals	45,687	100	31,111	100

Source: *Datamation,* July 1980, pp. 88–90 (data are for the top 100 firms).

Table S3.3 **Industry categories**

Mainframe manufacturers

The largest mainframe manufacturer in both 1978 and 1977 was IBM, which has dominated the industry since about 1956. It is noteworthy that the seventh largest mainframe manufacturer shown in Table S3.4 (Amdahl) is a manufacturer of mainframes that use IBM software. These machines can be substituted for IBM hardware. Their appeal is a higher level of job throughput and a lower price than the IBM equipment they replace. Of course, such plug-compatible manufacturers (PCMs) exist at the mercy of IBM. If IBM were to drop equipment prices or come out with a cheaper and more powerful system, the PCMs could lose their market. A third possibility is that IBM would reconfigure the hardware-software mix and convert an increasing portion of the system software into hardware. At this writing (1982), all these things have been occurring and a shakeout among the PCMs is well underway. Its beginnings are observable in Table S3.4 where Amdahl is shown to have fallen six positions in industry rank between 1978 and 1979. To be fair, we must also point out that part of the decline in rank by Amdahl is the result of gains by peripherals and terminal and minicomputer manufacturers.

The mainframe manufacturers in the second through sixth places are also old hands in the industry. Sperry Rand produced the first commerical computer in the early 1950s. Burroughs and NCR were familiar giants in the business machine field before they entered the computer industry in the middle 1950s. Control Data Corporation is a computer industry creation. Honeywell Information Systems expanded into computers from the production of control instruments and attained high ranking in the computer manufacturing business by taking over General Electric Company's computer manufacturing division in the late 1960s. It is interesting to note that

INDUSTRY RANK 1979	COMPANY	D.P. REVENUE 1979($M)	PERCENT OF TOTAL REVENUE	INDUSTRY RANK 1978
1	IBM	18,338	80	1
2	Burroughs	2,432	87	2
3	NCR	2,404	80	4
4	Control Data	2,273	70	5
5	Sperry Rand	2,270	49	3
7	Honeywell	1,453	35	7
21	Amdahl	300	100	15

Source: *Datamation,* July 1980, pp. 97–126.

Table S3.4 **The top mainframe manufacturers**

RANK	COMPANY	1979 DP REVENUES ($M)	PERCENT OF TOTAL REVENUES	OVERALL INDUSTRY RANK	
				1979	1978
1	Digital Equipment Corp.	2,032	100	6	6
2	Hewlett-Packard	1,030	42	8	8
3	Data General	540	100	10	11
4	Texas Instruments	425	13	14	16
5	Management Assistance	283	100	22	23
6	Wang Labs	280	68	23	26
7	Harris	210	20	28	27

Source: *Datamation*, July 1980, pp. 97–126.

Table S3.5 **The top minicomputer manufacturers**

General Electric retained its timesharing computer services business and, in 1979, ranked 17th in the total data processing industry, up from 20th in 1978.

Minicomputer manufacturers

Minicomputer systems is one of the growth areas in business data processing. Digital Equipment Corporation (DEC), the leading manufacturer of minis, (see Table S3.5) is growing more rapidly than the mainframers and may soon occupy second position in the data processing industry. The seventh-ranked minicomputer manufacturer had sales of about one-tenth of those of DEC, the leading mini manufacturer. Hewlett-Packard, second in minis, passed the milestone of $1 billion in sales in 1979, one of only eight companies attaining that level.

Microcomputer manufacturers

Although several minicomputer manufacturers also produce microcomputers, only three companies stand out as microcomputer manufacturers.

All three of these companies are relatively new entrants into the data processing industry and are growing at phenomenal rates. During 1979, Apple grew 650 percent, Tandy 131 percent, and Commodore 150 percent. Apple and Tandy sell their products through special retail stores. Commodore also markets its PET computer line through retail stores but has not established its own outlets. Data on the three major micro manufacturers is presented in Table S3.6.

RANK	COMPANY	1979 DP REVENUES ($M)	PERCENT TOTAL REVENUES	INDUSTRY RANK 1979	INDUSTRY RANK 1978
1	Tandy	150	12	39	58
2	Apple Computer	75	100	61	100
3	Commodore International	55	55	75	94

Source: *Datamation,* July 1980, pp. 97–126.

Table S3.6 **The top microcomputer manufacturers**

Peripherals and subsystems suppliers

The top ten suppliers of peripherals and subsystems are listed in Table S3.7. Notably, the top 6 firms in the group were among the top 20 firms in terms of revenue in 1979 and all 10 were included in the top 30 revenue producers. These facts clearly illustrate the importance of this market. One surprising result is that only the tenth-ranked firm has terminals as its major product. However, many of the subsystems provided by the higher-ranked firms include terminals and point-of-action recorders of various kinds. The major products for each of these companies is shown in the final column of Table S3.7.

RANK	COMPANY	1979 DP REVENUES ($M)	PERCENT TOTAL REVENUES	INDUSTRY RANK 1979	INDUSTRY RANK 1978	MAJOR PRODUCTS
1	Memorex	664	90	9	9	Disk drives, tape drives
2	Storage Technology	480	100	11	18	Tape drives, disk drives
3	Xerox	475	6.8	12	17	Rotating storage, printers, services
4	TRW	440	9.6	13	12	Terminals and subsystems
5	3M	310	5.7	19	19	Media and supplies
6	Northern Telecom	300	100	20	21	Telecommunications
7	ITT	260	1.2	24	24	Telecommunications
8	Datapoint	252	100	26	28	Network systems, telecommunications
9	Mohawk Data Sciences	198	100	29	29	Key-to-tape systems, supplies
10	Tektronix	195	22.2	30	32	Display terminals

Source: *Datamation,* July 1980, pp. 97–126.

Table S3.7 **The top peripheral and subsystems suppliers**

Summary

The computer hardware industry is dominated by one firm, IBM. IBM manufactures mainframes and minicomputers, peripherals of all types, and media and supplies and sells computer services through its own service bureau division. The major portion of IBM's data processing revenues arises from sale and rental of mainframes, however.

As IBM dominates the mainframe industry, so DEC dominates the minicomputer field. DEC, however, ranks only sixth in the industry although it is closing rapidly on the mainframers ahead of it.

No one company so clearly dominates microcomputer manufacture. There are only three major manufacturers, and the leader (Tandy Corporation) sells about 1.25 as much as the total of its two rivals.

No one company dominates the peripheral and subsystems suppliers. The top four firms had 1979 revenues that spread only from $440 million to $664 million. The tenth-ranked firm in this division of the hardware industry (Tektronix) generated almost 30 percent of the revenue of the division leader (Memorex).

DATA PROCESSING DISPUTE

Computer Buyers Beware

Perhaps nowhere should the first rule of purchasing—*caveat emptor*—be heeded more than in the fast-growing world of computer users. There have always been salesmen who promised what sounded like a data processing miracle and buyers who were surprised when the equipment delivered a lot less. But the number of users who are unhappy with their new systems is increasing rapidly, and this trend is straining the close customer-vendor partnerships that have nurtured the data processing industry.

A big part of the industry's problem is the expanding number of first-time users—small companies without the expertise to evaluate such complex systems—and the rapidly declining prices, which leave vendors a smaller margin to pay for the extra handholding that new users require. "About 50% of all computer users are disappointed [in their systems], if not angry," estimates Thomas K. Christo, a North Hampton (N.H.) attorney, who has represented more than 100 dissatisfied computer customers in the past six years. "It's a massive problem—and getting worse," he adds. These customers are grumbling about the cost of installation, which is considerably higher than they had anticipated or were led to believe. They also say that their new computers do not perform as expected. Moreover, they complain bitterly about unreliable vendors, often third-party companies that buy the hardware from the manufacturer, add the software, and market and service the system.

High stakes

Every industry, of course, has its share of unhappy customers, but there is increasingly more at stake in buying a computer than there is with most other capital equipment. A computer is the central nervous system of a growing number of companies. "If you buy a printing press that doesn't work, it won't ruin your business," says David C. Bauer, a Dubuque (Iowa) attorney who successfully represented one dissatisfied user in court. "But a computer that does not work can screw up your business records and bankrupt you."

Many computer users take their licks and suffer in silence, but now more are taking their vendors to court. As many as 500 cases are now in the courts, 10 times more

---

Source: "Computers: A Burst of Critical Feedback." Reprinted from the February 2, 1981 issue of *Business Week* by special permission, than a decade ago, estimates Dick Brandon, a New York management consultant who specializes in advising users on computer purchases. And these cases are only the tip of the iceberg, he adds, since most claims are settled out of court.

Those experiencing the pitfalls of computer buying range from the largest corporations to small businesses. Big companies have had their own computers for years, yet they still endure delays, cost overruns, and installation headaches with new systems. "You often discover you have more on your hands than you anticipated," concedes John R. Goodroe, vice-president for data processing at Equitable Life Assurance Society. Data-processing personnel know programming, he adds, but that "doesn't make them knowledgeable in how to install and operate the machines." The cost of installation—wiring and cabling and air conditioning—"are almost universally underestimated," Goodrow says. These costs can often run to as much as two and a half times the cost of the equipment.

Unrealistic expectations

Hardest hit, however, are small companies. Unlike large corporations, they lack an inhouse data-processing staff, and they often are least able to afford any cost overrun or losses that may result from installation delays or software glitches. No one knows this better than Robert Weinstein, president of Triangle Underwriters Inc., who claims that computer problems forced him to liquidate his $20 million business and lay off 82 of his 85 employees.

The New York company, an insurance middleman between a dozen carriers and 4,000 brokers, purchased a Honeywell computer to automate premium collection and commission payments. But Weinstein claimed that the software he purchased from Honeywell never worked: Commissions were paid twice to brokers and premiums were not passed on to the carriers. These errors destroyed his cash flow, says Weinstein, and he could not meet Triangle's credit obligations. A federal court jury last summer awarded Triangle a $1.1 million judgment against Honeywell, but the judge reversed its decision and Weinstein is currently appealing.

Problems such as Weinstein's are quite often exacerbated by the unrealistic expectations of first-time users. Conflicts arise, points out Roy N. Freed, a Boston attorney with Powers & Hall, because "suppliers often do nothing to dispel the customer's unreasonably high expectations."

Evaluating distributors

Vendors acknowledge the validity of such complaints and are increasing their efforts to educate first-time users on what to expect from a computer. "It's important [for first-time users] to have a clear understanding of what can be reasonably achieved and in what length of time," says James E. Dezell, vice-president of sales support for International Business Machines Corp.'s General Systems Div.

To help these less-sophisticated sales prospects, IBM has set up learning centers that teach how to use a computer. Data General Corp. is trying to educate first-time customers by offering its "Insiders' Guide to Small Business Computers." Nearly 35,000 copies at $6.95 each have been sold since last June. "We offer an analysis of the decision-making process and tell the prospect what questions to ask," explains Richard Brown, merchandising manager for the minimaker's General Distribution Div.

Many computer neophytes are not easily

reached by such direct methods because they buy their machines from third-party systems houses. And here the problems can multiply because of the large number of such companies. To cut down on these problems as much as possible, Digital Equipment Corp. began last year to evaluate systems houses before authorizing them to sell systems built around DEC computers. "We're trying to weed out those people not serious about the business and who won't represent us well," says Irwin Jacobs, a DEC vice-president. Before DEC began its program, as many as 30% of its distributors went out of business annually, Jacobs estimates. Only 6% have failed in the past year, when the manufacturer screened distributors and trained those accepted to manage their finances.

Pulling the plug

Vendors may be increasing their efforts to aid first-time users just in time. "There are too many war stories—the whole industry is starting to get a bad name," says Joseph Auer, president of International Computer Negotiations Inc. in Winter Park, Fla. One small-business operator who believes the industry deserves such a reputation is C. Robert Thonen, president of Wheeling Heating Co. in West Virginia. "When you go to buy a computer and you know nothing about it, you have to rely on the person who's selling it to tell you what it will do," he says. But that attitude got him into trouble, Thonen claims, when he tried to automate the financial operations of his air-conditioning and heating business with an NCR Corp. computer.

For one thing, Thonen says, hidden costs drove the price of his computer system from the $14,000 he expected to spend to nearly $130,000. The biggest chunk of additional expense, he says, came from having to build a special computer room—even though the salesman had originally told him the unit would fit in his existing office. Once the computer was up and running, Thonen claims, the accounting software constantly spewed forth incorrect invoices and payroll checks. The invoicing problem caused sales to decline to $140,000 in 1975, down from a record high of $834,000, recorded two years earlier, he maintains.

So Thonen pulled the computer's plug. "We went back to a pencil and paper, and we're doing much better," he says. By last year, sales had rebounded to $670,000. In the meantime, Thonen had filed suit against NCR for $10 million in actual damages and $30 million in punitive damages, charging fraud, misrepresentation, and negligence. NCR's Ben E. Olive, associate general counsel, denies that anything was amiss with its machine and points out there are "hundreds of the same model still in operation." The case is still pending, but meanwhile, Thonen's computer is sitting unused.

'One-sided' contract

For many users, however, legal recourse to redress computer problems is not an option because they sign the standard vendor contract that prohibits such actions. Surprisingly, these normally cautious businessmen, who would not think of buying property without consulting an attorney, never seek legal advice before signing a computer contract.

"In retrospect, we signed a very onesided contract," acknowledges Anthony B. Leisner, general manager of Quality Books Inc. The Northbrook (Ill.) publisher has taken Burroughs Corp. to court, claiming that the computer that it leased never performed as promised. Burroughs denies the charges and has countersued Quality to prevent it from publicizing its complaints. "The problem is a computer that didn't work," maintains Leisner, "but the difficulty of resolving the problems is the contract. If we were to do it again," he says, "we'd run the contract by an attorney—there is no such thing as a routine contract."

Despite the horror stories, no one in the industry expects the growing dissatisfaction with computers to slow industry growth. For one thing, the computer has become the crucial cog in most business operations. Wheeling's Thonen, for example, already plans to buy another computer to help manage his company's renewed growth. He explains: "I still believe a computer is faster and more accurate than a human being."

Part 3

Data Processing Software

Chapter 7 Computerized Data Processing Systems

Outline

Computer systems operation

Operating systems
- Job queuing
- Priority control
- Resource assignment
- Data access
- Data management
- System program library
- Overlapped functions
- Text editing
- Language translators

Applications programs

Types of processing systems

Batch processing systems
- Job-by-job system
- Stacked-job system

Multiprocessor and multiprogrammed systems
- Multiprocessor systems
- Multiprogramming systems
- Timesharing systems

Virtual storage

Data communication systems

Teleprocessing
- Multiplexors and concentrators
- Telephone lines
- Satellite transmission systems
- Types of data systems
  - Data acquisition systems
  - Data distribution systems
  - Data interrogation systems
- Decentralized data processing systems
- Distributed processing systems

System types and computer size

Realtime systems

Data processing devices are organized into systems that perform the sets of processing functions needed to accomplish a total task. This concept of processing systems has been illustrated in the payroll systems of Figure 4.7, page 79 and Figure 6.4, page 134. Our attention up to this point has been focused on the machines (the hardware) found in these systems. Now we will look at the procedures developed to direct the hardware in the execution of processing. These procedures are called computer **software**, the procedural instruction sets (programs) that control computer systems as they perform data processing.

Computer systems operation

As was explained in Chapter 2, computers are controlled by sets of instructions called programs. Without a program, a computer cannot operate as an automatic data processing system. It must be directed and controlled step by step in carrying out the individual operations of data processing. These step-by-step instructions are organized into sets (programs) of which there are three major types. **Operating systems** provide overall control and "supervise" all the hardware and software elements in the performance of their individual tasks. **Language translators** do what their name implies—they translate instructions written in a programming language into the internal language of the computer. **Applications programs** direct the step-by-step data processing required to carry out a task, such as hourly payroll processing. The purpose of this chapter is to explain what operating systems are and how they function in the organization and operation of different kinds of data processing systems. Later chapters will concentrate on applications programs and their development, and on language translators.

Operating systems

An operating system may also be called a supervisory program, supervisor, executive, or monitor. The most common term is operating system, usually abbreviated as OS, with an added letter or two to indicate the exact type of system. TOS refers to tape operating system, DOS to disk operating system, TSOS to timesharing operating system, and so forth. Simply put, an operating system is a set of programs or processing routines that manage the resources in the system as it carries out its operations. In other words, the operating system runs the computer system. It can range from one simple program loading and executing a stack of programs and their associated data to a complex set of interacting routines. The most complex operating systems direct the many varied components of both hardware and software in an interactive system, carrying out a multitude of processing tasks (jobs) arriving from a variety of sources at essentially the same time.

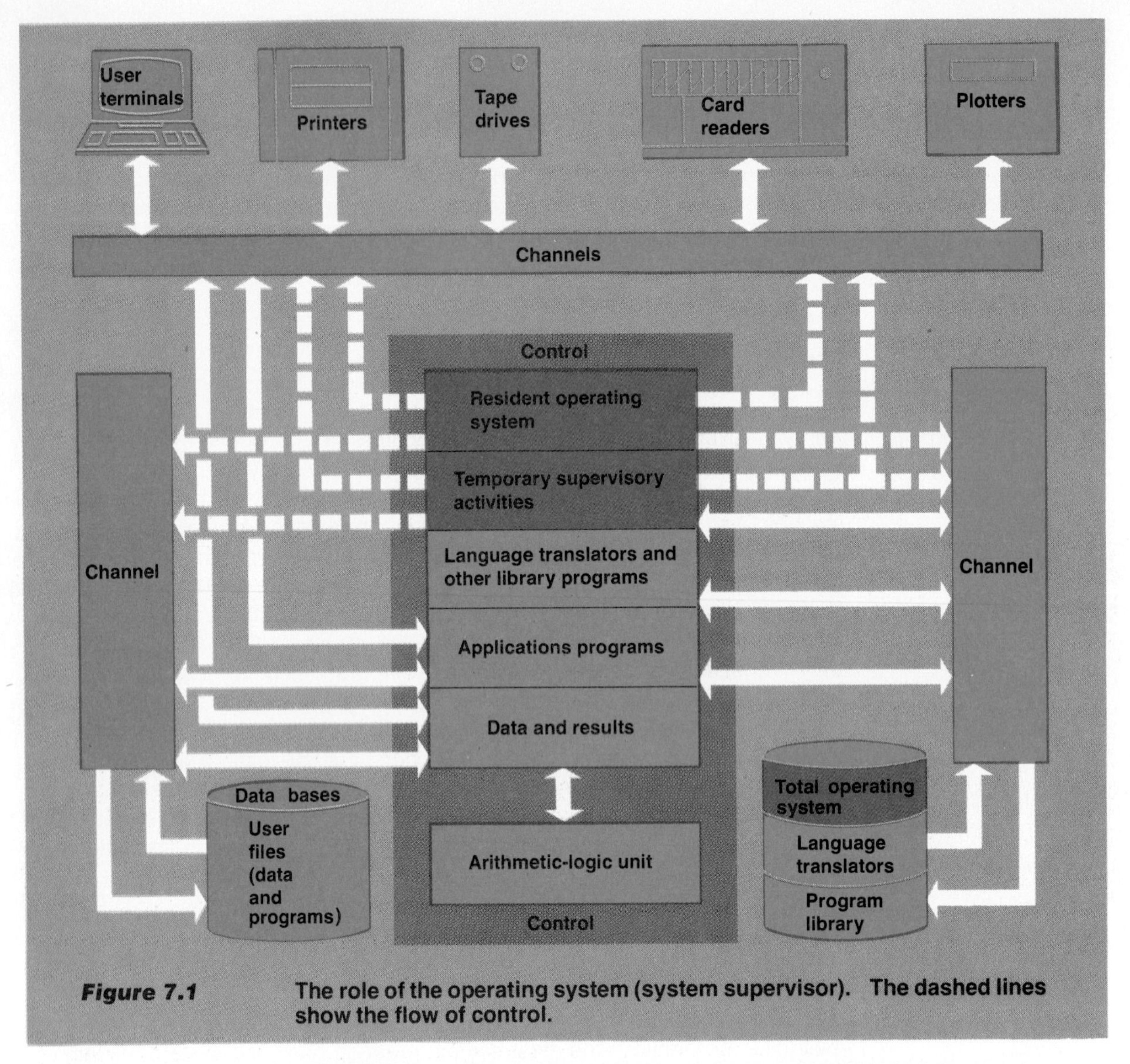

Figure 7.1 **The role of the operating system (system supervisor). The dashed lines show the flow of control.**

The purpose of the operating system is to use the speed of the computer itself in directing operations so that the amount of work accomplished by the computer can be increased. It is easy to see that a human operator could not respond in a fraction of a second to each of the many demands posed by a modern interactively shared computer system. Manually shifting processing control from user to user could not be accomplished in nanoseconds or even milliseconds. Recognizing availability of a resource (a printer perhaps) when one job was finished and shifting it to the next job in the (printing) queue would take seconds, not a fraction of a second. The operating system routines can do all these things so quickly as to seem to be doing them simultaneously. In this way the computer is kept productively busy. The specific tasks handled by the operating system are job queuing, priority control, resource assignment, data access, data management, management of a system program library, function overlapping, program loading, and text editing.

To accomplish all its jobs, the operating system (OS) is large and complex. As illustrated in Figure 7.1, not all the OS is resident in primary storage all the time; only a small portion is. This is the critical part of the OS, however, as it must prevent other programs from taking over its ultimate control authority. This core segment of the OS calls in other portions of the supervisor as they are required to control the many components of the system and the processing jobs flowing through them.

Job queuing

Before supervisory systems were developed, a computer stopped when it reached the end of a program. The operator then reset the controls, prepared input and output devices, and loaded the next program. Until the loading process was completed, the processor did not perform any productive work. With an operating system, this job-by-job approach is ended. The operating system can control the input of programs and data (jobs from many sources) and queue them up for processing as one overall stream of work.

Priority control

The operating system does not always process jobs in the order in which they are received. As jobs are entered, those jobs which are not of the highest priority are sent to secondary storage. Jobs placed in secondary storage are brought into the CPU and completed in an order reflecting the priority assigned to each of them.

Resource assignment

The hardware and software resources needed by a particular job are normally indicated (along with job priority) by a job description which precedes the job and by calls for resources within each program. The allocation of resources to individual jobs is controlled by the operating system. Hardware resources controlled in this process include all I/0 devices, secondary storage, and the CPU itself. Of course, the operating system never releases total control over the CPU. Rather, programs are given intermittent access to the processor and primary memory but overall control is retained by the operating system.

Software resources controlled by the operating system include language translators, utility programs, and other programs stored in the system program library.

Data access

Particularly in online interactive systems serving many users, individual users must not be allowed unauthorized access to the data files of another user. By restricting each job and each user to appropriate data only, errors are reduced, privacy protected, and security enhanced.

Data management

Modern operating systems often incorporate a set of programs for management of an online set of interrelated files (a data base). These data base management programs assist users in updating, correcting, modifying, and accessing data bases. Data base management systems are described in Chapter 14.

System program library

Among the resources of any computer utilizing an operating system is a system program library. This library is a set of routines and programs that can be used by applications programmers. (A routine is a series of program instructions that is not a complete program, but achieves a single purpose. Routines and their use will be discussed further in Chapter 9.) The routines are present on the system and each may be called upon at any time by an application program running on the system. The major types of routines are input/output utilities, transfer utilities, sort/merge utilities, and statistical/mathematical routines. The operating system must control access to and use of these programs to coordinate their use with two or more jobs running at the same time and to prevent the programs themselves from being modified or destroyed.

Utilities are generalized routines for performing specific data processing functions in an efficient way. Input/output utilities are perhaps the most important, since about 40 percent of most applications programs in data processing are involved in performing this function. Input utilities allow the programmer to describe the input file being read in terms of record and field lengths, field order, and the device (tape, disk, card reader) through which it is being read. The utility then furnishes the detailed instructions needed to actually read the file. Output utilities perform similarly in handling output. A description of the output file or report and its source is given to the utility, and the utility provides the detailed program instructions to handle the job of actually writing the file or report on the secondary storage or output device.

Transfer utilities provide for the transfer of data from one medium to another (card to tape, card to disk, tape to disk, disk to tape, and so on). Some of these transfer programs are really specialized output utilities (card to printer, tape to printer, disk to printer, for example).

Sort/merge utilities do exactly what their name indicates. After receiving descriptions of files or arrays (lists) of data, they provide detailed instructions to carry out sorting and merging of the files or arrays.

Statistical/mathematical routines are detailed instructions for performing statistical and mathematical analyses of files of data. They vary widely as to the routines provided and the formulas used to accomplish each task. An experienced mathematical analyst or management scientist should evaluate any of these packages before they are added to the system. If the algorithms (formulas) and the machine capabilities, such as length of word operated upon and precision of computation, are not carefully matched, errors can result.

Overlapped functions

The operating system makes use of the buffers and controllers (channels) for peripheral devices (secondary storage and I/O) to overlap input, processing, and output and keep the processor busy. This general process was explained in Chapter 2. What was not explained is that the operating system must contain routines for accepting and interpreting messages from peripheral devices (interrupts) in order to manage peripheral hardware.

Text editing

A **text editor** is a complex program that eases the job of modifying files stored on the system, particularly files of textual (alphabetical) materials. Operating under the control of the text editor, a series of simple codes are available for deleting, inserting, or changing characters, words, phrases, or even pages within a file. This system program is essential to efficient applications programming. It allows programs to be developed online and be treated as text files. After testing what has been written (see Chapter 11 for testing techniques), the programmer can, through use of the text editor, quickly carry out necessary changes. Suppose, for example, that in writing a large section of a program, a programmer has consistently referred to a name field in a record as Nme-In instead of Name-In. One command can be used to insert the omitted letter (*a*) in each of these references. The power of the text editor available on a system is very important to the productivity of applications programmers using the system.

These text editors are really low-level word processors. Although intended primarily for applications programmers, the text editor can also be useful to other users. For example, users can more easily correct data entry errors or correct programs they write for themselves.

Language translators

Language translators are the programs in the program library that translate programs from assembly or compiler language to machine language for processing. This process is illustrated in Figure 7.2. As indicated there, a program written in machine language (the combinations of 0s and 1s recognized by the hardware) is entered into the CPU and then reads and processes data to produce the desired output. When an assembly or compiler language (a programming language not in machine language) is used, an extra step is required. A language translator program is used to read the program prepared by the programmer and translate that *source program* into a machine-language *object program* that can process the data. Language translators are also called *assemblers* or *compilers.* These terms will be discussed in Chapter 9.

Figure 7.2

a. Machine language process

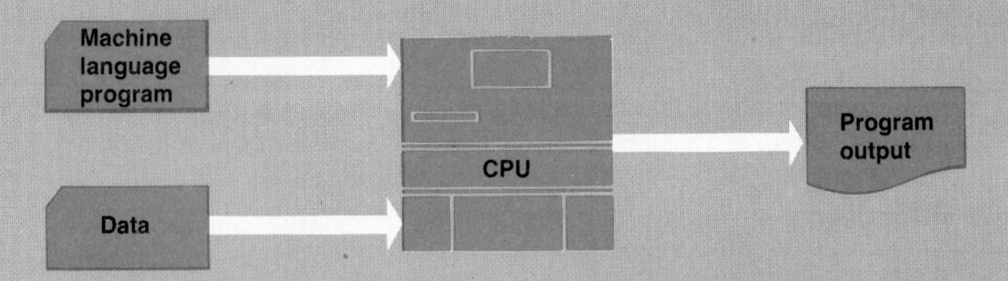

b. Assembler and compiler process Phase 1—compile source program written in compiler or assembly language into object program expressed in machine language

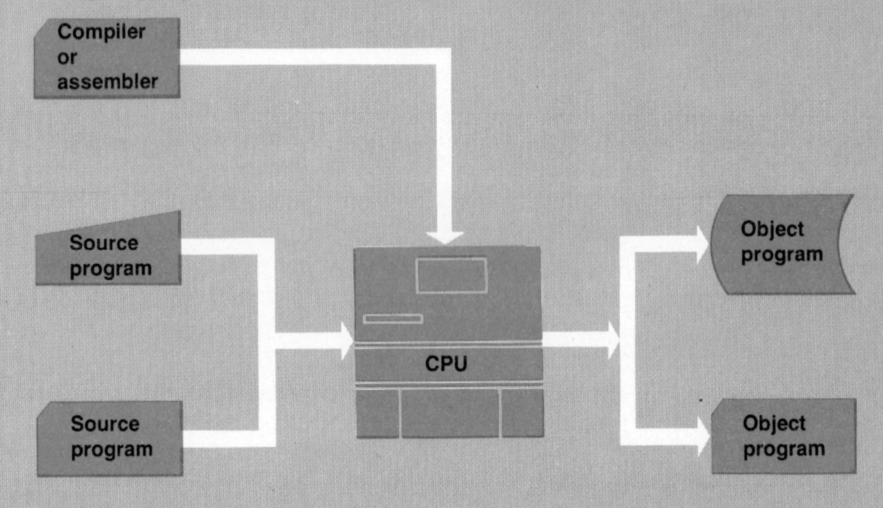

Phase 2—execute the object program

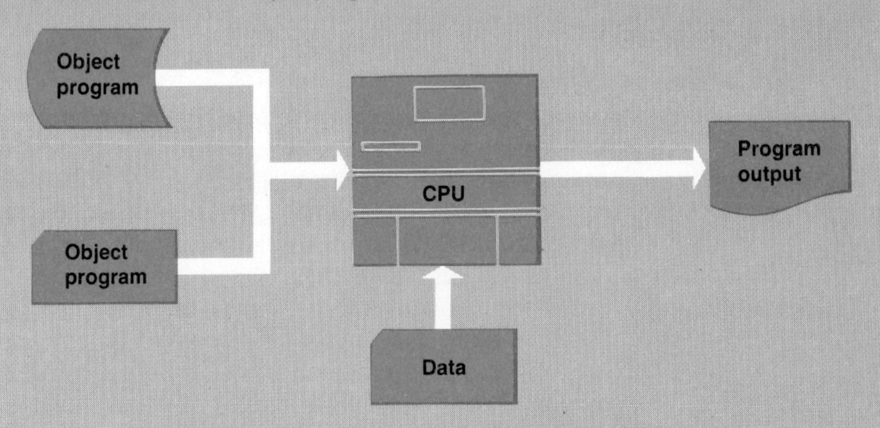

The machine language process and the assembler and compiler process

Applications programs

Applications programs perform specific processing jobs within a system, such as payroll, inventory accounting and control, or accounts receivable. Applications programs are most often written in a compiler language. Processes for designing and writing applications programs are described in Chapters 8-11.

Types of processing systems

There are four major types of data processing systems used in business. These are batch processing systems, multiprocessor systems, multiprogramming systems, and timesharing systems. In addition, there are different types of data communication systems and hardware configurations. The sections that follow describe each of the major processing and communication systems. Note at the outset that these system types are not mutually exclusive—that many of them may appear together in a single computerized data processing system.

Batch processing systems

When data from individual transactions are accumulated over a period of time and processed as a group at a later time, **batch processing** occurs. For example, the sales tickets representing the individual sales transactions at a department store may be collected during the sales day and used to update customer records and prepare reports during the night. Payroll timecards may be punched each day during the payroll period, but processed only at the end of the payroll period. Such batch processing is commonly used where the results of each transaction need not be reflected immediately in the affected master files.

Processing often costs less when data can be batched. The data from the transactions can be sorted into the same order as the master file and processed against a sequentially ordered master file. File processing procedures are less complex and therefore less costly. In addition, storage devices that provide direct or random access are normally more expensive than devices that provide sequential access. This means not only that storage for the current master file is cheaper, but that it is also cheaper to save earlier versions of the file and the transactions that have affected it in case of later problems. If the current master file were accidentially destroyed, it could be reproduced from the back-up files. Most batch systems preserve the two preceding versions of the master file (the "father" and "grandfather" files) and the transactions used to update them in case the current master (the "son" file) is destroyed (see Figure 7.3a).

Batch processing is not restricted to sequential processing, however. If the master file is stored on a direct-access device, as in Figure 7.3b, processing can be in line, that is, the transactions can be handled in the same order in which they occurred. Using a direct-access device to store the master file eliminates the need for sorting the transactions into master file order even though the batch mode of processing is used. Alternatively, the batch of transactions might be collected on an electronic medium such as a magnetic tape reel or cassette. This type of batching is becoming common in data processing networks for operations at geographically dispersed locations. For example, a retail store chain will record transactions at each store and cash register on a tape or disk during business hours each day. During the night, a central computer will "poll" the recording device at each location and retrieve the data on the day's transactions. The transactions will be processed against the inventory, sales, and ledger files at the central site to record the day's activities, make up orders for replenishing stocks of staple items at each location, and provide management control reports.

Job-by-job system

Although the simplest method of batch processing—the **job-by-job system**—is to load and process each job separately, a great deal of CPU time is wasted with such a system. It is still being used with small business systems, however, particularly those using punched-card input.

Stacked-job system

The more common method of processing batch jobs—the **stacked-job system**—"stacks" the jobs to be input. This requires an operating system capable of accepting jobs one after another from the job stack. To facilitate this, the supervisor program is able to call up a **job control program**. Each job is preceded by a **job control statement** that identifies the job and the resources it will use, including any applications programs or library routines stored online, as well as any hardware or peripherals. The job control statements are written in a **job control language (JCL)**, a set of short commands and identifiers that standardize commands from users and make communication of system resource needs more efficient. The job control program interprets the job control statements and is then directed back out of storage by the supervisor. The supervisor can then process the job according to the job control requirements. The advantage of the job control program is that it can be removed from storage when it is not needed and, therefore, does not have to tie up storage space permanently.

Stacked-job systems may or may not include the ability to assign priorities to each job. Priority systems require a mass-storage capability so that the job stack can be stored online and processed in any order.

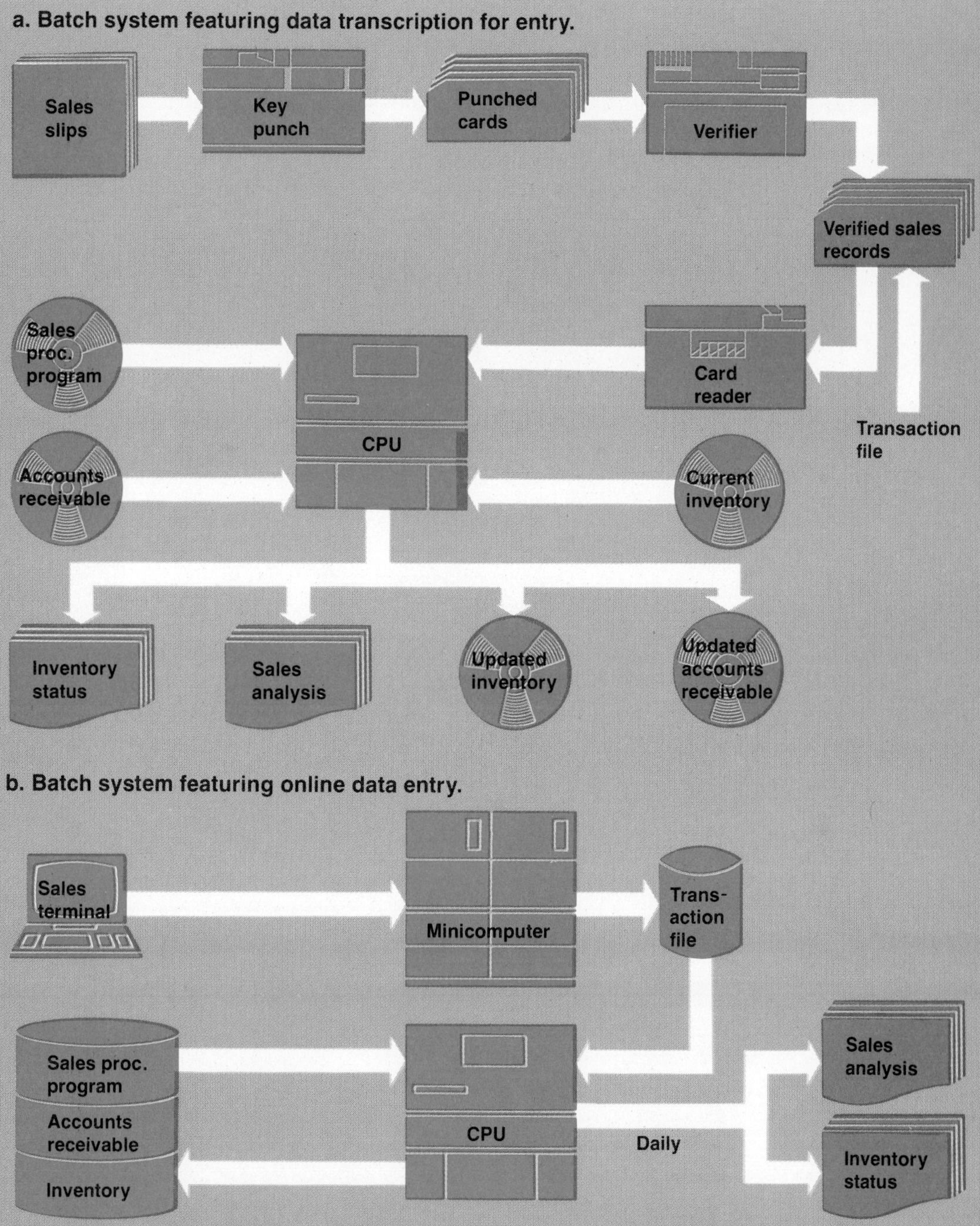

Figure 7.3 Two versions of a batch processing system, featuring key transcription of data and online data entry.

Multiprocessor and multiprogrammed systems

Multiprocessor systems

The system involving a master processor controlling a single slave processor was described in Chapter 2. In large-scale systems dedicated to serving many users in an interactive mode, the **multiprocessor system** can be very useful. For example, the large Cyber system produced by Control Data

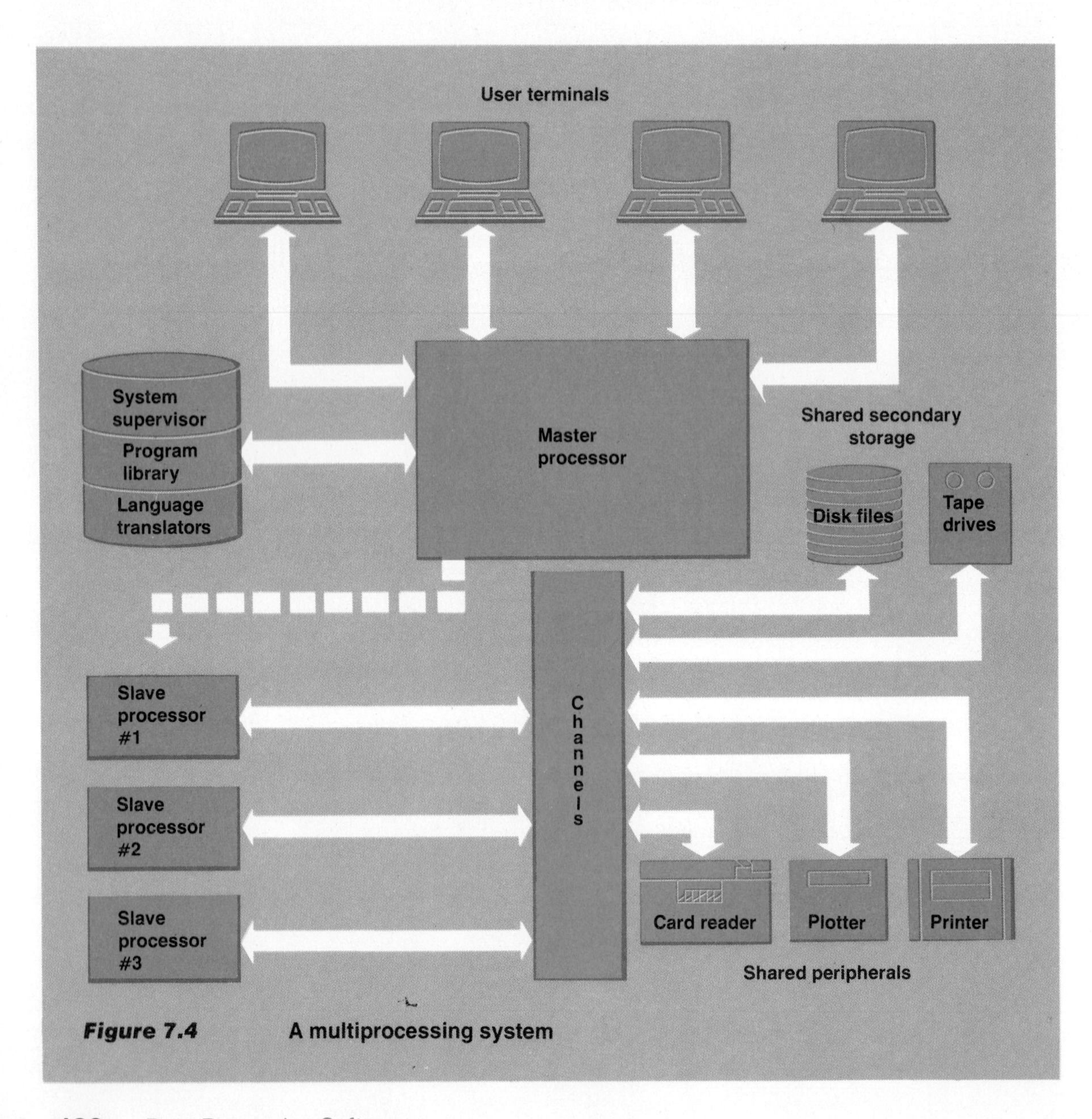

Figure 7.4 A multiprocessing system

Corporation serves hundreds of users essentially simultaneously. Such systems can provide for a single master processor to control as many as ten slave processors. With ten slave processors in the system, ten different programs could actually be processed simultaneously. More important, ten multiprogrammed or timeshared job streams could run simultaneously. When one realizes that it is not uncommon to serve over 100 simultaneous timeshare users with a single processor system, it is obvious that a system with ten processors operating should be able to serve many times more. Figure 7.4 illustrates the multiprocessor configuration.

Multiprogramming systems

Few computer users can afford a multiprocessor system. Many installations, however, do require the ability for many users to receive online interactive computer services. A process called the **multiprogramming system** has been developed that allows many users what appears to be simultaneous access to a single computer system. A multiprogramming operating system is controlled by a sophisticated program called an executive. This executive causes the machine to input from several sources simultaneously, placing unprocessed data streams (made up of programs and associated data) temporarily in secondary storage until the first job received has been at least partly processed. The second job then gets some processing, then the third, and so forth. Each job is retained in the CPU in its processing phase until processing is interrupted for either input or output. Whenever an **I/O interrupt** occurs in the current job, the next job in the queue immediately takes over the central processor. The CPU shifts automatically from job to job; the appropriate processing program and associated data are "rolled" into primary memory, and the program is given temporary control over the computer system as required for processing the data. No program, however, is allowed to override the operating system which retains ultimate control at all times (see Figure 7.5).

Multiprogramming systems are widely used for online interactive business data processing systems. For example, the processing required to update customer accounts at a savings and loan company as loans are repaid and shares (deposits) increased or decreased is frequently handled by an online multiprogrammed system. Please note, however, that simple multiprogramming is useful only when each transaction requires only minimal calculations. As can be seen in Figure 7.6, in multiprogramming, any job that involves lengthy computations after input and before output will cause processing on other jobs to be delayed. Program 1 in Figure 7.6 is such a process-bound job. Note how much waiting time programs 2 and 3 have in the multiprogramming process. This is caused by the lengthy processing time required for program 1.

Timesharing systems

Timesharing is a special form of multiprogramming in which the time each job is allowed to spend in the CPU (processing) on any one turn is limited. If an I/O interrupt has not been generated when that job has been in the CPU for its specified length of time, an interrupt is generated by the executive and

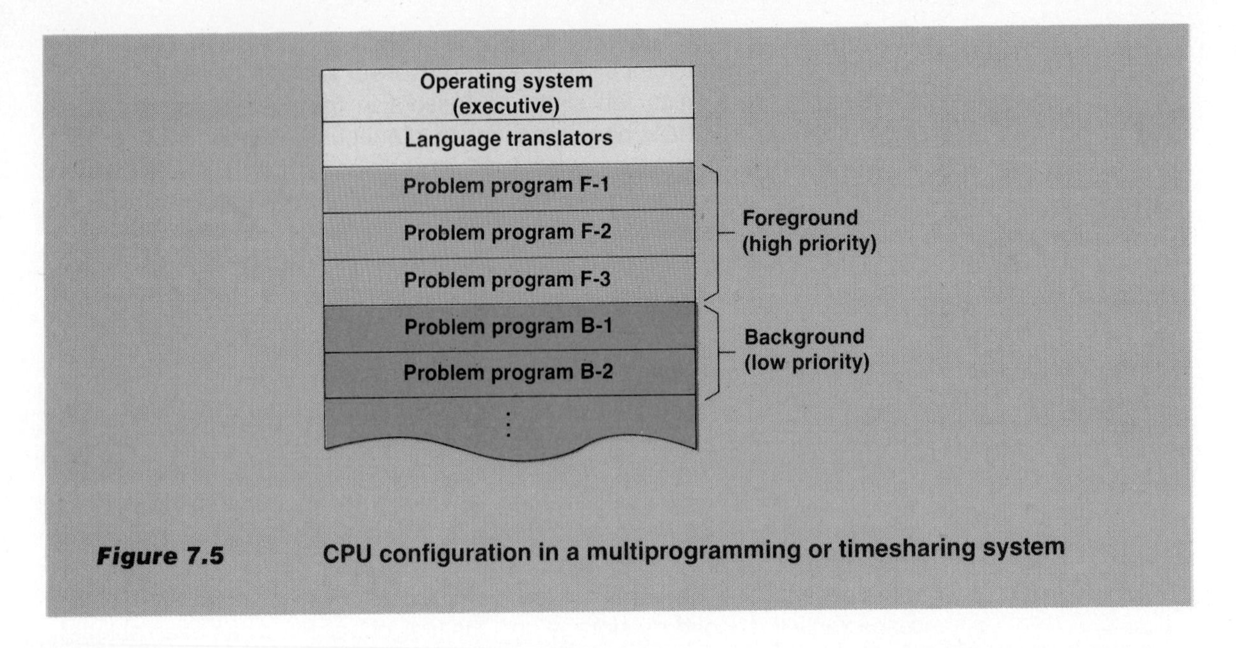

Figure 7.5 **CPU configuration in a multiprogramming or timesharing system**

the job is rolled out onto secondary storage to allow the next job waiting in the queue access to the CPU. The provision of the **time slice** (the limit on time in the CPU at each turn) is the difference between a timesharing executive and a standard multiprogramming executive. This process is illustrated also in Figure 7.6. Note how program 1, the process-bound job, now requires three turns in the processor before producing output. Note also how there is now waiting time for program 1, but less total waiting time for the three programs. As is shown, the I/O-bound job (program 2) does not really cause a problem since I/O operations can be overlapped with processing. Of course, if all three programs use the same output device (say a single printer), some delay in the receipt of output would be encountered. However, if sufficient secondary storage were available, output for the single device (the printer) would be queued up in secondary storage and the processor could continue to operate.

The differences between multiprogramming and timesharing are important to the design of data processing systems. Multiprogramming is cheaper and is the obvious choice where many jobs, each requiring very little in the way of calculation and comparison, are to be run online. If the online job stream contains some process-bound jobs, then timesharing is required. Timesharing has been widely used in educational institutions and in service bureaus, providing online service to all who desire it. Timesharing systems also have been used in large companies, providing administrative data processing and engineering or scientific computation services on one large computer system. Multiprogramming is more widely used for administrative and business data processing where each individual transaction (job) requires few calculations and comparisons before being outputted or before additional data are inputted.

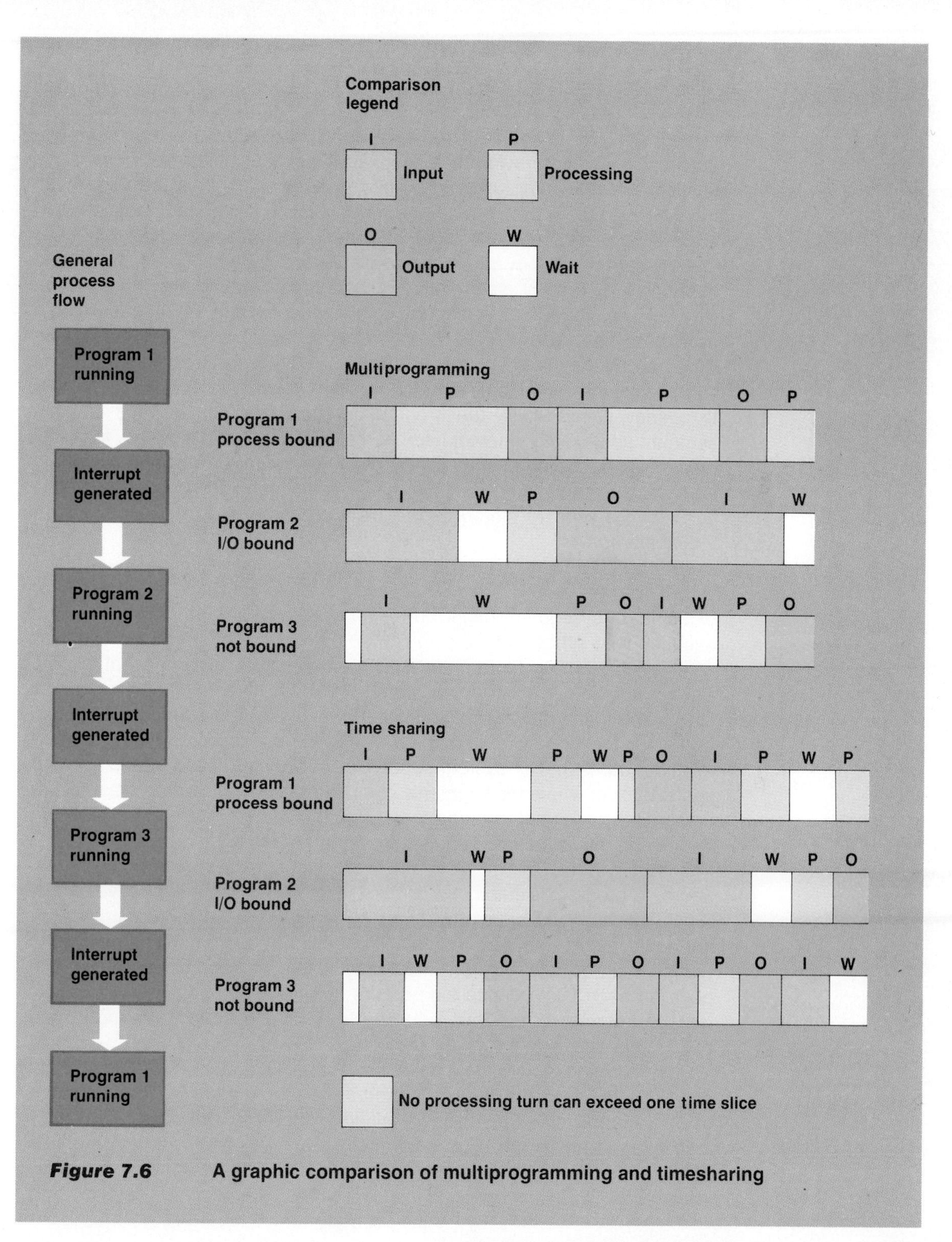

Figure 7.6 **A graphic comparison of multiprogramming and timesharing**

Virtual storage

During the second generation, Burroughs introduced a memory control process which has provided the basis for the successful use of timesharing and multiprogramming during the third generation. This is the concept of **virtual storage**. Prior to the development of this concept, programmers had to consider the capacity of primary storage when developing a program. If the program would not fit into the available space, the programmer had to break it into smaller segments. Each segment would then run as an independent program even if operating on the same data. All segments could be loaded into secondary storage, however, and run as a linked series. When a segment was completed in the CPU, the next segment would be written over the completed segment. This was known as **overlaying**. In order to overlay successfully, the programmer had to know the size of each segment and exactly where it had been stored in primary memory. In virtual memory, program segments are located in secondary storage and overlaying is taken care of by the operating system, and the programmer can consider the primary storage as virtually unlimited in size. Thus, the term *virtual storage.*

Burroughs used the **segmentation** approach in its virtual storage system. In this system, each program is separated into logical segments. For example, one segment might be for data used by the program, a second might be for a processing routine carried out within the program, and a third might be an input or output section. Segments need not be equal in size. Each instruction or data item within a segment is given a two-part address. One part is the number of the segment in which the item is found; the second part is the location of the item in relation to the beginning of the segment (a relative address). The system supervisor designates these addresses and keeps track of where the segments are in the system. If the program refers to a segment that is not in primary storage, the system interrupts processing and brings the requested segment into primary storage.

Current virtual storage techniques most commonly feature **paging**. In paging, a program is automatically divided into small segments called pages. A page is usually at least 1,024 bytes in length. All pages on a given system are equal in size. No more than a few pages of a program will be resident in primary memory at any given time. Many systems do bring in more than one page on each fetch, capitalizing on the fact that any one page will usually refer to nearby pages. This reduces the total time spent in rolling in and rolling out pages.

Segmentation and paging mechanics are illustrated in Figure 7.7. In segmentation, large blocks of the program are brought into primary storage at one time. Each segment is identified in the segment table by its initial location and its length. The segments would be stored as parts of the program in the virtual storage area. The addresses stored there would be relative addresses within segments. That is, the first position in each

Figure 7.7 a. Segmentation

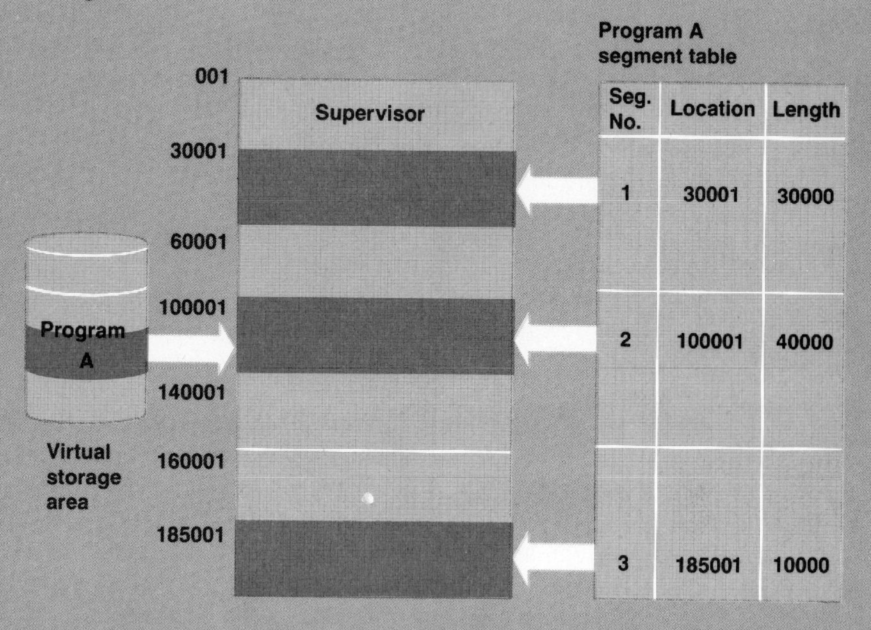

b. Paging

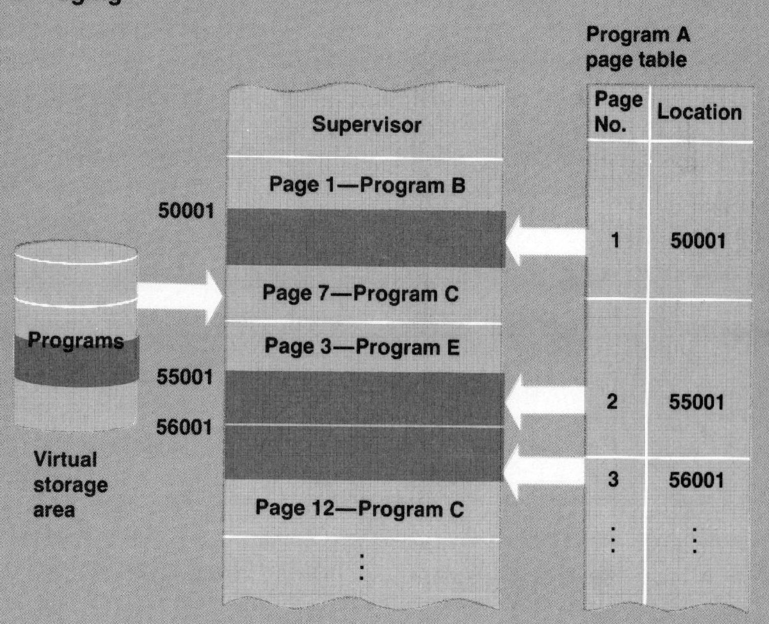

Virtual storage concepts. The mechanics of segmentation and paging.

segment would be the reference point for all other locations within that segment. As the segment was processed, a hardware register within the CPU would add the relative address for each instruction to the actual address of the first instruction in order to identify the appropriate instruction. To illustrate, suppose each instruction occupies two storage locations. The first instruction in the program would have the relative address of 000 (zero). The fifth instruction would have the relative address of 008 (eight). If this segment were segment 1 of program A in Figure 7.7, the address of the first instruction would be 30001. Therefore, the address of the fifth instruction would be 30009 (30001 plus 8) The segment table is maintained by the supervisory program.

Paging is essentially the same process as segmentation. The major difference is that the segments (pages) are all of the same length and are usually much shorter. In Figure 7.7 we have shown them to be 1000 locations in length merely for convenience. The paging table shows the location of each page resident in primary storage and is maintained by the supervisor. A reference to a page not yet present in the primary memory will cause an interruption in processing to bring the required page (and others, usually) from the virtual storage area where the total program is stored.

Segmentation and paging obviously make timesharing much easier. Segments or pages from a number of programs can be present in primary storage at all times. An I/O or time-generated interrupt can more easily transfer control to a page of another program. Total processing speeds are therefore faster. If whole programs or large segments had to be rolled in and out of primary storage each time the processor switched from one program to another, a lot of CPU time would be devoted to this transfer process. It is possible, however, that use of paging could result in lots of pages being rolled in and out. When the CPU spends excessive portions of its running time on such transfers, it is said to be **thrashing**. Several techniques have been developed to reduce thrashing. One method has already been discussed: Bring several pages into memory on each access. Chances are good that most references between pages involve adjacent pages. Having several adjacent pages in the CPU at the same time reduces the chance of a reference to a page not resident in the CPU.

A second method of reducing thrashing is to follow good programming techniques. This involves the use of structured programming, which is discussed in Chapter 10.

Data communication systems

Telephonic, microwave, and satellite transmission of data and programs has developed as a complement to multiprogramming and timesharing. Users dispersed over large geographic areas, even on different continents, are able to share the computational and decision-making power of a single computer.

Networks of computers are being developed so that users can share computing power with one another. Users possessing only a small computer can hook it into a network having a large computer in order to obtain automatic access to the computing power of the large computer. Businesses are using small computers as preprocessors and data acquisition units for larger machines that may be located anywhere on the earth.

Teleprocessing

When data are entered from remote locations via telephone and telegraph lines and are, perhaps, operated upon and results returned over the same lines, **teleprocessing** takes place. The use of special-purpose minicomputers has speeded the development of business teleprocessing systems, which often have featured multiprogramming or timesharing as well. Minicomputers have been used as "front end" communications controllers for such systems. They poll the individual data or inquiry stations and supervise development of a full message from one station before passing it along to the central computer over one of several high-speed channels. They temporarily store output messages until the proper terminals can receive them.

Multiplexors and concentrators

Minis have also been used in multiplexors and concentrators to concentrate line use and reduce the need for transmission lines. If we think of a transmission line as a complex pipe that is divisible into smaller pipes, then we can think of one type of multiplexor, called a **bandwidth multiplexor**, as dividing the pipe into a system of subpipes and sending simultaneous messages along each subpipe, as illustrated in Figure 7.8a(1). This provides more message-carrying capacity per unit of time. Unfortunately, the data-carrying capacity (speed) of a line is proportional to its bandwidth. Dividing the line into several parallel sublines divides the bandwidth of the total line in the same way. Each subline has a significantly reduced transmission capability.

A second type of multiplexor uses the full bandwidth for each message, but several messages are pulsed intermittently (spaced in time) along the line. This type is referred to as a **time division multiplexor** and is shown in Figure 7.8a(2).

Line concentrators differ from multiplexors in that they accept messages from a group of terminals and then pass them along (over the telephone or telegraph line) to the computer. As shown in Figure 7.8b, the concentrator involves buffering and may output less data in a single unit of time than is input to it during that time unit. In contrast, multiplexors are devices that allow several stations to share a single line simultaneously, and they accept input and deliver output at the same rate.

Figure 7.8

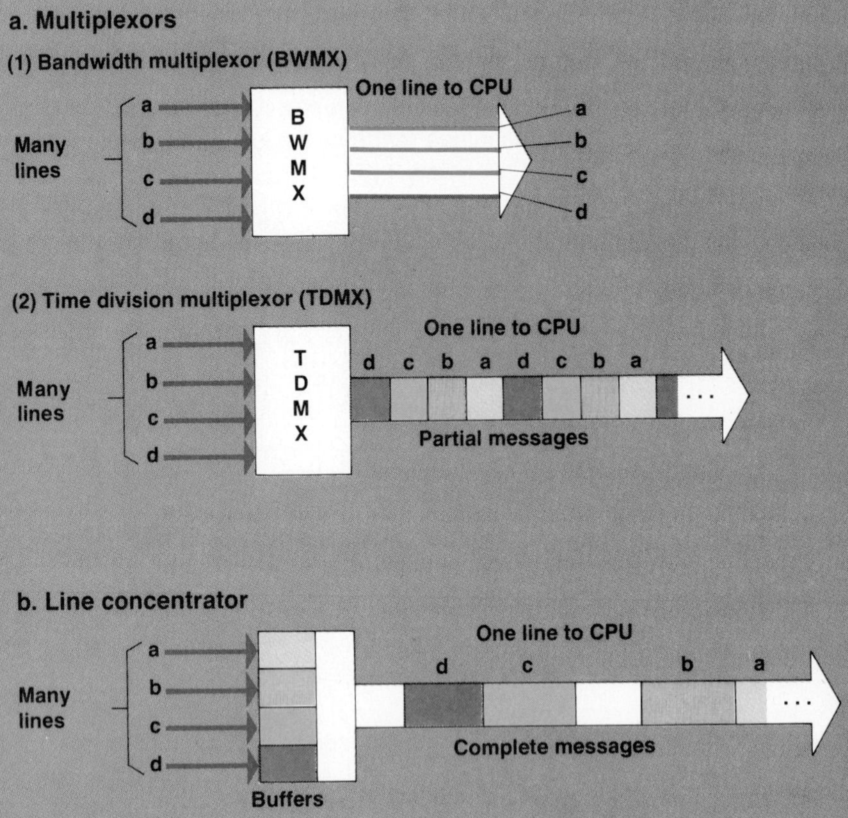

a. Multiplexors

(1) Bandwidth multiplexor (BWMX)

Many lines — a, b, c, d → BWMX → One line to CPU → a, b, c, d

(2) Time division multiplexor (TDMX)

Many lines — a, b, c, d → TDMX → One line to CPU: d c b a d c b a ... Partial messages

b. Line concentrator

Many lines — a, b, c, d → Buffers → One line to CPU: d c b a ... Complete messages

The bandwidth multiplexor, the time division multiplexor, and the line concentrator

Telephone lines Two basic types of telephone lines are available. **Dial-up** ("switched" or "direct distance dialing") **lines** provide flexibility, permitting contact with any party having access to the telephone network. **Leased lines** provide a continuous connection for two or more locations. These leased (private) lines can sometimes be shared with other users, which reduces the cost. In the same way, dial-up users can often save money by purchasing Wide Area Telephone Service (WATS). WATS allows unlimited calls to be placed (or received) within the prescribed service area without individual call tolls being paid.

The choice among standard dial-ups, WATS, and leased lines depends on the volume and nature of the messages. If there are many short message exchanges with numerous points, dial-up is more economical. Leased lines are used when lengthy messages must be exchanged with a few points. WATS becomes economical when messages are lengthy and frequent and are exchanged with numerous locations.

As indicated above, speed of transmission (characters per second) is controlled by the bandwidth of the line. Most lines in use today are so-called voice-grade lines designed to carry voice communications. The normal bandwidth is 3,000 cycles. Some lines—teletypewriter circuits, for example—are less than 3,000 cycles and are referred to as *narrowband lines*. High-speed transmission requires wideband or broadband channels of more than 3,000 cycles. Leased lines can also be conditioned to remove undesirable noise, or distortion, from the data transmission. Dial-up facilities cannot be conditioned. The maximum transmission rate for voice-grade lines is 2,400 bits per second as a dial-up line. Speeds of over 1 million bits per second are possible on conditioned leased lines. The greater the bandwidth and the more the conditioning, the greater the cost of a leased line.

Another factor to consider is transmission mode. A **full-duplex** line permits simultaneous transmission in both directions on the line. **Half-duplex** mode allows movement in only one direction at one time, although nonoverlapping transmission in both directions is possible. **Simplex**, the cheapest mode, allows transmission in only one direction.

The three factors—bandwidth, conditioning, and transmission mode—must be carefully considered in selecting a communication channel. Average data volume per period, maximum rate per period, calling distance, average call time, and need for fast response will determine what combination will be most cost-effective.

A final consideration in developing a cost-effective communication channel is the modem. Modems are required on each end of the line to make it possible to send data over lines designed for voice transmission. The *mo*dulator-*dem*odulator process converts the data signals to audio at the sending end and from audio back to data impulses at the receiving end. The modems on each end of the line must operate in phase with one another. Transmission involves sending a sequence of bits constituting a data message and containing not only the codes for the actual message but parity bits and control bits as well. Bits must be received in order and properly interpreted at the receiving end. This is accomplished by using a synchronous or an asynchronous timing process. The synchronous technique is more desirable. As the data comes out of the terminal, they consist of a sequence of pulses and no-pulses representing the binary 1s and 0s. Synchronous modems send pulses at regular, periodic intervals whether a message is being sent or not and no start and stop bits need be added to the message. Start and stop bits are required for asynchronous modems. Synchronous modems are faster but also more expensive. The transmission speed of a modem is also affected by whether it operates in serial or parallel mode. Parallel mode is faster and more expensive (see Figure 7.9).

Satellite transmission systems

The newest method of telecommunications involves transmission via satellite. Figure 7.10 provides an overview of the possible communication systems. Note that in the land-line system in Figure 7.10a, each user contacts remote sites over a physically connected wire. In the microwave

Figure 7.9 **A modem Although it looks unassuming, the modem is the key to data communications over telephone lines. (Courtesy IBM)**

system in Figure 7.10b, microwave transmission is substituted for land lines between systems exchanges; costs are significantly reduced. The use of satellites (Figure 7.10c) provides a more flexible system, however. Each user and remote site must be connected to ground stations only to transmit messages. Messages may be received directly over a wide area. The reason for the ground station in the sending loop is the size of the antenna required to direct the message to the satellite. The satellite and its solar-paneled power unit may weigh several tons, but it is quite a small target. Conversely, the satellite may send out a dispersed signal that can be picked up on much smaller antennas over a wide area. Through the use of microcomputers or minicomputers, each receiving site is capable of sorting out its own particular signal and retains only those messages intended for it.

Satellites are attractive as communications links between sites inaccessible by land lines or land-based microwave. Satellites can now be placed in synchronous orbit to circle the earth once in each 24 hours and thus appear to be stationary over a specific geographic location. The satellite is in a very high vacuum, out of the range of most human-produced interference, and is at a nearly constant temperature. The wear and tear of temperature-related expansion and contraction and atmospheric-born corrosion is absent. Thus

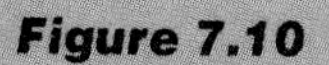

Figure 7.10

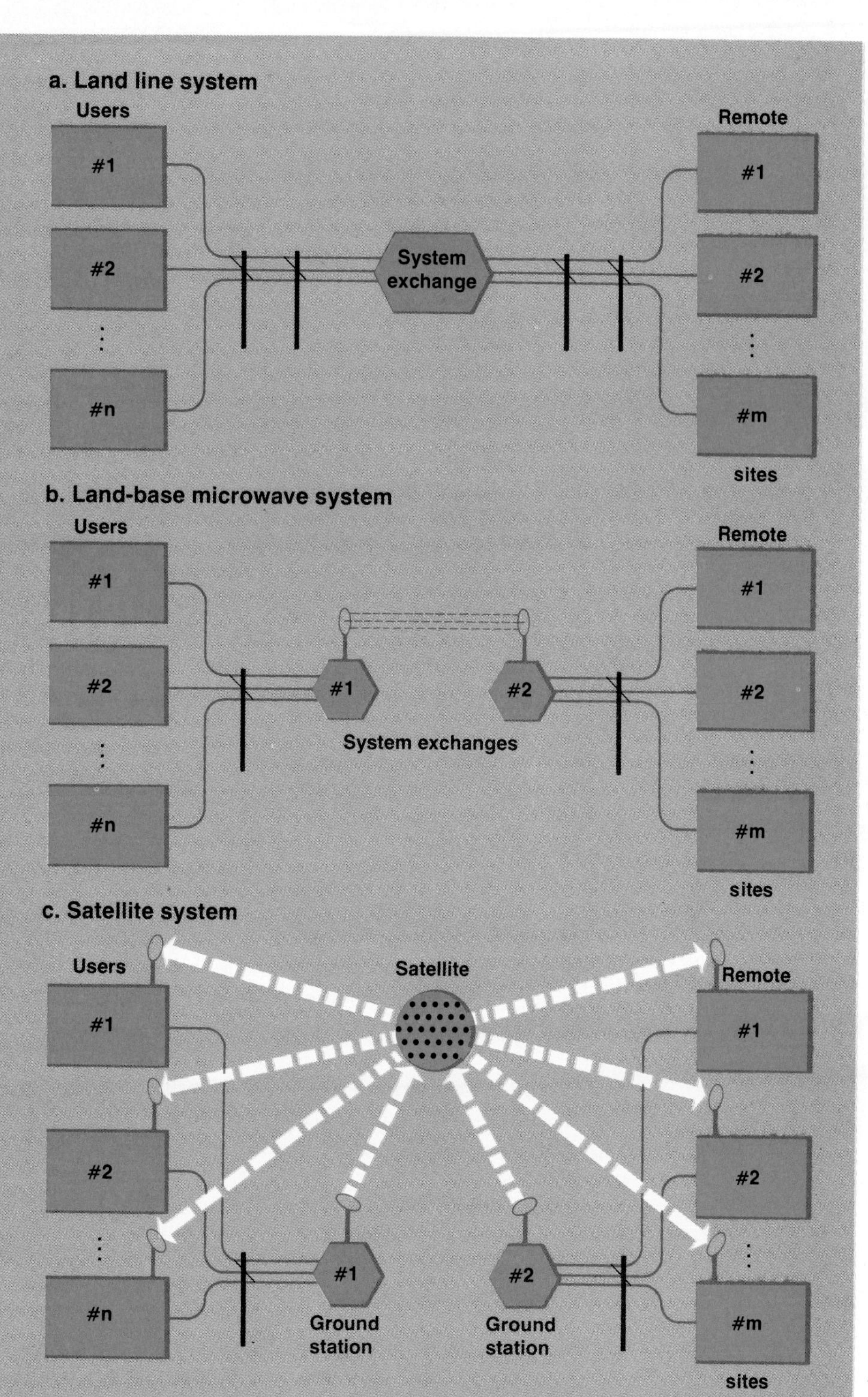

Three possible configurations of data communication networks the expensive satellite should outperform and outlast its earthbound electronic cousins. In this way, a satellite system can be less expensive than any land-based system when communicating over long distances. Satellite systems have an economic advantage on long-distance routes. Land lines and land-based microwave are more economic over shorter distances.

When systems are expanded to provide satellite-to-satellite links, any spot on earth becomes accessible. The minimum number of satellites required to give total coverage of the earth (other than the poles) is three. The only problem is that it takes a signal about one quarter of a second to travel to an orbiting satellite and back. This slight delay is increased by satellite-to-satellite links. Telephone users seem to notice only slightly the delays of up to one-half second. Persons using data networks would not be inconvenienced by delays of more than one second. (Timesharing systems are considered adequate if response times can be held to no more than three seconds.)

Two factors determine satellite performance. First, their power and sophistication is primarily dependent on their size. Second, the frequencies they use determine their signal-carrying capacity and the narrowness of their radiated beams. In order to have many satellites in orbit, the beam from each satellite must be narrow so that the signals do not become mixed. In general, as satellites get larger, the sending and receiving antennas on earth can get smaller. Eventually, each home will be able to receive television communications directly from a satellite. Similarly, each business location can now receive messages directly from a satellite (see Figure 7.11).

Types of data systems

Data communication systems may be simple two-terminal links (switched or leased lines), data acquisition systems, data distribution systems, or interrogation systems. Each of these systems can be online or offline. In the offline mode, the data transmission system is not connected to the computer processing system. Data would be transferred physically between the transmission system and the computer system, usually by use of punched paper tape or magnetic tape. In online systems, the communications link is attached directly to computer-controlled storage. Data may or may not be processed immediately, depending on the time constraints of the application.

Data acquisition systems Data acquisition systems are of two types, the star systems and the branched network. In the **star system**, each remote site from which data are sent is connected by a direct link to the central computer site. In the **branched network**, the message streams from individual remote sites are sent over tributary feeder lines to a major communication link connected directly to the central site. A number of slow links carrying low volumes of data are merged by zone concentrators onto a single but faster high-capacity line to the central computer site.

Data distribution systems Data distribution systems are the reverse of the data acquisition systems and are used to disseminate messages from a central site to many remote locations. Multiplexing is not usually used.

Figure 7.11

A communications satellite The solar "paddles" extending outward from the satellite convert light from the sun into power while the satellite is in orbit. (Courtesy Comsat)

Rather, each remote station is normally called onto the system whenever a message is to be sent to it. The entire message is then sent in a single transmission. Several remote sites can receive the same message simultaneously.

Data interrogation systems Data interrogation systems usually have been designed to enable remote users to access a central data base, usually one in which the stored data is being constantly updated. Examples would be a stock exchange price quotation system, a statewide welfare data base, and a statewide registry of automobiles and licensed drivers. Systems are now being developed that essentially reverse this process, allowing central sites and remote users to access several widely dispersed data bases.

Decentralized data processing systems

The development of relatively cheap computing power in minicomputer and microcomputer systems has encouraged **decentralized data processing**. Local users can afford a small computer system to meet their data processing needs at the local site. Users located away from the central data processing center find it advantageous to have a powerful processor at the local site to perform local processing under local control. For example, a production scheduling and control system for a single plant may be controlled by a minicomputer at the local plant. Special terminals on the factory floor, in the warehouse, at the receiving dock, and in the receiving department provide inputs to record materials received, goods in process, amount and cost of production, and so on. The minicomputer system provides all the processing necessary to plan and control plant operations to meet output and quality requirements at minimal cost. Evaluation and control reports are prepared and forwarded to the central offices of the company at another location. Telecommunications may or may not be involved in this communication.

Distributed processing systems

Central data processing organizations have been reluctant to give up all control over data processing at remote sites. However, they recognize the improved systems that result from increased local control over local processing. Also, the demand for specialized program development made on the central staff is reduced if computers are available to local users. These considerations have led to the development of **distributed data processing** systems. As can be seen in Figure 7.12, there are three types of networks used in distributed data processing. **Star networks** are built around a single CPU (much like the star system for data acquisition already discussed). This CPU controls all other components in the system, including any remote terminals. The **ring network** places all network nodes on the same communication system with no one node in control. The **hierarchical network** shown in Figure 7.12 is the most common form of distributed processing system. A large mainframe is at the top of the pyramid and communicates with and exercises some control over large multipurpose minicomputers or other mainframes at the regional or divisional level. The regional computers communicate with and exercise some control over local minicomputers to which are connected local terminals. These terminals are normally multipurpose, being used for data input, online inquiry generation, and for tapping the computer's processing power.

Distributed processing systems provide certain advantages.

1. Transactions processing is controlled at the local level.
2. Teleprocessing (communications) costs are reduced because only processed results are forwarded from the operational level to the central mainframe.
3. A more flexible and responsive system is in operation. Managers at all levels are provided with an increased ability to react quickly to problems.
4. The entire system is never without computing power. A computer breakdown merely means that the remaining computers temporarily carry larger workloads.
5. Quick response systems are more easily developed at any level. The computer network means that any online data bases can be accessed from any place in the system.

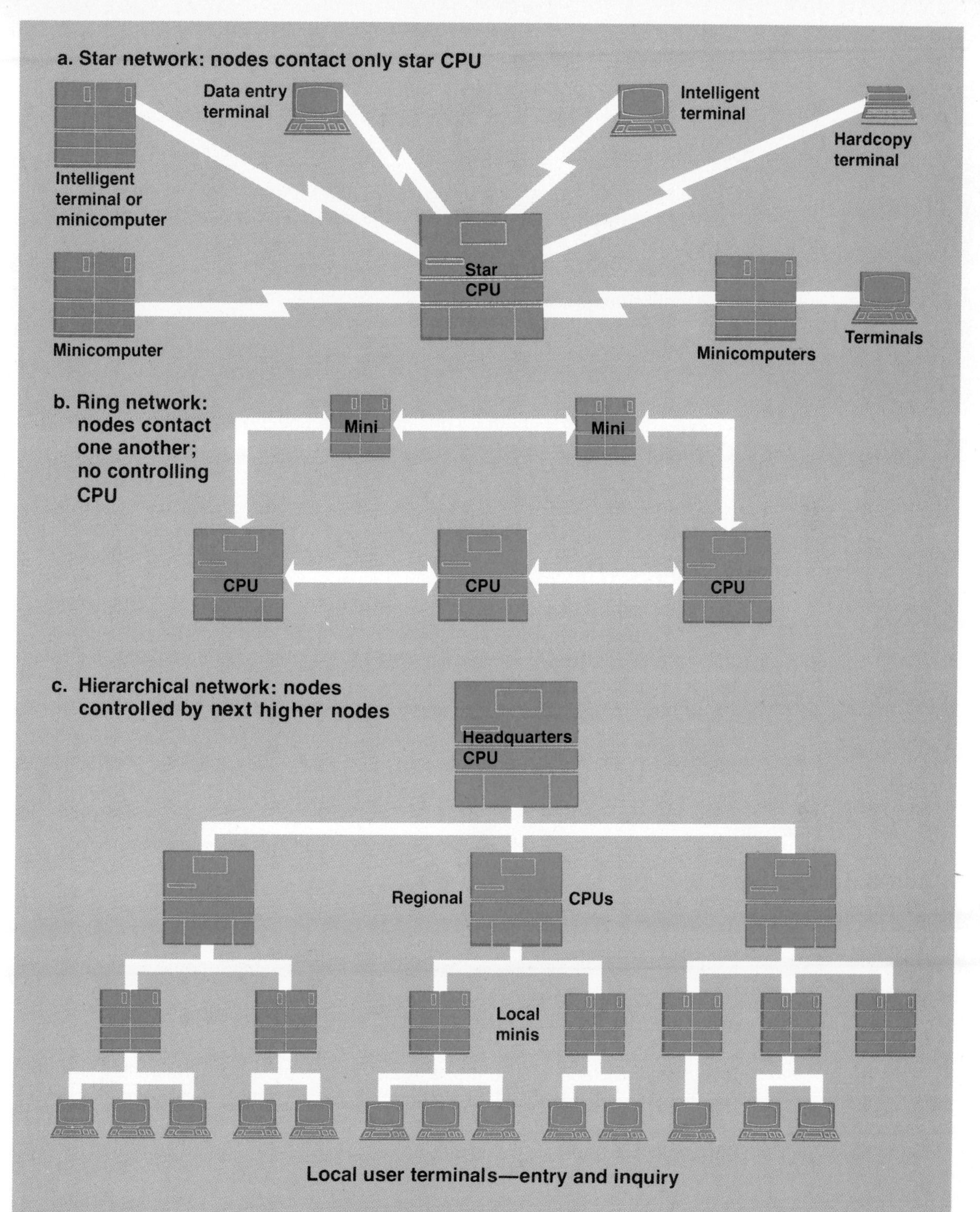

Figure 7.12 Distributed networks. The star network, the ring network, and the hierarchical network.

6 Local users tend to program their own special processing needs, so that the number of special requests handled by central data processing staffs is reduced.

Distributed processing systems also have some disadvantages.

1 Problems of data security and privacy are increased. We will have more to say about this in Chapter 15 and in the Special Option beginning on page 430.
2 Control of processing techniques and procedures to assure data accuracy and high-quality applications is difficult because of the many dispersed sites at which applications are being developed. Most firms using distributed data processing have felt it necessary to develop standards for designing and developing systems. All users, local and regional, must use the same computer language for a given application and may even be required to follow a standard design supplied by the processing experts at the central site.

System types and computer size

One important development in modern data processing is that almost any size computer can be found at almost any point in a network. Figure 7.12 only partially illustrates this point. It is further illustrated in Table 7.1. Even microcomputers are being used as limited timesharing systems. Minicomputers are commonly used for timesharing and are even showing up as the controlling node in star networks. Both minis and micros are common as intelligent terminals for teleprocessing and distributed processing systems.

Realtime systems

Many of the systems described above feature continuous interaction between users and the system. A transaction is recorded online and instantaneously reflected in all affected files. Such systems have come to be called *realtime* systems. However, as we learned in Chapter 1, a true realtime system is one in which facts are captured and processed in time to create information needed to control the ongoing process that generated the original data. In more technical terms, a realtime processing operation is (1) in a parallel time relationship with the ongoing activity that is generating the data inputs and (2) producing information quickly enough to maintain the ongoing activity in a desired steady state, that is, to provide adequate control over the activity. Loosely, then, the term *realtime* can be applied to any processing system that meets severe time limitations. Therefore, online, instantaneous response systems are called realtime systems.

Such systems allow users to enter transaction data and immediately

SYSTEM TYPE	COMPUTER SIZE: MAINFRAME				
	MAINFRAME		MINICOMPUTER		MICROCOMPUTER
	LARGE	MEDIUM	LARGE	MEDIUM	
Batch	C, LP	C, LP	C, LP	C, HP	C, HP
Multiprogrammed	C	C	C	O	S
Timeshared	C	C	C	O	S
Teleprocessing	C	C	C	IT	IT
Decentralized	S	O	C	C	C
Distributed	Center	Center	Center (O), IT	IT	IT

LP = low priority (runs in system background)
HP = high priority (runs in system foreground)
C = commonly used with system
O = occasionally used with system
S = seldom used with system
IT = used as intelligent terminal in system

Table 7.1 **System Types and Computer Size**

receive feedback on the effects of that transaction. Similarly, they allow access to online data bases for instantaneous response to inquiries as to the status of an entity in an ongoing activity. Thus, an inventory control clerk can use an online terminal to learn if a part is available in a warehouse. Similarly, a ticket clerk (or a hotel clerk) can immediately know whether a seat (or a room) is available for a prospective traveler. On a more sophisticated level, a financial manager can obtain an up-to-the-minute estimate of the amount of cash expected to be available six months in the future. Modern timesharing, teleprocessing, and communications technology means that these inquiries may originate half a world away from the computer providing the response as easily as they can originate from the room where the computer is located.

Summary

Data processing devices are organized into systems that perform the sets of processing functions needed to accomplish a total task. An important element of computerized data processing systems is the software in the system, the programs (sets of instructions) that direct and control the computer system as it performs data processing. The three major types of computer programs are operating systems, language translators, and applications programs.

Operating systems use the speed of the computer itself to perform job queuing with priority control, to assign system resources to individual jobs, to control data access, to assist in data management, and to provide overlapping of computer functions and text editing capabilities.

Language translators are the programs that translate source programs written in assembly or compiler languages to the object programs written in machine language. It is object programs that actually process data.

Conceptually, there are six types of data processing systems. Batch processing systems process jobs either individually, stopping between jobs, or in stacks of jobs. Job-stack processing may vary the order of processing jobs in the stack according to some priority scheme. Priority and resource needs are expressed in the job control language instructions preceding each job.

Multiprocessor systems use a master processor to control one or more slave processors. The workload of each slave is increased substantially in such systems. Also if two or more slaves are involved, different jobs may be run simultaneously on each slave.

Multiprogrammed and timeshared systems provide means for sharing one processor among several users. Users are given alternating turns in the central processor. The length of time a user can control the processor on each turn is limited in timeshared systems. In multiprogrammed systems, each user retains the central processor until computation is interrupted for input or output.

Virtual storage techniques make the primary memory of a computer seem unlimited to the user. Each program is automatically divided into pieces (pages or segments). As a page (segment) is needed, the supervisory program brings it from secondary storage and writes it over (overlays) a previous page (segment). The size of an individual program is limited only by the amount of secondary storage available. Virtual storage has made the sharing of a computer among multiple users more efficient.

As a complement to multiprogramming and timesharing, telephonic, microwave, and satellite transmission of data and programs (teleprocessing) has developed. Users dispersed over large geographic areas are able to share computer services of a single computer or of several computers formed into a network. Some of these networks form distributed data processing systems wherein small computers at remote sites perform some processing before sending the results to the central computer.

Decentralized data processing systems are also increasing. Remote users are taking advantage of the (relatively) low cost of minicomputers and microcomputers to acquire their own data processing units. Decentralized and distributed processing systems are being used by local users to program their own special processing needs and thus reduce the number of special requests handled by central data processing staffs.

Online instantaneous response systems provide realtime responses in activities faced with severe time constraints. Current status of inventories, effects of transactions, and updated analyses can be made immediately available to the user. Through the use of timesharing and teleprocessing, multiple users distributed over wide geographic areas can be served in these ways by a single computer.

Key terms

Define the following terms as briefly as possible and then, in a short paragraph, clarify each definition.

Applications program
Bandwidth multiplexor
Batch processing
Branched network
Decentralized data processing
Dial-up lines
Distributed data processing
Full-duplex transmission
Half-duplex tranmission
Hierarchical network
I/O interrupt
Job-by-job system
Job control language (JCL)
Job control program
Job control statement
Language translator
Leased lines
Line concentrator
Multiprocessor system
Multiprogramming system
Operating system
Overlaying
Paging
Ring network
Segmentation
Simplex transmission
Software
Stacked-job system
Star network
Star system
Teleprocessing
Text editor
Thrashing
Time division multiplexor
Timesharing
Time slice
Utilities
Virtual storage

Discussion questions

1 How are the minicomputer and the microcomputer affecting the design of business data processing systems?
2 What is the difference between a data acquisition and a data interrogation system?
3 What are the advantages and disadvantages of distributed processing systems?
4 Compare decentralized data processing systems and distributed data processing systems. What are their similarities? What are their differences? Do you see one as superior to the other in any way?
5 What are the types of data communication systems?
6 What are the three factors to be considered when choosing a communications channel?

7 Speculate on the reasons batch processing systems continue to be common in this age of online systems.
8 Speculate on how timesharing might be used in a distributed data processing network.
9 Compare multiprogramming and timesharing systems. What are their similarities? What are their differences? When should each be used?
10 Compare a multiprocessor system and a timesharing system. Could they be the same system?
11 How are applications programs affected by the operating system? Could the job of the applications programmer be reduced by adding utilities and other routines to the operating system?
12 Why is it important to have a good text editor as part of the program library on a modern computer system?

Exercises

1 Visit a local business data processing installation, and interview, if possible, a systems programmer and a lead applications programmer. Try to determine the following:
   a How many separate programs or routines are in the operating system and program library on their computer?
   b How does each use the operating system?
   c Does their system involve distributed processing?
2 Visit your school's computer center and determine the following:
   a How many separate programs or routines are in the operating system and program library on their computer?
   b Is there more than one computer in the system? If so, how are they organized?
   c Are there other computers on campus?
3 Compare the findings in Exercises 1 and 2. What do the differences suggest?
4 Visit a local retail outlet for microcomputers and collect any information available on the use of their microcomputers in processing networks.
5 Speculate on how distributed processing might be used by HFM Hardware Stores, a retail hardware chain with a total of 32 stores in five states in the Northcentral United States.
6 Speculate on how distributed data processing might be used by the auto parts wholesaler described in Exercise 2 of Chapter 5, page 124.

Distributed Minis Help Brew Beer

The acquisition of distributed minicomputer systems let the Olympia Brewing Co. of Olympia, Wash. avoid an expensive upgrade of its IBM 370/135 mainframe while improving the productivity of its systems staff and its production-scheduling systems.

Olympia Brewing is the country's seventh largest beer maker with sales of $372 million in 1978, according to Wendell Carlson, director of information systems. The company has three breweries—one each in Washington, Minnesota and Texas.

'Heartland' market

A few years ago, Olympia beer was sold only in the company's traditional West Coast "heartland" market. Today, both Olympia and Hamms are marketed in 26 states as far east as Florida, while Lone Star is sold throughout Texas.

According to Carlson, the minicomputer-based network has helped to make beer available when and where it's needed. This network of Data General Corp. Eclipse systems is the key to the distributed data processing (DDP) approach at Olympia's breweries in Olympia, Wash., and St. Paul, Minn.

By allocating production runs to incoming orders, Eclipse C/330s have moved the required order-scheduling information to the location where beer is produced and shipped, saving valuable time, Carlson said.

The C/330s are looked on strictly as "production machines," in that they support the daily plant-site operations. All development work for the minicomputer is done at the corporate information processing center. There the company has an IBM 370/135 mainframe, equipped with an IBM 3704 communications front end, and a DG Eclipse M/600 system.

Corporate CPUs

"We look on those two machines as the corporate computers. The M/600 is a market research tool that is used for interactive on-line problem solving," Carlson explained. This includes analysis of beer sales using graphics display terminals to project consumption trends in the brewery's product line. This research work on the M/600 is done using DG Dasher CRT terminals and Tektronix, Inc. 4014 graphics terminals.

Source: "Distributed Minis Let Brewer Avoid Costly Upgrade," *Computerworld,* July 28, 1980, pp. Special Report/24–25.

To streamline the order processing functions, Olympia is in the process of a major upgrade that includes moving the product and order scheduling out from the 370 to the C/330s. The minicomputers presently are operating under DG's RDOS, using an IBM 3270 emulation software package from an independent software house.

Conversion of the C/330s from RDOS to the Advanced Operating System (AOS) environment is scheduled for late this year. The conversion of the Eclipse C/330s to AOS will give the plant site managers greater control over their DP scheduling needs.

Up to now, this scheduling work had to be done on the 370, which is running more

(*Courtesy Computerworld*)

than 500 hours a month, handling between 4,000 and 5,000 batch jobs. The production scheduling work had to be fitted into the 370's crowded job stream.

But when the conversion is complete, the C/330s will do much of their own production work, and then the results will be transmitted to the 370 using bisynch communications.

Solutions near problems

The DDP approach being implemented on the C/330s is based on the philosophy that it is best to "put the solution where the problem is," Carlson explained.

Whereas marketing and financial work are done at the corporate computer center using the 370 and the Eclipse M/600, it is more efficient to give individual plant managers control of their own destiny in regard to their individual processing needs, he added.

In the past, users had to install DP equipment and then tailor their business to meet the capabilities of the equipment but with the distributed processing approach, "we can install the hardware functionally and geographically where it is needed from a business standpoint," he said.

The installation of the C/330s has had other benefits for Olympia. By adding smaller processors at specific locations, the company has avoided the need to upgrade its 370 mainframe.

With the installation of first the M/600 and then the C/330s, Olympia has "frozen" the 370 configuration for the past two and a half years. According to Carlson, this has resulted in a hardware savings alone of $300,000 to $500,000 in the company's DP expenditures.

When the AOS conversion is complete, the C/330s will be able to communicate through the IBM 3704 frontend processor to the 370/135. The 370 is the central point of the network, with the other machines exchanging data with the mainframe. . . .

Olympia has a staff of 13 programmers performing systems development work on the various applications. . . .

A total of 63 terminals are installed at Olympia with 47 Dasher CRTs, three Tektronix, Inc. graphics terminals and some IBM 3270 CRT terminals in use.

The M/600 will also be able to transmit data to the 370 in the same manner as the C/330s. With this approach, it will be possible to develop programs for the minis on the M/600, while all testing with the 370 can be done without tying up the production machines, Carlson said.

Chapter 8

Computer Programming— An Overview

Outline

This chapter defines the computer programming process and indicates in general how programs are designed and written. After thoroughly defining what a program is and explaining how program instructions are carried out (executed) by the computer, the logical structure of data processing programs is explained. Finally, general processes for designing and coding a program are laid out. Chapters 10 and 11 will explain actual program coding (the writing of the program) and getting the program to work (debugging procedures). Chapter 9 discusses the programming languages used in this process.

Program execution

A computer program consists of a set of instructions for accomplishing a specific task or set of tasks. As indicated in Chapter 2, the earliest programs were written in a language specific to the particular machine (computer) being used. Today, programs are developed in machine-independent, problem-oriented languages and then are converted to machine language by another program called a compiler. In all cases, however, a computer program consists of a set of instructions to be executed by the computer.

Computer instruction execution

A single computer instruction at the machine-language level usually accomplishes one minor step in a total processing task. Each of these small steps is executed in the sequence specified by the program as explained below.

A computer instruction is made up of two or more parts, an operation code and one or more addresses. All are numbers. The *operation code* of two or three digits identifies the specific detailed task to be accomplished. The address codes of four or more digits specify the location of the data to be operated on and/or the location of the next instruction to be executed. Instructions are examined and decoded in a set of special registers, or storage locations, called the instruction register.

The instruction register

The **instruction register** consists of one or more special-purpose storage locations within the CPU. One possible configuration is shown in Figure 8.1, which also details the steps in execution of a computer instruction. As indicated there, the first step in executing an instruction is to load it into the instruction register (step 1). The instruction register is composed of subsidiary registers. They analyze each instruction as it is chosen at the proper time in the sequence of processing steps to determine what detailed operation is to be performed (executed) during each CPU operating cycle. The instruction register shown in Figure 8.1 consists of a sequence register, an operations register, and two address registers.

Operations register

The **operations register** decodes the actual operational code of the instruction. It identifies the process to be carried out by the next CPU operating cycle and causes the selection and activation of the circuits designed to carry out the identified operation. As illustrated in Figure 8.1, the operations register sends instructions to the arithmetic-logic unit to activate the required processing circuits (step 2).

Address register

The storage address of the data to be operated on and/or the address of the next instruction to be executed are stored in one or more **address registers**. Depending on machine design, each computer instruction may contain one, two, or three addresses. In one-address instruction CPUs, the address normally refers either to the locations in storage containing data to be operated on or to the storage location where data are to be stored.

Sequence register

The instructions usually are stored sequentially in the primary storage, and the next instruction to be executed usually is found in the sequentially next word location. A special counter—the **sequence register**—keeps track of these locations by incrementing 1 (adding 1 to the address) each time a normal instruction is executed. This is shown as step 6 in Figure 8.1. Actually it is performed while steps 2-5 are carried out. Only if a branch is specified by the program will this sequential stepping process be interrupted. A **branch instruction** is a decision-making instruction that can cause the computer to execute some instruction other than the sequentially next instruction. In a branch instruction, one of the data addresses gives the address of the instruction to be executed next in the event the branch is actually made. For example, suppose that during an accounts receivable file update, one number (say 10) is to be subtracted from another (say 8). Then an instruction is used that tests the content of the register containing the difference to see if it is a negative value. In this case, the content is −2 and the condition specified is met. Since a negative account receivable will require special handling, the program specifies a branch, which is now executed, so the computer goes to the address named in the branch instruction for its next command. If the condition tested for by the branch instruction is not met (if 8 is subtracted from 10 and the result is +2), the normal sequential pattern is maintained and the next program step to be executed is located in the immediately following location, as specified in the sequence register.

Two-address instructions sometimes contain a data address (operand) and the address where the next instruction can be found. In such a system, instructions need not be stored in sequential locations. Branch instructions cause the computer to execute the instruction specified by the data (operand) address rather than that specified by the next-instruction address.

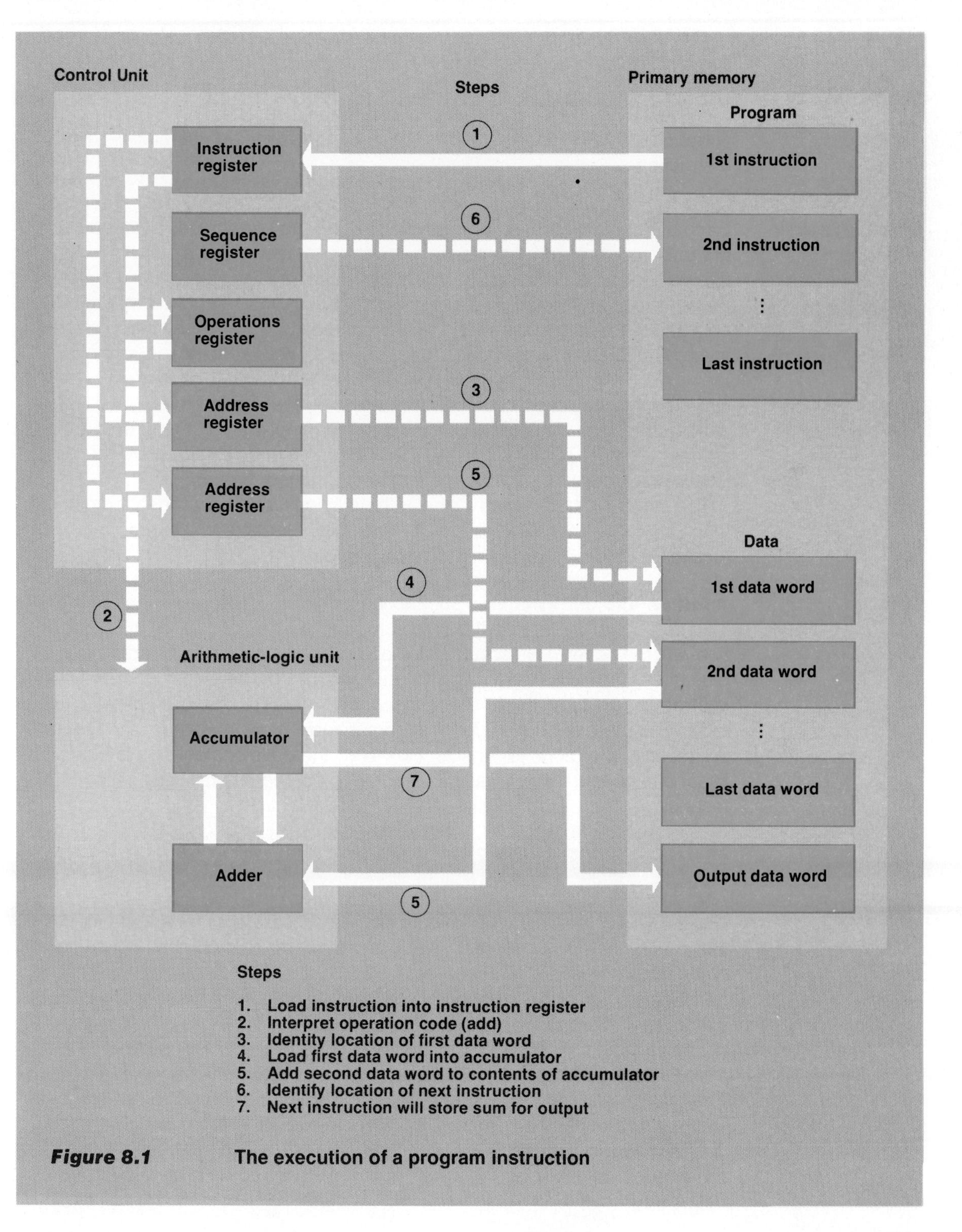

Figure 8.1 The execution of a program instruction

The three-address instruction normally contains two data addresses and a next-instruction address. The specification of two data addresses makes it possible to specify more complex processes with one instruction.

In Figure 8.1, we have shown two data address registers. Their job in steps 3 and 5 is to identify the locations of the data words to be operated on by the instruction.

Arithmetic-logic register

Each arithmetic operation is carried out as a form of addition. Two numbers are involved: two addendums for addition; a minuend and a subtrahend for subtraction; a multiplicand and a multiplier for multiplication; or a dividend and a divisor for division. The accumulator can provide temporary storage for only one of these numbers. The other must be stored in a second register in the arithmetic-logic unit or in a specially reserved word space in primary memory. In Figure 8.1, we assumed that the arithmetic-logic unit contained only one register, the accumulator. Therefore, the second number (addendum, subtrahend, multiplier, or minuend) was implied to come directly from primary storage. Actually, it would be placed in a special temporary storage location (register) before the operation was carried through.

The circuits and registers in the arithmetic-logic unit vary widely from one machine to another. There may be one major register or several, but the functions discussed below must be provided.

Addition and subtraction Subtraction is merely the complement of addition, so both are carried out by the same register (accumulator) in conjunction with the adder. This accumulator is most often as long as a storage word, plus the sign (positive and negative) and an overflow bit. Addition (as well as subtraction) is accomplished in *series,* one digit at a time, or in *parallel,* all digits at the same time. Parallel adders involve more hardware, are faster, and usually are more expensive. However, the development of microcircuit logic components has made them the most common type. With chip technology, there is little difference in hardware costs.

Multiplication and division Multiplication and division are carried out as repeated addition and subtraction, respectively.

Comparison Data items and instructions can consist of letters, numerals, special characters, or some combination of two or more of these character types. Characters are represented by combinations of binary digits and can be compared to find which comes earlier in alphanumeric sequence. For example, numbers can be compared to determine which one is greater; or letters of the alphabet can be compared to determine which one comes first in the alphabet. Most machines can compare entire words in one operation. The comparison process is the basis of branch instructions. That is, to know whether to branch, the computer must be able to tell which one of two given conditions exist. It does this by comparing data items to determine which of the possible relationships (greater than, less than, equal to, and so on) the data items have to one another.

Other instructions

Arithmetic and compare instructions comprise a minority of all the machine instructions available. Other major categories are shift, load, and store instructions.

Shift instructions move a word right or left one or more characters within a logic register. They are used to align words before comparison or addition and to accomplish rounding. Shifting far enough in one direction causes characters on that end of the word to "drop" out of the register and be lost while 0s are entered at the other end of the word.

Load instructions cause words to be entered into logic registers from general storage. Normally, loading does not change the content of the storage location in primary memory.

Store instructions are used to enter the content of the CPU register into a general storage location, replacing the previous content of the location. The content of the register normally is not changed by a store instruction.

I/O instructions control input and output processes. Special instructions recognize interrupts signaling the end of some I/O process or generate interrupts when signaled to do so by a CPU clock.

The instructions above, and others, make up the "instruction set" for a particular computer. Obviously, the more instructions, the more expensive the machine.

Knowledge of how a computer accomplishes basic operations can be important to programmers, especially those developing supervisory programs and compilers. For example, it is faster in most machines to ask the machine to add a value to itself (A + A) than to multiply the value by 2 (2 × A), because multiplication is repeated addition, which requires a control routine to be actuated to be sure the proper number of adds are carried out.

CPU operating cycle

An instruction execution cycle, or **operating cycle**, for a computer is the complete sequence of activities involved in carrying out an instruction, including fetching the next instruction from primary storage. To illustrate, we show in Figure 8.2 a computer executing an instruction located in storage location 0101. The next instruction is stored in location 0102. The instruction in 0101 is supposed to cause the content of location 1056 to be added to the arithmetic register (the accumulator—ADAC means *AD*d to *AC*cumulator). Note that we are now assuming a single-address machine. Assume that the content of 0101 has been entered into the instruction register. The activities making up an operating cycle would be:

1 Increase the sequence register by 1 to 0102, to indicate the address of the next instruction.
2 Decode the operation code (add).
3 Identify the location of the data to be operated on (1056).
4 Activate the circuits to cause the content of location 1056 to be added to

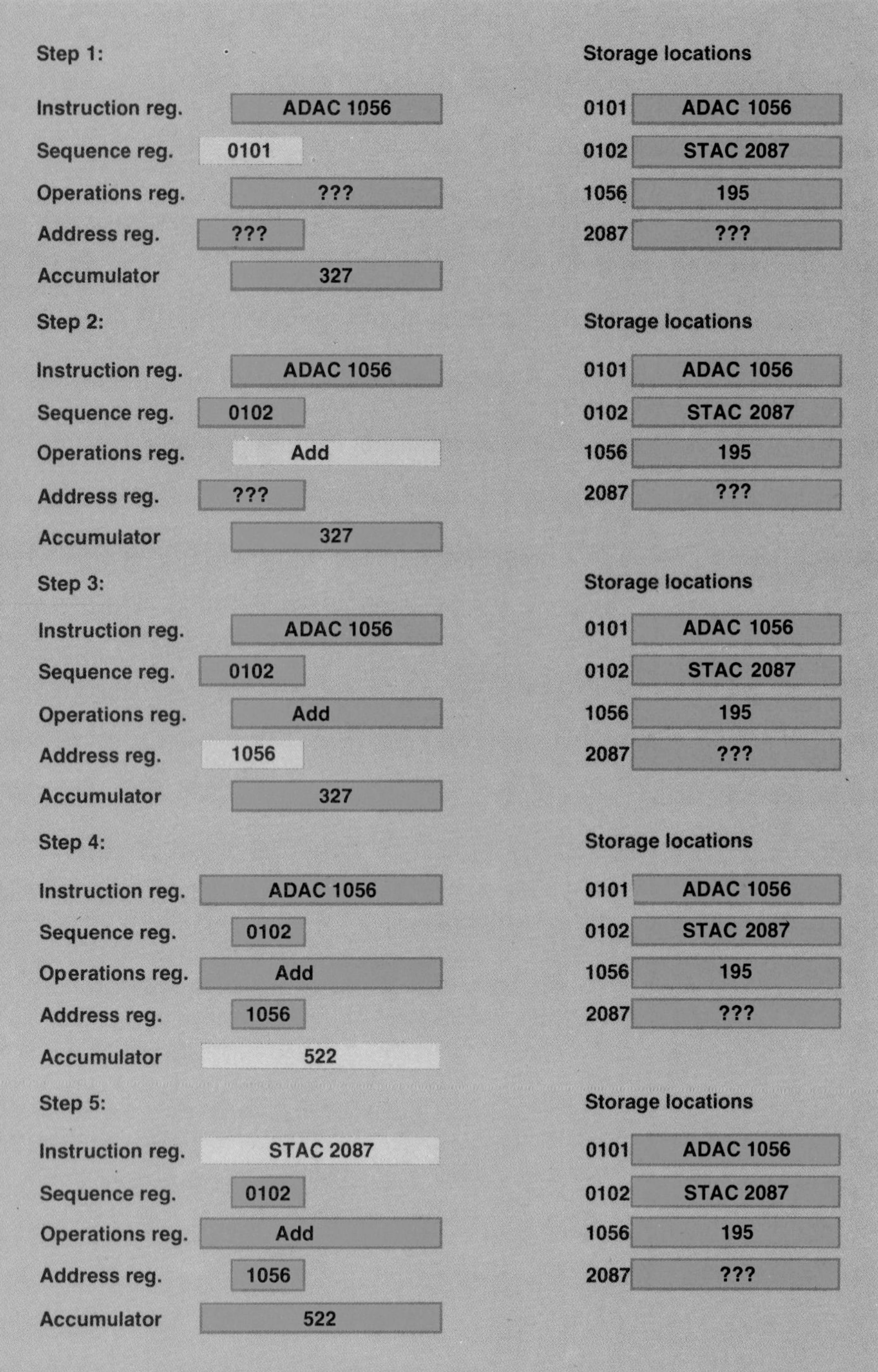

Figure 8.2 The instruction execution cycle

the content of the accumulator. (The result will be found in the accumulator.)

5 Load the content of storage location 0102 into the instruction register.

Note that some of the above activities could be accomplished simultaneously. Also, the cycle might be started at a different point to provide a fetch, execute sequence. In any case, to initiate any activity, the machine must receive an initial instruction that at least indicates the location of the next (first) instruction to be executed. This can be accomplished through switches on the control console or through action of the controlling operating system.

The control console

The operator communicates with the computer through the **control console**. This may be merely a set of switches and display lights but can include a typewriter and/or keyboard CRT and other items. By appropriate switch settings, the operator can enter an initial instruction to start the machine operating. The console also is used for "clearing" the machine in case of malfunction, bad data, or bad instructions. It can be used also, along with test equipment, to identify machine malfunctions and to initiate maintenance checks. Some machines have special maintenance consoles separate from the operating console.

The console can be used to enter data and to **debug** (test and correct) programs. These latter uses are rare, however. Modern systems are too fast and complicated to be harnessed to the slow keying processes of the control console.

In addition to their use in communicating instructions to the machine, the CRTs or typewriters at the console are used to keep track of what the machine is doing (jobs on the machine and status of each) and to record machine activity and operator interruptions. In modern multiprocessing systems, the machine operator usually receives instructions on the console typewriter or CRT for mounting and demounting tapes and disk packs and for changing forms on the printer.

Program organization and logic

Organization of data processing programs—general overview

In general, business data processing programs input transaction and/or change data and the master file record to which they relate, update the master record with the data, summarize and analyze the transactions and/or the current file status, and output the results. To accomplish these tasks, most data processing programs proceed through four or five steps.

1 *Initialize*—Identify files and set registers for totals and other values to zero. Consider, what is the first step in using an adding machine? Obviously, clear the machine so that the total will not reflect any leftover numbers in the machine.
2 *Input*—The process of entering the file and the data to be worked on.
3 *Process*—Perform the necessary replacement, addition, division, or other processing necessary to create the desired update of the file and/or to obtain information to be reported.
4 *Output*—The results of the previous steps must be made available to users. Even if the result is to be only an updated master record, that record in its updated form must be put back into the master file.
5 *Repeat by looping back to step 1 or step 2*—Usually, changes and transactions for a single record are used to update the master record, the updated master record is put back into the master file, and then the next master record is updated with its changes and transactions. Depending on the nature of the processing, some initialization of registers used for addition or other calculations may have to take place as processing begins for each record. At a minimum, we must loop back and repeat the process of obtaining the next set consisting of master record, changes (if any), and transactions involving that record. Printed output may be delayed until the end of the program if no custodial documents are being prepared.

The overall structure of a program—structure chart

To carry out the initialize, input, process, output, and loop-back sequence of data processing, a program must carry out many subtasks, each of which can be viewed as a **program module**, an integral unit of the overall program. Each module, in turn, is composed of various combinations of only three specific logic structures (sequence, selection or decision, and loop).

The major structure of a program is a hierarchical (ordered) series of modules to be executed one at a time. This is seen in Figure 8.3. The control level calls the major processing and control modules. The major processing and control modules then call specific processing modules. The processing modules are made up of the operational logic structures which carry out the detailed processing. The chart seen in Figure 8.3 is called a **structure chart**. Note how incomplete modules are represented as **stubs**.

This process can be illustrated best by a concrete example. Suppose we wish to develop a program to perform order processing. The program will receive input data on orders from inventory, current units on hand (from the item master record), reorder levels, and economic order quantities. Output

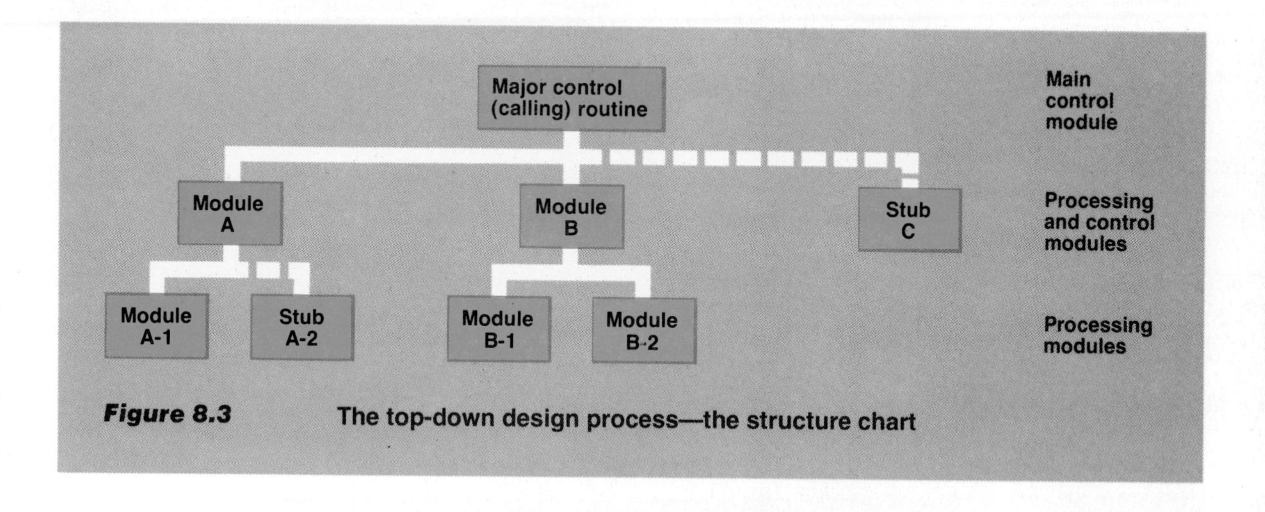

Figure 8.3 **The top-down design process—the structure chart**

will be backorders, reorders, and new balances (units on hand). It can be seen that the logic structure of the overall program will look like that illustrated in Figure 8.4. Note that there are three major branches (control modules) in the program but one controls no submodules.

The number of levels of processing and control and processing modules used can be varied as the program requires. In Figure 8.4, only four levels are required to complete the order processing. It is possible that other programs would require more than four levels of control and processing modules.

When the last processing block in each flow has been completed, control is returned to the major calling routine.

Program design

Computer programming is as much art as science, but some methods have been developed to guide in program development. The steps below have proved helpful to beginning programmers.

1 Define the problem.
2 Establish the general approach.
3 Specify the procedural detail.
4 Code the program.
5 Make the program work

Professional programmers do not agree on the specific techniques to be used at each stage. Again, the techniques suggested below have proved helpful.

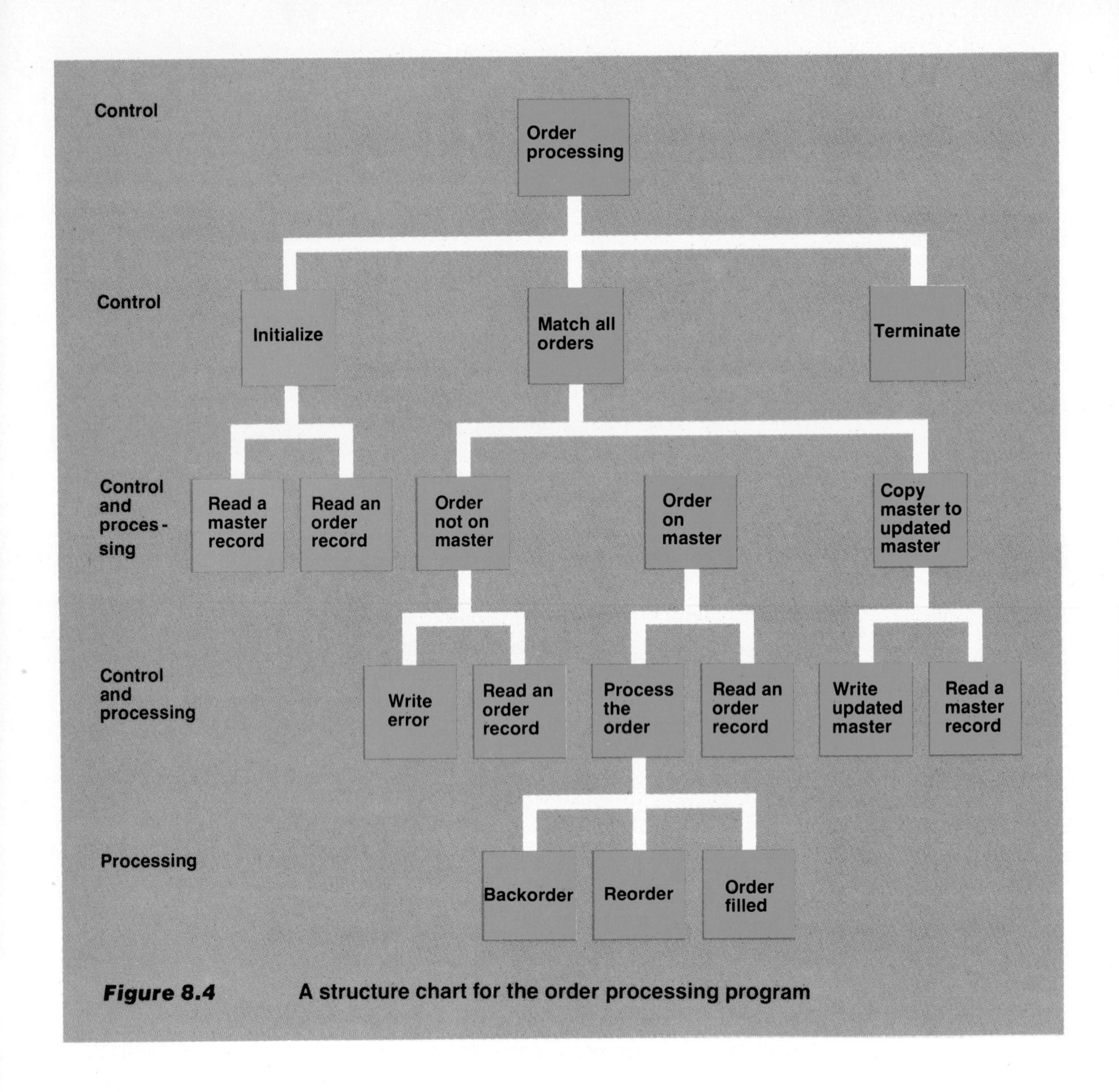

Figure 8.4 **A structure chart for the order processing program**

Defining the problem: verbal description

The obvious first step is to understand the task that the computer is going to be given. One advantage gained from learning to program any computer in any language is an improved ability to recognize the precise nature of problems and to more easily suggest a logical solution. In addition to the structure chart, tools useful here include the verbal description and the input-output schematic. The first step is normally to obtain agreement between the person with the problem and the programmer on a verbal description of the program, preferably in writing. The description need not specify solution algorithms or detailed steps.

Consider the program to perform order processing. The verbal description might run as follows:

"The general problem is to establish and maintain a sequentially ordered master inventory file containing a record for each standard inventory item showing number of units on hand, average cost per unit, units on order, units on backorder, year-to-date activity, reorder point, and economic order quantity. This program must process orders, updating the inventory on hand, units issued to date, and value of issues-to-date. In addition, this specific program must recognize and report when the number of units on hand of an item reaches or falls below the level at which a reorder should occur. If an order calls for more items than the number on hand, a backorder will be generated for the part of the order not filled. (Backorders will be filled when new additions to units on hand make it possible.) These updates and checks occur daily."

It is obvious that a complete verbal description is apt to be lengthy and can easily become hard to follow. The description can be simplified when a standard solution method (standard economic order quantity model, for example) is to be applied by merely calling for the standard method's use at that point. Still, the description of inputs and outputs can become tedious and confusing. Thus, the input-output schematic is probably a more easily understood way of describing the problem. This does not mean that the verbal description should be dropped, however. It is a starting point, even if it is never developed in full detail.

Establishing the general approach

The input-output schematic

The input-output schematic is particularly useful when developing custodial processing programs. It consists of listing *required outputs* and *specified inputs* in two columns and providing information connecting the columns to show that the required outputs can be obtained from the specified inputs. (See Table 8.1.)

Inputs are divided into two categories, data inputs and program inputs. Data inputs are facts about each transaction or problem that the program is to process. These data inputs, as defined here, include both transactions data and the master file records that are being modified by the transactions. Program inputs are numerical constants or algorithmic formulas used in processing data inputs.

Table 8.1 presents the input-output schematic for our order processing program. Data inputs will vary with each transaction. Program inputs are not affected by transactions but are an unchanging part of the program.

INPUTS	OUTPUTS
Data Inputs	*Direct Outputs*
MASTER ITEM RECORD	REORDER LIST
1. Date of Last Update	30. Date 20
2. Item No.	31. Item No. 21
3. Units on Hand	32. Units Ordered 5,14,22,25
4. Average Cost/Unit	*DIRECT AND INDIRECT OUTPUTS*
5. Units on Order	BACKORDER LIST
6. Units on Backorder	35. Date 20
7. Units Received-to-Date	36. Item No. 21
8. Value of Receipts-to-Date	37. Total Units, This Order 22
9. Units Issued-to-Date	38. Units Backordered 22,3
10. Value of Issues-to-Date	39. Total Units on Backorder 6,38
11. Units Returned-to-Date	40. Total Units on Order 5,32
12. Value of Returns-to-Date	UPDATED MASTER RECORD
13. Reorder Point	51. Date of Last Update 20
14. Economic Order Quantity	52. Item No. 2
ORDERS	53. Units on Hand 3,22
20. Date of Order	54. Average Cost/Unit 4
21. Item No.	55. Units on Order 5,32
22. Units Ordered	56. Units on Backorder 6,38
23. Price per Unit	57. Units Received-to-Date 7
PROGRAM INPUTS	58. Value of Receipts-to-Date 8
25. Reorder Formula	59. Units Issued-to-Date 9,22
	60. Value of Issues-to-Date 10,54,22
	61. Units Returned-to-Date 11
	62. Value of Returns-to-Date 12
	63. Reorder Point 13
	64. Reorder Amount 14

Table 8.1 **Input-output schematic—order processing program**

Outputs are also divided into two classes. **Direct outputs** are those obtained by direct manipulation of the inputs. **Indirect outputs** are derived from manipulation of direct outputs. Inputs may or may not enter directly into the development of indirect outputs. The distinguishing characteristic of indirect outputs is that they require the previous computation of direct outputs. Thus, in Table 8.1, the Reorder List is identified as a direct output. The remaining outputs in Table 8.1 (Backorder List and Updated Master Record) are, in part, indirect outputs. To obtain some items (for example, Units on Order, item 55), requires the previous calculation of the reorder amount (Units Ordered, item 32). This is learned by reading the numbers following the name of each output item. If the numbers refer only to items in the input column, the output item is a direct output item. If, however, the number for another output item appears, the item is an indirect output.

Block diagram

A careful examination of Figure 8.4 and Table 8.1 will reveal the general flow of processing. This can also be shown in a **block diagram**. Such a diagram is shown in Figure 8.5. It consists of a flowchart showing the modules (major task routines) that make up the program in the order in which they will be executed within the program. A **flowchart** is a set of processing blocks connected by flowlines and is described fully in Chapter 12. Here we are only illustrating the program development process.

Note that the block diagram is roughly analagous to the structure chart. They are merely alternative ways of showing the same thing. Note how the block diagram shows little processing detail. It reveals only the major tasks and the general order in which they are to be accomplished.

Specifying the procedural detail

The next step in program development is to take each module from the structure chart or each block from the block diagram and specify exactly how that subtask is to be accomplished. Tools to be used here are the detailed flow diagram or the HIPO diagram and pseudocode.

Detailed flowchart

A detailed flowchart showing the detailed processing required in the input module where the master item record and the order records are read and matched is shown in Figure 8.6. Note that orders are assumed to be entered in the same sequential order as the order of the master file.

HIPO diagrams

The acronym HIPO refers to *H*ierarchy plus *I*nput *P*rocess *O*utput. **HIPO diagrams** are used to expand structure charts and frequently are called IPO diagrams. The logic used is that the hierarchical structure is shown on the structure chart and only input, processing, and output need to be detailed. An example of a HIPO diagram is shown in Figure 8.7. Since this is a relatively simple program, the HIPO diagram for reading and matching master item records and order records is not at all complicated. In general, each processing block within the large processing block would be broken down into another HIPO diagram. That is, when the overall control module must pass control to a lower level module, that step is set inside a separate box inside the central "process" box. That box then becomes a lower level HIPO diagram.

HIPO diagramming will be detailed further in Chapter 10. For the time being, it is important to be aware that both HIPO diagrams and flowcharts are

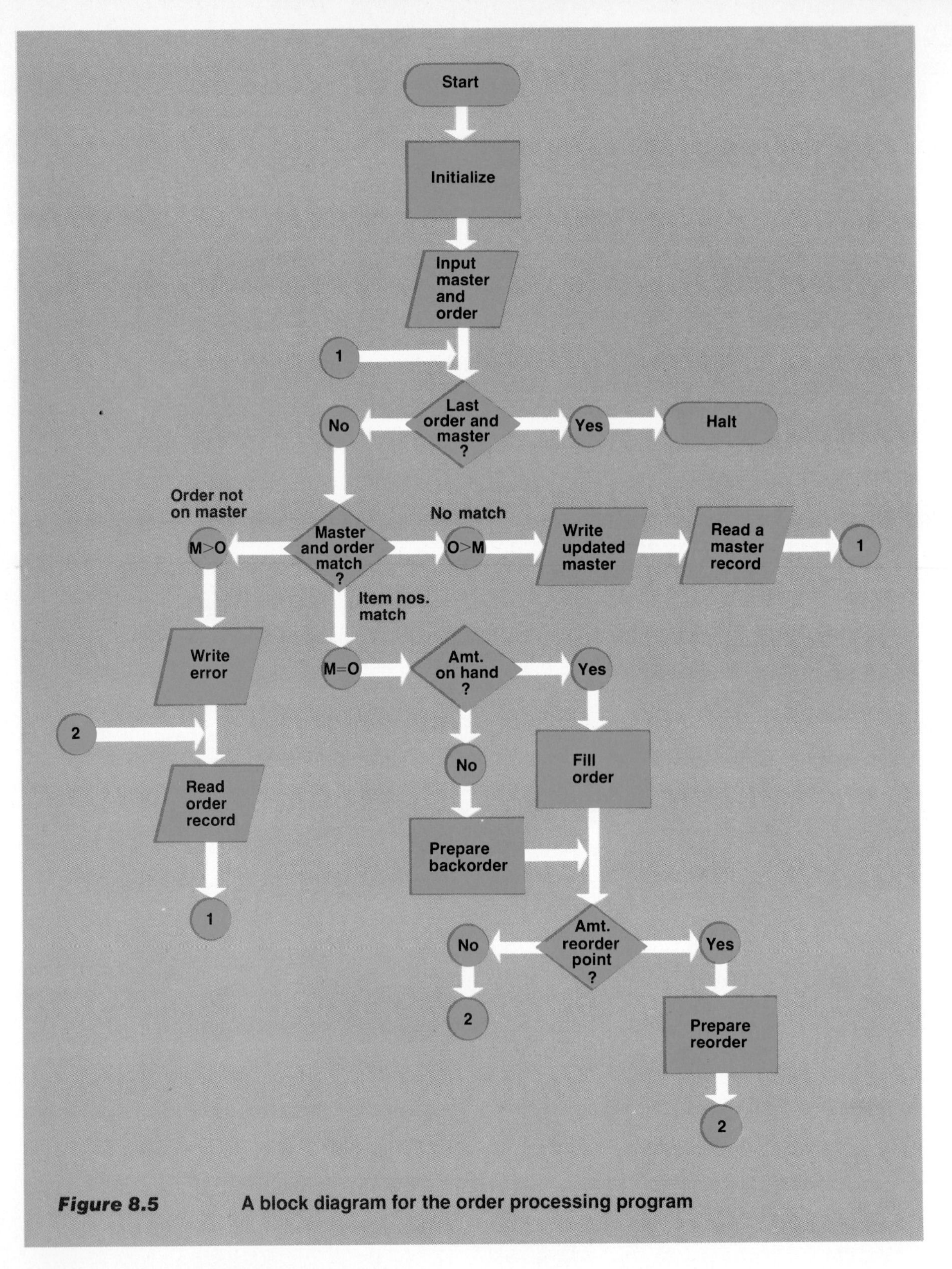

Figure 8.5 A block diagram for the order processing program

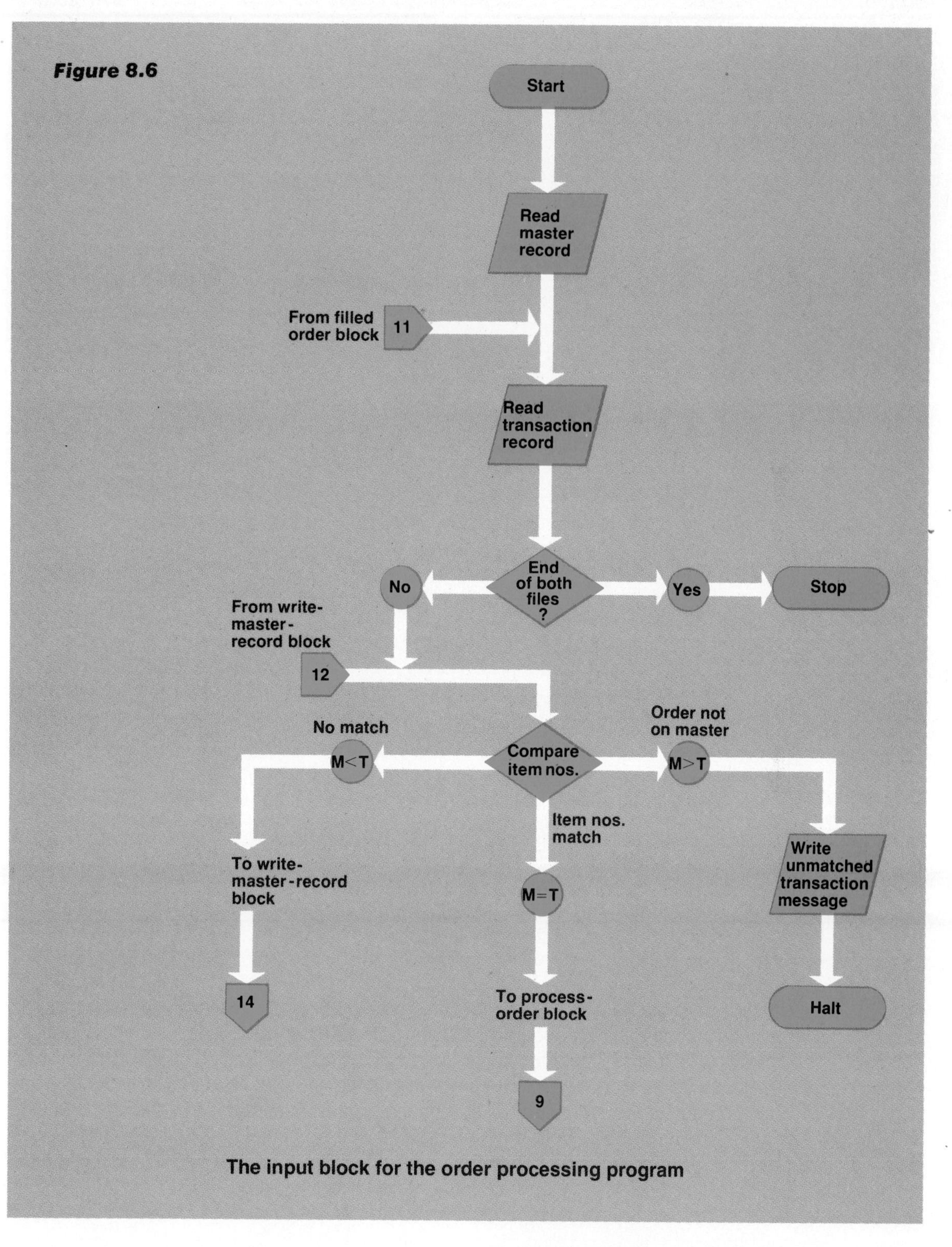

Figure 8.6 The input block for the order processing program

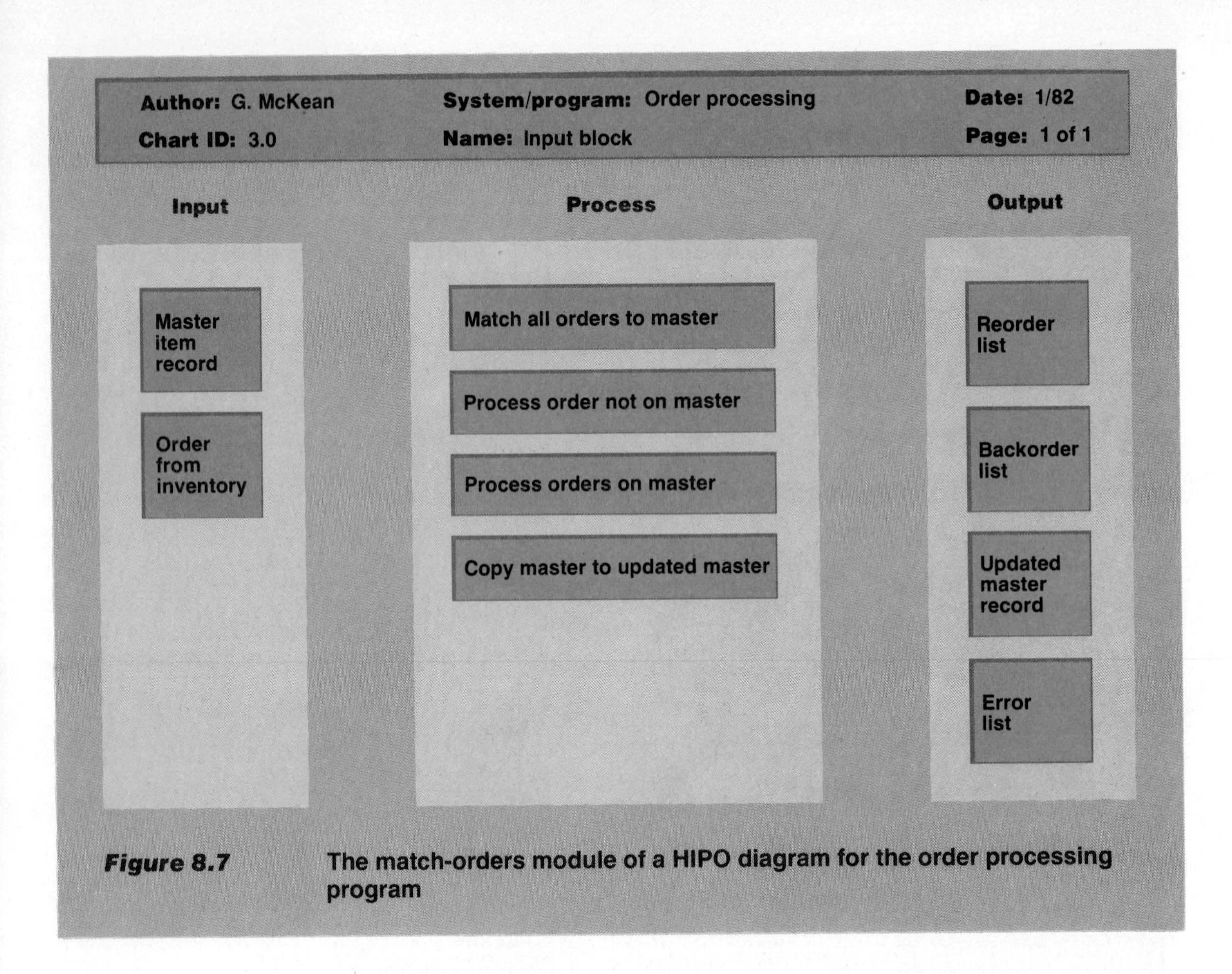

Figure 8.7 **The match-orders module of a HIPO diagram for the order processing program**

program design aids and program documentation procedures. Note also that the input-output schematic is similar in design to a HIPO diagram.

Logic structures of computer programs

Only three basic logic structures are required to develop any computer program. The most basic logic structure is the **sequence structure**. It provides for each of the processes in the program to be completed in the order in which they appear. A process, once started, must be completed before a new process or sequence can be begun. Practically, this means that branches in the program are avoided as much as possible. The sequence structure is illustrated graphically in Figure 8.8a.

The second logic structure is the **decision**, or IFTHENELSE, **structure**. It consists of a logical choice between processing sequences and is illustrated in Figure 8.8b. Note that one of the processes shown in the diagram may be a "null" process which merely passes control to the next module. Again, note that there is only one entry point and one exit point.

The third allowable logic structure is the **looping**, or DOWHILE, **structure**.

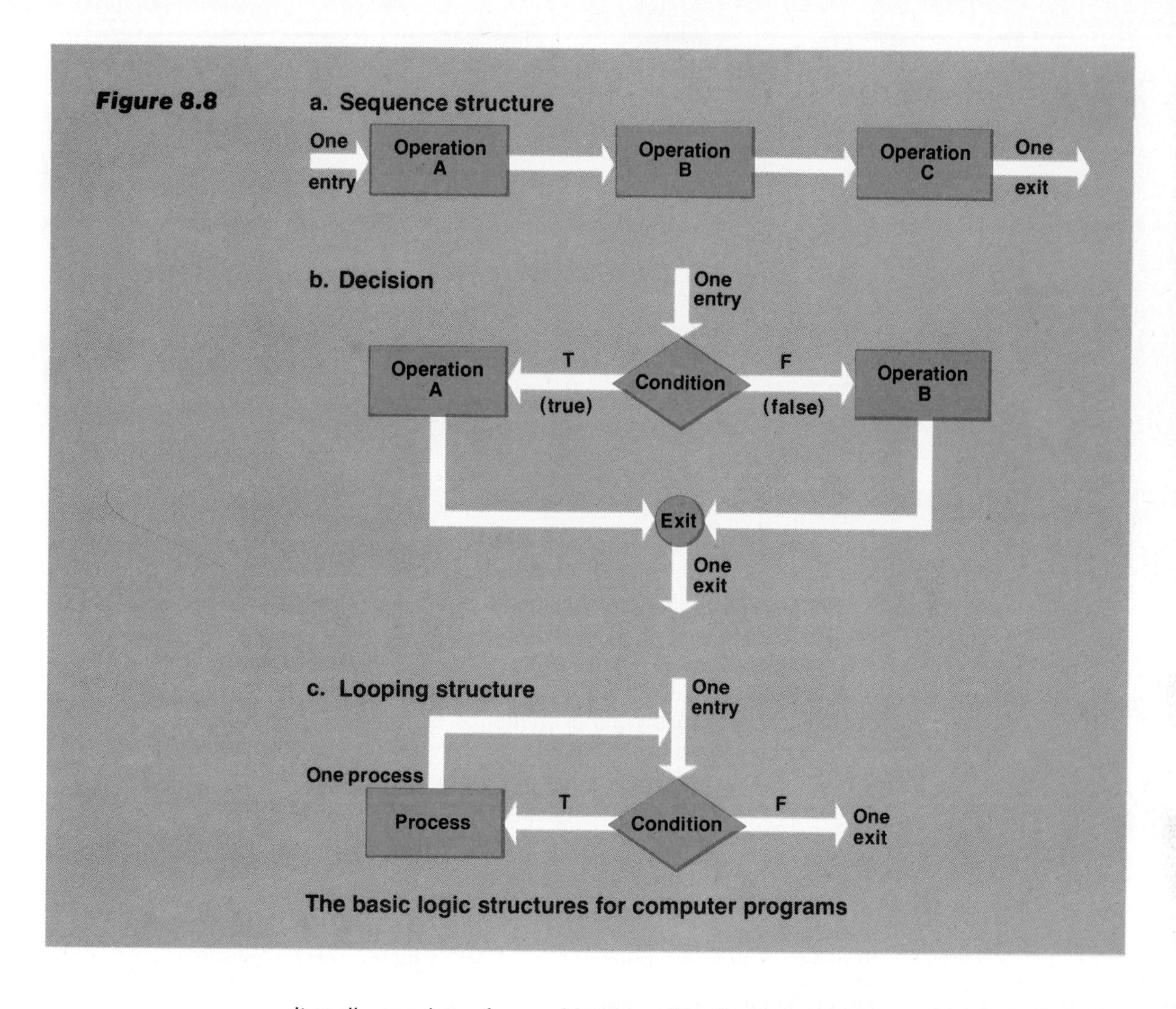

Figure 8.8 The basic logic structures for computer programs

It really consists of a combination of the first two structures which provides for repetition of a process, as is required in so many processing operations. The looping structure is represented in Figure 8.8c.

The three allowable structures may be combined in any order to perform any necessary processing. Restricting programmers to these three structures makes program modules easier to design. It also makes programs easier to read and understand. This results in easier debugging, easier maintenance, and easier control over program development and programmer activity. These structures are covered in more detail in Chapter 10.

Pseudocode

When structure and HIPO charts are used, **pseudocode,** is also used. Pseudocode is a substitute for detailed flowcharts. It is used to describe the detailed processing steps for completing a module. An example is shown in Table 8.2. There are no hard and fast rules for pseudocode. Each program

```
READ        first transaction record
READ        first master record
DOWHILE     transaction file and master file not empty
    IF      master item no. < transaction item no.
        THEN    Do order-greater-than-master
        ELSE
            IF  master item no. = transaction item no.
                THEN    DO process-the-order
                ELSE
                    DO  master-greater-than-order
ENDDO.
CLOSE FILES
```

Table 8.2 **Example of pseudocode description of detailed processing steps**

designer merely writes out the detailed steps of the program in English-like statements. (Note that important words, such as DOWHILE, and IF, THEN, ELSE, are capitalized.) These statements are then used as a guide by the programmer when the program is coded in some language. Pseudocode also provides excellent program documentation since almost anyone can read it. Can you follow the pseudocode of Table 8.2? (Hint: It applies to the order processing program we have been working on.)

Pseudocode resembles a programming language in that it can be used to express specific detailed operations such as:

Read next master item record
Add units received to units on hand

Pseudocode differs from most programming languages in that it can be used to express more complex or less detailed instructions such as:

Find matching master item record
Compute backorder amount

This is the second way in which pseudocode differs from a programming language. The first was its lack of formal rules for its structure or even for the words used. There are, however, a few guidelines that can be applied to the development of pseudocode.

1 Use a sequence structure; write each statement on a separate line.
2 Express decision structures as IFTHENELSE for efficiency in translation to a programming language. For example:

```
IF          units on hand is less than units ordered
    THEN    develop backorder
    ELSE    fill order
ENDIF.
```

Note how the alignment of the IF, THEN, and ELSE and the beginning of each condition or action makes the pseudocode easier to read.

3 Use DOWHILE to indicate looping. For example:

```
DOWHILE   item no.s equal
   READ   transaction record
     IF   units on hand is less than units ordered
       THEN   develop backorder
ENDDO.
```

Actually these guidelines merely specify using the structured approach to be explained in Chapter 10.

It may not be obvious that two general approaches to program development are being defined. They are as follows:

Approach 1

1 Verbal description
2 Input-output schematic
3 Block diagram
4 Detailed flowcharts
5 Code program
6 Make the program work

Approach 2

1 Verbal description
2 Structure chart
3 HIPO diagram(s)
4 Pseudocode descriptions
5 Code program
6 Make the program work

Note the similarity of the input-output schematic and the HIPO chart. Note how the block diagram corresponds to the structure chart, the detailed flowchart to the pseudocode description. It should be obvious that *both* approaches stress a top-down, modular approach (a structured approach). However, the second approach has been specifically designed to follow the structured approach. There are approaches other than the two presented here. Each data processing installation should specify an approach which will be used in the development of every program.

We are now ready for the last two steps which are common to both of the approaches that we are illustrating.

Coding the program

After the program has been fully defined and the processing solution completely described, the program can be written for the computer. The steps to be followed in coding the program are to select an appropriate language, code from the top down using a structured approach, and follow approved procedures while using standard forms for displaying the code.

The translation of a detailed flowchart or a pseudocode description into a working program is not as easy as it sounds. The program must be designed according to secondary objectives other than just obtaining a working program. The program may be written to be an efficient user of the computer, to be easy to understand and use, or to be easy to compile. It is extremely difficult for it to possess all these characteristics simultaneously. The programmer performing the translation needs a detailed knowledge of the language into which the process is being translated and a clear understanding of the process to be coded.

Making the program work

Programs seldom operate correctly, if at all, as initially written. Computers are very fast and powerful, but they are also limited. They cannot understand that a command RED D at a particular point in the program is *obviously* an input command telling the machine to input (READ) a variable (data word) called D. The computer would need to be specially programmed or designed to interpret RED as "READ" whenever it could be considered a program instruction. This too might cause problems. The simplistic consistency of the computer means that misplacing or forgetting a comma, transposing two characters, or other such simple errors can cause the program to malfunction partially or totally. The process of removing the errors, some of which may be logic errors, is called *debugging the program*.

The techniques described briefly here are useful in debugging the program and will be fully described in Chapter 11.

Desk debug This is the general process of reading the program to find errors.

Test data Programs may be tested with made-up (or actual) sets of data (master item files and transaction files).

Program tracing Techniques exist that trace out a trail through the program to check if the order of processing is correct and/or isolate where errors are occurring.

Diagnostics Most language translators provide identification of statements not in the proper form or obviously out of sequence according to the rules of the language being translated.

Structured walkthroughs Structured walkthroughs consist of the entire project team providing formal critiques of each module as it is designed and prepared by the programmer.

Programming guidelines

The basic guideline we favor is to use a structured approach to programming. This approach is explained in detail in Chapter 10. Within the structured framework, there are several specific guidelines whose use can improve the workability of programs and make programs easier to keep operating (easier to maintain).

1 *Document fully and carefully.*
   a Verbal description and/or input-output schematic
   b Block diagram or structure chart
   c Detailed flow charts or HIPO diagrams and pseudocode
   d Complete program listing keyed to the program descriptors
   e Sample inputs and outputs that illustrate exactly how the program is used
   f Complete instructions for the computer or terminal operator on how to run the program

   This last step is absolutely necessary, particularly if any tapes or disks must be mounted or outputs are provided in nonnormal ways. For example, if the output is via the line printer in the computer center for a program designed to be operated from a terminal, the user should know this. Similarly, if the program is operated from a terminal but can accept data from a file on an electronic storage device, the user should be given detailed instructions on how to use this alternative.
2 *Comments to the reader* as part of the program are provided for by most higher level languages. They should be used in the program to indicate sections where major and minor subtasks are performed. During program development, these comments can guide the programmer in placing temporary output statements for tracing program operation. Permanent comments that identify program modules are very helpful in maintaining an operating program. Modules needing correction or modification can be found quickly and identified without error.
3 *Make programs modular* and avoid interlocking modules as much as possible. Avoiding unnecessary complexity in program flow pays dividends in readability and ease of debug.
4 *Make each program loop unique.* Do not close two or more loops with the same command.
5 *Use* all possible *aids to readability* of the program.
   a Break up complex formulas into several commands.
   b Use parentheses liberally to provide clarity in arithmetic expressions.
   c Name program variables in as logical and natural a way as possible.
   d Avoid the use of two variable names for the same entity, and avoid giving two different variables the same name.

6 *Prepare* as much *documentation* as possible *before the program is written.* Complete documentation is required to prevent errors while running programs and to make program maintenance efficient or even possible.

Summary

Programming is the process of translating the steps in a problem solution into an ordered sequence of instructions for execution by the computer. Computer execution consists of bringing the instruction into the instruction register for decoding, activating the circuitry that will perform the operation specified by the instruction, and then identifying the next instruction. This process of fetch, interpret, perform, and identify the next instruction is repeated for each instruction in the program. The usual order in which the instructions are executed is sequential by location in the program. Branch instructions modify this usual sequential order whenever the condition specified for the branch (for example, a negative remainder) occurs.

Data processing programs exhibit an overall structure of initialization, input, process, output, and then loop back to process one record at a time. Each transaction (or change) record is used to update the corresponding master record. Information is accumulated for creating reports as each record is processed.

The internal detailed logic of computer programs consists of only three basic structures. These are the sequence structure, the decision structure, and the loop structure. Designing programs using only these structures is called structured programming.

The general approach to program development consists of five steps.

1 Define the problem.
2 Establish the general approach.
3 Specify the procedural detail.
4 Code the program.
5 Make the program work.

Two approaches for accomplishing these steps were presented:

Approach 1
1 Verbal description
2 Input-output schematic
3 Block diagram
4 Detailed flowcharts
5 Code program
6 Make the program work

Approach 2
1 Verbal description
2 Structure chart
3 HIPO chart(s)
4 Pseudocode descriptions
5 Code program
6 Make the program work

Tools for making the program work (debugging the code) are desk debug, test data, program tracing, diagnostics, and structured walkthroughs.

Program development should follow a structured, top-down approach that emphasizes modules. In addition, programmers should document their work fully and carefully, include comments in the finished program to guide the reader through it, make programs modular, make each program loop unique, strive for readability, and prepare documentation before the program is written.

Key terms

Define the following terms as briefly as possible and then, in a short paragraph, clarify each definition.

Address register
Block diagram
Branch instruction
Control console
Data input
Debug
Decision structure
Direct output
Flowchart
HIPO diagram
Indirect output
Input-output schematic
Instruction register
Looping structure
Operating cycle
Operations register
Program inputs
Program module
Pseudocode
Sequence register
Sequence structure
Structure chart
Stub
Verbal description

Discussion questions

1 What is modular programming?
2 How does structured programming relate to modular programming?
3 How does a HIPO diagram differ from an input-output schematic?
4 Compare a block diagram to a structure chart. How are they different? In what ways are they alike?
5 List the five-step structure usually found in a data processing program. Define each step.
6 List the major techniques used for program debugging.
7 Structured design emphasizes the top-down approach to program development. Could the first approach discussed in this chapter be considered top-down, structured design? Explain fully.
8 What are the three basic logic structures of any computer program? What characteristic do they have in common?
9 What are the types of inputs found on an input-output schematic? Why distinguish them?

10 What are the types of outputs found on an input-output schematic? Why distinguish them?

11 How do secondary objectives for the program influence the way it is coded?

Exercises

1 A program is being written for an industrial products firm to perform a sales analysis by cross-classifying sales by salesperson and product, by salesperson and customer, and by customer and product. The program is to be run at the end of each week. Sales orders are to be the data source for the program. They show customer name and salesperson, and for each product they list unit price, units, and total dollar amount. Finally, they show the total amount of sale. Assume at least 100 products, 25 salespersons, and 250 customers.

   a Prepare an input-output schematic for the program.
   b Prepare a block diagram for the program.
   c Prepare a procedural flowchart for the program.

2 Refer to Exercise 1 and prepare the following:

   a Structure chart for the program
   b HIPO diagram(s) for the program
   c Pseudocode description for the program

3 A program is being prepared to prepare checks to pay supplier invoices for a manufacturer. Payable invoices carry the signature of the accounts payable supervisor as authorization for payment. They also include vendor number, vendor name and address, and for each item on the invoice, the type of unit (pound, piece, pair, ton, and so on), the number of units, the price per unit, the total cost of each item, and the total amount to pay the vendor. They are arranged in vendor-number order for input to the program. The authorization signature is to be converted to a code and no check will be prepared unless the code is present in the input record. The program is also expected to scan all payable invoices for each vendor and prepare only one check per vendor. The calculations of amounts to be paid for each item and on each invoice are also to be checked. In addition to the checks, the program is to produce a list of paid and unpaid invoices as well as a list of total payments by vendor.

   a Prepare an input-output schematic for the program.
   b Prepare a block diagram of the program.
   c Prepare a procedural flowchart of one block of the program.

4 Refer to Exercise 3 and prepare the following:

   a Structure chart for the program
   b HIPO diagram for a module of the program
   c Pseudocode description of the module for which the HIPO diagram was prepared

5 Refer to the order processing program which we started to develop in this chapter and develop a complete structure chart for the update program. Note there will be the following transactions.
   Receipts of new items
   Returns of issued items
   Issues (orders from inventory)
   Adjustments (shrinkage reductions, new reorder amounts, new reorder points, and so on)

   Outputs should include:
   Updated Master Record
   Backorder List
   Reorder List

6 Refer to the order processing program which we started to develop in this chapter and develop a complete set of HIPO diagrams for the receipt of new items. Identify any assumptions you must make about processing rules.

COMPUTERS AT WORK

A Program for Lift Trucks

If you've ever felt like getting your lift truck fleet costs under better control, IBM's General Products Division in San Jose, California, may have the answer for you.

By using a computer program, they maintain excellent control of their fleet of 100 lift trucks. They know, for instance, when to avoid buying or leasing additional trucks. They know when an aging truck should be replaced rather than repaired. And they know when it should be "semi-retired" to a job that is less demanding rather than placed in an area of high usage.

"We control the fleet with the aid of a FORTRAN program that permits us to optimize truck utilization and allocation," says Jim Koenig, manager of distribution engineering at IBM. "As a result, we save the cost of buying or leasing about five extra trucks a year, at least one-half man-year of engineering support, not to mention the time saved gathering data and the time saved for all parties concerned who must decide what to do with particular trucks. Also, by keeping a closer watch on the trucks, we reduce downtime and safety hazards."

All in all, the program has been a valuable control device, enabling one person to monitor the entire fleet and quickly focus on existing or potential problems. It was also the prime aid in the recent justification and purchase of 40 new lift trucks. The program's output was used to show the financial review committees that the fleet was well utilized, but that it was very old, experiencing high downtime and rapid deterioration.

The computer program prints out graphs that show the utilization of individual trucks and of the fleet as a group, based on data collected every day from the trucks' hour meters.

The program output includes graphs that flag problem trucks and show an overall view of what's going on in the fleet. Other graphs show usage profiles and information on individual trucks that have been flagged as problems. Here's how IBM uses the graphs to optimize truck utilization and allocation.

Get the overall picture

"One thing we do is look at how the fleet is being utilized," says Koenig. "We are able to re-allocate certain trucks to optimize compatibility between the trucks and their

Source: Abridged from "Our Computer Makes Sure Each Truck Is on the Right Job," *Modern Materials Handling,* 35 (February 1980), 68–72. Reprinted by permission of Cahners Publishing Company, Division of Reed Holdings, Inc.

operations, in the sense that newer trucks are compatible with higher use and the older trucks are compatible with lower use."

The Fleet Utilization graph shows "compatibility" at a glance. It is an activity profile of the fleet as a group. It plots truck age versus weekly use, and divides the trucks into three categories: "high risk", which indicates high use of old trucks; "high potential", which indicates low use of new trucks; and "high compatibility", which indicates optimum use of trucks according to their age.

The objective is to assign trucks so they will have optimum utilization or "high compatibility" in their jobs. Newer trucks can be placed in high-use activities and older trucks can be moved to less demanding jobs. . . .

Find sudden changes in usage

IBM also looks at the entire fleet from a different perspective. This time they flag those trucks that are suddenly being used much differently than normal, to find out if they should be replaced or re-allocated.

The Utilization Summary table shows the entire fleet's operation for one week and how each truck compares to its average operation. . . .

Three pluses (+++) next to a truck's number means that it ran at least 20% more during the week than its average weekly running time, based on the last four weeks of data. Likewise, three minuses (−−−) next to a truck means that it was operated at least 20% below its weekly average.

Once these trucks are identified, IBM tries to determine a reason for the change in usage for the truck and whether that will alter its effectiveness. They do this by looking first at the other information on the table and then by looking at individual usage graphs of the trucks in question.

The Utilization Summary includes information about each truck's location, by department and building, its age in hours, average run hours, the standard deviation (or dispersion) of the data used to determine average run hours, the total hours run, and downtime data: hours and days down, and the percentage of down hours to total hours available.

Downtime data often explains sudden changes in usage. It identifies trucks that need repair and indicates the extent of repairs. "We feel that 10 to 15% downtime is the maximum tolerable amount. But even that is something we would want to correct immediately," says Koenig. "When we see that a truck has excessive downtime, we get in touch with the maintenance department and consider appropriate replacement or overhaul strategies."

Once IBM determines, from the Utilization Summary which trucks are experiencing a change in usage, they look at the recent history of each individual truck and find out what's behind the trend of increased or decreased use.

Investigate current trends

Individual Truck Usage graphs are used to confirm or investigate current trends or variations from an individual truck's average use.

For example, . . . [a] graph for Truck 520 was developed because that truck was flagged by the Utilization Summary table as running more than 20% *below* its average.

Here, you can see a definite trend of decreasing usage. And, referring back to the Fleet Utilization graph you'll find that it's in an area of high potential for increased utilization.

After checking with the department, IBM might find the trend is a result of decreasing production schedules in the department or it may be that the truck has recently been taken off some extra duties it had been assigned for the last few weeks. If the lower usage continued, they would make an effort to swap this truck with an older one.

"Without our program, the decreasing usage of this truck may have gone unnoticed for months before we would have found out," says Koenig. "Now with the print-out, we have a basis for rational discussion about what should be done. We can perform such an analysis for any truck at any time".

Data collection

IBM feels the program input is easy to collect and maintain on a routine basis. The only additional work that must be performed is the recording of truck hours at the beginning of a shift. They feel this can easily be absorbed into a normal day's activities. One person in each department spends about five minutes each morning recording the daily hour-meter readings from his trucks.

What's in store for the program

"This is really just the first step", Koenig says. "We plan to make the program easier to use in terms of data collection and interpretation by implementing an interactive plant-wide computer system which can be contacted on a CRT by the using departments.

"We will also incorporate preventive-maintenance scheduling. Here, we will be able to advise the maintenance department and the user's department a week in advance which trucks need preventive maintenance, and we will forecast maintenance activity for a given workload.

"We also plan to perform automatic lease/buy and optimum replacement evaluations using the data we are now accumulating on utilization, maintenance and downtime. Other planned enhancements include program algorithms which will predict future fleet requirements.

Chapter 9

Programming Languages

Outline

Computer software basics

Language types
- Machine language
- Assembly language
- Higher-level languages

Statement types in procedure-oriented compiler languages
- Input and output
- Arithmetic computation
- Decision making
- Other common language features
- Types of compilers

Some commonly available procedural languages
- COBOL
- FORTRAN
- BASIC
- APL
- PL/1
- ALGOL
- Pascal

Nonprocedural languages
- RPG
- Simulation languages
- List processing
- Data management languages
- Programming assistance

Type of program and type of language

Details of popular languages

BASIC

COBOL

FORTRAN

Choosing a programming language

Considerations for assembly language

Considerations for procedure-oriented languages

Considerations for nonprocedural languages

Criteria for language selection
- Language selection for a computer installation
- Language selection for a particular problem

Computer software basics

Without programs, computers would be expensive and not very useful playthings. A computer will do absolutely nothing without instructions to guide its operation. The process of translating a set of processing procedures into computer instructions is called programming the computer. This coding process can be carried out in many different languages. It is the purpose of this chapter to identify the major types of languages available and demonstrate their characteristics.

Language types

Four levels of computer programming languages can be identified:

1 Machine language—lowest level
2 Assembly language—second level
3 Procedure-oriented compiler language—third level
4 Nonprocedural compiler language—highest level

Each of these language types has strengths and weaknesses as discussed below.

Machine language

To illustrate **machine language**, consider a mythical two-address computer with a double-word-length accumulator for arithmetic and logic. Words are ten bytes. Instructions break down like this:

Operation code	Operand address	Next instruction address
01	1001	0005

Suppose we wish to code a program to add a series of number pairs. The steps to be accomplished are shown in Table 9.1 on the left. The code to accomplish each step is shown on the right. The instructions in steps 2, 3, and 4 refer to the lower half of the accumulator only. If we had wished to do this work in the upper half of the accumulator, the codes for steps 2, 3, and 4 would have been 15, 16, and 25, respectively. (Note how arbitrary the codes seem to be.) Machine language programming requires an intimate knowledge of the particular machine. The programmer must know the best way to accomplish each activity and how to take advantage of special machine features. However, knowledgeable programmers working in machine language can make programs use the machine in the most efficient way.

Another disadvantage of machine language programming is the need to learn the arbitrary operation codes. Why should a read command be 01?

STEP	DESCRIPTION	INSTRUCTION LOCATION*	CODED INSTRUCTION
1	Read first and second words.	0001 0002	01 0200 0002 01 0201 0003
2	Clear accumulator and enter first word.	0003	10 0200 0004
3	Add second word to accumulator.	0004	11 0201 0005
4	Store result.	0005	20 0202 0006
5	Print result and return to read next number pair.	0006	06 0202 0001

*The instruction locations are not part of the instruction. They are shown to facilitate following the program.

Table 9.1 **Machine language program to add pairs of numbers**

Why not 02? Also, each operation performed by the machine is a very small step in the overall process. For both of these reasons, programming in machine language takes an excessively long time and is impractical. Nowadays, programs are virtually never written in machine language.

Assembly language

The first step in making programming languages easier to use was the development of assemblers. An **assembler** is a program written in machine language that allows the programmer to write in a pseudoindependent language. Early assemblers required a one-to-one correspondence between the program written in assembly language and the program written in machine language. Assemblers in use today include **macroinstructions** (macros), which translate as more than one machine language instruction. A macro is made up of a series, or **routine**, of instructions, usually one that the programmer will encounter over and over again in preparing programs.

In any case, operation codes and addresses in **assembly language** are stated in alphabetic mnemonics, which are easier to remember. For example, the program of Table 9.1 has been restated in Table 9.2 in machine language form on the left and in a mnemonic assembly language form on the right. Note how much more easily the assembly language program can be read. RDD means "ReaD a Data word," RAL means "reset the lower accumulator and add a data word into it [Reset and Add Lower]," ALO stands for "Add to the LOwer," and so on. Only those instructions that do not follow in sequence need to be given names. The first instruction is named so that the last instruction can send the control back to begin the whole process over again.

You will recall from Chapter 7 that language translators, called assemblers or compilers, are used to translate programs written in assembly or compiler language into machine language. Assemblers are the translators used with assembly language. **Compilers** are used to translate higher-level (compiler) languages.

STEP	MACHINE LANGUAGE	ASSEMBLY LANGUAGE
1	0102000002	START RDD R01
	0102010003	RDD R02
2	1002000004	RAL R01
3	1102010005	ALO R02
4	2002020006	STL P01
5	0602020001	PRI P01 START

Table 9.2 **Machine and assembly language programs to add pairs of numbers**

Higher-level languages

The next refinement in languages made them procedure-oriented. Programmers were allowed to write in a language very near to the way they would state a problem. The compiler program accepted the program in the procedure-oriented language (called a **source program**) and converted it (compiled it) into machine language (an **object program**). Figure 7.2 (page 186) charts the general assembly and compiler process.

The latest movement is toward nonprocedural, problem-oriented languages. These languages allow the computer user to program a problem in the language of that problem. A few—RPG, some simulation languages, some auditing languages—have existed for some time. More recently, the attempts to develop easily used data inquiry languages and a more generally user-oriented environment have given real impetus to the development and use of nonprocedural languages.

Statement types in procedure-oriented compiler languages

The **procedure-oriented compiler language** differs from an assembly language in that each program statement in the procedure-oriented language is related to a procedural task and may compile as several machine language instructions. Table 9.3 restates the sample program of Tables 9.1 and 9.2. Note that the program requires only five statements, which have been placed opposite the steps in the original program that they replace. Note also that the fifth statement is a special statement whose purpose is to tell the compiler that the program is complete. Without such an ending statement, the compiler cannot complete all of its checks on program syntax (form).

Higher-level languages ease the task of writing a computer program. They speed program development and encourage programmers to pay more attention to getting a good problem solution than to writing a machine-efficient program. However, some compilers on some machines do compile slowly and do use the machine very inefficiently.

Although each compiler tends to be oriented toward a given class of

STEP	MACHINE LANGUAGE	PROCEDURAL LANGUAGE (BASIC)
1	01 0200 0002	100 READ A,B
	01 0201 0003	
2	10 0200 0004	110 LET C = A + B
3	11 0201 0005	
4	20 0202 0006	
5	06 0202 0001	120 PRINT C
		130 GO TO 100
		140 END

Table 9.3 **Machine and procedural language (BASIC) program to add pairs of numbers**

problems, the major procedural languages are general in nature and can be used to solve any problem. Obviously, each is most efficient when solving the types of problems for which it was designed. All these procedure-oriented languages perform each of the activities required for processing data. All of them therefore contain the same types of operational statements.

Input and output

Master files and transactions data must be input to storage elements of the computer to be available for processing. Input commands perform this activity. Output commands must be available so that managers and other users may obtain the results of processing. Input command words vary, but the most common are READ and INPUT. The most common output command words are PRINT and WRITE. Some languages essentially allow an entire file to be entered or outputted with one complex command.

Arithmetic computation

Languages must include commands making it possible to perform the arithmetic operations (addition, subtraction, multiplication, division, and exponentiation). All procedural languages have such capabilities.

Decision making

As noted in Chapter 7, the branch, or "transfer," commands make it possible to have the exact path of further processing depend on specified or calculated conditions. For example, the computer can decide if all items are processed or if the value of some variable is less than, equal to, or greater than some other variable or control constant. Looping instructions are another example of a specialized decision-making instruction. All higher-level procedural languages provide for looping in one or more ways. They also provide for decisions like a test for excess regular or overtime hours in a payroll program. Comparisons of alphabetic words can also be made to perform tasks such as identifying legal users of a timesharing system by name and/or password, identifying accounts by customer name, or using an alphabetic or mixed alphabetic and numeric key to arrange records in a desired order.

Other common language features

In addition to provision for input, output, arithmetic computation, and decision making (including looping), higher-level procedural languages usually contain several other common features. For example, variables usually may be called by mnemonic names, with the compiler converting these names to actual storage locations. The same generic (common) name may be assigned to a list or table of values, and provision is usually made for reserving storage space for such lists or tables when the source program is being compiled.

Provision is made for having subroutines or subprograms so that a process used several places in a program may be written once by the programmer and "called" wherever it is needed in the program. At least during development of a complex program, each module of the program can be designed as a subroutine, with the so-called main line program consisting primarily of a series of "call" statements.

Subroutines or subprograms should not be confused with mathematical functions that can be called for use at any point in a program to perform standard mathematical functions (such as extracting square root, obtaining an absolute value, or producing a random number).

Most procedural languages provide for the *exact* description of input and output records. They also require that language statements follow an exact format with spaces, commas, and symbols in an exact order in each statement line. The trend, however, is to remove such restrictions to make the programmer's job easier. Restrictions on the form of language statements and exact descriptions of data files are being eased in the new languages and in newer versions of the older languages. In BASIC, for example, statements are generally free format. The spaces between the words and symbols in the statements found in Table 9.3 are there only to make them more easily read by people. The compiler does not require them. Data to be read by BASIC programs are essentially free form, the general requirement being that data words be separated by a comma or a space. Current versions of FORTRAN also allow for inputting data files that have not been described in detail but include commas to separate data words. The standard mode of FORTRAN requires FORMAT descriptions of all input data, as will be described later.

Types of compilers

Language compilers are of two basic types. As indicated in Chapter 7, a compiler reads the source program and translates it into an object program in machine language. A "true" compiler reads the entire source program into primary memory before beginning to translate it. An interpretive compiler, or **interpreter**, translates the source program line by line as it reads it (as far as possible). A looping process, for example, cannot be completed until the end of the loop is found, but a statement to update the balance on hand by subtracting the amount ordered can be translated to machine language code immediately.

Object programs developed by true compilers are usually more efficient in use of machine time than object programs developed by interpreters. Interpreters are more useful in online program development because they immediately identify statements that are of illegal form. Neither compilers nor interpreters can catch errors in logic, however.

Some commonly available procedural languages

The procedural languages briefly described in this section are available for most large- and medium-size mainframe computer systems and for many minicomputer systems. Three of these languages, COBOL, FORTRAN, and BASIC, are also described in detail later in this chapter.

COBOL

COBOL was the first complete language developed for use in business. As its name, *CO*mmon *B*usiness-*O*riented *L*anguage, implies, COBOL is intended specifically for use in business data processing. COBOL is a file-oriented language whose structure assumes the processing of files of data to update other files and the outputting of reports and new files.

FORTRAN

The first complete compiler language, *FOR*mula *TRAN*slator was designed for use in scientific problem solving. Superficially, its processing instructions are similar to algebraic statements, but they have slightly different meanings. This remains the most popular language for scientific problem solving.

BASIC

BASIC (*B*eginners' *A*ll *P*urpose *S*ymbolic *I*nstruction *C*ode) is the most popular of the timesharing languages. It was designed to be used by students working at online terminals. Initially it was essentially a subset of FORTRAN with major omissions freeing the programmer from having to describe input and output records in detail. This is not an unmixed blessing, however, since well-organized output reports are difficult to produce using the simplest BASIC. Its biggest advantage is the ease with which it can be learned. Partly because of the interaction between the programmer and the interpreter, beginners produce complete, meaningful programs after as few as two hours of formal instruction. BASIC is available from most timesharing service bureaus and is being used in industry for both scientific problem solving and administrative data processing. Although its most common use is as a student programming language, it is gaining increasing acceptance for both scientific and business data processing. A so-called Business BASIC is available for some small business computers.

APL

Designed as a timesharing language, APL's greatest weakness for unsophisticated users is its use of mathematical notation including Greek letters. Its use requires a special terminal keyboard. It is a powerful language for scientific problem solving and has been used primarily in education and research applications. APL stands simply for A Programming Language.

PL/1

As a response to what was considered an undesirable proliferation of languages in the 1960s, PL/1 (Programming Language one) was developed at the International Business Machines Corporation and initially was available only on IBM computers. It is a very complex and sophisticated language designed to include the best features of ALGOL, COBOL, and FORTRAN. This strength is also a weakness, making PL/1 more difficult to master (or use) in its entirety than other procedure-oriented languages. One advantage of PL/1 from the user's viewpoint is the lack of rigid rules of form, so that no special coding forms are required. In response to user demand, PL/1 has been implemented on (programmed for) several computer families other than those manufactured by International Business Machines Corporation.

ALGOL

The arithmetic capabilities of ALGOL (ALGOrithmic Language) are similar in type and in operations to those of FORTRAN. ALGOL, however, is a more sophisticated mathematical language than FORTRAN. It is the most popular scientific programming language in Europe and has been used as machine language for one series of computers (Burroughs B-5000, B-5500, B-6000, B7100, B-8100).

Pascal

The Pascal language was developed by Professor Niklaus Wirth in Zurich, Switzerland, in the early 1970s. The language was intended to be efficient to implement on modern computers, to be useful in teaching the major concepts of computer programming, and to allow the development of structured programs. It is a procedure-oriented language that is applicable to a wide range of problems. Although it is most closely related to ALGOL, it does have similarities to both FORTRAN and BASIC, but has a much richer set of data types and available program statements. In this regard it is more similar to PL/1. Like PL/1 it is designed to handle problems involving numerical calculations such as those common in science and engineering and also to handle alphanumeric variables such as those encountered in business data processing. It also has file-handling and list-processing capabilities.

The major advantages for Pascal are that it is easy to learn and it is designed for structured programming. A possible disadvantage is the tighter structure it exhibits in comparison to BASIC. For example, types of variables (numeric, alphabetic, integer, and real) must be carefully defined at the beginning of the program. In addition, some symbols are used in unusual ways. To compute a value for the variable X would require a statement like this: X := A*B. The reason for using := instead of simply = is not obvious to the beginning programmer. On balance, though, the advantages it offers as a structured language definitely outweigh these minor complexities.

Nonprocedural languages

The exact number of programming languages that have been developed for different purposes is not known, but it is large. At least a score of special-purpose, or **nonprocedural languages**, are in general use. We will not attempt to identify all of them, but will give examples of major types.

RPG

As its name implies, Report Program Generator started out as a way to quickly and easily manipulate data files in order to prepare standard reports. Later extensions have expanded its capabilities, so that it is a general problem-solving language. However, it retains its report-generator origins, with three major sections in each program. The data file is described first, the necessary processing is detailed second, and the format of the output (report) is detailed in the last section. Note the similarity of this structure to the structure of COBOL. Both are business data processing languages.

Simulation Languages

The computer is a powerful simulation tool, and special-purpose languages designed to take care of the routine details and major (general) functions used in simulation are very desirable. In general, the languages provide the programmer with a set of modeling concepts (entities, events, levels, flows, and so on) by which to describe the system being simulated. These descriptions are then converted into a computer program by the language. Popular examples of system simulation languages are GPSS (General Purpose System Simulator), SIMSCRIPT, and DYNAMO.

List processing

A variety of languages have been developed that emphasize features making it possible to link up, or "chain," groups of interconnected items (lists). A "pointer" is attached to each data word or record identifying the next and/or previous item in the chain. Various ways of modifying lists are also added. These features make it possible to make chain searches of related files for information. One access of a set of files can retrieve all related facts from each file in the total set. Thus an inquiry directed initially to an inventory file to ascertain the availability of an item can obtain, in addition to the number of finished units in inventory, units in production and unfilled orders on file. The most popular languages of this type are LISP and SNOBOL.

Data management languages

In part a pragmatic development of list processing languages are the languages developed to handle large, integrated data base files. List processing languages ease the job of modifying all records in separate but integrated files. In addition, the data management languages provide automatic organization of data structures within files. (Data management languages will be discussed in detail in Chapter 14.)

Programming assistance

Computer scientists continue to work toward the goal of a computer that programs itself. At least, it is hoped that we can merely describe any problem in some simple fashion to the computer and the computer will develop a program to solve it. The special-purpose languages, in particular, are the result of efforts along this line. The ultimate goal is to allow the programmer to use natural language (English) to express problem solutions. Progress has been slowed by the ambiguities of the English language. COBOL is about as close as we've come, and it is far from the English language. A second approach has been to describe the solution procedure in a general way with flowcharts or decision tables and let the computer write the program code from this description. Work with flowcharts has not been too successful, primarily because of the difficulties of developing unambiguous input descriptions in flowchart form. Languages do exist that translate decision tables into machine code. The most widely used of these languages is called DETAB. DETAB translates decision tables into the COBOL language.

Programs do exist that develop flowcharts from source programs written in a higher-level language such as FORTRAN or COBOL. These programs can be helpful in providing documentation. However, flowcharts should be prepared *before* the program is coded, not after.

Type of program and type of language

In Chapter 7 we defined three major types of programs—operating systems, language translators, and applications programs. We found utilities, mathematical/statistical packages, and text editors in a system's program library. In this chapter we have defined four major types of programming languages—machine, assembly, procedure-oriented, and nonprocedural. Table 9.4 relates each of the program types to the language types, indicating which language type would be used in the development of each program type.

Table 9.4 clearly indicates that machine and assembly languages are not used much by the end users of computers. Applications programs, the programs written by end-users, are seldom written in machine language or assembly language. These lower-level languages are **machine-dependent** To use them efficiently requires intimate knowledge of the idiosyncrasies of the particular machine on which the program will run. The higher-level

TYPE OF PROGRAM	LANGUAGE TYPE			
	MACHINE	ASSEMBLY	PROCEDURE-ORIENTED	NONPROCEDURAL
Operating system	N	S	–	–
Utilities	S	N	–	–
Mathematical/statistical	–	N	S	–
Text editors	S	N	–	–
Language translators	N	S	–	–
Applications programs	P	S	N	N

Symbol Code: N = most usual language type
S = secondary language type
– = never or almost never use this language type
P = program "patches" are written in language type

Table 9.4 **Use of language type in creating different types of programs**

procedural and nonprocedural languages are generally **machine-independent**. That is, a program written in a higher-level language can be run on any machine for which an appropriate language translator has been written. Only minor revisions, usually in input/output statements and in some functions (random number generator, file identification, and so on), are required to run on a different computer.

Details of popular languages

The most popular and widely used procedural languages in use today are COBOL, FORTRAN, and BASIC. All these languages tend to make the program (and the programmer) machine-independent, that is, they allow the programmer to ignore (or not know) the characteristics of the specific computer on which the program will be run. Each language has been developed to meet a specific need and is therefore different from the others. The discussions below illustrate the similarities and differences of these popular languages. The same order processing program has been prepared in each of the languages so that comparisons of their characteristics are easier. Table 9.5 presents the data to be processed by the order processing programs. The languages will be discussed and illustrated in alphabetic order: BASIC, COBOL, and FORTRAN.

Table 9.6 presents the results to be obtained from running the order processing programs. These results are not printed out by the programs but are stored as files in secondary storage. An output utility was used to print out these files for reproduction here.

MASTER RECORDS

Date of Last Update	042081	032081	042081	043081	050181
Item Number	00010	00020	00030	00040	00050
Units on Hand	100	50	75	200	300
Average Cost/Unit	2.00	3.00	4.00	1.00	1.50
Units on Order	10	0	0	100	200
Units on Backorder	50	0	0	10	100
Units Received, Y-T-D	1,000	1,500	500	2,000	3,000
Value of Receipts, Y-T-D	2,000.00	4,500.00	2,000.00	2,000.00	4,500.00
Units Issued, Y-T-D	800	600	200	10	20
Value of Issues, Y-T-D	1,600.00	1,800.00	800.00	10.00	30.00
Units Returned, Y-T-D	10	20	30	5	0
Value of Returns, Y-T-D	20.00	60.00	120.00	5.00	.00
Reorder Point	70	25	50	100	200
Economic Order Quantity	500	800	100	10	100

ORDERS

DATE	ITEM NO.	UNITS	PRICE
052981	00010	50	3.00
052981	00010	20	3.00
052981	00015	10	7.00
052981	00030	10	6.50
052981	00030	20	6.50
052981	00030	50	6.50
052981	00035	100	5.50
052981	00040	300	1.75
052981	00050	100	2.25
052981	00050	200	2.25

Table 9.5 **Master records and orders to be processed by order processing programs**

BASIC

A BASIC version of the order processing program is presented in Figure 9.1, starting on page 256. Note the general organization of the program. Each program module is headed by a "remark" line which identifies the module. For example, line 100 identifies the initialization module and line 200 identifies the module to read a record from the master file. Can you see how these modules reflect the structure chart presented in Figure 8.4, page 224?

Let's look at some of the statements and see if we can understand the program.

The main control module is found in lines 40-70. Line 40 is the identifying

a. NEW MASTER FILE

Date of Last Update	052981	052981	052981	052981	052981
Item Number	00010	00020	00030	00040	00050
Units on Hand	30	50	0	0	0
Average Cost/Unit	2.00	3.00	4.00	1.00	1.50
Units on Order	510	0	100	110	300
Units on Backorder	50	0	5	110	100
Units Received, Y-T-D	1,000	1,500	500	2,000	3,000
Value of Receipts, Y-T-D	2,000.00	4,500.00	2,000.00	2,000.00	4,500.00
Units Issued, Y-T-D	870	600	275	210	320
Value of Issues, Y-T-D	1,740.00	1,800.00	1,100.00	210.00	480.00
Units Returned, Y-T-D	10	20	30	5	0
Value of Returns, Y-T-D	20.00	60.00	120.00	5.00	.00
Reorder Point	70	25	50	100	200
Economic Order Quantity	500	800	100	10	100

b. BACKORDER LIST

DATE	ITEM NO.	UNITS THIS ORDER	UNITS BACKORDERED	TOTAL BACKORDERS	TOTAL ON ORDER
052981	00030	50	5	5	100
052981	00040	300	100	110	100

c. REORDER LIST

DATE	ITEM NO.	UNITS ORDERED
052981	00010	500
052981	00030	100
052981	00040	10
052981	00050	100

d. ERROR LIST

DATE	ITEM NO.	UNITS ORDERED	PRICE PER UNIT
052981	00015	10	7.00
052981	00035	100	5.50

Table 9.6 **Results of running order processing programs**

remark and does no processing. Line 50 calls the initializing module, so we skip to line 100 which is another remark. Lines 110–160 are all alike. They each identify one of the files used by the program. Line 170 calls another subroutine (module) starting at line 200. Line 210 reads a master record. Line 220 says that if all the records have been read, we are to skip to line 240 and identify the item number as ZZZZZ. This "switch" is used later in the

(Text continues on page 258.)

Figure 9.1 **BASIC version of order processing program**

```
10 REM ******************THIS PROGRAM WILL PROCESS ORDERS AGAINST A
20 REM ******************SEQUENTIAL MASTER FILE
30 REM
40 REM *************MAIN CONTROL MODULE****************************
50 GOSUB 100
60 GOSUB 300
65 CLOSE #1,2,3,4,5,6
70 STOP
100 REM ************INITIALIZE MODULE****************************
110 DEFINE FILE #1='MASTER', ASCSEP
120 DEFINE FILE #2='ORDER', ASCSEP
130 DEFINE FILE #3='BACK', ASCSEP
140 DEFINE FILE #4='REORDER', ASCSEP
150 DEFINE FILE #5='ERROR', ASCSEP
160 DEFINE FILE #6='NEWMAST', ASCSEP
161 WRITE #3,'     BACKORDER LIST'
162 WRITE #4,'     REORDER LIST'
163 WRITE #5,'     ERROR LIST'
170 GOSUB 200
180 GOSUB 250
190 RETURN
200 REM **********************READ A RECORD FROM THE MASTER FILE***
210 READ #1,J$,I$,I1,I2,I3,I4,I5,I6,I7,I8,I9,J1,J2,J3
220 ON END #1 GOTO 240
230 GOTO 245
240 I$='ZZZZZ'
245 RETURN
250 REM ********************READ A RECORD FROM THE ORDER FILE****
260 READ #2,P$,O$,O1,O2
270 ON END #2 GOTO 290
280 GOTO 295
290 O$='ZZZZZ'
295 RETURN
300 REM ******************MATCH ITEM NUMBERS UNTIL I$ & O$ = ZZZZZ
310 IF I$<>'ZZZZZ' THEN 340
320 IF O$<>'ZZZZZ' THEN 340
330 GOTO 499
340 IF O$<I$ THEN 400
350 IF O$=I$ THEN 440
360 REM (ORDER # > MASTER #)
370 GOSUB 1000
380 GOSUB 200
390 GOTO 470
400 REM (ORDER # < MASTER #)
410 GOSUB 550
420 GOSUB 250
430 GOTO 470
440 REM (ORDER # = MASTER #)
450 GOSUB 600
460 GOSUB 250
470 GOTO 300
499 RETURN
550 REM *************ORDER ITEM # NOT ON MASTER*******************
560 WRITE #5,P$,O$,O1,O2
570 RETURN
```

```
600 REM *************PROCESS THE ORDER*****************************
610 IF I1 >= O1 THEN 640
620 GOSUB 900
630 GOTO 650
640 GOSUB 700
650 GOSUB 800
660 RETURN
700 REM *************UPDATE FOR AN ORDER**************************
710 J$=P$
720 I1=I1-O1
730 I7=I7+O1
740 I8=I8+(O1*O2)
750 RETURN
800 REM *************CHECK FOR REORDER****************************
810 W=I1+I3-I4
820 IF W<=J2 THEN GOSUB 850
830 RETURN
850 REM ************REORDER ROUTINE*********************************
860 I3=I3+J3
870 WRITE #4,P$,O$,J3
880 RETURN
900 REM ************BACKORDER THE ORDER****************************
910 B1=O1-I1
920 I4=I4+B1
925 B2=O1
930 O1=I1
940 IF I1=0 THEN 960
950 GOSUB 700
960 WRITE #3,P$,O$,B2,B1,I4,I3
970 RETURN
1000 REM **************WRITE UPDATED MASTER************************
1010 WRITE #6,J$,I$,I1,I2,I3,I4,I5,I6,I7,I8,I9,J1,J2,J3
1020 RETURN
2000 REM **************MASTER FILE FIELDS*************************
2010 REM J$=LAST UPDATE DATE
2020 REM I$=ITEM NUMBER
2030 REM I1=UNITS ON HAND
2040 REM I2=AVE. COST PER UNIT
2050 REM I3=UNITS ON ORDER
2060 REM I4=UNITS ON BACKORDER
2070 REM I5=UNITS RECEIVED YTD
2080 REM I6=VALUE OF UNITS RECEIVED YTD
2090 REM I7=UNITS ISSUED YTD
2100 REM I8=VALUE OF UNITS ISSUED YTD
2110 REM I9=UNITS RETURNED YTD
2120 REM J1=VALUE OF UNITS RETURNED YTD
2130 REM J2=REORDER POINT
2140 REM J3=ECONOMIC ORDER QUANTITY
3000 REM ****************ORDER FILE FIELDS*************************
3010 REM P$=ORDER DATE
3020 REM O$=ORDER ITEM NUMBER
3030 REM O1=ORDER UNITS
3040 REM O2=ORDER PRICE
3050 END
```

matching routine to let us know that unprocessed master records remain. If a master record were read, we would go directly to 245 and not set the no-data switch. At 245, control is returned to the calling routine. This module (subroutine) was called at line 170. Therefore, control is returned to the line after 170, or 180. Line 180 calls another subroutine (module) to read a transaction record (order). Note how closely this module (lines 250–295) parallels the module for reading the master record. At line 295, control is transferred back to line 190 (the line following the call at 180) which transfers control to line 60 which calls the first of the mainline processing modules (Match Item Numbers). Can you follow the control flow on through the program?

Look toward the end of the program starting at line 2000. This section identifies the fields (variables) on the master record. The last section starting at line 3000 identifies the contents of the order record.

Let's look at some of the logic statements. For example, line 340 says, if order item number is less than master record item number, control should be transferred to line 400. If this condition is not met (order item number is equal to or larger than master item number), statement 350 will ask if the two item numbers are equal. If so, control goes to line 440. If neither condition is true (that is, if order item number is larger than master item number), control goes to the subroutine starting at line 1000.

What about arithmetic? Line 720 says to reduce units on hand by the number of units ordered. That is, it says specifically: replace I1 (units on hand) by the amount I1 minus O1 (units on hand minus order units). Look at statement 740. What does it do? Do you see that it updates the value of units issued year-to-date?

Let's look more carefully at the input and output statements. Look at line 210 again. It says, read from file 1 a string of variables (J$,I$,I1, . . .) File 1 is identified in line 110 as the master file. Look at line 1010. The statement there says to write to file 6 a string of variables (J$,I$,I1, . . .). File 6 is identified in line 160 as 'NEWMAST', that is, the updated master file.

Figure 9.1 reveals some of the strengths and weaknesses of the BASIC language. One strength is that it is relatively easy to understand. A weakness is the way variables (data fields) must be named. Note that no data name used by the program is more than two characters in length. Numeric variables can be named with a single letter (the temporary amount W in line 810) or a letter and a digit (I1, the units on hand in the master record). Alphabetic or alphanumeric variables are named with a letter followed by a $ (see line 2010).

Given its purpose—to be used by students on an interactive timesharing system—BASIC is a workable language. It is easy to learn and not excessively complex. It has the power to handle simple processing problems well and can be used to solve complex problems. It has been extended to give it file processing and other capabilities that make it usable in business data processing. It is available on microcomputers, minicomputers, and mainframes and is quite popular.

Perhaps the biggest weakness of BASIC is that it is not designed for vigorous structured programming. Note the complexity of the calls in our simple program. A more powerful structured language would make possible a cleaner, more direct flow through the program.

COBOL

COBOL was designed specifically for use in business data processing applications and is therefore file oriented. Its structure requires the recognition of files and records as input and output structures. To illustrate the language, let's look at the COBOL version of the order processing program presented in Figure 9.2, which begins on the next page.

Every COBOL program is organized into four divisions. The *identification division* identifies the program and the programmer. This is done in lines 1 through 5 of Figure 9.2.

The second, the *environment division,* identifies the computer system or systems being used. In Figure 9.2 a Prime 550 is being used. The file structure of COBOL is first made specific in this division in the Input/Output Section (lines 10–17). The statements in lines 12–17 tell the computer that the files are being stored on a particular secondary memory device, in this case a disk drive.

The file orientation of COBOL is even more clearly apparent in the third division of the program, the *data division.* In the *file* section, each file is described in detail. Note there are really two sets of files. Described first in lines 20 through 76 are the input and output files. In lines 77 through 110, the working storage records are described. These latter records store the interim results before transferring the finished results to the output files.

It is particularly important to note how each file is described. Let's look at the description of the input master record, the old master. The file description in lines 20–24 tells us that the inventory master file contains one type of record of 80 characters. It also tells us the name of the file and that the name of the record is Master-Rec. (Note that the code FD indicates the beginning of a new file.) Master-Rec. is described in lines 25–41. Each field on the record is described independently. Note how a field description is identified by being indented and numbered 02. The total record is identified by being numbered 01. Parenthetically, if there had been two different record formats on the file, each would be identified by the 01 numbering followed by the record name.

Description of the form of each field is found in a picture (PIC) clause. For example, the date of the last inventory update is identified in line 26 as six alphanumeric characters: The X stands for an alphanumeric; the (6) says there are six of them. Contrast this to the description of units on hand in line 29. Units on hand is five numeric digits: the 9 identifies a numeric digit; the (5) says there are five of them. Consider line 30. The 9(3)V99 says this is a

(*Text continues on page* 264.)

Figure 9.2 **COBOL version of order processing program**

```
(0001)    IDENTIFICATION DIVISION.
(0002)    PROGRAM-ID.  ORDER-PROCESSING.
(0003)    AUTHOR.  GERRY MCKEAN.
(0004)    REMARKS.  THIS PROGRAM WILL PROCESS ORDERS AGAINST A
(0005)        SEQUENTIAL MASTER FILE.
(0006)    ENVIRONMENT DIVISION.
(0007)    CONFIGURATION SECTION.
(0008)    SOURCE-COMPUTER.  PRIME-550.
(0009)    OBJECT-COMPUTER.  PRIME-550.
(0010)    INPUT-OUTPUT SECTION.
(0011)    FILE-CONTROL.
(0012)        SELECT INVENTORY-MASTER ASSIGN TO PFMS.
(0013)        SELECT ORDER-FILE ASSIGN TO PFMS.
(0014)        SELECT BACKORDER-LIST ASSIGN TO PFMS.
(0015)        SELECT REORDER-LIST ASIGN TO PFMS.
(0016)        SELECT ERROR-LIST ASSIGN TO PFMS.
(0017)        SELECT UPDATED-MASTER ASSIGN TO PFMS.
(0018)    DATA DIVISION.
(0019)    FILE SECTION.
(0020)    FD  INVENTORY-MASTER
(0021)        LABEL RECORDS ARE STANDARD
(0022)        RECORD CONTAINS 80 CHARACTERS
(0023)        VALUE OF FILE-ID IS 'MASTER'
(0024)        DATA RECORD IS MASTER-REC.
(0025)    01  MASTER-REC.
(0026)        02  INV-LAST-UPDATE       PIC X(6).
(0027)        02  INV-ITEM-NO           PIC X(5).
(0028)            88  END-OF-INVENTORY-FILE VALUE HIGH-VALUES.
(0029)        02  INV-UNITS-ON-HAND     PIC 9(5).
(0030)        02  INV-AVE-COST-UNIT     PIC 9(3)V99.
(0031)        02  INV-UNITS-ON-ORDER    PIC 9(5).
(0032)        02  INV-BACKORDER-UNITS   PIC 9(5).
(0033)        02  INV-UNITS-REC-YTD     PIC 9(5).
(0034)        02  INV-VALUE-REC-YTD     PIC 9(5)V99.
(0035)        02  INV-UNITS-ISSUE-YTD   PIC 9(5).
(0036)        02  INV-VALUE-ISSUE-YTD   PIC 9(5)V99.
(0037)        02  INV-UNITS-RET-YTD     PIC 9(5).
(0038)        02  INV-VALUE-RET-YTD     PIC 9(5)V99.
(0039)        02  INV-REORDER-POINT     PIC 9(5).
(0040)        02  INV-ECONOMIC-ORDER    PIC 9(5).
(0041)        02  FILLER                PIC XXX.
(0042)    FD  ORDER-FILE
(0043)        LABEL RECORDS ARE STANDARD
(0044)        RECORD CONTAINS 21 CHARACTERS
(0045)        VALUE OF FILE-ID 'ORDER'
(0046)        DATA RECORD IS ORDER-REC.
(0047)    01  ORDER-REC.
(0048)        02  ORDER-DATE               PIC X(6).
(0049)        02  ORDER-ITEM-NO            PIC X(5).
(0050)            88  END-OF-ORDER-FILE VALUE HIGH-VALUES.
(0051)        02  ORDER-UNITS              PIC 9(5).
(0052)        02  ORDER-PRICE              PIC 9(3)V99.
(0053)    FD  BACKORDER-LIST
(0054)        LABEL RECORDS ARE STANDARD
(0055)        RECORD CONTAINS 132 CHARACTERS
```

```
(0056)          VALUE OF FILE-ID 'BACK'
(0057)          DATA RECORD IS BACKORDER-REC.
(0058)      01  BACKORDER-REC                 PIC X(132).
(0059)      FD  REORDER-LIST
(0060)          LABEL RECORDS ARE STANDARD
(0061)          RECORD CONTAINS 132 CHARACTERS
(0062)          VALUE OF FILE-ID 'REORD'
(0063)          DATA RECORD IS REORDER-REC.
(0064)      01  REORDER-REC                   PIC X(132).
(0065)      FD  ERROR-LIST
(0066)          LABEL RECORDS ARE STANDARD
(0067)          RECORD CONTAINS 132 CHARACTERS
(0068)          VALUE OF FILE-ID 'ERROR'
(0069)          DATA RECORD IS ERROR-REC.
(0070)      01  ERROR-REC                     PIC X(132).
(0071)      FD  UPDATED-MASTER
(0072)          LABEL RECORDS ARE STANDARD
(0073)          RECORD CONTAINS 80 CHARACTERS
(0074)          VALUE OF FILE-ID 'UPDATE'
(0075)          DATA RECORD IS UPDATED-REC.
(0076)      01  UPDATED-REC                   PIC X(80).
(0077)      WORKING-STORAGE SECTION.
(0078)      01  BACKORDER-DETAIL.
(0079)          02  FILLER                    PIC X(5) VALUE SPACES.
(0080)          02  BACK-DATE                 PIC X(6).
(0081)          02  FILLER                    PIC X(5) VALUE SPACES.
(0082)          02  BACK-ORDER-NO             PIC X(5).
(0083)          02  FILLER                    PIC X(5) VALUE SPACES.
(0084)          02  BACK-UNITS-ORDER          PIC ZZ,ZZZ.
(0085)          02  FILLER                    PIC X(5) VALUE SPACES.
(0086)          02  BACK-UNITS-BACKORDERED PIC ZZ,ZZZ.
(0087)          02  FILLER                    PIC X(5) VALUE SPACES.
(0088)          02  BACK-UNITS-ON-BACKORDER PIC ZZ,ZZZ.
(0089)          02  FILLER                    PIC X(5) VALUE SPACES.
(0090)          02  BACK-UNITS-ON-ORDER       PIC ZZ,ZZZ.
(0091)      01  REORDER-DETAIL.
(0092)          02  FILLER                    PIC X(5) VALUE SPACES.
(0093)          02  REORD-DATE                PIC X(6).
(0094)          02  FILLER                    PIC X(5) VALUE SPACES.
(0095)          02  REORD-ORDER-NO            PIC X(5).
(0096)          02  FILLER                    PIC X(5) VALUE SPACES.
(0097)          02  REORD-ORDER-QTY           PIC ZZ,ZZZ.
(0098)      01  ERROR-DETAIL.
(0099)          02  FILLER                    PIC X(5) VALUE SPACES.
(0100)          02  ERROR-DATE                PIC X(5).
(0101)          02  FILLER                    PIC X(5) VALUE SPACES.
(0102)          02  ERROR-ORDER-NO            PIC X(5).
(0103)          02  FILLER                    PIC X(5) VALUE SPACES.
(0104)          02  ERROR-ORDER-UNITS         PIC ZZ,ZZZ.
(0105)          02  FILLER                    PIC X(5) VALUE SPACES.
(0106)          02  ERROR-ORDER-PRICE         PIC ZZZ.ZZ.
(0107)      01  WORK-AREAS.
(0108)          02  WORK-BACKORDER-UNITS  PIC 9(5).
(0109)          02  WORK-ORDER-UNITS          PIC 9(5).
(0110)          02  WORK-UNITS-FOR-REORDER PIC 9(5)
```

```
(0111)    PROCEDURE DIVISION.
(0112)   ******************************************************************
(0113)   *               MAIN CONTROL MODULE                              *
(0114)   ******************************************************************
(0115)    MAIN-CONTROL.
(0116)        PERFORM INITIALIZE-MODULE.
(0117)        PERFORM PROCESS-ALL-ORDERS
(0118)                UNTIL END-OF-INVENTORY-FILE AND
(0119)                      END-OF-ORDER FILE.
(0120)        PERFORM TERMINATE-MODULE.
(0121)        STOP RUN.
(0122)   ******************************************************************
(0123)   *               INITIALIZE MODULE                                *
(0124)   ******************************************************************
(0125)    INITIALIZE-MODULE.
(0126)        OPEN INPUT INVENTORY-MASTER ORDER-FILE
(0127)             OUTPUT BACKORDER-LIST REORDER-LIST
(0128)                    ERROR-LIST UPDATED-MASTER.
(0129)        MOVE '       BACKORDER LIST' TO BACKORDER-REC.
(0130)        MOVE '       REORDER LIST' TO REORDER-REC.
(0131)        MOVE '       ERROR LIST' TO ERROR-REC.
(0132)        WRITE BACKORDER-REC AFTER ADVANCING PAGE.
(0133)        WRITE REORDER-REC AFTER ADVANCING PAGE.
(0134)        WRITE ERROR-REC AFTER ADVANCING PAGE.
(0135)        PERFORM READ-MASTER-FILE.
(0136)        PERFORM READ-ORDER-FILE.
(0137)   ******************************************************************
(0138)   *               READ ONE MASTER RECORD                           *
(0139)   ******************************************************************
(0140)    READ-MASTER-FILE.
(0141)        READ INVENTORY-MASTER AT END
(0142)             MOVE HIGH-VALUES TO INV-ITEM-NO.
(0143)   ******************************************************************
(0144)   *               READ ONE ORDER RECORD                            *
(0145)   ******************************************************************
(0146)    READ-ORDER-FILE.
(0147)        READ ORDER-FILE AT END
(0148)             MOVE HIGH-VALUES TO ORDER-ITEM-NO.
(0149)   ******************************************************************
(0150)   *      THIS MODULE MATCHES THE ORDER ITEM WITH THE MASTER ITEM *
(0151)   ******************************************************************
(0152)    PROCESS-ALL-ORDERS.
(0153)        IF ORDER-ITEM-NO < INV-ITEM-NO
(0154)           PERFORM ORDER-LESS-THAN-MASTER
(0155)        ELSE
(0156)           IF ORDER-ITEM-NO = INV-ITEM-NO
(0157)              PERFORM PROCESS-THE-ORDER
(0158)           ELSE
(0159)              PERFORM ORDER-GREATER-THAN-MASTER.
(0160)   ******************************************************************
(0161)   *    THIS MODULE IS ENTERED IF AN ORDER IS NOT ON THE MASTER   *
(0162)   ******************************************************************
(0163)    ORDER-LESS-THAN-MASTER.
(0164)        MOVE ORDER-DATE TO ERROR-DATE.
(0165)        MOVE ORDER-ITEM-NO TO ERROR-ORDER-NO.
```

```
(0166)         MOVE ORDER-UNITS TO ERROR-ORDER-UNITS.
(0167)         MOVE ORDER-PRICE TO ERROR-ORDER-PRICE.
(0168)         WRITE ERROR-REC FROM ERROR-DETAIL AFTER ADVANCING 2 LINES.
(0169)         PERFORM READ-ORDER-FILE.
(0170)     ****************************************************************
(0171)     *    THIS MODULE IS ENTERED TO DETERMINE IF THE MASTER FILE    *
(0172)     *         HAS ENOUGH UNITS IN INVENTORY TO FILL THE ORDER      *
(0173)     ****************************************************************
(0174)      PROCESS-THE-ORDER.
(0175)         IF INV-UNITS-ON-HAND NOT < ORDER-UNITS
(0176)            PERFORM UPDATE-FOR-AN-ORDER
(0177)         ELSE PERFORM BACKORDER-THE-ORDER.
(0178)         PERFORM CHECK-FOR-REORDER.
(0179)         PERFORM READ-ORDER-FILE.
(0180)     ****************************************************************
(0181)     *    THIS MODULE WILL UPDATE THE MASTER FILE FIELDS FOR AN     *
(0182)     *         ORDER THAT CAN BE COMPLETELY OR PARTIALLY FILLED     *
(0183)     ****************************************************************
(0184)      UPDATE-FOR-AN-ORDER.
(0185)         MOVE ORDER-DATE TO INV-LAST-UPDATE.
(0186)         SUBTRACT ORDER-UNITS FROM INV-UNITS-ON-HAND.
(0187)         ADD ORDER-UNITS TO INV-UNITS-ISSUE-YTD.
(0188)         COMPUTE INV-VALUE-ISSUE-YTD = INV-VALUE-ISSUE-YTD +
(0189)                 (ORDER-UNITS * ORDER-PRICE).
(0190)     ****************************************************************
(0191)     *    THIS MODULE WILL BACKORDER AN ORDER THAT COULD NOT BE     *
(0192)     *         COMPLETELY FILLED AND PRINT A BACK ORDER DETAIL LINE *
(0193)     ****************************************************************
(0194)      BACKORDER-THE-ORDER.
(0195)         COMPUTE WORK-BACKORDER-UNITS = ORDER-UNITS -
(0196)                 INV-UNITS-ON-HAND.
(0197)         ADD WORK-BACKORDER-UNITS TO INV-BACKORDER-UNITS.
(0198)         MOVE ORDER-UNITS TO WORK-ORDER-UNITS.
(0199)         MOVE INV-UNITS-ON-HAND TO ORDER-UNITS.
(0200)         IF INV-UNITS-ON-HAND NOT = ZERO
(0201)            PERFORM UPDATE-FOR-AN-ORDER
(0202)         ELSE NEXT SENTENCE.
(0203)         MOVE ORDER-DATE TO BACK-DATE.
(0204)         MOVE ORDER-ITEM-NO TO BACK-ORDER-NO.
(0205)         MOVE WORK-ORDER-UNITS TO BACK-UNITS-ORDER.
(0206)         MOVE WORK-BACKORDER-UNITS TO BACK-UNITS-BACKORDERED.
(0207)         MOVE INV-BACKORDER-UNITS TO BACK-UNITS-ON-BACKORDER.
(0208)         MOVE INV-UNITS-ON-ORDER TO BACK-UNITS-ON-ORDER.
(0209)         WRITE BACKORDER-REC FROM BACKORDER-DETAIL
(0210)                 AFTER ADVANCING 2 LINES.
(0211)     ***************************************************************
(0212)     *   THIS MODULE WILL CHECK TO SEE IF A REORDER IS NECESSARY *
(0213)     *        AND PRINT A REORDER DETAIL                          *
(0214)     ***************************************************************
(0215)      CHECK-FOR-REORDER.
(0216)         COMPUTE WORK-UNITS-FOR-REORDER = INV-UNITS-ON-HAND +
(0217)                 INV-UNITS-ON-ORDER - INV-BACKORDER-UNITS.
(0218)         IF WORK-UNITS-FOR-REORDER NOT > INV-REORDER-POINT
(0219)            PERFORM REORDER-ROUTINE
(0220)         ELSE NEXT SENTENCE.
```

```
(0221)     *****************************************************************
(0222)     *  THIS MODULE WILL UPDATE THE UNITS ORDERED BY THE              *
(0223)     *       ECONOMIC ORDER QUANTITY AND PRINT A REORDER DETAIL*
(0224)     *****************************************************************
(0225)      REORDER-ROUTINE.
(0226)          ADD INV-ECONOMIC-ORDER TO INV-UNITS-ON-ORDER.
(0227)          MOVE ORDER-DATE TO REORD-DATE.
(0228)          MOVE ORDER-ITEM-NO TO REORD-ORDER-NO.
(0229)          MOVE INV-ECONOMIC-ORDER TO REORD-ORDER-QTY.
(0230)          WRITE REORDER-REC FROM REORDER-DETAIL
(0231)                AFTER ADVANCING 2 LINES.
(0232)     *****************************************************************
(0233)     *  THIS MODULE WILL WRITE AN UPDATED MASTER RECORD TO THE *
(0234)     *       NEW MASTER FILE                                          *
(0235)     *****************************************************************
(0236)      ORDER-GREATER-THAN-MASTER.
(0237)          WRITE UPDATED-REC FROM MASTER-REC.
(0238)          PERFORM READ-MASTER-FILE.
(0239)     *****************************************************************
(0240)     *             TERMINATE MODULE                                   *
(0241)     *****************************************************************
(0242)      TERMINATE-MODULE.
(0243)          CLOSE INVENTORY-MASTER ORDER-FILE.
(0244)          CLOSE BACKORDER-LIST REORDER-LIST ERROR-LIST.
(0245)          CLOSE UPDATED-MASTER.
```

five-digit number with two decimal places. In other words, average cost per unit will not exceed $999.99. Compare the descriptions in these lines to the field values shown on the master records in Table 9.5 on page 254. Do they match up for you? They should.

Only one line in the description of the master record is unexplained. That is line 28 which starts with 88 and is indented under INV-ITEM-NO. Can you guess what it means? It obviously refers to the item number on the record. It also seems to apply only when the end of the file has been reached, that is, when all of the records have been read. It means that the highest-possible value of five characters will be inserted into this field when the end of file is encountered. The end of file is a special character placed at the end of the file on the file device on which the master file is stored. So line 28 merely does the same thing that lines 220 and 240 did in the BASIC program in Figure 9.1, where ZZZZZ is loaded into the item number after the last master record is processed. Note how line 50 does this same thing to order item number at the end of the order file.

Can you understand the description of the order file in lines 42–52? It describes the form of the order records shown in Table 9.5.

The description of the output files occurs in lines 53–76. Note how they each contain only one picture clause which merely reserves space for the entire record. The detailed description of each of these records is accomplished in either an input record description or a working-storage record description. There is no need to repeat the detailed descriptions in these cases.

But what about the picture (PIC) clauses for the working storage files? Some of them look different. For instance, lines 79, 81, 83, and so on, are all identified as FILLER. This means they are empty spaces. But what about line 84? The picture there is ZZ,ZZZ. This merely means that the maximum value of the number of units back ordered on this order is 99,999 and that if it is printed out, the comma will be there if the number is 1,000 or larger. Note how the decimal point is indicated in line 106. You should take a minute to compare how the descriptions of the files for backorders, reorders, and errors describe the output shown in Table 9.6.

The working part of the COBOL program starts on line 111. The *procedure division* is the processing part of the program. Note how headings have been inserted to identify each module. These headings are identified as nonoperable remarks by the beginning asterisk. Let's examine a few modules to see what they do.

First, the main control module. The module is identified to the COBOL compiler as the paragraph in lines 115–121. The paragraph is named for reference purposes on line 115. Each major submodule is called by the PERFORM statements on lines 116, 117–119, and 120. Note how the PERFORM calls a named paragraph. For example, line 116 calls the initialize module starting on line 125.

The initialize module starts by opening the input and output files. This instruction causes the compiler to locate these files in the secondary storage and makes them available to be read from (files identified as INPUT) or written to (files identified as OUTPUT). But what about the MOVE commands in lines 129–131? A MOVE command merely transfers a value from one location (variable) to another without destroying the content of the first location.

The sentence-paragraph structure of COBOL is particularly apparent in the procedure division. Each module is a named paragraph made up of sentences. The purpose of each paragraph is obvious to the careful reader.

A major strength of COBOL should now be clear. It is largely a self-documenting language. The identification and environment divisions identify the broad purpose of the program and specify the computer on which it will run and the file storage devices involved. The data division describes the input, output, and working storage records used. The procedure division describes the processing in an English-like language.

The weaknesses of COBOL can also be seen in Figure 9.2. A COBOL program is very structured; COBOL is highly inflexible in form. As much or more effort seems to go into description and form as into identification of the processing logic. Note that the first 110 lines are all descriptive and lines 111–218 describe the processing. If the fancy module naming were changed to one-line remarks, the procedure division would shrink by 22 lines and be only 96 lines in length, 14 lines shorter than the descriptive parts of the program.

FORTRAN

As indicated earlier, FORTRAN was developed to handle scientific problems. Like BASIC, which was initially developed from it, the processing statements in FORTRAN have a pseudomathematical appearance. The FORTRAN version of our order processing program appears in Figure 9.3, beginning on page 268. Comments (the lines beginning with the character C) have been used liberally to identify the parts of the program. Even so, the program is harder to follow than either the COBOL or BASIC version. This is due, in part, to the fact that FORTRAN is not intended to be a file processing language. It was developed assuming that a single data file was to be processed through one or more computational formulas. Look at the Set Up and Housekeeping section. These are all comments and do not define these files to the program. Note lines 100–180. These are FORMAT statements to be used in defining the form of input or output. Line 100 is to be used in reading a master record. It defines a master record as consisting of:

I6—a six-digit integer number (I means "integer")
I5—a five-digit integer number
I5—a second five-digit integer number
F5.2—a five-digit number with two decimal places (F means "floating point")
I5 (3 times)—three more five-digit integer numbers
F7.2—a seven-digit number with two decimal places
I5, F7.2 (twice)—two sets of a five-digit integer and a seven-digit, two-decimal number
I5 (twice)—two more five-digit integers

Check this description against the master record data in Table 9.5 (page 254). Do you see the correspondence? Line 110 is a similar description of the order record. Can you correlate it to the order data in Table 9.5?

The remainder of the FORMAT statements apply to output lines as follows:

Line	What it Does
120	Describes a backorder list line
130	Describes a reorder list line
140	Describes an error list line
150	The updated master record (compare this to 100)
160	A title for the backorder list
170	A title for the reorder list
180	A title for the error list

Compare lines 100 and 120. Note the 0 at the start of the description in 120. This is a carriage control that shifts to the next line before writing. The 1 in lines 160–180 causes a double space before printing the line. The three WRITE commands following line 180 write the headings (titles) on the backorder, reorder, and error files. Note that they are not numbered. Lines need not be numbered in FORTRAN unless they are referred to elsewhere in the program.

To illustrate the use of the FORMAT statement more fully, refer to the first READ command in the module, Read First Record From Both Files. It says, read from input device 5, the master file, using FORMAT 100, the named variables. If the end of file is encountered, go to statement 210. Line 220 reads the order record described in line 110 and goes to 230 if an end of file is encountered. Lines 210 and 230 set dummy variables to particular values and load 99999 as the item number for each record. These values are used to cause the program to transfer any remaining master records to the updated master after the last order is processed.

Let's look at some of the processing statements. Statements 210 and 230 look very much like their counterparts in BASIC. The content of the location identified on the left of the equal sign is to be replaced by the value of what follows the equal sign. Look at the first operable statement following line 600:

```
KBACKU = IOUNIT - IMUNIT
```

This statement causes the backorder amount for this order to be defined as the order amount minus the units on hand.

What about the decision-making statements? Line 300 says if I1 is not equal to 1, control is to go to 310. If this switch is equal to 1, then the last master record has been read and a test must be made to see if all orders have been read.

FORTRAN is harder to use with files than either BASIC or COBOL. Note also that the program in Figure 9.3 is less straightforward than the other two programs. To use subroutines in FORTRAN is more difficult because variables are defined separately in each subroutine. Any variables sent from the main program must be specifically transferred to the subroutine. On return, the variables are in effect redefined back to the main program. This is a confusing and tedious process. We chose not to use subroutines in this simple program.

FORTRAN is a good language if a single data set is to be processed through a set of computational routines. It is widely available. Compilers exist for almost every mainframe and minicomputer and most microcomputers. FORTRAN is not widely used for business data processing because of its structure. It is true, however, that versions of FORTRAN are now available that allow fairly efficient file handling and a more structured program design. With these modifications, FORTRAN is expected to continue to be widely used for all types of problems.

Choosing a programming language

As noted, four classes of programming languages can be identified: machine language, assembly language, procedure-oriented higher-level language,

(Text continues on page 270.)

Figure 9.3 **FORTRAN version of order processing program**

```
C     ************************************************************
C     *        THIS PROGRAM WILL PROCESS ORDERS AGAINST A        *
C     *        SEQUENTIAL MASTER FILE                            *
C     ************************************************************
C
C     ************************************************************
C     *         SET UP AND HOUSEKEEPING                          *
C     ************************************************************
C              FILE 5 = MASTER
C              FILE 6 = ORDER
C              FILE 7 = BACKORDER LIST
C              FILE 8 = REORDER LIST
C              FILE 9 = ERROR LIST
C              FILE 10= UPDATED MASTER
      I1=0
      I2=0
  100 FORMAT(I6,I5,I5,F5.2,I5,I5,I5,F7.2,I5,F7.2,I5,F7.2,I5,I5)
  110 FORMAT(I6,I5,I5,F5.2)
  120 FORMAT('0',5X,I6,5X,I5,5X,I5,5X,I5,5X,I5,5X,I5)
  130 FORMAT('0',5X,I6,5X,I5,10X,I5)
  140 FORMAT('0',5X,I6,5X,I5,5X,I5,5X,F5.2)
  150 FORMAT(I6,I5,I5,F5.2,I5,I5,I5,F7.2,I5,F7.2,I5,F7.2,I5,I5)
  160 FORMAT('1',10X,'BACKORDER LISTING')
  170 FORMAT('1',10X,'REORDER LIST')
  180 FORMAT('1',10X,'ERROR LIST')
      WRITE(7,160)
      WRITE(8,170)
      WRITE(9,180)
C
C     ************************************************************
C     *        READ FIRST RECORD FROM BOTH FILES                 *
C     ************************************************************
      READ(5,100,END=210) IMDATE,IMITEM,IMUNIT,FMCOST,IMORD,IMBACK,
     1IMRECU,FMRECV,IMISSU,FMISSV,IMRETU,FMRETV,IMREPT,IMORDQ
      GO TO 220
  210 I1=1
      IMITEM=99999
  220 READ(6,110,END=230) IODATE,IOITEM,IOUNIT,FOPRIC
      GO TO 300
  230 I2=1
      IOITEM=99999
C
C     ************************************************************
C     *            START OF MAIN LOOP                            *
C     ************************************************************
  300 IF (I1.NE.1) GO TO 310
      IF (I2.NE.1) GO TO 310
      GO TO 1000
  310 IF (IOITEM.LT.IMITEM) GO TO 500
      IF (IOITEM.EQ.IMITEM) GO TO 600
C     ************************************************************
C     *          ORDER # > MASTER #                              *
C     ************************************************************
      WRITE(10,150) IMDATE,IMITEM,IMUNIT,FMCOST,IMORD,IMBACK,IMRECU,
     1IFMRECV,IMISSU,FMISSV,IMRETU,FMRETV,IMREPT,IMORDQ
```

```
      READ(5,100,END=400) IMDATE,IMITEM,IMUNIT,FMCOST,IMORD,IMBACK,
     1IMRECU,FMRECV,IMISSU,FMISSV,IMRETU,FMRETV,IMREPT,IMORDQ
      GO TO 410
  400 I1=1
      IMITEM=99999
  410 GO TO 300
C     ******************************************************************
C     *     ORDER # < MASTER # - ERROR - ORDER NOT ON MASTER           *
C     ******************************************************************
  500 WRITE(9,140) IODATE,IOITEM,IOUNIT,FOPRIC
      READ(6,100,END=510) IODATE,IOITEM,IOUNIT,FOPRIC
      GO TO 520
  510 I2-1
      IOITEM=99999
  520 GO TO 300
C     ******************************************************************
C     *        ORDER # > MASTER # - PROCESS THE ORDER                  *
C     ******************************************************************
  600 IF (IMUNIT.GE.IOUNIT) GO TO 700
C     *        BACKORDER ROUTINE                                       *
      KBACKU=IOUNIT - IMUNIT
      IMBACK=IMBACK + KBACKU
      KSAVU=IOUNIT
      IOUNIT=IMUNIT
      WRITE(7,120) IODATE,IOITEM,KSAVU,KBACKU,IMBACK,IMORD
      IF (IMUNIT.EQ.0) GO TO 800
C     ******************************************************************
C     *        UPDATE FOR AN ORDER                                     *
C     ******************************************************************
  700 IMDATE=IODATE
      IMUNIT=IMUNIT - IOUNIT
      IMISSU=IMISSU + IOUNIT
      FMISSV=FMISSV + (IOUNIT * FOPRIC)
C     ******************************************************************
C     *        CHECK FOR REORDER                                       *
C     ******************************************************************
  800 KORDER=IMUNIT + IMORD - IMBACK
      IF (KORDER.LE.IMREPT) GOT TO 860
      GO TO 870
C     ******************************************************************
C     *        REORDER ROUTINE                                         *
C     ******************************************************************
  860 IMORD=IMORD + IMORDQ
      WRITE(8,130) IODATE,IOITEM,IMORDQ
  870 READ(6,110,END=880) IODATE,IOITEM,IOUNIT,FOPRIC
      GO TO 890
  880 I2=1
      IOITEM=99999
  890 GO TO 300
 1000 STOP
      END
```

and nonprocedural higher-level language. Each computer system has its own machine language. Except for limited "computer families," machine languages differ for each computer. Assembly language instructions usually bear a one-to-one relationship to machine language instructions, so they also differ from machine to machine, but they still have a great deal of similarity. In part, this is because machine language has tended to become more standardized. The higher-level languages are supposedly machine-independent, but do vary slightly from computer to computer, particularly in handling input and output. In addition, there are many candidates available as procedure-oriented higher-level languages. The purpose of this section is to guide the user through the maze to a suitable program-language match. (Note that we said *suitable,* not *optimal.*)

Considerations for assembly language

Assembly language has two levels. Assembly languages require, in general, that each assembly language instruction be assembled as a single machine language instruction. However, most assembly languages have been extended to include macroinstructions. Even so, all assembly languages are machine-dependent, generally indicating machine operations mnemonically and using symbolic machine addresses in each instruction. Like machine languages they tend to be detailed and arbitrary and therefore hard to learn. Program coding in assembly language tends to be a slow, tedious, and error-prone process. The programs are hard to read, so that program maintenance is difficult. However, assembly language programs can be more easily made machine-efficient. That is, they can be made to perform the required machine operations with a minimum of CPU time and with a minimum amount of total machine language (object) code.

Problems of any type of complexity can be coded in assembly language. The flexibility of the language is limited only by the architecture of the machine being used. Complex programs, however, are time-consuming to write and debug in assembly language. Assembly languages tend to be used to produce input/output and other data-handling utility programs. Compilers, timesharing executives, and most instantaneous-response systems also are written in assembly language. Production programs that require frequent and lengthy machine runs are sometimes written in assembly language, although most application programs are written in a higher-level language.

Considerations for procedure-oriented languages

These languages allow the user to prepare the program in a language procedurally oriented to the problem being solved. They are generally easier to learn and easier to use than assembly language. Programs can usually be developed and debugged with less effort. Maintenance is easier because the programs are easier to read and understand; that is, the higher-level languages are more self-documenting. Although any problem can be programmed in any procedure-oriented higher-level language, each language tends to favor particular problem types. COBOL is a business data processing language, FORTRAN and ALGOL are designed for scientific problem solving, and PL/1 contains elements of all three, including elementary list processing. PL/1, however, seems biased toward scientific rather than business problems. It looks more like FORTRAN or ALGOL than like COBOL.

Special problems arise with procedure-oriented languages. The compilers that convert the source programs to object code cannot be expected to produce optimal object code for all source programs. Object programs tend to be longer and to use more computer time than programs developed in assembly language to do the same job. In addition, some compilers can be quite slow at compiling the object code, particularly those compilers that attempt to optimize the object code. The additional machine time required to compile and execute the programs and the additional storage required to hold the additional object code are costs to offset against the lower costs of program development and maintenance.

Higher-level languages obviously are preferable to assembly language for programs that are to be run only once or at infrequent intervals. They, obviously, are favored by problem solvers who are *not* professional programmers but have a need to program. Most applications programming, even by professional programmers, is performed in higher-level languages. However, only when higher-level languages produce machine code approaching assembly language code in efficiency of machine use will the use of assembly languages for production programs completely disappear.

Considerations for nonprocedural languages

These special-purpose languages have the characteristics of procedure-oriented languages except for the limited scope of the problems they can be used on. They are, relatively, easier to learn and easier to use. They are also as easy to read as procedural languages and more self-documenting.

Criteria for language selection

The above discussions indicate the following criteria as appropriate for guiding language selection for a computer installation and for a particular programming problem. In each case, the object is to choose the language that will do the job at the least cost *in the long run.*

Language selection for a computer installation

To make a higher-level language available to programmers at a particular installation requires the acquisition (rent, purchase, or on-site development) of supporting software (assembler or compiler, manuals, and so on) and maintenance of that software. Factors to consider in justifying costs of these requirements include:

1. The type of problems being handled (number and frequency of programs of each type)
2. The cost of the software alternatives
3. The maintenance provided by the supplier, including the handling of any future changes in the language
4. Cost and availability of programmer training in the language
5. The efficiency of the compiler or assembler as evidenced by
   - a Satisfaction expressed by previous users
   - b Compilation speed
   - c Object code efficiency (run time and number of instructions in the object program)
6. Special hardware required to use the language efficiently, including costs of acquisition and of maintenance
7. The likelihood of a future change in hardware that could require machine-dependent programs to be rewritten

In general, the languages chosen for use in a computer installation will be determined by the major jobs to be accomplished. For example, assume a procedure-oriented data processing language, a simulation language, and a data management language are to be chosen. The languages in each of these three categories available for the computer system being used and capable of handling the work in each area must then be compared. Cost of acquisition and maintenance of each language, amount of programmer training required, cost of training programmers, the efficiency of each compiler available for the hardware in use, and costs for any additional hardware must be determined for each alternative. After all costs for each language alternative have been summed, the prime candidate is determined. If the prime candidate does not commit the installation to a language likely to become obsolete soon enough that the cost of the programming cannot be recaptured, that language should be chosen. Higher-level languages are less likely to be outdated by new hardware developments.

Language selection for a particular problem

In addition to the above factors influencing language selection for an installation, language selection for a specific problem should consider the following:

1. Programming skills available
2. Frequency of use of the finished program
3. Time available for program development

Choice of a language for a particular problem is simpler than choice of language for an installation. Higher-level languages that reduce program development effort are preferred for complex one-shot programs. Assembly languages can become competitive when jobs are run frequently and require a great deal of computer time and are usually preferred for developing utilities and other basic system software. However, a change in hardware can force reprogramming of jobs written in assembly language. A higher-level language procedurally oriented to the specific problem is usually the best choice.

Summary

A computer program consists of a set of instructions for accomplishing a particular task. Programs may be written in a machine language, an assembly language, or a compiler language. The computer directly executes only machine language. Programs written in an assembler or a compiler language (source program) must be translated into a machine language program (object program) by the assembler or compiler. Assemblers and compilers are programs that accept source programs as data and convert them to machine language for machine execution. Although procedure-oriented compiler languages differ in orientation, all must provide for input, output, and processing (arithmetic and data transfer, transfer of control for decision making, looping, and subroutines). Machine and assembly languages reflect the characteristics of the specific computer on which they are used. They are therefore more detailed and harder to learn and use than higher-level languages but tend to produce more machine-efficient object code. Higher-level languages have been developed to allow the user to concentrate on the problem without regard to the idiosyncrasies of the specific computer being used. They are usually not completely machine-independent, however, particularly with regard to input and output processes. Higher-level languages are preferred to prevent future reprogramming because of a change in hardware. Most applications programs are written in higher-level languages. Assembly language is still used for some frequently used or lengthy production programs and in preparing basic system software. Costs of program development effort, compilation, and operating runs must be considered in determining language selection. Programming skills on hand and time available for program development can influence choice of language for programming particular problems.

Key terms

Define the following terms as briefly as possible and then, in a short paragraph, clarify each definition.

Assembler
Assembly language
Compiler
Interpreter

Machine-dependent
Machine-independent
Machine language
Macroinstructions
Nonprocedural language
Object program
Procedure-oriented compiler language
Routine
Source program

Discussion questions

1 When should machine language be used for programming?
2 When should a procedure-oriented compiler language be used for programming?
3 When should a nonprocedural compiler language be used for programming?
4 What were called branch commands in this chapter have also been called conditional transfer commands. Justify the use of the latter term.
5 What three factors measure compiler efficiency?
6 Compilers furnished with several computer systems are imbedded in the hardware. That is, the compiler is executed by use of microprogrammed hardware instructions instead of being composed of the usual software assembly language instructions. What do you think the advantages and disadvantages of such a compiler would be?
7 Prepare a table ranking assembly language, procedure-oriented higher-level language, and nonprocedural higher-level language on each of the following factors (use 1 for best, 3 for worst of each factor):
  a Ease of learning
  b Ease of program development
  c Ease of debug
  d Ease of maintenance
8 Refer to the table prepared for question 7. What general conclusions can you draw from it?
9 What are the major differences between assemblers and compilers?
10 List the criteria for selection of a programming language. Briefly discuss each criterion, indicating what the criterion measures and its importance relative to the other criteria.
11 a Do you think a top manager of even a small firm should be expected to write programs? Explain.
  b If a top manager were to write programs, what kind of language should he or she use? Explain.
12 If programmer time is relatively more expensive than computer time, why are machine language and assembler language ever used?
13 Under what conditions would *all* computer programs in all installations be written in a higher-level, nonprocedural language?
14 Compare an interpreter and a regular compiler.

15 Compare BASIC and FORTRAN as programming languages. What are their similarities? How do they differ?
16 Compare COBOL and FORTRAN as programming languages. What are their similarities? How do they differ?

Exercises

1 The E-Z Sales Corporation sells industrial equipment. The company handles about 1,000 items used in precision manufacture. E-Z employs 20 salespersons to serve about 300 customers. Annual sales approximate $400 million. For each problem described below, state whether E-Z should use (1) machine language, (2) assembly language, (3) a higher-level procedure-oriented compiler language, or (4) a nonprocedural compiler language to prepare the program required. Briefly justify your choice in each case.
   a A weekly sales analysis report is needed to provide control by salesperson and by product group.
   b A quarterly sales analysis report is needed to provide control over individual salesperson and individual product by customer, and individual customer control as well (trends and other time patterns, unusually large or small sales, comparison to year ago, previous quarter and so on).
   c An analysis is needed to provide guidelines for locating two new sales territories and the realignment of existing sales territories.
   d The board of directors has asked the director of corporate research to define the relationship of the company to the total economy.
   e The controller has asked for a new credit and prepayment discount control system to provide control over the issuance of credit and to provide information on the effects on profit of cash and early-payment discounts. (An early-payment discount is a reduction in the amount owed by a customer which is given if the customer pays for the items within a specified time period.)
   f The company is developing an online inventory accounting and control system featuring automatic reordering in economic lot sizes, which are to be recomputed with current prices on at least a weekly basis as items are ordered.
2 Refer to the HFM Hardware Chain described in Exercise 5 of Chapter 7 (page 210) and specify the language you would suggest be used in developing the program(s) required to build an inventory accounting and control system for HFM. Briefly justify your choice.
3 Refer to the auto parts wholesaler of Exercise 2 and Chapter 5 (page 124) and specify the language you would suggest for building an online, interactive inventory accounting and control system for this wholesaler. Briefly justify your choice.

A Common Language for Computers

The data processing industry has long searched for a standard programming language for giving a computer the instructions to do a job. Because there is no such language today, a program written for one computer will not easily run on another model, so a second version of the program has to be written, duplicating costly software efforts. But help may be on the way—and from the Defense Dept., of all places.

A new standardized language called Ada is in the final stages of development for the Pentagon. Overwhelmed by the surge in the number of programming languages, the department discovered that an amazing 500 different types were being used for its computers. "Right now we have the Tower of Babel," admits Air Force Lieutenant Colonel Lawrence E. Druffel, director of Defense's Ada program office. The Pentagon, which now purchases some $4.5 billion worth of software annually, could begin buying programs in Ada by late 1982. Ultimately, the department is expected to require all of its software to be written in Ada.

The computer industry will move even faster. "There will be even more business in the commercial field than in the military," declares William H. Stevens, a marketing manager for Intel Corp., which has already chosen Ada as the primary language for its powerful new micromainframe computer (BW—Mar. 2). Although programmers will not have all the tools necessary to really begin using the new language for at least another year, 20% of the estimated $8.5 billion worth of software that will be sold worldwide in 1985 will be written in Ada, says George A. Heidenrich, a planning director in Saddle Brook, N.J., for Input, a California market researcher.

The race is on

The reason for such momentous growth is simple. "Our customers look at Ada as a way to reduce dramatically their software costs," says Intel's Stevens. The new language has features that will significantly increase the productivity of computer programmers. This in turn will slash software costs, and it also promises to ease the program-writing bottleneck that is now slowing the computer industry's momentum (BW—Sept. 1).

To meet the expected demand, Intel and dozens of other computer makers are racing to offer the required tools—compilers, editors, and analyzers, for example—needed by customers to write programs in

---

Source: "A Common Language for Computers," from the March 23, 1981 issue of *Business Week,* 84B, 84E.

Ada for their equipment. SofTech Inc., a Waltham (Mass.) company developing Ada compilers for the Defense Dept., expects to offer a commerical version in 1983. But TeleSoftware Inc., a startup software company in San Diego, boasts that in June it will begin selling the first Ada compiler, a product that enables a computer to understand the language.

Many computer users, in fact, are not even waiting for the necessary tools to be developed. For example, a number of Intel's customers are already busy using the new language for preliminary software design in such applications as industrial automation and process control. General Electric Co. may have consumer products such as microwave ovens, with the program for their microcomputers written in Ada, on the market as early as 1983, a research engineer at the company predicts. And Lee S. Maclaren, a software engineer at Boeing Co., says that within a few years "nearly all our new software—up to 90%—will be written in Ada."

Poetic beginning

Ada is the latest of what the data processing industry calls high-level languages. It was named after Augusta Ada Byron—the daughter of poet Lord Byron—who is credited with being the first computer programmer. The most widely used high-level languages are Fortran, Cobol, and Basic, and they all make it easier to program computers because they employ English-like commands instead of the esoteric and complex numeric codes that early computers "understood."

Unlike other high-level languages that work best for particular applications, Ada can be used for a wide variety of business or scientific tasks. "Ada combines the best points of the languages developed over the past 10 to 15 years," explains Patricia L. Eddy, manager of software technology in the Defense Systems Div. of Sperry Corp.'s Univac Div.

One key advantage that Ada has over any previous languages is its modularity. Programs can be broken into blocks or packages to make them easier to write; then they can be easily reassembled. Software users will also be able to build a library of basic blocks and reuse them, cutting software development costs. "Once a library is built up, it may only take the addition of 10% to 15% new work to finish many programs," says Warren J. O'Buch, president of TeleSoftware.

Key pentagon role

Ada is not the first example of a standard high-level language that has been promoted in the computer industry, but earlier attempts fared about as well as did the long effort to make Esperanto the world's universal human language. Ada will succeed, according to its many advocates, primarily because of the Penagon's backing. The government will spend nearly $20 million by the time Ada is finished—an investment that would normally come out of industry's pocket. "One reason I think Ada will have wide commercial applications is that the government is spending the money to develop a full line of support tools," says H. Gregory Schmitz, Ada program manager at Honeywell Inc. The company's French associate, CII-Honeywell Bull, developed Ada.

The Pentagon's urgent desire to standardize also will play a big role in popularizing Ada. Other recent high-level languages, such as Pascal (BW—April 23, 1979), that also promise substantial savings in programming time have not had such discipline imposed. They all exist in many incompatible versions, or dialects, which has scuttled any hopes of standardization. "I can't think of a stronger motivating force than the Defense Dept., and this may be Ada's most important feature of all," says Ruth A. Maulucci, president of her own Hudson (Mass.) computer consulting firm.

There are some software experts in the industry, however, who question the entire Ada project, partly, perhaps, because of the possible market dislocations that a standard software language could bring. "Standardization like this won't help because it takes a tremendous amount of retraining of programmers," argues John W. Backus, a research fellow at International Business Machine Corp.'s San Jose (Calif.) laboratory who headed the design team that developed the highly successful scientific language Fortran more than 20 years ago.

Another drawback, according to some, is that Ada has a larger variety of commands than do other high-level languages. Backus warns that Ada is so complex that "it might sink of its own weight." Ronald F. Hudler, general director of the systems development group at General Motors Corp., agrees: "We keep looking for a miracle [language], but we haven't found one. Ada isn't it."

European enthusiasm

One obstacle that will undoubtedly stop any universal move to Ada is the tremendous investment by business computer users in software written in other languages, primarily Fortran and Cobol, a specialized business language. For that reason, Ada will probably be employed only for new software in the coming years, primarily by minicomputer and microcomputer users who have not yet established a large library of programs.

Over the long run, though, Ada backers believe that their language will win out. "Ultimately, Ada will replace both Fortran and Cobol," declares Jean Ichbiah, who headed the CII-Honeywell Bull team that designed Ada. "There is not one thing Fortran does that Ada does not do better," he claims.

In fact, perhaps because many European nations regard Ada as a European language, it seems to be catching on faster in that commerical market than in the U.S. The European Community has awarded two contracts to develop Ada compilers and is considering designating Ada as its standard industrial process control language. For that reason, TeleSoftware expects to reap 40% of its Ada business from Europe.

U.S. observers predict, however, that it will not be long before American companies recognize Ada's superior features and adopt the new language for widespread commercial use. Says Intel's Stevens: "They are worried that, if they don't get on the bandwagon now with Ada, their competition will have a major cost advantage."

Chapter 10 Structured Design and Structured Programming

Outline

The **structured approach** to program development consists of using three specific techniques, top-down design, structured programming, and structured walkthroughs. When applied with understanding, these techniques have been widely acclaimed for improving programmer productivity, for increasing the chances of obtaining a working program, for making program maintenance easier, and for providing better control over the programming function. These gains are not solely due to the three techniques; they reflect the introduction of a systematic approach to the planning and execution of the program development process. The three basic techniques are only techniques. Applied without understanding, their use cannot guarantee such improvement.

Programming can be defined as the design and development of computer programs. Structured programming, then, is the design and development of computer programs following a prescribed pattern and with restrictions on allowable module design and allowable program logic structures. That is not, however, a very illuminating definition; it is the purpose of this chapter to make it understandable. To do so, we will explain the three techniques and the logic underlying them. We will show, also, how they interact to produce workable, maintainable programs that do what the user wants with a reasonable outlay of time and energy.

We should emphasize that we are striving for a **proper program**. A proper program has four important characteristics:

1 One entry point
2 One exit point
3 No unreachable code
4 No infinite loops

Structured programming is specifically designed to develop proper programs.

Top-down design

The major goal of **top-down design** is to obtain a program structure that is clear and easy to follow. Ideal structure will also reduce the size of complex programs. Because the program is easy to follow, debugging and maintenance are improved, and program development costs are reduced.

We were introduced to the process of top-down design in Chapter 8. We will now see the design in operation.

Control structure

The control structures used in top-down design, as we saw in Chapter 8, are the main control module, the control and processing modules, and the processing modules of the structure chart. Because all are types of modules, let us look at the module concept in more detail before we explain how to create each of these types.

The module concept

A program is a self-contained set of code that accomplishes a complete major task. It usually consists of several modules, each of which is an independent set of code for accomplishing a specific subtask. The concept of modules predates the concepts of top-down design, structured programming, and structured walkthroughs. Good programmers have always applied a modular approach to the task of program development. Basically, it consists of dividing the program into a set of logical subtasks, each of which can be attacked independently. In this way, a large complex task can be separated into a set of subtasks, logically simpler and therefore easier to develop and implement.

Advantages of modules The advantages of using the modular approach are as follows:

1 It simplifies design, making the program easier to maintain or modify.

For example, when preparing the order processing program of the previous chapter, it is easier to understand the module that checks for available inventory to fill an order than it is to envision the entire program.

2 It allows a large program to be worked on simultaneously by several people, thus making it possible to speed up program development by assigning more resources to the project.

This, of course, is limited by the number of modules that can be worked on simultaneously. Obviously, the more modules there are that interact with one another, the harder it is for different people to work on them. An obvious goal, then, is to design modules so that they interact as little as possible.

3 It provides a framework for more effective measurement of progress and for more complete testing of the program.

It is easier to finish and thoroughly test a module than it is to finish and test a complete program. If the modules are developed and tested in top-down order, the program is completely developed and tested when the last module is working.

4 It encourages the development of a library of commonly used routines.

When a program is broken down into modules, it becomes obvious that some modules are repeated in different parts of the program. It is also obvious that different programs contain very similar, if not the same, modules.

5 It simplifies design, making system overlay procedures (paging) more efficient and making it easier to maintain and modify the program later.

If the program is written as a set of independent modules, only one module needs to be in the CPU at a time, as the program will run module by module.

This one-module-at-a-time feature also makes it easier to discover errors and to know where to make needed changes. For example, if an added editing procedure is to be used to test input data more thoroughly, the input editing routine is the only routine that needs modification, unless the new edit is to be based on additional data inputs. In the latter case, the input module would also need to be modified.

Disadvantages of modules Modular programming has a few disadvantages, also. They are as follows:

1 Program execution time *may* be increased.
2 Compile and load times *may* be longer.
3 Communications between and among modules *may* increase program complexity and program size.
4 The program *may* be larger and thus require more storage space.

Note that all these negative results are not certain, they are only possible. Note also that three of the disadvantages (1, 2, and 4) involve additional computer time or resources (hardware), not additional time of program designers and developers. Since costs of computer time and effort are significantly lower than those associated with technical personnel, these three "disadvantages" can actually result in significant overall savings. Personnel costs continue to rise rapidly while hardware costs fall. On balance, the advantages of modular programming outweigh its disadvantages if programmers take care to keep communications between and among modules to a minimum. This activity *may* increase design time, however.

Desirable characteristics of modules Experience has taught us that, for best results, modules should possess certain characteristics.

1 Modules should be able to stand alone.

This means that a module is a self-contained entity. It should be possible to compile and execute (run) each module separately. Horizontally interlocking modules that transfer data back and forth in order to produce a specific output would not allow this.

2 A module may call other modules but only those at a lower level. A module should never call upward to a higher module.

If a module calls a higher module, this implies that the higher-level module is not complete and free standing or that it is misplaced in the hierarchy. A major objective is to preserve the top-down flow.

3 A module must return to its caller.

The main program will normally appear as a series of tests (decisions) and calls. The tests determine which module is to be executed at the next level. That module is then called and executed. Frequently, the results from that module must be tested to find the next lower module to call. For example, in the order processing program we have been working with, a transaction is read, and the available amount of the item is tested to determine if the order can be filled in whole, in part, or not at all. The main routine could call the module to read the transaction and then the module to check balance on hand, which could then call the proper processing routine. After the transaction is processed, control is returned to the main routine to test for last transaction (end-of-file condition) before reading and processing another transaction. If all transactions have been processed, then the remainder of the old master file must be transferred to the updated master file and the output reports printed.

4 A module should have a single entry point and a single exit point.

It is better to duplicate parts of modules than to have multiple entries or exits. The complexity of each module expands geometrically with the number of entry and exit points. Modular design is intended to reduce complexity. Having single entry and exit points requires smaller modules. Experience indicates that modules seldom contain more than 100 lines of code. Best results seem to accrue when modules contain 50 lines or less.

The advantages of smaller modules are many. Smaller modules are easier to code and easier to modify. The time required to design and code a smaller module is easier to estimate, which means project costs and project development times are more easily estimated and controlled. Smaller modules also encourage greater reuse of common modules, not only within the same program but also in other programs and systems. Finally, it is easier to effectively employ programmers with wide variations in skills. The easiest, most straightforward modules are assigned to the most inexperienced programmers. Highly skilled programmers are assigned the most complex modules.

Using small modules is not without its negative features, however. More design time is required to obtain smaller modules. More linkages are required if smaller modules are used because there are more modules to be linked up. As already indicated for modular programming in general, the time required for each compile and execution run tends to be longer. This, in part, arises from the fact that more lines of code will need to be written.

More modules can mean more time spent on documentation. The need for more documentation may be more than offset, however, by the greater ease of documenting simpler modules. Finally, simple modules do not provide as much creative challenge for the programmer, and therefore programmers may be less satisfied and less productive. It is more likely, though, that programmers will respond well to the ease of coding and the greater creative challenge in developing a clean top-down design of free-standing, small modules.

5 A module should have a single function (subtask) to perform and should perform all of that function.

It should be possible to describe the function of a module in a single simple sentence, for example, "match master item number and transaction item number," or "identify transaction code."

6 A module should not keep a history of what has occurred previously for the purpose of modifying its own actions or logic path.

As an example, consider the order processing program. There are three situations to handle: the required items are available in inventory, only part of the required items are available, or none of the required items are available. Each of these situations should be handled in a separate module. A test should be made once and control sent immediately to the appropriate routine.

Main control module

The **main control module** is the overall superviser of the other modules. Its purpose is to oversee the execution of the lower modules to attain the overall objective of the program. For our order processing program, the overall control module specifies its function to be simply

Order processing program

In order to accomplish this overall purpose, subsidiary activities must be carried out. These activities are first grouped by the next level of transaction, the control and processing modules.

Control and processing modules

The second-level modules are ordinarily **control and processing modules**. That is, they involve elements of control since they call lower level processing modules but they often do some processing as well. Turning again to the order processing program, we see the second-level modules as the second line of boxes in Figure 10.1.

Note that the termination module is a very simple one. The bulk of the

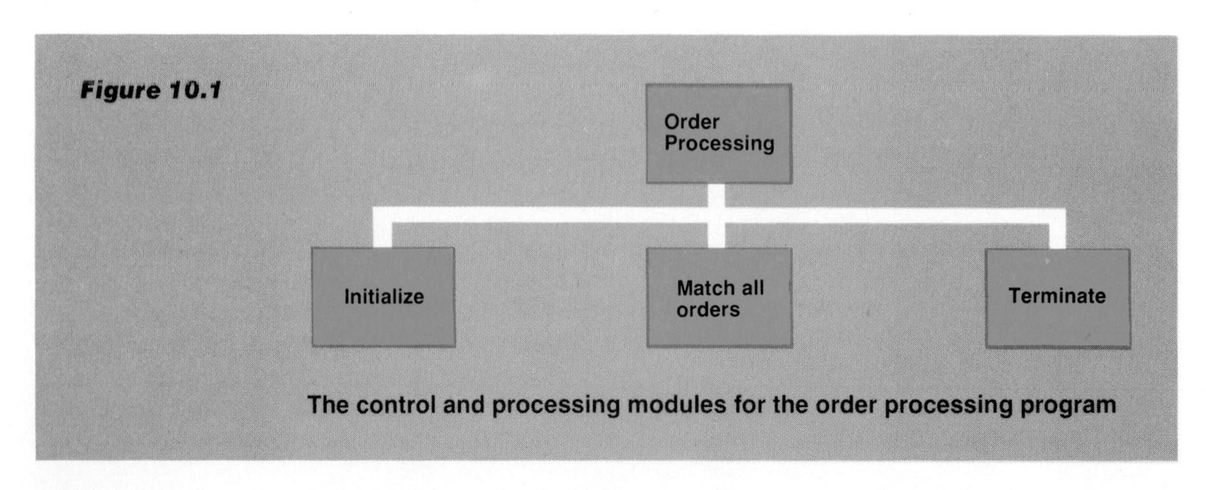

Figure 10.1 The control and processing modules for the order processing program

program falls under the matching branch. The initialize module merely reads the master and transaction records.

Processing modules

Each of the activities at the second level must be broken down further to be carried out. For this purpose, one or more additional layers of control and processing modules may be required. For example, the match-all-orders module is broken down into three modules, each of which has two submodules, as shown in Figure 10.2.

The process-order module would identify the added processes necessary to process the order. The lowest modules would each carry out a process. One would develop and write backorders; the second would develop and write reorders; the last would fill the order. By this process, each second-level control block is broken down to the point where each lowest-level module performs only processing and does not call any lower module. These lowest-level modules are called **processing modules**.

There is no single "optimal" solution to the development of a structure chart. The process of subdividing each subsequent level of the structure chart stops when all higher-level modules have been fully developed and further subdivision would require the splitting of a single function.

Order of processing

Note that the structure chart does not truly indicate order of processing. It is obvious, of course, that the input routine will run ahead of the processing and

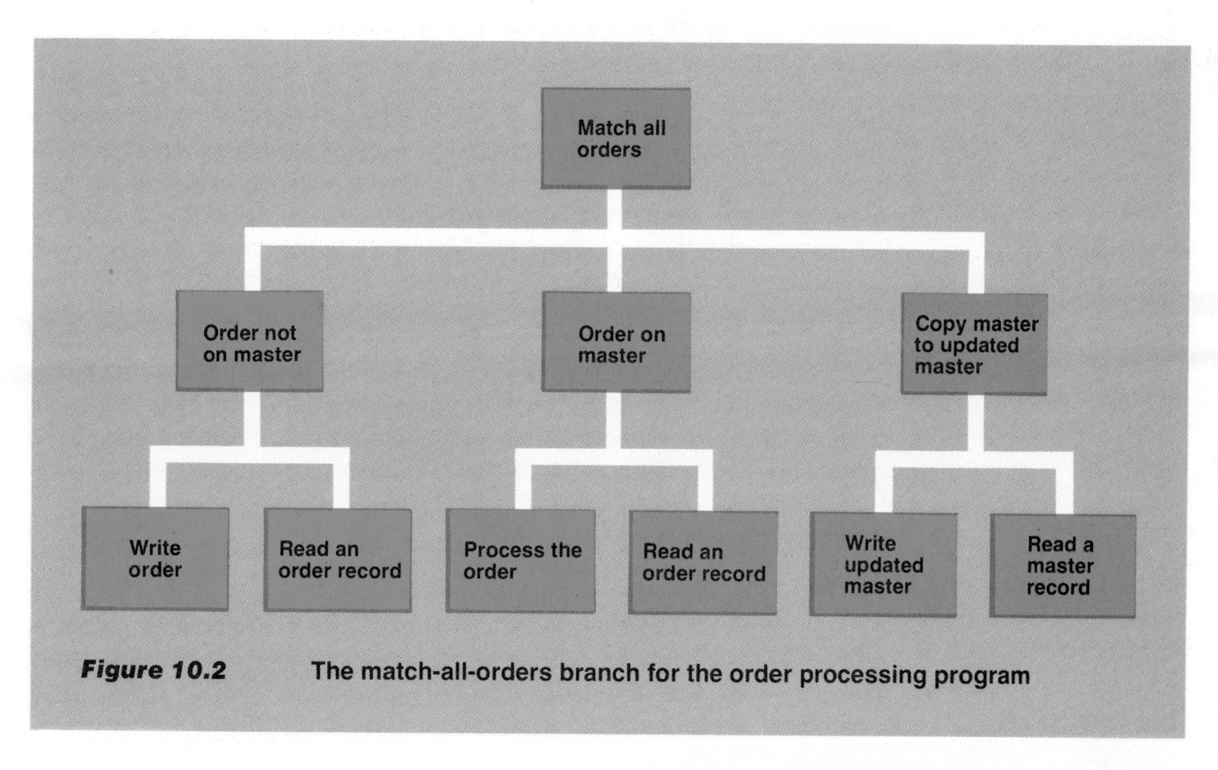

Figure 10.2 **The match-all-orders branch for the order processing program**

termination modules, but the chart does not indicate this. Neither does the structure chart indicate that order processing should be completed before termination. (The input/output schematic and the block diagram prepared in Chapter 8 did indicate that order.) Since people tend to read the structure chart in a conventional left-to-right mode, it is a good idea to allow left-to-right positioning to reflect order of processing. There is no "correct" order, however, and two major approaches can be defined: a hierarchical approach and an order-of-execution approach.

Hierarchical approach In the **hierarchical approach**, all modules at a given level are coded and tested on the computer before any lower-level modules are coded. Stubs are used to represent next-level modules which would be called by any of the current-level modules. Each stub contains only enough code to allow the higher-level module to operate. Some stubs merely output a message indicating the module was called before returning control to the calling module. If higher-level modules are dependent on lower-level modules for data or other results, then the stub must be more complex in order to allow the higher-level module to run to completion. Data dependencies are the primary factor that make the hierarchical approach difficult to apply.

Execution-order approach In the **execution-order approach**, the modules are developed in the order in which they will be executed when the full program is run. Figure 10.3 presents the structure chart for the order processing program with the order of development and execution indicated by the number above each module.

In many programs, the actual order of module execution is data-dependent. For example, if a program were designed to update the inventory master records with receipts and withdrawals, not every item would have all transactions every day. Some items might have receipts, some withdrawals, some both, and others no transactions at all.

A major advantage of the execution-order approach is that the data-dependency problem is reduced. Because each module is added in the order in which it would be executed, those modules that produce data for subsequent modules will have been completed before the using module is developed. The execution-order approach has the disadvantage of delaying development on each module until that module's "turn" comes up. This can present scheduling problems since the processing modules tend to be longest and most complex and also tend to be executed later in the program.

Combination approach Probably the best approach is a combination of the hierarchical and execution-order approaches. Five factors should be considered in determining the order of module development. These are data-dependencies, availability of resources, when a module's output is needed for testing other modules, the complexity of the module, and whether the module handles exceptions related to erroneous data.

Complex modules should usually be coded first. Design errors are most

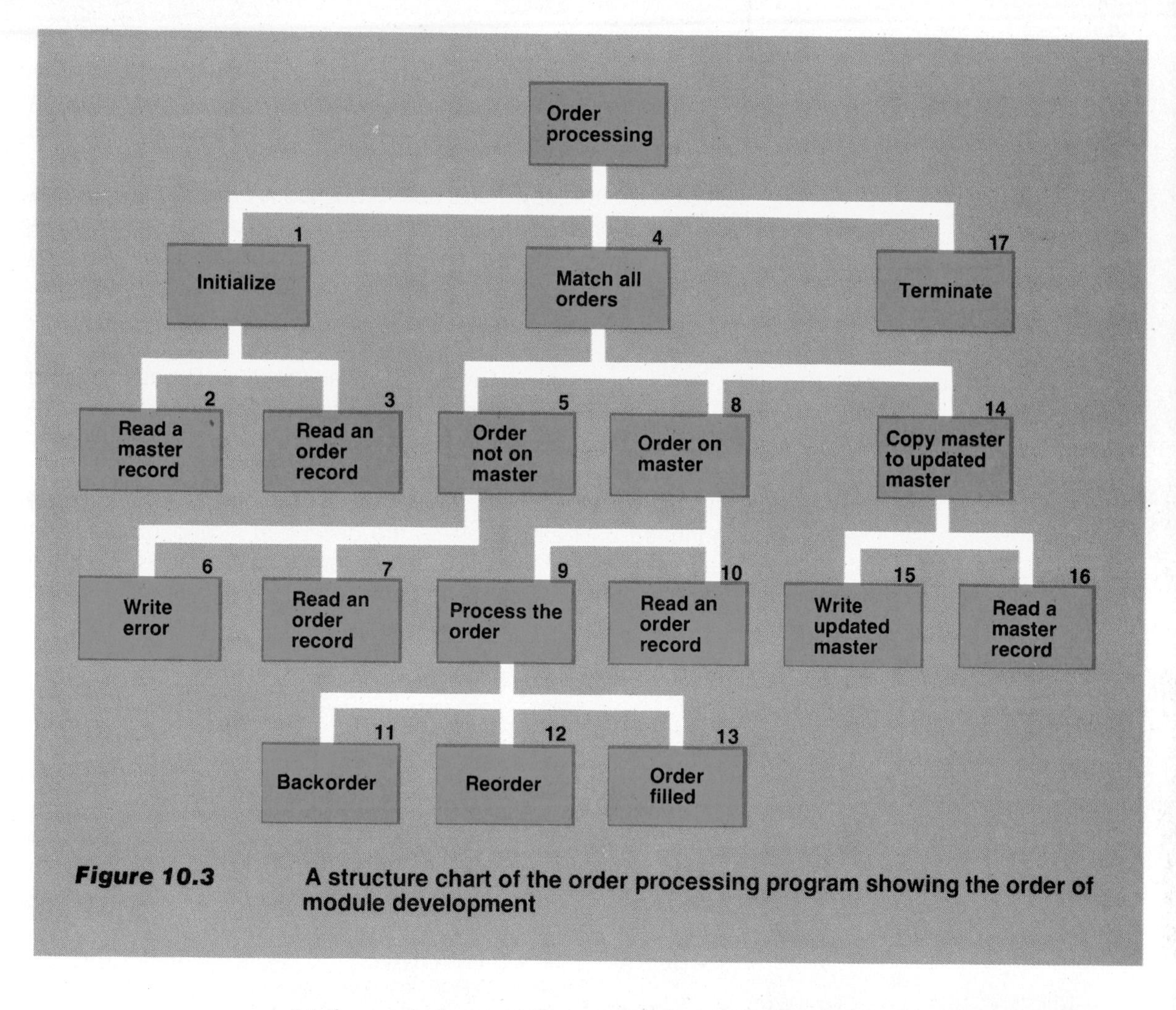

Figure 10.3 **A structure chart of the order processing program showing the order of module development**

apt to be made in a complex module because things can be overlooked more easily or can be inadequately defined. Coding the complex modules early should reveal such deficiencies. In the case of design errors, the structure chart must be corrected. If module specifications are incomplete, the missing items must be defined before continuing development.

Modules that process error-free data are usually coded and tested before any modules dealing with data found to have errors.

Procedural development

Designing and coding of procedural detail can be guided by the use of HIPO diagrams and pseudocode or by the development of detailed flow diagrams before coding. Either way, the job is to move from general procedures to the actual processing detail. HIPO diagrams are developed by level. Each higher-level diagram contains processing elements that must be developed in more detail in a lower-level diagram.

Overview HIPO diagrams

The vocabulary commonly used in this area is suggestive of the process. The structure chart is developed as a **visual table of contents** for the documentation. An **overview HIPO diagram** like that in Figure 10.4 is developed for each module shown in the visual table of contents (the structure chart).

Detailed HIPO diagrams

Whenever a module passes control to a lower-level module during its processing, that step is boxed in the process portion of the overview diagram. The backorder box in Figure 10.4 is an example. A **detailed HIPO diagram** is then prepared for each of these boxed processes. An example is the backorder process diagram in Figure 10.5. This top-down process is continued until all processes are described in enough detail so that they can be translated into pseudocode descriptions. Note how, in Figure 10.5, the variables have been given short, descriptive names in the parentheses.

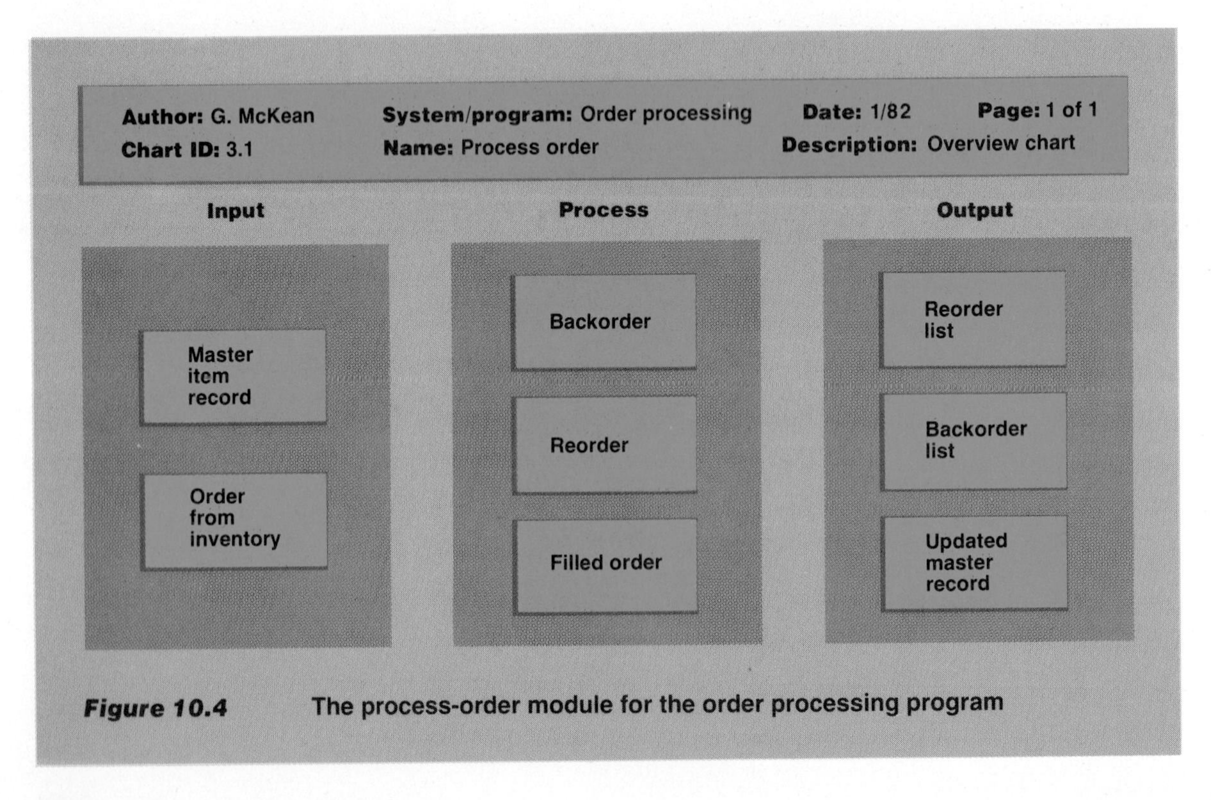

Figure 10.4 The process-order module for the order processing program

Pseudocode description

The pseudocode description of the backorder module is shown in Table 10.1. The process is straightforward. It involves no further decisions but only a process flow. This is illustrated clearly also in the detailed flowchart of Figure 10.6. However, note that the flowchart does not define the outputs of this module as clearly as does the HIPO diagram in Figure 10.3. This illustrates one of the reasons for the popularity of the detailed HIPO diagram. The detailed HIPO diagram also clearly identifies the variables that must be available to this module in order to obtain the required outputs. Note, also, that an input/output schematic could have been prepared for this module which would clearly define not only the inputs and outputs, but any required order of processing as well. Order of processing is generally indicated in both the detailed HIPO diagram and the pseudocode description by the vertical order of the processes. This ordering is not a requirement in developing the charts, however.

Structured programming

As was mentioned in Chapter 8, **structured programming** restricts the developing of a program to three basic structures. These structures (sequence, decision, and loop) are discussed in detail below.

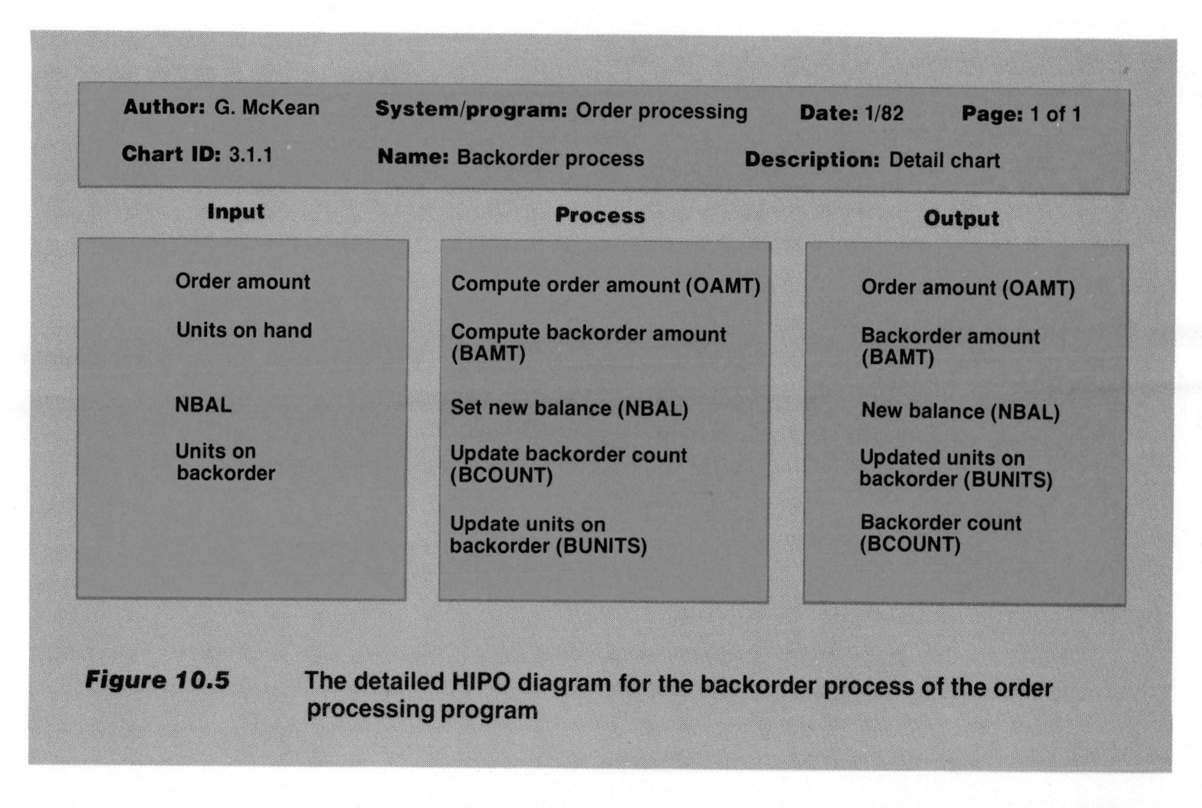

Figure 10.5 The detailed HIPO diagram for the backorder process of the order processing program

GET	New Balance on Hand (NBAL)
COMPUTE	Order Amt = Units on Hand
COMPUTE	Backorder Amount (BAMT) = − NBAL
COMPUTE	NBAL = 0
COMPUTE	Backorder Count (BCOUNT) = BCOUNT + 1
COMPUTE	Units on Backorder (BUNITS) = BUNITS + BAMT

Table 10.1 **Pseudocode description—backorder process**

Sequence structure

The sequence structure was defined in Chapter 8 (pages 230–231) and is clearly indicated in the detailed flowchart of Figure 10.6. Note however that each of the processes could be more complex than those shown there. As discussed more fully below, each process module could be a combination of one or more occurrences of each of the three possible program structures (sequence, decision, loop). For example, consider the detailed flowchart for the write-master-record block (module) shown in Figure 10.7 (on page 292). Note that there are three process blocks and one decision block in that chart.

Decision structure

This, the **IFTHENELSE** structure, is sometimes referred to as the selection structure. Note in Figure 10.7 how the decision block is used to select a processing procedure or branch of the program.

Loop structure

The words **DOWHILE** and **DOUNTIL** illustrate the two forms of the looping structure: first, a structure that checks for a condition at the beginning of the loop and branches out of the loop whenever the condition is not met (DOWHILE), and second, a structure that checks for a condition at the end of the structure and branches out of the loop whenever that condition is met (DOUNTIL). These two forms of the loop structure are illustrated in Figure 10.8 (on page 293). Nowadays, the DOWHILE structure is preferred because the test for condition is at the beginning of the loop rather than at the end. DOWHILE favors a design in which the main control module is a function-calling routine and each function module returns control to the module that called it.

Combination structures

It is worth repeating that one of the principles of structured programming is that a module will consist of any of the three basic structures or a combination of them. For example, note in Figure 10.9 (on page 294) that the decision "more master records?", if untrue, would select a process that

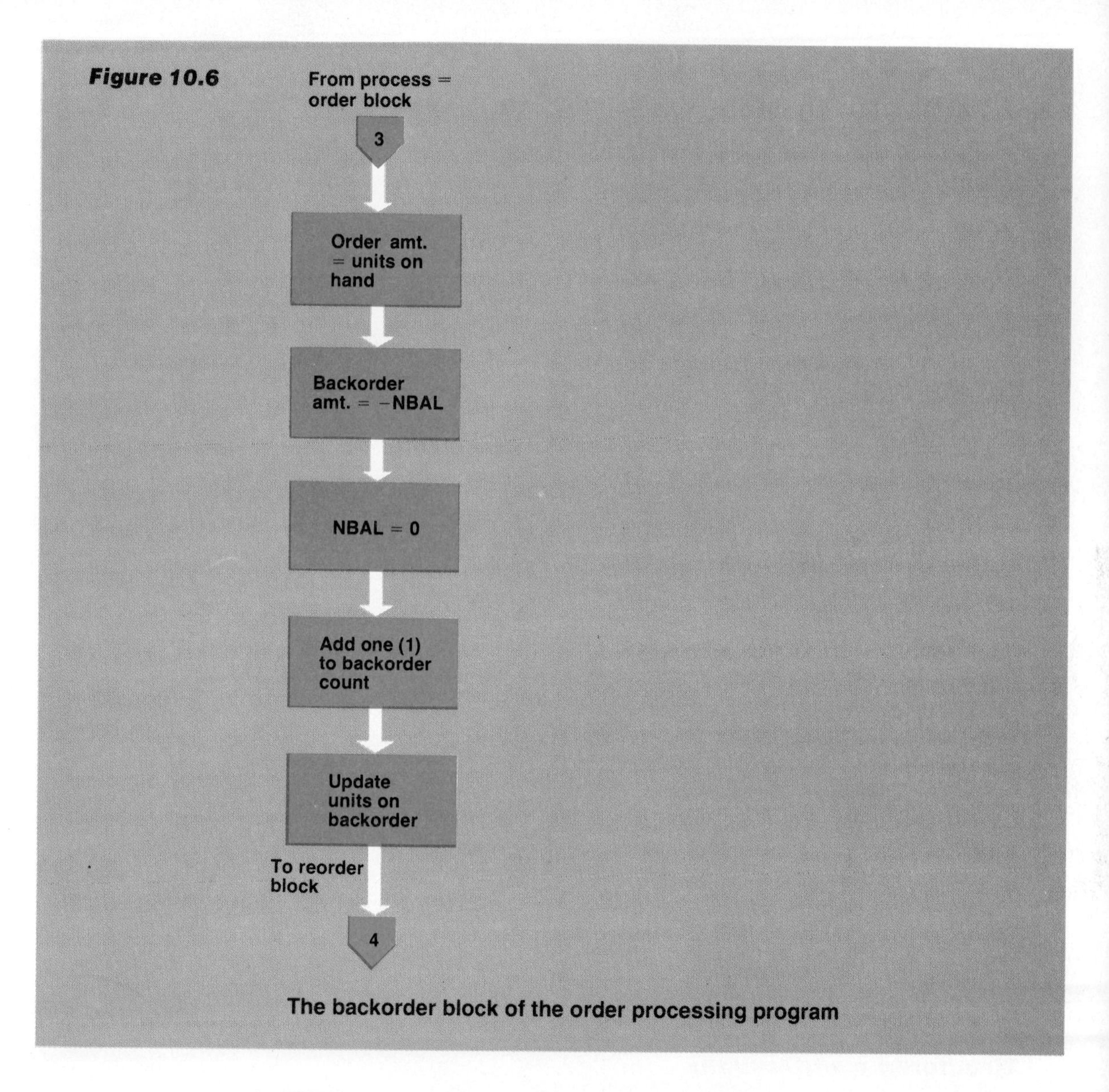

Figure 10.6 The backorder block of the order processing program

immediately must decide if there are more orders to be processed in order to determine which action will lead to a program halt.

Another important consideration is that each module should have only one entry and one exit point. This is critical if a *completely* proper program is to be developed. It is sometimes difficult to achieve, but it reduces the interdependence of modules and makes the program easier to understand and maintain. It helps greatly in this regard to try to avoid the GOTO statement, that is, the unconditional branch. Controlling all program branches with call statements reduces the likelihood of mistakes in programming and increases programmer productivity.

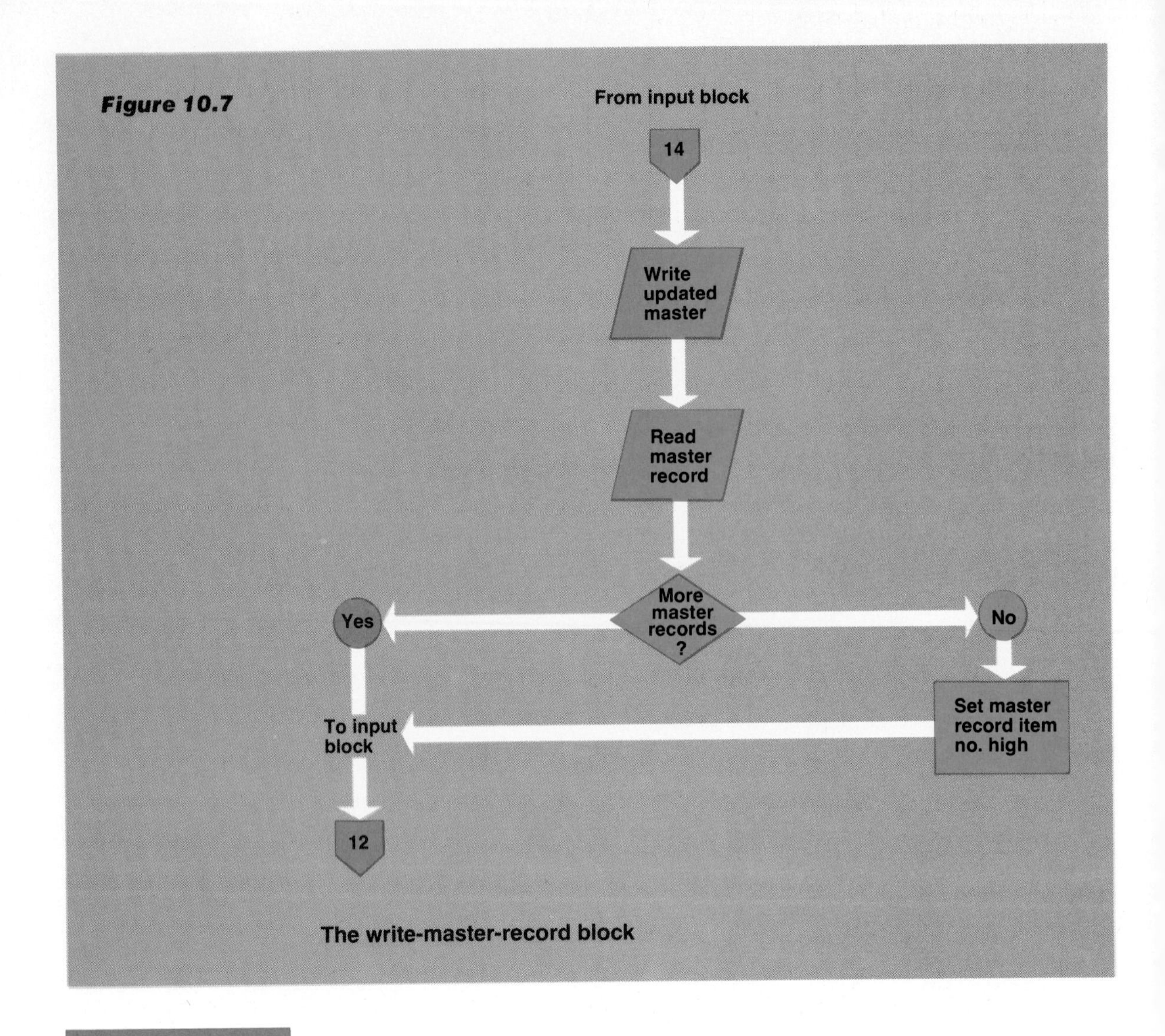

Figure 10.7 The write-master-record block

Structured walkthroughs

The **structured walkthrough** is a process for formal review of program development efforts at each major stage of that development. Walkthroughs are used to review program (system) specifications with the user, to review the design to ensure that the specifications are being met, to review coding to be sure that the agreed-upon design is being followed, and to review planned tests and test data to ensure their adequacy.

To illustrate the process, let us suppose that Susan P. Coder is assigned to code a module of a larger program. She knows the specifications the module must meet. When she is ready, she arranges a walkthrough session to review the way she is handling the data interfaces between her module and

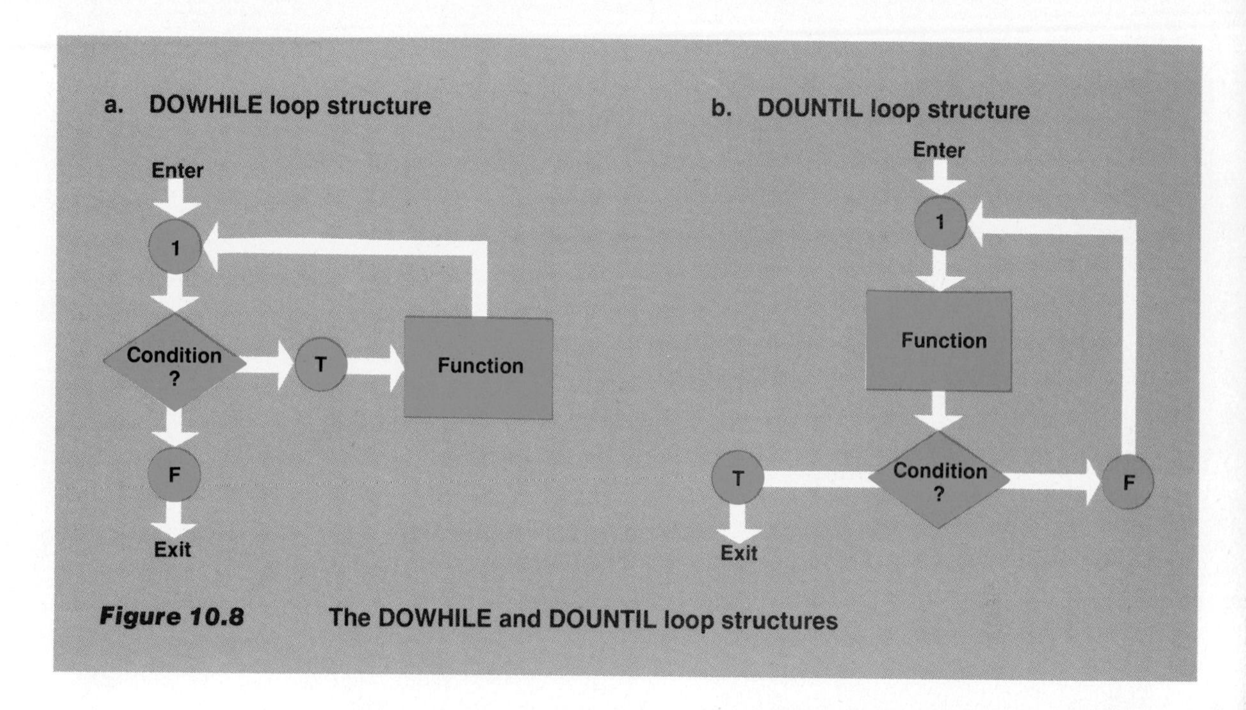

Figure 10.8 **The DOWHILE and DOUNTIL loop structures**

the other modules in the system. The walkthrough consists of the following steps:

1. A scheduled meeting is called, with all participants formally advised of the purpose of the meeting.
2. Each participant is provided with copies of all pertinent materials (specifications, assumptions, logic flows, and so on) to review *before* the meeting, and each participant is expected to be familiar with these materials.
3. The review session is conducted by a moderator. This may be Susan herself or one of the other participants. It is *not* Susan's supervisor, who does *not* attend the meeting.
4. Errors discovered during the session are recorded but not corrected. One participant acts as official recorder and develops a list of errors found. A copy of the list is given to each participant.
5. The above process is repeated as necessary until everyone is satisfied that Susan has properly designed and executed the data-handling interfaces in her module. Only then may Susan proceed to the next phase of development of the module she has been assigned.

There are several key characteristics that make the structured walkthrough effective. First, all participants understand the purpose and each is properly prepared to carry it out. Second, the walkthrough is a help session, not a performance review. Third, all technical members of the project team have their work reviewed at each stage of development before subsequent stages are begun. This structure provides protection against error. The walkthroughs contribute positively to progress and provide positive reinforcement

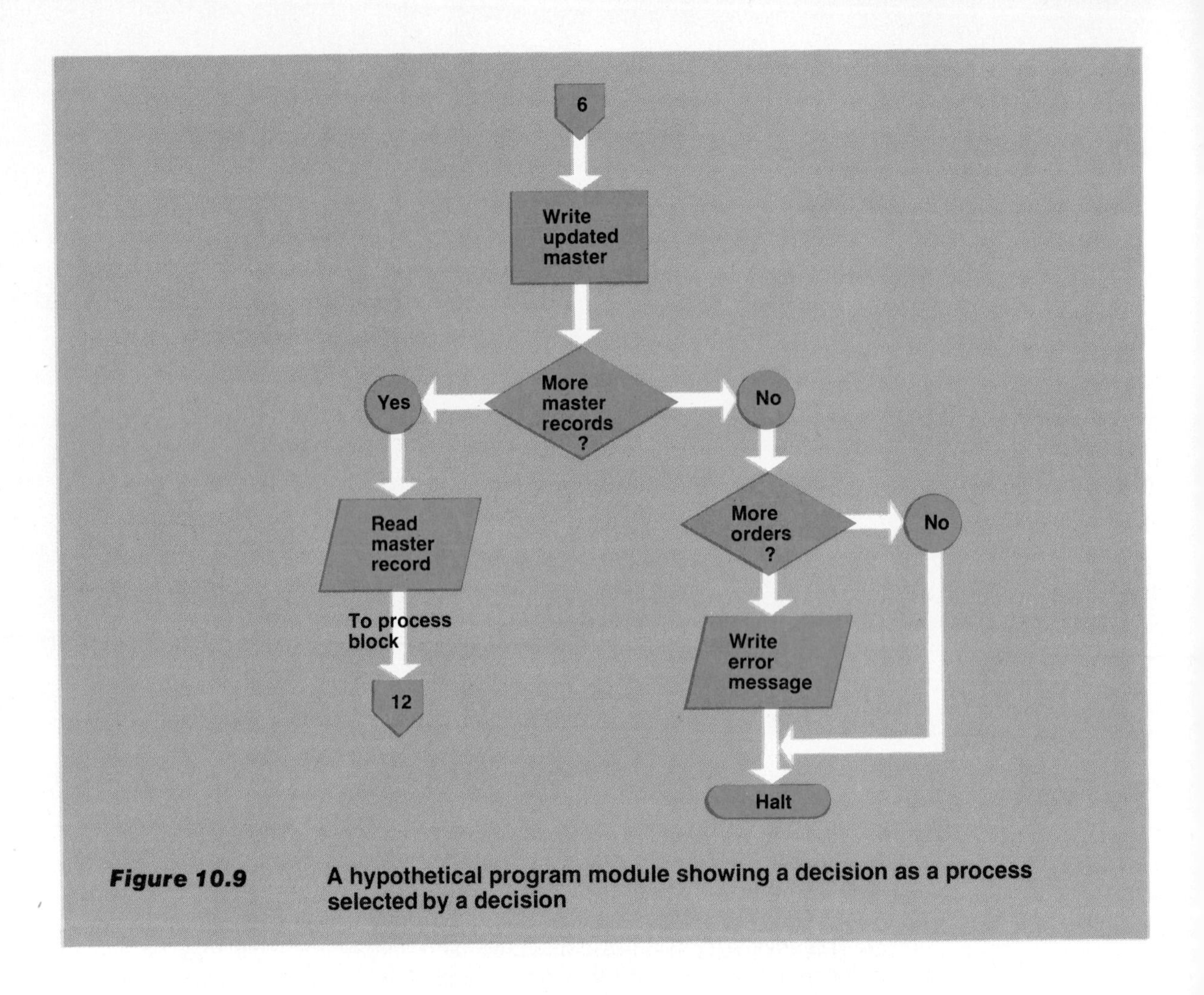

Figure 10.9 **A hypothetical program module showing a decision as a process selected by a decision**

of that progress. Perhaps because of the positive support it provides, the use of structured walkthroughs is reported to motivate personnel to higher levels of error-free performance.

A structured walkthrough should be held for each phase of program development. For example, for the order processing program we have been using as an illustration, walkthroughs would be scheduled *at least* at the following points:

1 Structure chart (the visual table of contents)
2 Overview HIPO diagram for *each* control module or control and processing module:
  a Control (order processing program)
  b Initialize
  c Match all orders
  d Terminate

3 Detailed HIPO diagram for each processing module:
   a Order not on master
   b Order on master
   c Process order
   d Backorder
   e Reorder
   f Order filled
   g Copy master to updated master
4 Pseudocode description for each module

Although it may appear that a lot of time is being wasted, these meetings uncover possible problems and future errors while they are easy to correct. For example, several walkthroughs would probably be necessary to develop the structure chart. There are details we have not considered. The names for each variable and the exact structure of the input files and the output reports would need to be known before developing and coding any module. We also must recognize that we have made some hidden assumptions in developing this program in order to keep the exposition simple. For instance, it is quite likely that a single customer order would involve several items. We have not even included a complete customer order as part of this system. Had you thought about that?

Advantages of the structured approach

Regardless of the specific documentation processes used for describing programs and their modules, the use of the structured approach has several advantages. Most important, it reduces development cost by increasing programmer productivity. Results to date indicate that the improvement varies from 35 to 45 percent, saving one-third to almost one-half of programming expense. At present, software costs for new systems are usually almost twice as high as hardware costs. Cutting software costs thus reduces the largest cost element. Of course, greater programmer productivity means faster program development, which can do more than cut costs.

Using a structured approach also makes programs easier to read and maintain. Bugs can be quickly isolated within a particular program module. Most required changes will directly affect only one or two modules. This makes structured programs easier to maintain. Concrete data on the improvement here is unavailable, but reported experiences indicate that savings may be as much as two-thirds of the cost of maintaining a nonstructured program. With maintenance currently absorbing 50 to 80 percent of the programming dollar, such savings would obviously be significant.

The use of the structured approach also increases the chances of obtaining a working program. The logical, hierarchical development process tends to reduce the complexity of the planning process. With a simpler job to do at each step along the way, success is more likely. The chances of success also increases with the lower rate of errors in design and coding that result from both simpler internal program structures and the structured walkthrough review process.

A final advantage of the structured approach is improved managerial control over the program development process. The structured approach breaks down the design and implementation process into a series of well-defined tasks with recognizable objectives. This makes it easier to estimate development time and to measure and evaluate progress.

Summary

The structured approach to program development consists of the use of three techniques—top-down design, structured programming, and structured walkthroughs. When properly applied, these techniques reportedly reduce program development costs by one-third to almost one-half.

Top-down design consists of developing and implementing the program in a hierarchical, from top-to-bottom, manner. The structure chart (the visual table of contents) is prepared and then broken down module by module into overview HIPO diagrams and detailed HIPO diagrams. The detailed HIPO diagrams are then described in pseudocode, and finally the program is expressed in a programming language (coded). At each step in this process, formal reviews (structured walkthroughs) are held which involve all members of the development team. These structured walkthroughs are designed to remove errors before they are implemented.

The internal logic structures of structured programs are restricted to the sequence structure, the decision (selection) structure, and the loop structure. Using only combinations of these structures and avoiding direct GOTOs as much as possible result in programs that are easier to read and maintain.

The advantages of the structured approach are increased programmer productivity, programs that are easier to read and maintain, a greater chance of obtaining a working program, and improved managerial control over the program development process.

Key terms

Define the following terms as briefly as possible and then, in a short paragraph, clarify each definition.

Control and processing module
Detailed HIPO diagram
DOUNTIL
DOWHILE
Execution-order approach
Hierarchical approach
IFTHENELSE
Main control module

Overview HIPO diagram
Processing module
Proper program
Structured approach
Structured programming
Structured walkthrough
Top-down design
Visual table of contents

Discussion questions

1 How is the module used in top-down design?
2 List and describe the three major elements in the structured approach to program development.
3 What are the advantages of the structured approach to program development?
4 What are the three internal logic structures of a structured program?
5 Describe the steps in a structured walkthrough.
6 How does the structured walkthrough contribute to improved programmer productivity?
7 What characteristics should a good program module have?
8 What is the difference between a control and processing module and a processing module?
9 What guidelines should be followed in designing a program module?
10 Why limit the complexity of a module?

Exercises

1 Refer to Figure 10.3, page 287, and develop an overview HIPO diagram and/or a detailed HIPO diagram for the order-not-on-master module.
2 Refer to Figure 10.3, page 287, and develop a detailed HIPO diagram for the filled-order module.
3 Refer to Figure 10.3, page 287, and develop a detailed HIPO diagram for the reorder module.
4 Refer to Figure 10.1, page 284, and develop overview HIPO diagrams and a detailed HIPO diagram for the initialize module.
5 Develop a pseudocode description for the detailed HIPO diagram developed for Exercise 1.
6 Develop a pseudocode description for the detailed HIPO diagram developed for Exercise 2.

MANAGEMENT ISSUES

Deskilling Programming

The structured methodology debate is alive and well and living in the pages of the professional press. Structured programming, especially, is taking its lumps and receiving its share of praises.

[James Martin] (*Computerworld Extra!,* Sept. 17) has entered the debate arena by asserting that structured methodology can contribute at best 10% to programming productivity. Martin believes that order-of-magnitude improvements are needed in the decade ahead and that they can be achieved only through nonprocedural, very high-level languages.

He is right, of course. We do need the benefits of better software tools, and slowly we are getting them. Natural languages for data base update and retrieval are available, although they are better suited to prototype development and on-line query than to batch production systems. Application development aids and a vast array of utilities are reducing coding redundancy.

But structured programming does have its place. It is available today, easy to learn and, contrary to many opinions, adaptable to Cobol, the most widely used procedural language. Furthermore, it has the potential of greatly increasing programming productivity, certainly not by tenfold, but probably more than the 10% quoted by Martin. . . .

Structured programming is a *standard* methodology for creating programs that are elegant because of their *simplicity, reliable* because of the reduction of the number of "moving parts," *maintainable* because of their modular structure and *minimally documented* because they are so explicit. . . .

If all these benefits accrue from structured methods, why then is there so much controversy? The answer is related to the people who must implement structured methodology and goes far deeper than just resistance to change.

Programmers are, in many respects, a breed apart. They are above average in intelligence, analytical and independent. Being mostly technical types, they are probably less knowledgeable and less concerned about the rest of the organization. Thus, they see their job as an end in itself and often as a source of amusement.

None of this is said in a derogatory sense. Dedication to the craft is an essential element of any technical job. The engineer also engages in "hobby shop" activities. Making work fun is necessary in order to improve the quality of work life and the quantity and quality of production. But the manager who lets these activities go on in

---

Source: Abridged from Durward P. Jackson, "Deskilling Programming: Management Issues," *Computerworld,* November 10, 1980, 49, 54.

an uncontrolled way is serving neither his subordinates nor the organization.

The dichotomy, then, is how to use structured programming to improve productivity while maintaining employee interest and motivation. Structured programming does involve deskilling the programming job. It does involve a lot of mundane work. It will turn off some programmers, even some very good ones.

On the other hand, it will allow a DP department to hire people with just average programming skills. There is a limited supply of super programmers in the world, and they are increasingly expensive and will leave at the drop of a better offer. Less skilled individuals can handle structured programming at far less cost and risk of turnover and still do a creditable job.

There are also benefits for the super programmer. Well-structured programs can substantially reduce the number of late-evening telephone calls so familiar to DP people. The resulting reduction in stress levels can only improve the quality of work life as well as home life.

Motivational problems

This is not to say that the motivational problems in a structured programming environment will not be serious. The manager must recognize the impact of deskilling on programmers' morale and motivation. How he handles this touchy issue will largely determine the success of any structured methodology program.

One thing the manager must do is understand the real purpose of structured programming—that is, to make people's weaknesses irrelevant. Few people in our society have the IQ to understand a spaghetti-like structure of GOTOs and multiply-nested IFs. On the other hand, there is a vast pool of talented people who can be very effective in a structured programming shop. Structured programming makes their weaknesses irrelevant to the job to be done.

But what of those high-powered programmers who resent being reduced to the lowest common denominator? One solution is to put them to work in areas where their talents are more useful. Programmers are logical candidates for jobs such as systems design, equipment or software evaluation, data base design, programming supervision, quality assurance and telecommunications. The manager must be alert to these and other career alternatives.

The manager who is convinced of the importance of structured programming must do four things to make it a reality. First, he must announce the decision forcefully so that there is no question as to the corporate direction. Second, he must develop and publish a set of guidelines or standards. Third, he must provide for the necessary training. Finally, he must ensure compliance with the standards while listening to the reasoned arguments of his staff.

Compliance with the standards must be aggressively pursued. During the initial implementation stages, programmers must be closely supervised. This means management must actually read the program.

Structured programming is not the panacea some would like to make it, but the basic principles make good engineering sense. The improvements in productivity will be substantial if the method is properly implemented. Problems in implementation involve primarily human issues, which must be overcome with firm but understanding management.

Chapter 11

Program Debug and Maintenance

Outline

As stated in Chapter 8, programs seldom operate correctly, if at all, as initially written. Computers are very fast and powerful, but also simplistic. They do *exactly* as they are told and they must be told in exact language. They cannot understand simple misspellings or other common errors. A computer would need to be specially programmed to understand that PRUNT NAME is obviously a misspelling of PRINT NAME. The simplistic consistency of the computer means that misplacing or forgetting a comma, transposing two characters, and many other common errors can cause a program to malfunction. Added to these **syntax errors** are possible **logic errors**. It may be obvious to a human clerk that you must compute net pay before you can print it in a check register. The computer, however, must be told in the correct order and the correct way. It is told with a program. The process of finding and removing errors in syntax and logic from a program is called debugging the program.

Even after a program has been developed and put into use, it may still malfunction. An unlikely combination of conditions may not be provided for in the program's initial version. Part of a program statement may be changed or lost while transferring a program between machine components. More likely, changes in data volumes, output requirements, or data magnitudes may necessitate a change in processing procedure. When a data processing program is used in an operating environment, it needs almost constant attention because of such changes. The process of keeping an operating program running and up-to-date in its procedures is called **program maintenance**.

The purpose of this chapter is to discuss in some detail the general processes and tools of program debug and program maintenance. Since program debug is a part of program maintenance, tools and procedures related to finding errors in a program are discussed first, then those related specifically to program maintenance are discussed. The last section of the chapter deals with the problems of selecting maintenance programmers.

Program debug

The most common tools available for program debugging are desk debug, diagnostics, test data, program tracing, memory dumps, modular programming, structured walkthroughs, and careful and complete documentation. We will also discuss the hierarchical testing process.

Desk debug

The process of reading through a program listing in search of errors in syntax and logic is called **desk debug**. Such proofreading can be successful only with concentration and close attention to detail. It is very easy to overlook missing or misplaced punctuation, misspelled words, and missing statements. Since most applications programs are written in an assembly or compiler language, errors in syntax are usually found by the assembler or compiler at the time the program is compiled for execution (translated into machine language for running on the computer). However, a careful rereading of the program can often spot some of these errors.

The most useful part of the desk debug technique is "playing computer." In this process, each instruction is manually executed in the specified order with sample data to see what results. It is helpful to use a table to keep track of what is happening, especially if looping is involved. Figure 11.1 shows an example of playing computer. Part a presents a flow diagram for a program to read five numbers, add each of them to get a sum, and then print the sum of

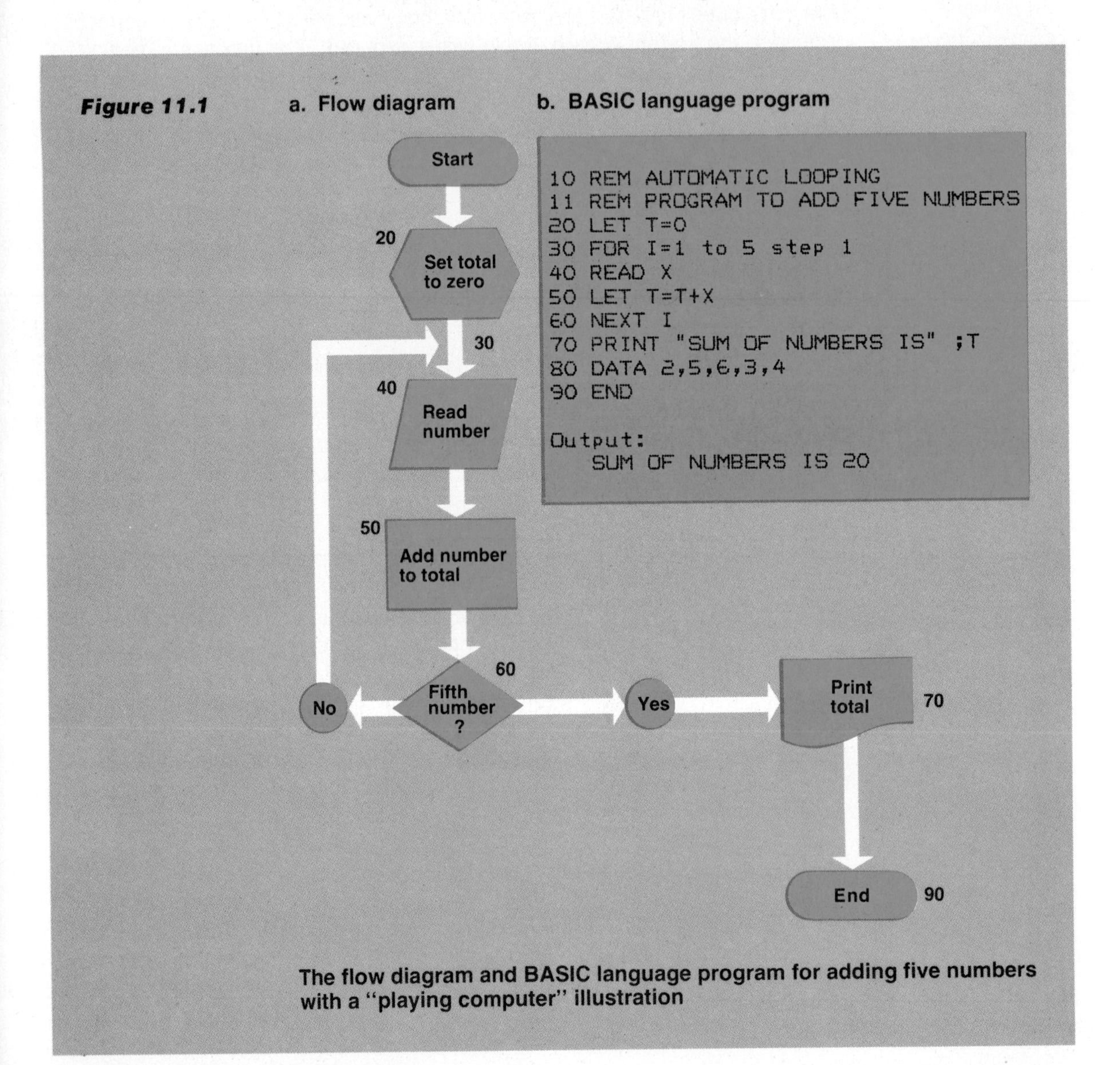

The flow diagram and BASIC language program for adding five numbers with a "playing computer" illustration

STATEMENT NUMBER	EXPLANATION OF STATEMENT	VALUES OF VARIABLES (IN ORDER OF APPEARANCE)		
		T	I	X
10–11	A "remark" to anyone reading the program.			
20	Clearing the adder.	0		
30	Open a loop to be repeated five (5) times.		1	
40	Set X equal to value of next data word in the data list (line 80).			2
50	Add X to Total (T).	2		
60	Close loop (change I by STEP value and repeat loop [go back to 30]			
30	if I<5).		2	
40	Define next X.			5
50	Add X to T.	7		
60–30	Return if I<5.		3	
40				6
50		13		
60–30			4	
40				3
50		16		
60–30			5	
40				4
50		20		
60	I = 5, so leave loop.			
70	Print output.			
80	Inoperable statement defining data.			
90	End of program—stop.			

c. Step-by-step explanation of the program

VALUE OF EACH VARIABLE IN LOOP AS I CHANGES:

I	X	T
		0
1	2	2
2	5	7
3	6	13
4	3	16
5	4	20

d. The normal playing-computer table

the five numbers at the end. The program written in BASIC is presented in part b. Note that each identifying statement number in part b has been placed alongside the corresponding flowchart symbol in part a. A step-by-step explanation of the program is given in part c along with the results of processing the data values found in the DATA statement at line 80. The normal form of a playing-computer table is given in part d. Note that what one does is to follow through each program step and indicate the result.

It can be seen that playing computer through a long, complex program could get very confusing. Usually, the playing-computer table is most useful for running through a specific loop or a short module of the program.

Diagnostics

Compilers and assemblers analyze programs to determine if they follow the syntactical rules of the compiler or assembler. They report the results in diagnostic statements or **diagnostics**, at the time compilation of the program is attempted. The diagnostic routines check for the following:

1 *Legal words:* Are the commands and variable names legal in this language? For example, READ, not RED, and variable names of the form and length accepted by the compiler or assembler.
2 *Statement form:* Statements must be written in the exact form specified. For example, refer to the BASIC language program in Figure 11.1b, statement number 50: that statement cannot be written LET T+X = T because the compiler would find two variable names where the result of the right-hand side (value of T) is to be stored. The location where the result is to go must appear unambiguously on the left side of the equal sign. The result to be stored there is defined in the statement to the right of the equal sign.
3 *Completeness:* Are formal program loops closed and does the program have an end? Refer to Figure 11.1 again. If one attempted to run the program without the NEXT command in statement 60, the compiler would respond with FOR WITHOUT NEXT IN LINE 30. Also, the END statement at 90 signals the compiler that the program is supposedly complete, and checking for open loops and other unfinished operations is appropriate. The END statement must also be the highest-numbered statement so that all other statements may be compiled. The compiler would warn us END NOT LAST AT 90 if we were to add a statement numbered 100.

Some diagnostic routines, particularly on older computers, identify some errors with almost incomprehensible messages. Only previous experience allows the programmer to recognize the possible source(s) of superficially incorrect diagnostics.

Diagnostic routines cannot check program logic, that is, cannot determine if the program completes its job. If all commands are legal in form and do not violate any syntactical sequencing rules, the program will be compiled without any diagnostics being printed. But the result may be no output or pure garbage if the internal logical processes of the program are not correct or input or output statements are missing.

Test data

After all errors that can be found by reading the program and by attempting to compile it have been corrected, its logic must be tested. The only way to be completely sure that the program actually performs as intended is to test it with data. The **test data** used must be carefully designed to test every part of the program. Every possible combination of data that may occur must be present. If a possible combination is omitted, the program may fail when such a combination is encountered in an operating run. The development of an adequate test deck for a large, complex program is a difficult task. It is best to develop specific data elements to exercise each error control in the program independently. After all seem to work, the ability of the program to handle combinations of errors in the same record can be tested.

Special care must be taken to test the error detection routines. For example, in an hourly payroll program, there would be routines that test for too many hours, too large a pay rate, negative net pay, and missing records. Each of these controls must be tested by the test deck if the program is to be considered complete.

The ability of the program to handle routine data inputs in the desired manner must also be tested. Here, the programmer must work through the required processing steps for each input record or record set and obtain the correct outputs. The outputs obtained from the program are then checked against the correct results. Any discrepancies in the two outputs must be carefully resolved. It is not unusual to find that the manual processing of test data contains errors and that the computer processing is correct.

Logic errors in a complex program can be difficult to isolate. Small things, such as the possibility of overflows or rounding errors, can cause significant errors in strings of calculations. Inconsistency in naming variables, or naming input variables in an order different from their ordering on input documents, or not allowing enough space for output of a number, all minor errors, can result in incomprehensible diagnostic statements.

Program tracing

One of the most common places for errors to occur is in the logical branches within the program. These errors are most easily found through **program tracing**, following the program through step by step to see the exact order in which it is proceeding. The simplest way in which to trace a program is by adding temporary (extra) output commands at intervals throughout the program. After the sequence is known to be correct, these extra commands can be removed. The placement of such temporary commands is crucial for success in finding errors. Obviously, there should be an "echo" print of what has been read immediately after each input (READ) statement. The results should be printed after each sub process (module) is completed. For example, if an hourly payroll program were producing erroneous results, temporary output statements would print out each transaction record and each master record immediately after it was read. The amount of gross pay would be printed at the end of the gross pay computation, the income tax deduction would be printed at the end of the income tax calculation, and so on. Care must be taken to identify clearly what each of these outputs is and exactly where in the program it is coming from.

Utility software routines that will perform a program trace and identify the exact sequence of activities are available for many compilers. Some of these can be triggered to output all interim results by the insertion of a single command. Some compilers also contain provision for "snapshotting" results at points in the program selected by the programmer. These snapshots identify the value of each variable that has been handled by the program to that point. These tracing routines are not freely available. They usually must be purchased from an independent software supplier or developed by the user.

Tracing through a program also can be assisted by liberal use of "comments" within the program. Comments that identify the beginning and end of each module and each specific task within a module are most helpful.

Storage dumps

Sometimes all the normal debug processes prove inadequate. The problem may be isolated to a particular program module, but defy further definition. In such cases, experienced programmers may resort to a **storage dump** which prints out a kind of map of the primary memory. Usually in hexadecimal notation, such a printout is difficult to read. However, it can provide a very clear picture of what is going on in the computer at that point. A sequence of such dumps can clearly reveal the sequence of changes carried out by the program.

Use of the storage dump is not recommended for beginning programmers. They are better off using simpler methods for tracing program operations.

Structured programming

As indicated in Chapters 8, 9, and 10, the use of structured programming reduces the problems encountered in developing a working program. Not only does structured programming speed up and simplify the process of program development, its use also makes program maintenance easier. In a structured program, a problem can usually be quickly isolated to one or two modules.

The greatest problem in using a modular approach is to find a logical way to divide the program into modules. The major block diagram and the structure chart are the most useful tools for identifying autonomous modules. Care must be exercised to avoid dividing the task into separate parallel flows. The use of several parallel modules, each operating in a different way on the same inputs and passing common outputs to a subsequent module or set of modules, compounds the problem of coordinating processing activities. It also encourages the development of inefficient processing procedures in the program. It is usually wise to divide a job into serially related cells, with each cell accepting inputs from the preceding cell and passing outputs to a subsequent cell.

Hierarchical testing

Probably the most useful approach to obtaining a working program is top-down structured design, development, and implementation. This process allows **hierarchical testing** of modules as each is developed. After each module is developed and tested as an independent entity, it is combined with the previously tested modules and the entire program to that point is tested. The questions to be answered are:

Is each control and processing module being called at the right time?
Does each module turn control back to the higher-level module that called it?
Does it return correct data elements?

Using this hierarchical top-down procedure, the entire program should run when the last module is added. If the entire program does not run or does not produce correct output, which module is in error? Only by following a specified hierarchical procedure can this question be answered. First test each simple routine (processing subfunction) within each module, then test the entire module, then the entire program.

Structured walkthroughs

As was explained in Chapter 10, the structured walkthrough is a powerful tool for locating errors before they are made, as well as after. Walkthroughs were fully described in that chapter.

Careful and complete documentation

Fully developed verbal descriptions, structure charts, input/output schematics, block diagrams, HIPO diagrams, procedural flowcharts, and pseudocode listings are obvious aids to program debugging. A **variable dictionary** which lists each variable name used in the program, its meaning, and its format (number and type of characters allowed for it) is also useful. For a complex program, desk debugging is next to impossible without documentation. Program traces must be compared to some detailed program description, such as a procedural flowchart or a pseudocode listing, to be useful.

Program maintenance

Reasons for changing operating programs

Changes are made in operating programs for several reasons. In the course of program maintenance, the most common changes are program improvements, refinements that improve the nature or utility of program outputs. Perhaps a new table or an added column on an existing table is considered desirable. A simple rearrangement of existing outputs may make them easier to use by making their meaning clearer.

Program enhancements are undertaken to improve operating performance. In order to shorten operating time, several independent steps or even separate programs may be combined. Data records may be reorganized so that elements are arranged in order of the frequency with which they are used in processing. Adjustments may also be made to speed up responses to inquiries from management.

Program changes may be necessary because of program failure caused by unforseen problems. Certain situations may actually cause the program to be unable to produce usable outputs. It is then necessary to correct the program so that it will handle the previously unrecognized problem. For example, we once encountered a payroll program that handled paid vacations in such a way that the program failed in the summer when the largest number of workers took vacations. A temporary table of pay records for workers on vacation exceeded the space allowed for it, and the program started to replace program instructions with the pay records. Naturally, payroll records do not correspond to computer operating instructions.

A third reason for making changes in an operating program is that there are changes in the business situation. Volumes or magnitudes of data may change as economic conditions change. Alternatively, the business may expand into new areas of activity through internal expansion, acquisition, or merger. Rates or formulas may be modified by new laws or by changes in agreements, such as labor contracts.

Programs may change because processing equipment changes. The addition of online mass storage and remote-access capability, for example, may require significant program modification to allow online inquiry of data files. Merely changing from a smaller to a larger computer or from one vendor to another can make it necessary to change some program statements even though the program is written in a higher-level language. Even with supposedly machine-independent languages such as COBOL or FORTRAN, it may be necessary to change input or output statements.

Control of changes

Changes in operating programs should be carefully controlled. Unauthorized changes can be expensive in many ways. One obvious way is embezzlement or theft of the assets of the firm by a dishonest employee.

Any change also carries a cost for the programming and testing involved. Left to their own devices, many professional programmers will strive continuously for perfection, often with little awareness of the cost. Managers should examine proposals for program enhancement as carefully as proposals for new systems. Even changes necessitated by problems in operation should be reviewed and approved by someone other than the maintenance programmer making the change.

Managers should also evaluate a proposal for program enhancement or change in the same *way* as proposals for new systems or programs. If expected benefits do not match the cost of the proposed change, then the change should not be made. Care should be exercised to evaluate benefits properly, however. Managers should recognize the value of such enhancements as making future maintenance efforts more productive or easing modification in response to foreseeable business developments.

Documentation of maintenance programming

Maintenance programming should be as carefully documented as the original program. The original documentation should be updated, either by issuing corrected verbal descriptions, input/output schematics, and flowcharts or by issuing addendums specifying the changes. Each new document or change should be numbered, dated, and recorded in a log so that the completeness of any document can be easily determined.

A log of maintenance activity, a **program maintenance history**, should be kept for each program and system. Not only should changes by date be shown, but also the reasons for each change and who authorized it. Such a log provides a valuable record of productivity in an environment where productivity is difficult to measure because of the creativity involved. A record showing which systems require excessive maintenance and which need only minimal maintenance is one indicator of the real producers among programmers and analysts.

The maintenance history should also indicate how difficult each change was to make and the most obvious reason for any problems. Sloppy or missing documentation is the most common problem. Often, a lack of documentation merely reflects a general lack of professionalism and the use of poor programming habits.

Periodically, the program maintenance histories should be summarized and evaluated. A report showing hours of maintenance effort for each system, program, and programmer is a valuable tool in managing the systems and programming function. Care must be taken, however, not to blame systems and programming personnel for management errors. Poorly defined requirements for a new system or program are often a primary cause of excessive program maintenance. Rushing a system or program into operation before it has been debugged adequately can be another cause of excessive correction and enhancement.

Choosing maintenance programmers

To find logic errors in a program is not easy, even if one wrote the program. Finding logic errors in a complex program written by someone else is much more difficult. To achieve high productivity, a maintenance programmer must be a well-trained professional with a detailed knowledge of the system or program involved and of the language in which it is written. It has been common practice to assign programmer trainees (inexperienced programmers) to maintenance so that they might learn systems approaches. Experience indicates, however, that it is better to assign maintenance of a program or system to one or more members of the original programming team.

There is no sure way to identify a good maintenance programmer except by trail and error. Programmers who do an excellent job in producing original programs may be unproductive as maintenance programmers. Productivity in each area requires strong logical ability, attention to detail, and controlled creative ability. There is a difference, though, between the internal motivation for chasing down an error and that for creating a new program. Some programmers assigned to maintenance programming regularly resort to rewriting whole modules rather than identifying and correcting particular logical errors. Although replacing a nonworking part is *sometimes* the best approach, it is not *always* best.

Good maintenance programmers should receive recognition and reward for their unique abilities. Maintenance programming should not be considered the lowest level of programming and assigned to the weakest programmers available. It can be a most productive role for exceptionally well-qualified professionals.

Summary

Developing a working computer program is a difficult process. Computers are very simple clerks that do exactly as they are told, but they must be told in very exact terms. Misplaced or missing punctuation, incomplete descriptions of input data, and simple misspellings can cause the computer to fail to understand. Such errors in syntax (form of instructions) are easier to locate than errors in the procedural logic of a program. Syntax errors (and some logic errors) may be found by the assembler or compiler as it attempts to interpret the source program, written in an assembler or compiler language. Such errors are revealed in diagnostic messages. Other tools for identifying errors in a program include reading a program (desk debug), program tracing, storage dumps, running the program with test data, using modular programming techniques, hierarchical testing, and insisting on complete documentation.

Operating computer programs are necessarily dynamic in nature, constantly changing. To carry out the necessary changes requires program maintenance. Programs are improved (enhanced) to make them more efficient. Changes occur because requirements change or the environment in which a business operates is modified. Laws and other regulations are not static, and operating procedures must fit the current business environment. Volumes of activity and the sizes of processed values are constantly changing for most business situations. Managers may have new or different reporting requirements as the business climate improves or declines, as the business itself changes in size, and as managers change their own responsibilities. The hardware (computer equipment) being used can change. Finally, an unusual combination of transactions data may cause a program failure.

Changes need to be controlled as carefully as any other system or application development. If assets are to be safeguarded, management should approve any change in a program. Proper management should also control costs of program maintenance like any other investment. Changes whose effects are less valuable than their cost should not be undertaken.

Good maintenance programmers are hard to find. Experience indicates that the program maintenance for a system or application should be assigned to one or more of the program team responsible for developing and implementing it. The practice of assigning beginning programmers to program or system maintenance has not been effective.

Key terms

Define the following terms as briefly as possible and then, in a short paragraph, clarify each definition.

Desk debug
Diagnostic
Hierarchical testing
Logic error
Program enhancement
Program maintenance
Program maintenance history
Program tracing
Storage dump
Syntax error
Test data
Variable dictionary

Discussion questions

1 Can diagnostic routines find logic errors?
2 How do the following pairs of items differ?
  a Logic errors and syntax errors
  b Program trace and storage dump
  c Program debug and program maintenance
  d Program improvements and program enhancements
3 How can a good maintenance programmer be identified?
4 List the reasons why an operating program might change after it has been put into use.
5 List the common tools available for debugging programs.
6 What is playing computer?
7 What are the three kinds of errors identified by diagnostic routines in assemblers and compilers?

Exercises

1 The program segment below is written in BASIC. Set up a playing-computer table and see what this segment does. What will be the final line of output?

```
100  REM LOOP
110  LET K=5
120  FOR I=1 to K
130  LET X=X+I
140  LET T2=I*I
150  LET X2=X2+T2
160  PRINT I,X,T2,X2
```

```
170  NEXT I
180  PRINT "TOTALS",X,"-",X2
190  END
```

Note: The FOR in line 120 and the NEXT in line 170 identify a DOUNTIL loop.

2 The program segment below is taken from a program written in BASIC. Set up a "playing-computer" table and see what it does.

```
10 DEFINE FILE #1='TESTSCORE'
30 I1=0
40 I2=0
50 READ #1,T
60 ON END #1 GOTO 100
70 I1=I1+1
80 I2=I2+T
90 GOTO 40
100 A=I2/I1
110 PRINT 'ANSWER = ';A
120 END
```

3 The program segment below is taken from a program written in COBOL. Only the Procedure Division is shown. You may assume all other divisions are properly written. Set up a "playing-computer" table and see what the segment does.

```
MAIN-CONTROL-MODULE.
    OPEN INPUT TEST-SCORE-FILE OUTPUT PRINT-FILE.
    MOVE '0' TO END-SW.
    READ TEST-SCORE-FILE
         AT END MOVE '1' TO END-SW.
    PERFORM PROCESS-AND-READ-SCORES
         UNTIL END-SW = '1'.
    PERFORM COMPUTE-ANSWER.
    CLOSE TEST-SCORE-FILE PRINT-FILE.
    STOP RUN
PROCESS-AND-READ-SCORES.
    ADD 1 TO TOTAL-SCORES.
    ADD TEST-SCORE-IN TO SUM-OF-SCORES.
    READ TEST-SCORE-FILE
         AT END MOVE '1' TO END-SW.
COMPUTE-ANSWER.
    DIVIDE SUM-OF-SCORES BY TOTAL-SCORES GIVING ANSWER.
    MOVE ANSWER TO ANSWER-OUT.
    WRITE PRINT-REC FROM ANSWER-LINE
          AFTER ADVANCING 2 LINES.
```

Note: The first PERFORM is a COBOL implemenation of a DOWHILE loop.

4 The program segment below is taken from a program written in FORTRAN. Set up a "playing-computer" table and see what it does.

```
C          FILE 5 = TEST SCORE FILE
C          FILE 6 = PRINTER FILE
      ISCORE=0
      ICOUNT=0
  100 FORMAT(I5)
  200 FORMAT('0',10X,F5.2)
C     ****************MAIN LOOP****************************
  300 READ(5,100, END=500) ITESTS
      ICOUNT=ICOUNT+1
      ISCORE=ISCORE+ITESTS
      GO TO 300
C     *************END OF JOB*****************************
  500 ASCORE=ISCORE/ICOUNT
      WRITE(6,200) ASCORE
      STOP
```

Note: Statement 300 uses the format at 100 and stores the data value in ITESTS. At end-of-file, control is transferred to statement 500.

5 Refer to any programs assigned in the programming laboratory for practice in applying debugging techniques.

DATA PROCESSING ERROR

Nuns Befuddled, Writer Corrected

Mild-mannered Sister Joan Mary, principal of the St. Alphonsus School here [in New Orleans], was a little befuddled and not terribly amused with a Western Union Mailgram she received last month.

It was from Gene W. Milner, chairman of Lanier Business Products, Inc. in Atlanta, and it read:

"I am counting on your tails being out in the field selling for the rest of this month and all of May. I don't want to hear nothing but that you are producing. Don't hire—don't do nothing else. Don't fiddle with papers, don't talk on the phone to your grandmother. Get the hell busy for the rest of the fiscal year."

Because of a computer-assisted error, Sister Joan Mary and about 500 other Catholic grade school principals received the front office edict originally intended for Lanier's 130 sales managers.

Western Union, obviously embarrassed over the situation, has refused to give any details explaining just what happened, saying only that it was a computer foul-up. The company sends out over 40 million Mailgrams annually, and a spokesman said the error "is like the dozens of other computer mistakes that make the papers all the time, except this one had a different twist."

Western Union makes extensive use of stored mailing lists in a computerized data base, and the spokesman hinted that a human data entry or keying error may have precipitated the misdirected mailings.

Whatever the case, many of the nuns and priests inadvertently reached seized the opportunity for a little tongue-in-cheek reprimand directed at Milner, who had arranged to follow up the first mailing with an apology and explanation from Western Union.

"I enjoyed this note," Sister Joan Mary wrote. "However, as a grade school administrator, I was offended by the use of the double negatives!

"The next time you are in New Orleans, please stop by," she continued, "I'm sure your tail comes to this field sometime."

Milner's reply

"Attached is my personal donation of 50 shares of Lanier Business Products stock (worth about $2,000) for your school," Milner replied.

"I had excellent grammar teachers, but unfortunately I still continue to use double negatives for emphasis. However, due to your reply to my missent Mailgram, I will be more careful in the future. I'm also trying to cut down on the use of expletives.

"This was not staged in any way but was a pure Western Union error and the very pleasant responses made me feel grateful for the collective sense of humor of Catholic elementary school principals." he continued.

"Yours is the winner because of your suggestion that I follow my own advice and get my tail out in the field and call on your school. I look forward to visiting with you on my next trip to New Orleans."

Special Option

Ready-Made Software

Introduction

Anyone can become a sophisticated computer user without becoming a sophisticated computer programmer. Modern operating systems, utilities, language translators, programming aids, performance monitors, data management systems, network controllers, and applications packages make this possible. These types of software, together with their documentation and maintenance, are available from computer vendors, independent software companies, and moonlighting individuals; and they can satisfy virtually every processing requirement involved in modern and sophisticated computer use.

Programs and packages

In order to discuss ready-made software intelligently, one must understand the difference between a program and a software package. A program is merely a logical set of instructions that accomplishes a task. A program is a single entity. It may be expressed in source code (BASIC, COBOL, FORTRAN, and so on) or it may be expressed in object code (machine language).

A software package may be only a program, but usually it is much more. A package is the complete program or set of programs and all future "support" of the program or set. Support may vary from none (here is the program, you take it and keep it running) to maintenance and enhancement. Major packages usually involve full support. The package is intended to solve, or help solve, a business data processing or decision-making problem. Business problems change and evolve. Even such a simple problem as payroll processing is subject to change. Changes in law (income tax rates, minimum wage, maximum hours of work, and so forth) and changes in union contracts (overtime rules, retirement or health benefits, and the like) can cause significant changes in payroll programs. Packages must be altered whenever changes in the social, economic, legal, or competitive environment cause changes in the business practices they affect.

Changes also arise out of changes in processing technology. Suppose a business decides to install a data base management system. Will the payroll package interface with the DBMS? Suppose a bigger, faster computer is obtained to handle an increased workload, or that wage data are to be collected on line. Will the package adjust? Even if the package can adjust, who will modify it? How will the modification be carried out? Will it require bringing in a different version of the package or will a single module be reprogrammed? If a module is reprogrammed who does it—the package vendor or the user? If a package is modified by the user, will the vendor continue to support it?

Sources of ready-made software

Ready-made software can be obtained from computer vendors and from independent software suppliers. Independent suppliers may be firms specializing in the production of software and software services, software marketers who only market products produced by others, and other users trying to recover their investment in a software product. At one extreme, a software firm may consist of a single programmer or computer hobbyist offering a program or a package to the local market. At the other extreme, the software firm may employ a staff of software specialists who develop and support packages and a marketing staff that carries out a full line of sophisticated marketing strategies.

Ready-made products

Eight basic types of software were identified in the introduction to this special option. We will now discuss each type more fully below and identify the source from which each type would normally be obtained.

Operating systems

Operating systems are most commonly supplied by the computer vendor. Since this software is a critical factor in determining the operating characteristics and the capabilities of a computer system, it has usually been priced with (bundled with) the basic hardware (CPU). This is beginning to change, however, as large software houses are starting to offer what are reputed to be more efficient operating systems. Software houses are offering operating systems for the more popular IBM computers, but for few others.

Utilities

As noted in Chapter 7, utilities are programs or routines that perform a particular function or task. These specialized routines are designed to perform certain repetitive tasks efficiently and accurately.

Utilities are offered by computer vendors, by software firms, and by other users. Utilities are a favorite product of the firms that locate and market packages developed by either users or software firms.

Language translators

The various compilers allow a programmer to work in a higher-level language. Assembly language assemblers and the most common procedural language compilers (COBOL and FORTRAN compilers, certainly) are provided by the computer vendor. Independent software firms also provide compilers for these and other procedural languages (APL, BASIC, PASCAL), but they are mainly a source of compilers for nonprocedural languages. The nonprocedural compilers most frequently supplied by computer vendors are those associated with data base management systems.

Programming aids

Various precompilers and application generators were developed originally by software firms. Precompilers are designed to remove obvious errors of format (supply missing commas, see that commands start in the proper column, correct improper variable names, and so forth). They remove some of the pressure for conformity designed into most procedural languages. Many of these precompilers are for use during online development of programs at a terminal.

Application generators are a different matter. An application generator assists in the design and coding of applications. Functions common to all applications (for example, data input) are provided by the application generator. The programmer is left to concentrate on the unique aspects of the particular application. Time and effort are not wasted on coding input, report generation, and file handling.

Most application generators are linked to a specific data base management system and a particular host language, most often, COBOL. Some application generators are designed for a particular class of business problems, usually financial problems. Common functions (for example, simple transaction input editing and development of control totals as well as logical sums) are only one feature of a complete application generator. Others are data management, design of screen formats, and report generation. In addition, a good application generator will provide a nonprocedural language for performing processing that is not available as part of the system software. Almost all of these languages interface with one of the popular procedural languages.

Application generators have been reported to increase programmer productivity by as much as 60 percent. They do reduce the amount of programmer-written code by 50 percent or more. Application generators also reduce program maintenance requirements and allow the employment of less experienced programmers. With application generators, all programs are structured in a common form and thus are easier to understand and modify. Programmers reportedly find it easier to shift from working on one application to a different application when using an application generator.

Almost every supplier of data base management systems has recently announced one or more application generators. They include IBM's Application Development Facility and Development Management System, Cincom Systems' TOTAL Information System, Cullinane's IDMS-based product line, and American Management Systems' Generation Five.

One important class of application generators are in the financial planning area. Over 30 packages are now available for use on mainframes and minis. At least 5 are available for microcomputers. Recognized leaders among mainframe packages are EIS (Executive Information Systems) from Boeing Computer Services, EXPRESS from Tymeshare, and IFPS from Execucom Systems Corporation. Packages available on a micro (Apple) include Micro-DDS/Finance from Addison-Wesley Publishing Company and RCS-The Micromodeler from Ferox Microsystems, Inc. Additional packages are appearing almost daily.

Performance monitors

Performance monitors are software routines designed to audit and record performance characteristics of computer systems. As systems become more complex—with high priority online jobs running in foreground and lower priority batch jobs running in background, with access being provided from remote sites, and with all these activities being performed in a computing network—the evaluation of computer efficiency becomes difficult. Performance monitors allow the user to fine-tune the system for maximum efficiency. They can also be used to develop a system for charging for use of the computer system and its components. Performance monitors are available primarily from independent software firms.

Data base management systems

Data base software can be purchased in a variety of configurations. Originally, such software was available almost exclusively from software vendors. Currently, almost all hardware vendors offer DBMS packages. They are even available for the most popular microcomputers.

Data base management software is sold in pieces as well as in entire systems. The user can purchase only data-access languages or data-dictionary languages (data definition languages) or, even, file maintenance packages. Total DBMS systems combining the three elements of data definition, data base maintenance, and data base access are becoming more common, however. These systems are usually sold separately as add-ons to a specific operating system. Some common sources are listed in Chapter 14., where there is further discussion of data base management.

Network controllers

A variety of systems are available for controlling distributed data processing, telecommunications, and other communication networks. Popular packages here include ENVIRON/1 from Cincom Systems, Inc.; CICS from IBM; ADR ROSCOE from Applied Data Research; Turnkey TASKMASTER from Turnkey Systems, Inc.; SNA from IBM; and DEC-NET from Digital Equipment Corporation. The latest entrants in this area provide both hardware and software connections for attaching microcomputers to mainframes.

Applications packages

There are many applications packages. The most common are accounting applications (accounts receivable, payroll, personnel, accounts payable, and general ledger). A major supplier in this area is Management Science America. MSA's most popular packages are ALLTAX tax tables, Payroll, and General Ledger. Payroll, general ledger, and accounts payable systems are available from IBM, NCR, Burroughs, and Honeywell Information Systems.

In addition to single applications, industry packages are also available. For example, banking systems are available from University Computing Co., Florida Software Services, and others. Insurance accounting systems are provided by Insurance Systems of America, Inc., Equimatics, Inc., and Policy Management Systems, plus others.

The most recent new packages are being developed in inventory and manufacturing control. Inventory control systems are available from Honeywell and IBM among others. Manufacturing control systems are also available from IBM and Sperry Univac.

Forms of ready-made software

Purchased software comes in several forms. It may be furnished in a source code (for example, COBOL). If so, it must be compiled before running. Some suppliers will only furnish object code and will allow no modifications by the user. Object code is difficult to maintain. Problems that are not the result of a design error in the original program are usually best handled by reentering (recompiling) the program.

Software can be purchased as-is with no further support. Such software should be received in source code and should be well-documented.

The amount of support necessary for a package depends upon package complexity. The best packages are easy to use and require little training for successful implementation. Complex packages that solve complex problems usually cannot be made so simple. A user purchasing complex software should receive adequate training in its use as well as complete documentation.

Advantages of ready-made software

Cost

The major reason for purchasing software packages is cost. The cost of developing a major package is substantial. A package can usually be purchased for a fraction of its development cost. This is partly because the cost of manufacturing additional copies of a package are minimal. The major expenses are initial development, marketing, and support. Current pricing tends to set the price of a package between 10 and 20 percent of its development cost. Maintenance usually costs from 8 to 15 percent of the purchase price per year. This, too, is a bargain, since in-house maintenance has tended to run upwards of 50 percent of total programming effort.

Immediate productivity

Purchased software provides several advantages other than cost. Most important, it can be used immediately. Development of a major application takes from several months to several years.

Reduced need for programmers

A further advantage of purchased software is that it reduces the need for programming talent. The increasing cost of programmers makes this a significant advantage. This reduction in use of programmers is due to reduced development activity and reduced time spent on maintenance.

Disadvantages of ready-made software

Ready-made software is not without its disadvantages. A major one is that it provides a general rather than a specialized solution to each problem. If the package provides for specialized versions, it is then more expensive both to buy and to operate. A generalized payroll package, for example, must allow for adjustment to different local payroll taxes at different rates. It also must allow for the possibility of every sort of payroll deduction, even though an individual user may need only a few of the possibilities. Thus, the package is apt to be larger than necessary and to require more computer facilities than the user really needs. In addition, it probably takes longer to run than a specially developed program.

Another obvious disadvantage of purchased software is that it is maintained from outside the user organization. If a problem is encountered, the maintenance programmer must be called in to fix it. This may take time.

A possible problem with purchased software is future support. A package is only as good as its support, particularly for unsophisticated users. Care must be taken to see that the vendor is capable of supplying continuous support in the future. This is a particular problem when dealing with very small vendors or firms just getting started. Young software firms can easily disappear because the key person who invented the package departs or because of general mismanagement. It has not been uncommon for firms to outsell their ability to provide support for individual users. Even if the package is well-designed, the unsophisticated user is then left in the lurch. "Let the buyer beware" is a good maxim when purchasing ready-made software.

Summary

Ready-made software can be the best buy in town. It allows users without sophisticated programming abilities to make sophisticated use of the computer at a fraction of the cost of in-house development. Packages exist that will perform almost any business data processing task. Packages also are available to provide interconnection of computer components in communication networks and distributed processing systems.

Users must look closely at the support to be expected from a software supplier. Small, young firms may fail due to mismanagement or loss of the key personnel responsible for the design and development of their software product.

COMPUTERS AT WORK

Marian: The Ready-Made Librarian

"The lowest priced on-line librarian on the market" has reduced programming maintenance by two-thirds, reduced disk storage by 50% and made a marked savings in paper costs for National Guardian Life Insurance Co. here [in Madison, Wis.], according to the company's DP manager, James M. Hartman.

Marian: The On-Line Librarian, developed and marketed by Computer Software Unlimited (CSU) of Memphis, was installed by Hartman and his staff after a thorough evaluation of available on-line librarian systems.

Needing to consolidate four different tape library systems maintaining some 900 programs, Hartman began searching for an on-line librarian compatible with his IBM 370/135, DOS/VS and Power VS configuration. By eliminating all systems that would not support his teleprocessing monitor (the Display Unit Control System [Ducs] from CFS, Inc.), Hartman was left with a choice between Marian, which supports any teleprocessing monitor, and one other system.

After ordering both systems on a free trial basis, "I was first impressed by Marian's smaller, more readable manual," Hartman said.

"I thoroughly read the other vendor's manuals, but afterwards still couldn't do anything with the system. After reading Marian's manual, however, I was able to install it."

In outlining the requirements he was looking for in an on-line librarian system. Hartman established a list of 14 selection criteria which were submitted to the prospective vendors. "CSU's president, Mike Pfaff, responded to each point individually, rather than just answering with a blanket statement as the other vendor did, and that impressed me," Hartman recalled.

Once both systems had been tested at National Guardian's DP site, Hartman and his staff had no difficulty making a decision. In fact, "my people got so enamored of Marian and kept slapping more and more programs into it that I had to take it. I could never have backed out of it."

Simplicity lauded

Now that Marian has been up and running for nearly six months, "there's no doubt in my mind that its most important advantage is its simplicity.

"Training time took no more than 30 minutes; Marian's approach to making changes eliminates the problem of learning multiple screens, and the traffic of program-

Source: "Many Savings Seen with On-Line Library Use," *Computerworld*, July 16, 1979, 74.

mers in the computer room has been eliminated," Hartman said.

That has a real impact on morale, according to Hartman: "My programmers feel more in control of their own destiny. Using Marian, they no longer need to worry about impacting background to do their testing."

The DP manager is also pleased with the system's time- and money-saving features: "Our programming maintenance has been reduced to one-third of what it was before the change. Keypunching, batching, compiling, testing and debugging frequently took two to three days. Now we can compile in a matter of minutes.

"Also, Marian's interface through the spooler queue allows programmers to look at output without printing compiles, so they can save two to three compilation printouts per day. And with paper prices going up, that adds up to a significant savings."

Disk storage space has been cut in half because of the systems's library compression techniques, according to Hartman. The programming staff has also gained a half-day of maintenance time per week, since the company's half-day Friday schedule previously allowed time only for production. With Marian allowing maintenance at any time, Friday mornings have been freed for his people.

Other features of the CSU software which have impressed Hartman are its "as of" date function, audit trail, documentation feature and speed of operation.

The "as of" date feature, which allows a member to be displayed, compiled or reproduced as it existed at any previous point in time, has been "very handy," Hartman said, when two people are working on the same program and it becomes necessary to back up to correct conflicting changes.

Marian's audit trail, which allows quick correction of erroneous program changes, has even been used by the company's external auditors to verify information, and the documentation feature enables easy updating of system documentation, he added.

"Marian's a fast system, too. It runs very quickly to pick up our entire library. We have about 250,000 statements, and Marian takes about eight minutes," he noted.

Faster maintenance

Even user departments at National Guardian have benefited from Marian, according to Hartman. Critical maintenance problems that were previously delayed by a long job being run can now be checked and corrected in one day.

The package is currently being used for systems-type work by Hartman's staff as well as source maintenance for the department's 14 on-line systems. Hartman has plans to develop additional on-line systems utilizing Marian.

Special Option

The Software Industry

Introduction

A computer system is made up of hardware components and programs. Software is more than just programs. It also includes the supporting manuals, user guides, program listings, flowcharts, and other materials required to make the program truly usable. In most computer installations, much of this software is obtained from outside suppliers. In addition, some business firms' programming jobs are actually carried out by independent programmers or software "houses" working under contract. The firms and individuals who develop and sell programs and programming services make up the software industry.

Software products

As we know from the preceding Special Option, it is possible to acquire ready-made software for almost every computing task one can name. Many software products are merely a single program (language translator, utility, and so on). A package is more than just a program or even a set of programs that will handle an application or task, however. It includes complete documentation, training, and support. Good package support includes more than simple maintenance to keep the package operating. Buyers of applications are purchasing a problem solution and most EDP problems are dynamic, changing in response to the changes in the social, legal, economic, and competitive environments in which the firm operates. Users also need and expect software that will adjust to hardware advances. If a bigger, faster computer system is obtained, the software that operated on the old system is expected to operate faster on the new, faster system. If a change in legal requirements or competitive relationships requires a change in the software, the user expects that either the supplier will make those changes or provide software that is easy for the user to modify. If new hardware features allow new, more efficient or effective approaches to the problem, the user wants the software to incorporate these new technologies. Thus a top-of-the-line package is a living, changing entity.

Software is available for all sizes of computers. Sometimes it even does the same exact job for different sized computers. For example, a BASIC compiler is available for mainframes, minis, and micros. A simple application such as a sort routine may be available for $5.00 or less for a micro. A sophisticated industry system featuring telecommunications and distributed processing (such as an insurance industry system) may cost as much as $500,000. In between are financial planning aids costing from $150 to $400,000, payroll systems costing from $150 to $50,000 and many more.

Industry Structure

The independent software products industry is a sector of the computer industry in which companies are typically small, with 80 percent generating less than $5 million dollars in sales each year and only a few with more than 100 employees or more than $15 million in sales. Less than ten firms sell more than $20 million worth of software products each year. Table S5.1 presents the software revenues of the top ten firms in the industry in 1979. With only a few exceptions (University Computing is one) these firms offer only one or two major products. International Computer Programs, Inc., published two product listings in 1978 which include more than 1,000 suppliers and over 6,000 products. Only a few of these products are really successful, generating total cumulative revenues of a million dollars or more during their lifetime. The top ten software products in terms of cumulative revenue are listed in Table S5.2. Comparison of Tables S5.1 and S5.2 reveals that some of the most widely used software products come from other than the leading software firms. For example, a popular utility (Westinghouse's Disk Utility) comes from a noncomputer firm. Most software companies were first formed to market a single product (SPSS, Software AG, Cincom Systems). Success in this initial venture lead to development of additional packages.

One sector of the industry is composed of the single entrepreneur with a

	1979 SOFTWARE REVENUES IN $MILLIONS		
	TOTAL	PACKAGES	OTHER
Informatics	102	35	67
Management Science America	35	28	7
Cincom Systems	31	26	5
Applied Data Research	30	26	4
Panasophic Systems	24	24	0
University Computing	83	19	64
Software AG	20	17	3
Rand Information Systems	21	16	5
Information Sciences	15	15	0
Cullinane	14	14	0

Table S5.1 **The top ten software companies**

single product. Moonlighting professional programmers and computer hobbyists seeking financial support for their hobby are significant in local markets. Individuals are particularly important sources of software for small business systems purchased through a retail computer store.

The retail computer store is becoming a source for increasingly sophisticated hardware and software systems built around a microcomputer. The major micro vendors now offer a wide variety of data processing programs on cassettes, disks, and as micro-chips. This should be an improving source of software for small business systems.

The independent software suppliers are only a portion of the software industry. A major segment of software is supplied by the vendors of computer hardware. IBM dominates this part of the industry with software revenues of 500 million dollars or more in 1979. IBM also influences the independents in that most software is designed and programmed for IBM equipment or plug-compatible systems that will run IBM software.

Software marketing

The marketing of this broad range of offerings also varies. As we have already stated, suppliers range from single individuals with a single program to sophisticated firms employing hundreds of software specialists and offering a variety of programs, packages and programming services. Some software is marketed by running advertisements in industry publications, *The Wall Street Journal,* or *Business Week.* Other firms employ a staff of marketing specialists and use the full spectrum of marketing tools.

Industry subsectors have developed in which firms provide catalogs of available software and make their living by bringing buyers and sellers

a. BY CUMULATIVE REVENUE

PRODUCT	SUPPLIER	NUMBER OF INSTALLATIONS	CUMULATIVE REVENUE (MILLIONS OF DOLLARS)
Mark IV Systems	Informatics, Inc.	1,300	50
TOTAL	Cincom Systems, Inc.	2,000	50
Insci Human Resource Systems	Information Sciences, Inc.	375	30
The Librarian	Applied Data Research, Inc.	4,500	20
MSA General Ledger System	Management Science America, Inc.	718	20
MSA Payroll Systems	Management Science America, Inc.	600	20
Scert	Applied Data Research, Inc.	530	20
IDMS	Cullinane Corp.	350	20
Adabas	Software AG	302	20
TALK	System Architects, Inc.	42	20

b. BY INSTALLATIONS

PRODUCT	SUPPLIER	NUMBER OF INSTALLATIONS	CUMULATIVE REVENUE (MILLIONS OF DOLLARS)
The Librarian	Applied Data Research, Inc.	4,500	20
Westinghouse Disk Utility	Westinghouse Electric Corp.	3,522	1
Panvalet	Panasophic Systems	3,300	10
CA-Sort	Computer Associates, Inc.	3,000	10
Autoflow II	Applied Data Research, Inc.	2,100	10
Fast Dump Restore	Innovation Data Processing	2,100	5
SPSS	SPSS, Inc.	2,075	2
TOTAL	Cincom Systems, Inc.	2,000	50
Syncsort	Whitlow Computer Systems Inc.	2,000	10
Easytrieve	Panasophic Systems, Inc.	1,650	10

*Compiled from data reported at March 1978 Seventh Annual ICP Million Dollar Awards Ceremony.

Table S5.2 **The top ten software products (1978 data)***

together. Some firms even seek out unique, marketable applications developed by computer users and seek to market them under a licensing agreement. Software is even given away, with program listings appearing in popular computer magazines. These giveaways tend to be concentrated in the microcomputer market at this time. Few programs for mainframes have been given away since software and hardware were "unbundled" (sold as separate products) by computer vendors starting in 1969. Most of the current giveaways are for the computer hobbyist, although some of the utility routines could be useful to business users.

Industry growth

The total size of the software industry is hard to judge. Estimates of total revenues of the independent software suppliers in 1979 vary from .5 billion to 1 billion dollars. Estimates of annual growth rates are more consistent however, clustering in the range of 25 to 28 percent.

The future of the software industry is being shaped by two forces. The economics of software (high cost of development, low cost of producing additional units) support increased growth. What is not clear is how the expanding use of firmware (software incorporated into hardware) will affect software sales. As hardware vendors incorporate features of operating systems into hardware, those features become unalterable and must be used. More important, they require changes in software that is to run on the new hardware. Since firmware is much harder to analyze and unravel than the software it replaces, independent software suppliers are at a disadvantage and must adapt their products to work with firmware features. Obviously, too, as the incorporation of firmware increases, the need for ready-made software decreases.

The move to added firmware and increased dependence on the computer vendor for software is countered by the existence of a large base of current installations. As indicated previously, the vast majority of software supplied by the independents is designed for IBM hardware. IBM cannot afford to abandon its 20,000 or so current installations. If all were forced to redevelop current applications to realize hardware savings or to implement more sophisticated systems, many would turn to other suppliers.

The long-run outcome of the above struggle is unclear. Software industry experts come up with varying answers. However, the estimates of revenues from independent software in 1985 vary upward from a *low* of 5 billion dollars. Technically competent software suppliers with good products do not seem to be in danger of falling by the wayside.

INDUSTRY TRENDS

Growing from the Inside Out

About twice each week, Ronald D. Palamara, chairman and president of Anacomp Inc., awakens during the night and spends as much as two hours dictating memos and business strategies that have come to him during sleep. Some might call this excessive. But for Anacomp, the company that Palamara co-founded in 1968, such dedication is paying off. Under the guidance of the hard-driving, 42-year-old former professor of engineering, Anacomp has become one of the fastest-growing companies in the rapidly expanding computer services and software industry.

Thanks to a voracious acquisition appetite—Anacomp gobbled up 15 smaller competitors in the last 34 months—the company has risen above the mom-and-pop status that still characterizes most of the industry. Anacomp's sales have grown at a rate of 51% compounded over the past four years. Net income last year topped $4.8 million on sales of $67.1 million and for the fiscal year ending June 30 revenues are expected to top $100 million. "They've put together a very successful, aggressive empire-building acquisition program," declares David A. Henwood, at Prescott, Ball & Turben, the Cleveland investment banking firm.

But now Palamara is planning to grow Anacomp from the inside out. The key to this strategy is a software package called CIS, (for Continuous Integrated System) a completely integrated retail banking system. The software will work on the International Business Machines Corp. computers installed at 95% of the banks with assets of more than $1 billion. CIS, when finished, will tie all of a customer's bank accounts—checking, savings, installment loans—into one master data file, enabling the bank to update instantly the appropriate account balance each time the customer makes a transaction. Current systems typically update separate files each night.

Significant risk

Even though the software will not be ready for delivery until early 1982, bankers are already enthusiastic. "It is going to change the whole way we deal with a customer, and it's got to save us big bucks, too," declares Paul B. Rossan, executive vice-president at First National Bank of Kansas City.

Indeed, CIS will be able to handle bank functions now carried out by a patchwork of software packages, enabling a bank to reduce software maintenance costs and to

Source: "Growing from the Inside Out," from the June 1, 1981 issue of *Business Week,* 108B, 108D.

adapt its computer operations more quickly to provide new services to customers. At Provident National Bank in Philadelphia, for instance, Anthony J. Cacciatore, senior vice-president, says it took almost nine months to convert the bank's demand deposit system to accommodate the new interest-bearing negotiable order of withdrawal (NOW) accounts. With Anacomp's CIS software, he figures, this time could be cut to two or three months.

Competitors wonder, however, whether the CIS project may prove to be more than Anacomp can successfully swallow. "What they're trying to do is doable," says Bernard C. Hogan, chairman of Hogan Associates Inc., a Dallas-based software concern that caters to banks. But, Hogan warns, "there's a significant risk [of failure]."

Just in case the task proves too difficult, Palamara has devised an innovative financing plan that would cushion the blow of failure. To finance the software project, Palamara put together a limited partnership of outside investors and Anacomp officers that will provide a total of $7.5 million. In addition, he recruited four banks, which kicked in $1.5 million and six programmers each. In exchange, the banks get free use of the software when it is completed, and the investors receive an immediate tax write-off for R&D expense and the right to royalties of as much as 70% of any profits.

$1 billion by 1990

To spread the risk beyond the software development effort, Palamara is counting on Anacomp's strong market position in computer facilities management; its on-line data processing services for banks, credit unions, and government agencies; and its micrographics business, which will account for close to half of Anacomp's sales this year, up from 35% in 1980.

Given the strong growth in micrographics and the expected revenues from banking software, Palamara is betting on a 30% compound growth rate for Anacomp over the next 10 years. "We should be a $1 billion company by 1990," he boasts. Outsiders say that his confidence in his company is not misplaced. "With the kind of track record he's had for the last five years," says Lawrence A. Welke, president of International Computer Programs, Inc., a neighboring software information bureau in Indianapolis, "there are few people around here anymore who doubt he's going to get the job done."

Part 4

Data Processing Systems

Chapter 12 Analyzing Data Processing Systems

Outline

The first step in designing a computerized data processing system should be a **system analysis** to determine whether a computer is to be used. The design of a computerized data processing system should not be undertaken until it has been demonstrated that the use of such a system is feasible. Are the volumes of data to be handled, the amounts and types of processing required, and the time available for carrying out the total process such that a computer is needed? Only after the feasibility of a computerized system has been demonstrated and the overall system defined, should the development of any computer program be started.

Steps in system analysis

Data processing systems dealing with a business activity (such as accounts receivable and customer billing) are complex. They usually process data from several sources and attempt to meet a number of objectives. The resources available for performing the needed processing are limited. Limitations also are imposed by company policy and organization and by available processing technology. It is best to have a set procedure to follow which will ensure careful attention to all these details. We suggest the following steps:

1 Define system objectives.
2 Define system components and boundaries.
3 Define system interfaces with other systems.
4 Define system procedures.
5 Define system volume and timing requirements.
6 Document the system.
7 Analyze system effectiveness and efficiency.
8 Suggest system improvements.

This chapter will describe these steps and the tools and procedures available for carrying them out.

Define system objectives

To determine the objectives of a data processing system, the objectives of the organization it serves must be understood. What is the organization trying to do? How are its resources arranged? Where does the data processing system being studied fit into the total picture?

Overall objectives for an organization are determined by top management, that is, the senior operating officers and/or the board of directors. In well-managed organizations, these objectives will have been formally recorded in statements of objectives and goals. In many organizations, however, such formal statements do not exist, are out of date, or are incomplete. Top management must then be asked to fill the gap.

Organization chart

A useful starting point in understanding relationships among the components making up an organization is the organization chart. As the following definition indicates, the organization chart is, in effect, a map showing where responsibilities are assigned within the organization. An **organization chart** is a two-dimensional schematic which, by showing the placement of individuals and groups and their reporting relationships, indicates the assignment of responsibility and authority within the organization. Figure 12.1 shows the major lines of authority and responsibility in a hypothetical firm. Figure 12.2 shows the organization of the financial function in more detail.

Organization charts must be developed and used with care. The true relationships between the persons making up organizational components may be different from those shown in a formal organization chart. In any case, the analyst must determine who is responsible for the activity being studied and can therefore identify the specific objectives and goals for that activity.

The objectives of a data processing system are indicated in part by its placement within the organization, by who controls it, and by who receives its reports, facts revealed by the organization chart. Usually, the higher it is placed in the organization the greater its emphasis on the creation of management information.

The supervisor of the system

The objectives of an operating data processing system are also reflected in the requirements of the system as understood by the person responsible for the system's operation. The system's supervisor obviously must have an idea of what the system is intended to accomplish. An in-depth interview with this person should provide valuable information on the system's objectives.

System inputs and outputs

The objectives of an existing processing system are further reflected in the system itself. What data inputs does it receive? What outputs (reports, documents, data files) does it create? These outputs indicate the system's objectives as they are understood by those currently operating the system. Top management should be able to specify if it desires any change in these outputs.

In summary, the objectives of a data processing system are found by consulting three sources.

1 Top management
2 The person supervising the data processing system (if a system exists)
3 The output of the system (if a system exists)

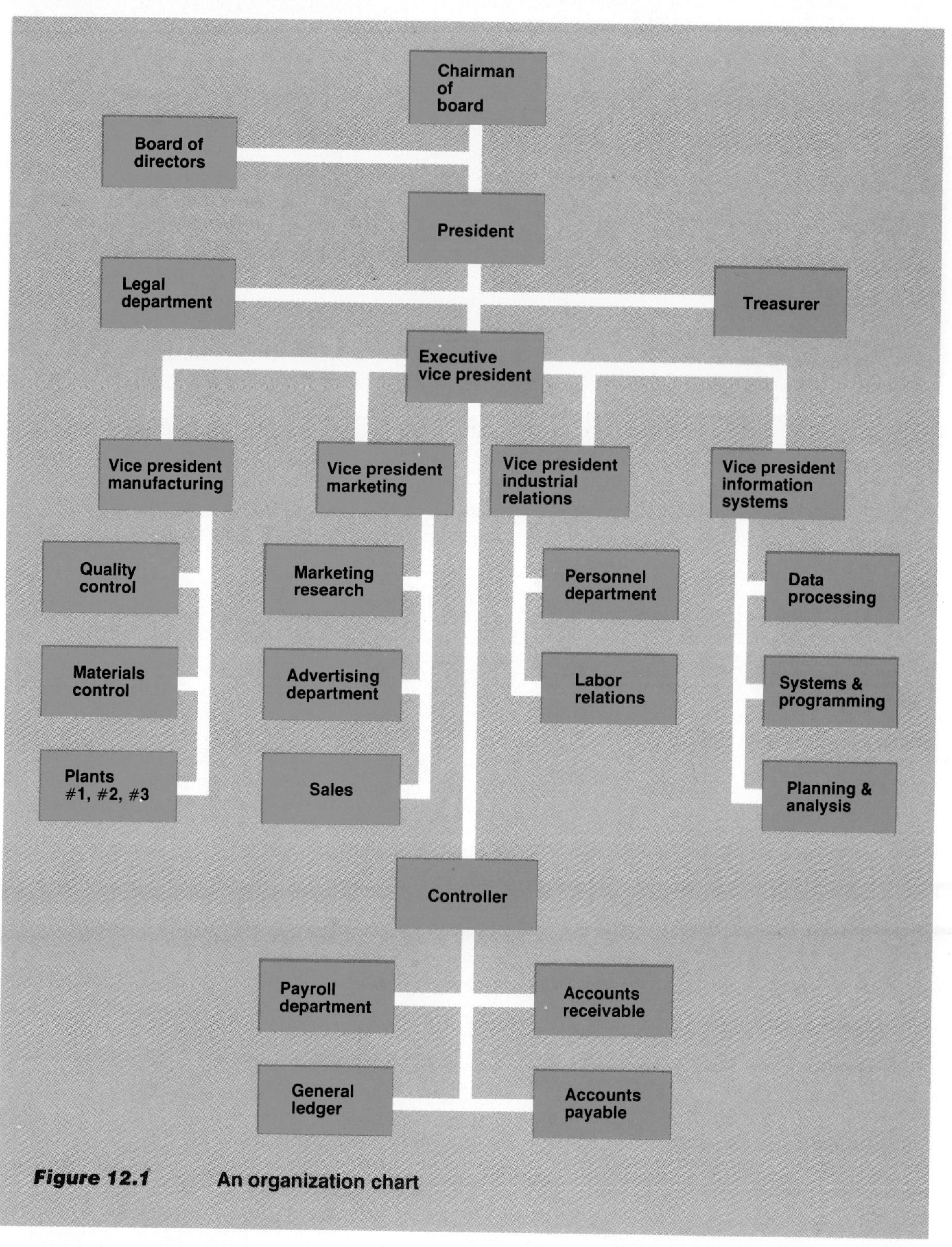

Figure 12.1 An organization chart

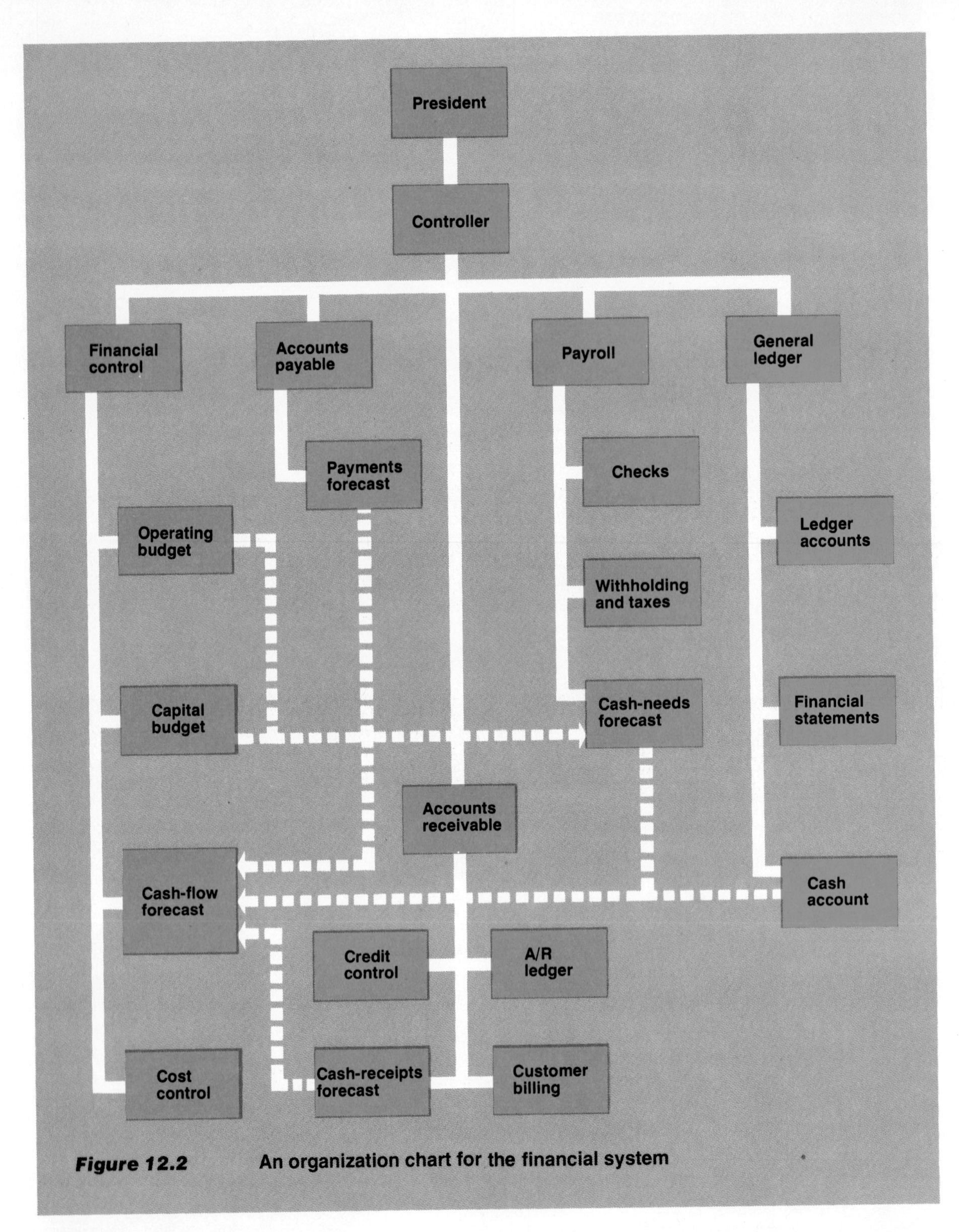

Figure 12.2 An organization chart for the financial system

Define system components and boundaries

All systems are part of a larger system. Consider, for example, a system for providing food to students living in a college dormitory. The immediate preparation and serving of the food usually occurs within the dining facility, but the raw materials, the unprepared foods, come from off the premises. How far along this delivery chain should one go in a study of the food delivery system? The local food delivery system can be considered as the last link in a system that includes retailers and/or wholesalers, farm-product processors, and farmers and their suppliers, including the sun's energy. Obviously, one would seldom have a real interest in the *total* system, nor would one attempt to reorganize or modify the entire system to make it more efficient or productive.

The components that need to be identified within a data processing system are the people, machines, and procedures accomplishing the data processing activities. A useful way to begin is to think in terms of the three basic data processing **system components**—input, processing, and output. How are data introduced into the system? What media are used for storage and transmission of the data within the system? What devices or machines are used in capturing, storing, transporting, and modifying data within the system? Are these devices special-purpose devices useful for accomplishing only a single activity or more general-purpose devices, capable of a wide range of activities? Who operates each of these devices and governs the data transfers between devices?

If the system being analyzed is only a part of the total data processing system, its purpose in the overall system must be known if its outputs are to be compatible with total system objectives. Thus it must be recognized that the payroll processing subsystem requires many of the same data inputs as the labor-cost control subsystem. These two jobs may be accomplished in part as an *integrated* processing activity. Data on labor time can be collected just once and used for both purposes. If the basic purpose of the total system is kept in mind, the integrated nature of subsystems and the need for fully processing each data input are more easily recognized.

In defining components, the total system is usually divided into subcomponents, or **work stations**, each responsible for a single activity or group of interrelated activities. In systems using electronic digital computers, these may not be physical work stations, but computer programs and related offline (noncomputer) activities. In such cases, the computer system is a major component and the individual programs are subcomponents of the total system being studied. In systems that are largely manual, a work station may be only a single desk or machine and the person assigned to that desk or machine. Alternatively, a work station may consist of a group of desks (machines) and the individuals performing a single detail operation or a set of related detail operations at those desks (machines).

The process of identifying system components necessarily includes the definition of system boundaries. **System boundaries** are defined to be all components that have a significant effect on the operation of the system. An effect is considered significant if it can change the system's results in a way that is important to the reason for studying the system. Obviously, in order for the boundary to include the components, the components must be identified.

The methods used to define components are numerous. Spending time with the system's supervisor can help to obtain an overall picture of the system. It is usually impossible to get a complete picture without spending time at the lowest functional level, however. The supervisor is often too far removed from daily operations to know the details of those operations.

An efficient way to gain an understanding of a system is to follow the basic system flow, simply taking note of any deviations from the main flow. Once the main-line system has been identified, each of the different **special-action paths** can be examined in detail. Failure to define adequately the special-action deviations from the main system will mean continual system failures and a need for constant revision of any new system that may be developed. At this stage, however, we are trying only to define what is contained within the system and are interested in the detailed activities carried on by components only to the extent that they help us to decide whether each component encountered is or is not in the system.

In summary, the analyst attempts to identify the groupings of productive factors (people and machines) whose activities affect the system's results in a meaningful way. At this stage, the analyst need not determine the detailed procedures followed by each group, but need only note each group's general task. The analyst need be concerned only with the major flow through the system that relates the components and thus identifies them.

Define system interfaces with other systems

As indicated above, the definition of system boundaries is somewhat arbitrary. Most business transactions affect several business functions. It is also clear, however, that attempting to analyze the total information and data processing system as a single entity is essentially impossible. The total system should be thought of as a "black box" with grossly specified inputs and outputs. Within that major black box are smaller black boxes with more clearly identified inputs and outputs. Each of these smaller boxes would normally receive inputs from or pass inputs to other black boxes. In addition, subsystems may use the same inputs or share a common master file. These areas where subsystems have contact are called **system interfaces**. It is important to identify them. In groupings of subsystems, it is often desirable to group together all those subsystems sharing common inputs or common files. Such interrelationships also affect transaction volumes in each subsystem. Integrating interrelated subsystems into a larger subsystem can reduce the total volume of processing transactions. For example, distributing labor costs to departments or projects while computing a payroll means that the inputs involved (hours worked, pay rates, and so on) need to be entered only once. Therefore, the number of input operations has been reduced.

Define system procedures

Once people and machines have been grouped into system components and the system's interfaces with other systems have been identified, the analyst can define the actual processing procedures carried out within the system. Again, a useful way to begin is to think in terms of the three basic components of any data processing system—input, processing, and output. What data enter the system? How, in general, are they modified? What reports and files are created by the system? At this stage, it can be useful to follow the input data representing a single transaction through the system and observe exactly what happens to it at each work station.

Work stations procedures

Identifying the actual tasks performed at each major work station is a good way to identify the major procedures carried out in the system. In processing for payroll and labor-cost analysis for workers paid on an hourly basis, we might find the following groupings in a large manual system:

Work Station	Tasks
1	Compute gross pay (hours worked times rate per hour, adjust for vacations, overtime, and so on)
2	Compute deductions, withholdings, and employer contributions for insurance, taxes, and so on
3	Distribute total labor costs (gross pay plus employer contributions) to cost centers
4	Compute net pay and prepare payroll register
5	Write checks

All these tasks might be performed by a single, complex computer program in a more automated system.

Special processing paths

In any processing system, some of the inputs are processed in a way different from the general flow. For example, what happens in the hourly payroll system if a worker is on paid vacation? Where is the payroll cost charged? It may be most appropriate to charge such costs to general overhead and redistribute them as an overhead cost. It depends on whether each employee has a single identifiable work station and whether his or her labor costs are always charged to a particular cost center. In any case, it must be recognized that a special transaction is being processed for which some processing steps depart from the usual routine. Failure to recognize such occurrences will result in an incomplete system.

Control procedures

Data processing systems must include controls to guard against mistakes. The most common mistakes are

1 Failure to process all transactions
2 Processing illegal transactions
3 Processing incorrect transactions
4 Processing transactions incorrectly

Specific control procedures will be discussed in Chapter 15. Here, we merely wish to emphasize the need for such controls and for their inclusion in the description of system procedures. Such things as use of prenumbered forms, audits of data before processing, control totals, record and/or transaction counts, sequence checks, checks for proper files, and other accuracy checks should be carefully noted in the description of system procedures.

Define system volume and timing requirements

The most efficient and economical processing procedures and devices to use in a processing system depend mainly on two factors: (1) the volumes of transactions and reports (including the number of records in the files found in the system); and (2) the length of time available for each processing operation.

The analyst normally starts with **master-file volume**. In the hourly payroll system, for example, we would ask, "How many hourly employee records are to be found in the master file?" and "How many characters are found in each master payroll record?"

How often the data and information in the file need to be referred to is also important. If raw or processed data for each transaction must be retained in easily accessible form for repeated reference or as a basis for daily operations, storage requirements can be substantially increased.

After file size has been established, the number of input transactions must be determined. A simple count of transactions by type may not be sufficient. To know only the number of hourly employees will not be enough. How frequently are they paid? How are their hours of work reported? For example, do all of them check in and record their arrival within a span of a few minutes each morning? If so, the system must be capable of accepting an input from each employee in that short time period. Is shifting between work stations or jobs permitted? If so, is the system responsible for recording these shifts? In other words, we need to know the **peak processing demands** that will be made on each part of the system, not just average weekly, daily, or hourly activity. Transaction counts must be related to the timing of inputs.

Transaction counts must also be related to the timing of outputs and, thus, to the length of time available for processing inputs. The question to be answered is, "How soon must the data be processed or analyzed; that is, how soon must custodial documents or analytic results of the processing be available for use within the operation or in the control of the operation?" A related question is, "Who is to receive the report, and how does that person use the results?" Normally, the closer the recipient of a report is to the actual physical operation, the more quickly that person must be made aware of the system's results. Those responsible for controlling day-to-day physical operations must receive frequent, detailed reports. Those responsible for planning and policy need more fully analyzed (summarized and organized) data and analytic results showing the relationship of the particular activity to other activities of the organization and to long-run plans and overall objectives and goals. For example, in a manufacturing business, those managing the production operation need to know the range of production rates, the product mix being run, the length of the run, and how efficiently each production unit is performing. Policy and planning management in the same firm needs only average costs and production totals, those data that reflect on the overall objectives and goals set by management. Operating management, on the other hand, must know detailed marginal costs and individual unit production to control the operation so it will reach management's goals. Planning and policy management is concerned primarily with whether or not the goals are being met. Operating managers must not only know the details of the operation; their information must also be current. Only when pursuing an explanation of unexpected or undesired results will planning and policy management be concerned with the day-to-day details of the operation. Actually, planning can operate effectively only if the day-to-day fluctuations in the data are not allowed to obscure trends and long-run averages.

Another dimension of the volume and timing requirements is the complexity of the processing required. More sophisticated and expensive processing devices can be justified at lower volumes when complex processing within a short period of time is required.

Documenting the system: flowcharts

Any data processing system accepts data inputs and transforms these inputs into desired outputs. This process can be shown as a flow. The transformations carried out at each work station can be represented as boxes or symbols and then be connected by flow lines. As we know, this is called *flowcharting.*

The black box concept

The overall premise underlying flowcharting is the **black box concept**. Each transformation process is considered to be a black box. Each black box can be further broken down until a level is reached where the process has been described in sufficient detail or the transformation process within the black box is described as completely as possible. The result is a flowchart.

There are two basic kinds of flowcharts. **System flowcharts** outline the system and identify the major inputs and outputs, the basic files, and work stations involved. Detailed **procedural flowcharts** are used to describe in detail the input, processing, and output activities involved in the system.

System flowchart

In the system flowchart, the process of breaking down the transformation boxes into greater detail is stopped at the point where the major work stations and files in the system have been identified. To illustrate, let's consider an inventory accounting and control system.

The term *inventory* includes a variety of subdivisions. In trading firms involved in wholesale or retail trade, the merchandise held for sale is the inventory. In a manufacturing firm, finished goods are held for sale, goods in the process of being produced form the goods-in-process inventory, the raw materials and parts held for future use in production are the raw materials inventory, and the consumables to be used to support future production and office activity are the supplies inventory. These inventories provide buffers between activities that vary because of transit and production time and seasonal irregularities in demand and supply.

The verbal description for an inventory accounting and control system might run as follows:

A master inventory file containing a record for each item is to be maintained. A record must contain the following:

Item identification
Number of units on hand
Cost per unit on hand
Number of units on order
Number and value of units issued this month
Number and value of units issued to date this year
Number and value of units on backorder
Number and value of units received this month
Number and value of units received this year
Reorder point
Economic order quantity

The system will receive as inputs inventory withdrawals, receipts, and returns, and will output stock-out notices, daily reorder lists, backorder lists, and purchase orders. At weekly intervals, the system will output an inventory status report showing the current balance of each item, and an open purchase order report showing unfilled and partially filled purchase orders. At monthly intervals, the system will output inventory activity reports showing the current balance for each item and number of units on order and on backorder.

The system will also maintain a vendor history file containing current data on the speed with which orders are filled, the extent of backorders, and the proportion of inadequate items received from each vendor. These data will be used to output a vendor evaluation report each month.

A simplified system flowchart for the inventory accounting and control system is shown in Figure 12.3. Note that the system, as shown, actually consists of two parts: a withdrawal (order from inventory) system and a receipts and returns portion.

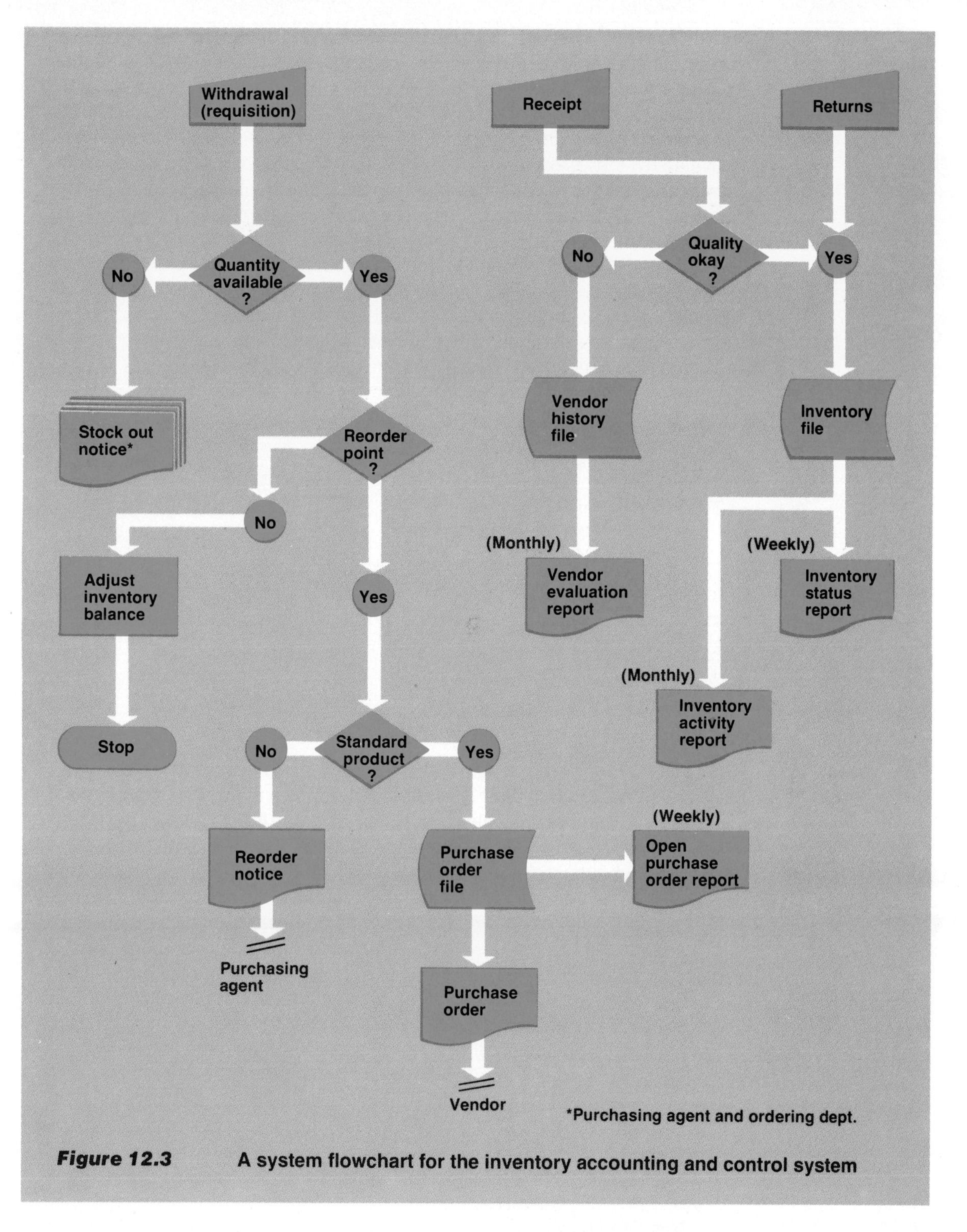

Figure 12.3 A system flowchart for the inventory accounting and control system

The symbols most commonly used in flowcharts are shown in Figure 12.4. The symbols shown are among the standard set adapted by the American National Standards Institute for flowcharting.

In addition to the symbols shown in Figure 12.4, there are other specialized symbols, some of which are shown in Figure 12.5, on page 348.

Note how the use of identifiable symbols in Figure 12.3 helps to clarify the system by clearly indicating the media on which each file is stored and which operations are online and which offline. In a complete system chart, annotation (notes) would be added to clarify the system by identifying major file content. Volumes are often supplied in notes also. A word of caution: At the earliest stages of system development, the analyst may not know what devices will be used and which processes and files will be online and offline. In that case the symbols used for each file would be those for online storage,

, or offline storage,

, from Figure 12.4.

To complete the entire inventory accounting and control system would require another flowchart, or two, to compute reorder points and economic order quantities (economic lot sizes for internally produced items). We also have not allowed for processes to add new items or delete old items from the inventory file.

Procedural flowchart

The specific detailed procedures followed at each work station to carry out the overall tasks also need to be defined. This is done with a procedural flowchart. The procedural flowchart evolves from the system flowchart to detail procedures at a work station within the system. The procedural flowchart is a sequence of processing steps and decision blocks connected by flow lines and connectors. Generally, the overall process again involves the three phases of input, process, and output. In business data processing, as indicated previously, files of transactions and change data are passed against a master file to update the master and create management reports. Usually, after a single transaction is handled and the resulting output created, the process loops back to handle another transaction. This feature is illustrated in the procedural flowchart of Figure 12.6, on page 350, where the process order module from the order processing program of Chapter 8 is detailed. A further illustration of a procedural flowchart is given in Figure 12.7, on page 351, where the reorder module for the program from Chapter 8 is detailed.

Note the sequence of decisions in Figure 12.6. This module is really only a

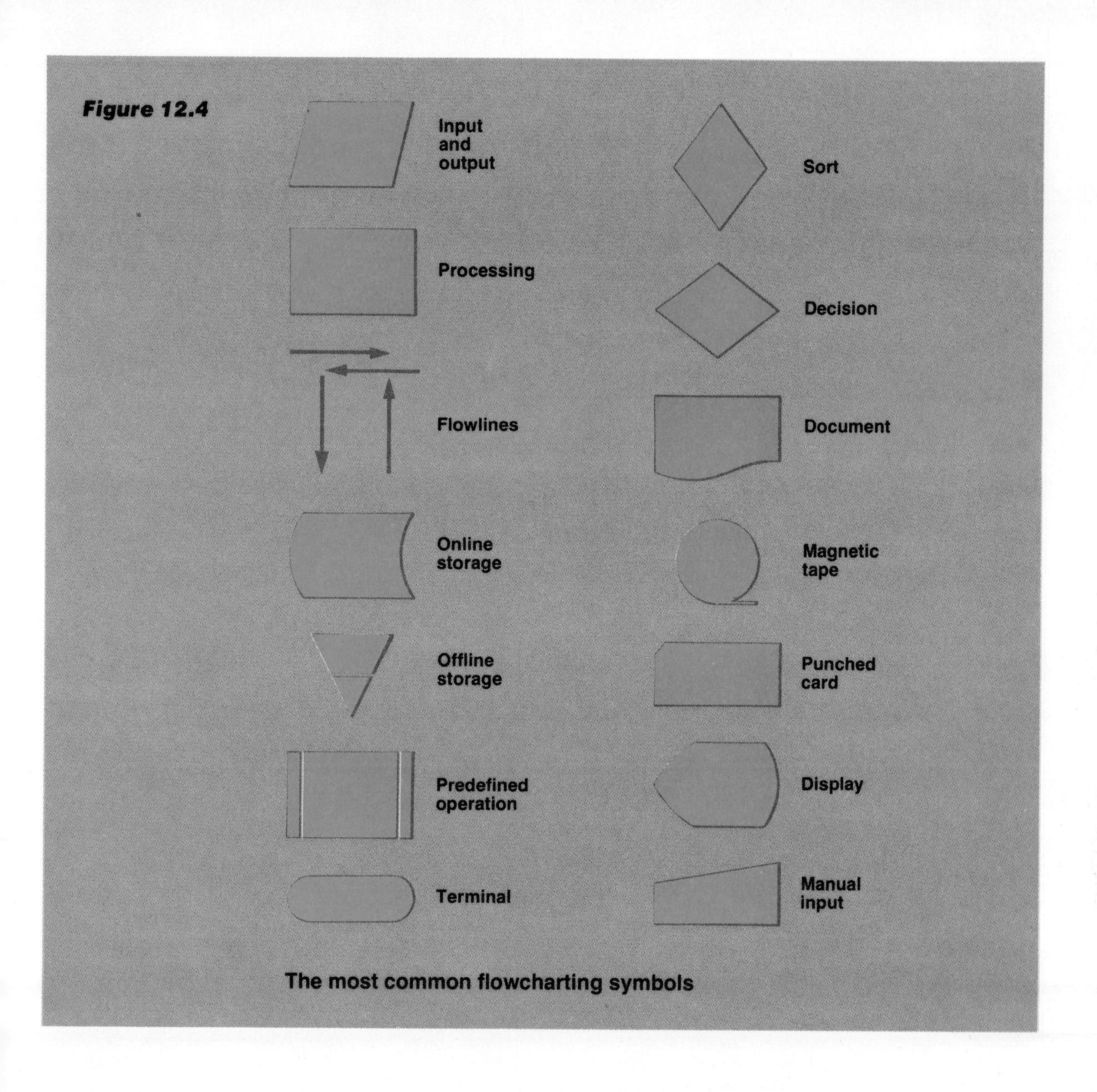

The most common flowcharting symbols

module for choosing submodules for processing. Figure 12.7, on the other hand, describes a processing module rather than a control module and therefore contains only a single looping instruction.

Flowcharting guidelines

The guidelines for system flowcharts and procedural flowcharts are roughly similar. They are summarized in the following list, which applies to *all* flowcharts:

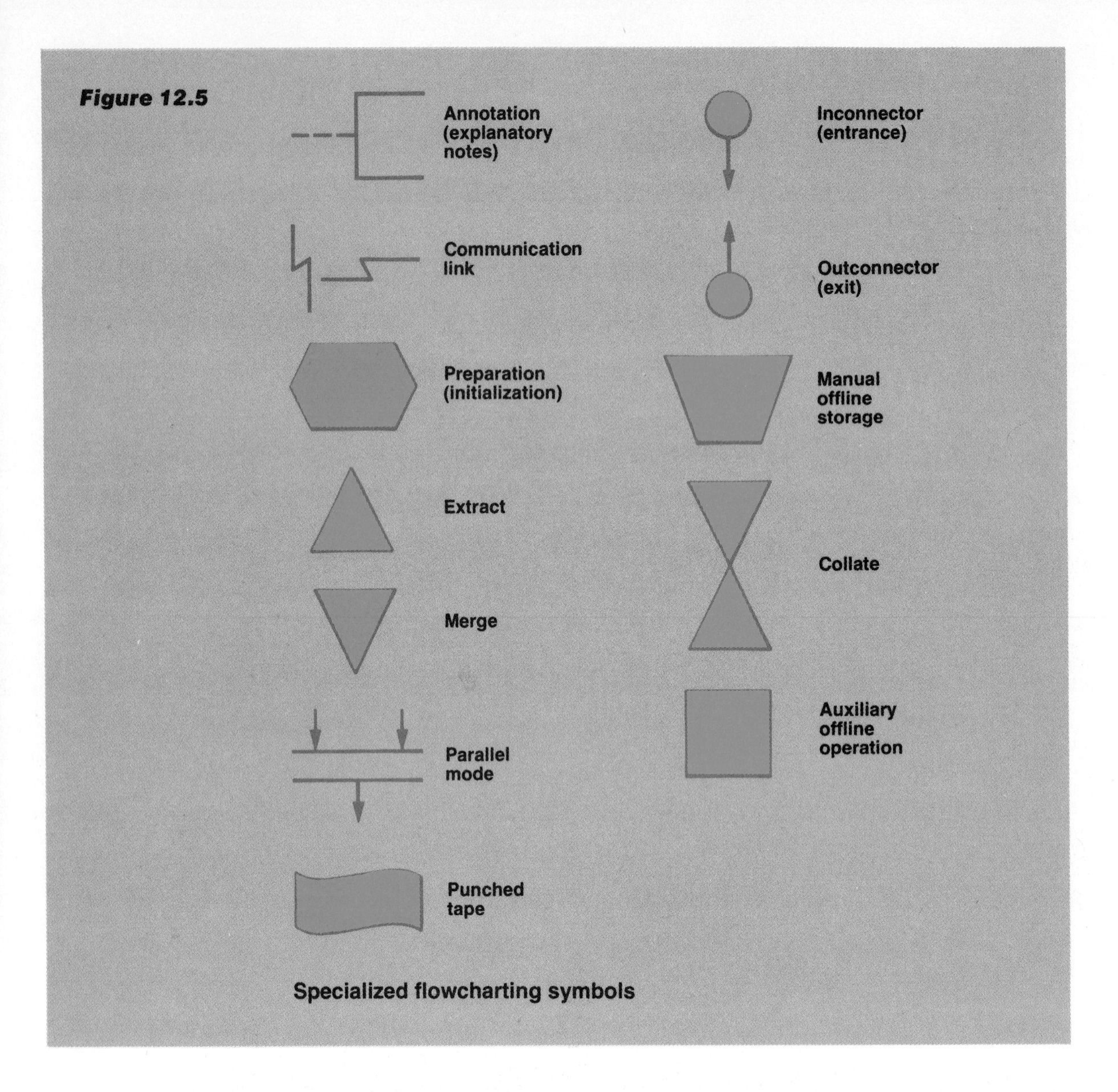

Figure 12.5 Specialized flowcharting symbols

1 Choose the wording within symbols to fit the needs of those who will use the charts, but charts using something close to common English are most easily understood. For example, note the use of words like *Backorder Amt.* in Figure 12.6. What about *NBAL;* what do you suppose it means? Maybe it should be *NUBAL.* It stands for "New Balance."
2 Hold to a consistent level of detail throughout each chart. The description of a system is usually developed in stages at successively more detailed levels. The reader is led into greater detail by each stage. This is illustrated best by the system chart of Figure 12.3, the block diagram in

Figure 8.4 (page 224), and the procedural flowcharts of Figures 12.6 and 12.7. These flowcharts describe the same program at different levels of detail.

3 Annotation (notes) can be helpful in providing clarity. Annotation can be used without the annotation symbol. For example, it is common to add a note giving volume and timing information at points where input or output occur. Thus, at the point where the master inventory records are read, we might find this note:

For notes without the annotation symbol, see Figure 12.3 where the timing of output reports is indicated by the notation above each output symbol. Other examples can be found in Figures 12.6 and 12.7 where a note is found with each page connector to clearly identify which module is found on the page referred to.

4 Use identifying names for variables and files consistently, that is, a specific name should refer to the same entity each time the name is used. Names should be brief, and English language names are preferred.

5 Keep the flowchart as simple and linear as possible. More cluttered charts are harder to read. Break them up if necessary (compare Figures 12.3 and 12.6). Flowlines should enter or leave near the center of a flowchart symbol. Whenever possible, collect flowlines so that only one line enters each figure.

6 Avoid crossing flowlines as much as possible. The use of connectors is helpful here.

7 Processing to be handled separately should be clearly separated. Thus, manual or electromechanical preprocessing of data before a computer run should be clearly specified separately from the computer program. Also, initial preparation of any processing device by an operator (for instance, changing plug boards, tapes, or disk packs and setting control switches) should not be included in the description of the internal process (the program) to be carried out, but should be shown in a separate preprocessing flow diagram.

8 Use cross-references liberally. Cross-references between different flows often serve to point out possibilities for greater integration of the system.

9 Flow should be from top to bottom and left to right. Initial entrances to a flow diagram should be at the top and/or left and final exits at the bottom and/or right. Preferably, intermediate entrances are from the left side and intermediate exits are to the right side.

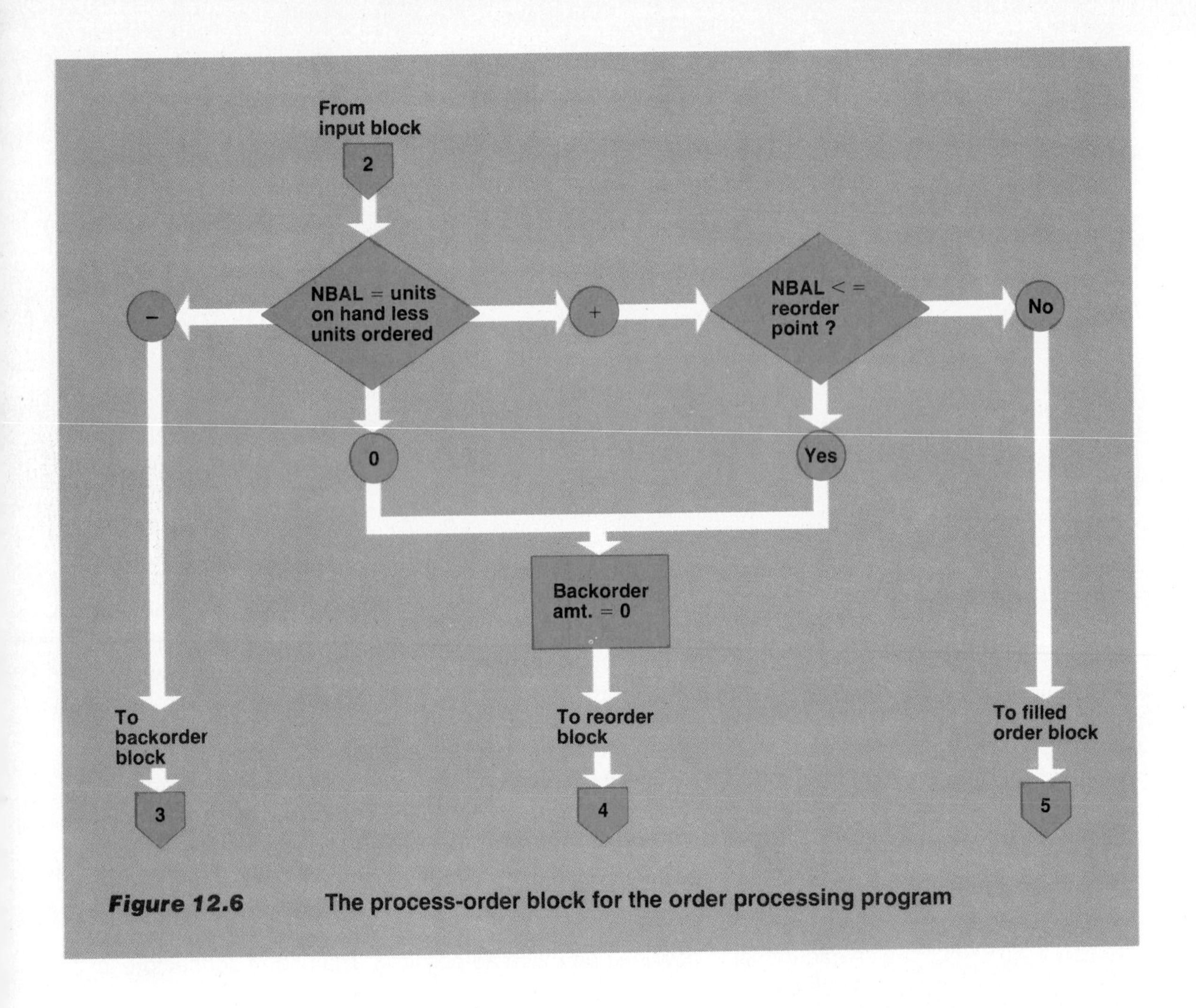

Figure 12.6 The process-order block for the order processing program

10 Use specialized symbols and annotation whenever appropriate to provide additional descriptive value to the flowchart. This is especially important on system charts. For example, the specialized symbols of Figure 12.3 tell us that the inventory master file is stored online in random-access storage, most likely a disk. For absolute clarity, we might have used the symbol for a specific device:

Core Storage

Magnetic Disk

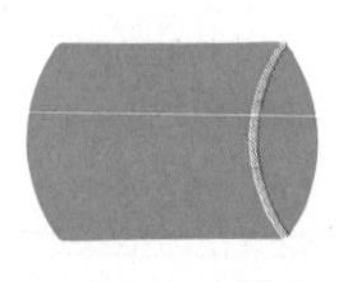
Magnetic Drum

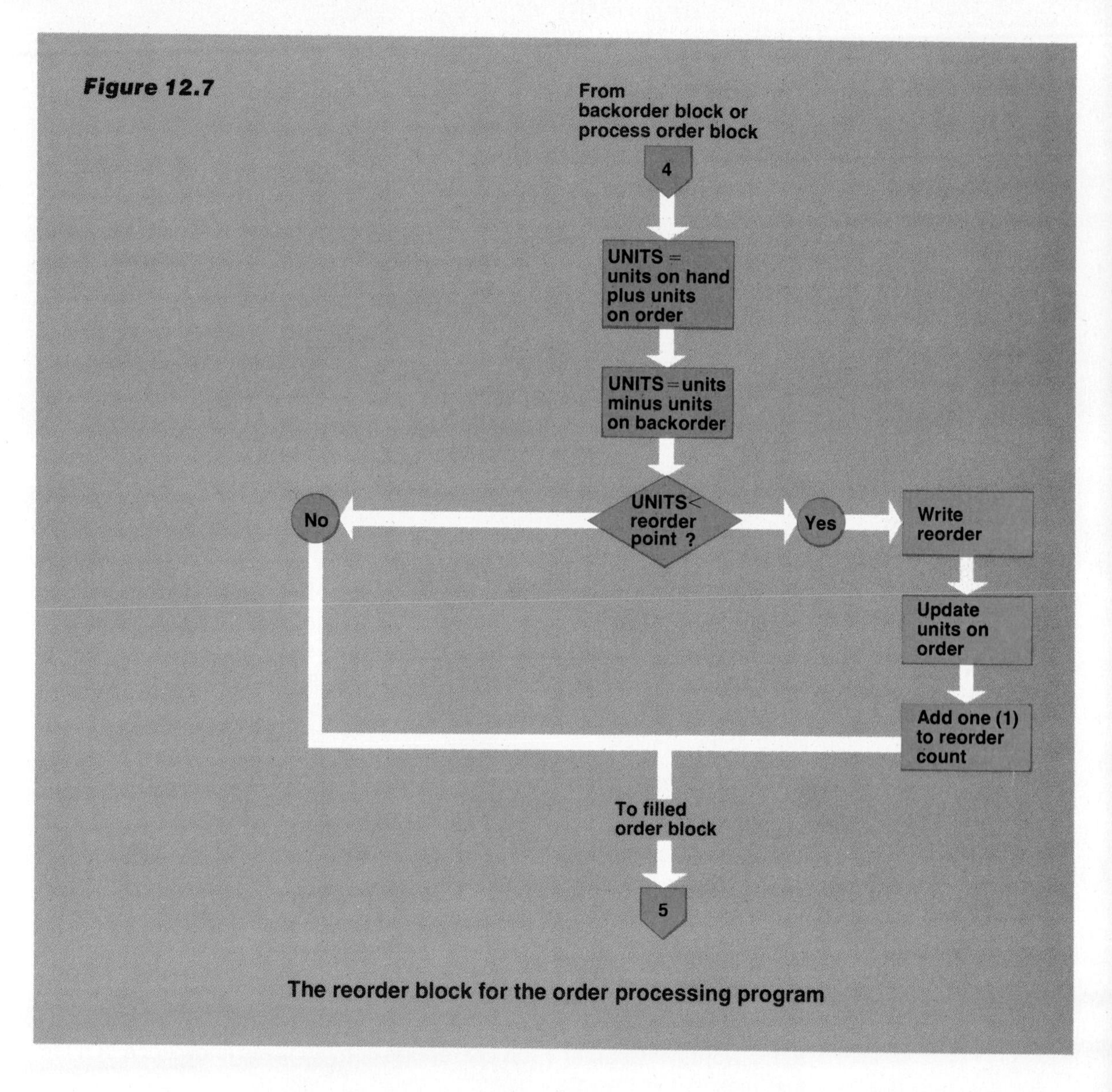

Figure 12.7 The reorder block for the order processing program

11 Stick to these guidelines and the standard flowcharting symbols; avoid all deviations.

Analyzing system effectiveness and efficiency

Adequate data processing systems provide the reliable processing and information that management wants and needs (*effectiveness*) at the lowest possible cost (*efficiency*).

System effectiveness

System effectiveness is measured by the degree to which the system meets its processing and informational goals. Three basic questions must be answered:

1 Does the system perform necessary custodial processing?
2 Does the system preserve the historical data needed as a basis for managerial planning and control and custodial reporting?
3 Does the system provide adequate information for managerial planning and control?

Basically, effectiveness is judged by the results (outputs) of the system in relation to the desired results.

Practical methods for assessing the effectiveness of a system in providing management information consist of asking, and answering, a series of questions:

1 Do managers use the reports they receive?
2 Do managers routinely perform data processing?

A look at the reports and related paper after the reports have been used by managers can be revealing. Managers and their assistants may be routinely performing further processing of reported data. Ratios and percentages are often scribbled in the margins of reports, or columns of comparative data for some past period are added. Key figures may be plotted on a graph or data from two or more reports combined to reveal changing relationships. If managers routinely process data further, the system is not doing a complete job of data analysis.

3 How frequently do managers find it necessary to go outside the formal system to get needed information?

Are the facts being solicited informally before the system supplies them in formal reports?

4 Does the same information appear in more than one report?
5 Do reports clearly identify problems and present the correct information for dealing with them?
6 Do reports arrive quickly enough to be useful in controlling the operation?

In the words of Chapter 1, do the reports communicate knowledge in a form that makes it immediately useful for decision making?

In summary, it must be determined whether the data from all transactions are properly recorded and processed on a timely basis to provide management with the information needed to keep the physical system operating correctly. Unless management has clearly specified measurable goals for the physical system and defined the information requirements for the processing system, this task can be almost impossible.

System efficiency

System efficiency refers to the ratio of outputs to effort and cost. That is, can the outputs from the system be obtained with fewer resources or can more outputs be obtained by rearranging the resources being used? There are two aspects of efficiency, technical and economic.

Technical efficiency Technical efficiency has to do with the methods and machines used for each job. That is, is the equipment being used correctly? Is there better equipment for the job? If a computer is involved, these can be difficult, highly technical questions. Analysis of technical efficiency is best carried out by a qualified computer scientist. For example, sorting with a computer can be done by a wide variety of techniques, each of which requires differing amounts of time and equipment components. The best technique to accomplish a particular sort depends on the system components available, the size and structure of the file to be sorted, the programming language being used, the speed of the computer, and the frequency with which the sort will be used—assuming, of course, that the sort is really desirable as a processing step in the system.

Basic questions to ask about computer-based data processing systems include:

1 Is the central processor well-utilized? What proportion of the time is it busy?
2 Is the system actually engaged in processing for a high proportion of the time? What proportion of the time is the system down for maintenance or repair? Is it down for any other reason?
3 Are the peripheral devices well-suited to the processing being done?
4 Is the system designed to minimize human intervention in the processing?
5 Is the programming language being used appropriate to the processing that is being done? (This question will be discussed further in future chapters.)

Economic efficiency Economic efficiency means that a system is getting the required processing done for the lowest possible cost. However, both long-run and short-run costs must be considered. The configuration of people and machines may provide necessary processing at the lowest cost at a given moment in time. But this will prove to be a false economy if the system must be totally replaced at great expense by a larger system when the volume of processing increases at a later date. If continuous growth in processing volumes is expected, excess capacity may be desirable. Alternatively, the modular nature of computer systems may suggest a flexible system whose capacity can be increased by adding components or replacing slower equipment with faster equipment.

Intimate knowledge of the types of available processing equipment (capacities, capabilities, and costs) and how these are changing is needed. Normally it will be necessary to consult a computer hardware specialist for this information.

A word of warning: Equipment vendor personnel are not always reliable as sources of information about what is available or technically feasible. Their primary job responsibility is, after all, to sell their employer's products, and their training is designed to fit them to that purpose. Their knowledge of alternative methods or new developments can be very limited, and their view of a competitor's products and services is likely to be biased. Sometimes they do not even know their own employer's total product line. They can be used as sources of information, but the information should be crosschecked and independently verified. They never should be relied upon as the sole source of technical or economic information for this aspect of a system analysis.

Suggesting system improvements

It is impossible to specify the exact nature of the improvements that might be suggested for a data processing or information system. A few examples must suffice as illustrations of the kinds of improvements that will occur to the analyst who has completed the steps described in this chapter.

Are there obvious duplications in the procedures carried out within the system? Can these duplications be eliminated?

What procedural changes might be made to make the system totally effective? Which of these seem to be worthy of consideration?

Are there underutilized components in the system? Are there ways to improve their utilization without increasing costs unduly? Are there any volume or timing bottlenecks in the system? Can inadequate components be replaced by units of greater capacity? Can underutilized resources be used to relieve any of these bottlenecks?

In summary, then, at this stage the analyst sits down and pulls together all the facts learned and sees if they indicate any obvious ways to improve the system. Apparently minor changes often have a significant impact. For example, throughput in one electronic data processing installation was significantly improved by having the receiving clerk take accumulated jobs from the receiving desk to the computer at more frequent intervals. Under the old system, as much as three or four hours of computer work would accumulate at the receiving desk during the first hour of operation. In the meantime, the computer had been idle because no jobs had been delivered to the computer room. Similar rush hours just before and after coffee breaks and the lunch hour and just before closing also contributed to the development of long waiting lines in the computer room at certain periods during the day. Shortening these lines led to faster service and discouraged users from bunching their deliveries at these times. The net result was a decline in average job turnaround time from about eight hours to a little less than two hours.

Common sense is the analyst's greatest ally here. In many cases, application of the analyst's reason, supported by suggestions from people operating the system or from users of the system outputs, will make significant improvements possible.

Summary

The first major task in system analysis is to describe the system (components, boundaries, interfaces with other systems, volumes handled and the time required to handle them, and system procedures). The second major task is to evaluate the system's success in meeting its objectives (effectiveness) and its efficiency (technical and economic) in doing what it does. The third and last major task is to suggest system improvements.

The components, boundaries, volumes, timing requirements, and procedures must be documented (written down). This is most frequently done by preparing flowcharts with careful annotation of volumes and timings on the charts. A system flowchart clearly identifies system inputs, major work stations (centers where major tasks are performed), and system outputs. The exact procedures carried out at each work station are described in detail flowcharts. When flowcharting, care should be taken to follow the approved guidelines presented in this chapter. It is particularly important to use standard symbols to increase the readability of the charts.

Key terms

Define the following terms as briefly as possible and then, in a short paragraph, clarify each definition.

Black box concept
Economic efficiency
Master-file volume
Organization chart
Peak processing demands
Procedural flowchart
Special-action path
System analysis
System boundaries
System components
System effectiveness
System efficiency
System flowchart
System interfaces
Technical efficiency
Work station

Discussion questions

1 List the steps in system analysis.
2 How may the objectives of a system be defined?
3 How does the analyst determine where the boundaries of a system are?
4 How does the analyst determine whether a component is part of the data processing system being studied?
5 Why are simple counts an insufficient indication of volume to be handled in a data processing system?

6 What is (are) the difference(s) between a system flowchart and a detail flowchart? Make your answer exhaustive.
7 Relate the black box concept to flowcharting.
8 How does economic efficiency differ from technical efficiency?
9 Why is it necessary to pay close attention to special processing paths when analyzing a data processing system?
10 How is the work station concept related to electronic data processing?
11 How does the work station concept relate to the black box concept, the system flowchart, and the detail flowchart?
12 What techniques are available for measuring the effectiveness of data processing systems? Make your answer exhaustive.
13 Define and discuss the way(s) in which system volumes and system timing requirements are related.
14 Why is it so important to look for special-action paths when analyzing a system?

Exercises

1 Prepare a system flowchart for the credit card procedures of the Open Sesame (OS) Credit Card Company. OS uses the following procedures:
  a Each customer is supplied with a credit card containing his or her name, address, account number, and expiration date.
  b The customer presents the card each time a credit purchase is made and receives a sales invoice of the sale which shows the date of purchase, what was purchased, unit prices, total item amounts, and total amount of the purchase as well as full customer identification (from the card) and full identification of the seller (name and address).
  c At the end of each week, the seller batches the accumulated invoices, sums the total amounts on an adding machine, and sends two copies of each invoice and a copy of the adding machine tape to OS. The total amount is verified by OS and a check for that amount less 3 percent is sent to the seller. Individual invoices are also checked for validity.
  d At the end of each month, OS sorts the accumulated invoices by customer, microfilms them as a permanent record, adds the invoice amounts to each customer's account on the customer tape file, computes any interest charges due, adds any interest to the account balance, and mails a statement to each customer, along with a copy of each individual invoice charged to that customer.
  e Upon receipt of payment from the customer, the amount is verified against the payment stub returned by the customer (or the customer account if there is no stub), sorts the stubs (or the stub duplicate prepared from the account record), and updates the customer record on the tape file.
  f Each customer account is checked for payment status each month just before the billing run, and accounts needing delinquency letters are

indicated. Accounts over 90 days delinquent are also put in a "stop-charge" category. Accounts over 120 days delinquent are canceled and the account sold to a collection agency.

2 You are developing an inventory control system for which the following rules have been specified:

a In general, a replacement order for a product will be sent if (1) units on hand is at or below the reorder point, and (2) the item is still being sold.

b If there have been no sales in the last month, the item will be reordered only if approved by the materials control manager, regardless of inventory level.

c If there have been no sales in the last three months, the item will be removed from active inventory.

d After 60 days or more in inactive inventory with no further activity, any remaining units will be considered for sale at auction. The materials control manager and the sales manager must both sign a retention order to prevent the auction sale at this point. This action is reviewed monthly.

(1) Develop and draw a system flowchart for this system.

(2) Draw the detail flowcharts for this system.

3 Refer to Exercise 1. Can you suggest any improvements in this processing system? Justify your suggestions.

4 Refer to Exercise 2. Can you suggest any improvements in this processing system? Justify your suggestions.

5 **a** Develop a detail flowchart for the process of crossing the street. Assume there is a traffic light.

b What if there were no traffic light?

COMPUTERS AT WORK

Getting the Most from a System

Using text-editing equipment to combine WP [word processing] with data processing functions is like killing two birds with one stone. With some planning, it can even help an organization tackle "birds" it never could before.

The case in point is Apple and Bernstein, a Pittsburgh law firm specializing in commercial collections and insolvency proceedings, which uses a shared-logic system not only to handle text preparation chores, but also to provide users with information for day-to-day and long-term management decisions. Under the direction of Bob Bernstein, office administrator, the system:

Prepares all documents and correspondence while simultaneously recording all pertinent data on the system's three disk drives for subsequent data processing.

Compiles and analyzes data recorded in the text-editing cycle for internal management reports.

Various documents and letters are used to make commercial collections. It requires an average of four letters and two legal documents for each of the 3,500 cases which Apple and Bernstein handles annually. These documents are all prepared on a Compu-text shared-logic system.

With a customized version of Compu-text's new claims software programming package, Bob has established a procedure which simultaneously generates the necessary preliminary correspondence and starts both a physical and computerized record when a case is opened.

An operator uses any of four typing stations to access the system. Following a standard routine, the name of the client, the name of the debtor, the debtor's county of residence, and amount owed are entered.

At this point several operations are carried out automatically. The system records the data in its new claims and name/address files while, at the same time, a letter with the appropriate figures, names, and addresses is printed for the debtor to inform him that Apple and Bernstein is on the case. A second letter of acknowledgement is ordered for the client.

Meanwhile, two three-part carbon forms are printed. They provide a gummed label for the case file and index cards for company records. The cards are indexed alphabetically according to client and debtor names, and numerically according to file and client number. "This way we can retrieve a file using any of four criteria," Bob explains.

Source: Abridged from Geoffrey C. Lewis, "WP Does Double Duty at Apple and Bernstein," *Word Processing World,* 5 (September 1978), 12–13. Reprinted with permission from Word Processing and Information Systems.

As the case proceeds, the system assembles additional correspondence and documents from among 1,500 stored paragraphs and 500 legal passages. . . .

The system also prepares 1,500 documents and letters annually for the firm's general practice. This often includes writing corporate minutes which run 75 to 80 pages and are composed of standard texts.

Prior to installation of the shared-logic system last December, all text-editing was done on mag card equipment with each card holding only one paragraph. Document assembly was such a laborious task that in order to achieve acceptable turnaround time, Bob was forced to use preprinted forms. "Even if two identical letters from the same file were being sent to two different debtors at the same address and the name was the only revision, the operator would still have to keyboard all the variables twice," Bob recalls.

Although the system has been a boon to productivity in the text-editing operation (output has almost doubled while one clerical worker has been reassigned and two new users have been added), the major benefit for the firm may be the system's records management and data processing capabilities which automate additional functions.

Bob utilizes the system's minicomputer intelligence for manipulating the data collected during the text-editing cycle to compile reports on all phases of the collection practice.

The system keeps a daily record of all new cases and indicates the value of the collections as well as the identity of the client. This file is continuous and can be accessed to compile data for weeks, months, quarters, and years. "I can instantly compile information on clients, listings, and debtors' counties, specifying the range which includes time spans, amount of the collection, and disposition of the case," Bob reports.

This enables management to determine whether or not a particular client has been a profitable account. Bob can see quickly whether the efforts required to complete a collection were justified by the final fee. "The real benefit is to be able to look at the record when a client calls asking us to take on a special case as a favor. We look at the figures and can say to him, 'We haven't really been getting the business we think we should from you and we will not be able to help you in this case,' " he explains. . . .

Similar data processing helps the firm determine long-range goals. Because its clients tend to specialize in collections within a particular industry, Apple and Bernstein analyzes collections by industry. "This way," Bob explains," we can pinpoint where we could gain more expertise to better serve a profitable client. We can also decide, based on this data, if it would be worthwhile to concentrate on a certain industry."

Bob also uses the manufacturer's docket and calendar program to keep the company's daily business on schedule. This lists deadlines including statutes of limitations and renewals of judgement for various cases. In addition, it provides a daily printout of all appointments and deadlines for two days. Each Wednesday the program puts out an updated 12-day schedule to help users organize schedules.

Another important function is maintaining records in the name and address file on the network of connections which the firm has established throughout western Pennsylvania. Bob has built this file in such a way that the firm can actually keep an accurate tally of the people it owes favors and those indebted to the firm. Because the file also includes data about these people, Bob can use the sort function to find, for example, all contacts over 50 who live in Beaver County and have police experience.

Finally, the system automates some of the firm's public relations functions and helps maintain ties with professional groups. This has been useful for Bob who is active in IWP, the Commercial Law League of America, and the Association of Legal Administrators. He maintains contact with colleagues in these groups by including their names in the computer file and accessing these lists (and sublists) when he has information to share.

These factors—the tangible increase in text-editing productivity and the intangible benefits of precise management information—have made Bob a successful administrator and have helped the firm outgrow similar organizations of the same size.

Chapter 13

System Design and Implementation

Outline

Designing the new or improved system

System analysis is ordinarily undertaken to find a better way of doing the job. Usually, a changed system results. This chapter presents a reasoned approach to system design or redesign.

Steps in system design

In order to design a new or improved system, certain things must be accomplished.

1 Analyze the system (as described in Chapter 12).
2 Choose system components.
3 Reanalyze system effectiveness and efficiency.
4 Establish back-up procedures.
5 Make allowance for growth.

The discussion immediately following is organized around the last four steps. The first of these steps, choosing system components, is divided into four parts. Each part relates to one of the functional components of a data processing system, storage, input, processing, and output.

Choosing system components—storage

Business data processing systems are oriented toward file processing. This orientation means that storage files are a critical component of any data processing system. File structure and file access determine which input, processing, and output devices can be employed most effectively. File access methods are identified in the section that follows. Then, file design criteria are identified. The final section of this discussion relates these concepts to the actual selection of storage components.

File access

The order in which records are *accessed* (selected from the file) in processing may or may not be directly related to their ordering in the file. Access method is related primarily to the device used to store the file. The two basic access methods are random (direct) access and sequential access.

Sequential access Sequentially accessed devices, such as punched paper tape and magnetic tape, are not intended to provide random access. The time required to find and retrieve an item will depend on where the read head is positioned on the tape when the search for the specific item is started. If the next item sought is next on the tape, it can be retrieved quickly. If, however, the next item is located on the opposite end of the tape from the last item retrieved, the entire tape will have to be moved by the read head in order to find the desired item.

Random access For *true* random access, the storage device must allow direct retrieval of each and every item in the same amount of time per item, regardless of the location of the last item retrieved. Few purely random-access file devices exist (magnetic core is an example).

A directly accessible file is one in which each record in the file can be found and recovered in *about* the same length of time. Although very few purely random-access devices exist, many file devices allow direct access. These *modified* random-access devices usually feature direct access to blocks of records and sequential access within the blocks. An example of a direct-access manual device is the tub file where the files are contained in a rotating "tub" which allows easy access to each record. The most common electronic modified random (direct) access devices are magnetic disks and drums.

File design criteria

The storage device used to store a file and the method chosen to process transactions and changes depend on many criteria. The most important criteria are the processing hit rate, the processing mode, and the frequency with which the file is to be consulted (accessed).

Processing hit rate Processing hit rate refers to the proportion of records that are selected for processing during each processing run. For most applications, not every record in a master file must be changed during every processing run. For example, at a department store, less than 25 percent of all charge customers are likely to make charges or returns during a given period. Processing every record in the master file at each daily or weekly updating run may be overly expensive since most records do not change. At the end of each billing period, however, each customer may get a bill, even if the balance due is zero. In such systems, expenses may be lower (because of less processing) if the master file is stored on a direct-access device such as a disk rather than on a sequential-access device such as a magnetic tape. Customer records can be arranged sequentially but accessed randomly, so that updating runs are handled more efficiently and the billing process is handled efficiently in a sequential file order.

Processing mode Obviously, immediate online processing requires random-access storage for the master file. Batch processing, on the other hand, can allow time to resequence transactions and changes so that processing in file order (sequentially) is possible. Note that the decision on processing mode depends to a great extent on the timing requirements that the system must meet.

Frequency of access Files that must be continuously consulted (such as airline seat inventories) to carry out a business function must be stored on a random-(direct) access device. If there is infrequent need to consult records in the file (year-to-date payroll file, for example), then its records need not be instantaneously available. Not all files for which access is frequent need contain up-to-the minute facts. For example, credit-rating data can normally be updated at intervals rather than as items are charged and bills are paid or default occurs. However, the need for fast access indicates that the file should be stored on a direct-access device. Thus, the decision to store a file on a direct-access device should depend more on the nature of the business activity supported by the file than on routine processing modes used to maintain the file.

Choosing storage components

The choice of storage devices for a processing system is central to total system design. Storage files may be online (connected to and under the control of the CPU) or offline. They may be sequentially or randomly (directly) accessed. Note that the data input process and the file storage components must match. Random-access storage is required for online entry, for example. In fact, random-access storage is required for any system designed to process transactions in line, that is, in the order in which the transactions occur. Sequentially accessed storage devices serve best when the file is updated periodically and most of the individual records in the file are affected on each processing run. If the hit rate on each processing run is low, even a periodically updated file may best be stored on a direct-access device.

Data storage devices may be manual, machine-assisted manual, or electronic.

Manual storage devices The most common manual device is the ordinary file cabinet found in every office. Manual files are used primarily for storing paper documents. They tend to be very bulky and are also subject to errors in filing, since human beings control the process. Moreover, access is slow. However, they are a flexible storage medium which can be used for storing a wide variety of files.

Machine-assisted manual storage devices It is possible to substitute electric motors and electronic selection for human effort. Systems are available for storing file folders, punched cards, magnetic tapes and tape cassettes, microfilm rolls and cartridges, movie film, and so on, that provide ready access to each individual element through key control (see Figure 13.1). These systems also tend to be bulky. Since initial entry and re-entry are controlled by human beings, errors in filing are common. Nevertheless, machine-assisted manual storage systems do speed filing and make it possible for a single person to maintain a larger set of files. However, the number of individual elements that can be accessed in a short period of time is not very large in comparison to electronic storage devices.

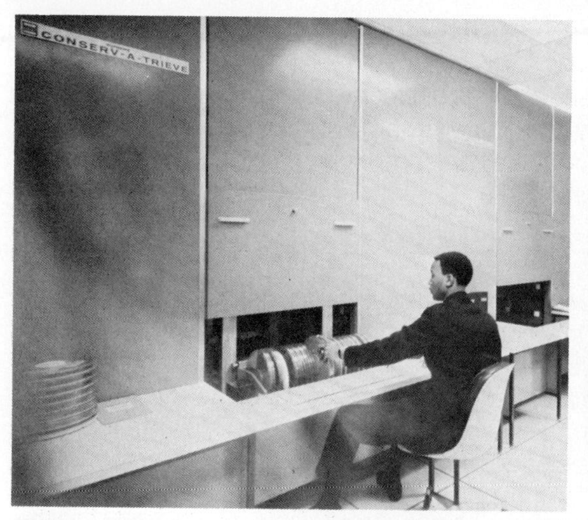

Figure 13.1 **A machine-assisted manual storage device** **This system is used to store magnetic tapes offline. The photo on the right shows the inside of the machine, with the storage bins and the retrieval mechanism. On the left is the machine's operator. (Courtesy Supreme Equipment & Systems Corporation)**

Electronic storage devices Of course, we have already discussed electronic storage devices at length. The systemwide advantages of electronic storage under computer control are speed of recording and ease of retrieval. Disadvantages include cost and the technical knowledge needed to devise and maintain such systems.

Choosing system components—input

There are numerous media and devices available for capturing data on each business event (transaction).

Manually prepared forms

It is common to capture (first record) data on manually prepared forms. This method has several advantages.

1 Manual processes are easy to set up and use in most business situations.
2 The tools (devices) required are simple (pen or pencil and a preprinted form).
3 Mistakes are easy to correct.
4 A permanent record of the transaction is created.

Manually prepared forms also have disadvantages.

1 Preparation is relatively slow when compared to automatic processes.

2 Mistakes are easily made; human beings tend to be more error prone than machines.
3 Transfer to another medium, such as a punched card or a magnetic tape, is usually required for entry into machine processing systems. The use of devices, such as optical readers, as short cuts in this process is not yet very reliable.

Machine-assisted manual processes

It is also common to use machines to assist in the manual entry of data. Plastic identification cards are combined with manual (key) entry to record credit sales at department stores, automobile service stations, restaurants, hotels, and other places accepting credit cards. Plastic cards identify the customer and the place of business and/or sales clerk. The variable data elements identifying items sold, quantities, and amounts are entered by the sales clerk. The chance for mistakes in recording customer name and address is thereby reduced. Cash sales are more fully recorded with a machine, the cash register. Buttons on the register are used to identify the department or category for each item sold and the amount of money received from the customer. A record of the transaction is created on a paper tape within the cash register.

Advantages of machine-assisted systems are

1 Reduced errors.
2 Speedier processing.
3 A record of the activity, for later machine or manual processing, can be produced as a by-product of the machine cycle.

The primary disadvantages of machine-assisted manual recording are

1 Inflexibility in the processes used.
2 Limited alternative processing approaches.

Each machine is usually designed and built to do its job in a specific way. Alternative processes are limited, and there is a limited ability to change the machine. The latter limitation is not as dominant in new freestanding electronic machines such as electronic cash registers, however.

Online input

Special-purpose devices or remote terminals are increasingly used for data input. Devices vary from key-driven terminals with either visual display or typed hardcopy to very exotic special devices. Badge readers and plastic card readers are common on the shop floor. Point-of-sale recorders of several types are found in retail stores. It is becoming common for electronic cash registers to be online terminals. Even voice input is being used for quality control systems in manufacturing.

Advantages of online input reflect the use of electronic devices.

1 Speed—because data becomes immediately available in the computer system, processing can begin immediately.

2 Greater integration of the system is fostered. For example, when a sale is rung up on a cash register terminal in a retail store, inventory and other accounting records are usually updated. Items reaching the reorder point can be identified and purchase orders written. Sales totals by register and by type of item can be developed for daily sales analysis to spot developing sales trends.
3 Operating costs are reduced. There is no need for handling input documents nor for transcription from transaction documents for computer processing.

The disadvantages of direct entry fall primarily in the control area, but cost is also a factor.

1 Records of individual transactions are not usually preserved. The transaction data disappear immediately from direct human view and are used to update inventory and other records. Tracing individual actions through the system may be virtually impossible.
2 Controls to catch errors and fraudulent entries before they affect system records must be carefully developed. Progress is being made in this area. This problem is discussed further in Chapter 15.
3 Development costs are high. The systems are necessarily complex and require a large investment of time and effort by highly skilled analysts and programmers. This problem is addressed by the "turnkey" systems available from software firms and equipment manufacturers. These systems provide a total working system operable by retrained current personnel. The cost is often little more than the cost of the hardware used in the system.

Choosing system components—processing

Actual manipulation of data (and media) can be carried on manually, manually with machine assistance, by electromechanical machines, and by electronic computers.

Manual processing

It is not uncommon to process data captured on manually completed forms by manual processes. The major advantages of manual processing systems are as follows:

1 They are easy to install and change.
2 They are usually easy to understand.
3 Human beings recognize some errors, particularly when individual data items do not exhibit the proper relationships to each other.

The disadvantages of manual processing systems arise in part from their advantages.

1 They are *too* easy to change. Manual systems tend to change continuously, evolving into less tightly structured and more loosely controlled systems as workers within the system strive for greater speed and more individual autonomy.
2 They are the slowest method. People are not as fast as machines.
3 They exhibit high error rates. Human beings have a tendency to make mistakes.
4 Complex analysis in a reasonable amount of time is difficult if not impossible.
5 Operating costs are high in relation to workload accomplished.

Machine-assisted manual processing

Machines can be used to assist manual processing. Examples include the use of manually operated calculators, adding machines, and cash registers to perform some processing functions (see Figure 13.2). The advantages of machine-assisted manual systems are as follows:

1 The work is speeded up. Machines can perform arithmetic functions faster than people.
2 Errors are reduced. Machines have greater reliability in performing arithmetic and other functions. However, in most cases, people are still responsible for entering the data and controlling the processing sequence.
3 A clear hardcopy record of the processing is usually prepared and can be used in controlling the processing to prevent mistakes.

Figure 13.2

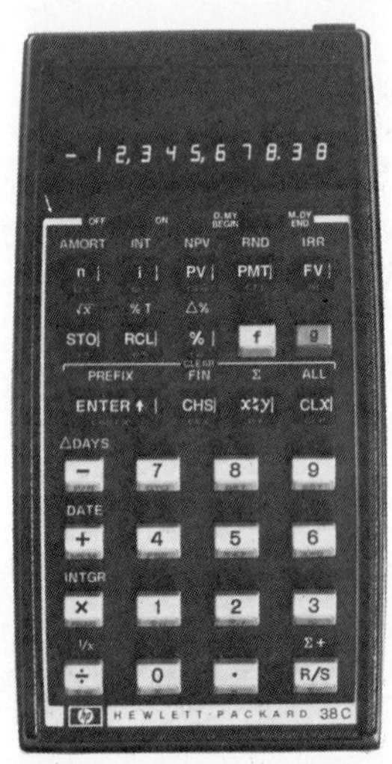

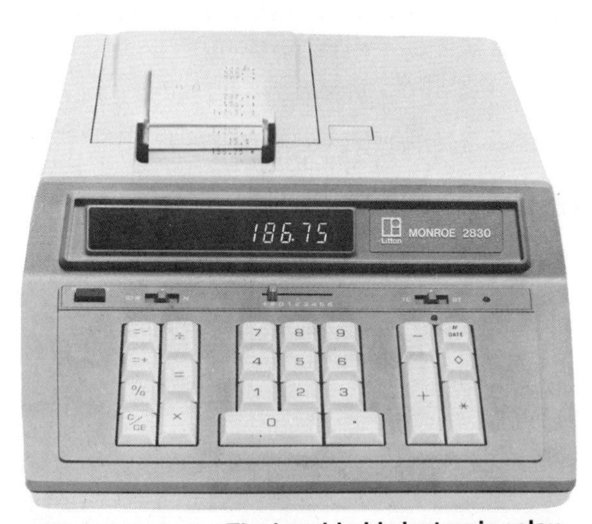

Two machines that assist manual processing **The hand-held electronic calculator on the left can be programmed to perform useful business and financial calculations. The desk-top calculator on the right is less portable, but it is more versatile and provides a printed record of calculations. (Photo on left courtesy Hewlett-Packard Company; photo on right courtesy Monroe, the Calculator Company)**

The disadvantages of machine-assisted manual processing include the following:

1 The processing is still relatively slow because human beings and the machine must interact with the person in control of the sequence and speed of starting each step, even though machines are usually faster than people.
2 Cost per transaction is high.
3 These systems are not well adapted to truly complex analyses.

Electromechanical machine processing

Slightly more complex machines (accounting machines) speed routine processing still more. These machines perform standard accounting functions, such as posting to individual accounts, computing discounts on payables and receivables, calculating simple payroll deductions, and accumulating totals by categories.

The most numerous of the electromechanical machines are the so-called unit record punched-card systems. As noted in Chapter 4, the label *unit record* comes from use of the punched card as a record of each transaction or account (each *unit* of data).

Unit record equipment is being replaced by computers. A few small business systems still use card input, but most use some form of direct entry. Larger computer systems running batch processing use key-to-disk systems to translate input documents for processing. Cards are too bulky, too slow, too easy to damage, and too expensive to prepare to remain a viable input alternative. With cards disappearing, the electromechanical card processors are also disappearing.

Computer processing

The automatic electronic digital computer is a fast, accurate, and flexible *machine*. As such, it is not able to do anything it has not been programmed to do. Even so, the computer serves to extend people's calculating and decision-making powers. As a data processing device, it tirelessly performs highly complex analyses or simple, repetitious calculations with speed and accuracy. The computer will follow a program automatically and correctly with speed and accuracy. The program can be changed and the machine shifted to another job. Modern computers can even switch back and forth among several stored programs at a speed that makes it appear all are being performed simultaneously.

Disadvantages of computers are initial cost and the fact that they utlize such basic logical processes that few people can perform the programming necessary to harness their great capacity. In business data processing, many are used at a level well below their full capability. Coupled with their high cost, such misuse can easily make the computer appear to be an expensive device only capable of speeding up clerical processes. Faulty attempts at sophisticated use lead to missed schedules, erroneous billings, and processing bottlenecks. Such mistakes in system design lead to errors for which the machine is blamed. When used effectively and efficiently where volumes are large, timing requirements severe, or needed analysis complex, computers have proved themselves to be effective processing devices in information and data processing systems. Smaller firms can avoid the computer's disadvantages through timesharing or by sending their data to independent service bureaus.

Choosing system components—output

Capturing data, storing them, and processing them are not enough. The results of processing activities must be delivered to final users in a form and in time to make those results useful. We have already discussed the wide variety of media and devices that are available. Data and information can be presented on paper, on film, or as pictures on a cathode ray tube. The time required to respond to a request for data can vary from a fraction of a second to many hours.

In addition to standard management reports, data processing systems must prepare a variety of custodial documents, such as checks to reimburse employees and suppliers, invoices to order items from suppliers, and receipts to acknowledge payments made by others or shipments received from vendors. The need for custodial documents may require a paper-handling capability whose cost dictates that paper will provide the medium for all information and data presentations from the system. Even so, many different devices are available for preparing paper documents.

Paper is the medium most widely used for presenting data and information outputs from data processing and information systems. Devices for preparing paper documents vary from pen and pencil to sophisticated chemical and photographic printing processes capable of preparing multiple copies of a document at a speed of thousands of lines per minute. The most commonly used devices were discussed in Chapters 4 and 5 and will be mentioned only briefly here.

Probably the most familiar hardcopy report preparation device is the typewriter, a key-driven printing device. The typewriter is slow, error prone, and relatively expensive on a per copy basis. Its advantages are flexibility and ease of use. Modern versions coupled with electronic control devices featuring magnetic tape, magnetic card, or floppy diskette storage decrease per copy costs of documents (such as letters) for which several original copies are required. The use of tape or disk storage and electronic control decreases initial preparation time. The maximum printing speed of such a device is more than double that of the manually controlled electric typewriter.

Printers are output devices that present data and information outputs on paper. The major types for printing text and reports were discussed previously, but (listed in order of speed from slowest to fastest) they are as follows:

1 Typewriter and typewriter-like devices (600 to 1800 characters per minute)
2 Line printers (300 to 3000 lines per minute)
3 Page printers (nonimpact printers) (15,000 to 23,000 lines per minute)

The major special output devices include plotters, microfilm devices (see Figure 13.3), and visual displays. Plotters should be included with the document producers. Microfilm devices and visual displays both produce images that can be converted into documents by special hardware.

Reanalyze system effectiveness and efficiency

Having examined the options available and chosen system components, we must pause to assess the kind of system we propose to create. Will it satisfy managerial objectives at a minimal cost? As the question indicates, we would ask the same questions as in a system analysis but slightly differently. For example,

Will managers find it necessary to do further processing or to go outside the system to obtain the information required to carry out their responsibilities?
Are the proposed system components the best for the tasks for which they are intended?
Can the proposed system handle the necessary processing volumes?

In addition to repeating the questions asked of the old system, some new questions concerning the relation of system benefits to system costs should reveal whether the new system is truly desirable.

The cost economies of new systems are often hard to demonstrate, however. New systems usually are sold by the additional benefits they provide. Ideally, the new system should provide the same or more information for less money or more information for the same money. If costs are to increase, the increase must be justified by added benefits. Benefits and costs are of two types, *tangible* and *intangible.* However, care must be exercised to be sure that both the costs and the benefits are completely enumerated. The lists below are helpful in this regard.

Tangible benefits

Tangible benefits are measurable cost benefits to be obtained from a new data processing or information system and are fairly easy to define.

1 Reducing the number of employees involved in data processing
2 Reducing the total investment in data processing equipment
3 Reducing the cost of maintaining data processing equipment
4 Reducing the amount of physical space devoted to data processing

Figure 13.3

Using microfiche In the foreground is a microfiche reader printer in use. In the background is a microimage processor that processes COM. (Courtesy Kodak)

Tangible costs

Offsetting the tangible benefits are complementary **tangible costs**.

1 Added employees needed with the new system
2 Training employees to work in the new system
3 Lease or purchase of new equipment
4 Maintenance of new equipment
5 Cost of physical space used by new equipment, including remodeling and/or environmental controls

A common mistake is to underestimate system development time. Setting up a new system can be time consuming, particularly if machine processes are involved. Computer and accounting machines have to be programmed. Forms and/or procedures for data capture and for output reports have to be created. Personnel have to be trained in the new way of doing things. Often, basic data files have to be transferred to a new medium. Too many times, an enthusiastic salesperson leads the inexperienced and untrained to believe that when the new machine comes in the door, all problems will disappear. Unfortunately, system development has hardly begun when the new machine arrives.

Intangible benefits

Intangible benefits are nonbudgetary and are more difficult to measure, but they are frequently the most important effects that a new system can have.

1 Improving control over the physical operation.
2 Allowing expansion of profitable activities by removing volume limitations in processing capacity.
3 Allowing expansion or increasing operating efficiency by reducing the time required for processing.

(Note that these first three benefits overlap, particularly the second and third.)

4 Positive effects on employee morale arising from a recognition that the system is effective and efficient. (Note: Employees must feel involved in the system design effort if this effect is to be fully realized.)
5 Positive effects on external public relations. Customers and business associates like to work with an organization whose data processing systems are efficient and effective.

Intangible costs

Complementary to the intangible benefits are a set of **intangible costs**, all of which can be avoided if the system is properly designed and implemented. They include the following:

1 Loss of control over the activity by operating management.
2 Negative effects on employee morale and a consequent drop in employee productivity, an increase in errors, and general inefficiency. (Note: This usually arises from *not* involving key employees in the system design effort and *not* keeping employees informed of progress in system design.)
3 Negative effects on external public relations. (Note: This can result from trying to switch abruptly to an untried new system. Keeping the old system running until the bugs have been worked out of the new system can result in a long-run saving. Also, the system should be responsive to the ultimate user. Keep customers and business associates in mind when designing systems.)

Most of the intangible costs result from poor system design and/or poor management of system implementation. The following three points can pay big dividends in gaining intangible benefits and avoiding intangible losses:

1 The rule of KISS—Keep It Simple Stupid. The simpler the system is, the less can go wrong with it and the easier people, including employees and customers, will find it to work with.

2 People operate systems; don't build systems to operate people.
3 Informed and involved employees are productive employees; don't shroud system changes in mystery. If outside experts must be brought in, explain why and use them to educate your own people.

Establish back-up procedures

It is wise to provide alternate means for accomplishing system tasks. This is particularly important when a processing system is being computerized. What will be done if the computer suffers a major breakdown? What about power failures, fire, flood, or sabotage? How will data be processed in such situations? Because these interruptions are possible, provision should be made for processing on another machine, preferably one running on another power source. Alternatively, emergency power can be supplied by a diesel generator or a battery pack. In any case, something should be done to continue in business and to protect against the loss of important data.

It is particularly important to provide back-up for online systems. If an online system goes down (fails), input data cannot be collected and operations must stop.

In particularly sensitive or pervasive systems, a dual system may be justified. Then, if one computer fails, the other can cut in and assume the load. Supplemental power sources are called for whenever a dual system can be justified.

Sources of back-up are varied. Service bureaus may provide time on the same computer model. Other firms that are reasonably close by may have excess time available on a compatible system. With modern transportation and communication systems, back-up may be provided from another division or regional center anywhere on the continent. Some national service bureau firms may be able to temporarily absorb critical parts of an online system into a commercially available timesharing network.

Make allowance for growth

It is usually false economy to install a system that can barely handle the expected processing load. Even if growth is not expected, additional uses are almost certain to be found. As a rule of thumb for business firms, it is recommended that a minimum of 10 to 25 percent excess capacity be attainable without changing the CPU. If a firm is growing rapidly, even more excess capacity may be justified. Normally, only the CPU need be larger in order to provide this flexibility. Additions to primary memory and peripheral devices can be made as needed if the processor has sufficient capacity.

Another rule of thumb is to install enough capacity to handle fully all processing for at least the next three years. Again, this flexibility may be attained fairly cheaply by buying a larger CPU but only a modest amount of primary memory and a limited set of peripherals.

Installing the new or improved system

It has been implied that a system is developed, tested, and then put into use (installed). The process of installing really should begin in the development phases by involving in the design of the system the operating managers and others who will use the system and its outputs, for their participation will make them familiar with the system. As the system is being diagnosed for errors or omissions (debugged), operating personnel can be particularly valuable. Their knowledge of the details of the operation, especially of the nature and likelihood of unusual events, can assist in developing system tests.

Obviously, not all of the operating personnel to be affected by a new system or a system change will be involved directly in the development of the new system. Attempts to keep the nonparticipants informed through periodic briefings, documentation review, and consultation can be helpful, however. A formal training program is desirable. The extent of training will be determined by two things, (1) the complexity of the new system, and (2) the degree to which the new system differs from the system to be replaced.

The actual implementation is accomplished by one of four basic methods.

1 A brand new system is installed as part of a new operation or organization. The problem here is to train new personnel in the new system.
2 The old system is stopped and replaced by the new. This **sudden system cutover** may produce a gap in operations while the cutover is being made. For this reason and because it is difficult to develop complex systems without errors, this process is recommended only for small systems and/or proven turnkey installations.
3 The new system is substituted in stages in **phased system cutover**; it is phased in one minor subsystem at a time. The fact that such phasing in is possible, however, can be a clear indication that the new system is no more integrated than the old. Phasing in is usually impossible when a computerized, online system is replacing a manual operation or a computerized batch system.
4 The new system is operated in parallel to the old system before complete cutover. In **parallel operation**, the new system processes the same transactions as the old for a period of time. As soon as the new system proves to be working properly, the cutover is made. The duplication in manpower and other operating costs makes this an expensive method. However, in sensitive operations involving people-related activities such as charging or billing customers or payroll, it is strongly recommended.

Regardless of the method used, several activities must be included.

1 Any new data files must be generated.
2 System personnel must be selected and trained.
3 The site (operating facilities and offices for personnel) must be prepared and new equipment obtained and installed.
4 The operation of the system must be checked for completeness, freedom from error, and reliability.
5 Procedures for checking system performance (error rates, effectiveness, efficiency) must be developed and continuously applied.

Generating new files

The specifications for any new master files to be used in the system will be developed as part of the detailed design for the system. In the creation of the initial master file or files the system will maintain and use, the initial data must be entered onto the storage medium according to the design format. This can be a tedious, time-consuming task if the files are to be moved to an electronic device from a document file. Errors must be carefully avoided, and it is advisable to develop tight controls in order to do so. For example, the old file can be grouped and totals for significant fields developed for each group. After transfer, the totals can be developed from the new file as a check on transcription errors.

New forms and/or procedures for data collection must be developed also. Each data item to be captured will have been identified and described in some detail. An example of a data element description form is provided in Figure 13.4. The general methods for recording, storage, and retrieval (including the necessary indexing) will already be specified. The implementation phase will be involved with developing specific forms and putting into practice the designed procedures for updating files and creating reports.

Selecting and training personnel

Introduction of new data processing and information systems can require wide-ranging changes in the organization and in operating procedures.

1 Changes usually occur in decision-making practices and in the techniques and organization of processing activities.
2 If a computer is being introduced into the organization, new positions come with it: computer operators, computer programmers, data control personnel, and systems analysts.
3 Personnel employed in the operating areas generating the input data or using the outputs must be retrained in the new procedures.
4 Special security procedures are required to deal with the concentrations of sensitive data and information and to prevent either the disruption of computer operations or unauthorized access to the data being processed.
5 The introduction of a computerized data processing or information system will influence and probably change the activities of all employees who contact or work with the system, from the top management level down to the lowliest clerk preparing data inputs. All of these personnel must be

Figure 13.4

Organization ______________________ Date __________

Element name ______________________

Element number ______________________

Maximum length ______________________

Form: Alpha ________ Numeric ________ Alphanumeric ____

Units ______________________ Initial value: __________

Source: System name ______________ System no. ________

Document name ______________ Document no. ______

File name ______________ File no. ________

Retention criteria ______________________

____

Edit criteria ______________________

____

Update procedure: Source ______________________

Frequencey ______________________

Comments ______________________

Other comments ______________________

____

____

Data Element Description

informed of the changes, be made to understand why they are necessary, and be trained to operate in the new system.

New positions can be filled with employees from outside the organization or with present employees. In implementing a new system within an organization or one that will cause a reduction in the organization's current work force, recruiting from within is preferred. Machine operators, data control personnel, and applications programmers, particularly, are positions for which available employees can be profitably retrained. Highly skilled technicians, such as systems programmers, who implement and maintain the executive programs that control overall computer operations, and maintenance engineers, who take care of system hardware, may have to be hired from outside or contracted as consultants.

Regardless of the source of personnel, each position in the system must be identified and a job description and job specification prepared. A job

description describes the work to be performed in detail, including such things as machines to be operated, special skills to be applied, the amount of supervision to be given or received, and general working conditions. A **job specification** identifies the physical skills, education, training, and experience required for successful completion of the job. Job descriptions and specifications provide valuable guidelines for personnel selection and training.

Site and equipment preparation

New systems usually involve new equipment. A major revision of facilities and offices may be required to house the added equipment and staff. A new layout of work space may be needed to adjust to a revised work flow. Whatever the reason, space planning is a must. The spaces to be occupied by people and equipment must be compatible with exits, utilities, and storage areas. Special requirements for environmental control (temperature, humidity, cleanliness of air, lighting, and so on) must be considered. Safety requirements relating to fire, flood, general working conditions, and so on, must be met.

The relationships between people and equipment should be determined early. Training is more successful if it is based on the exact way in which each employee will interact with equipment.

Testing the system

Tests to be performed during the installation of a new system are component tests, subsystem tests, and total system acceptance tests.

Component tests In **component tests**, components are tested more or less independently rather than in conjunction with the system as a whole. Equipment, whether old or new, must be checked for proper functioning. Data collection forms and procedures must be tried under operational circumstances to prove their adequacy. New reports must be tested for effectiveness in supplying needed information. All data controls must be tested. Some incorrect data inputs must be designed that will challenge the controls over accuracy, allowable ranges of values, and data placement errors (data in the wrong fields). New computer programs and modules of the programs can be checked outside the system as well. Even parts of the complete software for online, interactive systems can be tested in modules.

Subsystem tests Independent modules of the total system can also be tested independently in **subsystem tests**. Thus, in a total accounts receivable accounting and control system, the following subsystems and their components could be identified for independent testing:

1 Accounts receivable accounting
   a New account development
   b Charge to an account
   c Payment on an account (including prepayment)

- **d** Refund for returned or damaged items
- **e** Changes to existing account records (changes in address, credit limit, payment dates, and so on)
- **f** Removal of accounts due to cancellation or customer withdrawal

2 Credit control
- **a** Establishing credit limit
- **b** Checking on credit limit when charge sale is made
- **c** Aging of accounts to identify overdue accounts
- **d** Cancelling accounts because of inadequate payments

3 Customer billing and collections
- **a** Customer billing process
  - (1) Current accounts
  - (2) Overdue accounts
  - (3) Delinquent accounts
- **b** Collections process
  - (1) In person
  - (2) By mail
- **c** Cash flow forecasts

Each subcomponent of the above system can be tested independently and then in increasingly larger subsystems until, finally, the entire system has been tested.

Total system acceptance tests All components and subsystems may work fine as individual units, yet fail to operate as a single unit. There are interactions between subsystems. Thus, in the accounts receivable example, the accounting operation must interact with credit control and customer billing. These subsystems feed data back and forth and the system will fail if they do not identify common data elements in the same way or properly exchange data. Total **system acceptance tests** determine if the system will work as a whole.

System acceptance standards There should be standards for acceptable operation of the system, and they should be established as part of the system design.

1. *Volume and timing standards* should specify the number of transactions the system must handle in a given period of time—in other words, the amount of work the system will do.
2. *Error standards* refer to the percentage of transactions with mistakes that will be accepted. The size of undetected mistakes allowed by the system is also important.
3. *Reliability standards* for machine components in a system are also important. The length of time each component operates between breakdowns is measured by the "Mean Time Between Failures" (MTBF) rate. Reliability can also be measured by *uptime,* the percentage of the total operating time that the component or system operates successfully.

4 *System effectiveness standards* should be developed by those managers receiving outputs (reports) from the system. Specific criteria appropriate to each manager's responsibilities should be identified. The system should be tested for its ability to improve management control or planning. For example, a new accounts receivable system should reduce the number and amount of delinquent accounts receivable. It should also lead to improved estimates of cash receipts from receivables as input to cash flow estimation and control.

5 *Standards for ease of use* are important. For example, customers should find it easy to get billing errors corrected. Employees responsible for developing data inputs to the system should find the job easy and *not* unpleasant. Managers should receive reports organized and developed for easy interpretation by *each* manager. In other words, remember three points: (1) people operate systems, (2) systems operate *for* people, and (3) systems must not operate people.

Summary

Designing a new or improved system involves system analysis, choosing system components, reanalyzing the effectiveness and efficiency of the proposed new system, establishing back-up procedures, and making sure that the proposed system will adapt well to growth. System components are chosen for storage, input, processing, and output. File structure and file access must be considered when deciding which input, processing, and output devices will work best in the system. File access methods are random (direct) access and sequential access. In deciding on file design, the analyst should consider processing hit rate, processing mode, and frequency of file access. Files may be stored online or offline but, in any case, file storage components must be compatible with the data input process.

Input, storage, and processing may be carried out manually, with machine assistance, or by electronic means. Output can be on paper (typewriters or printers) or on film, or it can be displayed on a CRT tube.

When the choice and configuration of system components has been finalized, the proposed system should be analyzed. Intangible (nonbudgetary) as well as tangible (budgetary) benefits and costs must be identified and compared to determine if the new system pays its way.

When designing a new or improved system, it is wise to establish back-up procedures for accomplishing system tasks in the event of a major breakdown. For computerized data processing systems, particularly online systems, it is advisable to arrange access to alternate machinery run by another power source in case the main system goes down. Sources of back-up include service bureaus, neighboring computer installations, and other centers in a distributed network of processing centers.

A new or improved system should be designed with a built-in allowance for growth. For business firms it is recommended that a minimum of 10 to 25 percent excess capacity be attainable without changing the CPU, or that capacity be sufficient to handle all processing for at least the next three years after installation.

Installation of a new system requires the generation of new files, the selection and training of personnel, site and equipment preparation, and system testing to be sure the system operates at acceptable levels in terms of workload accomplishment, error rates, reliability, effectiveness, and ease of use.

Key terms

Define the following terms as briefly as possible and then, in a short paragraph, clarify each definition.

Component test
Intangible benefits
Intangible costs
Job description
Job specification
Parallel operation
Phased system cutover
Processing hit rate
Subsystem test
Sudden system cutover
System acceptance test
Tangible benefits
Tangible costs

Discussion questions

1 What factors should be considered in the selection of input media and devices?
2 What are the major advantages and disadvantages of online input?
3 Why is direct input of data into electronic processing systems increasing? Make your answer exhaustive.
4 Why are punch card–oriented electromechanical accounting systems referred to as unit record systems?
5 Are tangible benefits and tangible costs more important in measuring system effectiveness or system efficiency? Explain fully.
6 Are intangible benefits and intangible costs more important in measuring system effectiveness or system efficiency? Explain fully.
7 In each pair below, which element is likely to be more important in justifying new data processing or information systems?
   a Tangible or intangible benefits
   b Tangible or intangible costs
   c Benefits or costs
   Justify your choices.
8 Prepare a table summarizing tangible and intangible costs and benefits to be considered in evaluating a new system design.

9 What are the major weaknesses of manual processing of transactions data?
10 Why might workers deliberately sabotage factory floor data collection terminals that were suddenly installed without explanation? What could be done to reduce the chances of such sabotage?
11 If it is true that top managers (as a group) do not wish to use a computer directly, how does this affect the design of computerized management information systems? Does this mean that direct-access devices cannot be used in such systems?
12 Contrast system analysis and system design.
13 Why should excess capacity be designed into a data processing system?
14 Why should a back-up system be available to replace any data processing system?
15 How may back-up be obtained for data processing systems? (Include techniques for both online and batch systems.)
16 What criteria should be used to decide between inline instantaneous updating of a file and batched sequential updating?
17 What are the factors critical to choice of file design?

Exercises

1 Locate a document such as a regular billing from a store or credit card company or a tax return supplied by the Internal Revenue Service. Is the form well designed from the user's standpoint? What changes would you suggest? Why?
2 Prepare a four-column table listing data-recording media and related devices in the first two columns on the left, advantages of each medium-device combination in the third column, and disadvantages of the medium-device combination in the last column. Include manual, machine-assisted manual, and automated devices in your table.
3 Prepare a four-column table listing storage media and devices and the advantages and disadvantages of each combination. (See Exercise 2 for suggested format.)
4 Prepare a four-column table listing output media and devices and the advantages and disadvantages of each combination. (See Exercise 2 for suggested format.)
5 Prepare a table showing, for the input, the processing, and the output areas, the critical characteristics of media, devices, and the system that should be considered in choosing components for a system.

How to Buy Enough Computers

Corporate managers who have long insisted on 10-year strategic business plans and 5-year plans for their marketing and production operations have rarely required similar projections from their data processing departments. Yet information processing budgets are now growing as large as those of other corporate operations, and more important, the function they perform is rapidly becoming critical to large companies. "There is an absence of recognition of how important data processing is," says John M. Thompson, vice-president of Index Systems Inc., a Cambridge (Mass.) management consulting firm. But, he adds, "Just try turning the computers off, and any company will see how important they are."

Some companies are getting the picture, however, and data processing is taking a seat at a growing number of annual planning meetings. At Ford Motor Co., for example, more sophisticated planning for data processing activities alerted management to the need to maintain computer capacity for 1980 at the same level or higher than last year, even though the auto maker's business is down by 20%. "In the past, I presented [top management] with a progress report. [But now it] is designed more like a strategic plan," says Mayford L. Roark, Ford's executive director of systems.

Getting into the guts

The change in management's attitude toward computers may be coming just in time. Data processing has been considered merely a support function that was part of administrative overhead. But the move to interactive systems that process orders, maintain inventories, and perform other financial transactions is making computers an integral part of doing business, says Robert P. Goldberg, vice-president of BGS Systems Inc., a Lincoln (Mass.) marketer of computer planning tools. "In the last three years computers have gotten into the guts of business," he adds. Today, Goldberg points out, companies "are essentially betting their business on their computer systems."

Companies also are paying more attention now to data processing expenditures because the size of computer budgets is growing just when business activity is falling

Source: "How to Buy Enough Computers," from the December 8, 1980 issue of *Business Week,* 83–84.

off. "Because of the increasing bottom-line orientation of the company, there is more pressure to keep costs down," says John R. Goodroe, vice-president for data processing at Equitable Life Assurance Society.

Until now, planning for the future of a computer center has been haphazard. "Over the years, data processing people have depended on the vendors to determine their equipment needs," says Kenneth W. Kolence, president of the Institute for Software Engineering, a data processing planning firm in Palo Alto, Calif. And computer manufacturers' efforts to educate the users, such as International Business Machines Corp.'s Systems Science Institute, were aimed primarily at computer personnel, who Kolence says, "were red-hot technicians bent on proving how good these things were, not on managing them."

For the most part, top management has not moved to correct the lack of planning. "Data processing strategy has been considered separate from the business strategy of an organization," says Index's Thompson. "The gap between the two cultures is getting wider," he warns, because "chief executive officers are more terrified [of data processing]. They don't understand it." Indeed, Warren F. McFarlan, a Harvard Business School professor considered an expert in data processing management, says, "By and large, it takes a crisis for people to wake up." Only now are "companies in the process of figuring out how to include data processing managers in the planning process," says Richard L. Nolan, chairman of Nolan, Norton & Co., a data processing management consulting firm.

Cooperation

A first step at many companies is a corporate steering committee (BW—Apr. 2, 1979). Typical is Deere & Co., the Moline (Ill.) equipment maker. Even though data processing managers have tried since 1963 to project capacity needs, it was not unusual for top management to go ahead with plans to build a new plant without consulting the computer department. Finally, a computer systems council including the top officers and directors was formed, and since then, says Robert A. Bulen, director of computer systems, "We've been working pretty closely together." . . . Such cooperation is vital to Bulen, because it enables him to keep the corporation's four computer centers equipped to handle a work load that has been growing by 30% to 35% annually.

Data processing managers and consultants agree that successful planning begins with a view of the computer center as a small business within a business in the same way that operating divisions and other corporate profit centers are looked upon. Equitable's Goodroe, for instance, charges other corporate departments for his group's data processing services. In this way, he recoups Equitable's entire investment in computer equipment. Goodroe even goes so far as to publish an internal annual report for his $40 million-a-year data processing operation. "I'm in competition with outside computer services companies and new technology that enables departments to set up their own minicomputer operations," Goodroe says, "so planning is important. If I am overconfigured in hardware or people, my costs will not be competitive. And if I underconfigure, then performance isn't satisfactory."

Knowing the risks

Despite the growing recognition of the need for more sophisticated planning for information processing, developing detailed strategies for computer configurations remains very much a black art. "The techniques are relatively limited," admits Thomas P. Gerrity, president of Index. "Data processing management is just starting to borrow techniques from other management disciplines."

Making the planning process especially arduous is the large number of subjective questions that must be answered: How much money should be spent on data processing? Is the manager competent? Is the data processing organization properly matched to that of the corporation? Stresses Equitable's Goodroe: "It's not just the capacity of machines but also of the people and procedures that must be planned."

Planning is more difficult, and more essential, when computers are being applied to operations of an enterprise for the first time. This is primarily because exact costs and data processing loads cannot be determined. "The computer changes your whole way of working, so you can't extrapolate from past experiences," says one manager now planning to install a multimillion-dollar interactive terminal system.

One skill that Gerrity of Index views as essential to computer capacity planning is risk management. More often than not in data processing operations, Gerrity explains, "risk was implicit rather than explicit." Now managers must be aware that they are taking chances before they attempt a computer project. They need to analyze the type of risk involved: Is it simply a chance that the project might take longer or cost more than expected? Or will the failure of the project interfere with the daily business of the company and result in financial losses? "A good manager brings risks up front," says Gerrity. "You don't want to avoid risks, but you want to make sure the benefits justify the risks."

One of the best tools, in fact, for helping managers plan for future data processing needs is the computer itself. Just as computer-based models help managers formulate and evaluate long-term strategic business goals, similar models will help them to determine how much computer power they will need to help the company meet these goals.

BSG, for example, sells a software planning package called Best/1 that mathematically models computer systems. It permits a user to examine how a particular arrangement of equipment will perform without actually having the equipment on hand. Thus a user can "test drive" alternate arrangements of various models of equipment before actually purchasing and installing the hardware. But as with all computer modeling, the Best/1 results are only as good as the estimates of the demand for data processing power on which they are based. Warns BSG's Goldberg: Best/1 "is only as good as the [corporation's] general business strategic plan."

Soaring demand

The payoff from proper planning, however, can be dramatic. James D. Callaway, senior systems programmer at Utah Power & Light Co., says BSG's planning software "paid for itself in the short time we've used it." The computer model showed the Salt Lake City utility how to improve the overall performance of its computer system simply by shifting work between the processors in its computer center. Says Callaway: "It showed us that we could make do with what we had, so that we didn't have to lease another computer for $19,000 a month."

The promise of such a savings is sending demand for data processing planning aids soaring. At Index, for example, phone calls from prospective customers averaged one a week three years ago. Now the consulting firm recieves 20 such inquiries weekly. And IBM says that demand from its customers for planning instruction and consulting grew 33% last year.

To be sure, professional planning for data processing is still in its infancy. But those in the field are confident it will make rapid progress. After all, says Index Vice-President Gerald Loev, "Accounting has been with us for 300 or 400 years, and we're just starting to get the hang of it. Data processing has only been with us for 25 years, and it is already as important as other corporate functions with longer histories."

Chapter 14 Integrating Business Data Processing Systems

Outline

Data processing system orientations

Applications-oriented data processing systems

An **applications-oriented system** emphasizes the efficient handling of each subsystem. For example, one system could record charge sales and update customer accounts. The same sales record would then serve as input for several other separate systems. Totally separate systems would bill customers and age accounts receivable, account for and control inventory activities, and analyze sales.

As another example, consider the order processing system we have been working with. Receipts and returns might be handled in one program, withdrawals in a second program, and reorders in a third program. It is undoubtedly more efficient for all these transactions and triggered activities to be handled in a single program.

Integrated data processing systems

An **integrated system** tries to view the different applications as a total system. Seldom is the ideal of a totally integrated system achieved, however. There are many degrees of integration. Technically, integrated data processing occurs when there is a single recording of the data from each transaction or change in a common classifying code for the purpose of making maximum use of the data with a minimum number of human operations. A beginning in integrated processing occurs when multiple copies are made of an input document, such as the sales slip at a department store. Each copy is used as input in a different application subsystem (accounts receivable accounting, customer billing, inventory accounting and control, and sales analysis). In a *fully* integrated system, the data from each sales transaction would be entered only once and all files updated and all reports prepared in one complex operation.

In a *partially* integrated electronic system, the transaction document (sales slip) would be converted to a machine-sensible input medium (punched card, magnetic tape, magnetic disk) that would be used separately as input to each subsystem (accounts receivable, billing, sales analysis, inventory). Two or more of the basic subsystems could be combined in one computer program for a higher degree of integration.

Fully integrated electronic systems are available for department stores in which each sales transaction is entered directly into the computer system and used to update customer, inventory, and sales records. When preset conditions such as a reorder point for an inventory item are encountered, the system automatically provides exception reports or may even prepare purchase requisitions to replenish stock items. The number and scope of such integrated systems for all types of businesses are increasing as the cost of computer hardware continues to decline, computers become physically smaller and require less power to operate, and programming is made easier.

When the initial development expense can be justified and when the volume is large enough to reduce per unit operating costs, fully integrated systems tend to be more efficient and less costly than applications-oriented systems. This is because the fully integrated system eliminates duplication of master records and input and reduces the processing time required to update all the files affected by each transaction. One of the largest savings with fully integrated systems arises from the decrease in data preparation and input costs.

Regardless of the system orientation, operating data processing systems are very complex activities. In order to understand what happens in such systems, one must understand how they are put together. All systems cannot be built in exactly the same way. The remainder of this chapter is devoted to understanding the different file structures and file processing techniques, data bases, and data base management systems (DBMS) used in business data processing.

File organization

A file is a collection of records on similar entities or transactions and can be organized in several ways. All ways involve ordering the records into file storage through use of a file key.

File keys and file order

A **file key** is a field within a record that is used in ordering the records in some way. The **major record key** is used as an identifier of the record. An example of major record keys is the employee number or employee name in a payroll file. The major key also is referred to as either the *control field* or *control key* of the record since it is used to control the positioning of the record in the file.

Secondary record keys are fields other than the control field (major record key) that are used in ordering the records for some purpose other than positioning them in the file. For example, the department number might be used in selecting employee records to prepare a departmental payroll listing.

Records within a file are usually accessed by the major key for routine processing activities. Any field (or word) within the record can serve as a **sorting key**, however. For example, in preparing a report on overtime paid, it might prove desirable to list the employees receiving overtime in order of hours worked on overtime in the study period. Overtime hours then would be the sorting key. Similarly, a study of inventory outages might arrange the items involved by the frequency with which outages have occurred to identify clearly the inventory items for which the supply has been inadequate most frequently. Number of outages in a given time period would be used as the sorting key.

Sequential file order

Sequentially ordered files are arranged and stored in some logical order with relation to the control key. For example, a payroll file could be arranged in alphabetic order using employee names as the control key. A file of items in inventory might be arranged in order by the item number. Using an appropriate alphabetically related coding scheme to establish the identifying numbers for either employees or items could result in a numeric ordering by the identifying number and an alphabetic ordering by name at the same time. Since numbers can be more easily sorted by machines (including computers), processing costs can be reduced while obtaining an alphabetic ordering which is more pleasing to people using the files.

Indexed-sequential file order

An **indexed-sequential file** is arranged into sequence by the control key and grouped into blocks for storage. A **block index table** is created which contains entries for each block. The first entry indicates the starting point of the block. The second contains the control entry (major key) for the last record in the block. Within the block, the records are arranged sequentially according to control field content. Access to an individual record is gained by looking up the block location in the block index table and then reading sequentially through the records in the block until the desired record is found. A sequentially ordered file stored in a set of steel file drawers is a common example of an indexed-sequential file. Each drawer is labeled with the major-key identifier of the first and last records the drawer contains. The labels on the outside fronts of the file drawers form the block index table. The labels on the tabs of the folders within the drawers are the sequentially indexed keys within each block.

Indexed-nonsequential file order

A nonsequential file can be indexed as easily as a sequential file. The index must contain an entry for every item in the file, however, and is therefore larger. The most familiar example of an **indexed-nonsequential file** is the library card catalog. Each volume in the library is assigned a key (code number—Dewey Decimal or Library of Congress) that is related to its content. The volume is then shelved according to that coded key. It is indexed in the card catalog by author and title. Each author and title card identifies the location of the item by its coded key. Note that the index does not give an exact *physical* location for each volume but rather a *symbolic* location. Each shelf unit is identified as to its contents by use of these same symbolic addresses, the catalog number. This is a real advantage because the books change their specific physical location on the shelves as volumes are added or deleted. If all the volumes in the library were arranged alphabetically by author or title, a large number of books would need to be moved each time a volume was added to or deleted from the library stock.

Random file order

The location of each record in a **randomly ordered file** is computed by a special formula. The major key is often the basis for this computation. A record is retrieved from the file by recomputing its location by use of the major key and the computational algorithm. Such methods do not locate records randomly over the possible storage locations but make direct access of each record feasible.

The simplest method of direct file access assigns the location of the record on the storage device as the major identifying key of that record. The main advantages of this **direct relation address** system is its simplicity and the ease of locating records. However, it has several disadvantages. First, the location of each record is not related to the content or frequency of use of the record. Second, if the logical major record key is not numeric (name, for example), a second major key is being created. Third, since a block of storage locations (usually in a contiguous series) must be set aside for the records, it is possible many of them will remain empty and valuable storage space will be unused.

A second form of direct addressing locates the address of the record through logical calculation of its **relative address** and conversion of the relative address to an actual physical address. This method is particularly useful when the file is in the form of a matrix of two or more dimensions. For example, suppose a firm sells 10 products through 5 distributors. The sales of the 8th product (P = 8) by the 4th distributor (D = 4) in the 12th week of the 1st quarter of the year is being located (W = 12 and Q = 1). Each weekly record contains 150 bytes or characters (L = 150). The relative byte location (R) of the beginning of the record would be:

$$
\begin{aligned}
R &= 10(D-1)(L)13Q + (P-1)LWQ + 1 \\
&= 10(3)(150)13(1) + 7(150)12(1) + 1 = 71101
\end{aligned}
$$

This relative address could be added to the first physical byte location of the file to obtain the actual machine location of the first byte of the record being located.

An alternate to the direct relation or logical calculation method of addressing is the **key transformation** technique. Two methods of key transformation are illustrated in Table 14.1. In the first, the division method, the key is divided by a number, the quotient discarded, and the remainder becomes the address of the record. Usually, the divisor is the number of storage locations in the physical file, although a prime number is also a common divisor. In the example, there are 2000 locations in the physical file. Note that the smallest remainder would be 0 (zero) indicating the first location in the file. The largest possible remainder is 1999 which would indicate location 2000 (the last location in the file) as the record location. Note also that the location obtained is a relative address and only locates the relative position of the record within the locations containing the file, not the actual address on the physical device.

The second transformation technique extracts digits from the record key to determine the record location. In some forms of this technique, the record key is divided into two numbers by extraction, and the sum of these two numbers is the record location.

To overcome the inflexibility of the direct addressing techniques, the physical file is often divided into groups of locations referred to as **buckets**.

1. Division: The record key is divided by a number, the quotient is discarded, and the remainder (plus 1) becomes the storage location of the record.

Example: Record key = 9,763

Range of locations = 2,000

$$\begin{array}{r} 4 \\ 2000\overline{)9763} \\ \underline{8000} \\ 1763 = \text{remainder} \end{array}$$

1763 + 1 = 1764 = location of record

2. Extraction: The storage location is derived by selecting a set of digits from the record key.

Example: Record key = 819763

Extract second, fourth, and fifth digits to obtain storage location: 176 is the location of the record.

Table 14.1 Two examples of random record location through key transformation

The direct addressing technique is used to find the physical address of a bucket and the record is added to the content of that bucket. In the event that bucket is full, the record will be placed either in the next contiguous bucket or in an overflow bucket whose address is recorded in a pointer at the end of the full bucket.

List organization Retrieval of data from storage files presents the most severe problems for file organization. Even random organization assumes a logical sequence of processing or inquiry from a single file. The use of sequential and indexed-sequential file organization makes it difficult to relate information from two different files. Only by creating a temporary new file with data from the two or more independent files can direct comparison of elements from separate files be accomplished. The first alternative to sequential or random organization designed to overcome this deficiency was **list organization**. In a list organization, logical relations among records are identified by pointers attached to each record. A **pointer** is a data item in a record which gives the address of the next related record. There can be several pointers within a given record to reflect the relation of that record to several other records. In this way, intersecting lists can be obtained. The most common list organizations are simple lists, ring lists, and inverted lists.

Simple list In a **simple list,** an entry in an index points to the first record in the list. The first record contains a pointer to the second record, the second record points to the third, and so forth. The last record in the logical sequence contains a special character as its pointer to identify it as the last record in the list. The physical location of each record is immaterial. Addition or deletion of a record in a list merely requires changing the pointer in the previous record. Of course, if a record is a member of several lists, the pointers must be changed for all lists. Backward pointers can be added to allow searching in either direction.

As an example of a simple list, suppose we wanted to identify all employees who are electrical engineers. In the index under electrical engineers would be found a pointer pointing to the first employee who is an electrical engineer. A pointer in the record for that employee would point to the next electrical engineer, and so on.

Ring list A **ring list** has a pointer linking the last record back to the first. Most rings contain pointers pointed in both directions so that retrieval can proceed in either direction from any record in the ring. The ring organization is very useful in answering logical queries. For example, suppose we found one customer who had ordered item number 27863. To find all other customers who had ordered the same item using a sequentially ordered file, we would need to examine all records in the file. If a ring list were maintained for all customers ordering this item number, we could merely follow around that ring until we returned to the record we started with.

Inverted list In another way of locating items in a file, the **inverted list,** we create a partially or fully inverted file. The inverted file is just what it sounds like—the roles of data elements (characteristics) and keys (identifiers) are reversed. In a standard file, each record is identified by its major key and the physical location of the file is dependent upon that file key. The contents of a record are called **record characteristics** of that record. For example, the inventory record for item 16093 is identified and located by the item number (the major key). The characteristics of the record are the units on hand, backorder amounts, and so forth, found in the data fields on the record. In an inverted file, the characteristic is taken as the file key and the identifiers of all records possessing that characteristic make up the content of the record. For example, the inventory file might look like this in its normal form:

		Characteristics		
(Key) item no.	**Item description**	**Units on hand**	**Units on backorder**	. . .
10176	Flat-Head Metal Screw #8, $\frac{1}{2}''$	0	26	. . .
10177	Carriage Bolt, $\frac{1}{4}'' \times 2''$	100	0	. . .
10178	Flat-Head Metal Screw #10, $\frac{3}{4}''$	24	0	. . .
⋮	⋮ ⋮ ⋮	⋮	⋮	. . .
21063	Round-Head Wood Screw #8, $1\frac{1}{4}''$	6	0	. . .

Suppose we set up a record to identify all items that are flat-head metal screws:

Key	**Characteristics**
Flat-Head Screw	10176, 10178, . . .

This latter file is an inverted file. Note that the index could be expanded to include every characteristic in the file. The result would be a fully inverted file.

Integrated data bases

Integrated sets of basic data files where each data element appears only once, where related data are cross-referenced, and where related data elements can be located by starting from any one of the individual elements don't just happen, they must be planned and created.

Data as a resource

The increasing prevalence of electronic processing has made management aware that data comprise an organizational resource. This concept of data as a resource is made very clear when attempts are made to integrate data processing applications to reduce duplication of effort. If the same data on hours worked, pay rates, and work accomplished can be used to determine payroll, to assign labor costs to different activities or projects, and to establish standards for use in controlling efforts of workers, the desirability of capturing these data once and holding them for use in each of the three activities is obvious. In addition, the data would be available for recall by any manager interested in examining the productivity of a particular employee or group of employees (section, department, project).

The integrated data concept

Historically, a data element (hours worked) belonged to the application or department (payroll) that captured or created it. As new applications (labor cost standards) were developed, often in a different department (production), the same data elements might be recaptured or recreated all over again. The integrated data base *philosophy* turns this historical process around by assigning each application that uses a data element as an attribute of that data element. In effect, the application is seen as belonging to the data.

Creating an integrated data base

Creating and using an **integrated data base** is a four-step process of inventorying data resources, analyzing data uses, designing the data base, and establishing the necessary procedures to maintain the data base.

The data inventory Each data record is made up of fields, or **data elements.** Historically, two applications often used the same data elements, but they were captured differently and therefore could have different values. As analysts tried to reconcile these differences and integrate the applications using a particular set of data elements, they found it necessary to define each element, its meaning, and its source clearly and unambiguously. This led to the creation of lists of data elements used in each application. As new applications were developed, analysts found that duplication could be reduced and integration fostered by referring to data lists for previously developed applications. Out of these beginnings grew the idea of a single listing of all the data elements available in the organization. This listing, or **data dictionary** as it is called, provided an inventory of available data which could be drawn upon for any new application or as a guide to pertinent information for any manager with a problem.

The data dictionary, therefore, is a listing of all the data elements found in the organization and usually shows the following items (with examples of each):

1 The name of the data element (employee name)
2 The form of the data element (alphabetic)
3 The size of the data element (the number of characters in the name field, often 26)
4 The primary source of the data element (the employee master record)
5 The location of the primary source (the master employee inventory file created by the personnel department and stored on tape number EMP 1000–1)
6 The applications that use the data element (payroll, personnel evaluation, promotion eligibility listing, and so on)

Analysis of data uses As already indicated, how each data element is used is listed in the data dictionary. However, at the time an integrated data base is first being developed, each data element may not be fully exploited. There may be additional beneficial ways in which a particular data element could be used. To determine the data and information needs of an organization or function that is being integrated, a **data use analysis** must be made. Each use listing must identify the following:

1 The form of each data or information element in each of its uses (a graph, a table, a document, a ratio, or simply a listing)
2 The frequency with which each use (report or recall) occurs by individual item as well as by category. (Monthly, weekly, daily, intermittently)
3 The speed with which recall or presentation must be made.

Data base design Conceptually, the data base can be conceived of as including all the data found in the organization. However, the data base must be segmented into parts according to whether it is manually or electronically recorded, stored, and maintained. Manually stored and maintained data typically consist of correpondence, memoranda, special reports, individual activity reports, and other infrequently used documents. These data are usually managed and maintained by personnel trained in office and records management. In this text, the term *data base* refers only to data stored and maintained on electronic devices with the aid of a computer and including two or more interrelated files.

Technically, a **data base** is a set of two or more interrelated files, each of which contains at least one data element in common. Data base design involves the exact definition, selection, and coding of the data elements to be stored, the determination of the media and devices to be used for the storage process, and the organization of the stored data for retrieval and use. For most business organizations, the sheer volume of data to be stored and the differences in the uses of the various master files mean that seldom will all the data stored on electronically controlled devices be arranged in a single integrated data base. Also, because of the cost in relation to the value of such storage, not all possible data can be stored on computer-controlled devices (online in a computer system).

The determination of which data elements to store and in what level of detail specifies the capacity of storage required. These determinations should be based on the value of each of the uses to be made of the resulting file. For example, is it worth the cost to record that an item sold in a particular sales transaction was a pair of men's shoes, oxfords, dark brown in color, 8½ B in size, with cap toe, rubber heels, leather soles, and a 1½-inch heel, purchased from the All-American Shoe Company? How much of this information should be stored will depend on how it is coded as well as how it will be used. For example, the item type, style, color, and supplier may be included in the item number and a lot number which can be stored as two data elements. But can the complex code required to identify the item as a pair of men's oxfords of a particular style and dark brown in color be justified? The more facts the number contains, the longer and more complex the number. Also, an index description of the code will have to be stored in the file if users are to receive an uncoded translation.

The decision as to what devices will be used to store the data will depend on the volume of data, the hit rate in processing the file, the frequency of retrieval, and the mode of processing (as already indicated). Care must be exercised to balance cost of the storage device and the value of the service the stored data provide.

Maintenance of the data base Maintenance of the data base consists of capturing the data, recording the data in the files to keep the records up-to-date, purging outdated data and information, modifying the record and file structure to insert new data elements (fields), expanding or contracting existing fields to reflect changes in data element coding, and removing fields no longer required. Procedures must be established for each of these processes as well as for data retrieval. These procedures must be carefully designed to perform the required task and to protect against accidental destruction or rearrangement of any file element.

Data base management

Data base management involves both an organization and the use of a hardware or software data base management system.

The data base administrator

The job of designing and maintaining (managing) an integrated data base requires a high degree of technical skill. A person possessing such skills is usually designated as the **data base administrator**. This person is given responsibility for data base design, creation, and maintenance and will usually be involved with the design of data processing systems and the selection of hardware and software as well as with the day-to-day redesign required to keep the system up-to-date. The technical skills of this person will largely determine the technical efficiency and reliability of the integrated data bases used in any organization. It should be recognized, however, that the effectiveness of the integrated data base in providing the right information in the right form to the right manager at the right time is not just a technical problem, and the data base administrator should not be accountable for system effectiveness. The system users are primarily responsible for seeing that effectiveness is designed into the system (Figure 14.1).

The data administrator

If data are to be treated as an organizational resource, they must be managed. The data base administrator (DBA) provides the expertise for the technical design and management of any integrated data bases in the organization. The DBA should not also be responsible for the data dictionary, for the prevention of unneeded duplication, or for the effectiveness of data

Figure 14.1

Data management System users are primarily responsible for seeing that effectiveness is designed into the system. (Courtesy Tektronix)

systems. This latter job is given to a data administrator, to whom, ordinarily the DBA reports. The **data administrator** (DA) should be a high-level manager responsible for the overall management of the data resources of the organization. The DA will create and maintain the data inventory and see that data use analyses are properly carried out. The DA will also bear prime responsibility for determining the need (desirability) and economic feasibility of establishing each integrated data base.

Specifically, the DA is responsible for the following:

1 Documenting and analyzing existing data systems
2 Accessing data and information requirements
3 Developing a model of the organization's data which makes data sharing possible and reduces duplication of capture, storage, and processing to a minimum
4 Interfacing with data users to develop efficient and effective procedures for data capture, storage, and retrieval, and for information dissemination to management.

The DA is first of all a manager. He or she does not require the same degree of technical knowledge and skill as the DBA. The DA will make the managerial analysis and decisions used to control the DBA's efforts. The DA must interface with other managers in the organization and assist them in identifying and meeting their data resource requirements. The level of technical knowledge possessed by the DA must be sufficient to understand and evaluate the technical decisions of the DBA, but the DA must manage the total data resources of the organization. In carrying out this responsibility, the DA will be involved with the non-computer-related aspects of data processing, particularly in providing a strong interface with its users.

Data base management systems

Programs designed to work with integrated data bases must be complex and very detailed. Starting with list-processing concepts, software experts have built **data base management systems (DBMS)** or languages (DBML). These languages free the programmer from the need to know all the details of how the files in a data base are structured. All that need be known is what, in logical terms, is in the file and what logical relationships have been set up. The DBML handles such details as specific locations and the number of characters in each data element. The programmer is left free to concentrate on logical (meaningful to the user) relationships and how to use them to get the information that is wanted from the data base.

Over a score of file management systems are available for purchase or lease. Languages can be found that are based on COBOL, FORTRAN, PL/1, or some unique special language. The value of such systems is great. They reduce programming cost, reduce time required to respond to special data requests, and ease the job of keeping an electronic data base up to date.

Additional data management systems are being introduced frequently. The most widely used complete data base management systems are TOTAL (Cincom Systems, Inc.), IMS (IBM), ADABAS (Software AG), and IDMS (Cullinane Corporation).

A complete **data base management language (DBML)** really consists of three major elements, each designed to carry out one of the major functions of data management.

1 A data definition language (DDL)
2 A data manipulation language (DML)
3 A data base inquiry language (DIL)

Each of these elements is described below.

Data definition language

The purpose of the **data definition language (DDL)** is to create a data dictionary describing the data elements found in the data base.

Data manipulation language

Data manipulation languages (DML) are programs designed to provide the procedures for maintaining integrated data bases. These languages provide the detailed processes to insert new fields and to shorten, lengthen, or delete existing fields. Data elements can be referenced for storage, retrieval, or manipulation by name alone. The same is obviously true for entire records. The DML relieves the applications programmer of a great deal of detailed programming. Thus, program development is simpler, faster, and less costly. Redesign of records within the file is also simplified. The language is used to transfer data between a data base and applications programs. It interfaces between the user and the data base.

Data base inquiry language

A language that provides the ability to access data stored in a data base by reference to the logical organization and meaning of the stored data is called a **data base inquiry language (DBIL)**. Its purpose is to allow users to search a data base to retrieve data defined only by its logical name. Logical relationships among data elements in the data base are used to control the retrieval process. For example, suppose we wish to interrogate the sales order file, retrieve all orders for less than $100 in a particular area, and print out a list showing, by customer name, the name of the item, the number of units ordered, and the value of the order. The order in a data base inquiry language could look something like this:

File is Orders
If Order-Amt. is less than $100 and area is 17
Sort on Cust-Name
Print Cust-Name, Item-No., Units-Ordered, Order-Amt.

Data base inquiry languages can thus make online data much more accessible to the nonprogrammer.

DBMS data base structures

There are three basic ways in which DBMSs structure data bases—hierarchical, network, and relational. With the increased availability of random-access, mass-storage devices in the 1960s and 1970s, the usual choices were the hierarchical and network structures. Now (1982), relational DMBLs are beginning to emerge.

Hierarchical data structures Various methods can be used to represent data. For example, in a simple one-to-one relationship of record and content, a flat file may be used. This is a collection of records of the same size, each containing data about two related entities. Thus, a customer and the amount he or she owes could structure as a simple one-to-one flat file. Unfortunately, almost no business files exhibit this simple one-to-one relationship. Rather, it is more often a one-to-many relationship, for example, a customer and events like credit purchases made by the customer, payments received from the customer, when the customer last paid, and the current amount owed. This more complex relationship can be represented in a tree structure, or **hierarchical data structure**.

The weaknesses of the hierarchical structure are revealed when elements from two files are to be compared or used as simultaneous sorting keys. For example, we would like to relate finished goods and goods-in-process to customer orders for a particular item. Three different files are involved—the customer order file, the finished goods inventory file, and the goods-in-process inventory file. This is, in reality, an example of a many-to-many relationship. Such relationships are difficult to handle in a hierarchical structure.

Hierarchical trees are sometimes hard for users to understand. This is especially true when an inverted tree structure is required. In addition, all possible relationships must be known when file structures are established.

Network data structures Many-to-many relationships, such as all customers who have ordered one or more of a set of items versus the inventories (finished and in-process) for those items, are usually represented by **network data structures**. The networks are developed using list processing techniques. The major weaknesses of the network parallel those of the hierarchical organization: they can be difficult to understand, and all relationships must be specified when the files are established in order to set the pointers.

Relational data structures The newest data base organization is the **relational data structure**. The relational structure was conceived by data base theorists as early as 1970 as an answer to the limitations of hierarchies and networks. The concept is simple: Consider a relationship between elements in the data base as a two-dimensional table. Each record is considered a row in a table. Relational operators from mathematical set theory are used to manipulate relations. The model is simple but also precise. It allows an organization's data to be viewed as a collection of tables defined by a precise set of rules and procedures for gathering, updating, and using the data.

Simple in concept, the relational model has been difficult to implement. Relational DBMS did not become available until 1979 and 1980. The announcement in December 1980 of IQL by IBM has given impetus to the movement toward relational DBMS.

Relational structures have a number of advantages. First, they are easier for users to understand. Second, because they reflect precise mathematical processes, the relations can be used to determine the size of the completed data base, something that was very difficult with networks and hierarchies. Thus, storage requirements can be precisely computed. It is also claimed that the relational design is efficient in its use of computer resources. Storage requirements are not greater than with hierarchies or networks and operation is faster. Finally, since relations are automatically maintained, changing relations by adding or deleting fields is simplified.

Hardware DBMS

Another important announcement of 1980 concerned the introduction of hardware data base management systems. These electronic boxes are a firmware version of a DBMS. They have two major advantages. They are easy to add to a host system to manage a particular data base and their use adds little to the workload of the host system. This could be an important direction of development for DBMS in the future.

Summary

Business data processing systems can be applications oriented and emphasize the efficient handling of each subsystem (application). Alternatively, they can emphasize the integrated nature of the overall system. Regardless of their orientation, business data processing systems are complex. Each master file is ordered onto or into a storage device, using a major identifier for each record. This major identifier is known as the major record key, and is normally used to identify each record when retrieving records for processing. The records may be arranged in sequential, indexed-sequential, or random order within the file. They also may be processed as simple lists, ring lists, or inverted lists.

Integrated data bases underlie integrated data processing systems and are necessary for a high degree of integration. As analysts and managers have worked to develop integrated systems, they have come to recognize that data comprise an organizational resource and must be managed if full value is to be obtained from their capture and use.

Creating and using an integrated data base involves four steps: (1) inventorying data resources and preparing a data dictionary; (2) analyzing data uses; (3) designing the data base; and (4) maintaining the data base to keep it up to date. Managing an integrated data base requires an organization and the use of a hardware or software data base management system.

The technical task of designing and managing integrated data bases is the responsibility of the data base administrator. The data administrator, on the other hand, has responsibility for inventorying the data elements available in the organization, analyzing their uses, and recommending needed additions to and improvements in systems for data capture, storage, analysis, and use.

The data base administrator's job is eased by the use of data base management languages, the software or firmware interface between an integrated data base and the applications programmers or other users working with it. Data base management systems organize data in hierarchical, network, or relational structures. Relational structures are preferred.

Key terms

Define the following terms as briefly as possible and then, in a short paragraph, clarify each definition.

Applications-oriented system
Block index table
Bucket
Data administrator
Data base
Data base administrator
Data base inquiry language (DIL)
Data base management language (DBML)
Data base management system (DBMS)
Data definition language (DDL)
Data dictionary
Data element
Data manipulation language (DML)
Data use analysis
Direct relation address
File key
Hierarchical data structure
Indexed-sequential file
Indexed-nonsequential file
Integrated data base
Integrated system
Inverted list
Key transformation
List organization
Major record key
Network data structure
Pointer
Randomly ordered file
Record characteristic
Relational data structure
Relative address
Ring list
Secondary record key
Sequentially ordered file
Simple list
Sorting key

Discussion questions

1 Can a sequentially ordered file be randomly accessed?
2 Explain why an applications-oriented system can or cannot include:
 a Batch processing b Online processing

c Inline processing
d Realtime response
e Integrated data base
f Buckets
g Random access

3 Could a randomly ordered file be sequentially accessed?
4 How is the major record key related to
   a File ordering?
   b File access?
5 If this book were considered a file,
   a What is the major record key?
   b What file order is used?
6 Does the use of the computer favor integrated or applications-oriented data processing systems? Explain.
7 When would integrated data processing systems be better than applications-oriented systems? Explain.
8 What are the duties of a
   a Data administrator?
   b Data base administrator?
9 When should a data base management language be used?
10 What is data base management?
11 How does data base management differ from file management?
12 Compare the advantages and disadvantages of hierarchical, network, and relational data structures.
13 What are the advantages of a hardware DBMS?
14 What is the basic data processing philosophy that supports the use of integrated data bases? How does it differ from the data philosophy underlying applications-oriented data processing?

Exercises

1 Refer to the order processing program described in Chapters 8, 9, and 10 and prepare a data inventory of the data elements in that program. (Note: You must decide on the size of each data word.)
2 Visit the data processing department of your school and determine the following:
   a Is a DBMS in use? If not, why not?
   b If a DBMS is in use,
      (1) What data structure is involved?
      (2) How do each of the following feel about the DBMS?
         (a) Analysts
         (b) Programmers
         (c) Nontechnical users
3 Visit the data processing department of a large firm in your area and find the answers to the questions posed in Exercise 2.
4 Compare the results for Exercises 2 and 3. (Note: Exercises 2–4 might be assigned as a class project with teams of students visiting different organizations.)

Success with POS

Precise control with overnight results available to top management is a combined benefit gained by Macy's New York Inc., through the installation of an on-line, point-of-sale (POS) network.

The network has "long ago paid for itself," although it was installed about three years ago at 15 retail stores in Metropolitan New York City and now handles about 120,000 transactions per day through 1,775 terminals, according to William Klein, vice president and assistant controller of this New York division of giant retailer R.H. Macy & Co.

"We're constantly growing; finding new ways to use what we bought," Klein told *Infosystems* in an exclusive interview. "We're not anywhere near the end of the potential of this system," Klein said. . . .

"With improved accuracy and timeliness of information, the problem areas can be identified and we can move in quickly to plug the holes," said Klein, who supervises the data processing department for the New York retail operation from offices at 7th Avenue and 34th Street near midtown Manhattan. The point-of-sale (POS) system is almost a turnkey network for retail stores that is comprised of computer and communications equipment manufactured, installed and maintained by NCR.

Prior to conversion to the on-line POS network, Macy's New York was using about 450 Class 52 NCR optical-scan cash registers and hundreds of cash registers that produced only journal tapes that had to be processed manually. Once the conversion decision was made, and Massapequa, a Long Island unit of Macy's, was equipped with NCR POS terminals for a test run, the installation proceeded to a portion of the Herald Square store on 34th Street and 7th Avenue for a two-week test run. . . .

"After that, we did one store a week. . . . It was a record-breaker, faster than anybody has ever done it. If we had gone slower, it would have been harder. We had the momentum," Klein said, recalling the rapid installation of more than 1,600 NCR 280 point-of-sale terminals in the 15 stores, including some 500 in the Herald Square store alone, which is one of the largest retail stores in the world.

The number of installed POS terminals has subsequently been increased to 1,775 partly because of "an aggressive modernization program." . . .

"We would be hard pressed in this market area (New York City) without point-of-sale terminals," Klein said. "We have a flexibility we never had before. In the networking

Source: Abridged from "Aggressive Modernization Pays Big Dividends," reprinted from *Infosystems,* 25 (October 1978), 16–18. Copyright, Hitchcock Publishing Company.

concept, with one mesh we cover everything, all aspects of our business," Klein explained. "It controls all types of transactions from beginning to end, starting with the point-of-sale terminal."

The "coverage" includes about 20 classes of merchandise in each of 300 departments within each of 15 store locations, including four furniture/clearance stores. Not included are the several restaurants within the Macy's stores and a warehouse in which two-day sales are held four times a year. At sale time, 60 POS terminals are installed to handle the volume.

"The point-of-sale is the source of data for the company." Klein said. "It provides credit authorization for our more than two million charge account customers, authorization for American Express cardholders, authorization for cashing checks drawn on almost any bank, control of inventory in hard goods, and basic accounting information for our sales and returns.

"Controls are extremely tight now," he emphasized, but added, "although our primary concern is increasing control, we never lose sight of the fact we need to provide more timely information for merchandising decisions (by the buyers and management). . . .

Until late September, the primary processor in the system was an NCR Century 201, but this was replaced with the newer, more powerful, and physically smaller Criterion 8570 processor. Being phased in now are NCR 7200 keyboard/CRT units with cassette tape drives. These are being used in each store for off-line entry functions as part of Macy's move further into networking and distributive data processing, Klein indicated.

"We're moving more and more standalone intelligence out to the point where the data is first entered," he said. "The person most able to correct an error is the person sitting right where the data is. It's extremely expensive to try to search out the paperwork and correct an error after the fact. The element of control is greatly enhanced. The operator can't leave something out that we need—the terminal is almost a teaching machine," Klein said.

These terminals are used to record merchandise received at each store at the time it is received. Capturing data there, Klein explained, provides two benefits—information for the accounts payable file and information for merchandisers and buyers who track reorder points.

One of the principal benefits of the POS system to Macy's is the credit authorization capability provided at each of the 1,775 terminals operated by store clerks. More than half of the store's business is handled through the firm's own credit card system or American Express. And it is growing steadily. "This is a 100 percent positive authorization file," Klein explained, noting that all credit card customers, their credit limits and sales history are stored in the file.

"If a sale is approved, it is automatically recorded (by the NCR 280 terminal)," he said. "If it's not and we want to talk to the customer, the sales person sends the customer to a service desk. There, a CRT is used to make an on-line inquiry into the authorization file to determine why a sale was referred to the service desk."

The POS system, because it provides much tighter control of credit card usage, has greatly reduced the possibility of fraud in the Macy's store, Klein indicated. This can be extremely critical during peak sales periods when daily transaction volume more than triples to 420,000.

With the POS system, Klein said that 99.98 percent of the data required by the company is captured in each transaction, resulting in an extremely low .02 percent that must be re-entered because of clerical errors or problems in the network. In the previous system, the error rate was relatively low, but because of high daily transaction volumes even this small error rate required a large number of people to identify and re-input data. . . .

With the POS network, Macy's has automated the sales audit function, and Klein said the computer system now does "everything an auditor would do to verify that transactions are complete and correct," including balancing individual cash register/POS terminals.

The NCR network system, with its overnight processing of POS data, also provides each of the 15 stores with a series of control reports to help that store detect and correct any of the previous day's errors before the store opens in the morning, he explained. These reports, and others planned for implementation in the near future, are transmitted to the stores over the remote inquiry network, which becomes an administrative broadcast network after the stores are closed.

The "big payoff" for Macy's in the use of its POS system is "control of credit and credit authorization," Klein acknowledged, but added, "we're capturing other very valuable information as a by-product—100 percent unit sales information, captured in many areas and department/class sales information in the remainder of the company, with ability to monitor and control selling floor procedures and reports on a timely basis with elimination of delays. The system also facilitates personnel scheduling and productivity reviews."

Klein noted that each Monday, the management of both the New York division and the R. H. Macy chain receive audited sales and activity figures for the previous week, current through Saturday night closings, plus a "flash report" on Sunday sales of the previous day. Delivery of such critical merchandising information was previously impossible to obtain in such a short time, if at all, Klein indicated. The POS system also has allowed Macy's to implement tighter control over furniture orders and shipments to customers, because information now is available through an on-line delivery tracing system.

The delivery tracing system maintains complete records of every aspect of big-ticket delivery transactions. The record includes financial data captured at the point of sale and separately keyed alpha information (name, address, phone number, etc.) entered the same day into each store's 7200 visual display terminal.

"This is a difficult business," Klein said of the "big ticket" items such as furniture, but "this makes it a little bit easier and greatly enhances the element of control so that we don't forget to deliver something that has been ordered or try to deliver something twice." (During the INFOSYSTEMS interview this furniture system proved its worth by quickly resolving a dispute concerning the delivery of a $400 sofa to a woman in a fashionable East Side apartment.) . . .

But what about the salespeople using the new POS terminals? Klein was asked. He answered, "They took to the terminals very quickly. The machine leads the clerk through the proper steps of the sale. We've reduced the time it takes to train new sales people and the time it takes to handle a customer properly. The salescheck produced for our customers fully describes, in English, the type of merchandise selected. Our customer account statement shows the same description. POS has reduced a lot of areas of confusion for the sales person and the customer," Klein concluded.

Chapter 15 Controlling Business Data Processing

Outline

Control systems

The concept of control systems

The objective of a **control system** is to keep the operations it controls performing according to some recognized plan. Unlike planning, which is concerned with what will happen in the future, control looks at what is happening in the present and what has happened in the recent past. As long as activities are proceeding in a desirable manner, the operation is allowed to continue operating as it has been. If, however, the level of any part of the activity (sales amount, inventory levels, numbers and rates of errors) changes in an unexpected or undesired way, the control system recognizes and reports that fact.

Corrective action may be automatic. As examples, an input error would be corrected or more widgets would be added to available inventory. Such automatic actions have been referred to as **programmed decisions**.

Corrective actions may also be nonautomatic, or **nonprogrammed decisions**. For example, if sales in the men's shoe department of a department store suddenly fall well below expected levels for a quarter (three months) what should be done? Are all clothing sales down? Are sales personnel performing inadequately in the department? Is inventory inappropriate? That is, does the mix of colors and styles of inventory match what customers want? Are prices out of line with competitors? Until a reason for the change in sales level is determined, the proper corrective action is unknown.

Steps in the control process

Regardless of what is being controlled, a control system operates in four steps.

1 Standards are set.

Standards, or predetermined goals for the operation (sales levels, inventory levels, error rates) must be set to give the system a basis for recognizing departure from the desired activities. These goals are usually in numeric form (quantitative). Thus, the desired error rate is 1 percent, the desired sales level for the quarter is $75,000, or the desired inventory level is 64 units.

2 Performance is measured.

Once a standard is set, performance must be measured in the same terms as that standard. Note that in order to get realtime control, the measurements must be available before the physical operation is completely out of control. For example, knowing the inventory of men's oxfords is lower than desired because none are left in stock does not allow for timely control. Customers will go elsewhere for their purchases during the time a new supply of shoes is being obtained. Such a lack of adequate supply, if repeated, will drive away regular customers, and men's oxfords will be sold only to casual, drop-in customers with no loyalty to the store.

3 Performance is compared to the standard.

Again, results must be available in time to take corrective action *before* a serious problem is created. For example, the fact that an automatic filling machine in the packaging department of a cereal manufacturer is consistently overfilling cereal boxes by a significant amount should be discovered fairly rapidly since the margin of profit on each box is small. Overfilling a few boxes will add little to costs; overfilling several thousand boxes could result in a loss for the operating period.

4 Appropriate control action is taken.

If the process is under control, it is operating as desired or planned. In that case, the decision would be to take no corrective action, but to allow the process to continue operating as it is. If actual performance deviates to a significant degree from the standard, corrective action is called for. Such action can take at least three general forms.

a It may be automatic (programmed).
b It may require further analysis to discover the cause of the deviation.

As indicated earlier, the reason for a drop in sales of men's oxfords can be one of many factors. Examples already cited are

A drop in all clothing sales
Inadequate performance by sales personnel
Inappropriate styles and colors in stock
Noncompetitive prices

Other possible causes include

Traffic through the store is down because of new competition or poor location.
Advertising has been inadequate.

c It may show the standard to be unrealistic.

Refer again to the sales of men's oxfords falling well below planned levels. The real problem may be that planned sales levels are too high, that is, the standard is wrong. Standards that result from the planning of future activities in a poorly understood environment often are wrong. The manager of the shoe department may not have properly assessed the factors that determine the level of sales of men's oxfords. There are many factors to consider: Style, price, color, general economic conditions, the level of traffic through the store, location (accessibility) of the shoe department, advertising, fashion trends, and performance of sales personnel are the most obvious. A slump in the general level of economic activity may not have been foreseen. A decline in the popularity of the store because of new competition or a shift in consumer traffic patterns from downtown where the store is located to suburban shopping centers may be under way. Men's styles of dress may be shifting away from oxfords. All these reasons could make forecasts of sales based on past data too high. Sales may, in fact, be very good in relation to what is realistically possible. If so, the standard (desired sales level) should be changed.

Types of control systems

There are two general types of control systems, managerial and internal.

Managerial controls Those systems designed to control overall levels of activity and results, such as the general level of sales, profits, or return on investment, are **managerial controls**. Such controls, obviously, are revised on a regular, periodic basis as the result of strategic and tactical planning, that is, planning whose purpose is to determine what is to be done and how it is to be accomplished. Strategic and tactical controls deal with the overall performance of a firm, a division, a department, or a project. The control of total sales in the shoe department is a tactical control. Control of the sales of men's oxfords is an operational control. Checking the sales made by each sales clerk in the department is an example of a supervisory control relating to an individual operator.

Internal controls Operational and supervisory controls are called **internal controls**. These controls apply to control of specific activities and have four major purposes.

1 Checking on and maintaining the accuracy of business data
2 Safeguarding the firm's assets against fraud, embezzlement, and theft
3 Promoting operating efficiency
4 Encouraging compliance with the established policies and procedures of the firm

Data processing system controls are internal control systems. Therefore, general internal control processes and specific data processing controls will both be discussed in some detail.

General internal control processes

The processes used in applying internal controls to data processing activities include separation of physical control and accountability, written procedures, standardized documentation, preset procedures for making system changes, a data security system, protection against outside intervention, and a well-developed audit program.

Separation of physical control and accountability The general procedure of separation of physical control of an asset from the responsibility for accounting for that asset is reflected in data processing, in that no one individual performs all aspects of data capture, processing, and output. This also applies to design, particularly if a computer is involved. Allowing one individual to design and program an application, prepare the input data, run the program, and proof the output gives that person ample opportunity to implement a system that converts company assets to his or her own use. No employee should have unrestricted access to all data files and programs. A records librarian with no operating responsibilities should keep and control computer programs. Machine operators and other personnel should be rotated in their assignments in such a way that no person consistently controls a complete processing cycle.

Written procedures Good documentation provides a means for the auditor (external or internal) and management to keep control of procedures. It promotes operating efficiency and adherence to established policy. All data processing systems, whether manual or machine based, automated or nonautomated, fully integrated or applications oriented, must be designed and documented with control and audit considerations in mind. The participation of an auditor in systems design is imperative.

Standard format and standard symbols in system documentation Documentation is supposed to describe the system clearly and completely. Adherence to a standard organization for the system description is a first step in assuring a complete description. Items to be included in the description of data processing and information systems were indicated in Chapters 12 and 13.

Procedures for making changes in the system Changes in system procedures should not be possible without prior authorization by a responsible authority. For example, it should not be possible to make changes in an operating computer program without written approval from the affected department and the data processing supervisor. The internal auditor should receive automatic notification of such changes if that auditor's prior approval is not required. Changes should be completely documented and made part of the system procedure file.

Data security program Definite procedures should be established to control access to all data files. In addition, data files should be protected against accidental or deliberate destruction by outside forces, human or natural. Master files should be protected against destruction by fire or water. Fireproof storage vaults for the most important files should be considered. Adequate insurance should be provided to compensate for any loss. Proper identification of and control over paper or magnetic tape files, disk packs, and so on, should be established. Waste disposal control procedures should guard against accidental destruction of important files while assuring the destruction of carbon paper, abandoned punch cards, and so on, to prevent vital company information from falling into the hands of competitors. Access to processing areas, particularly computer centers, should be strictly controlled.

Protection of processing procedures and equipment against outside intervention Only authorized personnel should be allowed to operate processing equipment, including computers. Access to processing sites, particularly computer centers, should be carefully controlled. Only trained, authorized personnel should be allowed access to data and programs. Changes in processing procedures should require management clearance before implementation.

Well-developed auditing procedures Auditing procedures should be developed that take advantage of system characteristics while not placing an undue burden on the system. The primary purpose of an audit is to check on the effectiveness of internal control procedures. The audit technique will vary in accordance with the manner in which the processing is performed. In largely manual, nonintegrated systems, controls will be people-oriented, depending largely on crosschecks of data between people and departments. In a computerized system, processing tends to be more centralized, and controls must of necessity be more system oriented and included in computer programs. Checking for the presence and adequacy of such controls will differ in the two situations. (A more complete discussion of the auditing of computerized data processing systems may be found in the Special Option on p. 531.)

Specific data processing controls

Data processing procedures must include procedures adequate to ensure that all data items are recorded and processed correctly and that the resulting output is complete and correct. The three major areas of data control are input, processing, and output. Some of these controls can be built into computer hardware.

Input controls **Input controls** are established to ensure that data from all authorized transactions are correctly recorded at the right time and that all these data elements enter the processing system at the right place. Many specific control techniques can be used in controlling input data. The most commonly used techniques are listed and described below.

1 **Prenumbered forms** Serially numbered forms are effective in preventing the loss of input documents. An example used by most persons with a checking account is the prenumbered check.
2 **Control totals** When batch processing is used, totals can be used to prevent the loss of transactions. Either totals of meaningful data fields (such as hours worked) or "hash" totals (such as sums of employee numbers) can be used.
3 **Record or transaction counts** Counts of the records at each processing station can help to prevent loss of a record or introduction of illegal records.

Initial number: 97822

1. Beginning with first digit, multiply every second digit by 2:

   $9 \times 2 = 18$

   $8 \times 2 = 16$

   $2 \times 2 = 4$

2. Add these products together with the digits not multiplied by 2:

   $(18 + 16 + 4) + (7 + 2) = 47$

3. Subtract the units digit of this sum from 10 to obtain the check digit:

   $10 - 7 = 3$

Table 15.1 **A common method for computing a check digit**

4 **Data pre-audits** Data can be checked before processing. Computer programs as well as manual processes can check for the following:

- a Data in the proper format. These controls determine whether data items are properly entered on the form. Are there numeric data in alphabetic fields or alphabetics where numbers should be? Is the proper data element entered in each field? For example, is the customer's name entered in the address field, or the price of an item entered in an amount field?
- b Is the record complete? Are all appropriate fields filled? Has any part of the form been left blank?
- c Limit checks. Do the data values in each field fall within reasonable limits? For example, are regular hours worked in one week no greater than 40? Are total hours worked in a week less than the maximum possible, perhaps 72?
- d Check digits. Check digits can be used to check for transposed or incorrect numerics in an identifying number, such as a customer account number. In this process, a check digit is computed from the number itself and then carried with the number. At each processing station (desk or computer program, for example), the check digit is recomputed and checked to ensure data accuracy. The calculation process is designed to recognize most common recording errors, such as transposing (reversing) adjacent digits and dropping a digit. A common calculation procedure that is designed to catch about 98 percent of such errors is shown in Table 15.1.

5 **Identification records** Identification of data inputs and files before processing is important. In batch processing, all files (change files, transaction files, and master files) should carry as their first (leading) record and as their last (trailing) record an identification record. The

identification record should specify what is contained in the file including the type of data (change, transaction, master), the date on which it is to be processed and/or destroyed, the program or work station that is to do the processing, the number of records, and any control totals to be used in processing.

Failure to identify files properly can result in large losses. Think how easily a master file of accounts receivable could be destroyed by using it as a "scratch" tape, a tape that is no longer in use and therefore can be used as a blank tape. Destroying a file before its scheduled expiration date can cause at least a lot of extra work. It might lead to disaster. A good procedure here is to preserve three generations of files for each transaction at all times. That is, the current version (the son), the immediately preceding version from which the son was created (the father), and the version from which the father was developed (the grandfather).

Destroying a father or grandfather master file may cause no problem unless something goes wrong with processing the current son. Early destruction of previous transaction or change files will create no problem unless they are needed to reproduce the next generation. Without proper file identification and checking of the file "label" during each run, it would be possible to destroy the master file for an entire application. How many businesses could absorb the loss of their accounts receivable files? How many customers would cooperate in the rebuilding effort that would be required?

In online systems, it is very important to identify the exact nature of each incoming transaction. Addition or deletion of records, changes in the fixed data contained in a record, reversal of entries, and ordinary transactions would each be handled differently. Failure to use proper identification codes could cause significant error. Also, reversal of entries and deletion of records from the file should require special clearance. Such actions should not be possible from an ordinary sales terminal in a department store, for example.

Processing controls **Processing controls** should ensure against loss of data or failure to process a data item and should check the accuracy of processing arithmetic and procedures. They are implemented as part of the processing system and include some of the same controls used as input controls. These include record counts, limit checks, and control totals. Obviously, the count and control totals would be developed from processed units and the limit controls applied to computed values such as a pay amount.

Control techniques used as processing controls not previously described include the following:

1 **Structural checks** are based on the fact that some data values have predictable relationships. For example, the total of all deductions, for income tax, Social Security payments, and other purposes, when added to the total of the net pay amounts should equal the total of the gross pay

amounts. More subtle but useful structural relations can also be used. As examples, the total units produced should not depart significantly from the product of total hours worked and standard production per worker hour; total withholding for income tax should not exceed a reasonable proportion of gross pay; deductions for Social Security should never exceed the withholding rate times gross pay.

In sophisticated statistical or mathematical analysis, computed values often have distinct relationships. The apparent violation of such relationships may be the first warning of hardware malfunctions, rounding errors, or improper programming. Careful checking of data elements or processing when such checks fail can help to ensure processing accuracy.

2 **Sequence checks** can be used to discover missing or misplaced items and prevent out-of-order processing which may cause false exception signaling or the application of transaction or change data to the wrong master record.

3 **Dual processing** can be used to discover errors in calculation. Carrying out the same arithmetic operations independently or computing the same values by a second process can be used to check on the accuracy of arithmetical calculations. Rereading or proofreading data or information, particularly when transfer between media occurs, can catch many errors.

Dual processing is expensive, but it is used in systems producing critical results. In electronic systems, two processors or repetition of calculations can be used if the additional cost can be justified. It is not uncommon for tape and disk controllers to check the accuracy with which data are magnetically recorded by automatically reading each data item after it is recorded and checking it against what was to be recorded.

4 **Operation monitoring** is used to check for illegal access or tampering with computer programs. Operating logs prepared by the computer itself can help to ensure that regular processing procedures are followed. They are invaluable in spotting unauthorized processing or illegal interference in processing procedures. Computer executive programs of the current generation usually include this automatic logging of all jobs performed by the machine and of all actions by the operator. Other machines usually can be fitted with a meter that registers the amount of use in hours or operating cycles performed. Unauthorized machine time should always be investigated.

Output controls **Output controls** apply to the final reports, documents, and data files prepared by the processing system. They include several of the same controls applied as input and processing controls. These include record counts, limit checks, control totals, prenumbered forms, sequence checks, and structural checks. At this point, the totals and limits apply to outputted results (for example, calculated net pay to an employee cannot be negative). Prenumbered forms and sequence checks prevent the loss of data in custodial processing and can also help to prevent introduction of unauthorized documents. Structural checks are applied to final results in the same way they were during processing.

Procedures unique to output controls are review of interested parties and transaction sampling.

1 **Review of interested parties** can spot inconsistencies and other signals of input or processing errors. The data processing department should welcome the review of those who supply its inputs and use its outputs and should follow up on any reported problems to correct file inaccuracies or other errors.
2 **Transaction sampling** involves the random selection of transactions to be reprocessed; all affected outputs are checked for the same results. This technique is useful to internal auditors if done on a regular basis. In online electronic systems, this technique can be included in the processing program to produce an "audit trail" of a sample of activities within the system by printing out interim results as processing of each sample transaction proceeds. The auditor can then follow this trail of readable results through the system to check the results.

Computer hardware controls Quite a number of controls can be built into computer hardware to recognize equipment failure during input, processing, or output. These include parity checks, dual read or write heads, echo checks, overflow and sign checks, and dual wiring.

Parity checks are designed to recognize that one or more bits have been dropped from or added to those representing a character. As we already know, within the computer each character is represented by a sequence of 1 bits and 0 bits. One bit space is used as the parity bit. It is used to make the number of 1s in the character either odd or even, depending on the design of the particular machine. As each character is transferred between components of the system, a check is made for the required odd or even parity. If parity is not found, an error is signaled.

Dual heads are used to check on the reading of data from or to input, output, or storage media. As the second head reads each character, comparison to the first read is made. If the second head does not read the same character as the first head, an error is indicated. On output, the second head reads what the first head has written on the medium and comparison is made. Again a difference indicates an error.

Echo checks are similar to dual reads. At data transfer points (either local or remote) within the system, a feedback mechanism echoes each character back to the source from the receiving point. The source checks for any difference between the character that was sent and the character echoed back. A difference would indicate a failure of the equipment.

Overflow and sign checks are used during processing in the CPU. If a number is developed that is too large for the receiving register, the excess digits may overflow out of the top of the register and be lost. Such an overflow signals a processing error. The significant digits are held so that corrective action is possible. The sign check is used to signal that the result of a particular arithmetic operation has the wrong sign. This can be a form of a limit check since many business values cannot logically assume negative values.

Dual wiring is used to perform operations twice simultaneously and compare the results, and is a generalized form of dual heads. In its most sophisticated form, the entire processing section of the CPU is duplicated, allowing all program steps to be completed simultaneously in each processor.

The addition of any of the hardware controls described above necessarily adds to the cost of producing the computer hardware. The additional cost is most easily justified when handling sensitive data or when designing online systems. Some of these controls (parity checks and overflow checks) are now standard on almost all computer systems.

Accounting for computer use

If any resource is to be efficiently utilized, the cost of each alternative use of that resource must be known. Most computer suppliers provide some sort of job accounting information as part of their executive control programs. A number of independent software suppliers have developed various accounting programs or extensions to suppliers' software to assist in accounting for computer use on large systems. These normally supply data in the three areas of job accounting and control, resource utilization monitoring, and individual user billing.

Job accounting and control

The flow of jobs through the system can be traced. Jobs can be suspended or modified on the basis of variations from predetermined system use standards or computed run times. Resource utilization data and job billing based on resources used can be obtained from most of these programs. Billings are computed on the basis of rates established by the computer operations department. A control useful here is the checking of authority for requesting particular priority levels for each job (based on budget account number).

Resource utilization monitoring

Resource utilization can be controlled only if data on resource use is summarized for each major device in the system. Such data can provide the basis for planning for and control of resource acquisition and future hardware systems design. For example, an expensive set of tape drives and a controller linking them to the computer might be found to be used very seldom. The cost of these unused resources might be used to add a heavily used resource, perhaps a disk drive on which floppy diskettes could be mounted for online access. Cross-classifying resource use by job and programmer can assist analysts in planning for more efficient use of the total system (Figure 15.1).

Individual user billing

Computers are seductive creatures. The unwary can easily be trapped into using the computer to perform jobs that could be done much more economically in other ways or that might better not be done at all. Charging users can help to curb the misuses. The allocation of costs, by job and by department, is routine on most large computer systems. Costs of each resource and how to charge for each are not standardized, however. The vendor-supplied programs merely keep track of usage and allow the user to add the per unit dollar cost data if they are desired.

Chargeable items vary among the various job accounting and control programs. Most programs make provision for costing the following:

1 *CPU time.* The user pays for processor time plus interrupt processing charges.

In timeshared systems, the number of interrupts (and the associated charges) will vary with the number of users on the system. The user thus pays a higher fee for running the same program when the system is particularly busy. Unfortunately, a timeshare system user can pay for more time when the other users on the system are of higher priority even though there are few users on the system.

Figure 15.1

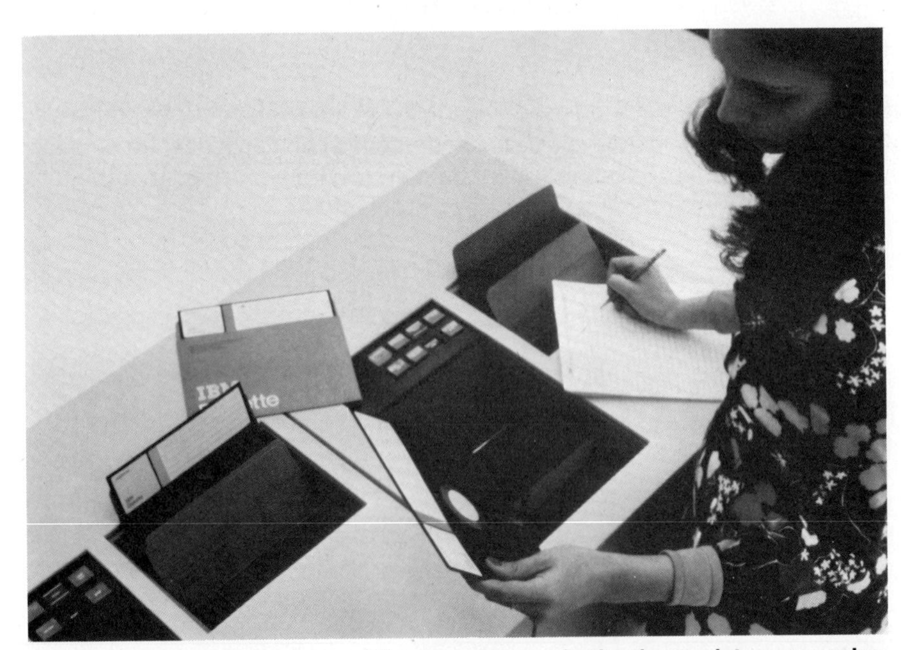

Keeping track of resources All components of a business data processing system should be subject to control activities. (Courtesy IBM)

2 *Input/output* (also called *spooling*). The user is charged for cards or records read and lines printed.

Input/output charges often include necessary job control statements, the number of which is determined by the system executive.

3 *Media mounting.* A charge is made for each tape or disk mounted by the operator.
4 *Other resource use.* Elapsed time of use of peripherals (tape and disk drives) and volume of storage required can also be priced. Special surcharges may be included for resource use over an established limit when such use affects performance capabilities of multiprogrammed or timeshared systems.
5 *Priority.* Basic usage charges for each element can vary depending on the speed of response or throughput requested.
6 Currently, most timesharing and multiprogramming systems provide for billing for *connect time* (time the remote user is online) and for *memory use.* Memory use charges are variable and include any or all of the following: total space used, number of references, and time spent in the primary memory.

Most of the available programs are relatively inadequate in providing billing information. Not all systems provide itemized billings by programmer, job, and date within multiple levels of account numbers. Some do not even provide totals by this level of detail for an accounting period. Many systems are inflexible in the length of accounting period used.

Setting charges for each part of the computer resource can usually be varied easily. Most billing systems allow the charge coefficients to be changed but do not allow for modification of the billing algorithm. That is, the basic formula stays the same, only the coefficients can change. This is unfortunate since modification of both the formula and the coefficients may be necessary in order to establish a billing system that leads to efficient and effective allocation of the resources making up a particular computer system.

In general, once a computer component is in place, charges should be set so that maximum benefits are derived from that component. If the component is idle, its cost is being wasted. Any job whose value is greater than out-of-pocket running expenses will provide some return on the fixed cost of the component. The computer department should, ideally, set internal use charges at the level that causes total user demand to equal the total resource availability.

Summary

The process of control involves setting standards, measuring performance, comparing actual performance to the standards, and taking appropriate control action. Managerial control systems are devoted to control of the performance of the firm and its components. Internal controls are designed to check on and maintain the accuracy of business data, safeguard business assets, promote operating efficiency, and encourage compliance with established policies and procedures. Internal controls for data processing include separation of physical control and accountability; use of written procedures, standard formats, and standard symbols; controls over system changes; a good data security program; protection against outside intervention; developing adequate auditing procedures; and data processing controls over input, processing, and output.

Accounting for computer costs is a developing field. Accounting programs currently available as part of system executives provided by computer vendors are not complete. They do provide valuable information on resource utilization and the capability to turn this into highly useful cost data.

Key terms

Define the following terms as briefly as possible and then, in a short paragraph, clarify each definition.

Control system
Control total
Data pre-audit
Dual heads
Dual processing
Dual wiring
Echo check
Identification record
Input controls
Internal controls
Managerial controls
Nonprogrammed decision
Operation monitoring
Output controls
Overflow and sign checks
Parity check
Prenumbered forms
Processing controls
Programmed decision
Record or transaction count
Review of interested parties
Sequence check
Standards
Structural check
Transaction sampling

Discussion questions

1 Explain the difference between managerial control and internal control.
2 What are the purposes of internal controls?
3 How is separation of responsibility used in internal control in general and in data processing in particular?
4 There are eight major processes used in internal control. What are they and what is the purpose of each one?
5 What is a data security program?

6 What are the five major areas of input controls? List them and briefly define each one.
7 What is a data pre-audit?
8 Why is identification of data files so important?
9 What are the major controls used in processing that are *not* used as input controls?
10 What are the major controls used to check on processing?
11 What are the major controls used to check on outputs? Which of these are unique to this stage?
12 What is (are) the purpose of accounting systems for computer use?
13 Ideally, where should internal use charges be set? Why?
14 Prepare a table which classifies each of the data control techniques discussed in this chapter as input, processing, or output data controls.
15 What are the four steps in the control process?
16 Corrective control action may take three general forms. What are they?

Exercises

1 Sell-All Department Stores is considering switching to online entry devices at all cashier stands in their 102 stores. Charge customers already carry plastic charge cards. In the new system, these cards would be changed to contain magnetically encoded identification which the terminal would read. What input controls would you suggest? Make your answer exhaustive.
2 Use the formula given in Table 15.1 to compute the check digit for each of the following employee numbers:
  a 36817
  b 24365
  c 11928
3 A program is being written for an industrial products firm to perform a sales analysis by cross-classifying sales by salesperson and product, by salesperson and customer, and by customer and product. Assume at least 100 products, 25 salespersons, and 250 customers.
  a What input controls would you suggest? Justify your choices.
  b What processing controls would you suggest? Justify your choices.
  c What output controls would you suggest? Justify your choices.
4 You are developing an accounts payable program to pay vendors for materials and parts. What controls would you suggest in each of the areas listed below? Justify your choices.
  a Input
  b Processing
  c Output
5 The Black Oil Company uses the following credit charge procedures:
  a Each customer is supplied with a credit card containing his or her name, address, and account number.

b Each time the customer makes a purchase at a Black Oil service station, the credit card is presented to the attendant, who completes the sales invoice, giving one copy to the customer.

c At the end of each week, the station manager batches the accumulated invoices with an adding machine tape and sends them to Black Oil. The amount is verified by the company, and the station account is credited with the amount of the batch.

d At the end of each month, the company sorts the accumulated invoices by customer number, microfilms them as a permanent record, adds the invoice amounts to each customer's account on the customer tape file, prints a billing statement for each customer, and mails each statement and the individual invoices to the customer.

e Upon receipt of payment from the customer, the amount is verified with the payment stub, the stubs are sorted by customer number, and the payment is subtracted from the customer record on the tape file. Partial payments and overpayments are input on a special card. Please specify the input, processing, and output controls you would suggest. Justify your suggestions.

COMPUTER CRIME

Superzapping in Computer Land

The customer, calling from Ottawa, was furious. Someone, he complained to officials of Telenet, a telecommunications network based in Vienna, Va., was using its lines to penetrate his company's computer. As a result, his operations were fouled up. The next week another computer network, named Datapac and tied to Telenet, got a similar call from a firm in Montreal. Its circuits too were being plagued by electronic interlopers.

Operating out of unknown terminals, possibly hundreds of miles away, the intruders had tapped into—or "accessed," in computer jargon—one of the company's computers. Even worse, they had actually "seized control" of the electronic brain, blocking the network's legitimate users from getting on line, and were systematically destroying data. The raids continued for more than a week. During one foray, 10 million "bits" of information, almost one-fifth of the computer's storage capacity, were temporarily lost.

It was an electronic sting with international repercussions: the Royal Canadian Mounted Police joined with the FBI to catch the criminals. By tracing phone calls, they soon got their man. Or rather boys. The culprits, only 13 years old, were four clever students at New York's Dalton School, a posh private institution on Manhattan's Upper East Side.

The bit-size bandits, perhaps the youngest computer con men ever nabbed, had obtained the Telenet phone number, coupled their school terminals to the line, and probably by nothing more than trial and error punched out the right combinations—in this case only five letters and numbers—to link up with the computers. More shrewd guesswork got them the "password" to log onto and operate the machines.

It was a schoolboy lark. None of the Dalton gang, even its eighth-grade leader, was prosecuted. But computer specialists were not amused. Besides costing the firms thousands of dollars in computer time, the incident was one more irritating example of the vulnerability of systems that can have price tags in the millions and store information of incalculable value. It was also a sign of the growing incidence of computer crime.

No one can say exactly how much such crime costs; often the losses are not even reported by embarrassed companies. But the larceny clearly is far from petty. It may well run to hundreds of millions of dollars a year. Last January, California became the first state to enact a computer-fraud law, allowing fines of up to $5,000 and three years' imprisonment. Still, warns Donn Par-

Source: Frederic Golden, "Superzapping in Computer Land," *Time,* January 12, 1981, 76.

ker of SRI International, a leading scholar of electronic theft: "By the end of the 1980s, computer crimes could cause economic chaos."

An exaggeration perhaps. But as computers spread into all facets of life, from controlling the flow of money to manning factories and missile defenses, the potential for troublemaking seems boundless. Already computer thieves, often striking from within, have embezzled millions of dollars. In 1978 a consultant got a Los Angeles bank's computer to transfer $10.2 million to his out-of-town account. Only a confederate's tip led to his discovery. To be a computer-age thief, you need nothing more than an inexpensive home computer, a telephone and a few light-fingered skills. As in the Dalton case, computer passwords are often short and simple. Besides, computer networks like Telenet or Datapac, frequently publicize their numbers to attract customers. Once into the computer system, there are other barriers to crash, and other techniques for purloining information.

Computer crooks have developed a whole bag of electronic tricks. One is the so-called Trojan Horse. Like the famed ruse used by the Greeks to penetrate Troy, it helps an interloper get into forbidden recesses of a computer. The mischiefmaker slyly slips some extra commands into a computer program (the instructions by which the machine performs a given task). Then when another programmer with higher clearance runs the program, he will unwittingly trigger the covert instructions. These unlock the guarded areas, just as the Greek soldiers hidden in the horse unlocked Troy's gates. The culprit might then transfer money to his own account, steal private information or sabotage the system itself. Other colorfully named ploys: superzapping (penetrating a computer by activating its own emergency master program, an act comparable to opening a door with a stolen master key); scavenging (searching through stray data or "garbage" for clues that might unlock still other secrets); and piggybacking (riding into a system behind a legitimate user).

Faced with such ingenuity, some computer owners are resorting to complex coding devices that scramble information before it is transmitted or stored. They are also changing passwords. Some even rely on detectors that identify legitimate individual computer users by fingerprints or voice patterns.

Yet as the safeguards go up, so does the urge to crash the barriers, especially among students. In a celebrated Princeton University case, students snatched grades and housing data from the school's computers and, by their account, briefly shut them down. Last September, two Illinois high school students dialed their way into one of DePaul University's computers and threatened to immobilize it unless they got access to a special program that would have let them communicate with the machine more directly. Said an investigator who helped catch the teen-agers: "They did it because everyone said it couldn't be done." Maybe so. But computer owners wonder: Where does the fun end and the crime begin?

Special Option

Ready-Made Systems

Introduction

Systems able to perform the specialized data processing functions for a particular small business or for a particular business function in a larger firm are available from a wide variety of firms. These turnkey systems are a combination of hardware and software needing only to be plugged into a power supply to take over the data processing application for which they have been designed. Thus the designation as turnkey, turn them on and they perform.

Turnkey systems are available for handling almost every one of the basic accounting systems. Specialized accounting and/or control systems are available in the areas of total accounts receivable, customer billing, inventory or general materials control, order processing and sales analysis, payroll, labor cost control, and general ledger accounting. These ready-made packages of hardware and software serve both large and small firms.

Turnkey systems are also available that provide a fairly complete data processing system for a particular type of firm. Systems are available for automobile dealerships; medical and dental clinics; wholesale distributors (automobile parts, electrical supplies, and so on); retail stores; and many more. These systems eliminate the need for small firms or divisions of large firms to design and program their own data processing and information systems. Maintenance for both the hardware and software are provided (for a fee) by the system vendor.

The quality of turnkey systems varies widely. Some are packaged and sold by large, stable firms with a history of success in software development. Some are being developed and sold out of someone's garage. Great care should be exercised when purchasing such systems to be sure that the firm is solvent and stable enough to continue to supply support over the life of the system.

Turnkey systems developed on mainframes are also available. For example, total packages for Medicare and Medicaid processing at the state level are now available. Complete data processing and information systems for large wholesalers, automobile dealers, and other industries can also be purchased.

Advantages of turnkey systems

Turnkey systems offer small firms the opportunity of automating record keeping with a relatively low start-up cost. In addition, the turnkey vendor provides system maintenance services, which means that the user need not hire technical experts for maintenance. These systems are usually designed to be operated by a clerk with no special knowledge of computers or programming. A final advantage of turnkey systems is their almost immediate availability. There is no system development period. The vendor brings in the hardware, installs the software, and trains operating personnel, and the system is in operation.

Disadvantages of turnkey systems

The major disadvantage of turnkey systems is that they are designed to solve a data processing problem in a general way. This usually means that the user must adjust procedures to fit the turnkey system. Unique features that give a small business an advantage over its competitors may be lost. For example, an accounts receivable system may automatically send rather harsh collection letters to delinquent accounts. This could be bad business for, say, a retailer in a farming community, who may need to carry farmers on credit for several months until their crops mature and can be sold. Great care must be exercised in selecting a turnkey system to see that it fits the particular situation where it will be used.

Another disadvantage of turnkey systems is that they are accounting oriented. Many systems provide only bookkeeping with few, if any, management control features.

A final disadvantage of turnkey systems is their limited expandability. This is particularly true for the small firm possessing no programming talent. It may be better to acquire a hardware system and buy ready-made software to get started. In the meantime, employees can learn to program the system and thus start to tailor it to the unique needs of the firm.

SYSTEM AT WORK

Marketing Support from the Computer

One of the main reasons for General Mills' prominence in the food processing industry is its dedication to sophisticated marketing principles. Now, the giant food firm's efforts have been enhanced with the ability to generate vital market data quickly for management decision-making in the easily-understood form of charts and graphs. These illustrations are then reproduced as 35mm slides, pen plots, transparencies, and microfilm.

According to Raymond E. Jacques, time-sharing manager, this high-speed information capability became possible with the installation of a computer graphics software system two years ago. The system is used in six major types of applications to track such information as a product's market share, production and manufacturing statistics, shipment details, and company financial data.

About 200 black-and-white and 25 color hard-copy charts are produced each month at General Mills through this system, for both internal and external reports and presentations. Furthermore, 35mm slides are generated periodically and 40 color charts are produced quarterly for the firm's quarterly financial report.

General Mills

The corporation is a leading producer of packaged consumer foods such as Gold Metal Flour; Cheerios, Wheaties, and Total ready-to-eat cereals; Betty Crocker cake mixes and frostings; Bisquick variety baking mix; and Hamburger Helper and Tuna Helper main dish mixes. Other food lines include Tom's snacks, Gorton's seafood products, Saluto frozen pizzas, Yoplait yogurt, and institutional food products.

The software package which the firm is employing is called DISSPLA®, developed by Integrated Software Systems Corporation (ISSCO), San Diego, California. DISSPLA is a system of FORTRAN subroutines which transforms virtually any data into graphics arts-quality bar, curve, and pie charts, maps, and 3-D plots, with customized annotation. The software system can be operated on most mainframe computers

---

Source: "Software Draws the Performance Picture," *Modern Office Procedures,* 25 (© December 1980), 102, 106.

and produces plots on any graphics device including monochrome and color video display terminals, pen plotters, electrostatic printer/plotters, and computer output microfilm (COM) units.

About the system

"We chose DISSPLA because it allowed us to program in color, use different fonts, and even generate three-dimensional plots—in short, its capabilities and options were exceptionally suited to the applications we had in mind," Jacques notes.

The system is being used with Hewlett-Packard equipment—a Model 3000 host computer, a 7221A four-color flatbed plotter, and a 2648A graphics display terminal. Recently General Mills purchased a Zeta continuous roll plotter.

General Mills also devised in-house a front-end program in FORTRAN called PLOTIT so that individuals without FORTRAN knowledge can use the system. It is an interactive program which prompts questions which are answered by the operator. A graph can be created by answering a series of questions. Approximately 80 to 90 percent of their business graphs are produced by way of this program. . . .

The firm is also investigating the possibility of licensing TELL-A-GRAPH®, ISSCO's English-access computer graphics software system, which will enhance their business graphics capabilities and enable non-computer staff to produce plots.

Graphics applications

1. "Of the six major types of graphics applications at General Mills, marketing tracking is one of the biggest areas for DISSPLA," said Jacques. "This application consists of tracking brand product market share information, as well as sales volume data, to measure product performance. These graphs are produced mostly as black-and-white hard copy."
2. "In production and manufacturing tracking," Jacques explained, "the color hard-copy graphs that are produced illustrate the production status of each of our products. For instance, one graph may display Wheaties planned versus actual production on a daily, weekly, or monthly basis."
3. Jacques noted that in the third application area, transportation tracking, the graphics system helps to present the percentage of on-time customer shipments from General Mills' various packaging plants. "This enables us to pinpoint problem areas so that we can better service our customers," he stated.
4. DISSPLA is used to produce 35mm slides for customer presentations. For example, slide presentations are given by General Mills personnel to discuss products with management of supermarket chains, he pointed out.
5. The fifth application area, financial reporting, provides graphs of such functions as tracking the number of days of working capital and the company's profits by division—actual versus planned.
6. "Finally, we use DISSPLA in the production of color transparencies for in-house presentations. The transparencies play a major role in our management presentations," Jacques said.

Benefits

Because the DISSPLA software system offered the maximum applications flexibility, according to Jacques, General Mills has reduced the time it takes to produce business graphs by more than 30 percent.

Jacques stated, "Management can receive data much more quickly now and, in turn, make more timely decisions. What used to take two or three days to produce now takes just a few hours."

In addition to saving a vast amount of time, the in-house capability also helps to save the company money because more data can be processed in a shorter period of time. Jacques also noted that the in-house system provides confidentiality to their data, thereby tightening company security.

"Because the DISSPLA system has helped to achieve marketing analysis and time management, effective financial planning, and improved company security, we consider the graphics software system a valuable asset to our operation," he concluded.

Special Option

Security of Online Systems

Types of threats to security

There are numerous threats to the security of an online data base. Not only is the system subject to all the abuses associated with physical penetration of the computer area, but it is also subject to penetration from outside the area via communication lines. Five general types of damage that must be guarded against are (1) system errors, (2) fraud and theft, (3) sabotage, (4) mechanical failures, and (5) natural disasters. Control processes for controlling system errors, fraud and theft, natural disasters, and ordinary vandalism and sabotage were discussed in Chapter 15. Loss from mechanical failures is protected against by adequate preventive maintenance and the availability of system back-up. The purpose of this Special Option is to discuss the problems of illegal penetration of the online system by illegal users.

Penetration techniques

There are four major techniques for gaining illegal access to online systems. They have been given the colorful names of masquerading, eavesdropping, piggybacking, and line grabbing.

Masquerading The illegal user may pretend to be an authorized user, thereby gaining access to the system. Of course, the perpetrator would have to know a user's identification number(s) and password(s).

Eavesdropping This technique consists of tapping in on a communication line (land line, microwave, or satellite system). All communications over the tapped link can then be monitored, or illegal messages can be entered into the system.

Piggybacking This is a sophisticated version of eavesdropping in which a special terminal is entered into the line in such a way that all messages must pass through the terminal. The user's input and the system's responses can then be modified. Frequently, after logging in, the user receives a message indicating that the system is not available or has broken down. The perpetrator then operates as the legal user.

Line grabbing This is a form of piggybacking in which the user is allowed to carry through the legal operation but is not allowed to sign off the system. The sign-off message is intercepted by the penetrator, and the proper response is returned. The penetrator can then continue to access the system on the legal user's credentials.

Controls and safeguards

The controls and safeguards against system penetration are physical security, data encryption, transaction serial numbering and time stamping, wiretap and bugging checks, call-back for connect, restricted uses, logging illegal requests for access, and automatic terminal disconnect.

Physical security It is common to provide physical security for the computer center but to leave terminals and communication circuits easily available. Whenever possible, terminal access should be controlled.

Illicit wiretapping can be easily accomplished at only a few places in a communication system. One of the most obvious is the telephone terminal box or "telephone closet." Not only are these terminal boxes easy to get at in most buildings, but the communication lines and terminals are usually carefully labeled. It is therefore important to control access to the telephone closet.

Direct communication lines are most secure when buried in metal conduits in concrete-filled trenches. Lines outside the property of the firm cannot be treated in this way, however.

Encryption

Data to be sent over long-distance communication lines and public networks can be coded. For full protection, the encryption process should be changed frequently and, ideally, randomly. Encryption is particularly important for protecting sensitive data transmitted over microwave or satellite systems. It may also be valuable for protecting particularly sensitive data and information stored in an online data base.

Encryption processes include transposition of characters in the data or message, substitution of other characters for characters in the data or message, and logical or mathematical manipulation of the characters in the data or message. Such changes are designed to make the data unintelligible to anyone who does not know the coding scheme.

Transaction serial numbering and time stamping

The host computer can be programmed to assign a unique sequential identification number to each transaction or message. In addition, the time the transaction or message arrived can also be added. The transaction or message is recorded in a log or journal along with these identifiers. Some systems also record the source of the transaction or message. It is then possible to trace back illegal messages and discover wiretaps, piggybacks, or other interventions.

Wiretap and bugging checks

At the first sign of anything suspicious, communication lines should be thoroughly checked for wiretaps or bugs. These checks should be run periodically even if there is no indication of anything amiss.

Call-back for connect

One method for verifying a legal user is to have the host computer collect the identifying number(s) and password(s) from a terminal that is calling in, then disconnect the terminal and call back to the legal terminal identified. This can prevent a terminal with an assumed identification code from getting online, simply because the intervening user's terminal can't have the same phone number as the legal terminal.

Restricted uses

Each legal user should be restricted to certain uses of the system. For example, applications programmers may be restricted to use of higher-level languages. System controls are usually written in assembler language. Only systems maintenance personnel should be given access to that level and then only under stringent controls. A terminal intended to be used for online data entry in a particular application should not be open for use for programming or system maintenance.

Logging of illegal requests for access

Whenever an illegal request for access to any part of the system occurs, that request should be logged as to time, source, and access requested. Persons searching for "trap doors" into the system can often be spotted before access is gained.

Automatic terminal disconnect

A common method for gaining illegal access is to wait for a user to leave a terminal without signing off. To prevent this occurrence and to prevent a port into the system from being needlessly tied up, most systems disconnect a terminal after a period of inactivity. Terminal users should be trained not to rely on this feature but to sign off immediately when a session is completed.

Conclusion

Even though modern online systems are particularly vulnerable to illegal use, exercising care can prevent most of these abuses. An intelligent, knowledgeable computer expert with sufficient finances can probably break through any safeguard. However, it should not be easy, and the invader should be made to leave some evidence of the visit. Certainly, the worst abuses to date have come from amateurs and insiders where systems controls were loose or nonexistent.

COMPUTER CRIME

Programmed for Stealing

A former programmer is behind bars after admitting he stole more than $100,000 in money orders from a minicomputer system he had programmed for his own illicit ends.

Michael Murray, 30, is being held without bail while he awaits formal sentencing. He could receive up to 10 years in state prison and a $3,000 fine for the computer-assisted heist from National Bonded Money Orders here [in Shreveport, La.].

Murray began writing applications programs for National Bonded's new Datapoint Corp. 5500 system last August. At the time, he was an employee of Digital Electronic Services, Inc., a systems house from which National Bonded had bought the packaged system.

National Bonded's office manager, Bobby Marrs, said Digital Electronic Services fired Murray shortly after the applications programs were completed. Murray, a personal friend of Marrs, was then retained by National Bonded to "help work some of the remaining bugs out of the system," Marrs said.

According to Murray's testimony and a recent investigation by the district attorney's office of Caddo Parish, Murray began tinkering with the program so that checks he wrote to fictitious people and cashed himself were ignored by the system after the canceled checks were returned.

"He was in on writing the programs from the very beginning, and being a friend I trusted him completely," Marrs said. "He knew the business from top to bottom and just altered the software so that he could do his own thing. And believe me, he did his own thing."

Losses noticed

Early this spring, the company reportedly began to notice inordinately large paper losses and summoned an auditor to investigate the situation. On May 7, during the investigation, the company was burglarized; the computer printout records and check code numbers were stolen, the firm said.

A probe of the break-in revealed that more than 1,000 money orders had been stolen throughout the preceding months and that the system was programmed not to reveal the losses. The investigative trail reportedly led to Murray, who in turn led police to the evidence lifted in the burglary.

"We know he was using some of the stolen checks to pay off his Visa charge card, among other things," said Assistant

Source: Bill Laberis, "CPU Programmed to Hide Theft," *Computerworld,* June 8, 1981, 2.

District Attorney Robert Gillespie. Those "other things" may have included gambling debts as well as investments in a satellite communications capture dish company in which Murray had interests, sources close to the investigation said.

"At any rate, it is clear to us that his intent in going into the place was to manipulate the computer so that it would not show up the theft," Gillespie said. He added that state Judge Eugene Bryson has the option of handing Murray a suspended sentence in return for demanding that full restitution be made to National Bonded, which is not insured for the loss.

Part 5

Data Processing and Management

Chapter 16

Applications: Information Systems

Outline

Management information systems
- The nature of a firm
- The information system as an organizational construct
  - Idealistic hierarchical
  - Worst-case hierarchical
  - The true hierarchical MIS
- The information system as a feedback and control system
- The information system as a data processing system

Functional information subsystems
- Functional subsystems
- The financial information subsystem
- The marketing information subsystem
- The production information subsystem
- The materials control information subsystem
- The personnel information subsystem
- The planning information subsystem

Management reporting
- Realtime control
- Types of reports
  - Status reports
  - Activity reports
  - Exception reports
  - Analytical reports
- Timing of reports
  - Periodic reports
  - Triggered exception reports
  - On-demand reporting

Effects of computers on management practice
- Special capabilities of computers
  - Speed
  - Accuracy
  - Complexity of analysis
- Changes in management practice

Organizational effects of computers
- Overall organization
  - Centralized management
  - Decentralized management
  - Computers and centralization
- Effects by management level

Placement of the information function

Management's interest in data processing is twofold. First, the data processing systems are information systems, providing management with the factual basis for planning and control decisions. Second, the data processing system must itself be managed if the resources used in data processing are to return benefits in excess of their cost. This chapter deals with the first of these two topics.

Management information systems

A **management information system (MIS)** is merely a *combination of people, machines, and procedures organized to produce information for management.* In order to understand this concept, we need to understand the firm itself. We also must remember the definition of information we established earlier: *Information is communicated knowledge expressed in a form that makes it immediately useful for decision making.*

The nature of a firm

Any institution, whether business, government, or educational, is composed of at least three kinds of interrelated factors, or elements. First, there are the resources and productive factors controlled by the institution. In a business organization, these are people, materials, and money that the organization controls. The second classification of factors is the specific activities to be carried on by the institution. In a business organization, these might be manufacturing, marketing, personnel management, and financial operations, for example. The third and final set of factors is the activities of management. Managers establish objectives and translate them into plans. Managers then attempt to execute these plans and evaluate the results as a basis for further planning.

The above classification is illustrated in Figure 16.1. Although this figure's representation of all the components in each element is inadequate, it does illustrate two important implications for MIS development. The first is the complexity of the organization and the many points at which data and information must be available to guide and ease the interaction of the many diverse elements of the firm. The second implication is more subtle but equally important. It requires the recognition that the individual elements of the firm are controlled and operated by *people.* The job of executing done by management consists largely of coordinating and controlling people. Without sufficient knowledge of what is being done and how it is being accomplished, people do not perform well. Part of the job of the information system must be to get the right data and information to each point where people interact so that they will be sufficiently informed to perform their individual functions effectively.

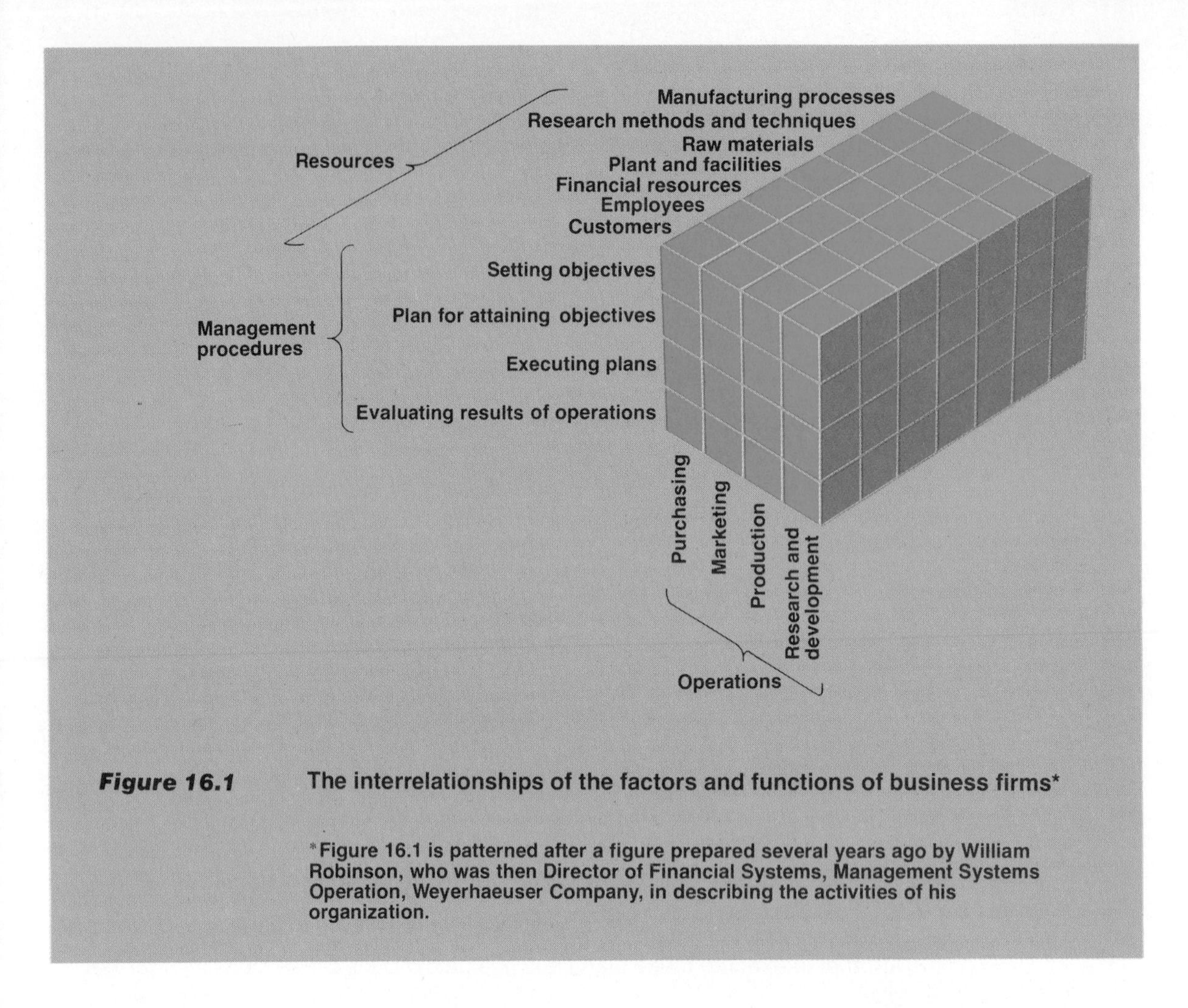

Figure 16.1 The interrelationships of the factors and functions of business firms*

*Figure 16.1 is patterned after a figure prepared several years ago by William Robinson, who was then Director of Financial Systems, Management Systems Operation, Weyerhaeuser Company, in describing the activities of his organization.

The information system as an organizational construct

The information system of an organization obviously reflects the structural organization of the firm. The MIS can thus be viewed as an organizational construct. The organizational structure of information systems can be represented by at least three different organizational patterns.

Idealistic hierarchical The first pattern reflects an idealistic organizational pattern and is represented by the two-dimensional pyramid in Figure 16.2a. As information about activities moves from the production line or sales room to the chief executive or top executive body of the organization, the information passed upward is continually condensed. Information on individual customers, employees, facilities, and transactions goes to the first-level manager (the first-line supervisor). This supervisor then summarizes the detailed information and passes on the summary to the next management level, his or her departmental or division manager. Administrators at this next level then summarize and analyze information concerning their individual

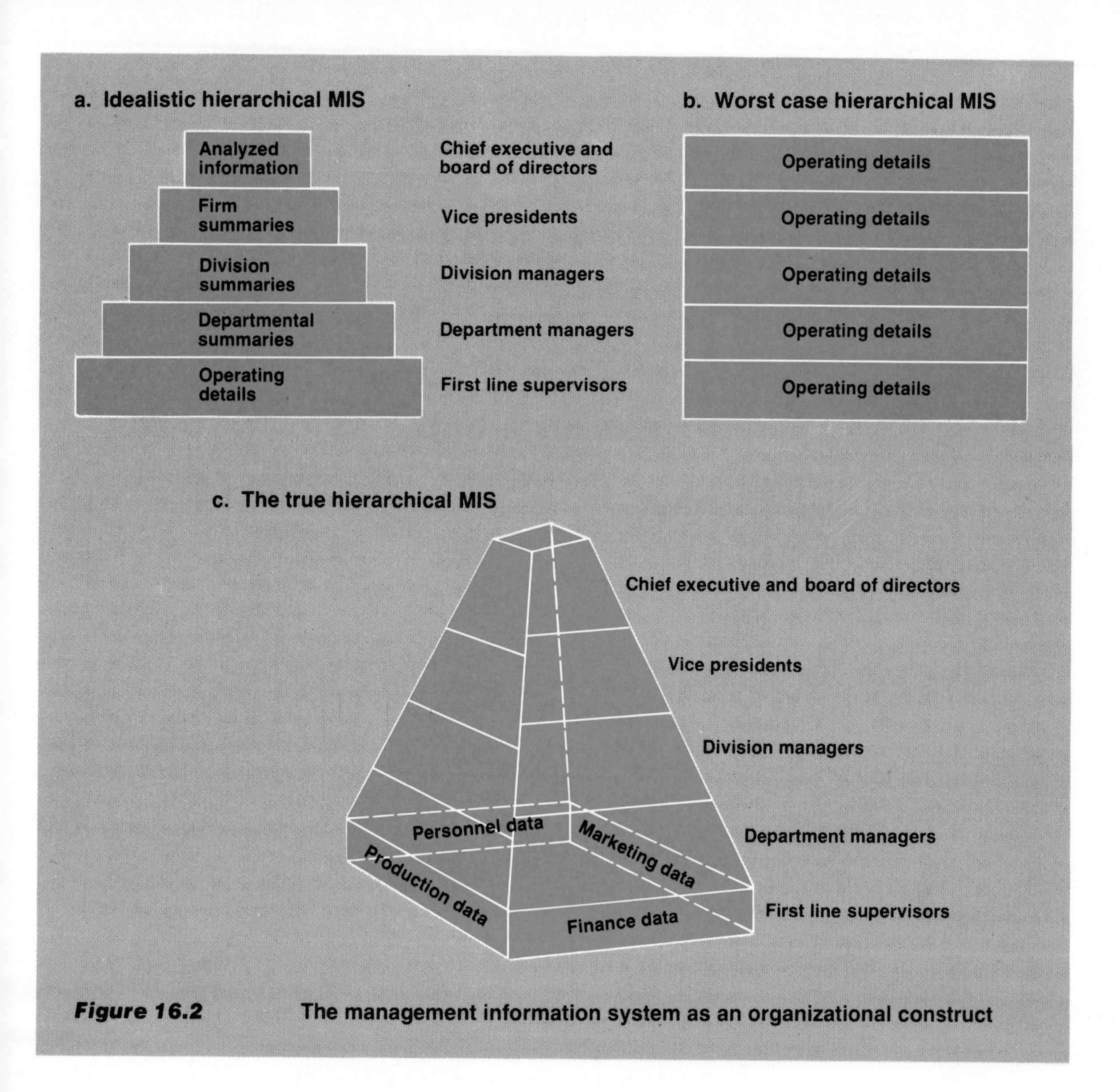

Figure 16.2 **The management information system as an organizational construct**

departments or divisions and pass it on up the chain of command. So it goes, until finally the chief executive or chief executive body receives analyzed information for the entire organization or for major activities within the organization. The information at the top level supposedly is in a form useful for assessing overall performance and trends and for setting major goals and policies for the organization. The confusion of detail existing at the first-line level has been sifted and analyzed (refined) to reveal the essence of its overall meaning.

Worst-case hierarchical Contrasted to the idealistic hierarchical type of information system is that illustrated by the cylinder in Figure 16.2b. In this system, the detail available at the first-line level is passed upward through the chain of command without analysis and summarization. Managers at each level feel that they can adequately assess the performance of the managers reporting to them only if they themselves have all the detail used at the level below. This system obviously is ineffective and does not really exist except in very small organizations.

The true hierarchical MIS A third organizational pattern for the information system is probably nearer a true picture of existing systems. It is represented by the three-dimensional structure in Figure 16.2c. The figure indicates that the detailed data generated by the activities carried on by the organization form a base from which the various levels of management extract information for purposes of decision making. The varying widths of the horizontal strata of the pyramid are intended to indicate that the differing levels of management reduce (distill) the information flowing upward to varying degrees. All levels do not contribute equally to the data analysis necessary for putting information in a form suitable for decision making at the higher levels. When the information flow reaches the top level (chief executive and board of directors), much analysis still remains to be done. The lack of a point on the top of the pyramid indicates that not all the information contained in the data base has been distilled. If this had been done, the pyramid would reach a sharp point.

Most firms have semi-independent information subsystems for each function, division, or product, depending on the way they are organized. The different functional subsystems perform at differing levels of efficiency and effectiveness from firm to firm. Some firms have a better marketing information subsystem, others do better with finance, and so on.

There are obvious relationships between manager's positions in an organization and the type and form of information they should receive. As shown in Table 16.1, the higher in the organization the manager is located, the less detail should be contained in the reports received. The higher in the organization the manager, the less he or she is involved in execution of plans (supervision); rather, this manager is concerned with setting goals and planning their attainment. Top-level managers have primary responsibility for **strategic planning**, deciding *what* should be done. Middle-level managers have primary responsibility for **tactical planning**, deciding *how* it should be done. Lower-level managers have primary responsibility for **operational control**, carrying out the plans. This means that the higher the manager is in the organization, the less the need for detailed data and the greater the need for summarized and analyzed information. This also means that the higher the manager is in the organization, the more that manager is involved with how the organization interacts with its environment.

Top-level managers must be aware of how the environment is changing. They must be aware of information that can be drawn only from sources external to the firm. The informational needs of top management can be fully

LEVEL OF MANAGER	LEVEL OF DECISIONS	INFORMATION REQUIRED	
		SOURCE	LEVEL OF DETAIL
Top	Strategic and basic tactical (what to do and the basic outline of how to do it)	Firm activity	Summaries for firm and projects
		Environment	Summaries of economic conditions, market sizes, overall competition
		Special analyses	Potential efficiency and effectiveness of alternative strategies and tactics
Middle	Tactical and operational (how to carry out the strategies and how to control the process)	Firm activity	Summaries by departments, activities (projects), products
		Environment	Standards of performance (sales/inventory ratios, labor/production ratios, etc.)
		Special analyses	Alternative methods of performing a task; effectiveness of operational controls
Lower	Operational (supervisory)	Firm activity	Detailed results by unit (person, machine, product, etc.)
		Environment	Almost none (some standards)
		Special analyses	Minimal (time and motion studies; unit efficiency)

Table 16.1 **Relationship of level of manager and information needs**

satisfied only by an information system that captures data about all activities of the organization and about its environment and then combines those data to show not only the outcomes of past actions but also the expected results of future actions. The decisions in this area tend to be individually unique and the related information requirements difficult to predict.

Middle managers attempt to optimize relationships between resource inputs and product or service outputs. They deal with problems like the scheduling of tasks, determination of optimal inventory levels, allocation of resources among different tasks, and cost control. The informational needs of these managers require more detail on results of past actions but are more predictable than the informational needs of top management. The decision process for many such situations can be fully described and turned over to a staff clerk or a machine (inventory control, for example).

Lower-level managers are primarily responsible for supervision of employees as they carry out day-to-day tasks. Planning is minimal; the focus is on individual tasks and techniques of performing those tasks. The information needed at this level relates to performance measurement (relation of actual results to previously specified standards for both quantity and quality of output).

The timing of system response also differs by management level. Planning the distant future does not *require* as current information on past results as does the planning of tomorrow's production schedule. More time can be afforded for analysis of data to be used in long-range (strategic) planning. Tactical planning requires more immediate feedback on operating results. Adequate control of operations requires immediate feedback on quantity and quality rates.

Another important factor in determining a manager's information needs is the manager's functional responsibility; that is, what the manager is responsible for getting done: administration, financial control, marketing, production, and so on. Even though each business transaction normally affects more than one function (Figure 16.2c reflects this fact by showing no vertical divisions), it is still true that most managers do have a functional (or project) responsibility. The information they receive must pertain to that responsibility.

Other factors that affect the informational needs of managers relate to their *management style.* Management style (directive, supportive, task oriented, participative, and so on) is most directly the result of education, experience, and personality. Education and experience also are major determinants of a manager's ability to take advantage of technology and science (for example, computers and management science).

The information system as a feedback and control system

A different but equally instructive view of the information system is provided by cybernetics. In this view, each organization or part of an organization is viewed as an operating feedback and control system. As shown in Figure 16.3, each of these systems consists of three elements: the planning and control element, the operating element performing the activity, and an evaluation element monitoring the results of the operation and reporting back to the planning and control element. Planning and control receives inputs from outside the organization (economic conditions, market trends, activities of competitors, and so on) as well as information from within the organization by way of the evaluation element. On the basis of this information, planning and control sets goals, develops policies and operating guides, and issues directives to the operating element. The resulting activity is monitored by the evaluation element and matched against the goals, plans, and directives established by planning and control. Deviations from desired results are reported so that corrective actions can be formulated and undertaken.

There are at least two key relationships in the feedback and control loop we have just described. The first of these is *timing,* the second is the nature of the *monitoring* function. It is necessary to know how rapidly feedback must be developed in order to keep the process under control. Second, we must know what information must be developed, that is, what elements are critical in providing adequate information for effective planning and control.

The speed with which feedback must be developed depends upon the *cycle time* of the physical operation being controlled, that is, how long it takes the physical operation to run from start to finish. For example, the cycle time on a stock transaction on the New York Stock Exchange is very short. In most instances, when a trader (customer) places an order, it is sent

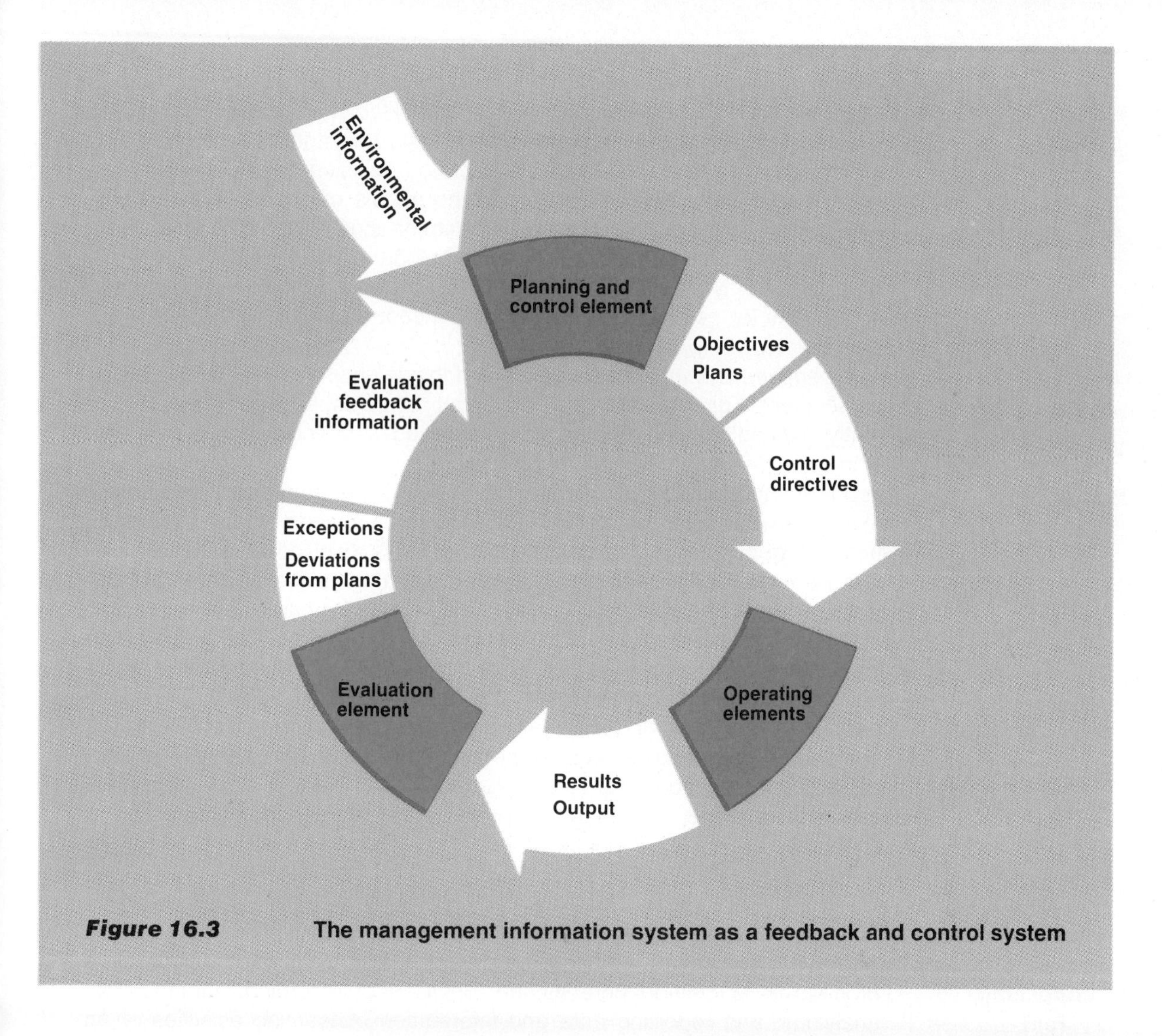

Figure 16.3 **The management information system as a feedback and control system**

immediately to the trading floor and executed. The cycle time for this physical operation can be less than one minute. On the other hand, a cattle rancher breeding cows to obtain calves which are to be raised and sold as beef cattle has a complete cycle time of three to four years. There are, however, decision points within that overall cycle. The first could be at the time of birth of the calf. The calf is marketable at that point. It might also be marketed at weaning time, as a yearling, or as a mature animal. Even in the last case, the rancher has a choice of marketing the animal as grass-fed only or as fattened (grain-fed) beef. For control of the process, information on ancestors' size and health and on the weight gain of each animal at each decision point would need to be considered in developing a feedback and control system for the rancher. However, there would not be any severe time constraint on the system.

Not all data that are recorded about an operation must necessarily be communicated to those responsible for the operation in order for them to adequately plan for and control that operation. Rather, it is apparent that data should be distilled, that their essence should be captured, and that only information that has immediate impact for decision-making or planning purposes should be communicated to the people responsible for planning and control functions. Most of our information systems tend to look pretty much like the three-dimensional pyramid of Figure 16.2c. We have tended to report too many details at all levels. One very important concept has been noteworthy for its absence. This is the concept of *control by exception,* or *management by exception.*

Exceptions are unusual or unexpected things and have very high information content. For example, knowledge that the salespeople who are consistently exceeding their quotas have received a specific type of training, whereas salespeople without that training often fail to achieve their quotas is important information for planning future training programs. As another example, knowledge that certain individuals in management are successful because of specific attitudes, concepts, or skills received from their education is a very important piece of information for selecting management trainees. As a final example, knowing that sales of a particular product are considerably above (or below) expected levels has significance for future production and inventory levels. Knowing the detailed distribution of these sales by area and salesperson can be important in deciding on the permanence of the high (or low) level of sales. On the other hand, knowing such details about sales that are meeting expectations in total and by area and salesperson would not be as valuable. In this latter case, no corrective action is required, and planning procedures can apparently remain unchanged.

The information system as a data processing system

Still another way to view the MIS is as a data processing system involved with the capture and processing of data to obtain information. *Data processing* is defined here as the functions of recording, summarizing, analyzing, and reporting data and information concerning activities of an organization (with *data* and *information* defined as in Chapter 1).

Perhaps the most important concept involved in this area is the principle of integrated data processing discussed in Chapter 14. In integrated data processing, the attempt is to record each piece of data once, to record it correctly, and then to use it in that same form in every way possible to elicit information for the planning and control purposes of the operation. Thus, we need to proceed on a twofold basis when designing an adequate information system. On one hand, we need to look at the media requirements for the establishment of an efficient, unified set of basic data files. On the other hand, we need to take a look at the information requirements for efficient administration of current operations and also design routine analytic studies of the proper kinds of correctly captured data to provide the information necessary for future planning.

For an effective information system to be developed, information should be available to all parts of the system. The MIS is a mix of information on employees, products, customers, facilities, and finances. Supporting information must be available on competitors, market conditions, government activities, and general economic conditions. Thus, we need files of data about employees, facilities, current products and production processes, customers, budgetary and financial information, and research and development activities. Stated simply, we need to establish a **data bank** for the organization, a library of files containing all data and information relevant to the organization.

Figure 16.4 gives a diagrammatic view of a data bank. The total cylinder is the total file system. Each slice of the cylinder represents a different file (or set of files) relating to a different area of the system. Figure 16.4 also indicates the different parts of the decision-making milieu most deeply interested in different aspects of the data bank. We must recognize, however, that each functional activity interacts with other functions; no transaction is solely a "marketing," "production," "finance," or "personnel" activity.

It is obvious that a desirable characteristic from this point of view is that

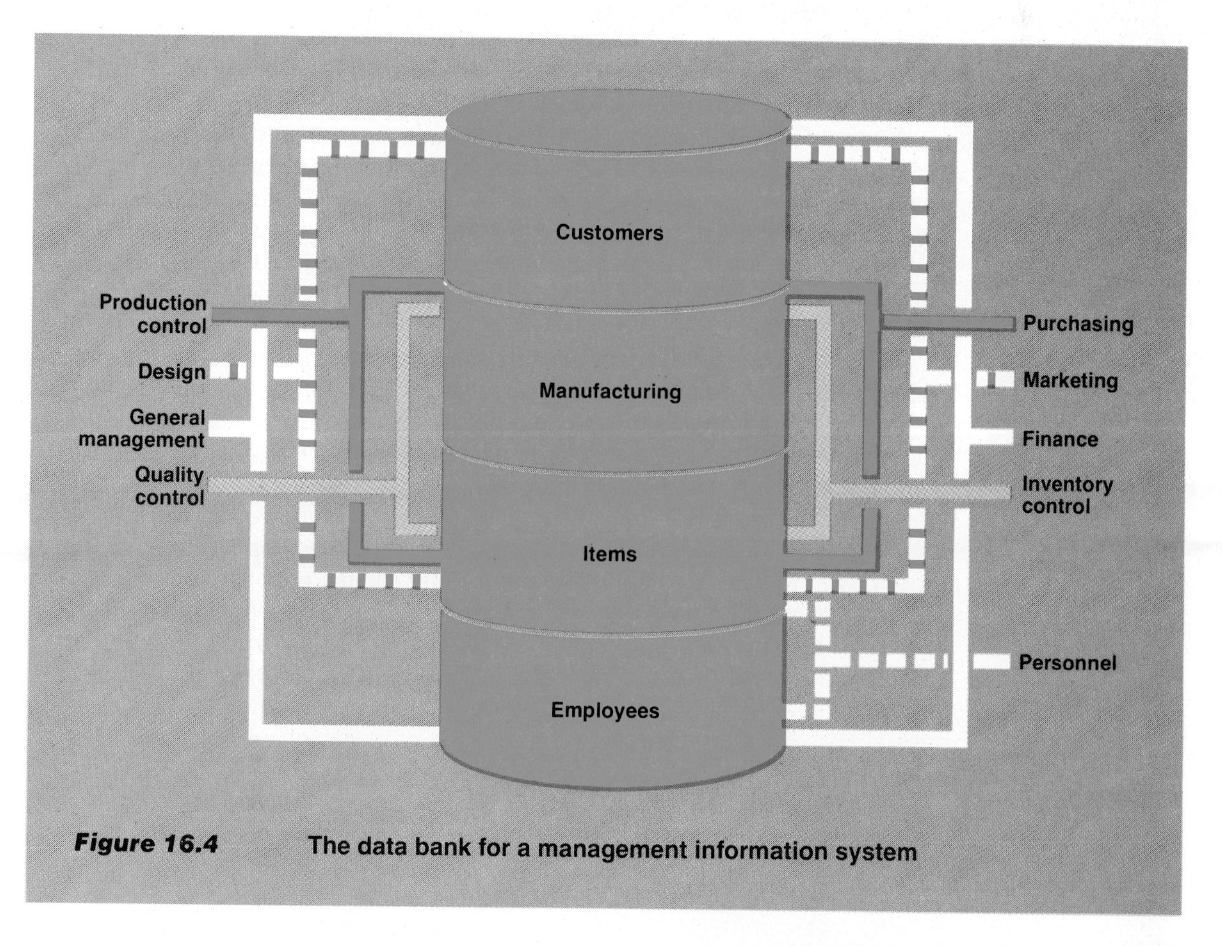

Figure 16.4 **The data bank for a management information system**

each piece of original data be captured once, placed in its proper file, and held there until needed or until changed by other transactions. The information system would incorporate that datum with the other facts in its home file, relate these facts properly to the facts in other files, and thus produce information for management.

This data processing view of an MIS thus recognizes three tasks to be carried out.

1 The data bank (sets of interrelated master files) pertinent to the system must be established.
2 Procedures must be developed to capture relevant data from transactions and from the environment to update the data bank.
3 Processes must be developed to access the flow of transactions and environmental data and the changing status of the data bank to create management reports.

One area of controversy in the data processing view of the MIS is what should be put into the data bank. Some experts argue that it is appropriate to capture all possible data in the data bank in the expectation that someone in the organization will find a use for each data set included. Others suggest that it is necessary to define what the information outputs will be before the data bank is established, that only those data elements necessary to the provision of the required information be captured and stored in the data bank.

A second area of controversy concerns the accessing of the data bank for development and retrieval of its information content. One group believes that all informational requirements must be fully defined and included in a regularized system of formal reports. A second group believes that managers should define most of their informational requirements as the need arises. Reports would tend to be unique and be developed on demand in such a system.

It seems rational to adopt an intermediate position on both of these controversies. All data that can be expected to be useful at some time should be recorded and retained. Data sets not being used immediately might be stored in a less easily accessed form. Access to the data bank should be on a regularized basis for standard reports, but provision should be made for on-demand access for obtaining guidance for unexpected problems or one-of-a-kind decisions.

Another problem in establishing and maintaining the data bank is the level of detail in which data are to be maintained. Should we aggregate sales information into totals by product, salesperson, and territory? Should the permanent record of customer visits include only the number of visits per period (week, month), or should it include the names of firms visited, the actual persons contacted, and the specific products or product lines discussed? It is not always easy to foresee future control or analytic processes that may require such detail. Most data base experts are now encouraging the storage of detailed data at least on a less expensive medium, such as microfilm or magnetic tape.

In summary, the basic data processing view of MIS is that of a set of basic files (a data bank) that is modified by current transactions. Ideally, fixed data in the files are captured once and retained, and variable data describing each transaction are captured and used to update all files affected by that transaction. The informational content of the data bank and the flow of transactions are reported according to management's requirements for that information. Finally, the data should be organized and stored in such a way that processing and reporting applications can be changed without totally redesigning even a single data base within the data bank.

Functional information subsystems

It should be clear that there is no such thing as a *single* totally integrated management information system. Rather, there is a collection of subsystems, each integrated in varying degrees into the overall information system of the organization. These subsystems are most frequently organized around each of the functions making up the firm. Identification of each of these functions and the information subsystem that serves it should provide a clear picture of current management information systems.

Functional subsystems

We are making the following assumptions in the discussion that follows:

1 We are dealing with a firm that manufactures and sells a set of related products.
2 The firm is functionally organized.

We have chosen to describe a firm involved in the manufacture and sale of a set of related products because service firms can be viewed as manufacturing and selling services. For example, a financial institution, such as a commercial bank, can be viewed as manufacturing and selling loans to consumers and businesses, demand deposit and time deposit services, and money management (trust) services.

We have assumed a functional organization because other organizational functions (product or project and matrix) normally include functional subdivisions under the project (product) or as one element of the matrix.

The subsystems can be defined in many ways. We have chosen to identify six functional subsystems.

1 Financial subsystem
2 Marketing subsystem
3 Production subsystem
4 Materials control subsystem
5 Personnel subsystem
6 Planning subsystem

Note: Most of the symbols used to describe the functional subsystems and their information subsystems have been taken from a flowcharting template.

These special symbols are used partly for clarity and partly for convenience. They should not be interpreted literally. Neither all files nor all processing must be online to a computer, as these charts seem to indicate. Further, all input need not be captured online and all outputs need not be on display terminals. The use of the symbol for an online display terminal is intended to indicate a need for fast response, which could be obtained in other ways.

The description of each subsystem will identify the objective of the function, graph its structure, and present a brief picture of the information subsystem that serves it.

The financial information subsystem

The basic objective of the **financial subsystem** is to meet the firm's financial obligations as they come due, using the minimal amount of financial resources consistent with an established margin of safety. The diagram in Figure 16.5 illustrates the activities of the financial function. Basically, it monitors and controls the flow of money through the firm. The specific tasks it must accomplish include the following:

1. Financial control—capital and operating budgets, cash flow forecast, and cost control
2. Accounts payable—including a cash needs forecast
3. Accounts receivable—including credit control, customer billing, and a cash receipts forecast
4. Payroll—including a cash needs forecast
5. Financial accounting—general ledger and financial statements

Two major data bases would underlie the financial information subsystem. One would be the budget file containing capital and operating budgets, plus budgeting models, cost data, and cash flow data. The second data base would contain general ledger accounts, including accounts receivable and payable, payroll, and ownership accounts.

The marketing information subsystem

The objective of the **marketing subsystem** is to facilitate the flow of goods and services from the firm to satisfy the perceived wants and needs of customers in support of the objectives and goals of the firm.

Note that the marketing function has two somewhat conflicting responsibilities. On the one hand, it attempts to identify and satisfy the needs and wants of customers. On the other hand, it is trying to obtain an amount of sales that will maximize the firm's profits, which usually translates into maximizing sales of the firm's products.

The schematic in Figure 16.6 outlines what it is that the marketing function does. Note that it is primarily an information flow process operating at the place where the firm interfaces with its customers. The heart of this information flow is the marketing intelligence data bank containing all the

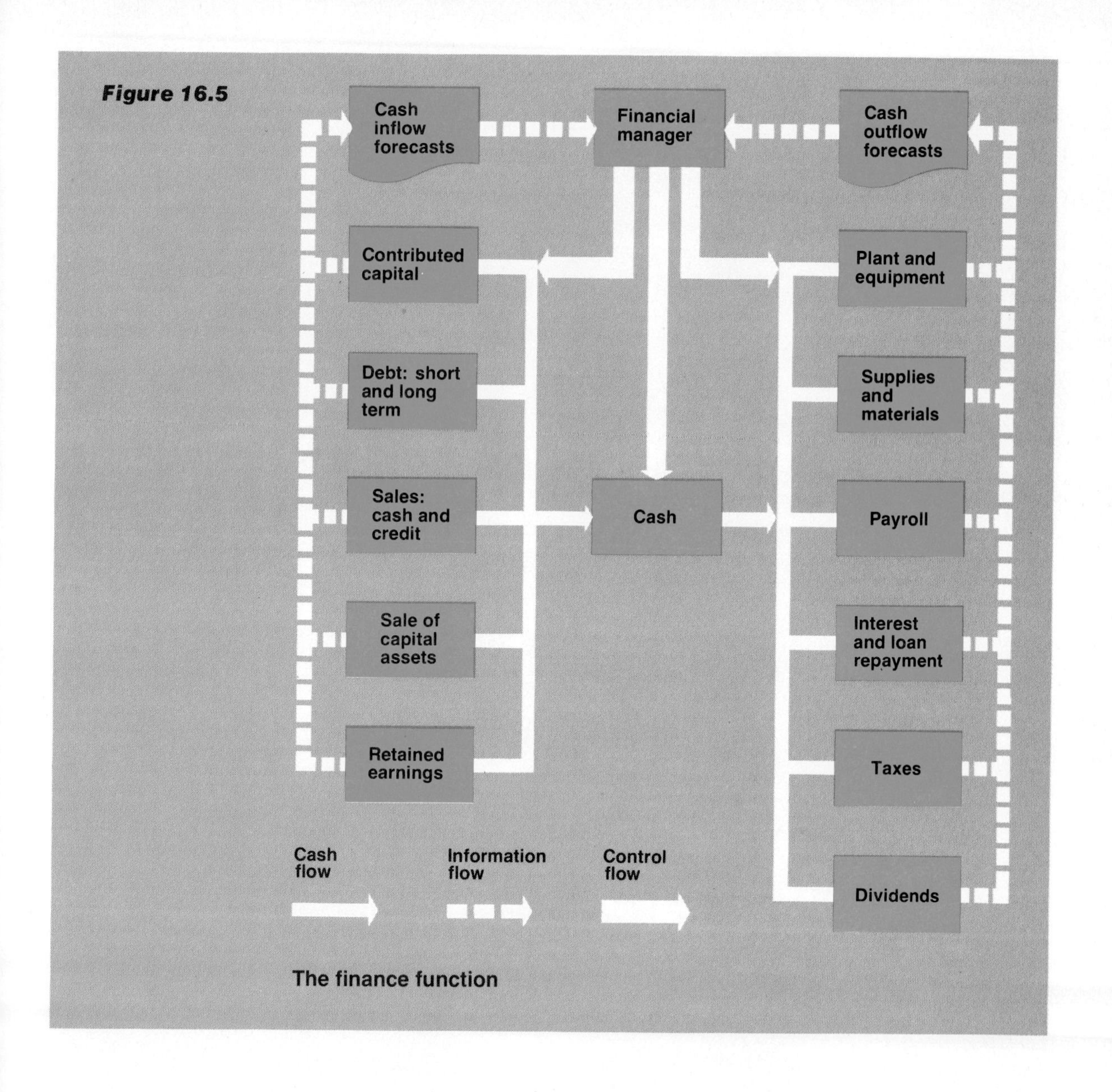

The finance function

information needed to make rational decisions in choosing and developing products and planning and carrying out marketing plans.

The intelligence data bank would be supported by a market research function using a model data base (statistical methods, market models) and providing interaction with the intelligence data bank and the sales and advertising data bases.

A subsidiary data base organized by product, salesperson, area, and campaign would be needed to support the sales control function. A similar

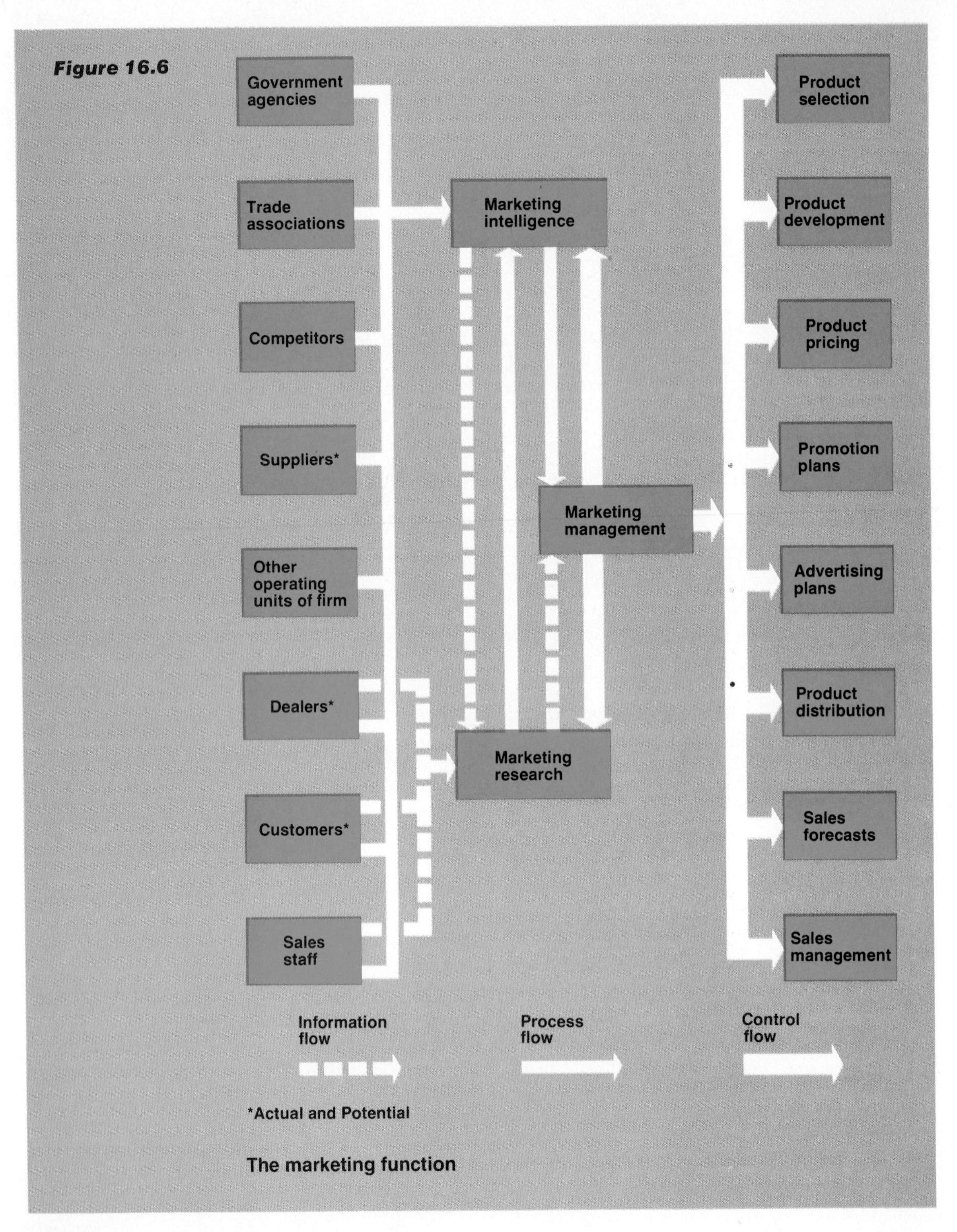

The marketing function

data base organized by campaign, product, media used, and results obtained would be needed to support the advertising function.

The production information subsystem

The objective of the **production subsystem** is to produce the goods and/or services provided by the firm at the least cost consistent with the firm's goals of quality and quantity.

This function is the process by which raw materials, parts, and supplies are converted into finished goods as illustrated by the schematic in Figure 16.7.

The production information subsystem is a dual system, one for production planning and one for production control. The production planning information subsystem is depicted in Figure 16.8. Note how this system "explodes" orders into material requirements, production requisitions, and production

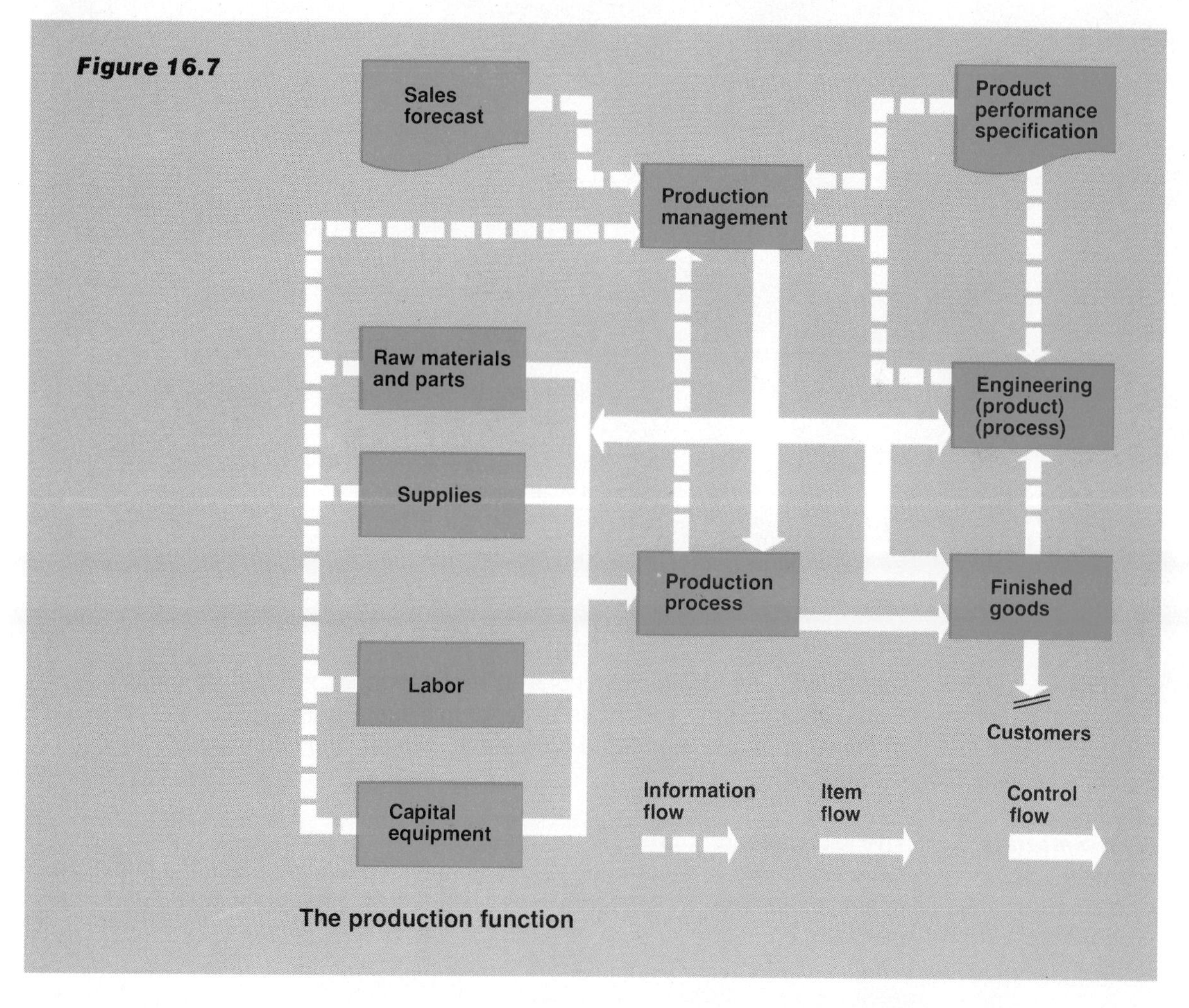

Figure 16.7

The production function

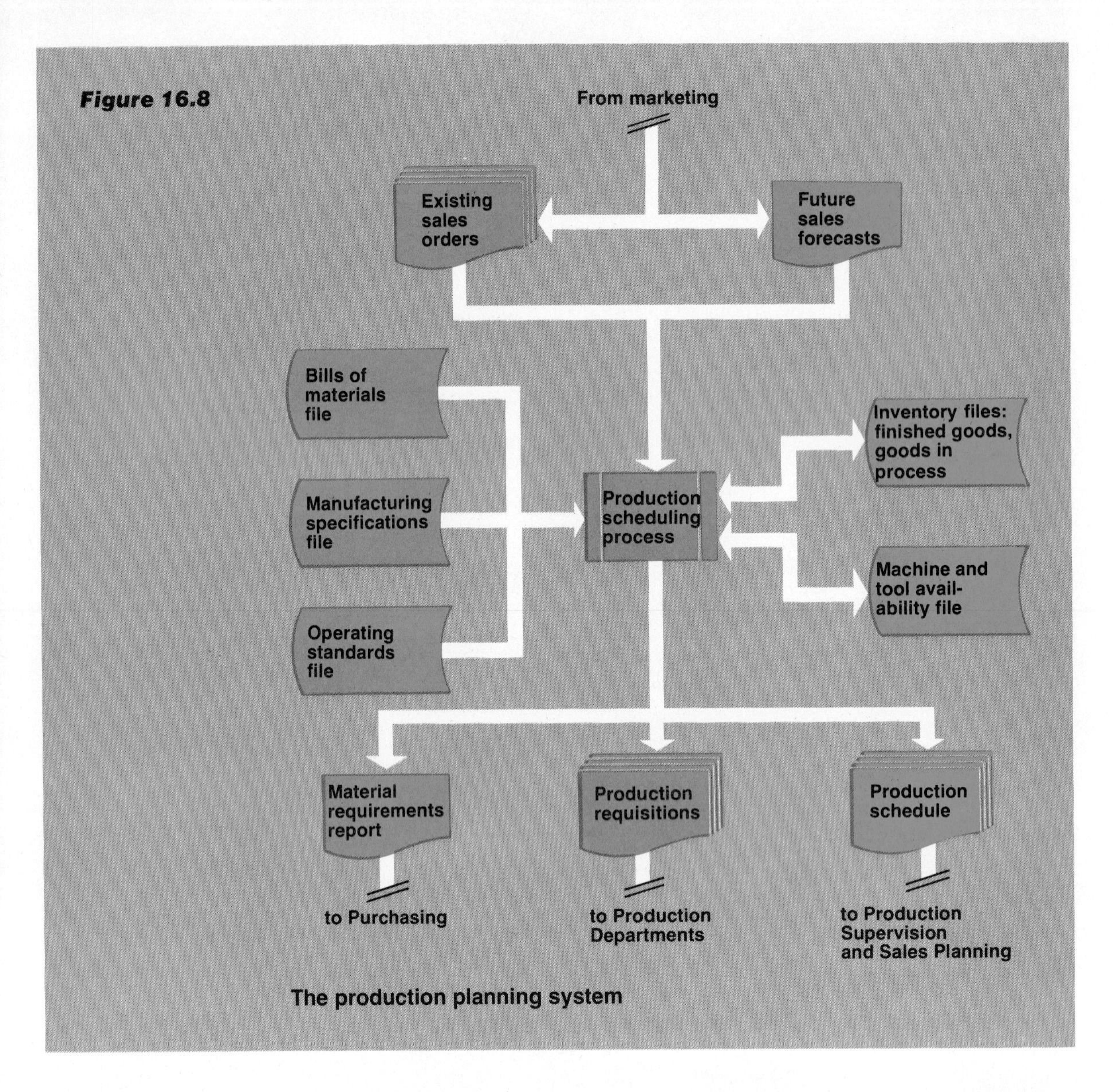

Figure 16.8 The production planning system

schedules. The production control information subsystem is depicted in Figure 16.9. Examine the data base for this subsystem. Notice the reflection of the various activities to be carried out in production control.

The materials control information subsystem

The objective of the **materials control subsystem** is to provide and maintain stocks of raw materials, parts, and supplies of adequate quality in quantities sufficient to accomplish the objectives and goals of the firm at a minimum cost.

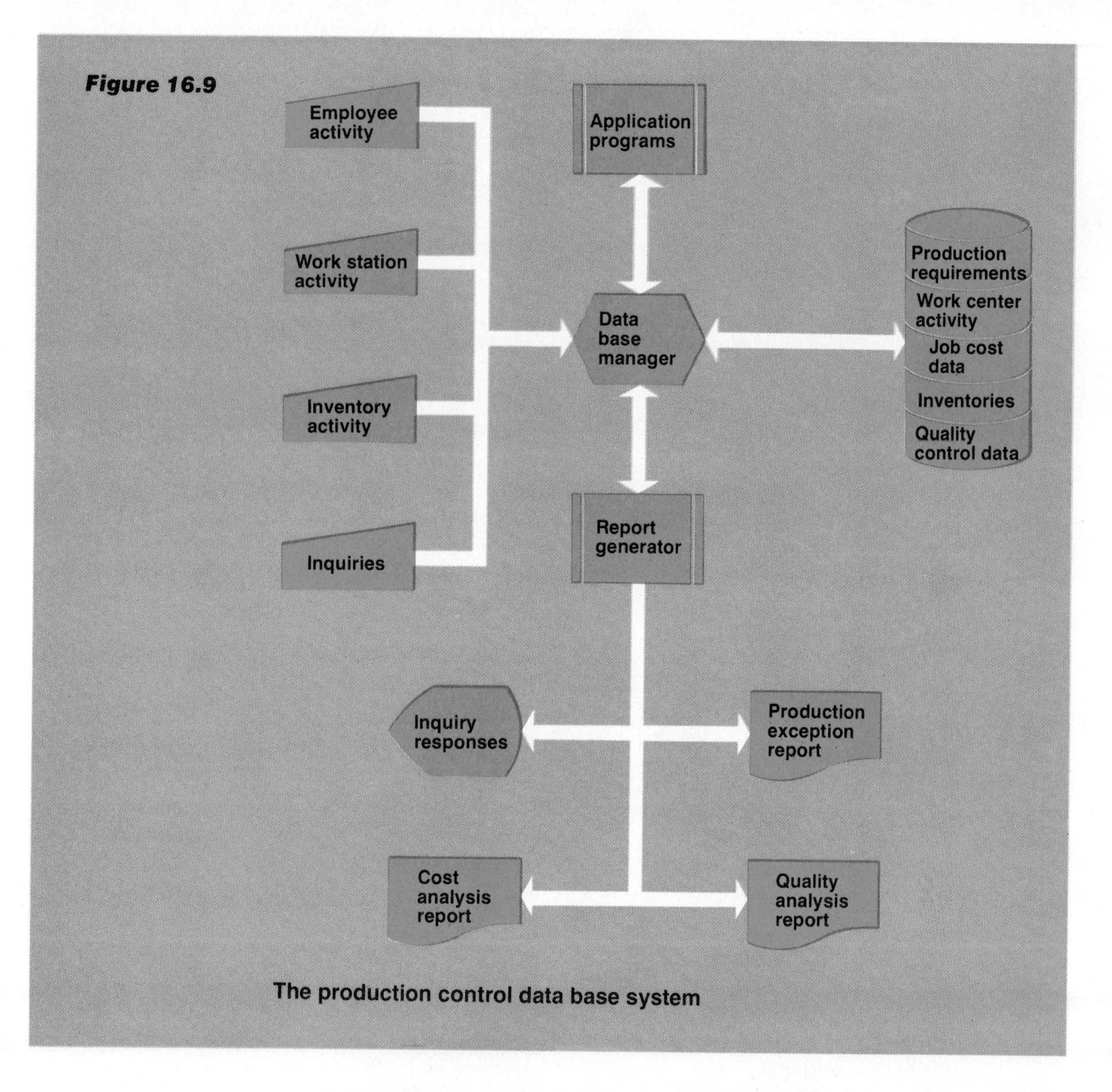

Figure 16.9 The production control data base system

The structure of this function is shown in Figure 16.10. Note that the materials control process receives its basic inputs from production and marketing. This is, in part, due to the fact that it is providing service to these two functions by selecting, ordering, and storing items (raw materials, parts, supplies, and finished goods) to be used in production or to be resold. The major subsystems are inventory accounting and control and purchasing. The primary data base is comprised of the inventory files and the order file. The primary activities are procurement, inventory control, receiving and warehousing, and material requirements planning.

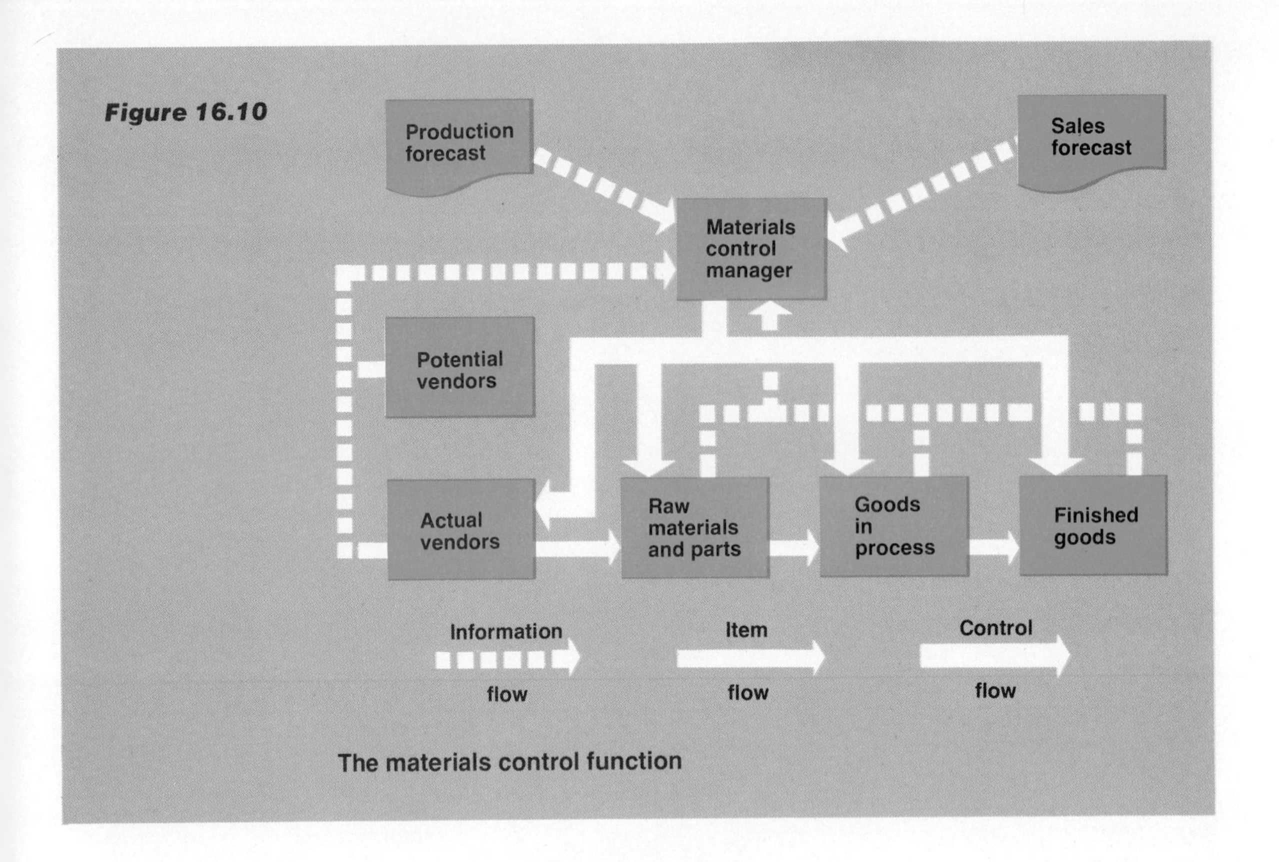

Figure 16.10

The materials control function

The personnel information subsystem

The objective of the **personnel subsystem** is to provide and maintain at a minimum cost the human resources for accomplishing the firm's objectives, while ensuring satisfaction and personal development for the individual employee.

The personnel function interfaces between the firm and its employees (actual or potential). The nature of this function is clearly spelled out in Figure 16.11. One thing that should be emphasized is the responsibility of the personnel function for promotion of employees' development. Note that the personnel activities include many designed to help employees reach their full potential.

The structure of the information system for personnel is revealed in Figure 16.12. Note the contents of the data base and the various outputs.

The planning information subsystem

The objective of the **planning subsystem** is to set the objectives and goals of the firm and the paths of action that will be followed in seeking to attain those objectives and goals.

The results of planning are predetermined courses of action and the expected outcomes from taking those actions. As can be seen in Figure 16.13, inputs to the planning system are objectives, environmental data, and

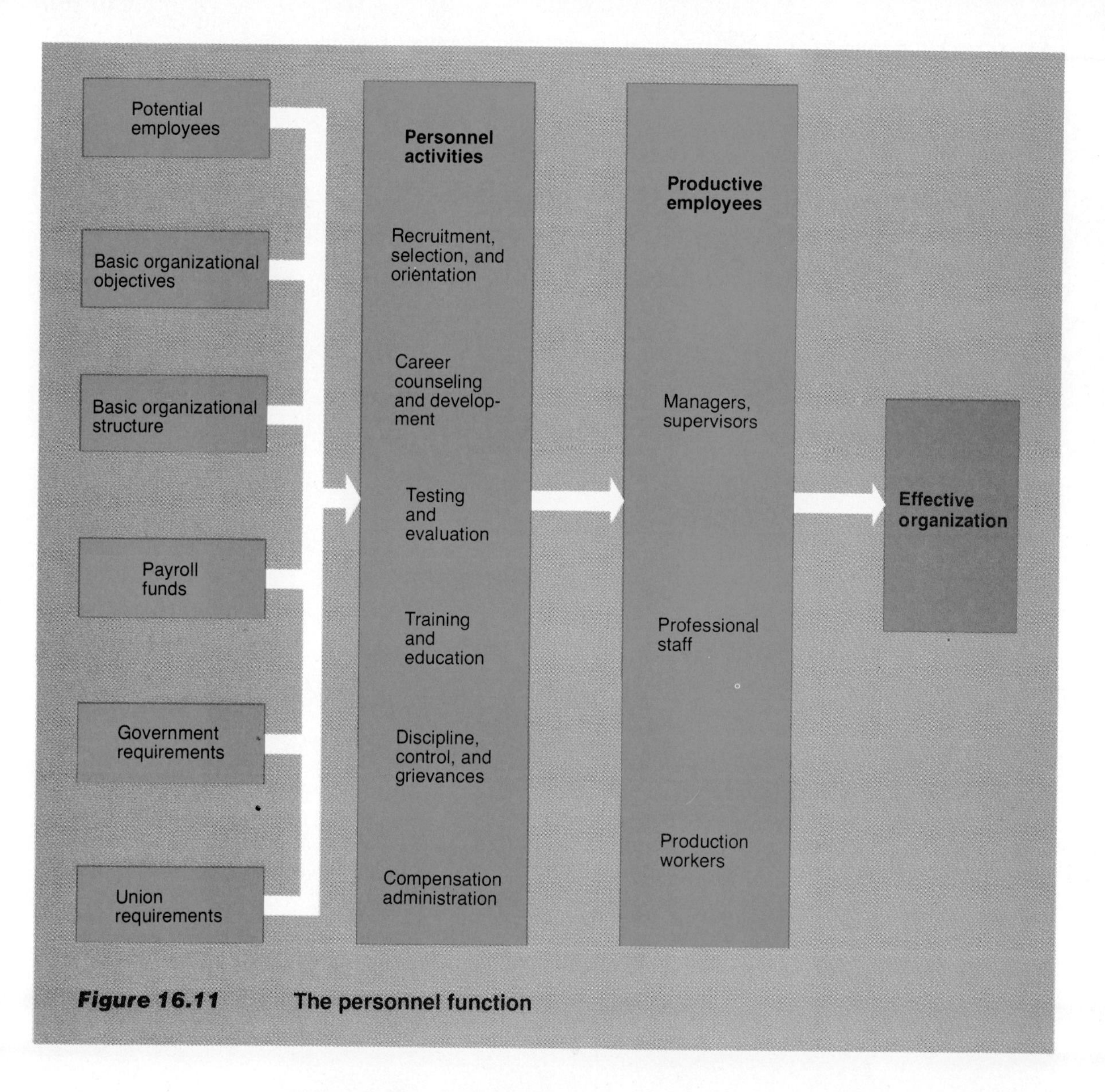

Figure 16.11 **The personnel function**

financial data. These inputs are used to assess strategic alternatives or general directions of activity, to develop strategic plans, and then to express these decisions in operating plans for the other functional areas.

The planning information subsystem is depicted in Figure 16.14. Note the overlap at the bottom of the chart with the other basic functions. Operational planning is best accomplished by the operating units.

The two data bases supporting the planning information subsystem are for environmental and internal data. The third major file is the model bank containing the various analytical and resource distribution models available to support planning activities.

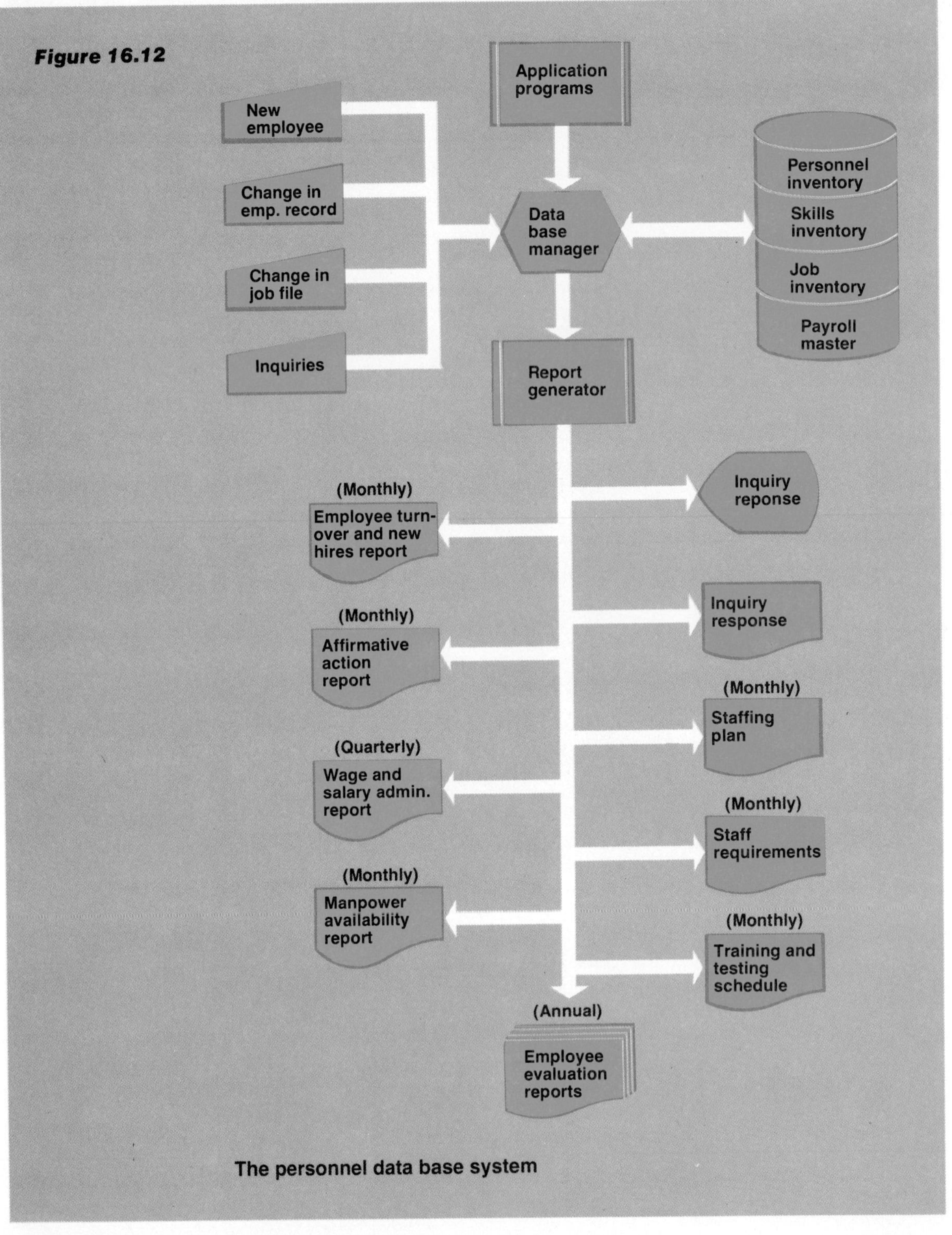

The personnel data base system

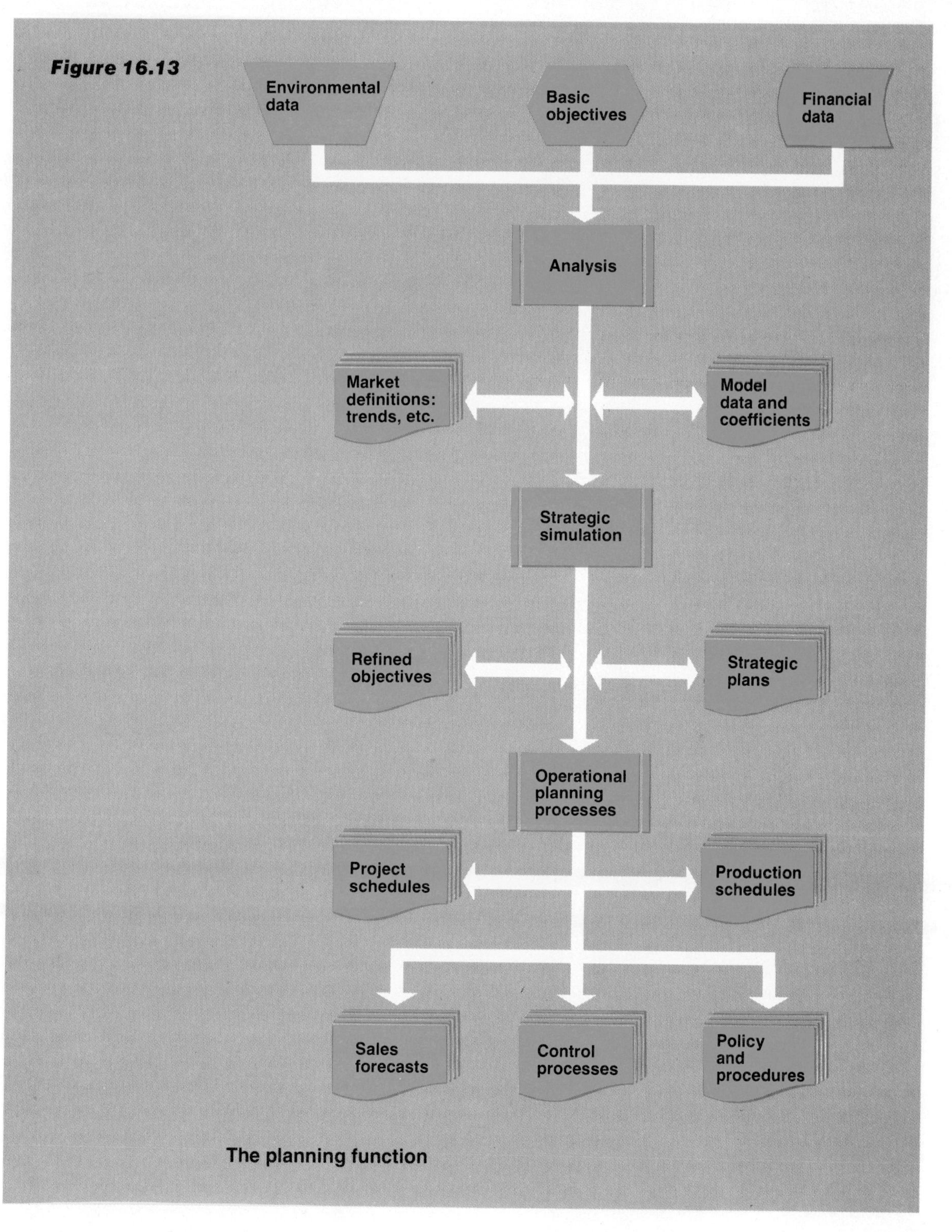

The planning function

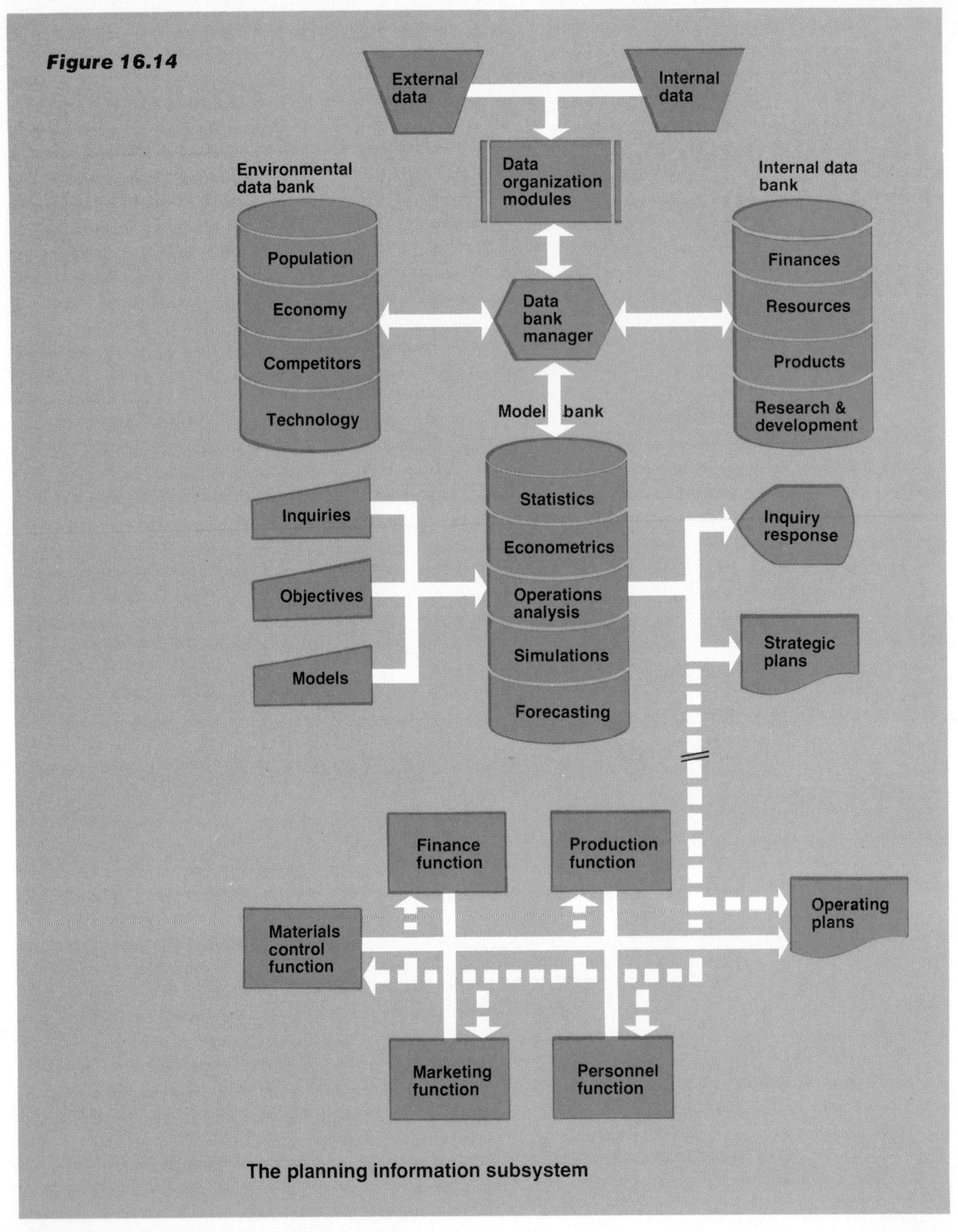

The planning information subsystem

Management reporting

As was indicated earlier, a data processing system is not complete unless the reports it produces are adequate to provide the knowledge about the underlying business operation that will allow effective managerial decision making (unless *information* is created). This implies that the reports prepared must be responsive to management's needs (Figure 16.15).

Realtime control

In Chapter 1, timeliness was indicated to be a desirable characteristic of business data processing systems. Data should be processed into information fast enough to provide adequate control of the physical operation that generated the data. Such a system was identified as a realtime data processing system (page 12).

Historically, reporting to management has been *periodic.* Processing has been largely in the batch mode after the close of an operating cycle or an accounting period. At that point, transactions were processed, all files completely updated, and the condition of the organization or operation

Figure 16.15

Using data   A data processing system is not complete unless information is created. (Courtesy Monsanto)

determined. The length of time required to determine the condition of the organization or operation usually meant that reports were available some time after the operating or accounting period being reported on had ended and the next period was well started. Actions taken in response to revealed problems were often incorrect. The nature of the problem had changed, the problem was already solved, or it was too late to do anything about it. The delayed reaction often reinforced and overextended natural corrective actions. Thus the delayed reaction tended to create an unnecessary oscillation in the operation. Overcoming this problem is the **realtime response**, a response in time to affect (in a desirable way) an ongoing physical operation.

The speed with which reports must be developed depends on two factors.

1 The total time required for the physical operation being controlled
2 The time between points where decisions must be made in completing the operation

For example, consider the timing requirements associated with controlling the inventory of seats available on an airline. A customer wishing to make a reservation for a seat on a particular flight wants to know quickly whether a seat is available. When it is recognized that numerous persons scattered across the country may want seats on that flight, the need for up-to-date information is apparent. The time required for a seat request to go by surface mail to a central point so that a reservation can be made is too long. Customers want faster action. They may even be trying to get on a flight that leaves only a few minutes from the time of their request. Thus, the airlines have developed electronic systems that provide instantaneous responses to online inquiries and allow immediate confirmation or denial of a seat reservation. Realtime response in this case must be instantaneous.

Not all systems require feedback so quickly in order to provide realtime control. For example, suppose a department store decided to make a special purchase of a carload of electric clothes dryers and sell them in a special sale. The entire operation may take several weeks to set up and carry out, and its total success cannot be judged until it is over. Having a complete summary of the results the instant the sale is finished would be nice, but it is not *required* to provide adequate control over the operation. As a matter of fact, analysts could take several days to pinpoint the reasons for the success or failure of the operation without upsetting store management. Only if the store's buyers were waiting to decide whether to move on another similar purchase and sale would the information need to be *immediately* available. Once the merchandise is ordered and the initial advertisements placed, the store is committed to follow through. Canceling would probably cause customer alienation to a degree that could adversely affect sales for some time and would therefore be uneconomic.

As a further example of realtime, consider the farm manager growing crops. Information on the economic success of a particular cropping operation in a given season is not needed for control until the planting decisions are being made for the following season. This could be several months after the earlier crop has been harvested and sold.

Types of reports

The reports that go to management can be classified in many ways. One useful way is by the type of information they carry. The four types of information are status information, activity information, exceptions, and analytical results.

Status reports Reports that indicate the condition of a business operation (its status) at a point in time are called **status reports**. The balance sheet shown in Table 16.2a is such a status report, as is the inventory status report shown in Table 16.2b. Status reports do not show how the operation reached the given condition, only what that condition is. It can be useful, however, to contrast status at two points in time to judge progress. Thus, comparing the balance sheet in Table 16.2a with the balance sheet for an earlier point in time would indicate whether conditions have improved or not. Unfortunately, comparison of status reports for different times will not tell us *why* conditions are better or worse.

Activity reports To determine what has happened over a period of time, an **activity report** is useful. The income statement shown in Table 16.3a (page 465) is an example of an activity report. The inventory activity report in Table 16.3b (page 466) is another example. These reports tell us how much activity took place within a given period of time.

Comparing activity reports for different time periods lets us compare rates of activity, but most activity reports do not identify the reasons for any changes in the rates.

Exception reports Some reports require action. The most common example is the **exception report**. An *exception,* as the term is used here, is a deviation from desired levels of activity. One obvious example of an exception report is the inventory status report shown in Table 16.2. Note that some of the inventory amounts could be identified as at or below the reorder point. That is, the amounts of these items have dropped to the point where more should be ordered if the item is to be continued in stock.

Another example of an exception report is the sales analysis report shown in Table 16.4 (page 467) where certain sales amounts have been identified as being above or below the planned level.

Again, exceptions may not tell management why something is happening. They do, however, direct attention of management to the problems by identifying the unexpected, unusual, and/or undesirable events. True exception reports have the further advantage of reducing the total amount of reporting that is required, since only the exceptions need be reported in any detail.

a

CSFM CORPORATION
BALANCE SHEET, 1980

	1980		1979	
Assets:				
Cash	$ 21,000		$ 14,002	
Accounts Receivable	41,003		30,102	
Building and Land	84,000		84,000	
Supplies on Hand	350		425	
Sales Inventory	96,026		72,019	
Total Assets		$242,379		$200,548
Liabilities:				
Accounts Payable	$ 4,926		$ 4,543	
Taxes Payable	954		954	
Total Liabilities		$ 5,880		$ 5,497
Owners' Equity:				
Capital Stock	$ 50,000		$ 50,000	
Retained Earnings	186,499		145,051	
Total Equity		236,499		195,051
Total Liabilities and Owners' Equity		$242,379		$200,548

b

CSFM CORPORATION
INVENTORY ON HAND, DECEMBER 31, 1980

ITEM	NUMBER OF UNITS	UNIT VALUE	TOTAL VALUE
Model I-343	3	$ 4,026	$12,078
Model I-570	4	6,039	24,156
Model I-870	1	42,000	42,000
Total Value of Models			$78,234
Repair Parts			17,792
Total Value of Models and Parts			$96,026

Table 16.2 **Two examples of status reports**

Analytical reports If management is to make the right adjustments to changing conditions or unrealized plans, the reason for things turning out the way they do can be learned through **analytical reports**. The success or failure of the special sale of the carload lot of electric clothes dryers referred to earlier could depend on a number of factors.

1 Bad weather may have kept customers at home. Extremely good weather may have sent everyone to the lake, the beach, or the mountains.

a	RSFM COMPANY	
	INCOME STATEMENT FOR THE YEAR ENDED DECEMBER 31, 1979	
Revenues:		
Net Sales	$563,215.91	
Interest Revenue	13,142.09	
Total Revenue		$576,358.00
Expenses:		
Cost of Goods Sold	$303,650.00	
Selling Expenses	151,216.65	
Administration	78,608.32	
Interest Expense	10,004.28	
Income Tax	8,792.31	
Total Expenses		552,271.56
Net Income for Year		$ 24,086.44

Table 16.3 **Two examples of activity reports**

2 Promotion may have been faulty, so that customers' perceptions of quality/price relationships were adverse. That is, customers may have felt that defective merchandise was being offered, and therefore it was not a bargain.
3 Sales personnel may have unwittingly tried too hard to sell customers the more expensive models already available, thus creating a "bait and switch" atmosphere in which customers perceived that the bargains were not really available.
4 Customer demand was just not adequate to move all the dryers.

A careful, scientific study of the situation, including, perhaps, interviewing actual and potential customers, may reveal which of these factors, if any, were operating. Such a determination cannot usually be made from routine reports. This does not mean that analytical reports cannot be routinely produced, however. Analytical planning reports are produced at regular intervals in well-run business organizations. Most analytical reports, however, are done as special studies which search for a solution to a particular problem.

Timing of reports

Reports can be produced at regular, periodic intervals, be triggered by the occurrence of some exception, or be produced in response to a request from management (on demand).

Periodic reports Most **periodic reports** are accounting reports. It is not unusual, however, for inventory status reports to be produced on a daily or weekly schedule to be used to identify items to be reordered. The president of a small bank, for example, receives a combined balance sheet and income

b	MSFM COMPANY INVENTORY SUMMARY JANUARY 1—DECEMBER 31, 1979		
Beginning Inventory:			
Materials		$ 26,543.17	
Parts		22,045.62	
Finished Goods		18,111.78	
Total			$ 66,700.57
Purchases:			
Materials		$159,259.02	
Parts		110,669.01	
Transportation In		23,380.38	
Subtotal		293,308.41	
Returns to Supplier		1,072.74	
Net Purchases			292,235.67
Finished Goods Produced			438,275.98
Total Beginning Inventory, Purchases and Finished Goods			$797,212.22
Issues:			
Materials		$137,360.89	
Parts		96,904.04	
Finished Goods		398,415.95	
Subtotal		$632,680.88	
Returns			
From Factory	$ 8,602.55		
From Customers	7,488.63		
Total Returns		16,091.18	
Net Issues			$616,589.70
Ending Inventory			
Materials		63,181.63	
Parts		52,980.45	
Finished Goods		65,460.44	
Total Ending Inventory			$181,622.52

Table 16.3 (Cont.)

statement daily. He or she also receives a report of all new loans, new accounts, accounts closed, and accounts overdrawn by $50 or more. These two routine reports allow the president to exercise tight control over the bank's daily activities.

Periodic reports, which most frequently are status reports but can be activity or analytic reports as well, normally relate to a particular point in time or a particular time period. The time between reports is known as the *reporting period.* Activity reports reflect the amounts of activities occurring

CSFM CORPORATION ANALYSIS OF NEW MODEL SALES FOURTH QUARTER, 1979								
	AREA							
	SOUTHWEST		YOUNGSTOWN		NORTHWEST		TOTALS	
Model No.	Units	Dollars	Units	Dollars	Units	Dollars	Units	Dollars
I-343	2	$ 8,663.88	3	$12,931.16	3	$ 12,931.16	8	$ 34,526.20
I-570	5*	35,901.60	4	28,721.30	3**	21,540.99	12	86,163.89
I-870	1	56,070.00	1**	54,810.00	2	112,098.00	4	222,978.00
Total	8	$100,635.48	8	$96,462.46	8	$146,570.15	24	$343,668.09

Table 16.4 **Sales analysis report (*over quota; **under quota)**

over the reporting period. Status reports normally reflect conditions at the end of the reporting period. The best of both the status and activity reports usually contrast current period data with values for the preceding period and/or for the same period a year earlier.

Triggered exception reports The occurrence of an unexpected or unusual event can lead to a **triggered exception report** to management. This can vary from noting that the inventory of some item has reached the reorder point to a report that certain goals (sales levels, money flows, and so on) have not been reached or have been overshot. It is certainly useful to have the system so designed that unusual and/or unexpected results (outputs or sales levels) will be brought to the attention of management as soon as they are identified.

On-demand reporting The use of the computer has led to **on-demand reporting,** wherein reports are developed and delivered on command. Many computerized systems, particularly online systems, include this feature. Predefined reports (balance sheets, income statements, inventory status or activity reports, and others) are put together from the various online files and delivered whenever they are requested. The programs that produce the reports are always resident on the system and are activated whenever a request is received.

Another type of on-demand report is the *inquiry response.* For example, the marketing vice president has just been informed that the veteran salesperson assigned in France has entered the hospital because of a major illness that may well sideline the salesperson for weeks. A potential French customer is undecided about placing a large order with the company for one of its technical products. The manager requests a printout of all salespeople with experience in selling the technical product who are also fluent in the French language. As another example, the credit manager wants to know what percentage of the current accounts receivable are delinquent by as much as 90 days, how much money is involved in these accounts, and how long each of the delinquent customers has been dealing with the company. Such requests for information cannot be satisfied by a standard report, but require a specially tailored inquiry into the data files.

Effects of computers on management practice

Special capabilities of computers

Computers have three particular capabilities that have affected the content of managerial jobs. These are the speed with which computers perform, their accuracy, and the complexity of analysis they make possible.

Speed The ability to perform millions of calculations in one second has obvious implications for management practice. Transactions data can be summarized, compared to historical trends, checked for other relationships, and reported quickly. This means the managerial control cycle can be shortened. At least two things must be present for this effect to be realized.

First, operational data must be entered into the computer system and processed in time to make realtime control possible. Even though the computer collapses the processing time, the change is not significant unless the processing system will provide information in time to reflect the current status of the physical operation.

Second, the system output must be designed as *information* in the sense we have described: communicated knowledge in a form that is immediately useful for decision making. To meet this definition, the output must be in a form that the recipient is willing and able to use for guiding decisions.

Accuracy Modern computer hardware is extremely reliable. If properly programmed, computers can be safely assumed not to make mistakes in processing. Note, however, that we said *if properly programmed.* Computers do as they are told and will produce bad results with great speed if incorrectly programmed. Also, hardware failure is possible, though infrequent, and procedures for recognizing and recovering from such failures should be provided. Software failure is much more likely, however. Failure to provide recovery procedures can mean lost records, inaccurate billings, lawsuits by irate customers, and so on.

It is true also that the input must be correct for output to be correct. The computer can be programmed to edit incoming data, checking format, structural relationships, and so on, in order to recognize and reject (or even correct) as many erroneous entries as possible. Experience has shown that computerized processing systems generally commit fewer errors than manual processing systems. Machines are more reliable than people. They are designed that way.

Complexity of analysis Because of their speed and accuracy and their decision-making capabilities, computers can carry out very complex analyses in brief periods of time. Management can apply the complex mathematical tools of management science (statistics, operations research, mathematics, decision analysis, and so on) as a routine part of operational data processing. Answers to questions, such as what mix of products should be produced with available materials and productive capacities to attain a maximum net return or to fill available orders at minimum cost, can now be available daily, weekly, or monthly. Changes in product prices and costs of materials can be combined with modifications in productive capacities to determine optimum operating mixes. Warehouse locations can be found that minimize storage and transportation costs and also reduce chances of failing to satisfy customer demands in each area. The number of equipment repair centers and their locations can be so determined as to minimize all costs, including the cost of required service and the cost of downtime while equipment is out of service. Complex projects ranging from constructing a large building to preparing a computer-based data processing system can be so scheduled that it can be expected that the project will be finished on time and within allowable cost limits.

Computer simulation has been valuable when none of the available analytic solution models fit the situation. For example, simulation is valuable in studying the realistic but complicated queuing situations for which analytic models do not exist. In computer simulation, how the situation (problem, organization, market) operates is described as fully as possible. Important relationships are stated explicitly and then "programmed" in a computer language. The simulation model is then operated by the computer. Inputting changes in model parameters and observing the results allow an analysis of the effects of different policies on outcomes.

Changes in management practice

The implications of these new capabilities for managers are obvious. To compete effectively with their counterparts in other firms and other industries, today's managers must be able to utilize the results of management science tools. They must ensure that their information systems take advantage of the new techniques made available by the computer. They do not need to become mathematicians, statisticians, or operations researchers. They do need to become aware of the new tools that are available and how to use them. They must assure themselves that they are receiving competent technical advice and assistance in applying and interpreting these new analytic techniques. The manager must not fall into the trap of abrogating responsibilities in this regard by depending *totally* on the knowledge and skills of trained specialists. To the professional specialist, all problems *tend* to be seen from the perspective of his or her specialty. Problems tend to be narrowly and incompletely analyzed. Hard-to-quantify factors, often of overriding importance, can be assumed away and erroneous results obtained. Unless the manager knows enough about the tools of the specialist to ask proper questions and to participate in the development of analytic models, the results will most likely be inadequate.

Organizational effects of computers

The organizational effects of computers are twofold. First, the potential effects of the computer on the placement of decision-making power in an organization must be understood. Second, the importance of the location of the information system function must be recognized.

Overall organization

Two general philosophies of management organization exist, and a debate has developed over whether the use of computerized information systems favors a centralized or a decentralized management structure.

Centralized management The philosophy of **centralized management** is to push all decisions as high in the organizational structure as possible. Authority and responsibility are centralized in the managers or executives at the top of the organizational hierarchy. Supervisors do not participate in planning or goal setting activities. Middle managers tend to be involved almost entirely in operations and participate little in planning and goal setting. They carry out plans and strive after goals developed almost entirely by top management.

Decentralized management The philosophy of **decentralized management** is to push all decisions as low as possible in the organizational structure. All levels of management participate in planning and goal setting to the maximum extent possible. Each manager then attempts to attain the plans and goals that have been developed. Middle managers tend to run autonomous departments.

Computers and centralization of management A debate has developed about whether computers favor (promote) centralized management. It is asserted that computers centralize and speed up data processing. Data for the entire organization tend to be collected and analyzed at one location. Therefore, centralized (top) management can stay abreast of operational details for all parts of the organization. Proponents of this view believe that authority is given up by any manager only reluctantly. Without the computer, top management of large enterprises had no choice but to give some authority to lower-level (operating) managers. Lower-level managers were the only ones close enough to the situation to know what was going on. With computerized, quick-response, realtime systems, however, the top-level manager can be made aware of lower-level problems and be given the information necessary to make the required operating decisions. Many students of management believe that top managers will be unable to resist the opportunity to recentralize decision making.

The arguments in favor of decentralization also recognize the ability of the new information systems to provide better and more complete information to top management. It is argued that the computer can be used to improve the performance of the lower-level manager. Use of automatic control by exception designs in the electronic information system will improve control of routine operations and give operating managers more time to concentrate on planning, goal setting, and personnel relations. Top management can therefore have greater confidence in the ability of lower-level managers to use wisely any authority delegated to them. Top managers also can be more confident of their own ability to control the performance of lower-level managers, because better information can be obtained more quickly about the effects of the decisions made by lower management. The conclusion, then, is that decentralization will be supported and promoted by the use of computerized information systems.

Careful analysis of the arguments leads to the conclusion that the computer itself favors neither centralization nor decentralization. Where decisions are to be made is determined by where authority and responsibility are assigned. Information from a computerized system can be reported to whoever is to use it. In fact, if the definition we've established for *information* is to be realized, the pertinent, useful, timely facts *must* be reported to the person or persons responsible for using them in decision making. Otherwise, information is not created!

When the current increasing uses of teleprocessing, particularly distributed networks, and timesharing and multiprogramming are considered, no *distinct* trend toward decentralization or centralization can be clearly identified. Centralization and decentralization of processing are both occurring. All forms of processing are being used to support centralized and decentralized management structures.

Effects by management level

All managers perform the functions of planning, organizing, staffing, and controlling. The computer is expected to take over more of the controlling function, primarily through application of the concept of control by exception. Responses to many exceptions (reaching the inventory reorder point, for example) can be predetermined and left to the computer. Routine planning (such as work scheduling) can also be programmed for accomplishment by the computer. Managers will have more time to recognize opportunities and plan to capitalize on them. More time can be devoted to personnel relations and communication. Employee morale and productivity should therefore improve.

The effects of these developments on the different levels of management are being debated by students of management. One group sees a greater challenge for managers at the middle level. Lower-level managers are not expected to be affected as much because their jobs are primarily supervisory. Middle managers, however, will be expected to exercise closer control over operations and react more quickly to both problems and opportunities. It may well be that middle managers, generally, will be given greater responsibility and authority for planning and for making strategic policy decisions. The conclusion of the group of management experts who feel this may happen is that middle-management jobs will be made more challenging and candidates for those positions will have to be better educated, more creative, and ready to assume responsibility for strategic decisions.

Another group of management experts sees the middle-manager job as composed in large measure of the application of standardized responses to repetitious problems. Computers will tend to perform these routine functions while increasing the planning and decision-making capabilities of top management. The number of people employed in routine clerical activities supervised by middle managers will also decline as the computer takes over these activities. Those positions that remain will be highly specialized. At the lowest level will be the production-level employees who prepare data and material inputs and supervise machine functions in data processing and production. A higher-level group will be specialists performing systems analysis and design, engineering design, programming, and nonroutine data and material processing. At the top will be the top managers who receive informational outputs and make planning and strategy decisions. There will be limited transfer among these three levels. Middle managers will virtually disappear.

An intermediate view is held by the majority of management experts. These people agree that management jobs will become more challenging (including those of middle management) and the number of middle managers will decline, perhaps significantly. (However, those authorities who believe that computers will result in greater decentralization of authority actually see an *increase* in the number of middle managers.)

Placement of the information function

Historically, the information function has tended to be fragmented, with each functional component of the organization (production, marketing, finance) responsible for its own information system. The pressure for integration of these systems brought by the computer has tended to concentrate the information function in a data processing department. Recent developments in networking, the increasing capabilities of minicomputers, and timeshared or multiprogrammed systems may be modifying these trends. The evidence is not completely clear. However, one thing is clear: the location of the *responsibility* for the information function is changing.

The most common organizational placement of the electronic data processing (EDP) department has been to locate it in another department, usually finance. The location of the computer in the finance area usually results when the computer is initially acquired to perform large-volume clerical applications, such as hourly payroll or customer billing. In firms involved with large scientific research or engineering projects, the computer has been located in the engineering or research department because that department provided the initial impetus for acquisition.

There are several disadvantages to having the computer located in the sponsoring department even if that department is and will continue to be the major user. First of all, the operation tends to be staffed by personnel drawn from or with the same viewpoint as the host department. This leads to a less than companywide viewpoint and a lack of objectivity in selecting applications and setting job priorities. Location in a user department also reduces the status of the data processing operation. Because their authority derives only from the host department, the manager of data processing and the systems analysts find it difficult to design technically efficient systems and to enforce high standards for data preparation.

The second most common location of the EDP department is as an independent "service center" department. Often the center reports to a committee representing the using departments. This can give objectivity (depending on how the manager is selected and on the charge given to the department). However, the department usually has no authority for rational planning or long-term development of the information system. Jobs are brought to the department by the operating departments. Integration of systems is not fostered. Systems work is directed toward individual applications for customer departments. Chaotic and costly development of overlapping applications that do not use the full capabilities of the computer are the almost inevitable result.

A third alternative is being used to an increasing degree. This involves the establishment of the information system function (ISF) as an independent department reporting at the top level of the firm. Although clearly not best for all firms of all sizes in all industries, this location tends to overcome the weaknesses of the other two locations. First of all, the establishment of a separate, major department headed by a member of top management reflects the importance of the information system function. It also promotes a companywide viewpoint that promises an unbiased evaluation of project proposals. Job priorities set by such a department can be expected to reflect company goals. Integration and continual improvement in the information system are encouraged. Personnel within the department are encouraged to think in innovative terms and to seek continually for improvement of the current system.

The independent major department is not without some drawbacks. Hardware and software technicians can easily get carried away with innovation and the desire to have control of a big hardware system. "Empire building" can occur in the area of computer hardware or online information systems just as in other areas. That is why great care must be exercised in the selection of subdepartment managers within the function and the top-level executive to whom they report. The department should be subjected to the same controls as any other function, clearly justifying whatever system it may seek to develop. On balance, however, the advantages appear to outweigh the disadvantages for this location of the information system function.

Summary

Data processing systems are information systems for management. As such, they must provide the information to guide and facilitate the complex interactions of the human beings carrying out the functions of the organization. The information system can be viewed as a reflection of the hierarchical structure of the organization, as a feedback and control system, or merely as a data processing system. The data processing jobs to be accomplished are to establish a data bank of interrelated master files, develop procedures to capture relevant data to keep the data bank files current, and establish processes to extract the needed information for management planning and control from the flow of data and the changing status of the data bank records.

There is no single management information system right for every firm. Rather, there is a set of subsystems, each of which is usually designed primarily to serve a specific functional part of the firm. The functional information subsystems for finance, marketing, manufacturing, materials control, personnel, and planning have been described and discussed. These descriptions should lead the reader to recognize that these systems have more in common than might be supposed. Each of these subsystems tends to consist of a set of basic records (a data bank) and a method of extracting from business transactions and activity in the environment data that is used to update those data banks. The flow of data and the master files are accessed to develop information for management to use in decision making.

For any information system to be useful the reports it fosters must be responsive to management's needs. Realtime response takes place in time to affect an ongoing physical operation in a desirable way. Types of management reports include status reports that indicate the condition of a business operation at a point in time, activity reports on what has happened over a period of time, exception reports that alert management to the need for action, and analytical reports that give reasons for why things turn out the way they do. Management information can be reported periodically at regular intervals, as is usually the case with accounting reports. Reports may also, however, be triggered by an unexpected event, or they may be produced in response to a specific request from management (on demand).

Because of their speed, accuracy, and ability to facilitate complex analysis, computers have become important to management practice. Today's managers need to be familiar with data processing tools and how they can be used for management information. This does not mean that they need to become technical experts, but that they should know enough to participate in the development of electronic information systems.

It is not very clear what effects computers have on the overall organization of management structure. What is clear is that computers will probably take over more of the controlling function in business operations. This will free managers for other activities, such as planning and personnel relations.

Finally, the placement of the information function in a business organization varies. Most commonly the EDP department has been placed in another department, usually finance. Another common EDP position is that of an independent "service center" department. A third approach, which is on the increase, is the creation of an information system function (ISF) as an independent department reporting to the top level of the firm.

Key terms

Define the following terms as briefly as possible and then, in a short paragraph, clarify each definition.

Activity report
Analytical report
Centralized management
Data bank
Decentralized management
Exception report
Financial subsystem
Management information system (MIS)
Marketing subsystem
Materials control subsystem
On-demand reporting
Operational control
Periodic report
Personnel subsystem
Planning subsystem
Production subsystem
Realtime response
Status report
Strategic planning
Tactical planning
Triggered exception report

Discussion questions

1 State as briefly as possible the objective of each of the functional subsystems listed below:
   a Financial
   b Marketing
   c Production
   d Materials control
   e Personnel
   f Planning
2 Contrast the objectives of the personnel and the materials control subsystems. In what respects are they the same, and in what respects do they differ?

3 Identify the four inventories controlled by the inventory control subsystem.
4 How can the efficiency of the production systems be measured?
5 How can the efficiency with which the personnel function is carried out be determined?
6 Compare the objectives of the marketing function with the objectives of the personnel function. In what general ways are they the same? In what specific ways are they different? Can you draw any general conclusions from this comparison? Explain.
7 Some firms do not establish an identified planning unit. Why might this be an acceptable organizational structure?
8 How might the effectiveness with which the planning function is performed be determined?
9 What are the operational effects of computers on management?
10 What are the organizational effects of computers on management?
11 How have the new capabilities of computers affected management practices?
12 Argue that the use of computers favors
   a centralized management.
   b decentralized management.
   c neither centralized nor decentralized management.
13 Several studies of the effects of introducing computers into business organizations have indicated that the activities of top managers of medium-sized and large firms are affected very little, if at all, by the introduction of computerized data processing into the firm.
   a Is this an expected result? Explain.
   b Is this a desirable result? Explain.
   c Would you expect this to continue to be true? Why or why not?
14 How is a manager's information needs related to
   a the *level* of the position occupied?
   b the functional responsibility of the position occupied?
15 What are the data processing jobs necessary to the establishment of a management information system?
16 What are the advantages and disadvantages of using on-demand reporting as opposed to using periodic, regularly scheduled, standardized reports?
17 What are the advantages and disadvantages to locating the computer in each of the following:
   a Major user department
   b Independent service center department
   c Independent major department
18 Why is the concept of control by exception important to the development of management information systems?
19 Exception reporting has several advantages. How many can you identify? What are they?
20 Why do exceptions have a high information content?
21 Why might managers prefer on-demand reporting?

Exercises

1 Speculate on additional resources and additional operations that might be used to extend Figure 16.1, page 440.

2 Visit a local wholesale distribution firm and ask to have their inventory control processes explained to you. Try to determine the following:
   - **a** Is the system computer based?
   - **b** Are economic order quantities used in the system?
   - **c** How are purchase requisitions triggered?
   - **d** How are vendors selected? How often do they change?
   - **e** What are the major control reports received by the chief executive officer?

3 Visit a newly opened manufacturing plant in your area. Try to obtain answers to the following:
   - **a** What determined the location of the plant in this community? at this specific location?
   - **b** Who made the decision to build this plant?
   - **c** What factors were considered in making the decision to establish this plant?
   - **d** Was a computer involved in carrying out the analysis that led to the decision to build this plant? If so, how?

4 A manufacturer of industrial machine parts provides inventory, quality-control, and cost analysis as triggered exception reports and income statements and balance sheets when requested by a manager. Would a reporting period be involved for each of the two sets of reports? Explain.

Corporate "War Rooms" Plug into the Computer

Boardrooms and executive suites are being deluged with corporate operating data despite the best efforts of management information specialists, computer programmers, and designers of visual display units. They are desperately trying to channel only as much information from a sea of statistics as executives and board members can absorb. For a diversified company such as Gould Inc., which acquired I-T-E Imperial Corp. this spring and saw its sales spurt by two-thirds to $1.3 billion, the problem is particularly knotty. But Gould's proposed solution is especially innovative.

Gould is combining the visual display board, which has now become a fixture in many boardrooms, with a computer information system. Information on everything from inventories to receivables will come directly from the computer in an assortment of charts and tables that will make comparisons easy and lend instant perspective. The information also will be instantly available on individual video terminals in the offices of senior managers.

"This system gives us the control to stay on top," says William T. Ylvisaker, chairman and chief executive officer at Gould, who ordered up the $300,000 system for Gould's plush boardroom in its new headquarters at Rolling Meadows, Ill., a Chicago suburb. "With this, our margins will be higher, and our decisions will be better because we have more information available and we'll be analyzing situations more frequently," he says.

Touch of a finger

Starting this week Ylvisaker will be able to tap three-digit codes into a 12-button box resembling the keyboard of a telephone. "SEX" will get him sales figures. "GIN" will call up a balance sheet. "MUD" is the keyword for inventory.

About 75 such categories will be available, and the details will be displayed for the company as a whole, for divisions, for product lines, and for other breakdowns, which will also be specified by simple digital codes. In this way Gould hopes to overcome the psychological problem that many executives have in sitting down at a more conventional terminal keyboard that resembles a typewriter and can be somewhat complicated to operate. Later this year the system will automatically show significant deviations from operating plans to facilitate management by exception. Ultimately directors and executives will be able to ask

Source: Abridged from "Corporate 'War Rooms' Plug into the Computer," from the August 23, 1976 issue of *BusinessWeek,* 65, 67, "what if" questions and see the anticipated consequences of various ploys.

Gould, of course, is only one of a growing number of companies that are becoming aware of the potential uses of visual displays hooked directly to information stored in the computer. This fall IBM will throw its marketing muscle behind a similar concept, called Trend Analysis 370. This will be the 15th software package that IBM has developed in the past five years for management information systems (MIS), and it will be the first capable of producing color graphs. Unlike the Gould system, the information in its first application will be displayed only on a video screen, not on a wall screen.

The display question

"The use of color helps to present data better," explains Gale R. Aguilar, director of systems marketing for IBM. "Colored graphs are the way you'd present the information if you did it manually. It really is the form that senior business managers are used to looking at in their chart rooms."

IBM has worked nearly four years with First Chicago Corp. to construct an executive information system that will also serve as a prototype for the Trend Analysis 370 package. Much of that time was spent analyzing the information that First Chicago executives asked for and how they asked for it. The resulting system, which has been tested for a year at First Chicago, provides easy access to large banks of data in forms that executives can use and permits fast comparisons of different sets of data. It can store everything from Federal Reserve data on all banks to economic statistics on various industries and information on First Chicago's own customers. And a special screen next to the cathode ray tube will display information in line graphs and bar charts in bright green, red, and blue.

Already users include such executives as Treasurer David Vitale, who as secretary of the bank's assets and liabilities committee had found that information for analysis in that area was hard to obtain. With the new information system he can now tell in seconds, for example, how stable various purchasers of liabilities are and where they are located. Recently the system helped to show that the bank was not attracting many fund investors on the West Coast, so the bank set up a new issuing facility there.

Simpler approach

Many companies have found that video systems and display screens in corporate boardrooms, or "war rooms," can be effective in communicating information to hurried executives even if the displays are not tied to a computer. In 1973, for example, Transamerica Corp. installed a $60,000 electronic video display system in its 26th floor boardroom in San Francisco. It included two slide projectors, a movie projector, a reel-to-reel tape system. But each slide must be drawn and photographed manually. If someone wants additional information, it is available only in printed form. Similarly, Atlantic Richfield Co. has seven wall display systems at its Los Angeles headquarters, has installed one in Philadelphia this summer, and is putting another in Dallas. Transamerica originally intended to link its display with a computerized information system but has not done so.

One company that hopes to computerize its diplays is Motorists Mutual Insurance Co. of Columbus, Ohio. It devised a system that enables participants to feed information into video displays as well as to receive it. Each executive has a video screen in front of him in Motorists' boardroom, and an overhead TV camera allows the system to pick up charts and even computer data exhibited on a cathode ray tube. But, says Dorothy Penny, who operates the system, "The picture is shaky. We would have better reception if we could move the computer data directly to the TV screen." Motorists hopes to adjust the system to accept data directly from the computer and to enable it automatically to form graphs.

A long buildup

Gould was able to link its elaborate display to its data base because it already had spent considerable effort under Ylvisaker, a former securities analyst, in fine-tuning its reporting system. Gould has rebuilt the charts of accounts for each of its operations, which range from its original battery business to electronics and metallurgy, so that financial data are correlated among all divisions.

When Ylvisaker joined Gould eight years ago, its sales were $115 million, earnings were $2.8 million, and top executives made do with monthly summaries of such factors as sales, back-logs, receivables, and payables for each operation. As the company's sales grew to $891 million and earnings to $45 million in the fiscal year ended in June (not taking account of the I-T-E acquisition), the summaries began coming out weekly instead of monthly. Now, with the new system, the information comes instantaneously, either on TV screens at various Gould offices and outposts or on the big 4 ft. by 5.5 ft. screen in the Gould boardroom.

Too much or too little

The problem with most management information systems is that they give out too much information, too little information, or the wrong information. Ylvisaker has spent years refining his theories of what operational figures are crucial and building a system that is capable of producing them. His analytical nature and academic training in mechanical and industrial engineering at Yale helped to fit him for the task. And his first job was in banking, which made him think in terms of financial statements and balance sheets.

Ylvisaker and in-house systems experts have been experimenting with the best way to focus executive's attention on trends and fluctuations. He already has made some trial runs on the graphic display system in his boardroom, and not all have been successful. At first, color was used extensively to distinguish patterns. Green lines were used where results were up to budget, red lines where they were not. Orange lines indicated forecasts, blue lines budget figures.

"The theory was that if we looked at these for two or three months, we would get used to reading them," explains Edwin C. Parker, vice-president for finance. "But after several months of using them with the board, they didn't get any clearer." So when the system goes on line, displays will be simplified, showing trend lines plotted against plan lines.

Zeroing in

Since Ylvisaker is a management-by-exception enthusiast, a computer program will automatically tabulate all key items for any division that are more than 10% off budget, that are off budget by any amount for two months in a row, or that have moved in an unfavorable direction for three months in a row even if they are still within the budget. Each item will be displayed on the screen in sequence for 30 or 45 seconds so that Ylvisaker can pick out areas where problems exist.

"Our core report now shows the administrative costs of a division," says Ylvisaker. "But our new system can show all the costs so that we can examine why they may be out of line."

The system is expected to be a time-saver, of course. Parker notes that at one point Ylvisaker noticed that the working capital requirements of two divisions appeared to be getting way out of line. "He asked me why," says Parker. "I had to ask the comptroller. He had to ask three or four people to work on it. It took eight days to get back to me. With this equipment, the thing could be settled on the screen in five minutes."

Down the road, the system should graphically display the consequences of actions that are only contemplated. Says Ylvisaker: "We'll be able to ask what will happen if we raise prices 2% or 3% or 4% on a product. Or what will be the effect of getting working capital down to a certain amount. We ask such questions now, but it takes a lot of time to handle them."

Spreading the system

While terminals will eventually be installed in offices of managers both at headquarters and in the field, one of the system's first tests will be in the boardroom. Gould's directors have already come away impressed by trial runs of the graphic displays. "The advantage of the new visual setup is the ability to present things to the board in a manner that will not require so much digging and will emphasize things management wants to emphasize," says Gould director Keith R. Potter, executive vice-president of International Harvester Co. He points out that a staff could never prepare slides with the array of data that the Gould system can draw from the computer and display visually.

"Very frequently when a topic comes up at a meeting, you have to defer discussion until another meeting or wait until figures can be obtained," adds Potter. "That is not nearly as satisfactory as being able to pull the data immediately and have the discussion then and there when the question is hot."

For Ylvisaker the important improvement will be the ability to analyze more situations more rapidly. "The two most important factors in business are time and cost," he says. "Timely information is the biggest asset a manager can have. You can't ask other managers for everything. This way you can do it yourself."

Chapter 17 Managing the Development of a Data Processing System

Outline

Selecting the hardware and basic software, designing the system, and implementing the final product is a complex process. We have already learned in earlier chapters (12–15) how to design a data processing system. However, the procedure was based on some unspoken assumptions. We were assuming, first, that it would pay to computerize the system we were dealing with; second, that a computer was available; and finally, that the language to be used in programming the system had been chosen. In this chapter, we are going to consider those assumptions, outlining a complete logical procedure for the entire process.

The project life cycle

Projects have a **project life cycle,** the major phases of which are a feasibility study, a system design phase, a system development phase, a system implementation phase, and system operation.

The feasibility study

Before design or development of a project, it must be determined in a **feasibility study** if the expenditure of time and effort is justified. Users and data processing experts must agree on the general nature of the system to be developed. Alternate solutions must be identified. Preliminary estimates must be made of the time and cost required to develop the system. These costs can then be compared to the estimated tangible and intangible benefits of the proposed system. If the benefits outweigh the costs, more precise plans are developed.

Typically, there are several outputs from the feasibility study. The user organization has been described, and the current flow of data and information in the organization has been documented. Alternative system designs worthy of serious consideration have been identified. Most important, a specific proposal for further action has been developed. This proposal contains a description of the project team and its general responsibilities and a preliminary timetable for completion of the project.

The study team

The feasibility study should be performed by a group composed of operating managers from the affected system and technical experts with knowledge of available hardware and software.

Responsibility of operating personnel The operating personnel should understand that they are a vital part of the team. Their specific responsibilities are as follows:

1 They should provide information about the application(s) being considered for computerization. Items included are volumes to be handled, timing

requirements, and reporting requirements. Future growth must also be considered.

2 They should ensure that the study considers user needs and the responsiveness of the system to its users. This includes more than ensuring that the informational needs of management are met. It also includes ensuring that the system is designed to be operated by people rather than designed to operate people.

3 They should ensure that the benefits to be derived from computerizing the system are higher than its costs.

Responsibility of technical personnel The technical personnel on the feasibility team are obviously responsible for providing the information that makes for good technical decisions. Their specific responsibilities are as follows:

1 They should provide technical information about potential hardware and software. Care must be exercised to be sure *all* potential designs are considered, from pencil-and-paper systems up through online systems. There is a tendency for technical personnel to consider only computerized systems and try merely to pick the best computerized approach.

2 They should provide the technical expertise needed to document the current system at the system-chart level to be sure that all needed information on desired system capabilities is obtained.

The user representatives should be managers from the operating departments that will be affected by any change in the system. They should not hesitate to include on an ad hoc basis employees who are familiar with the details of the business operation. These persons can best determine the effects of any proposed change on the people who come in contact with the system. However, managers should be participative team members to provide users with the prestige and power to ensure a responsive system. The worst mistake that can be made here is to allow the system design to be determined exclusively by the technicians on the team. System design is not totally a technical problem. Systems responsive to users are not usually the result of the application of only technical data processing knowledge.

Once it has been determined that computerization appears feasible, a preliminary system flowchart should be prepared. This preliminary system flowchart together with the timing and volume requirements established earlier are the basis for selection of hardware and software.

The system design phase

The purpose of the **system design phase** is to analyze the processing requirements of a project and to design a system (or systems) to meet those requirements. Top-down design should be used, starting from general requirements and ending with detailed system specifications for guiding program development.

The products of the design phase include more than program specifications. Functional specifications of the system defining what the system is to accomplish precede the program/module specifications. All system procedures (data collection, data preparation, order of processing, and so forth) must be specified in detail. A plan for conversion to the new system also should be included, as well as initial specifications of the testing process.

The system development phase

The **system development phase** includes program design and coding in accordance with the specifications developed in the design phase. Testing processes need to be worked out in detail, system documentation must be prepared, and the training to be given to system users must be specified.

The outputs of the development phase should be obvious from our discussion.

1 Test plan for programs, jobs, and the system
2 Tested programs
3 System documentation
4 A final installation (conversion) plan
5 Training plans

When all these things are complete, system implementation can take place.

The system implementation phase

The objective of the **system implementation phase** is a working system. Jobs to be completed are as follows:

1 Fully test all aspects of the system to ensure that it correctly meets all requirements for the system.
2 Educate users to make them capable of working effectively with the system.
3 Finalize system documentation and have it reviewed and accepted by the system users.
4 Install the system as an operating system.

System operation

System implementation is not complete until the **system operation** has proven itself. Acceptance testing during conversion is not a foolproof process. It is extremely difficult to foresee and test for every possible ordering and magnitude of transactions that can occur during normal operation. Design errors may not show up for months. That is why it is important to plan for continuing system testing and maintenance during operation of the system after conversion.

Choosing system hardware

The steps in choosing system hardware are obtaining good estimates of the system characteristics critical to hardware selection, determining performance requirements, and defining the alternatives available.

Critical system characteristics

The critical system characteristics can most easily be considered under the four major components of any computerized data processing system—input, processing, storage, and output.

Critical input requirements The questions to be answered here include:

1 How many different inputs will there be? How many different transactions and changes are to be handled by the system? This will depend primarily on the degree of integration planned for the system. The more integration, the larger the number of different inputs.
2 What is the volume of each input type?
3 How are each of these inputs distributed over time? The absolute number of inputs may not be as important as their time distribution. A smaller number of inputs all arriving in a short period of time can require input media and devices with higher rated capacities than a larger total volume arriving in a constant flow.
4 How are the inputs created and can the form of the input-carrying medium be changed? For example, if an input is to be created as part of a transaction procedure, is there enough flexibility in the procedure to consider online input?
5 Where are the inputs coming from? That is, what are their physical locations? If inputs are created in a constant flow at several widely dispersed locations, processing can be accomplished much faster with online input than with batching of inputs.

Nature of the processing The nature of the processing can give valuable guides to determining the size of the primary memory and the access time it should have. For some applications, such as large-scale simulation, the primary memory may need to be larger to accommodate large-scale mathematical manipulation and comparison of many variables. Cycle time of the computer, the time required to carry out an instruction, should be low if number-crunching processing jobs are many and large; but cycle time can be higher for custodial processing. Primary memory access time should be balanced with the CPU cycle time so one element does not wait on the other.

Large-scale custodial processing or accounting applications involve large volumes of input and output with little computation. For such situations, primary storage requirements are dictated primarily by the configuration of system software rather than processing volumes. Such applications also create a wide variety of reports and documents, which means a flexible printing capability must be provided. A mix of number-crunching and administrative data processing applications may indicate a need for a fast CPU, a fast and large primary storage, large online and offline secondary storage capacity, and high input/output speeds. Such a configuration allows both types of processing to be efficiently carried out.

Depending on system design, magnetic tapes or disk packs will be required for secondary storage and for efficient sorting of large files. The secondary storage requirements may be met by other devices (drums or fixed disks), but if batch processing is involved, with files inactive for days at a time, magnetic tapes or strips and disk packs are more efficient, since they can be stored offline when not in use (Figure 17.1).

A requirement of multiprogramming or timesharing capability usually will require a large primary memory capacity to provide simultaneous storage for the executive and the several compilers and/or applications programs. A fast CPU is needed to handle the management of the system. Otherwise, response times for individual users may not be sufficiently low to make the system feasible.

The volume of each type of processing should be established for a different reason. If one type of use is very limited, it may be less costly to obtain a leased or purchased system for the major use and then farm out the other use. Computer time can be purchased in a variety of ways on almost the full spectrum of machine configurations. Raw time can be bought at some service bureaus, and the purchaser's own employees can operate the system to perform the processing. At the other extreme, the entire job from data preparation to final output can be contracted out to a full-service computing organization. Timesharing services make a full range of computing power available through terminals. Common prudence should be exercised regarding the reliability, capability, and continuity of any service used.

The amount of computing power needed at one time is useful in determining CPU and primary memory speeds, primary memory capacities, number and kinds of I/O peripherals and their speeds, and the possible usefulness of multiprogramming or timesharing. However, it should be recognized that satisfaction of peak load demand can mean excess capacity at other times.

Figure 17.1

A data processing installation **Magnetic tapes or disks are the most efficient type of secondary storage for batch processing of large volumes of data. (Courtesy Digital Equipment Corporation)**

Storage and retrieval requirements The storage and retrieval requirements indicate the volume of online storage capacity required and the type of I/O needed to obtain responses to inquiries. For immediate response, some form of terminal I/O is indicated, probably for sites away from the data processing center where the computer is located. Four levels of response speeds can be identified.

1 *Instantaneous response,* within less than two seconds, requires fast online storage (drum, disk, or slow core) and a fast CPU and primary storage (cycle time and access time of one microsecond or less).
2 *Fast response,* within ten seconds, can be accomplished by a slower CPU and almost any type of online random-access store (disk, drum, slow core, or magnetic strip).
3 *Intermediate-speed response,* within five minutes or so, can be accomplished by several microfilm retrieval systems as well as all computer systems.
4 *Slow response,* within several hours or longer, can be accomplished with manual or machine-aided manual systems and need not involve the computer.

Response time requirements must be related also to volume of requests. The lower the frequency with which response requests are received in *any* system, the lower the average response time, down to the minimum of which the system is physically capable. Type of data stored and retrieved also influences storage device selection and input/output capability. For example, are data records short or long? Is each data input lengthy? is it coded? How much of each input or output message is really redundant, that is, not required to make the meaning of the message clear?

Inquiry stations also change with desired speed of response, volume of inquiries, and average length of each response. If each response is short (for example, Yes or No, an account balance, or O.K. or Reject), almost any terminal device can be used, including voice response. When response is more voluminous, either a CRT or a typewriter-like printing terminal is more apt to be required. CRT terminals are generally faster, but message length should be limited to what can be displayed on the screen at one time.

Remote use is important in determining the need for terminals or other remote I/O devices or provision for several computers in the system. The nature of the processing at the remote sites and the demand for use of central computer resources (primary and secondary storage and I/O peripherals) at each site will determine if one central computer should be shared or if several smaller computer systems might be installed at different locations. The provision of remote job entry facilities and batch output terminals may be sufficient for satisfying many remote-use requirements. The ever-increasing capabilities of minicomputers cannot be ignored: timesharing and multiprogramming uses are common; virtual memory capabilities are not unknown; cycle times, access speeds, and length of instruction sets rival the large number crunchers. As a stand-alone system or as part of a distributed processing network, the minicomputer can provide large amounts of custodial processing and problem-solving computation at remote sites. These systems are fast, reliable, and inexpensive. If remote input and output (teleprocessing) is considered, a distributed network should be investigated. It may be less expensive to perform the bulk of the routine jobs at the activity sites, sending only the large jobs to a central computer. Data bases may be common to the remote sites and the central facility.

Critical output requirements The output capability required is determined by the kinds of custodial processing carried on and the nature of the reporting system. If exception reporting is the primary type of activity report, the volume of reports to be printed will be much lower than if all details are reported and users must search out the exceptions.

If reporting on demand is a feature of the system, output devices needed will be determined by how reports are to be requested. If remote terminals at each manager's location are to be used to request reports and follow-up analyses, the terminals should be capable of producing most of the reports requested. This suggests a faster printing device as part of the terminal. Large-volume reports would probably still be printed on a fast printer in the computer center and delivered to the requesting manager.

Task specification

At the completion of the feasibility study, the basic system flowchart, and the input, processing, storage and retrieval, and output studies, a specification of tasks to be accomplished by the system will be available. Certain minimums for the configuration will also be established. These include minimum numbers of input and output devices by type, capacity of online secondary storage, response times expected, and capacities of output devices. If multiprogramming is planned, what applications are to run concurrently? If timesharing is involved, how many simultaneous users are to be supported, and what will be the total number of terminals? If direct entry of data is planned, has the nature of the direct-entry device been established? In this regard, will the system interface in any way with other systems?

What about future growth in volume of activities or expectations for more sophisticated use of the computer system? Being able to expand volumes of transactions or file data without extensive modification of current software (programs) can be important to a dynamic, growing organization. Similarly, a change to more sophisticated forms of use (remote data entry, online response, timesharing, and so on) may be desired at a later date. No computer system can grow indefinitely, although most systems can grow over a wide range of capability. However, not all can economically provide services such as multiprogramming and timesharing.

Finally, what about reliability? Minimum performance standards for the system must be decided. Average length of time between failures and proportion of allowable downtime (time the system is broken down and not functioning) should be specified. This also involves questions of technical maintenance. For example, must maintenance be available on site or within one hour? Such questions must be related to the costs of downtime at different periods and the cost of preventing the downtime.

Defining system options

If the general system specifications in terms of tasks and minimum capabilities are complete, the available systems that can meet these general specifications can be defined. Of course, the flexible nature of computer configurations means that many systems can be made to perform the tasks specified. The problem is to find the configuration that performs the prescribed tasks at the lowest cost while providing the potential for any expected future growth. The first step is usually a request for bids on the system by computer manufacturers.

Request for bids The request for bids ordinarily takes the form of a letter to vendors indicating an intent to acquire (buy or lease) a system meeting the established specifications. These specifications should be carefully and completely stated in as succinct a manner as possible. A due date for the acceptance of preliminary bids should be established. One person in the organization should be designated to answer prebid questions and to assemble additional information for bidders where it appears desirable. Choose this person well—someone with knowledge of your needs and of computer and data processing concepts and terms and with the strength of character to resist the blandishments and special pleas that are apt to come from the computer vendors.

In situations where completely new or quite different computer systems are sought, the initial bid specifications may need to be modified. Also, changes in hardware or software capabilities unknown to the persons preparing the specifications may give less costly configurations the ability to do the job. For this reason, the bid specifications should put more emphasis on the tasks to be performed than on the hardware minimums.

Bid requests should be extended to as many potential vendors as possible. It may even be advisable to encourage bids on only a part of the system. In any case, vendors should be encouraged to bid separately on each part of the system, including software. Definitely, bidding should not be restricted to only a few vendors.

Recognizing functional trade-offs Particularly in business data processing applications, fast input can be traded for online random-access storage of files. Transactions can then be input as they occur instead of in batches. This can reduce the need for data transcription to a machine-sensible medium in a batch operation and decrease the need for a fast input device to handle the batched transactions on the medium to which they were transcribed. When costing out system alternatives, the analyst or study team must recognize trade-offs in reduced data preparation and offline data storage available from larger online systems and from systems involving direct data entry from each operating area. The analyst must also recognize that such online input can increase the cost of detecting and correcting errors in data entry.

Larger primary memories may be replaced by larger and slower secondary memories. Sophisticated address modification hardware and virtual storage software can reduce the need for a large primary memory.

The necessity for functional balance One of the most uneconomical computer configurations is one in which inadequate, slow I/O devices are hung on a fast processor and used for only custodial data processing. Better system balance would involve greater online storage and a larger number of direct-entry devices. Such a system could make a small but fast CPU productive. In any case, care must be taken to match functional components so that they balance—that is, so that all components are about equally productive. This should not be taken to mean that no component (or even the whole system) should ever be idle. However, an imbalance between size and type of storage, CPU size and speed, and I/O capability means some components will be worked very hard while others are idle. Many times the whole system is only as fast as its slowest component.

Sampling the experiences of other users Valuable information can be obtained from past users of similar systems. Not only hardware and software performance but the integrity and reliability of particular suppliers can be evaluated. Suppliers will normally provide a list of satisfied customers to contact. Ask competitive suppliers for names of users who have switched suppliers. Their reasons may provide valuable warnings that will prevent future problems.

Choosing system software

There are several levels of system software. Most basic is the operating system, or system executive. Usually chosen with the operating system are system utilities. Data base management languages also can be considered as basic software today. If the DBML uses a host language, it would not be chosen until the procedural host language (COBOL, PL-1, and so on) had been chosen. Nonprocedural languages are normally the highest order of software. Not all types of nonprocedural languages are available for all computers, however.

Usually, only three basic choices are available. One is the operating system to be used. The second is the higher-level languages that are to be available. Third is the choice of a data base management language. The sections that follow discuss these three problems.

Selecting the operating system

The operating system will be determined largely by the tasks to be performed. From the most to the least complex, the tasks to be considered include the following:

1 *Multiprogramming or timesharing.* This depends primarily on the number of users and their locations. It also depends on the number of interactive applications and their complexity. For batch processing from a distance, remote job entry can meet the need. If, however, there are numerous tasks to be performed for widely dispersed users, some form of multiprogramming is to be preferred. If some tasks are computebound, timesharing may be preferred.
2 *Types of secondary storage and file structures.* The most popular secondary random-access memory (RAM) in use today is disk. Therefore, most data processing systems will be disk oriented. The operating system should reflect this fact by making disk-oriented operations easy.
3 *The nature of the hardware.* Changes in hardware design have made the choice of hardware less critical than in the past. Hardware is decreasing in cost while increasing in sophistication and reliability. Mini and micro computers are putting computer power within the economic range of almost all businesses. And it is now fairly simple to purchase hardware-software packages (turnkey systems) that can virtually be plugged in and turned on. The critical factors in obtaining an effective and efficient data processing system are the system design and the software. Therefore, great care should be given to the selection of system software. A major problem in this selection process is obtaining a hardware-software match. Software systems involving either timesharing or multiprogramming require hardware properly designed to perform the necessary system management function efficiently. Usually, the adequacy of these kinds of hardware-software combinations is easily determined by testing, but as indicated previously, care must be exercised to be sure one is testing *exactly* the same system that is being purchased.

A newer development affecting the choice of software is the increasing availability of compilers that are "imbedded in" (part of) the hardware. The microcomputer, that is, microminiaturized circuit board technology, has made such hardware compilers possible. Modern technology allows the creation of almost any logical structures on a very small silicon chip. By mounting several chips on one circuit board, manufacturers can create a specialized digital computer for little cost if the production is done in enough volume. This process, which is the basis of the hand-held calculators and digital watches selling for under ten dollars, can provide hardware "compilers" that make a computer "speak" COBOL or some other higher-level language. The microprocessor compiler actually converts COBOL statements into machine instructions on an interpretive or line-by-line basis. Thus, the machine operates in COBOL.

Selecting programming languages

Specific rules for choosing the programming languages for an installation were covered in Chapter 9, pages 267–273. Readers are urged to review those pages at this time. A few supplementary remarks are in order, however.

To be efficient in use, programming languages should support structured programming. Most procedural languages now exist in a structured form. Programs written in a structured form are easier to maintain and modify. They are also more likely to reflect users' needs. Users can more easily understand exactly what the program is doing and, therefore, judge if it is doing what it should.

Selecting data base management languages

Data base management languages (DBMLs) should be chosen for what they can do. The DBML should be logically complete and should perform all the tasks one is interested in (get, put, replace, and so on).

As indicated in Chapter 14, DBMLs are differentiated primarily by their structural approach (hierarchical, network, or relational) and by whether or not they require a host language. Data base experts recommend a relational structure and an independent nonprocedural language.

Negotiating the contract

Choosing between buying and leasing

Computers and computer components can be purchased outright, leased, leased with an option to buy, or acquired through a sale and lease-back arrangement involving a third firm. The firm or agency contemplating the acquisition of computer equipment must decide which method is best for it. This, of course, is all part of the larger decision whether it is best to acquire a configuration or to rent computer services from a service bureau or timesharing service. The objectives are to obtain the needed computing services at the least possible cost while giving appropriate attention to considerations of privacy and control and of reliability and continuity of service.

Contracts for rent or purchase of a computer or computer components are variable documents. Lease contracts are more complicated documents than purchase contracts. The discussion below is organized around the items that should be specifically provided for in purchase and lease contracts. Contracts for maintenance services are also discussed.

Purchase contracts

Contracts for purchase of computer systems or components should provide specifically for performance on the part of both the buyer and the manufacturer. The exact configuration is included, with components designated by name, manufacturer's part number, and capacity, speed, and other performance measures. Overall performance levels for the total configuration should also be specified. Penalties against the manufacturer for performance below specifications should be provided. The date of delivery or turnover by the manufacturer of an operating configuration should be stated, again with penalty for nonperformance and with the provision of alternative means of processing provided for. The manufacturer should insist on availability of the computer site with an appropriate lead time. Again, penalties should be paid for late availability. Payment terms should be clearly spelled out and not left to any verbal agreement.

Leases

Rental terms are more complex than purchase agreements. They should, however, contain the same description of the total system, component by component, and provide for delivery of a working system on the agreed date the same as purchase contracts. Additional provisions should specify the contractual period, the exact nature of the rental charges and how they are computed, standard periods of use, extra use charges, and any purchase options.

The contractual period The length of the lease and the length of notice required to cancel the total configuration or any part of it are referred to as the contractual period. Nongovernment users are normally required to retain equipment at least one year, but can cancel at any time from then on with 90 days notice.

Rental charges Lease prices are usually stated in terms of monthly payments for a one-shift operation (176 hours). Additional use may or may not require the payment of additional fees. Users should be aware of the exact provisions. A few manufacturers compute rental charges entirely from use. Meters installed on the equipment measure the amount of time each component is in operation.

Purchase options Most manufacturers offer the alternative of applying portions of the rental payments to purchase of the equipment at any point in time. The percentage of the payment that can be applied varies with the length of the lease and the length of time the equipment has been installed. The user should check this provision carefully.

Other services Any services or software to be supplied by the equipment manufacturer should be completely and clearly described. Many services in this area used to be supplied as part of the lease or purchase agreement. Generally, this is no longer true. Each service or program is separately priced and must be contracted for. If the vendor promises to train employees or assist in developing information or data processing systems (including programming), the exact nature and amount of these services should be spelled out in the contract. Otherwise the user is apt to receive a bill for the services provided or not get the services as expected. The time to clear up potential misunderstandings is when the contract is being negotiated. Unsophisticated users acquiring a major, modern computer system would do well to hire a consultant with knowledge of available services and software and experience in contract negotiation.

Maintenance contracts

Usually, basic monthly maintenance charges cover parts, preventive maintenance, and remedial maintenance performed during normal working hours. For large computer systems, the maintenance services are provided by workers stationed on site. For small systems, remedial maintenance is usually provided on call. Payment for maintenance outside normal working hours is usually at a higher rate. However, users can choose as the "principal period of maintenance" an eight-hour period outside normal working hours but usually falling between 7 A.M. and 6 P.M. For large systems, maintenance is at the regular rate 24 hours per day but service at times outside the principal period of maintenance is on an on-call basis. Maintenance services either are obtained from firms other than the manufacturer or are provided by the user. Maintenance of mixed vendor systems is usually contracted from the group of vendors, with each vendor providing maintenance for the equipment it furnished. Questions concerning the validity of manufacturer guarantees of equipment performance can then be encountered, however. In a mixed vendor system it is often difficult to attain unequivocal assignment of equipment failure to a specific component in order to receive corrective service from the equipment supplier involved.

Controlling the system development process

The discussion of the project life cycle above has indicated that time schedules are to be developed and development costs estimated before development begins. These estimates should be used to control project development. Also important to the success of this process is the organizational structure for the project team. Several common techniques for team organization, schedule monitoring, and cost control are discussed below.

Project management

Project management consists of the processes used to control any ad hoc project like data processing system development. The important elements of project management are the project team, controls over time schedules, and cost controls.

Project team The project team can be organized many ways, but should contain a high-level representative of the user. This person should have the knowledge and authority to speak for the user organization in questions of requirements and of design to meet those requirements. Some firms insist that a user representative chair the project committee as project manager.

In addition to user representatives, the project team obviously must include personnel with skills in the areas of systems analysis and design and programming. Personnel knowledgeable about hardware and software are also important, particularly if a new computer is to be acquired.

In any case, a project team headed by a responsible person who understands the problem must be given responsibility for carrying through the system development. This group must be held accountable for the results, both in terms of obtaining a working system and in terms of development costs.

Project schedule control Project management should establish careful time parameters for the project development effort. These time estimates should provide the management of the firm with feedback on progress toward an operating system. Periodic status reports will indicate if the time schedules are being met. One technique that has been rather widely used for controlling project schedules is the **program evaluation and review technique (PERT)**. PERT involves defining the tasks necessary to complete a project and setting them in a **critical path network**. An example of a PERT network is given in Figure 17.2. The network shown is the general network developed for the feasibility study for a project intended to develop an inventory accounting and control system. All paths converging at a point must be completed before the next task can be started. Note that all paths must be completed to get to the end at point 8. The longest path is 6.8 man-weeks in length:

Leg	Man-weeks
1–2	0.2
2–4	1.2
4–5	3.6
5–6	1.4
7–8	0.4
	6.8

This longest path is the *critical* path. Any slippage in performing any of the tasks on this path will add to the total time required to complete the feasibility study. Taking added time to complete legs not on the critical path will not affect the completion date unless the time is lengthened to the point of establishing a new critical path. Also, the critical path could be shortened by assigning additional people to tasks on the critical path in order to complete them faster.

Organization of programmers

There are three commonly used methods for organizing programmers during the late design and development phases of the project.

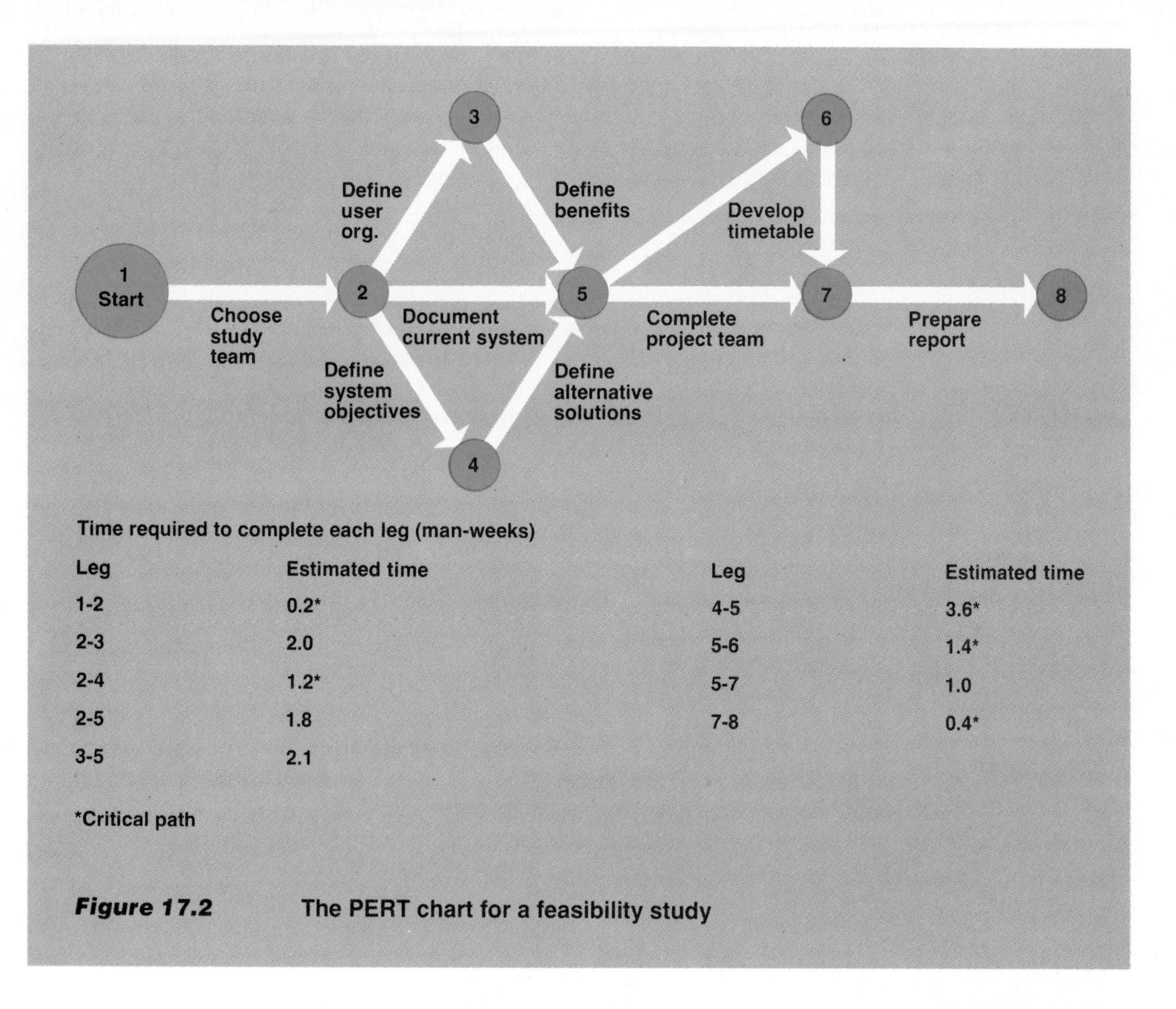

Time required to complete each leg (man-weeks)

Leg	Estimated time	Leg	Estimated time
1-2	0.2*	4-5	3.6*
2-3	2.0	5-6	1.4*
2-4	1.2*	5-7	1.0
2-5	1.8	7-8	0.4*
3-5	2.1		

*Critical path

Figure 17.2 The PERT chart for a feasibility study

Hierarchical grouping The hierarchical grouping is a traditional organization that is headed by a programming manager who assigns tasks to one or more levels of subordinates. The manager may be responsible for the management of programming on several projects at the same time and is not active in the program coding. Ordinarily, each programmer individually designs and codes any program or module for which he or she is responsible, and each ordinarily documents and tests the program or module assigned.

Chief-programmer teams In the chief programming team, each programming project is assigned to a team. The team consists of a senior-level chief programmer, a skilled back-up programmer, and a librarian. Additional applications programmers may be assigned to the team on large projects. The chief programmer has complete technical responsibility for the project and is the principal designer and key coder of the program or programs being developed. The back-up programmer supports the chief programmer and is ready to take the chief programmer's place if necessary. The back-up programmer is often called upon to develop important elements (programs or modules) of the system. The librarian relieves the chief programmer of administrative detail by gathering, organizing, and maintaining the records and documents associated with the project. Any application programmers assigned to the team codes specific modules as they have been designed by the chief programmer.

The chief-programmer organization is often associated with the use of top-down design. The chief programmer writes the code for the top-level control modules and defines the ways in which lower-level modules and components will interface with each other and with the top level. The chief programmer also assigns the lower-level modules and programs to the applications programmers.

Egoless programming teams In the hierarchical-grouping and chief-programmer organizations, each programmer is made responsible for the design and coding of a program or a module. That program or module then becomes an extension of the programmer's ego, and if there are problems with it, defensive reactions can be expected from the programmer. In the **egoless programming team**, there is no chief programmer and each team member does that part of the job for which he or she is best suited. One team member may lead during program design, but take a subordinate role during coding. Team members are expected to check the work of others during coding to learn what they are doing and to catch errors early so they can be easily corrected. The programming team is designed to be a close-knit, democratic group, and members should be willing to accept peer review. Each completed program is the responsibility of the entire team rather than being the product of a single person's efforts. Problems are seen as challenges to the team rather than as errors made by one person.

Controlling project costs

The processes for controlling project costs are related to controlling project time schedules. Careful estimates made early in the project are used as control standards as the project proceeds. Time schedules can be met by adding resources (more people) to the project team. This, of course, will mean that initial cost estimates cannot be met. If time schedules are critical, then greater flexibility in resource use and costs must be allowed. If it is critical that costs estimates not be exceeded, time schedules may have to be more flexible. In any case, cost should be controlled during a project.

Performance standards

Cost control and time schedule control both require the use of performance standards for the project team. There are few general standards that can be applied, but control is possible. It is obviously true that each program or program module will consist of an estimatable number of program instructions in a given language. A programmer can be expected to produce some number of working instructions in that language in one working day. Then, using this data, the time (and cost) required to produce a program can be estimated. Suppose, for example, that we have a program module estimated to contain 80 statements. How much time would we allow a programmer to obtain a debugged version of this module? The number of instructions produced in one day will depend, of course, on the language used, the skill of the programmer, and the complexity of the module. Past experience should give us some indication of how these factors operate. Suppose we find that the production rate for programming in the chosen language has varied between 10 and 22 lines per day with an arithmetic average of 14. Further research may indicate that skill is built through experience and that experience and its lack (on the average) add or subtract a couple of lines per day. Suppose we are using an experienced programmer. We would expect, at this point, an average of 16 lines per day. Analysis of complexity at the level of this module suggests a loss of 1 line per day. By this analysis, we have arrived at an estimate of 15 lines per day, constructed as follows:

Overall average	14
Adjustments	
Experience	+ 2
Complexity	− 1
	15

The next step would be to break these estimates down by the major events involved. That is, how much of this time will be spent on design, how much on coding, and how much in debugging?

Such figures will vary by installation and job. The point is that experience can provide the basis for standards to use in time and cost control.

Control over the quality of work is attained by following proper procedures. Use of top-down design, structured programming, and structured walk-throughs are vital to obtaining quality systems which accomplish system objectives and are easy to maintain.

Controlling system implementation

Implementation consists of organizational change as well as technical change. Organizational change must be managed as much as technical change to have a successful system implementation.

Managing organizational change

This requires more than personnel acquisition and training. Most of the time, a new data processing or information system requires significant changes in operating procedures. To change procedures successfully requires that attitudes change along with actions. The attitude shifts required to accomplish this can be difficult to achieve. The organization, that is, its people, must be prepared for change (the organization must be "unfrozen") before it can be "moved" to a new set of attitudes and actions. The final step is to be sure that the new control and evaluation procedures reinforce and continue the change ("refreeze" the organization into its new mold).

Unfreezing the organization is best accomplished by keeping all employees aware of potential and actual changes as they are planned, including any plans for personnel displaced by the new system. The need for and advantages of the new system should be shared with employees. Involving current operating personnel in planning for the new system is particularly important. It is much easier to accept and support changes one understands. It should be obvious, then, that implementation should begin with the feasibility study, not after the design is set.

Moving the organization is accomplished primarily through training. Training should start as early as possible and proceed on a regular schedule that does not require the trainee to try to take a drink from a fire hose. It is difficult to absorb information presented in large doses at high rates of speed. Control in this area is provided by the training schedule and by regularly scheduled and nonthreatening evaluations of trainee progress.

Refreezing the organization into its new structure and operations requires that control and evaluation processes be altered to reflect the changes that have been made. Equally important, employees must understand the new control and evaluation criteria and procedures and appreciate why they have changed. Clear communication of expectations removes uncertainty. Uncertainty is the worst enemy of morale and productivity in an organization.

Managing technological implementation

Technological implementation consists of hardware and software acquisition, conversion, and testing. Carefully developed time schedules must coordinate these activities with training, programming, preparation of the physical site, development and/or acquisition of forms, and delivery of supporting supplies and materials. Written procedures and close supervision are needed. Special care must be exercised to prevent loss of data during the changeover. Time must be allowed for generation of new files, particularly if manually maintained files are to be placed on electronic online storage. Performance standards can be used to control much of this activity. For example, a trained operator can key data into magnetic storage at the rate of about 8,000 key strokes per hour, including corrections.

Some flexibility should be built into these schedules. Illness of key employees, late deliveries of equipment or supplies, lost orders, and other unplanned developments can cause minor or even major delays. It is better to have a site available a month early, for example, then to have equipment arrive when there is no place to put it. The conversion schedule should be made final only after all preconversion tests are completed with satisfactory results. The schedule should allow time for corrections arising from inadequate test results.

Testing should continue after conversion. Test specifications defining the objectives of the tests and the acceptable results should be carefully prepared. Test procedures also should be prepared in detail. Finally, formal reports of test results should be required. Difficulties experienced during testing can require major design changes to obtain satisfactory results.

Part of implementation planning is provision for continuing system maintenance after conversion. Operating schedules must include time and procedures for preventive and ad hoc maintenance activities. Space must be provided for storage of test equipment and spare parts as well as working room for maintenance personnel.

Summary

The life cycle of a data processing system starts with the feasibility study, the objective of which is to determine if it is economically and technically feasible to develop a new or revised system.

If the decision to develop is positive, the system design phase begins. Functional specifications defining what the system is to accomplish form the basis for developing system design, program specifications, and system procedures.

In the system development phase, programs are designed, coded, and debugged. System testing procedures and conversion plans are completed during this phase. System documentation is largely completed as well.

The implementation phase carries out the remaining activities required to obtain an operating system. The major processes involved are testing and conversion. System documentation is also completed. The final phase of the life cycle is system operation. But remember, maintenance and testing continue throughout the life of the system.

Choice of system hardware and software is a basic feature of system design. The hardware and software used largely determine the technical feasibility of alternate designs. Hardware and software must complement one another and support the approved system configuration. Hardware selection depends on such factors as volume and timing requirements and the nature of the processing required (batch or online, interactive, and so on).

Software selection starts with the operating system and proceeds to specific languages, including the data base management language. The availability of turnkey systems and compilers imbedded in the hardware have made software selection easier for some business users. This is particularly true for small businesses. The user can obtain a hardware-software package (turnkey system) designed to provide the necessary data processing for a particular business application. Also, hardware compilers are beginning to be offered that make the computer on which they are installed "speak" a higher-level language such as COBOL.

Contracts negotiated with manufacturers and other firms offering computers for sale or lease now include penalty provisions for failure to perform as specified. Care should be exercised in negotiating contracts to be certain that the computer investment is adequately protected. Contracts for equipment maintenance are also necessary unless the user supplies maintenance.

The system development process is normally organized under a project team, which is composed of users (operating personnel) and data processing technicians (systems analysts and programmers). The operating personnel are responsible for assuring the effectiveness of the new system. Technical personnel have the responsibility for its economic and technical efficiency.

Project management techniques require that resource and time requirements for the system development process be estimated as a basis for project scheduling. The project time schedule and cost schedule are then used to measure project progress as revealed in regularly scheduled reports.

Key terms

Define the following terms as briefly as possible and then, in a short paragraph, clarify each definition.

Chief programming team
Critical path network
Egoless programming team
Feasibility study
Hierarchical grouping
Program evaluation and review technique (PERT)
Project life cycle
System design phase
System development phase
System implementation phase
System operation
Technological implementation

Discussion questions

1 How does the nature of the processing required affect the specification for
   a CPU cycle time?
   b primary memory cycle time?
   c primary memory capacity?
2 When selecting a computer system, why is it important to know the physical locations of the system users?
3 What are the advantages and disadvantages of each of the following methods of acquiring a computer system:
   a Outright purchase
   b Straight lease
   c Lease purchase
   d Sale, lease-back
4 What things should be included in a
   a purchase contract?
   b lease contract?
   c maintenance contract?

5 Why is software documentation important?
6 Compilers furnished with some computers are part of the hardware. That is, they are a permanent part of the computer system and can be changed only by changing the hardware. What are the advantages and disadvantages of such an arrangement?
7 If a computer costs several hundred dollars per hour and a programmer costs only about $15 per hour, why are higher-level languages so popular even for professional programmers?
8 What factors should be considered in selecting a computer programming language for
   a a computer installation?
   b a particular problem?
9 Should a top manager be expected to write programs
   a in a small firm?
   b in a large firm?
   c in a specialized, research-oriented firm?
10 If a top manager were to write programs, what type of language should he or she use? Justify your choice of language type.
11 On the feasibility team, what are the specific responsibilities of
   a the technical specialist?
   b The operating personnel representing users?
12 On the project team, what are the responsibilities of
   a the technical specialist?
   b the operating personnel representing users?
13 List each of the phases in the data processing project life cycle and indicate the major outputs of each phase.
14 What are the three types of software to be chosen for a new data processing system?

Exercises

1 Develop a PERT chart for the design phase of a system development effort.
2 Develop a PERT chart for the development phase of a system development effort.
3 Develop a PERT chart for the implementation phase of a system development effort.
4 Refer to Exercise 1 at the end of Chapter 14 and specify what language you would prefer for programming the system described there. Justify your selection.

MANAGEMENT ISSUES

Choosing a Computer

Hopefully through this article I can pass on to property owners and managers a few of the lessons I've learned while setting up my own computer system.

At Brennan & Associates we specialize in managing the mechanical portion of large office complexes in the Cleveland, Ohio area. We act as the mechanical agent directly for the property owners and in some cases for their management firms. In either case our function is the same—we perform all preventive maintenance functions, diplomatically answer all tenant heating and air conditioning complaints, provide 24-hour emergency service, subcontract for all major repairs or installations, perform all minor repairs and installations, provide the owners with a monthly report detailing all work performed, material used, labor hours, and lastly provide the owners with year-to-date figures on all the above information.

As you can imagine, it takes a tremendous amount of toil and paperwork to provide the service and the reports required. Our solution, at least with the reports and with some of the service-related problems, was a computer system we developed over a three-year span.

Three years is a long time to devote to a project, and now that it's complete, I'm glad I've done it. However, along the road many painful and sometimes costly lessons have been learned.

The hardware

My first step was to contact the large computer manufacturers and see what they could offer as a solution. By and large they all had good, reliable hardware that can do anything you want it to, provided you want it to do accounts payable, receivable, inventory and a host of related general business applications. Well I wasn't looking for that.

Another drawback was that their mini-systems were not generally compatible with their larger systems, which means that if you run out of core memory, the only solution is to lease or buy one of their big crunchers in two years or load your office up with floppy disks. In the second case you lose and in the first case they win—not a good solution.

Source: Patrick T. Brennan, "Choosing a Computer." Reprinted with permission from the January/February 1979 issue of the *Journal of Property Management*, the official publication of the Institute of Real Estate Management of the NATIONAL ASSOCIATION OF REALTORS®.

Next in line were the service bureaus. In most cases they will custom design all the software and generate all the reports you need in any fashion. Super. However, their schedule of charges look like it was written by a group of attorneys (which it probably was) bent on becoming another utility company.

There's a hookup charge, an equipment rental charge, a time charge, a line charge and a monthly base charge. Most of the charges go up as time goes on so that two years down the road, when you are thoroughly dependent on the system, the new rate schedules might be much more than you can afford or are willing to pay, besides the fact that you never own anything.

Hobbyist gear at the time of my investigation was getting more professional and much more sophisticated, so my next area of research was directed toward this marketplace. Again I found we would be locking ourselves into floppy disks, which might be fine for a dentist's billing needs or a home computer system, but for a true business system they aren't feasible.

The only attractive feature was the price, which all things considered would amount to about $10,000. The final drawback was the system language, which in all hobbyist gear is BASIC. The only acceptable language for a true business system, I've learned, is COBOL or some derivative of it.

My final choice was to buy a computer on a lease-buy arrangement from one of the major minicomputer manufacturers. Our system has ten million bytes of online storage residing on two disk packs, one fixed and one removable. The operating language is COBOL. We have a CRT and a keyboard for input and output and a 60-character-per-second printer for hard copy or reports—beautiful hardware. It should fill our needs for size and speed regardless of how big we grow in the future.

The software

Our computer still had to be programmed, however, to make it spit out the reports we needed, along with year-to-date figures on labor, material, travel time, plus work order forms, scheduling sheets, etc.

The range of programming possibilities was even greater than the hardware types and manufacturers. Our solution was to enlist the service of a professional software house with a good track record, whose range of experience bridges all businesses and computer languages—absolutely the only way to go! I've learned that first, there was no stock program available from anyone that would keep track of preventive maintenance functions on a frequency, skill level, owner or property basis and secondly, to design such a system, although very costly, is much more difficult and time consuming than anyone not familiar with the computer industry can imagine, clearly an impossible task for an amateur.

The complete system we ended up with included hardware and software leases for less than $950 per month—a great investment considering the fact that it more than replaces two secretaries and it can work around the clock, never stops for lunch, requires no hospitalization, sick days or periodic raises and after five years it will work for free.

The computer has become an integral part of our operation, and regardless of who feeds it information, whether it be a secretary, a field supervisor or myself, it always asks for the same information in the same way. No one can feed it information that it cannot act upon and it always acts upon information in the same way, never making a mistake.

It has been a long three years and I don't

envy anyone beginning the task of computerizing their operation. In general I would offer the following tips.

When chooosing hardware

1 Everyone and his brother manufactures hardware these days. Stay with a company that has been around and will be around in the future.
2 Be sure that service is available in your area, but don't buy a maintenance contract. The equipment is extremely reliable and may never need servicing.
3 Buy a system that can handle your future needs. It's amazing how many things you can think of to add as time goes on, and the difference in original cost between a "small" system and a "medium sized" system is minimal.
4 Be sure the system can use some form of COBOL. Most manufacturers have their own derivative of it.
5 Buy all system components from the same manufacturer. Remember, you are not setting up a stereo system.
6 Disk packs, usually 5 megabyte disks, have everything floppy disks and tape systems don't—reliability, speed and volume. Tapes don't have speed, and floppy disks don't have volume.

When choosing software

1 Very few stock software packages will work well if at all. The exception to this are packages that relate to general business categories like payroll, ledger, accounts receivable, accounts payable, inventory, etc.
2 Decide beforehand exactly what information you want to receive from the computer and in what format. The amazing thing about computers is that they can tell you instantly and accurately anything you want to know—if you let them and your programmer know what you want.
3 Be prepared to spend some money on custom software. The machine itself is useless without software and stock packages, unless these are made specifically for the exact machine you've bought and the exact purpose you have in mind [won't solve the problem].

I'm personally aware of some horror stories regarding the installation of computer systems. Since ours went relatively smoothly, I hope I've saved someone some agony through what is normally a long and trying experience. Remember though, when a computer is finally working for you, it's well worth the effort.

Chapter 18 Managing Data Processing Operations

Outline

Data processing activities are a significant element in business firms. The acquisition and use of a computer can easily cost several million dollars per year in a large firm. The information output derived from this outlay is used to guide decisions involving many more millions of dollars of income and expenses each year (Figure 18.1). For this reason, it is important that data processing activities be managed well. It is the purpose of this chapter to provide some guidelines for organizing and operating this important function. In our discussion, we will assume that top management recognizes the importance of data processing operations and has established basic policy guidelines. The guidelines will have answered questions such as the following:

1 What is the mission of the data processing operation?
2 Which data processing decisions will be made by top management, which are to be made by users, and which are to be made in data processing?

Figure 18.1

A teleprocessing network control room **This control panel is the nucleus of a vast data processing network on which depend most of the business activities of one of the nation's larger insurance companies. (Courtesy John Hancock Mutual Life Insurance Company)**

3 What is to be the size of the data processing budget?
4 Who will be expected to suggest new applications?
5 Will users be allowed to go outside the firm to obtain computing services?
6 Will data processing be centralized or decentralized? Will data bases be centralized or distributed?
7 Where will computer services be located in the firm? To whom will the operation report?
8 What criteria will be used in judging whether or not to approve the development of a new system?

Our concern will be directed toward the day-to-day operations within these policy guidelines. We will start with a look at the major parts making up the total data processing function. Then we'll look at the personnel who perform each function, what qualifications they should possess, and how they may be selected, trained, and supervised.

Business data processing organization

The common major functions in business data processing are as follows:

1 Systems analysis and design
2 Computer programming
3 Data processing operations
4 Data management

The most common organizational structure reflects these divisions of function as shown in Figure 18.2 but there are many variations, as we shall see.

Systems analysis and design

As defined earlier, the specific activities carried out in this subfunction are as follows:

1 Feasibility studies
2 Analysis of operating systems
3 Design of new or improved systems (including the selection of computer hardware and software)
4 Supervision of system implementation

Physical location of systems analysts is highly variable. In many firms, particularly smaller ones, this function is combined with computer programming under a single manager. Analysts are being increasingly viewed as a separate group, however. The emergence of data processing personnel as an elitist group has given them almost monopoly control over information systems development in many organizations. Data processors have frequently ignored basic tenets of management and organization in designing

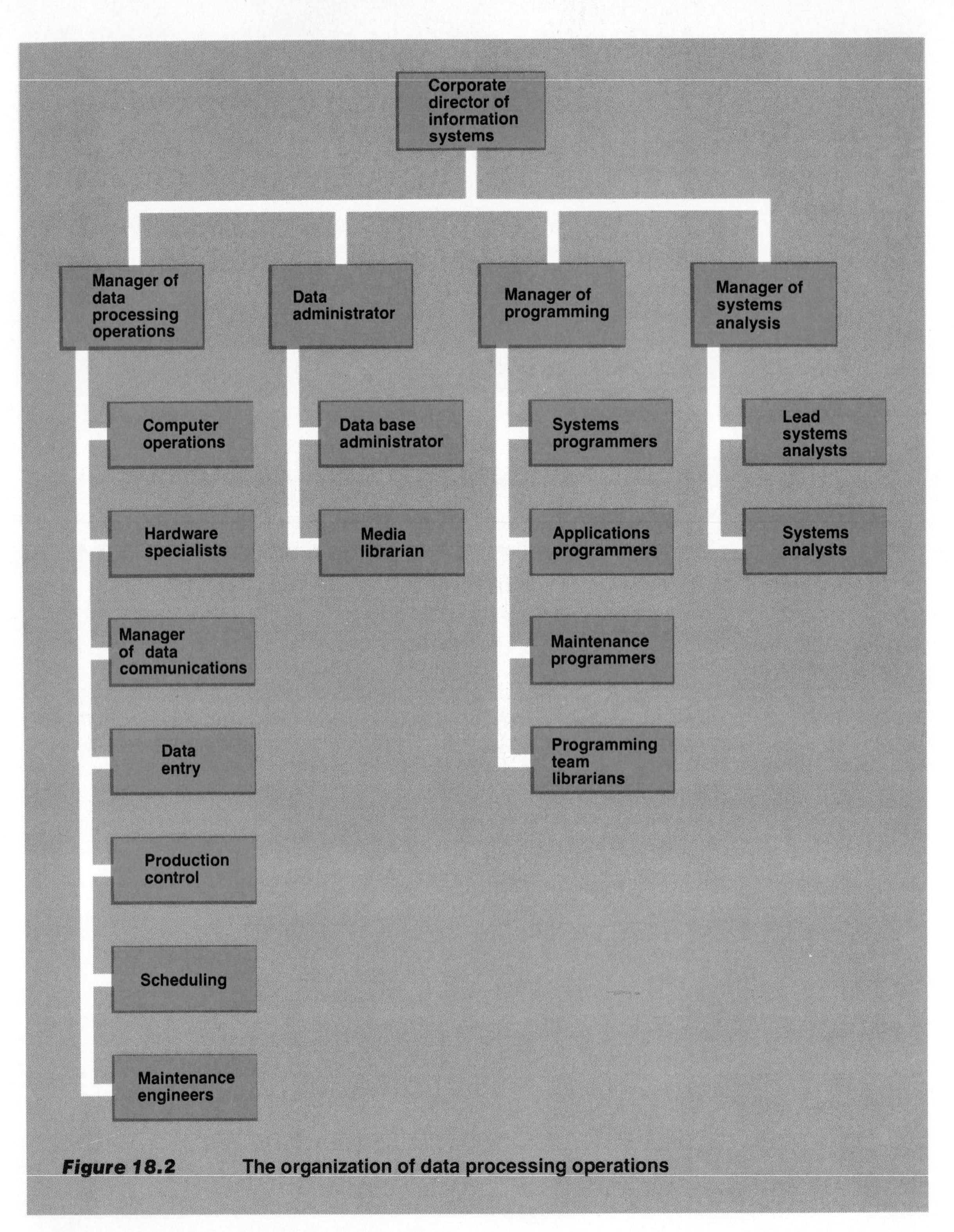

Figure 18.2 The organization of data processing operations

the processing systems that serve as the basis for the management information system. More loyal to their elitist discipline than to the organization that employs them, these people have often striven for the latest (and biggest) hardware utilizing the fanciest software. Some, unfortunately, appear merely to have striven to delay balanced development of the information system function, preferring the comfort of outmoded and managerially ineffective but easy-to-operate data processing systems. Information systems have been oversold, overdesigned, and underdeveloped. Projects have been started or abandoned with little regard to their worth to the organization. Operational departments lacking in data processing knowledge have been at the mercy of the data processing elite.

An attempted solution to the unresponsiveness of the data processing elite has been to place one or more systems analysts in each operating department. These analysts, hired by and responsible to the manager of an operating department, are, it is argued, loyal to the interests of that department. Also, the analyst(s) in each operating area can fully understand the processing and informational needs of that home department. The systems designed by a resident analyst reflect the procedural and informational requirements of that operation. Training and experience within the departments create analysts attuned to and responsive to user needs. This alleviates the past tendency to design systems for technical efficiency but with little regard for the intended function of supporting the decision-making activities of management.

Among supporting arguments for locating analysts in operating departments is the alleged inability of computer personnel to work effectively with each of the many functional (operating) departments of an organization. Because of their training and their position as part of the data processing elite, systems personnel tend to think of their work as dealing with data processing problems, not business problems. Many systems analysts and programmers were originally trained in nonbusiness fields such as engineering and mathematics. Their subsequent training in systems analysis often omitted practical business orientation, emphasizing data processing procedures instead. Even the analyst who has received business training has seldom had any practical experience in most of the operating areas where he or she is expected to work.

Disadvantages of user departments acquiring their own systems analysts do exist. Integration within the information system is hindered. Improvements in methods for processing data are slow to be adopted. Standards for documentation, design, and programming are hard to enforce. Decentralized personnel tend not to keep up with technical developments in their field. Activities within a centralized processing department (economies of scale still favor a single department) are difficult to schedule when user departments determine development schedules and systems timing features. Of course, a data processing department that does not adjust its schedules to the needs of users is labeled unresponsive and finds expansion of processing systems is inhibited. Nevertheless, the need for some central coordination of information systems is undeniable. Standards of quality must be enforced for the work of every analyst. Analysts must be kept informed of what is being done elsewhere. Knowledge of the current systems in related areas is vital to efficient and effective design of processing or information systems in a given area.

Project management is widely used to control development projects in data processing. It involves the planning and carrying out of an integrated effort leading to the attainment of a specific limited objective. A special organization (project team) is established to plan and carry out the activities required to meet the specific objective and to dissolve after the objective is attained.

Project management initially involves planning of the work to be done and development of the team required to carry it out. Objectives, schedules, and budgets must be set out in considerable detail. First, the total project must be broken down into measurable work units. Expected cost, completion schedule, performance quality, and resource requirements are then developed as standards for each work unit. Organizational units of the project team are assembled and assigned responsibility for particular work units. It is desirable that all work groups (especially systems analysts and programmers) participate in the development of the performance standards for the work units assigned to them. During project implementation, a project management control system monitors progress in terms of the established standards.

Computer-based techniques, such as linear programming and critical-path planning, including PERT, are valuable in this phase. Computer programs are available that make personnel assignments on the basis of job requirements and skill levels for systems analysis and programming personnel.

Except on small projects, the use of a computer program to keep track of schedules, costs, and personnel assignments is required. The entire project starting with the feasibility study can be planned and monitored by some programs. These programs incorporate planning techniques such as critical-path analysis (PERT) to schedule projects, develop detailed budgets, and then assess progress against these schedules. These so-called project management systems differ widely in effectiveness. Some are highly inflexible, making the modification of project schedules difficult. In the performance monitoring area, some systems report performance in detail and provide little real information about deviations from projected schedules. A good project management system, whether computer based or not, should provide for participation of project personnel in setting goals, time schedules, and individual personnel assignments and provide continuous project status information (work units completed and costs incurred) while assuring orderly completion of the project.

Project teams are usually led by a senior systems analyst and involve one or more representatives of operating management in the user departments affected by the system. Small systems with clear-cut objectives may be designed by a single analyst and programmed by a single programmer. As already mentioned, in many instances the analyst and programmer may be the same person. This approach is most common in small organizations.

Computer programming

The three types of computer programming (systems, applications, and maintenance) are usually functionally separated in large data processing installations. The systems programming and program maintenance functions are sometimes assigned to the operations function. Applications programming may be assigned to a systems development department along with systems analysis.

Data processing operations

This function includes a variety of activities, and large installations often separate them completely as subgroups. Scheduling is done by the operations manager or a staff assistant. Computer operators comprise a subgroup. Data entry and production control are sometimes supervised by one person but are most often separated in a large installation. Computer hardware specialists and data communications specialists are often assigned to this area. In very large installations, these people plus some top analyst talent may be assigned to a planning section.

Data management

Data management is carried out by the data administrator, who oversees the activities of the data base administrator and the media librarian. The responsibilities of persons in these three positions will be discussed fully in the section that follows.

Data processing personnel

The entire information system function (ISF), not just the data processing function, has been affected by computers. Data processing personnel are not the only members of a business organization who speak a technical language and use sophisticated skills. Market researchers, management scientists, operations researchers, control statisticians, and economists use the computer to apply sophisticated analytical tools in assisting managers to carry out their planning and control functions. Because of the nature of this book, however, we will restrict ourselves to the technical personnel involved with computerized data processing and the special problems that arise in recruiting, training, and supervising these technicians.

These special personnel problems are not the only challenge faced by managers while planning and controlling modern systems. The problems associated with system acquisition and development were discussed in Chapter 17. Controlling errors in data processing was discussed in Chapter 15. The discussions in Chapters 15 and 17 have touched upon some of the personnel problems discussed here. The emphasis now, however, will be on position descriptions (what the position does) and specifications (what qualifications are required to hold the position).

The data processing manager

Historically, **data processing managers** came primarily from two sources. Some worked their way up through operations or programming and systems analysis. Others were chosen from the major using department and, most frequently, were accountants. The increasing emphasis on information systems and the recognized importance of the ISF to the organization have led to a change. Professional managers from all operating areas are being placed in charge of the extended information system departments. They are being charged with objectively developing plans and an organization that promises a profit-oriented information system and close managerial control over the costs of developing and operating that system. This means that these new managers must possess the following knowledge and skills:

1 A complete knowledge of the organization, its objectives and goals, the physical or economic activities it is engaged in, how it is organized to carry on those activities, and the rationale for its organizational structure
2 The knowledge and skills to motivate and control a group of highly skilled technicians; in other words, the manager must understand the personal motivations and aspirations of all types of information systems personnel and know how to lead and control them in the application of their specialized skills
3 A working knowledge of management practices, including the tools of management science and accounting
4 A general knowledge of data processing techniques, including types of available hardware and software

Data management

There are three major positions in this area—the data administrator, the data base administrator, and the media librarian.

Data administrator The person occupying this position is responsible for the overall process of data management. This position interfaces with all parts of the firm in developing and maintaining an adequate, up-to-date inventory of data in whatever forms and degrees of access that may be required by users. The data administrator is not responsible for the technical aspects of file and data base design and maintenance, however. That task is reserved for the data base administrator. Any competent administrator familiar with the firm and possessing some knowledge of data processing and information systems can serve as data administrator.

Data base administrator The person occupying this position needs a high level of technical expertise in file structure and file handling. This person is responsible for the technical aspects of design and maintenance of individual files and data bases in the firm. Only if this individual performs at a highly expert level will a firm be able to approach the ideal of a single integrated management information system.

Media librarian Someone must maintain control over tape, disk, and card files of data and programs. This person, the **media librarian**, should be separated from programming and machine operation to provide adequate control. Access to stored master files and programs by programmers and operators should be closely controlled.

Systems analysis and design

Systems analysis and design have already been described in Chapters 12 and 13. Because of the nature of their duties, systems analysis and design personnel require more education than other data processing personnel; usually, they hold a college degree.

Systems analysts should possess the following characteristics:

1. A general knowledge of the organization, including its objectives and goals, the physical or economic activities it is engaged in, how it is organized to carry on those activities, and the rationale for that organizational structure
2. A knowledge of management practices, including the tools of management science and accounting
3. A working knowledge of data processing techniques, including computer programming
4. An up-to-date, broad knowledge of data processing hardware, including both electronic and nonelectronic devices
5. A high level of disciplined creativity, including the ability to express ideas clearly and persuasively in person or in writing
6. An orientation to detail work that does not inhibit creativity
7. An ability to work cooperatively and effectively with technical (programmers) and nontechnical (operations) personnel and managers

Systems analysts must be able to develop innovative improvements to current systems and sell those improvements to data processing management and the managements of operating departments. They should have a broad knowledge of currently available equipment of *all* types. Given such knowledge, they are less likely to uneconomically restrict the systems to electronic equipment.

Experienced analysts are often assigned the responsibility of project leadership. **Project leaders** are responsible for the analysis, design, development, and implementation of an application system. They lead a team of analysts and programmers doing the technical work. They also work closely with the operating personnel in the departments impacted by the system. Leadership abilities are just as important as technical skills for such persons. If analysts are to be expected to assume such responsibilities, they should be given opportunities to develop leadership skills.

Systems analysts as a group aspire to management positions. Encouraging them to train for functional or systems management positions is helpful in keeping them on the job. Closing of such career paths to them encourages systems analysts to seek these positions in other organizations. Management training also tends to improve their ability to understand the problems of operating managers and to be able to establish effective communication with such managers.

Computer programming

There are three levels of programmers at work in most installations: **systems programmers, applications programmers**, and **maintenance programmers**. All these programmers should possess certain characteristics.

1 A thorough knowledge of the language or languages in which programs will be written at this installation
2 A knowledge of general programming techniques and general relationships between program and hardware features

All programmers should understand and be able to use general techniques such as modular and structured programming. They should also be aware of significant interactions that can exist between programs and hardware and between programs and the system executive. For example, for the use of virtual storage systems to be most efficient, programs run under the executive must be properly designed. To prevent excessive executive overhead, swapping of program "pages" between primary and secondary memory should be minimized. Programs must be designed to reduce interactions between widely separated portions of the program. In some instances (for some executive operating systems), it may pay to reproduce frequently used subroutines at several points in a program. Hiring programmers only on the basis of their knowledge of a specific language or set of languages can lead to ineffective use of hardware.

Failure to use good programming techniques will lead to problems. All programmers in an installation must understand and follow a consistent and rational set of programming guidelines.

3 A strong orientation to detail

Programmers must possess the patience to spend the time to assure that every symbol in a program is correct. A misplaced comma, reference to the wrong variable in a little-used subroutine, or failure to include an infrequently exercised control routine can all cause expensive system failure or a managerially ineffective system. This detail orientation is especially important during program debugging and maintenance.

4 A disciplined, logical creativity

Programmers must translate flowcharts or HIPO diagrams into computer code without unauthorized embellishment. An excessive desire to develop innovative coding will lead to programs that are extremely difficult to maintain at best and can cause system failure at worst. At the same time, a lack of creative development in new programs makes the development of innovative new systems impossible.

Programmers tend to fall into two categories as to career aspirations. One group desires to become systems analysts and, eventually, managers. The other group enjoys the technical challenge of programming. These latter persons tend to avoid social interaction, including receiving close direction, and have no interest in a management position. Systems programmers tend to fall in the second category.

In addition to the common characteristics outlined above, each type of programmer should possess certain special characteristics.

Systems programmers Systems programmers should have the following characteristics:

1 A detailed knowledge of the hardware system and the system software that controls it

In addition to maintaining the system software, systems programmers should be involved in decisions concerning hardware additions and deletions. They also help to train applications and maintenance programmers in the use of system software and provide them with assistance in debugging complex applications programs.

2 A thorough grounding in the theory of computer language structure and syntax

Systems programmers are expected to maintain compilers and assemblers, develop enhancements to them, and develop needed utilities. A knowledge of the principles of language development and structure is essential to the efficient performance of such duties.

In short, a systems programmer should be a full-fledged programming professional trained in computer science. Care must be exercised to be sure the systems programmer has a sufficiently pragmatic orientation to be interested in furthering the objectives of the organization, not just an interest in pushing back the frontiers of computer science. Experimentation with esoteric and untried software techniques of doubtful productivity can be very costly. It is true that a computer can be made to do almost anything in the way of symbol manipulation, but that does not mean that it should be put to every task that might be suggested. Dedication to achieving optimal fine tuning and enhancement of the system executive for a multiprogrammed or timeshared system containing features such as dynamic storage allocation and virtual storage can lead to excessive experimentation. The resulting downtime and loss of production are often of greater cost than the benefits realized from the successful software changes.

Applications programmers These programmers should possess the following characteristics:

1 A general knowledge of the objectives of the organization and the activities involved in pursuing those objectives

2 At least an introductory knowledge of accounting and management science if involved with administrative data processing or management information systems

With only a knowledge of coding techniques, programmers can experience difficulty in properly interpreting flowcharts or HIPO diagrams. Lack of communication among management, systems analysts, and programmers often can be traced to lack of knowledge of the organizational activities by the programmer. In one installation, the hourly payroll program required excessive maintenance. It had been designed and programmed by two systems analysts—programmers with backgrounds in teaching high school mathematics and English literature. Pay scales were written into program instructions rather than being entered as variable parameters subject to change. Obvious control checks were omitted from the program, resulting in one employee receiving a check for a negative amount for a pay period in which he worked only a few hours. Unfortunately, neither the employee nor the bank where the check was presented for payment was bothered by the minus sign on the amount. The later adjustments that were required had to be carried out entirely by hand. Reprogramming would have been required to perform all the adjustments on the computer. The payroll program had to be completely redeveloped to correct these and other deficiencies.

Maintenance programmers Program maintenance activities are highly important. An enormous number of elements are involved in most computer systems. Most large programs are *never* completely debugged. There is a continuing need for enhancement or repair of major programs. Skills of value in maintenance programming include:

1 Experience in program development
2 A high level of analytic ability

Almost nothing of substance has been written on debugging techniques. Substantial skill and experience are required to develop an excellent maintenance programmer.

Program maintenance is made feasible by complete and consistent documentation supplemented by a program maintenance history. The history describes each corrective or enhancement change, with emphasis on the techniques used to isolate any bugs discovered. Since some bugs are a result of corrections of other bugs during maintenance, the corrections made should be described in detail. Major computer programs interact in complex ways with themselves, with system software (executives, compilers, and utilities), with the hardware, and at times with other application programs. Small changes in a major program can result in failure of some other software element. Careful collection of bug types, their frequencies of occurrence, and the isolation and correction techniques proved to be successful can pay dividends in improved maintenance.

Programming team librarian The **program librarian** is responsible for keeping track of program revisions and program documentation. This can be the first project assignment for an applications programmer trainee.

Data processing operations

Data processing operations consist of three subgroups—computer operations, data entry, and production control—all involving a variety of positions.

Data entry and processing control These clerical workers and machine operators are responsible for preparing data for entry, for preparing jobs for entry into the computer system, and for checking and distributing output.

Machine operators who key data onto cards, tapes, or disks for batch applications will probably continue to make up the bulk of these workers. Also involved in card-using systems are the operators of the other card processing machines (sorters, reproducers, tabulators, and so on). In online systems, data are entered directly from operating stations. Regardless of the entry point, all workers involved in data entry should be carefully trained to reduce the incidence of errors in data entry. In online systems, the systems designers must give special attention to simplifying data entry and developing intensive editing procedures that forestall the entry of erroneous data to the maximum extent feasible.

Production control clerks assigned to postprocessing operate forms bursters and decollators for separating output pages and multiple copies. They also operate binding equipment to bind output reports before routing.

Scheduler A person—the **scheduler**—who plans daily work flows in data preparation and batched computer processing may be required for large installations.

Computer operator **Computer operators** set up the machine and mount and remove tapes, disks, and printer forms as required by jobs being processed. On multiprogrammed and timeshared systems, control over a large part of this activity is channeled from users through the system executive program. The operator appears to perform as directed at the console (by messages on a typewriter or CRT). However, operators of modern, complex computer systems are trained technicians interacting with a sophisticated operating system to attain maximum efficiency from the hardware. Even so, they usually receive their training as apprentice operators and seldom have a college education.

Maintenance engineers Electronic equipment requires preventive maintenance on a regular schedule as well as repair in the event of breakdown. The technicians responsible for this activity, the **maintenance engineers**, require background training in electrical engineering and mechanical maintenance and specific training in routine maintenance procedures for the equipment in the system being maintained. Generally maintenance is obtained on contract from the equipment supplier, but it can be provided by user personnel. If maintenance is to be supplied by employees of the user, the employees should be intensively trained by the equipment supplier or suppliers. In mixed vendor systems where components from a number of suppliers are intermixed, fewer problems are encountered when maintenance is carried out by user employees.

Career ladders in data processing

In its 1980 survey of salaries in data processing, *Datamation* magazine identified 55 different positions. Most of the positions discussed above exist at several levels in large installations, as shown in Figure 18.3 which depicts career ladders in information systems. In general, entry into the field is by way of one of the jobs at the bottom of each career ladder. For example, in data processing operations (Figure 18.3b), the entry-level job would normally be computer operator trainee, data entry operator trainee, or production control clerk trainee. In smaller installations, the trainee positions might not exist. New people would start as full-fledged operators and clerks and be trained on the job.

Obviously, especially talented persons may not need to climb all levels of each job on their way to the top. Often they will be moved laterally through a series of jobs to better prepare them for supervisory and management positions. (Some common lateral shifts are indicated in Figure 18.3.) Indeed, some positions tend to be filled most often through lateral shifts. For example, the hardware and communication specialists in DP operations (Figure 18.3b) usually transfer from computer operator and from systems analysis. Other common shifts are from data entry or production control to computer operator, from computer operator to programming, and from programming to systems analysis.

The distinctions between different occupations shown in the figure do not always exist. It has been common, for example, to combine programming and systems analysis into a single set of positions called programmer analysts. Most experts seem to prefer keeping these two activities separate, however.

To clarify the titles shown in Figure 18.3 refer to Table 18.1 where the definitions used by *Datamation* in their salary survey are found.

As one moves toward the top jobs in data processing, the opportunities for advancement obviously decrease. For this reason, it is not uncommon to see analysts, supervisors, and managers moving out to line management positions which allow more opportunity for advancement to the ranks of top management. This is particularly common for analysts at the senior- and lead-analyst levels.

Managing business data processing

Business data processing should be planned and controlled much like any other business activity. Objectives and goals for the overall performance of the function should be established and used as yardsticks to measure its performance. Standards of performance should be established for each subfunction (systems analysis, programming, operations) and the performance on each project and by each employee should be measured against these standards. The technical nature of the work performed should not be used as an excuse for not providing as tight control for data processing as for any other activity. Nevertheless, the *special* problems of staffing (selecting and training personnel), organizing, and controlling data processing activities cannot be ignored.

Selection of personnel

The first step in successful recruiting of appropriate personnel is the preparation for all positions of complete, detailed job descriptions and job specifications, which were discussed in Chapter 13. As noted there, a job description describes the work itself, and a job specification identifies characteristics job applicants must possess. Job descriptions and job specifications are also useful in carrying out wage and job evaluations and in defining career paths (promotional opportunities for employees) during manpower planning.

Positions in DP operations may be filled from within the organization or with outside applicants. In a new installation and in implementing new systems that will result in work force reductions, recruiting from within is preferable, particularly for machine operation, data preparation, and applications programming. The danger in filling systems analysis positions initially from within is that most of the employees to be removed will have had experience only in a single department of the company and will possess very limited knowledge of data processing equipment and processes. The training courses provided by computer vendors and most private short-term schools concentrate on EDP systems. Often all that is learned is an ability to develop flowcharts for use in programming an application and a rudimentary knowledge of some programming language. The result is an employee with limited knowledge of alternatives.

If personnel are recruited from within the company, the positions available should be announced and all interested employees allowed to apply. Review of personnel records to develop a list of qualified persons will undoubtedly miss interested persons with qualifications as good as those on the selected list. Knowledge of the best background for each job in data processing is not definitive. Who would believe that a person trained to teach American history in secondary schools would develop into a top-flight systems programmer (largely through self-study) within three years after being accepted as a

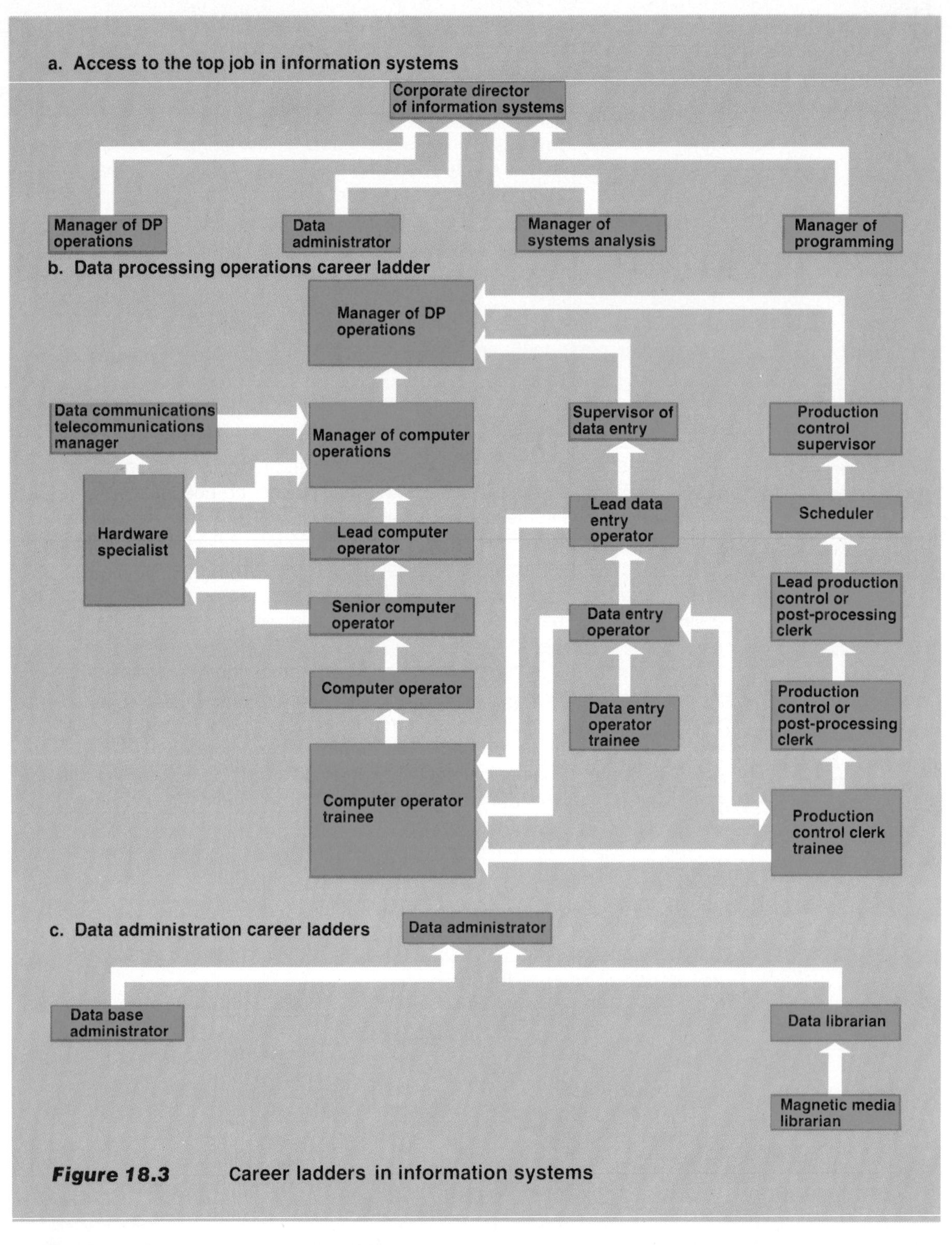

Figure 18.3 Career ladders in information systems

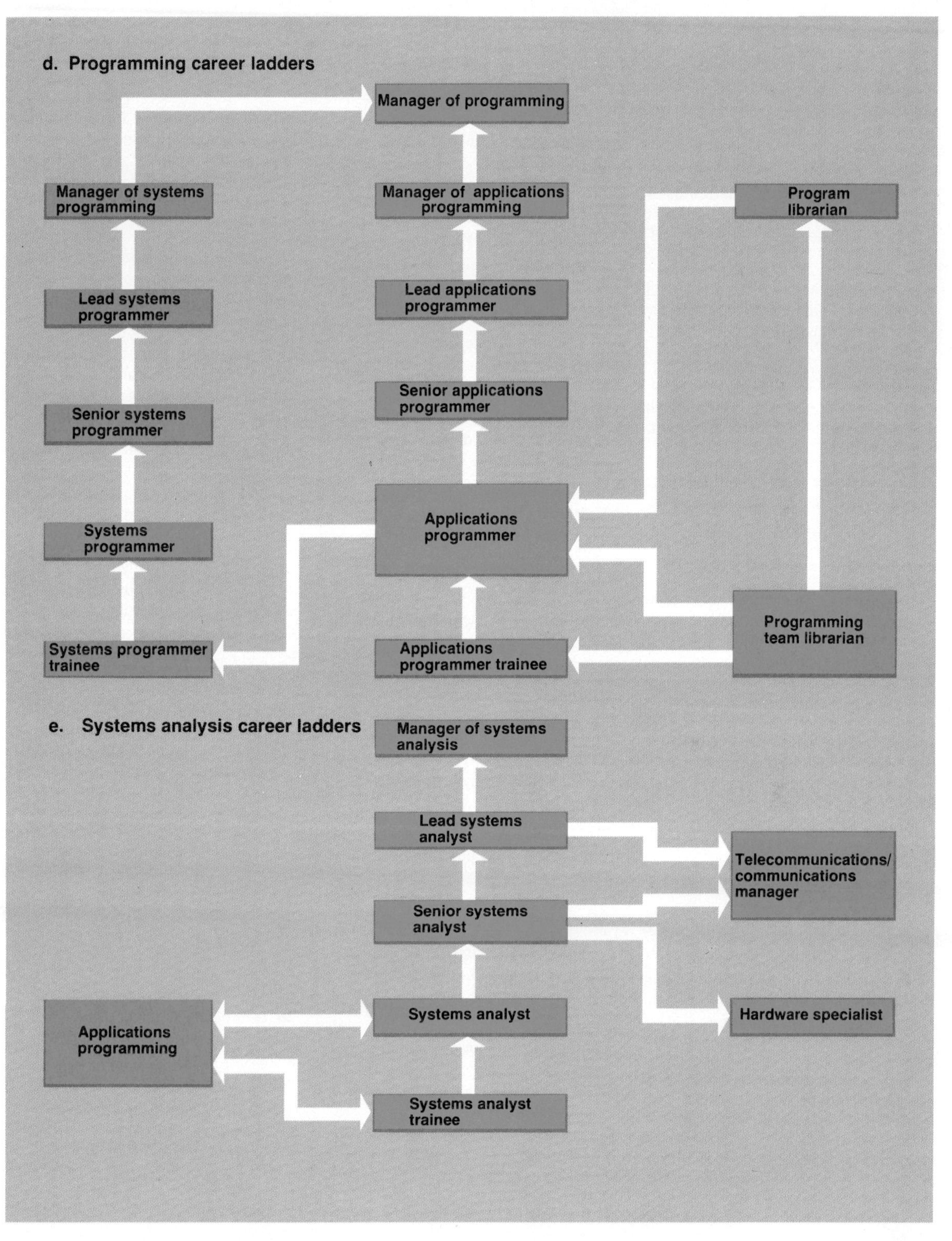
d. Programming career ladders
Manager of programming
Manager of systems programming
Manager of applications programming
Program librarian
Lead systems programmer
Lead applications programmer
Senior systems programmer
Senior applications programmer
Systems programmer
Applications programmer
Systems programmer trainee
Applications programmer trainee
Programming team librarian
e. Systems analysis career ladders
Manager of systems analysis
Lead systems analyst
Telecommunications/ communications manager
Senior systems analyst
Applications programming
Systems analyst
Hardware specialist
Systems analyst trainee

The following 55 job descriptions were used as the basis for our salary survey questionnaire. DP managers were asked to match their job categories as closely as possible.

1 Corporate Director of Data Processing or MIS: The top executive for all computer processing.

2 Administrative Assistant: Primarily concerned with money matters and sometimes with personnel administration.

3 Technical Assistant: A member of the corporate director's staff. Usually the head of advanced planning for the DP function.

4 Services Coordinator/User Liaison: Coordinates DP activities with those of other functions or departments.

5 Division or Department Director of DP or MIS

6 Administrative Assistant

7 Technical Assistant

8 Services Coordinator/User Liaison: 5–8 are in the division or department staff; they are directly parallel to 1–4 but their influence may be less.

9 Manager of Systems Analysis: Analyzes how DP is applied to user problems, designs effective and efficient DP solutions.

10 Lead Systems Analyst: Assists in planning, organizing, and controlling the activities of the systems analysis section.

11 Senior Systems Analyst: Confers with users to define DP projects, formulates problems, designs solutions.

12 Systems Analyst: Works with users to define DP projects or project segments or iron out details in specifications.

13 Systems Analyst Trainee: Usually has some DP experience. Expected to spend a good deal of time learning rather than producing.

14 Manager of Applications Programming: Responsible for the development of effective, efficient, well-documented programs.

15 Lead Applications Programmer: Assists in planning, organizing, and controlling section activities.

16 Senior Application Programmer: Works with program designs or specifications.

17 Applications Programmer: Usually works on only one or a few applications.

18 Applications Programmer Trainee: Is learning to program. Usually works under direct supervision.

19 Programming Team Librarian: Keeps track of program revisions.

20 Manager of Systems Analysis/Programming

21 Lead Systems Analyst/Programmer

22 Senior Systems Analyst/Programmer

23 Systems Analyst/Programmer

24 Systems Analyst/Programmer Trainee: 20–24 positions cover both the analysis and programming functions.

25 Manager of Systems Programming: Plans and directs the activities of the OS programming section, assigns personnel to projects.

26 Lead Systems Programmer: Assists in planning, organizing, and controlling the activities of the OS programming section.

27 Senior Systems Programmer: May specialize in the support, maintenance, and use of one or more major operating systems. Is able to work at the highest levels of programming.

28 Systems Programmer: May specialize in the support of one or a few operating system components or subsystems.

29 Systems Programming Trainee: Has a good background in DP and knows or is learning assembler language.

30 Program Librarian: Responsible for maintaining the online and offline libraries of production programs in source and object form.

31 Manager of Data Base Administration: A still relatively new position which has the functions of planning, organizing, and scheduling the activities of the data base administration section.

32 Data Base Administrator: Analyzes the company's computerized information requirements, coordinates data collection and storage needs, organizes data.

33 Data Communications/Telecommunications Manager: Responsible for design of data communications networks and installation and operation of data links.

34 Data Communications Analyst: Specializes in network design, traffic analysis, and data communications software.

35 Technical Control Specialist: Primarily concerned with hardware selection, operation, and maintenance.

Table 18.1 **Job description guide**

36 Manager of Computer Operations: Responsible for the operation of computers including scheduling, assignment of operators, and monitoring of efficiency.

37 Manager of Data Processing Operations: In charge of computer operations, data entry, production control, and post processing, but not of systems analysis or applications programming.

38 Lead Computer Operator: May be responsible for the operation of large-scale computers for the duration of an eight-hour shift or the operation of a remote site.

39 Senior Computer Operator: May be responsible for all operations on a medium-scale computer or for console operator of a large machine.

40 Computer Operator: Assists in running the computers and may operate the central console in the absence of the senior operator.

41 Computer Operator Trainee: Usually assigned to mounting magnetic media, loading printers, or working on a peripheral subsystem, always under direct supervision.

42 Magnetic Media Librarian: Maintains the library of magnetic tapes, disks, and/or cartridges.

43 Post Processing Clerk: Operates forms-bursting, decollating, and binding equipment. May also deal with microfilm and microfiche output.

44 Production Control Supervisor: Responsible for setting up and scheduling jobs for processing.

45 Lead Production Control Clerk: Responsible for the data control function for the duration of an eight-hour shift or the data control function of a single site in a multisite organization.

46 Production Control Clerk: Prepares jobs for processing, enters the appropriate job commands, gathers output for routing.

47 Production Control Trainee: Learning the production control function and works under direct supervision.

48 Data Entry Supervisor: Responsible for a staff which performs data entry and verification functions.

49 Lead Data Entry Operator: Responsible for data entry during an eight-hour shift or for data entry at one site in a multisite environment.

50 Data Entry Operator: Qualified to operate one or more data entry devices, requires only general supervision.

51 Data Entry Operator: Has not yet become fully qualified to operate one type of data entry device.

52 Staff Consultant/Trainer: Helps in debugging and in understanding system messages.

53 Librarian: Responsible for the library of technical documentation.

54 Word Processing Supervisor: Responsible for a staff that operates word processing equipment.

55 Word Processing Operator: Qualified to operate intelligent typewriters, WP systems, terminals for text editing/WP.

Table 18.1 (cont.)

programmer trainee? As another example, one of the best systems programmers the authors have ever met had only a high school education.

In a new installation, highly skilled technicians (systems programmers, maintenance engineers) may have to be hired from outside. Other personnel can often be selected from present employees who can then be specifically trained for the positions they will fill. Machine operators and clerical personnel are easy to train and usually require no more than a high school education. Systems analysts and programmers are in a different category. If the installation is to involve a large, complex system, some of these people must have a background in the work. In a small system restricted largely to routine processing, the advantage in having analysts and programmers who know the business may well outweigh the disadvantage of lack of technical skill. Experience seems to indicate that the technical skills can be learned quickly but knowledge of the business takes time to acquire.

Identification of potential programmers and systems analysts is difficult. Inexperienced candidates for programming or systems analyst positions are often given an aptitude test, and those scoring sufficiently high are interviewed and their educational and work records checked carefully. Aptitude tests have not proved to be an infallible indication of programming ability. Proficiency tests are sometimes administered to experienced programmers, but personal interviews, examination of work and training records, and direct contact with former employers are more common.

Tests measuring manual dexterity, mechanical aptitude, and/or clerical aptitude have generally yielded satisfactory results in choosing computer operators and data preparation personnel.

Personnel training

All employees at the supervisory level and above, whether or not they are involved in computer processing, should receive some information systems training. In fact, it would be well to include key personnel in all operating departments in this group. This training should include an introduction to basic concepts of information systems, computer hardware and programming, and the implications of computer usage for management practice and operating procedures. Such training can be important in reducing resistance to new systems. Training programs of this type are available from consulting organizations, computer vendors, professional associations, and colleges and universities. They also can be provided within the organization when employees with proper skills are available to teach the courses.

Programmers and programmer trainees also can receive training in courses offered by computer vendors, technical schools, consulting firms, professional societies, and colleges and universities. However, much more training is given within user organizations. Experienced programmers and analysts train their less experienced colleagues while they are involved in projects or in formal classes.

Systems analysts have more limited opportunities for training. A review of the skills and knowledge required by analysts indicates they cannot be easily obtained in part-time or short-term study. A college degree in business administration supplemented by intensive training in data processing techniques and equipment seems a reasonable prerequisite. Working under an experienced analyst on several projects after formal training is completed is recommended before an analyst is considered fully trained. Training programs are being developed in a few colleges and universities that involve actual project experience along with classroom training. However, familiarity in a particular industry and firm gained from two or more years of experience is advisable before considering the analyst to be fully trained.

Summary

The data processing operation is staffed by specialists speaking a cryptic technical jargon and engaged in highly technical work. Special problems arise in recruitment, training, and supervision. The management of data processing must recognize the differing skill levels required by systems analysts, programmers, and operating personnel and must also be aware of the differing career aspirations of individuals within these job classifications in order to obtain maximum effort and cooperation from them.

Internal organization of data processing has usually been along functional lines. The exact organizational groupings are not critical as long as the need for planning and analysis, system analysis, programming, machine operation, and data control are provided. Some organizations have found that locating systems analysts in user departments makes for a more responsive data processing function, one more clearly oriented to the solution of management problems than to achieving technical efficiency.

Project management has proved to be an effective means of organizing systems development efforts. This process involves the creation of a special organization (team) for planning and carrying out an integrated effort leading to attaining a specific limited objective such as developing a particular processing subsystem.

Key terms

Define the following terms as briefly as possible and then, in a short paragraph, clarify each definition.

Applications programmer
Computer operator
Data processing manager
Machine operator
Maintenance engineer
Maintenance programmer
Media librarian
Production control clerk
Program librarian
Project leader
Project management
Project team
Scheduler
Systems analyst
Systems programmer

Discussion questions

1 What are the specific skills that should be possessed by the person occupying each of the following positions?
  a Systems analyst
  b Systems programmer
  c Applications programmer
  d Maintenance programmer
  e Data processing manager
2 Argue that systems analysts should be placed in user departments rather than a centralized department.
3 How should computer scientists be used in data processing operations?
4 What are the advantages and disadvantages of using the project management approach to design and installation of new processing systems?

5 There are three reasons why systems analysts should receive management training. What are they?
6 What are the differences in skills needed by the data administrator and the data base administrator?
7 Turn to Table 18.1, page 524, and study the various levels of programmer positions listed there. Why would so many levels be used, even in a very large organization?
8 How do the responsibilities of lead systems analyst differ from a senior systems analyst as described in Table 18.1?
9 Draft a position specification describing the education and experience requirements you would think appropriate to the position of lead systems analyst.
10 Identify what *you* consider to be the major problem in managing business data processing. Justify your choice.
11 What are the major subfunctions in business data processing? Briefly describe each of the subfunctions.
12 Why should career paths in data processing be clearly spelled out?
13 How does a programming team librarian differ from a media librarian?
14 How would one expect the personality and work habits of a systems programmer to differ from those of an applications programmer?
15 Some experts believe that programming and systems analysis (particularly systems design) require different skills and interests.
   a Develop justifications for this view.
   b Develop arguments against this view.

Exercises

1 Suppose it takes an entry-level systems analyst an average of two years to work through each of the levels on the career ladder. How long will it take the analyst to become manager of systems analysis in a very large organization? (See Table 18.1, page 524–525, for job levels.)
2 To whom would you assign each of the following specific tasks?
   a Entering a new working program into the program inventory and physically securing the master copy of the program and related documentation
   b Providing physical security for the master copy of the latest version of a developing program and its related documentation
   c Project manager of a project to develop an inventory accounting and control system
   d Responsibility for coding the order processing program of the inventory accounting and control system
   e Responsibility for designing the order processing module of the inventory accounting and control system

3 Visit a large data processing installation and a small data processing installation in your area and collect the following information from each of them.

a How many positions are there for

(1) systems analysts?

(2) programmers?

(3) computer operators?

b How many levels of positions are there in each of the career areas listed in a?

4 Compare the results of your findings in Exercise 3 for the large and small installations. What general conclusions do you feel are justified?

Note: Exercises 3 and 4 can be assigned to teams of students as a class project with several sizes of installations included.

MANAGEMENT ISSUES

Holding On to Data Processors

If your DP department is beginning to resemble a revolving door with more people going out than coming in, maybe you should try Lourie Davis' approach.

Davis began training clerical employees as programmers, added career path and technical training for all levels of employees, threw in a competitive salary program —and slashed turnover by 83% in three years at Blue Cross and Blue Shield of Oklahoma's Computer Services Division here [in Tulsa].

The division had a 50% turnover rate in 1977. The new policies were instituted in 1979, and the rate dropped to less than 9% in 1980.

Nine employees are halfway through the company's programming trainee course, and five of them have already been placed in better jobs. Three will move into teleprocessing openings, one will be a DP auditor and another will join Davis' department, Planning and Control. Davis said the remaining four probably will be placed soon.

Every employee in the Computer Services Division is required to enroll in at least 40 hours of career path training every six months during office hours. These courses include introduction to IMS, DL/1 programming, cost benefit analysis, technical writing and project management concepts.

During 1980, employees earned 2,881 hours in 29 individual subjects. This includes technical training contracted for with Advanced Systems, Inc. (ASI), as well as in-house courses taught by Blue Cross personnel in their own specialties. Over 140 employees completed at least one course.

When workers complete training in certain areas, they are eligible for advancement, Davis said. This is in addition to a regular six-month salary review conducted by the company's personnel department which attempts to bring wages "in sync" or perhaps a little higher than those offered for equivalent jobs in the Tulsa area. Salaries and grade levels of Blue Cross employees are adjusted, as needed, after each six-month review, Davis said.

Commenting on the effectiveness of the training programs, Davis said that some employees who have been with the company only three and a half years have advanced to the systems analyst level and are performing very well in this position.

She attributes the drastic reduction in turnover directly to the company's new training and salary policies. "A lot of the people feel that as long as they are being challenged and trained, have the opportunity to

Source: Abridged from Lois Paul, "High Turnover? Try Lourie Davis' Approach," *Computerworld,* March 9, 1981, 7. Copyright 1981 by CW Communications/Inc., Framingham, MA 01701—Reprinted from COMPUTERWORLD.

do interesting work and are being paid well, there is not much reason to go somewhere else."

Davis became head of planning and control in 1979. Her first move was to organize an executive training session that brought in IBM representatives to teach Blue Cross vice-presidents about computer usage in management. . . .

Davis and several other Blue Cross DP professionals teach the bulk of the programming trainee course. The students are learning COBOL, assembler language coding, JCL, Easytrieve and systems analysis. Upon graduation, they will be considered trained to the associate degree level, she said.

Next on the drawing board for Davis is an expansion of the training program to include major systems training for all employees responsible for interfacing with each of the company's major production systems. This will include over 200 people in as many as 10 different departments in four major corporate divisions.

"We want to train them to make the most effective use of the systems," Davis said, noting that this should result in higher quality, increased productivity and enhanced customer service.

Special Option

Auditing Online Systems

The nature of online systems

Online integrated systems feature random-access storage and direct data entry. Transactions data are captured by online devices and used to keep all online files updated. Very few systems are totally integrated online systems, but many large subsystems (inventory and customer orders, for example) are. In the online system, the computer performs all the functions of the bookkeeper and the accounting clerk, keeping the accounts updated and preparing reports. Normally, the computer also handles all random inquiries to the system and is responsible for proofing input data and recognition and reporting of unusual or unwanted developments. Of course, the computer must be programmed to do these things, which can be a difficult and costly task.

System controls must be built into online systems to a greater degree than in unit record systems. Online integrated systems tend *not* to retain transactions data in any form. Ledger accounts frequently contain only a summarized account balance. Not only do transactions data disappear after being entered into an online system, but certain external controls, such as batch totals and interdepartmental crosschecks, cannot be used.

Two basic problems must be faced in using an online system. The first is the problem of correctly identifying each transaction at its point of capture. If more than one type of transaction is carried out at an activity station, transactions must be kept clearly separate. For example, an online terminal on the receiving dock at a warehouse is used to enter both receipts from outside vendors and returns from using departments. Although both transactions result in an increase in inventory, they must be handled differently.

The second problem is the problem of control. If data are entered directly into the computerized system, how do we prevent errors? How do we catch and correct errors? That is, how do we audit the system?

The first step is to do all we can to prevent erroneous entries. Data entry should be carefully supervised and controlled by the system. Each item should be edited for form and for reasonableness. Attempts to enter alphabetics for numerals (or vice versa) or a value that is unreasonable should not be accepted by the system. The presence of proper confirmation or authorization codes should be checked *before* accepting the input as valid. All errors should be carefully recorded as a check on operator training and system procedures.

The problems faced in attempting to audit online electronic systems are easily identified.

1 Data and records are captured and stored as invisible magnetized spots on magnetic tapes, disks, and strips.
2 Interdepartmental and interpersonal crosschecks on data accuracy are no longer present.
3 The processing procedures are stated in computer programs that also carry them out. These programs are written in special languages and stored on a machine-sensible medium.
4 Online integrated systems retain only the current status on each account. Transactions documents and daily journals usually do not exist to provide an audit trail.
5 Electronic accounting systems are frequently developed by nonaccountants (systems analysts and programmers) as part of a total information and custodial processing system.

Auditing techniques

Early batch systems were often audited by proofing input controls and then checking the computer outputs for correctness. The assumption of this "around-the-computer" technique is that if inputs are correct and outputs are also correct, the processing in between must be okay. This technique cannot be used with online systems since all records are stored on the system and updated on the system. The computer *is* the entire physical data processing system. Therefore, if one audits around the computer, one audits *around* the system, that is, one does not audit the system.

The next attempt was to audit "through the computer." The input and the internal processing is proofed and the output is assumed to be correct. The most common tools for this technique are reading programs and running test data. Since programs other than one's own are usually very difficult to follow, reading programs to find errors can be unsuccessful.

Running test data is a necessary part of acceptance testing for a new system, but is difficult to use as an auditing technique for online systems. To be effective, the test data should be run as part of the ordinary system input.

Entries to online records would then need to be reversed. Since the tests should exercise system controls, some records would need to be put into a condition that was either an error or that triggered control actions. For example, in checking the operation of an inventory system, one would want to learn if reorder points were being honored. Therefore, balances for some items would be driven below the reorder point. The resulting order would have to be intercepted and reversed. In addition, the fictitious orders from inventory would have to be reversed; the routines for receipts and returns would need to be reversed. A series of adjusting entries would be needed to return the affected accounts to their correct balances. In an operating online system, it would be easy to create some real problems with these activities. In addition, some of the reversing entries might be missed. Most important, procedures for reversing such entries are not normally a part of the system. Further, it must be possible to make test runs unannounced. Ideally, test data would go through the system as part of the normal input stream. The use of special false accounts for system testing is inadequate since real accounts are then open for manipulation.

The techniques used in auditing around and through the computer have proven inadequate for very large, complex systems, particularly those involving online input, quick-response, and on-demand management reports. It is now recognized that some of these difficulties can be overcome by engaging the computer as an ally in the auditing process. Much of the detailed checking performed by auditors can be carried out by the computer. In fact, the computer can often do a better job than people. It does not get tired or bored and it is very fast. Even before online systems were common, auditors who had learned computer skills started to use the computer as an aid in the auditing process. Two basic approaches have been developed, use of auditing programs and continuous audit processes.

Auditing programs are really nonprocedural languages. They allow auditors to easily perform auditing functions, such as sampling accounts for internal or external verification, and to compile totals and other check statistics. Continuous audit processes usually involve some form of sampling. A complete audit trail is provided on a random and/or judgemental sample of transactions. The sample normally includes all transactions on an adequate sample of records and all transactions involving reversing or adjusting entries. The computer can be programmed to perform continuous audit processes automatically.

Conclusion

Online systems have two basic problems, identification of transaction entries and control of errors. Effective auditing of online systems starts with careful editing of inputs. It ends with use of the computer as an ally in the auditing process. Purposeful and random sampling can be used to preserve an audit trail of critical transactions and an adequate sample of routine transactions.

COMPUTERS AT WORK

Reducing Errors

"With good risks taken in 15 minutes, our underwriters have to make fast decisions," says Bill Conway, who is president of US Facultative Management Corp. (USFMC), a New York City-based reinsurance firm. A better way had to be found to provide his producers with the service they demanded while ensuring that his company was protected from errors that could damage reputation and profitability.

A combination of perseverence and ingenuity brought the answer with a Basic Four System 610 computer and customized applications software developed expressly for Mr. Conway's business. The program, called Underwriting Assistance Program (UAP), has spelled accuracy, convenience and speed for USFMC. Since it began operation in its first-phase configuration two years ago, the UAP helped reduce the company's error rate to less than 1%. "Everyone is encouraged to use it because of its ease of operation," says Mr. Conway. "It's a working tool that's used from top management to the clerical level."

Mr. Conway knew that the large mainframe at the parent company's offices was already preempted by numerous ongoing projects. "It's difficult to get individual projects handled on a mainframe," he says. "I would have had to submit my needs well in advance and simply wait my turn. Once it was in operation, I couldn't have the personal access I needed. Having my own computer was the only answer."

The dedicated computer in the USFMC office provides the underwriters with the information they need, when they need it. In ten seconds, for example, an underwriter can learn if his company is already committed on the same account. This prevents incurring excessive liabilities. Once specifics are obtained from the caller, the system is interrogated to learn the account's status. An answer is quickly flashed on the terminal's screen.

This information directs the underwriter on a course of action. If the company is already committed, even if the commitment was made only minutes earlier at a branch office, he knows the level of commitment. The UAP was designed to provide control over four operating offices. To ensure a complete data base, data on each discussion is entered in the system—specifically whether the account was authorized and under what terms, bound or declined.

Aggregate limits of liability carry important meaning in the reinsurance industry. In

---

Source: "Reinsurance Firm's Computerized Record-Keeping Reduces Errors," *The Office,* July 1980, 84, 90.

two geographic areas, earthquake-prone and hurricane-prone, companies like USFMC must know at all times precisely how much total liability they have incurred. Excessive liability in an earthquake zone, for example, could spell financial disaster for the reinsurer if a quake should strike. These factors were built into the UAP. As certificates are added or dropped, the records stored in the data base change automatically, reflecting up-to-the-minute status of liability in these areas.

Before Mr. Conway applied EDP technology to his operation, things were a lot different. As each call came in, three clerks searched through mammoth files to find an account's status and supply the information to the underwriter who waited on the telephone. This laborious task was repeated many times throughout the day.

According to Mr. Conway, "There were no computer programs available for our work. Nobody was doing what underwriters needed." With their computer system, combined with the application software, "The underwriters now have all the answers they always wanted but could never get," he says.

Many of these answers were supplied by Paul Helfner, an analyst-programmer, and approved Basic Four software vendor. It was his effort that made possible the successful UAP. Engaged by the computer supplier to work with Mr. Conway in applications programming for his computer, Mr. Helfner first had to learn what the reinsurance industry was all about: its jargon, paperwork and operation. All figured prominently in the software development.

Mr. Conway stresses the importance of creating a system that relates to people in their own language rather than that of the programmer. "I insisted that only terms readily understood by underwriters could be used in the program. The only compromise I had to make was in the use of the word 'input,' " he says. "Other than that, Paul Helfner developed a program that required no words unfamiliar to underwriters."

Working with a standard data base package he had already developed, Mr. Helfner made the necessary modifications to suit the needs of USFMC. "I have had an excellent relationship with Bill Conway," he says. "He knows what he wants and says exactly what he means. This made my job a whole lot easier. The computer also is easy to work with, and it's very reliable."

The host computer, located in Manhattan, has multiple video-display terminals, a central processing unit, disc memory and a line printer. Through the Basic Four remote communications capability, the system "talks" to video terminals in Chicago, San Francisco and Atlanta. According to Bob Borab, account manager, both he and George Cotsonas, Basic Four branch manager, consider the USFMC computer their finest installation.

Planning for the future is the surest way to avoid unpleasant hindsight discoveries. Mr. Conway looked well ahead when he began developing the UAP. "Just about everything on the system was planned from the first day," he points out. "This way we were certain that problems wouldn't be encountered later on in succeeding phases. We expected to make our operation completely self-sufficient someday."

Originally, three phases of development were anticipated. However, the UAP's success has yielded additional, more ambitious projects. A claims program under test at present, for example, will allow an underwriter to determine the complete history of an account. All claims settled against the account in the past, at any point in its history, will be available for instant retrieval.

According to Mr. Conway, the future of the minicomputer is secure in American business. "The summary-type information, however, must be produced on mainframes at corporate headquarters," he said. "Only they have the capacity needed for handling large amounts of information and synthesizing it into top-level management reports. What we'll be seeing more of is the use of minis to control everyday operations. These, in turn, will be linked through communications to mainframes. The low cost of minis, and their suitability to fit into the office scheme, have earned them their place."

Special Option

The Social Impact of Computers

Introduction

Computers are being hailed as the basis of a postindustrial revolution. The industrial revolution substituted mechanical power for human effort in the production of goods. The computer substitutes electronic power for human brain power. Its ability to store, retrieve, and manipulate data to produce information gives it some powers previously thought to be uniquely human. It has already allowed us to solve problems we could not solve on our own because of the multitude of calculations they involved. It is impossible to think of an area involving human thought where the computer has not been applied. It keeps our accounts, plays games with us, directs our machines, helps us explore our universe, and solves complex mathematical problems in a few seconds. It is even used in creative ways—writing music, drawing pictures, creating unique paintings, and illustrating books. It also tutors students and tests their knowledge, writes poor poetry and worse novels, checks student themes for correct spelling and grammar, and helps us speak foreign languages.

Such a general-purpose, powerful tool has a significant impact on our society. All of us are affected whether we realize it or not. The too-brief discussion below attempts to trace some of these effects. It only hints at some of the problems computers have created. A complete treatment would fill several books the size of this one.

Data and information processing

Data processing

The computer is unmatched in its ability to collect, store, analyze and disseminate data and information. As computer systems have become cheaper, the computer's use as a data processor has spread to all levels of society. It is hard to believe that in the early 1950s computer experts were predicting that less than 100 computers could be sold in the United States! Its use as an accounting tool was not foreseen. Without this processing power we could not adequately clear the checks used to transfer money within our society. Neither could we have the convenience of credit cards.

Decision support

Computers are increasingly involved in providing information in support of managerial decision making. Simulations provide managers with answers to questions such as "what if?" and "how much?" that allow the manager to weigh the implications of different actions *before* a choice is made. Even the homemaker is able to use a home computer to assist in menu planning to obtain the proper balance of nutrients, taste appeal, and cost.

Teleprocessing and communications

Access to computers through terminals is now commonplace. Transactions data are input directly from the checkout counter in the supermarket and from the factory floor. Executives, salespeople, and other employees can access the computer's store of data and its computational power from any remote site. Computer programmers are now working from their homes, linked with the computer at the office by terminal and telephone line. Through electronic message systems and teleprocessing networks, executives can contact fellow executives, issue directives to workers, and perform complex decision making tasks from any place with a telephone.

Consumers are able to shop and pay bills without leaving their homes. The power to transfer data and information between computers may soon bring us a checkless society. Electronic transfer of funds will replace paper checks. The technology is available, it only requires acceptance by society for implementation. You could buy an automobile without writing a check for even the down payment. Your purchase could be financed by the automatic extension of credit from your bank, all handled by computer-to-computer messages triggered by a properly identified request from you through a terminal at the auto sales agency. You could make a purchase at any major retail store by dialing your telephone and you could have the purchase immediately paid for by an electronic transfer of funds from your bank account to the bank account of the retail store.

Home computers are able to perform consumer data processing, maintain tax records, balance your checkbook, help monitor your diet, and schedule social events.

Computer-assisted design and manufacture

Computers are given graphic capabilities and used to assist in the design of products. Whether this will lead to better designs that are more fully adapted to individual needs remains to be seen. Some experts are now predicting this result.

Computer systems now control manufacturing processes. Machines can be run by control messages that are either read from a magnetic tape produced on the computer or received directly from the computer itself. Some experts foresee the joining of computer-assisted design and computer-assisted manufacture to make custom products, each unit produced to order for an individual customer. At the very least, computer-controlled robots should take over many dangerous and monotonous jobs now performed by humans.

Government data processing

Computers have increased the efficiency of many government operations. Payroll records, budget data, social security records, and income tax data are all examples. Without computerized record keeping, the social security system would be impossible to administer. Use of the computer makes it possible for the Internal Revenue Service to process the millions of income tax returns received each year. State and local governments also use the computer for processing income, retail sales, and property tax forms. The volume of records involved in these systems would be almost impossible to handle without computers. They are also used in welfare systems and in setting up and controlling budgets.

Military data processing

Computers were initially developed to handle the computational problems associated with artillery and military logistics. In addition to these tasks, they are now used by the armed forces in payroll and inventory control and for all types of accounting. They also provide control over military weapons such as the DEW (Defensive Early Warning) line and other military intelligence systems. Large and complex simulations are used to train military personnel and to assist in stategic planning and the design of weapons, aircraft, and other military equipment.

Legal data processing

Lawyers now receive legal searches for precedent cases conducted by computers. Word processing computers assist in preparing briefs, wills, contracts, and other legal documents. Laws themselves are codified and stored on computers for ready access, both as they are being prepared in legislative bodies and for reference purposes after they have been enacted.

Medical data processing

In addition to keeping the accounting records for doctor's offices (micros), clinics (minis), and hospitals (mainframes), computers are deeply involved in the practice of medicine. They maintain patient records for quick access and monitor the progress of critical patients. They assist in laboratory work, supervising blood tests and other analyses. They even analyze symptoms and suggest possible diagnoses. They also keep track of drugs, analyze poison symptoms, and monitor drug use. There is practically no area of medicine in which computers are not involved.

Entertainment

Computers play games with us at home and in bars, restaurants, and amusement arcades. They also create many of the visual effects we see on our TV sets and at movie theaters. They aid in developing background music for our science-fiction movies. They draw pictures and create all kinds of visual images. Computers have become indispensable in the entertainment industry.

Social issues in computer usage

Depersonalization

Standardization of records and transaction inputs are required to obtain efficiency in computerized processing systems. Numerical codes are easier to process than personal names. As individuals in society go on record in more and more computerized systems, the use of numerical codes for identification must expand. There will be increasing pressure for use of a common identifier such as the social security number. Already, the IRS, the armed services, universities and colleges, state driver's license departments, insurance companies, banks, credit bureaus, most hospitals, and many other organizations are using the social security number as a common identifier. The danger of the use of a universal identifier is that the separate records can easily be consolidated to create massive personal dossiers on individuals.

Standardization also leads to inflexibility. Personal needs are ignored in favor of system efficiency. Individuals are often made to feel helpless and frustrated when trying to deal with such systems.

Data integrity

Data entered into computer systems must be entered correctly, stored securely, processed properly, and reported responsibly.

Data should not be gathered without a legitimate reason. The temptation to gather data that is not really needed can be strong. For example, knowing the age, marital status, occupation, education, and political affiliation of each customer is not necessary to process each customer's charge account. Obviously, these facts might prove useful in studying demographic patterns associated with different types of buyer behavior. Is this a strong enough reason to invade the privacy of every customer?

Data should not be used for purposes other than that for which they were collected. For example, data on individual expenditures available from an electronic funds transfer system should not be revealed. Would you like everyone to know every expenditure you have made this year?

Data error should be controlled. Invalid data should be purged quickly when discovered. Horror stories abound of citizens arrested for stealing their own car because, after being stolen, it was recovered and returned to them, but still listed as stolen in an uncorrected data file. Not only have citizens been falsely arrested, but some have had their record of arrest for "grand theft, auto" turn up in their file long after the unfortunate incident was over. Similarly, one person had a new car repossessed because the check covering the monthly car payment bounced. The person's account number had been incorrectly coded at the bank and the check was charged to a nonexistent account. It has been found that incorrect data entered into a credit file might stay there for years without correction. Some systems provide no process for correction of errors in billing systems. The firms involved seem to have concluded it is cheaper to acquire a new customer than to retain an old one.

Data security

As we have previously discussed, businesses must control the processing of and access to data stored in their files. Access to files of business data by competitors or their agents can compromise trade secrets and other proprietory data. Data on individuals not only need to be accurate but also must be protected from unauthorized scrutiny, manipulation, or destruction. Our society expects that confidential data on individuals will be protected from unauthorized or malicious access and manipulation. We also expect that businesses will not allow others to steal our money. For example, there have been several occasions when enterprising individuals have opened bank accounts merely to steal. They have taken the batch of computer-coded deposit slips that come with the account and distributed them to deposit form boxes in the bank lobby. Other customers have used them to make deposits, writing in their own name and account number. Unfortunately, the computer only reads the coded account number. In one case, the thief reportedly closed out his account and escaped with over $60,000 after having distributed his slips on a payday for the largest employer in the area where the bank was located.

Individual privacy

Private and public organizations build files on individuals. Most people have a medical history with the doctor and/or hospital. Their history as a student follows through to the highest degree earned. A history of debts, payments and, possibly, defaults is found in an individual's credit file. Tax records trace income and some expenditure patterns. Bank records reveal monetary wealth. An electronic funds transfer system would list all expenditures by amounts, dates, and to whom paid. Just imagine how much would be revealed if all these records could be combined. With modern computer systems and a standard identifier (social security number?) this *is* possible.

Who has access to these individual data files? Only those with an authorized need to know should have access to any particular file. Certainly, casual perusal of such files should not be possible. Most of these files are accessible from a computer terminal anywhere in the world, subject only to knowledge of access methods and a few authorizing codes. How easy it would be for government organizations to practice individual surveillance. The idea that someday Big Brother could easily be watching all of us no longer seems far fetched.

Hopefully, the dangers of improper consolidation and access to personal data files will be resisted. All of us must remain alert to protect ourselves. Our most important contribution to our own privacy is to see that the business files *we* control are adequately protected.

Economic effects of computers

What is the impact of computers on our economy? One of the reasons for using computers is to replace human effort. Won't this lead to mass unemployment? Studies to date are not definitive but it seems safe to conclude that computers and office electronics provide a net addition to employment. A quick look at the help-wanted advertisements in your local paper will reveal that programmers, operators, systems analysts, and maintenance engineers are in strong demand. In addition, thousands are employed in the production of computers and computer components and in the maintenance and repair of such systems.

It must be recognized, of course, that the people replaced by computers cannot all become operators, programmers, systems analysts, or maintenance engineers. Office workers replaced are normally clerks and typists. Can they be retrained to move up to higher-level jobs as EDP specialists? Similarly, the production workers replaced by a computer-controlled robot cannot all find employment producing and maintaining computer-controlled robots. The effects of computer-assisted manufacturing are just beginning to appear and have not been studied.

In the office, studies to date have indicated that only a fraction of the computer installations result in direct lay-offs. A definitive study has not been made, but it does appear that over 80 percent of the time computers are installed they do not replace people directly. They are known to have slowed or stopped the growth of clerical staffs in many offices, however. Whether these results are offset by the added employment in production and maintenance of computers and computer-using products has not been determined.

Conclusion

Computers are said to be bringing an information revolution to modern society. They have invaded every area of human endeavor involving the processing and dissemination of data and information. They are now invading the factory in the form of computer-controlled machine tools and robots. All aspects of our lives, social, political, economic, and technical are affected. Computers are even changing the way we are entertained and educated.

Computer use has raised some important social issues. It is said that our society is being depersonalized, that individuality is being supressed and conformity encouraged. The integrity of data contained in computer systems must be maintained. The data contained in these files must be pertinent and needed. It must be entered correctly, manipulated properly, and reported responsibly. Information must be protected against malicious use by controlling its accessibility and how it is used. Individual privacy must be protected at all times.

Computers are a significant factor in our economy. Some fear that they will cause mass unemployment as they take over office and factory jobs. The evidence to date, while incomplete, does suggest that the introduction of computers into an office results in a direct reduction in the workforce in only about one-sixth of the cases. It seems safe to conclude that, up to this time, the net effect of computers on employment has been positive. The use of the computer has upgraded the quality of the work force required however, and displaced workers from standard clerical tasks to computer operation, programming, systems analysis and maintenance engineering. These trends are expected to continue in the near future.

DATA PROCESSING DISPUTE

Computers and Our Privacy

Now that computers have been used extensively for two decades in the management of personal data files by government and private organizations, just how does the American public view the impact of computer systems on society, especially in terms of computers and privacy? How do these attitudes compare with the views of key business and government leaders (including computer industry executives)? Are there demographic, ideological or other social factors that help explain the shape of public opinion? And, most important of all, what does current public and leadership opinion suggest about the environment in which computer uses will be unfolding in the 1980s?

Data for answering these questions is now available from a national survey conducted by Louis Harris & Associates, in a public service project sponsored by Sentry Insurance. The public survey consisted of a representative sample of 1,513 adult Americans interviewed in November and December of 1978. The leadership survey was composed of 618 interviews with representatives of 11 selected groups: public sector representatives (Congress members, federal regulatory officials, law enforcement officials, and state insurance commissioners), and leaders from the private sector (business employers, computer industry executives, life insurance executives, credit card company executives, credit industry executives, commercial bank executives, and doctors). The computer industry interviews were with executives from 34 computer hardware or software firms selected from Standard & Poor's Directory.

First, some of the good news. The Sentry survey found that the public and most leadership groups held some highly positive views about the value of computers to society. Sixty percent of the public feel that "computers have improved the quality of life" in the United States. Demographic groups that scored substantially higher than the public average (5% or more) included younger adults (18 to 29), the college educated, professionals, Easterners, males, those earning over $25,000 annually, and liberals.

Those groups scoring substantially lower than the public in seeing such value to computers were people over 50, those with only eighth grade educations or lower, those earning under $7,000, and women. All the leadership groups, both business

---

Source: Abridged from Alan F. Westin, "The Impact of Computers on Privacy." Reprinted With Permission of *DATAMATION*® magazine, and governmental, scored substantially higher than the public's 60% in seeing computers as improving the quality of life. Not surprisingly, 97% of computer executives believe that computers have had this effect.

The survey also asked whether those interviewed agreed that "because they can use more personal details, computers make possible more individualized service to people." Almost two of three members of the public (64%) agreed with this statement. This view was especially strong among males, executives, and higher income groups, and was less accepted by the eighth grade educated, lower income earners, proprietors, and political liberals. All the business executives, law enforcement officials, and state insurance commissioners held this view more strongly than the public, while federal regulatory officials, Congress members, and doctors were more skeptical. Again, computer executives supported this view fervently, at 86%.

At the same time, both the public and leadership groups see some clear and present dangers in the way that computers are being used to process personal data. Eighty percent of the public believe that "computers make it easier for someone to obtain confidential information improperly on individuals." Higher income groups, professionals, and proprietors held such a view even more strongly than the public average, as did all the government leaders and doctors. Though they scored lower than the public, majorities of all business executives and law enforcement officials still registered such a sentiment. And 67% of computer executives saw that their own technology as having this effect today.

Turning from the general tendency to immediate dangers, the survey asked whether respondents "believe the present uses of computers are an actual threat to privacy in the U.S." Fifty-four percent of the public said yes, a jump from 34% who recorded such a view when the same question was asked in 1976. Somewhat surprisingly, 53% of computer executives—a majority and only a point off the public view—adopted the same judgment. Among other leaders, all government officials believed computers threaten privacy today more strongly than the public did, while all business leaders scored below the public.

A final measure of negative judgment came from the question asking respondents whether they believed privacy was adequately safeguarded today in computer systems. Fifty-two percent of the public replied that they felt it was not, and 53% of computer executives expressed the same view. Government officials and doctors felt much more strongly that safeguards today are not sufficient.

The survey also listed a number of situations in which computers might be used and asked the respondent to indicate whether such uses seemed justified or not. An overwhelming 87% of the public feel it is justifiable to use computers to match employment records with welfare rolls to detect improper welfare payments. Business and government officials were about the same or even higher in expressing support for such practices, and 92% of computer executives held this view. Somewhat surprisingly, 92% of the public who classified themselves as political liberals also said that this use of computer systems was justified. Only Southerners, blacks, and persons with eighth grade educations scored substantially lower than the general public. . . .

Several uses of computers drew opposition from majorities of the public. Sixty-eight percent of the public said it was not justifiable for employers to have access to a central computer file of people who had been treated for mental health problems. All business and government officials held such a view even more strongly, with computer executives at 83%. Similarly, 51% of the public said it was not justifiable for the state to have a central file of individuals given prescriptions for addictive drugs, a position held by 61% of computer executives and by higher-than-public-averages by all the business and government officials. . . .

In a question that tapped people's general feeling about the balance between computer benefits and computer dangers, the survey asked for agreement or disagreement with the statement "If privacy is to be protected, the use of computers must be sharply restricted in the future." Almost two out of three members of the public (63%) expressed their agreement with the statement, a view especially strong among white collar workers and union members.

Not surprisingly, such a position did not sweep the computer executive sample. Only 8% of computer industry officials believed that sharp restrictions on computer use are needed to assure privacy protection in the future. On this issue, business and government leaders were substantially less in agreement that restrictions were needed than the public, though still considerably higher than computer officials. . . .

The Sentry survey demonstrates that while the public is most immediately worried about issues such as energy, inflation, and war and peace problems, most Americans now see privacy as one of the central quality-of-life issues of our time. For want of a better term, "privacy" has been adopted as the way to express the public's demand that powerful institutions engage in open, equitable, and procedurally fair relationships in dealing with individuals as consumers, employees, and citizens. To do this, the public wants a better balance to be created between information subjects and information keepers in both the private and public arenas, and especially where high technology information systems are involved.

Though the survey shows that the public generally appreciates the positive contributions of computer use, it also reveals a deep-seated fear that computer uses are not yet sufficiently controlled and safeguarded. When almost two out of three Americans say that computers will have to be sharply restricted in the future—far ahead of what leadership groups feel—the minimum conclusion is that the public does not believe that existing privacy protections are dealing adequately with the basic problem.

Furthermore, had the study been conducted *after* the Three Mile Island nuclear mishap, I believe a majority of the public—not just 43%—would have said that technology is almost out of control. Similarly, I think more than 63% would have said that computer use will have to be sharply restricted in the future.

Thus there may well be trouble ahead for some large new federal information system projects that have been proposed for the next decade, such as the IRS Tax Administration System, the FBI's Criminal History Project, and the Future Process Design of the Social Security Administration. The same may well be true of state and local government "big system" projects, as well as private sector developments such as EFT (Electronic Funds Transfer) proposals, and some of the plastic card, personal data base plans that are being discussed.

The reasons will be not "only" concerns over privacy of the kind explicitly registered in the Sentry survey. Public concern will expand outward to uneasiness over the effect of very large systems on equitable administration and provision of meaningful fair procedure rights in decision-making, and in the very capacity of such complex systems to be managed successfully in the real world of government and private organizations.

On this aspect, the Sentry survey offers a warning to the computer industry, computer users, and public policy makers. The privacy issue is not solved and fading away. It is going to become more intense in the next decade, as "privacy" serves as the handle with which a still considerably alienated public seeks to define and install greater measures of individual or social control over an organizational system whose powers have been vastly increased by computer uses in the last 20 years.

Glossary

Access Method Refers to the process used to locate a data item in storage or on an input medium. *See also* **Direct (random) access, Sequential access.**

Access time 1. The time required to locate an address on a storage device and return its content to primary memory. 2. The time required to locate a storage location in order to transfer data into it.

Accounting machine 1. A machine that prepares accounting records and usually is key-activated. Automatic accounting machines read data from offline storage media such as cards or tapes, and automatically produce accounting records or tabulations, usually on continuous forms. 2. A punched-card lister with the ability to sum fields as it lists the card contents onto a paper form.

Accumulator A register in which the result of an arithmetic or logic operation is formed.

Accuracy The degree of freedom from consistent error in a given direction (bias). Contrast with **Precision.**

Action data Data that require a response. For example, a customer request for delivery of a specific item.

Activity report A report that shows the amount of activity in a firm over a period of time.

Address An identification, usually a number, for a specific location in storage. *See also* **Relative address.**

Address register A register in which the address of data to be operated upon or of the next instruction is stored.

Alphanumeric A character set containing letters, digits, and, usually, special characters such as punctuation marks. Also called alphameric.

American Standard Code for Information Interchange (ASCII) An 8-bit data code comprised of a 4-bit binary zone code on the left and a 4-bit binary numeric code on the right developed by the American National Standards Institute in cooperation with a number of major computer manufacturers.

Analysis The methodical examination of data to reveal their underlying relationships.

Analytical report A report that attempts to identify for management why some events have occurred.

Annotation A descriptive comment or explanatory note added to a flowchart.

APL (*A Programming Language*) A powerful timesharing language used primarily in education and science.

Applications-oriented system A system that emphasizes the efficient handling of each subsystem without regard for subsystem overlap.

Applications program A program that directs the step-by-step data processing required to carry out a complete task, such as hourly payroll processing.

Applications programmer A person involved in design, development, and implementation of applications programs.

Arithmetic-logic element The set of registers and circuits of a computing system that perform arithmetic and logical operations.

Artificial intelligence The capability of a machine to perform functions that are normally associated with human intelligence, such as reasoning, learning, and self-improvement.

ASCII *See* **American Standard Code for Information Interchange.**

Assembler A computer program written in

machine language that allows the programmer to write in a pseudoindependent language.

Assembly language A source language that substitutes alphabetic mnemonics for operation codes and storage addresses and assumes automatic sequencing of program statements.

Auditing The process of checking source data, processing procedures, and output documents for validity and error control (accuracy).

Audit trail The visible (hard-copy) trail or path left by a transaction as it is processed.

Automatic data processing (ADP) Data processing that is carried out mostly by automatic machines and, by extension, the discipline that deals with methods and techniques involved in automatic-machine data processing.

Automatic electronic digital computer A machine that utilizes electronic circuits to manipulate data expressed in a symbolic (digital) form according to specific rules in a predetermined but self-directed way.

Background processing The execution of lower-priority computer programs when higher-priority programs (foreground processing) are not using system resources. Contrast with **Foreground processing.**

Bandwidth multiplexor A type of multiplexor that divides the total bandwidth of a line or channel into a set of smaller bandwidths and sends a message simultaneously along each of the smaller bandwidths.

Bar printer An early printer that printed by positioning character-carrying bars and striking them against the paper and ribbon. For line printing, a vertical bar at each position carried all possible characters.

BASIC (*B*eginners *A*ll-purpose *S*ymbolic *I*nstruction *C*ode) An easy-to-learn procedure-oriented programming language designed for interactive use at a terminal.

Batch processing A technique by which data items or transactions and programs are accumulated over a period of time and processed as a group in a single computer run.

BCD *See* **Binary-coded decimal.**

Bias A consistent error in reported figures in a given direction. For example, to consistently include some sales from a men's clothing department in the sales of a notions department.

Binary-coded decimal 1. A 4-bit system of number representation in which each decimal digit is represented by the 4 binary digit positions representing 1, 2, 4, 8 (or 0). 2. A 6-bit system of data representation in which a 2-bit zone code is added to the basic 4-bit numeric code to allow representation of 64 characters rather than only the 16 represented by the 4-bit code.

Binary number system A basic data-representation method used in computers, which is a base 2 system involving the digits 0 and 1.

Bit The smallest unit of information, particularly in a binary system; a bit is a binary 0 (turned off) or 1 (turned on). The word is a contraction of *binary digit.*

Black box concept Premise underlying flowcharting: each transformation process is thought of as a black box; each is broken down until description is complete.

Block 1. A set of data elements (bits, characters, words) handled as a unit. 2. A set of records handled as a unit.

Block diagram A graphic representation of a system or program showing major modules and the general flow through them.

Block index table A table in which two entries (identities of the starting point and of the last record) identify each block in an indexed-sequential file.

BPI Bits per inch.

Branched network A data acquisition system in which messages from individual remote sites are sent over tributary feeder lines to a major communication link connected directly to the central site.

Branch instruction A decision-making instruction that can cause a computer to execute some instruction other than the sequentially next instruction.

Bubble memory An electronic data storage device that stores binary digits as microscopic spots (bubbles) in a thin film on garnet crystals.

Bucket A group of contiguous locations within a physical file (on a storage device).

Buffering process A process whereby a storage reservoir connects two devices and compensates for the difference in speed with which each device can send or receive data.

Bug An error or malfunction in a computer program.

By-product recording Capturing data in machine-sensible form (punched card, punched paper tape, magnetic tape, magnetic disk, or optically readable printout) as a secondary operation of machines used to perform a business action.

Byte A collection of bits, usually 8, representing a numeric, alphabetic, or special character.

Cache memory *See* **Scratch-pad (cache) memory.**

Capacity The amount of data in bytes that can be stored in or on a medium or device.

Card collator A device that can merge, merge with selection, or match two decks of cards.

Card keypunch A keyboard-actuated machine that punches holes in a card to record data.

Card reader A device that accepts punched cards, senses the holes in each card, and translates them into machine data codes.

Card sorter A device that separates a stack of cards into pockets according to the punches in a specific card column.

Cathode ray tube (CRT) terminal A device (which looks like a TV screen with a keyboard attached) that presents data in visual form electronically.

Centralized management The philosophy of management that specifies that all decisions be made as high in the organization as possible, so that authority and responsibility are concentrated in the managers or executives at the top of the organizational hierarchy.

Central processing unit (CPU) The basic operating elements of a computer: the control element, arithmetic-logic element, and primary storage element. It does not include the input and output elements nor secondary online storage.

Chain printer A line printer that uses a rapidly moving chain to carry the character set. As the chain moves across the paper, the hammer at each print position strikes when the proper character is at that position.

Change file A temporary data file containing changes to be made in the records of a master file during a particular processing cycle.

Channel A hardware device and the associated communication links that control and accomplish the flow of data and information between the primary storage in the CPU and the peripheral I/O and storage devices.

Character printer A device that prints a single character on each machine cycle.

Character reading An input method whereby a machine reads a human-sensible document, allowing people to use familiar methods to record data.

Chief programming team A method of organizing the programming activities in the system development process wherein each program is assigned to a team working under the direction of a senior-level chief programmer.

Classification and sorting Separating recorded data by type and then physically arranging them into meaningful sequences or groupings. For example, sales records can be classified and sorted by department, by salesperson, by specific item or item type, and by size of order.

COBOL (Common Business Oriented Language) A procedure-oriented higher-level programming language designed to be used in processing business data files.

Code 1. A set of unambiguous rules for representing data, for example, the American Standard Code for Information Interchange (ASCII). 2. To write a routine in a programming language.

COM *See* **Computer output microfilm.**

Communication Sending processing results to someone who can use them.

Compiler A program that accepts source programs written in a higher-level (procedural or nonprocedural) language and translates them into machine language object programs.

Component test In system testing, a test that is applied more or less independently to a single component.

Computer The automatic electronic digital computer is a machine that utilizes electronic circuits to manipulate data expressed in a symbolic form according to specific rules in a predetermined but self-directed way.

Computer family A set of computers, graduated in size and produced by one manufacturer, that can be programmed using the same numerical instruction code (machine language).

Computer operator Person who sets up the machine and mount, and removes tapes, disks, and printer forms as required by jobs being processed.

Computer-output microfilm (COM) Pertaining to a process for placing computer output on microfilm to speed output and reduce output-media storage needs.

Computer program A series of instructions or statements prepared in a form acceptable to a computer that will yield a planned result.

Computer word A sequence of bits or characters treated as a unit and capable of being stored in one computer location.

Continuous form Paper for impact printers which comes as one long sheet that folds like a fan; perforation lines separate individual forms.

Control and processing module In top-down design of a computer program, a module that calls lower-level modules and also performs some processing of data.

Control console The part of the computer through which the operator communicates with it.

Control element The operator's console, control registers, and related control circuits that select instructions in proper sequence, interpret them, and activate required operating circuits.

Control module In top-down design of a computer program, a high-level module which does no processing of data but only calls lower level modules for processing.

Control system A system designed to keep the operations it controls performing according to some recognized plan.

Control total A meaningful or nonsense (bash) total used to prevent loss of transactions from a batch.

CPU *See* **Central processing unit.**

CPU operating cycle The complete sequence of activities involved in carrying out a computer instruction.

Critical path network A network that defines the time relation of tasks required to complete a project and, specifically, identifies the longest (critical) path through the network of tasks.

CRT *See* **Cathode ray tube.**

CRT/photographic technique A nonimpact printing technique that starts with the formation of characters on a cathode ray tube (CRT). The lighted characters are exposed to photographic film or paper which is then developed by the ordinary photographic process.

Custodial processing Data processing the purpose of which is to carry out organizational operations, usually involving the creation of custodial documents like customer billings, employee paychecks, purchase orders, and so on.

Cylinder A vertical set of coordinated tracks, one on each recording surface of the disks in a disk pack or a multiple-fixed-disk unit.

Data Raw facts and their representations deriving from business activity and a firm's environment and used for communication or processing. (May or may not be information.)

Data administrator The person responsible for the overall management of the data resources of an organization.

Data bank A comprehensive library of files or data bases. The totality of files and data bases for an organization.

Data base A set of two or more interrelated files, each of which contains at least one element in common.

Data base administrator The person responsible for managing the technical aspects of data base design, creation, and maintenance in an organization.

Data base inquiry language (DBIL) A language that provides the ability to access data stored in a data base by reference to the logical organization and meaning of the stored data.

Data base management language (DBML) A computer language that provides for addition, deletion, modification, and retrieval of data stored in a data base by reference to the logical organization and meaning of the stored data. Includes one or more of the following: a data definition language, a data manipulation language, and a data base inquiry language.

Data base management system (DBMS) A software or hardware system that interfaces between the data bases on a system and users and programs to provide for addition, deletion, modification, or retrieval of data elements, records, and files by logical reference to them.

Data definition language (DDL) A language used to describe or define the data elements included in a data base. It is used to create and maintain the data dictionary for the system.

Data dictionary A listing of all the data elements available in an organization which describes each data element and identifies its source, location, and uses.

Data element A field within a data record.

Data input In an input-output schematic, a fact about a transaction or problem that the program is to process.

Data manipulation language (DML) A program designed to provide procedures for maintaining integrated data bases.

Data pre-audit Check on the correctness of data before processing. Can include checks on format, completeness, ranges of values, and check digits.

Data processing The recording and manipulating of data. Also called information processing.

Data processing managers Charged with developing plans for, and an organization leading to, a profit-oriented information system under close managerial control.

Data use analysis An analysis of the uses of all data elements available in an organization which identifies each as to its form, frequency of use, and speed of recall; also identifies additional ways elements might be used.

DBML *See* **Data base management language.**

DBMS *See* **Data base management system.**

Debug To find and correct errors in a computer program.

Decentralized data processing Dispersed data processing with independent computers at local sites.

Decentralized management The philosophy of management that specifies that all decisions be made as low in the organization as possible, so that all levels of management participate in planning and goal setting to the maximum extent possible.

Decision structure A basic structure in structured programming which provides for selection of one of two processing sequences based on a condition. Also called IFTHEN-ELSE.

Decollator A machine that removes carbons and separates copies of multiple-copy forms.

Density The number of characters or bits that can be stored in a given unit of length.

Desk debug Reading a program to find errors in syntax and logic.

Destructive read A reading that also erases the data in the source location.

Detailed flowchart *See* **Procedural flowchart.**

Detailed HIPO diagram A HIPO diagram prepared from one processing box on an overview HIPO diagram.

Device A machine or unit that performs a data processing function.

Diagnostics Reports from compilers and assemblers of program analyses, made to determine if syntactical rules have been followed.

Dial-up line A common telephone line accessed by the normal dialing process.

Direct (random) access Refers to the ability to access directly each location in a storage with almost no variation in the time required to obtain data from each data location. Contrast with **Sequential access.**

Direct-entry device A device for entering program statements or data into a computer without first recording it on an external (offline) medium.

Direct output In an input-output schematic, an output element obtained by direct manipulation of program inputs.

Direct relation address A direct file access system that assigns the location of a record on the storage device as the major identifying key of that record.

Disk cartridge A disk or disks sealed inside a plastic housing containing a read-write mechanism.

Disk drive A device on which one to eight removable disk packs may be mounted for use as secondary storage in a computer system.

Diskette A small disk 6 to 8 inches in diameter.

Disk pack A stack of magnetic disks that can be removed from the disk drive and stored offline.

Disk track Rings on a magnetic disk in which data are recorded.

Distributed data processing Geographically distributed computers (usually minicomputers) connected in a network with each other and (usually) with a central computer (most often, a large mainframe). Local processing is carried out by local processors, and the results are transmitted to the central computer for further processing.

Documentation 1. The written and diagrammatic descriptions of a data processing operation, for example, verbal descriptions, flowcharts, program listings, run instructions. 2. The creating, collecting, organizing, storing, citing, and disseminating of descriptions of data processing operations.

DOUNTIL A form of looping structure that checks for a condition at the end of the structure and branches out of the loop when that condition is met.

DOWHILE A form of looping structure that checks for a condition at the beginning of the loop and branches out when the condition is not met.

Downtime The portion of operating time during which a device or system is inoperable.

Drum printer A line printer that uses a drum embossed with the character set. As the drum rotates, a hammer at each print position strikes the paper from behind when the desired character is in position.

Dual heads A control method used to check the accuracy of calculations and the reading of data; results from two read or write heads are checked against each other.

Dual processing A processing control method used to discover calculation errors; two independent results are checked against each other.

Dual wiring A control method whereby operations are performed twice simultaneously and the results compared; a generalized form of dual heads.

EBÇDIC *See* **Extended Binary-Coded Decimal Interchange Code.**

Echo check A hardware or software control process in which the receiving element or device sends a copy of the signal received back to the sender to confirm that it is correct.

Economic efficiency Refers to whether a system is getting the required processing done for the lowest possible cost; both short-run and long-run costs are considered.

Economic feasibility In data processing, refers to the economic burden a system places on the operation where it is applied. This burden must not be so high that the operation cannot absorb it.

Effectiveness In systems analysis, refers to the degree to which the system meets its processing and informational goals.

Egoless programming team A method of organizing the programming activities in the system development process in which there is no chief programmer and team members contribute according to their abilities; no one person is totally responsible for a program.

Electrostatic imaging A nonimpact printing technique in which the character shapes are charged onto the paper in the form of dots of static electrical charges and then exposed to ink.

Electrothermal imaging A version of matrix printing in which characters are formed on heat-sensitive paper by touching it with heated rods.

Exception report A report that identifies unexpected, unusual, and/or undesirable events, any deviation from desired levels of activity.

Execution-order approach An approach to processing order in which the modules are developed in the order in which they will be executed when the full program is run.

Extended Binary-Coded Decimal Interchange Code (EBCDIC) An 8-bit data code comprised of a 4-bit binary zone code on the left and a 4-bit binary numeric code on the right developed by International Business Machines Corporation.

Feasibility study A preliminary system analysis whose purpose is to determine the potential for cost savings, time savings, increased capacity, and improved managerial control resulting from the design or redesign of a system, particularly where computer processing is being considered as one alternative.

Field In a record, a specified area used for a particular data element, for example, a group of character spaces used to represent a customer's name.

File A set of records relating to a specific business activity. For example, the accounts receivable file of a department store made up of the individual records of the store's credit customers. *See* **Change file, Master file, Transaction file.**

File key The field within a record that is used to order the records in some way.

Financial subsystem That part of an organization whose basic objective is to meet the firm's financial obligations, using the minimal amount of financial resources consistent with an established margin of safety.

Firmware Software translated into hardware in microprocessor form.

First generation Refers to computers manufactured in the period 1946–1960 whose basic hardware component was the vacuum tube and whose operations were timed in milliseconds.

Fixed disk A storage device with a set of disks permanently mounted on a spindle, usually with a set of read-write heads for each disk surface.

Fixed-word-length storage A storage organization in which each addressable storage location contains a fixed number of bytes or characters.

Floating-point binary Refers to a numeration system in which each number is represented as one numeral multiplied by a power of a fixed positive integer base. Common notation: .03456; floating-point notation (base 10): 3456E-05.

Floppy disk A flexible plastic platter with one or more iron-oxide-coated surfaces.

Flowchart 1. A graphic representation of processing in which symbols are used to represent data flow and system components. 2. A set of processing blocks connected by flowlines.

Font Refers to a set of printing characters of a particular size and style.

Foreground processing The preemption of computer facilities for the highest priority programs while lower priority programs (background processing) are forced to wait. Contrast with Background processing.

Forms burster A machine that separates individual sheets from a continuous form and removes pin-feed edge holes.

Fortran A procedure-oriented higher-level programming language designed for use in solving scientific problems.

Fourth generation Refers to computers manufactured since about 1973 whose major hardware components are large scale integrated and very large scale integrated circuits and whose operations are timed in nanoseconds and picoseconds.

Hardcopy terminals Interactive typewriters and typewriter-like devices capable of producing printed copies of output in humanly readable form.

Hardware The physical equipment used in data processing; in electronic data processing, the machine devices in a computer system, including the central processing unit, devices for data preparation, data input, secondary storage, and output, and devices for intercommunication among hardware components.

Head crash The abrasive contact between a read-write head and the magnetizable surface due to contaminants breaking up the film of air on which the head rides above the surface.

Head-seek time The average time it takes for a read/write head to be positioned over the desired track on a magnetic surface.

Hexadecimal system Refers to the number system with 16 counting symbols (0 through 9, A, B, C, D, E, F) and a base of 16.

Hierarchical approach An approach to processing order in which all modules at a given level are coded and tested on the computer before any lower-level modules are coded.

Hierarchical data structure A tree-like structure used to identify logical relationships among data elements in a data base.

Hierarchical grouping An organizational structure in which the programming function is headed by a programming manager who assigns tasks to one or more levels of subordinates and retains responsibility for all projects but usually does not participate in actual coding.

Hierarchical network A teleprocessing network in which each computer is controlled by the computer immediately above it in a hierarchical structure.

Hierarchical testing A program debug technique used with top-down design in which each module is developed and tested as an independent entity and then combined with previously developed higher-level modules so that the entire program to that point can be tested.

HIPO diagram A chart showing the hierarchical input-process-output structure of a program module. (HIPO stands for *H*ierarchy plus *I*nput, *P*rocess, *O*utput.)

Hollerith 80-column card A key-input medium, which is a punched card utilizing twelve rows per column and, usually, eighty columns per card.

Identification records An input control method in which data inputs and files are identified before processing.

Idle time A period of time during which available hardware is not being used.

IFTHENELSE *See* **Decision structure.**

Impact printer A device that prints by forcing (impacting) the type against the ribbon and paper.

Inaction data Data that require no action. For example, the cashing of a paycheck by an employee.

Indexed-nonsequential file A nonsequential file that is indexed in groups. The index must contain an entry for every item in the file.

Indexed-sequential access An access method in which the location of a block of data is identified in an index. Access to the beginning of the block is direct, but access through the block is sequential.

Indexed-sequential file A file that is arranged into sequence by the control key and grouped into blocks for storage.

Indirect output In an input-output schematic, an output element derived, at least in part, from the manipulation of direct outputs.

Information Communicated knowledge expressed in a form that makes it immediately useful for decision making.

Initialize To set counters, switches, addresses, and variable values to starting values usually at the beginning of a computer routine.

Ink jet printer A printer that prints with a spray of fine droplets of ink. The most common type uses magnetic or electrostatic "steering" to direct the ink through matrix character positions. Another type uses magnetically formed characters behind the paper to attract the ink.

Inline processing Processing of data transactions in the order in which they occur.

Input Data that is recorded.

Input control A control applied during the input phase of the input/process/output cycle to ensure that all authorized transactions are correctly recorded and that all data elements enter the processing system at the right place and time.

Input element The element that translates data from the symbols of human language to the symbols used by the machine.

Input-output schematic A table listing required outputs and specified inputs for a program; it provides information to show that the required outputs can be obtained from the specified inputs.

Instruction A statement that specifies an operation and the locations of its operands.

Instruction register A register consisting of one or more special-purpose locations that store instructions for interpretation and execution.

Intangible benefits Nonbudgetary benefits only indirectly measurable in money to be gained from a system.

Intangible costs Nonbudgetary costs of a system that are only indirectly measurable in money.

Integrated circuit (IC) Electronic circuits containing a number of components in miniature form placed on a single silicon chip. *See also* **Large-scale integration (LSI)** and **Very large-scale integration (VLSI).**

Integrated data base A set of basic files where each data element appears only once, related data are cross-referenced, and data elements can be located by starting from any one of the individual elements.

Integrated system A data processing system that minimizes the overlap of subsystems to decrease redundancy of data and processing operations.

Integration In data processing systems, the single recording of data from each transaction or change in a common classifying code for the purpose of making maximum use of the data with a minimum number of human operations.

Intelligent terminal A combination of a minicomputer or a microprocessor on a chip with a terminal (usually a CRT) to allow the use of programming to perform tasks, such as input editing.

Interactive Refers to computer systems where the person at a terminal interacts with the computer by exchanging questions and answers with the machine.

Interblock gap A space on a data medium used to separate blocks of records.

Internal controls Operational and supervisory controls designed to check on and maintain the accuracy of business data, safeguard business assets, promote operating efficiency, and encourage compliance with established policies and procedures.

Interpreter A compiler that translates the source program into machine language line by line as it reads it (as far as possible).

Interrecord gap A space on a data medium used to indicate where one record stops and another begins. Also called *record gap.*

Interrupt 1. To stop processing in such a way that it can be resumed. 2. The signal for accomplishing an interrupt.

Inverted list A list in which a data element (characteristic) is used as the control key and the original file key appears as the data element (characteristic).

I/O-bound job On a computer system, a job that requires lengthy inputs with very little intervening processing.

I/O interrupt Refers to the stopping of processing for input or output.

JCL *See* **Job control language.**

Job-by-job system The simplest method of batch processing in which each job is loaded and processed separately. Contrast with **Stacked-job system.**

Job control language (JCL) A language that provides a set of short commands and identifiers that standardize job control commands from users in a stacked-job system.

Job control program The program used by an operating system to interpret the job control statements preceding each job in a stacked-job system.

Job control statement A set of commands written in a job control language which precedes a job to identify it and the system resources it will use.

Job description A detailed description of the work to be performed, special skills to be applied, amount of supervision to be given or received, and general working conditions of a job.

Job specification A description of the physical skills, education, training, and experience required for successful completion of a job.

K In automatic data processing, loosely, 2^{10} (two to the tenth power), 1,024 in decimal notation.

Key-to-disk device A device providing the capability of entering data onto magnetic disk packs by use of a keyboard. Usually involves multiple key stations.

Key-to-tape system A system providing the capability of entering data directly onto magnetic tape by use of a keyboard. Usually involves multiple key stations.

Key transcription The creation of a machine-sensible medium by operators using machines with typewriter-like keyboards to punch data into cards or paper tape to encode data on magnetic tape or disks.

Key transformation A process that calculates the storage location of a record by transformation of the record key.

Language translator Translates an instruction written in a programming language into a computer's internal language.

Large-scale integration (LSI) Refers to miniaturized circuits, each containing hundreds of electronic circuits on a single silicon chip.

Laser/xerographic imaging A nonimpact printing process which uses a low-power laser beam to paint the mirror image of characters on the light-sensitive surface covering a rotating drum in the form of dot matrices.

Leased line A telephone line providing a continuous connection between two or more points.

Light pen A pen-like device that is used to input data through a cathode ray tube (CRT) terminal by touching it to the tube face. The pen contains a photo cell which is activated by lighted areas of the screen to tell the computer where it is being pointed.

Line concentrator A device for concentrating line use by accepting simultaneous messages from a group of terminals, storing them in a buffer, and then passing them along over a single line to the computer.

Line printer A device that prints a line of characters with one machine cycle.

List organization A file organization structure in which the logical relations among records are identified by one or more pointers attached to each record.

Logic error An error in ordering or method in programming which leads to incorrect processing or a failure to process some data items.

Looping structure A basic structure in structured programming which provides the ability for repetition of a process within a program module. Also called DOWHILE and, less frequently, DOUNTIL.

LSI *See* **Large-scale integration.**

Machine-dependent Refers to a computer programming language designed for a particular computer.

Machine-independent Refers to a higher-level programming language that can be run on any computer for which an appropriate language translator has been written.

Machine language The lowest-level programming language. It is a set of instruction codes that a computer can execute directly and is usually expressed in binary 0s and 1s.

Machine operator Person who keys data onto cards, tapes, or disks for batch applications.

Macroinstruction An instruction in a source language that will translate into several machine language instructions.

Magnetic disk A flat round platter with at least one oxide-coated surface which can be magnetized. Also spelled *disc.*

Magnetic disk pack *See* **Disk pack.**

Magnetic drum A cylinder with a magnetizable outer surface on which data can be recorded by magnetizing portions of the curved surface.

Magnetic ink character recognition (MICR) The machine recognition of characters printed with magnetic ink.

Magnetic strips Lengths of flexible plastic material with a coated surface organized like short pieces of magnetic tape either hung independently on racks within the storage device or placed in groups in cartridges hung in the device.

Magnetic tape Mylar tape coated with a magnetizable substance, so that bits may be recorded in channels running the length of the tape.

Main control module The overall supervisor of the other modules. Its purpose is to oversee the execution of lower modules to attain the overall objective of a program.

Maintenance engineer Technician responsible for repair of electronic equipment and preventive maintenance on a regular schedule.

Maintenance programmer A person responsible for maintenance of operational application programs.

Major record key A record identifier used to determine the primary order of records in a file.

Management information system (MIS) A combination of people, machines, and procedures organized to produce information for management.

Managerial control A control placed upon overall levels of activity and results, such as the general level of sales, profits, and return on investment.

Marketing subsystem That part of an organization whose objective is to facilitate the flow of goods and services from the firm to satisfy the perceived wants and needs of customers in support of the objectives and goals of the firm.

Mark reading An input method involving codes or use of special forms that make the meaning of the marks clear; allows use of human-sensible documents.

Mass-storage systems Large-capacity storage devices designed to provide online access to very, very large amounts (masses) of data and information.

Master file The file containing primary and relatively permanent records for an application. For example, the complete set of permanent records for credit customers at a department store is the master file for the accounts receivable system.

Master-file volume The amount of transactions and reports, including the number of records in files, in a processing system.

Materials control subsystem That part of an organization whose objective is to provide and maintain stocks of raw materials, parts, and supplies of adequate quality in quantities sufficient to accomplish the objectives and goals of the firm at a minimum cost.

Matrix character printer A character printer that uses a matrix of wires or tiny rods to form characters.

Matrix line printer A line printer with a character matrix at each print position across a line; all are activated on a single machine cycle.

Media librarian The person who maintains control over tape, disk, and card files of data and programs in an organization.

Medium The physical material, or configuration thereof, on which data are recorded and stored. For example, paper tape, cards, magnetic tape.

MICR *See* **Magnetic ink character recognition.**

Microcomputer A computer built around a microprocessor by adding circuitry and devices to provide memory, input/output, and control functions.

Microprocessor A general processor created using microcircuit technology (LSI and VLSI) without any of the supporting circuitry and devices to provide memory, input/output, and control capabilities present in a computer system. Contrast with **Microcomputer.**

Microsecond One-millionth of a second.

Millisecond One-thousandth of a second.

Minicomputer A size category of computers that overlaps both microcomputers on the small end and mainframes on the large end. It tends to have smaller word sizes than a mainframe and larger word sizes than a microcomputer. Its instruction set tends to be larger than that of a microcomputer but smaller than that of a mainframe.

MIS *See* **Management information system.**

Modem (*mod*ulator-*dem*odulator) A device that converts electronic impulses representing data into sound impulses (data tones) for transmission over a telephone line and then converts the sound back to electronic machine impulses at the receiving end.

Modularity Expanding the functional capacity of computers by adding units (modules).

Module 1. In programming, an independent set of code for accomplishing a specific subtask in a program. 2. An independent functional hardware unit designed for use with other components.

Multiplexor channel A channel that can be active with several devices at one time. Contrast with **Selector channel.**

Multiprocessing The use of a system involving two or more central processing units.

Multiprocessor system A computer system in which a master processor controls one or more slave processors.

Multiprogramming system A process that allows many users what appears to be simultaneous access to a single processor by accepting simultaneous inputs from many sources and switching from job to job as processing is interrupted for input or output.

Nanosecond One-billionth of a second.

Network data structure A data base structure in which list processing techniques are used to identify logical relationships among data elements in the same and in different files contained in the data base.

96-column card A punch card that is smaller than the 80-column card but uses smaller holes and a binary-coded decimal code for compact data representation; for use with minicomputers.

Nonimpact printer A printer that uses a process other than forcing (impacting) the ribbon and paper against the characters.

Nonprocedural language A highest-level computer programming language designed to allow easy development of special-purpose programs using relatively natural forms of language.

Nonprogrammed decision A decision which cannot be fully specified in advance.

Nonvolatile storage A storage device whose data content is not lost when electrical power to the unit is removed. For example, magnetic core storage.

Object program A fully compiled or assembled program that is ready to be carried out by the computer.

OCR *See* **Optical character recognition.**

Octal number system A number system in which each position represents a power of 8 and is counted 0 to 7 times.

Offline Pertaining to equipment or devices not physically attached to and under the control of a CPU. May also refer to data processing activities peformed off the computer.

OMR *See* **Optical mark recognition.**

On-demand report A report developed and delivered whenever commanded.

Online Pertaining to equipment or devices physically attached to and under the direct control of a CPU. Also refers to data processing activities performed on the computer.

Operand That which is operated upon. In computer processing, an operand is usually identified by an address in the instruction.

Operating cycle The complete sequence of activities involved in carrying out a computer instruction.

Operating system The system that provides overall control and "supervises" all the hardware and software elements in the performance of their individual tasks.

Operational control A control applied in carrying out a plan.

Operation monitoring Checking operating logs to spot illegal access or tampering with programs.

Operations register A register that decodes the operation code in a computer instruction to identify the process to be carried out by the next CPU operating cycle.

Optical character recognition (OCR) Refers to the use of light-sensitive photoelectric cells to identify printed characters.

Optical mark recognition (OMR) Refers to a device that reads marks (lines) rather than characters photoelectrically.

Organization chart A two-dimensional schematic which, by showing the placement of individuals and groups and their reporting relationships, indicates the assignment of responsibility and authority within an organization.

Originating (recording) Capturing data regarding a transaction or a firm's environment for processing.

Output The results (management information, custodial documents, or historical records) generated by processing input.

Output controls Controls applied during the output phase of the input-process-output cycle to ensure completeness and accuracy of the output from a processing system.

Output element The element that translates the results of processing (output) from the symbols of the machine to human-sensible forms or forms used by another machine.

Overflow check A control method used to signal processing errors. Excess digits from a too-large number are held for correction.

Overlap The simultaneous performance by a computer of two or more functions. For example, input and output or input, processing, and output.

Overlaying The process of bringing individual segments of a large program from secondary storage into primary storage as needed, replacing (overlaying) segments of the program that have already been completed.

Overview HIPO diagram In structured program development, a nondetailed HIPO diagram developed for each module shown in a structure chart.

Packed binary 1. A special form of hexadecimal representation of numbers in which the zone code occurs only once for each number rather than once for each decimal digit. 2. The representation of two numeric characters in 8 bits in either the EBCDIC or ASCII codes by use of hexadecimals.

Page A piece of a program or a block of data of a fixed size created automatically in a virtual storage stystem.

Page printer A printer that prints a complete page in each machine cycle.

Paging An automatic overlaying technique used in timesharing and multiprogramming in which a program is automatically divided into segments called pages which are transferred from secondary storage into main storage whenever required in processing a program.

Parallel operation When a new processing system is operated in parallel to an old system before complete cutover; duplicating transactions checks the new system.

Parity bit A binary digit added to a set of bits to make the number of 1 (*on*) bits in a character always even or odd, its purpose being to detect errors.

Parity check A test to see if the number of on (1) bits or off (0) bits in a set of bits (byte) is even (or odd).

Pascal A procedural language designed for the creation of structured programs.

Peak processing demand The maximum number of input transactions during a given time period required of a processing system.

Periodic report A report produced at regular, periodic intervals of time.

Peripheral device In a data processing system, a piece of equipment, distinct from the central processing unit, that provides the system with additional capacities or communication. For example, a disk or tape drive.

Personnel subsystem That part of an organization whose objective is to provide and maintain at a minimum cost the human resources for accomplishing the firm's objectives.

Pert *See* **Program evaluation and review technique.**

Phased system cutover When a new processing system is substituted for the displaced system one phase (subsystem) at a time.

Picosecond One-trillionth of a second.

Planning subsystem That part of an organization whose objective is to set the objectives and goals of the firm and the paths of action that will be followed in seeking to attain those objectives and goals.

PL/1 (*Programming Language one*) A higher-level compiler language developed by IBM as an all-purpose procedure-oriented language intended to replace COBOL and FORTRAN.

Plotter A special-purpose printer that outlines drawings.

Pointer In list organization, an address attached to each word or record to identify the next related record.

Point-of-action entry device A device that records data at the location where a transaction takes place. Also called point-of-sale (POS) device.

Port A path along which data flow into or out of primary storage.

Portable terminal A hardcopy CRT terminal designed to be carried about and used for remote access to computer systems, usually via telephone lines.

Prenumbered form A serially numbered form used as an input or output data control.

Primary memory In computers, the memory (storage) contained within the central processing unit. Contrast with **Secondary storage.**

Procedural flowchart A diagrammatic representation of the input, processing, and output activities of a system.

Procedure-oriented compiler language A language in which each program statement is related to a procedural task and may compile as several machine language instructions.

Process-bound job On a computer system, a job that involves lengthy computations after input and before output.

Processing controls Controls applied during the processing phase of the input-process-output cycle to ensure against loss of data or failure to process a data item and to check the accuracy of the processing arithmetic and procedures.

Processing hit rate The proportion of records in the master file that are accessed during a processing run.

Processing module In top-down design of a program, a low-level module that performs only the processing of data and does not call any other module.

Production control clerk Person assigned to postprocessing, who operates forms bursters, decollators, and binding equipment.

Production subsystem That part of an organization whose objective is to produce the goods and/or services provided by the firm at the least cost consistent with the firm's goals of quality and quantity.

Program 1. A finite sequence of allowable individual computer operations designed to carry out a processing operation. 2. To design and develop (plan, code, and test) a computer program.

Program enhancement A change in an operating program undertaken to improve its operating performance, usually the speed of its operation.

Program evaluation and review technique (PERT) A process for defining the tasks necessary to complete a project and setting them in a critical path network.

Program inputs In an input-output schematic, the numerical constants or algorithmic formulas used in processing data inputs.

Programmable read-only memory (PROM) A read-only memory whose content can be changed by special procedures but not by the use of standard programming processes.

Program maintenance A process during which changes may be made in an operating program to improve and refine it.

Program maintenance history A log of the maintenance activity for each program and processing system which contains full documentation of each change (date, what was done, and who authorized it).

Program maintenance librarian Person responsible for keeping track of program revisions and program documentation.

Programmed decision A processing decision which is automatic.

Programming The process of translating a problem solution into an ordered sequence of instructions for execution by a computer.

Programming flowchart *See* **Procedural flowchart.**

Program module An integral unit for accomplishing a specific subtask within an overall program.

Program tracing Following through a computer program step by step to check the order of processing and to isolate errors.

Project leader In systems development, the person who heads the project team responsible for the analysis, design, development, and implementation of a system.

Project life cycle The phases in the design, development, and operation of a project. For data processing systems, the major phases are feasibility study, system design, system development, system implementation, and system operation.

Project management 1. The processes used to control any ad hoc project, such as data processing system development. 2. The process of creating and controlling a special organization (team) for planning and carrying out an integrated effort leading to attaining a specific limited objective.

Project team In system analysis and design, a team led usually by a senior systems analyst and including representatives of operating management in user departments.

Pseudocode An informal design language written in English-like statements to describe the detailed processing steps for completing a module.

Punched card A card punched with holes in patterns that represent data.

Punched paper tape A paper tape punched with holes in a pattern that represents data.

Purge In data processing, to remove inactive or unused records from a master file.

Random access *See* **Direct (random) access.**

Randomly ordered file A file in which the location of each record is computed by a special formula.

Read To enter data from a storage device, from a data medium, or another source.

Read-only memory (ROM) A device used to store data (or instructions) that are not alterable by computer instructions. Thus, contents are protected against accidental destruction.

Read-write head A device that utilizes a magnetic coil to create a magnetic force field either to magnetize spots on a magnetizable surface or to sense the presence of such magnetized spots.

Realtime data processing system 1. A processing system that feeds back information in time to affect the situation from which the raw data were generated. 2. A processing system that meets severe time constraints in updating the master file and/or in providing response. 3. Loosely, any processing system featuring online data entry with immediate update and/or instantaneous response.

Realtime response In system control, a response in time to affect an ongoing physical operation in a desirable way.

Record A collection of related items of data, treated as a unit. For example, a charge sale may form a transaction record; a complete set of such records for a given period of time may form a transaction file.

Record characteristics The contents of a record.

Record count A count of records at a processing station designed to prevent loss of a record or introduction of illegal records. Also called *transaction count.*

Recording density The number of bits in a single linear track per unit of length of the recording medium, for example, bits per inch.

Record length The length of a record, usually measured in words or characters.

Register A device capable of storing a specified amount of data, such as one word.

Relational data structure A data base structure in which each logical relationship between data elements in the data base is represented as a two-dimensional table.

Relative address A storage address that locates a record relative to the beginning of the file.

Remote access Access to a data processing facility via a station or stations located outside that facility.

Reproducing punch A machine that reproduces a deck of cards exactly, or reproduces all or part of each card with rearrangement or with constant added data on each card. Also called a *gang punch.*

Retrieval The act of finding and returning data from storage.

Review of interested parties An output control to spot inconsistencies and other signals of input or processing errors.

Ring list A list in which the last record contains a pointer identifying the first record. Most rings contain pointers pointing in both directions from each record so retrieval can proceed in either direction.

Ring network A teleprocessing network in which all the nodes are located on the same communication line with no one node in control.

ROM *See* **Read-only memory.**

Rotational delay The time required for the beginning of a desired data location to move under the read-write head after the head has been positioned over the track containing the desired location.

Routine An ordered set of instructions that may have some general or frequent use. (A routine may be a program.)

Scheduler Person who plans daily work flows in data preparation and batched computer processing.

Scratch-pad (cache) memory Temporary interim storage devices used to speed processes in the central processing unit.

Secondary record key A field other than the major record key that is used for ordering records in a file for some purpose other than positioning them.

Secondary storage Auxiliary storage, that is, online storage other than primary storage and offline storage on a machine-readable medium. Also called *auxiliary storage, peripheral storage, secondary memory.*

Second generation Refers to computers manufactured in the period 1960–1964 whose major hardware component was the transistor and whose operations were timed in microseconds.

Segmentation The process of dividing a program into logical segments, such as I/O and processing routines, for automatic overlaying in virtual storage.

Selector channel A channel that can handle only one device at a time. Contrast with **Multiplexor channel.**

Sequence check A check on the sequencing of processed items used to discover missing or misplaced items and prevent out-of-order processing which can cause false exception signaling or application of transaction or change data to the wrong master record.

Sequence register A special counter that keeps track of the sequentially next CPU storage location where the next instruction is usually found.

Sequence structure One of the three basic structures in structured programming which provides that modules be executed in the order in which they appear in the program.

Sequential access A storage access that requires that data locations be accessed in their positional order in sequence. Contrast with **Direct access.**

Sequentially ordered file A file whose records are organized in some logical order with relation to the control key.

Sign check A control method used to signal that the result of an arithmetic operation has the wrong sign.

Simple list A list in which an index entry points to the first logical record, the first record points to the second, the second to the third, and so on.

Simulation The representation of features of behavior of a physical or abstract system by the behavior of another system, for example, the representation of physical phenomena by means of a set of mathematical functions or by operations performed by a computer.

Software The procedures developed to direct hardware in the execution of processing.

Sorting key Any field within a record that is used for rearranging records in a file.

Source document A data-carrying medium that is entered into a manual or machine processing cycle.

Source program A program written in a procedure-oriented language.

Special-action path A deviation from the main flow of a data processing system in which some of the inputs are processed in a way different from the general flow.

Special character A graphic character that is not a letter, not a digit, and not a space character.

Stacked-job system A batch processing system in which the controlling operating system is capable of accepting jobs one after another from a job stack. Contrast with **Job-by-job system.**

Standard A predetermined goal for an operation (for example, sales level, inventory turnover rate, error rate).

Star network A teleprocessing network in which each remote terminal is connected by a direct link only to a central computer.

Star system A data acquisition system in which each remote site from which data are sent is connected by a direct link to the central computer site.

Status report A report that indicates the condition or level of a business operation at a point in time.

Storage 1. A device into which data can be entered and retained for retrieval and use at a later time. Also called *memory.* 2. The act of retaining data on or in a storage medium or device. *See* **Read-only memory, Secondary storage, Volatile storage.**

Storage capacity The amount of data that a storage device or system can contain.

Storage dump A printout which is a kind of map of the primary memory, showing what is going on in a computer at a given point. Used in debugging.

Storage element The element that stores program instructions, input (raw) data, intermediate results from processing, and final results (processed data) for output.

Stored program The characteristic of the computer that allows it to store the instructions for a process (a program) in its memory and follow them through unaided by further supervision and direction. The stored instructions can be replaced with a different set (a different program) or modified by results obtained during processing.

Strategic planning The process of deciding *what* should be done.

Structural check A control procedure based on the fact that some data values have predictable relationships.

Structure chart A graphic representation of a program or system that displays program modules and the relationships between modules.

Structured approach An approach to program development that uses three specific techniques—top-down design, structured programming, and structured walkthroughs.

Structured programming The design and development of computer programs following a prescribed pattern and with restrictions on allowable module design and allowable program logic structures.

Structured walkthrough A process for formal review of program development efforts at each major stage to prevent errors in design or development.

Stub In structure charts, the symbol used to represent an incomplete program module.

Subsystem test In system testing, a test applied independently to a subsystem within the total system.

Sudden system cutover When a new processing system completely replaces the displaced system in a sudden and complete shift to the new system.

Summarization Accumulating details to obtain totals, including averages (rescaled sums).

Syntax The structure, form, and required organization of expressions in a language.

Syntax error An error—such as a misspelling, a misplaced comma, or character transposition—in a computer program.

System A combination of elements, their attributes, and their interrelationships that are organized in the pursuit of some objective.

System acceptance test A test applied to a total system to determine if it will work as a whole.

System analysis A detailed step-by-step investigation of a system for the purpose of determining what it does and how it can best do it. It determines the objectives of a processing system, its organization, and its procedures.

System boundaries All components that have a significant effect on the operation of a system.

System components The people, machines, and procedures accomplishing data processing activities within a system.

System design phase One phase of a project life cycle the purpose of which is to analyze the processing requirements of a project and to design a system to meet those requirements. Top-down design should be used.

System development phase One phase of a project life cycle which includes program design and coding, and development of testing, system documentation, and user training programs.

System effectiveness The degree to which a system meets its processing and informational goals.

System efficiency The ratio of a system's outputs to effort and cost.

System flowchart A graphic representation of a processing system which outlines it and identifies major inputs and outputs, basic files, and work stations.

System implementation phase One phase of a project life cycle the objective of which is a working system.

System interface A point where a subsystem has contact with another subsystem.

System operation The final phase in a project life cycle during which a system proves itself in a program of continuing system testing and maintenance.

Systems analyst Person engaged in system analysis and design.

Systems programmer A person involved in design, development, implementation, and maintenance of basic system software (operating system, language translators, DBMLs, utilities).

Tactical planning The process of determining *how* what is to be done will be accomplished.

Tangible benefits Obvious cost benefits to be obtained from a data processing or information system.

Tangible costs Measurable costs, the obvious additions to expenses arising from a system.

Tape density The number of byte positions (characters) on 1 inch of tape.

Tape drive A device that reads from or writes onto magnetic tape. Also called *tape transport.*

Technical efficiency Refers to the efficiency of the methods and machines used in a processing system.

Technological implementation Consists of hardware and software acquisition, conversion, and testing.

Teleprocessing A process in which data are entered from remote locations via telephone and telegraph lines and are, perhaps, operated upon and results returned over the same lines.

Terminal A device for entering data into or outputting data from a communication network or computer.

Test data A set of made-up or actual data used to test the correctness of a computer program.

Text editor A complex program for modifying stored files by providing a series of simple codes for deleting, inserting, or changing characters, words, phrases, or even pages within the files.

Third generation Refers to computers manufactured in the period 1964 to about 1972 whose major hardware components were the microcircuit and whose operations were timed in nanoseconds.

Thrashing When a computer spends excessive portions of its running time rolling in and rolling out programs and data under control of a virtual storage executive.

Time division multiplexor A type of multiplexor in which the full bandwidth of a line is used for each message, but several messages are pulsed intermittently (spaced in time) along the line.

Timesharing A special form of multiprogramming in which the maximum time any job can spend in the CPU (processing) is limited to a specified amount of time—a time slice.

Time slice The maximum length of time that each program using a CPU in timesharing is allowed to retain control over the central processor at each turn.

Top-down design An approach to the design of systems or programs in which design starts with the major objectives and proceeds to the lowest-level detailed processing procedures.

Track The path on a moving storage medium such as a drum, tape, or disk, along which data are recorded.

Transaction count *See* **Record count.**

Transaction file A file containing data pertaining to a related set of business transactions to be processed in combination with a master file. For example, in a billing application, a transaction file of credit sales might be processed with a master file containing customer name, amount owed, and so on.

Transaction sampling A control process in which a random sample of transactions is reprocessed, and all affected outputs are checked for the same results.

Transfer rate The number of characters (or bytes) that can be read out of (or off of) or accepted into (or onto) a device or medium in one second.

Translation The process of translating data from human-sensible symbols to symbols used by the computer.

Transmission mode The kind of transmission—full-duplex, half-duplex, or simplex—permitted by a specified telephone-line service.

Triggered exception report A report that is developed and delivered upon the identification of an exception.

True binary A coding system in which each component state represents a binary digit (bit), a 0 or a 1.

Turnaround document A document that is sent out and returned for processing.

Turnkey system A data processing system, including hardware and software, capable of performing the data processing functions of a small business or of a particular business function in a larger business.

Type wheel A wheel on which the characters are mounted in some character printers.

Typewriter-like terminal A machine by which users enter data via a keyboard connected to a computer by a direct cable or telephone line.

Unit record system A data processing system using punched cards and card processing equipment.

Update In data processing, to change a record in a master file to reflect current transactions or changes. For example, to increase the amount owed in the accounts receivable record for a customer who makes a credit purchase.

Utility A generalized routine for performing a specific data processing function in an efficient way.

Variable dictionary A listing of all variable names used in a program with the meaning and format (number and type of characters allowed for it) specified for each variable.

Variable-word-length storage Storage in which each word is identified by the address of the byte or character at one end of the word and a special character (word mark) at the other end of the word, thus allowing word length to vary.

Verbal description A written description of the general purpose, primary inputs, and desired outputs of a program or system.

Verifier A machine used to check the correctness of a punched card as an operator keys the card contents a second time. The machine stops if an error is indicated.

Very large-scale integration (VLSI) Refers to miniaturized circuits, each containing thousands of electronic components on a single silicon chip.

Virtual storage A storage and program control process in which program segments (or pages) are located in secondary storage and are automatically brought in to overlay the previously used program segments in primary storage as required to continue processing a program.

Visual table of contents A term expressing the function of the structure chart.

Voice response A device used in computer-controlled inquiry systems to provide responses that do not require an operator to read the response; makes telephone inquiry possible.

Volatile storage A storage unit whose data content is lost when electrical power to the unit is removed.

Word length The size of a word, usually measured in characters or binary digits.

Work station The subcomponent responsible for carrying out a single activity or group of interrelated activities within a data processing system.

Zone bit 1. In the ASCII and EBCDIC codes, the 4 left-most digits which are used to distinguish positive from negative numbers, alphabetics from numbers, and special characters. 2. In packed binary, the final 4-bit code which represents the common code for the preceding numeric digits.

Index

ABCDEFGHIJ-H-898765432